AMERICAN
WRITERS
Classics

VOLUME I

ISSN 1541-4507

AMERICAN WRITERS
Classics

VOLUME I

EDITED BY JAY PARINI

CHARLES SCRIBNER'S SONS®

THOMSON
—★—
™
GALE

New York • Detroit • San Diego • San Francisco • Cleveland • New Haven, Conn. • Waterville, Maine • London • Munich

THOMSON
GALE

American Writers Classics, Volume I
Jay Parini, Editor in Chief

© 2003 by Charles Scribner's Sons. Charles
Scribner's Sons is an imprint of
The Gale Group, Inc., a division of
Thomson Learning, Inc.

Charles Scribner's Sons™ and Thomson
Learning™ are trademarks used herein under
license.

For more information, contact
Charles Scribner's Sons
An imprint of The Gale Group
300 Park Avenue South, 9th Floor
New York, NY 10010
Or you can visit our Internet site at
http://www.gale.com

Permissions Department
The Gale Group, Inc.
27500 Drake Rd.
Farmington Hills, MI 48331-3535
Permissions Hotline:
248 699-8006 or 800 877-4253, ext. 8006
Fax: 248 699-8074 or 800 762-4058

Since this page cannot legibly accommodate
all copyright notices, the acknowledgments
constitute an extension of the copyright
notice.

ISBN 0-684-31248-4 (volume 1)
ISSN 1541-4507

Printed in the United States of America
10 9 8 7 6 5 4 3 2 1

Editorial and Production Staff

Project Editor
ALJA KOOISTRA COLLAR

Assisting Editor
MARK DROUILLARD

Copyeditors
JANET BYRNE
LISA DIXON
GRETCHEN GORDON
ALAN V. HEWAT
TERESA JESIONOWSKI
MARCIA MERRYMAN MEANS

Proofreader
ANNA SHEETS NESBITT

Indexer
CYNTHIA CRIPPEN

Permission Researchers
MARGARET CHAMBERLAIN
UMA KUKATHAS

Compositor
GARY LEACH

Manufacturing Buyer
STACY MELSON

Publisher
FRANK MENCHACA

Acknowledgments

Acknowledgment is gratefully made to those publishers and individuals who have permitted the use of the following material in copyright. Every effort has been made to secure permission to reprint copyrighted material.

Beloved
Excerpts from *Beloved,* by Toni Morrison. Plume, 1988. Copyright © 1987 by Toni Morrison. All rights reserved. Reproduced by permission. Excerpts from "Revisions, Rememories and Exorcisms: Toni Morrison and the Slave Narrative," by Cynthia S. Hamilton. *Journal of American Studies* 30 (December 1996). Reproduced by permission. Excerpts from "Violence, Home, and Community in Toni Morrison's *Beloved,*" by Nancy Jesser. *African American Review* 33 (summer 1999). Reproduced by permission. Excerpts from "Models of Memory and Romance: The Dual Endings of Toni Morrison's *Beloved,*" by Mary Paniccia Carden. *Twentieth Century Literature* 45 (winter 1999). Reproduced by permission.

The Catcher in the Rye
Excerpts from *The Catcher in the Rye,* by J. D. Salinger. Back Bay Books, 2001. Copyright © 1945, 1946, 1951 by J. D. Salinger. Copyright renewed © 1979 by J. D. Salinger. All rights reserved. Reproduced by permission.

Death of a Salesman
Excerpts from *Death of a Salesman,* by Arthur Miller. The Viking Press, 1949. Copyright © 1949 by Arthur Miller. All rights reserved. Copyright renewed © 1976 by Arthur Miller. Reproduced by permission. Excerpts from Introduction to *Collected Plays,* by Arthur Miller. Viking, 1957. Copyright © 1957 by Arthur Miller. All rights reserved. Copyright renewed © 1985 by Arthur Miller. Reproduced by permission. Excerpts from "The Shadow of the Gods," by Arthur Miller. *Harper's* 217 (August 1958). Copyright © 1958 by Harper & Brothers. Copyright renewed © 1985 by Harper's Magazine Foundation. Excerpts from *Arthur Miller and Company.* Methuen Drama, 1990. Copyright © 1990 by The Arthur Miller Centre for American Studies. All rights reserved. Reproduced by permission. Excerpts from *Christian Science Monitor,* February 14, 1949. Copyright © 1949 by Christian Science Publishing Society. Copyright renewed © 1976 by Christian Science Publishing Society. Reproduced by permission. Excerpts from *New York-World Telegram,* April 28, 1949. Reproduced by permission. Excerpts from "Tragedy and the Common Man" and "On Social Plays," by Arthur Miller. In *The Theater Essays of Arthur Miller.* Edited by Robert A. Martin. Penguin Books, 1978. Copyright © 1978 by Arthur Miller. All rights reserved. Reproduced by permission. Excerpts from "*Salesman* at Fifty," by Arthur Miller. In *Death of a Salesman, Fiftieth Anniversary Edition.*

Viking Penguin, 1999. Copyright © 1999 by Arthur Miller. All rights reserved. Reproduced by permission.

"Howl"
Excerpts from *Howl and Other Poems,* by Allen Ginsberg. City Lights Books, The Pocket Poets Series Number 4, 1956. Copyright © 1956 by Allen Ginsberg. All rights reserved. Reproduced by permission.

Lolita
Excerpts from *The Annotated Lolita,* by Vladimir Nabokov. McGraw-Hill Book Company, 1970. Copyright © 1955 by Vladimir Nabokov, All rights reserved. Copyright renewed © 1970 by McGraw-Hill Inc. Revised edition, Vintage Books, 1991. Reproduced by permission. Excerpts from *Playboy,* 1963. Copyright © 1963 by HMH Publishing Co., Inc. Copyright renewed © 1991 by Playboy Enterprises Inc. Reproduced by permission. Excerpts from unspecified interview. Reprinted in *Strong Opinions.* McGraw-Hill, 1973. Copyright © 1973 McGraw-Hill International, Inc. New edition, Vintage Books, 1990. All rights reserved. Reproduced by permission.

Long Day's Journey into Night
Excerpts from *Long Day's Journey into Night,* by Eugene O'Neill. Yale University Press, 1989 (corrected edition). Copyright © 1989 by Yale University Press. All rights reserved. Reproduced by permission. Excerpts from "Concerning the Boom," by Arthur Miller. In *Echoes Down the Corridor: Collected Essays 1944–2000.* Edited by Steven R. Centola. Viking, 2000. Copyright © 2000 by Arthur Miller. All rights reserved. Reproduced by permission. Excerpts from Walter Kerr, Review of *Long Day's Journey into Night. New York Herald Tribune,* November 8, 1956. Reproduced by permission. Excerpts from "Trying to Write the Family Play," by Jean Chothia. From *The Cambridge Companion to Eugene O'Neill.* Edited by Michael Manheim. Cambridge University Press, 1998. Copyright © 1998 by Cambridge University Press. All rights reserved. Reproduced by permission.

My Ántonia
Excerpts from "The Literary Situation in 1895," by Willa Cather. In *The World and the Parish: Willa Cather's Articles and Reviews, 1893–1902.* Edited by William M. Curtin. University of Nebraska Press, 1970. Copyright © 1970 by University of Nebraska Press. All rights reserved. Reproduced by permission.

On the Road
Excerpts from *On the Road,* by Jack Kerouac. The Viking Press, 1957. Copyright © 1955, 1957 by Jack Kerouac. All

Rabbit, Run

The Red Badge of Courage

A Streetcar Named Desire

The Sun Also Rises

The Waste Land

List of Subjects

Introduction . . . . *xi*

List of Contributors . . . . *xiii*

THE ADVENTURES OF
HUCKLEBERRY FINN
   by Mark Twain 1
Richard Wakefield

BELOVED
   by Toni Morrison 19
Pauls Harijs Toutonghi

THE CATCHER IN THE RYE
   by J. D. Salinger 35
Ted Weesner Jr.

DEATH OF A SALESMAN
   by Arthur Miller 53
Dominic Oliver

"HOWL"
   by Allen Ginsberg 71
Sharon Bryan

LOLITA
   by Vladimir Nabokov 89
Lydia Rainford

LONG DAY'S JOURNEY INTO NIGHT
   by Eugene O'Neill 109
Jason Gray

MAIN STREET
   by Sinclair Lewis 125
Ted Sutton

MY ÁNTONIA
   by Willa Cather 143
Clare Morgan

MY BONDAGE AND MY FREEDOM
   by Frederick Douglass 163
Mark Richardson

ON THE ROAD
   by Jack Kerouac 183
Stephen F. Soitos

THE PORTRAIT OF A LADY
   by Henry James 199
Jonathan Freedman

RABBIT, RUN
   by John Updike 219
Patricia B. Heaman

THE RED BADGE OF COURAGE
   by Stephen Crane 237
Mark Richardson

THE SCARLET LETTER
   by Nathaniel Hawthorne 257
Ellen Weinauer

THE SOULS OF BLACK FOLK
   by W. E. B. Du Bois 281
Mark Richardson

A STREETCAR NAMED DESIRE
   by Tennessee Williams 303
Philip Parry

THE SUN ALSO RISES
   by Ernest Hemingway 321
Stephen Amidon

TALES OF THE GROTESQUE AND
ARABESQUE
    by Edgar Allan Poe................. 339
    Thomas Wright

THE WASTE LAND
    by T. S. Eliot...................... 359
    Jay Parini

Index................................*375*

Introduction

American Writers Classics, Volume I is the first volume in a series that we hope will continue for a long time to come. It represents a further development of American Writers, a series that had its origin in a sequence of monographs called the Minnesota Pamphlets on American Writers. These biographical and critical monographs were incisively written and informative, treating ninety-seven American writers in a format and style that attracted a devoted following. It proved invaluable to a generation of students and teachers, who could depend on the reliable and interesting critiques of major figures that were offered in those pages. The idea of reprinting the Minnesota pamphlets occurred to Charles Scribner Jr. (1921–1995). Soon four volumes, entitled *American Writers: A Collection of Literary Biographies* (1974) appeared, and it was widely acclaimed by students, teachers, and librarians. The series continues, with volumes added yearly as supplements and retrospectives. The articles in these collections all consider the whole career of an important American writer, supplying biographical and cultural context as well as taking careful look at the shape of the individual achievement.

American Writers Classics will provide substantial articles that focus on a single masterwork of American literature, whether it be a novel, a sequence of stories, a play, a long poem or sequence of poems, or a major work of autobiography or nonfiction. The idea behind the series is simple: to provide close readings of landmark works. These readings, written by well-known authors and professors of literature, will in each case examine the text itself, explaining its internal dynamics, and consider the cultural, biographical, and historical dimensions of the work. Some effort will be made to place the work within the author's overall career, though the main focus in each essay will be the chosen text.

In the past twenty-five years or so, since the advent of post-structuralism, the emphasis in most critical writing has been largely theoretical. What was called "close reading" during the days of the so-called New Criticism—a movement that had its origins in formalist criticism of the 1920s and 1930s, and which reigned supreme in university English departments for several decades—was often immensely useful to students and teachers, who wanted careful and detailed analyses of individual texts. Every effort has been made in these essays to provide such useful and patient readings of important works without sacrificing theoretical sophistication.

Our hope is that students and teachers, as well as the general reader, will find these essays both informative and stimulating. Each will introduce a reader to a major text and offer a subtle analysis of its formal properties without ignoring the historical and cultural dimensions of the work. The bibliographies attached to the end of each essay offer a guide to further reading on each work.

This first volume examines *The Adventures of Huckleberry Finn, Beloved, The Catcher in the Rye, Death of a Salesman,* "Howl," *Lolita, Long Day's Journey into Night, Main Street, My Ántonia, My Bondage and My Freedom, On the Road, The Portrait of a Lady, Rabbit, Run, The Red Badge of Courage, The Scarlet Letter, The Souls of Black Folk, A Streetcar Named Desire, The Sun Also Rises, Tales of the Grotesque and Arabesque,* and *The Waste Land.* These are all major texts of the nineteenth and twentieth centuries, ranging across the genres. Not one of them could be called less than a masterwork of literature. They were chosen precisely because of their cultural centrality.

The intent of American Writers Classics is that it will encourage readers to return to the texts of these American classics, thoughtfully, and better informed than they were before. That is, after all, one of the traditional functions of criticism. My own sense is that we have achieved a good deal in this first volume, and that readers will go away pleased and edified.

——JAY PARINI

Contributors

Stephen Amidon. Novelist whose books include *Splitting the Atom, Thirst, The Primitive,* and *The New City.* His criticism has appeared in numerous publications, including the *Atlantic Monthly, Guardian, New York Times Book Review, London Sunday Times,* and *Times Literary Supplement.* THE SUN ALSO RISES

Sharon Bryan. She is the author of several volumes of poetry, most recently *Flying Blind* from Sarabande Books. She is also the coeditor, with William Olsen, of *Planet on the Table: Poets on the Reading Life* and the editor of *Where We Stand: Women Poets on Literary Tradition.* She is currently completing a volume of poems (*Stardust*) and a memoir (*Double Vision: A Life in and Out of Poetry*). She teaches as a visiting writer at universities around the country. "HOWL"

Jonathan Freedman. Author of *Professions of Taste: Henry James, British Aestheticism and Commodity Culture* and *The Temple of Culture: Assimilation, Anti-Semitism and the Making of Anglo-America.* He is professor of English and American Studies at the University of Michigan and has also taught at Yale University, Caltech, and the Bread Loaf School of English. THE PORTRAIT OF A LADY

Jason Gray. A graduate of the Writing Seminars of Johns Hopkins University. His poems and book reviews have appeared in *Poetry, Threepenny Review, Sewanee Theological Review, Literary Imagination, Prairie Schooner,* and others. He has been a Tennessee Williams Scholar at the Sewanee Writers' Conference. LONG DAY'S JOURNEY INTO NIGHT

Patricia B. Heaman. Professor Emerita of English at Wilkes University, Wilkes-Barre, Pennsylvania. She is the author of numerous articles and reviews. Most recently, she has published essays on George Eliot, Elizabeth Gaskell, Flannery O'Connor, Mary Wollstonecraft, Dorothy Richardson, Katherine Mansfield, and others in *Women in World History.* RABBIT, RUN

Clare Morgan. Tutor in English at Oxford University. She has published a novel, short stories, and poems as well as articles on Virginia Woolf, A. S. Byatt, and Welsh writing in English. She is a regular reviewer for the *Times Literary Supplement* and is presently writing a book on poetry and strategy for the Boston Consulting Group. MY ÁNTONIA

Dominic Oliver. Lecturer in English Literature at St. Peter's College, Oxford University. He teaches and writes on British and American Drama from the sixteenth century to the present day, with a dual concentration on Shakespeare's contemporaries and writing from the mid-twentieth century onward. Current projects include an examination of the dramatic representation of treason in early-modern England and a study of Marlowe's *Doctor Faustus.* DEATH OF A SALESMAN

Jay Parini. Poet, novelist, biographer, and the Axinn Professor of English at Middlebury College. His six novels include *The Last Station, Benjamin's Crossing,* and *The Apprentice Lover.* His recent volumes of poetry include *Town Life* and *House of Days.* He has published biographies of John Steinbeck and Robert Frost. The latter won the Chicago Tribune-Heartland Award in 2000. THE WASTE LAND

Philip Parry. Lecturer in Drama at the University of St. Andrews in Scotland, where he specializes in twentieth-century British and American drama. He has published articles on Shakespeare, William Wordsworth, and Tom Stoppard. A STREETCAR NAMED DESIRE

Lydia Rainford. Junior Research Fellow at St. Hugh's College, the University of Oxford. She has published articles on T. S. Eliot, Samuel Beckett, and feminist theory. She is currently coediting a book on literature and cinema, titled *Literature and Visual Technologies.* LOLITA

Mark Richardson. Associate Professor of English, Western Michigan University. He is the author of *The Ordeal of Robert Frost: The Poet and the Poetics* and coeditor (with Richard Poirier) of Robert Frost, *Collected Poems, Prose & Plays.* MY BONDAGE AND MY FREEDOM; THE RED BADGE OF COURAGE; THE SOULS OF BLACK FOLK

Stephen F. Soitos. Author of *Blues Detective: A Study of African American Detective Fiction.* He has published many articles on African American literature and art as well as various aspects of popular culture. He is a landscape painter who lives in Northhampton, Massachusetts. ON THE ROAD

Ted Sutton. Teaches a broad range of subjects to students from third grade to graduate school in the Boston area. He is also an editor and fiction writer. MAIN STREET

Pauls Harijs Toutonghi. Lecturer at Cornell University. He is the author of short fiction, poetry, criticism, and several novels. His work has appeared in a variety of nationwide periodicals, including the *Boston Review, Pittsburgh Quarterly, Glimmer Train,* and *Crab Creek Review.* He was the winner of the *Zoetrope: All-Story* Short Fiction competition and was awarded a 2000 Pushcart Prize. His research

interests include contemporary Latvian literature and hybrid literatures. BELOVED

Richard Wakefield. Teaches American Literature at the Evergreen State College–Tacoma Campus, Tacoma Community College, and the University of Washington-Tacoma. He is the poetry critic for the *Seattle Times.* THE ADVENTURES OF HUCKLEBERRY FINN

Ted Weesner Jr. Lecturer at Tufts University and Emerson College in Boston, Massachusetts. He has also taught in the Czech Republic and at Rutgers University. He is the author of articles, reviews, and essays published in the *Boston Globe,* on National Public Radio, and elsewhere. His fiction has received the PEN/ New England Discovery Award, a St. Botolph's Club grant, and a Somerville/Massachusetts Arts Council grant, and he is currently at work on a novel, titled *The Modern Lovers.* THE CATCHER IN THE RYE

Ellen Weinauer. Associate Professor of English and Director of the Women's Studies Program at the University of Southern Mississippi. She has published articles on a variety of nineteenth-century authors, including Nathaniel Hawthorne, Herman Melville, Elizabeth Stoddard, and William Craft, and is currently at work on two books: an edited collection of essays on Elizabeth Stoddard and a study of the relationship between gothic narrative and debates about property in the antebellum United States. THE SCARLET LETTER

Thomas Wright. Freelance Writer. Editor of the recently published *The Collection,* an anthology of Peter Ackroyd's journalism and miscellaneous writings. He has published a book, *Table Talk Oscar Wilde,* and a number of essays on the 1890s. TALES OF THE GROTESQUE AND ARABESQUE

Mark Twain's
The Adventures of Huckleberry Finn

RICHARD WAKEFIELD

THE CIVIL WAR destroyed the world that was the setting for much of Twain's work, especially his four "Mississippi writings." He believed the South had made the war inevitable by clinging to the institution of slavery and by embracing a Romantic sentimentality. Although the Civil War was a victory over slavery, the situation of blacks in the South was seriously undermined following the presidential election of 1876 and the end of Reconstruction, which had promoted the rights of blacks but was resented by southern whites.

When *The Adventures of Tom Sawyer* was written, in 1874–1875, Twain believed the antebellum South was truly laid to rest. Ten years later, as he worked on *The Adventures of Huckleberry Finn,* the oppression of blacks in the South was worse than ever, and Twain wrote his story—set on the Mississippi River of the late 1840s—with a sense of failed promise that tainted his view of the Old South.

Joel Chandler Harris (1848–1908), the author of the Uncle Remus stories, was another important influence in the writing of *Huckle-* *berry Finn.* Harris, whom Twain met in 1882, reproduced the speech of southern blacks and preserved their folk wisdom. Many writers used regional vernaculars for humor, but Harris recognized the speech of black southerners as the necessary medium for conveying their experience.

The first Uncle Remus story appeared in 1879, after the publication of *Tom Sawyer* and before Twain began *Huckleberry Finn;* the first collection of Uncle Remus stories (*Uncle Remus: His Songs and His Sayings*) appeared in 1881, during Twain's long hiatus from the novel. In letting Huck tell his story in his own words, Twain followed Harris' example and departed radically from his approach to *Tom Sawyer.* Here, from *Tom Sawyer,* is the first description of Huck Finn:

> Presently Tom came upon the juvenile pariah of the village, Huckleberry Finn, son of the town drunkard. Huckleberry was cordially hated and dreaded by all the mothers of the town, because he was idle, and lawless, and vulgar, and bad—and because all their children admired him so, and

delighted in his forbidden society, and wished they dared to be like him.

Compare this with Huck's first words in his own book:

> You don't know about me, without you have read a book by the name of *The Adventures of Tom Sawyer*, but that ain't no matter. That book was made by Mr. Mark Twain, and he told the truth, mainly. There was things which he stretched, but mainly he told the truth. That is nothing. I never seen anybody but lied, one time or another, without it was Aunt Polly, or the widow, or maybe Mary.

The anonymous narrator of *Tom Sawyer* loves gaudy adjectives and adverbs: "juvenile," "cordially," "perennial." His grammar is perfect. In contrast, Huck prefers bare nouns and verbs, and he modifies his thoughts as people do in spontaneous speech, adding clauses that refine his meaning: "without you have read a book," "but that ain't no matter," "mainly," "but mainly he told the truth," "one time or another," "without it was Aunt Polly," "or maybe . . . ." He also commits solecisms: "without" for *unless,* "ain't" for *isn't,* "was" for *were,* "seen" for *saw.*

Jim's speech is even less refined: "Goodness gracious, is dat you, Huck? En you ain' dead—you ain' drownded—you's back agin? It's too good for true, honey, it's good for true. Lemme look at you, chile, lemme feel o' you." The use of "dat" for *that,* "you's" for *you is* (which is in turn dialect for *you are*), and "chile" for *child* were characteristic of southern black dialect, which was often parodied in entertainment for white audiences. Minstrel shows featured white performers in blackface whose dialect jokes and songs promoted the racist stereotypes. The Jim Crow laws, legislated after Reconstruction to reestablish the subjugation of blacks, were named for a character in a minstrel song. In *Huck Finn,* however, Jim's dialect is used for the same reason that Huck's is: to give his character authenticity.

CHRONOLOGY

1835	Samuel Langhorne Clemens, later known as Mark Twain, born in Florida, Missouri.
1837	Father, John Clemens, moves family to Hannibal, Missouri.
1843	Financial difficulties force sale of much of the property in Hannibal.
1851	Samuel begins working as a typesetter for his brother, Orion, who runs a newspaper. Publishes his first article, in Orion's paper.
1855	Samuel moves with Orion to Keokuk, Iowa, to set up a printing shop. Publishes sketches and stories in the Keokuk *Post.*
1856	Samuel works as a typesetter in Cincinnati, continues to write for the *Post.*
1858	Samuel becomes a cub pilot on a river boat, earning his license a year later.
1861	Outbreak of the Civil War curtails steamboat activity on the Mississippi. Samuel joins a group of Confederate volunteers. Soon leaves the group and accompanies Orion to the Nevada Territory, of which Orion has been appointed secretary. Over the next several years travels extensively in California, to Hawaii, and across Central America.
1863	Publishes several letters in a Nevada newspaper under the name Mark Twain.
1867	Gains nationwide fame with *The Celebrated Jumping Frog of Calaveras County and Other Sketches.* Begins career as a lecturer. Travels to Europe and the Holy Land as a correspondent for several newspapers. Meets Olivia Langdon.
1869	Meets William Dean Howells.
1870	In February, marries Olivia.
1871–1874	Travels as a lecturer throughout the United States and Europe.
1874	Begins work on *The Adventures of Tom Sawyer.* Begins publishing articles on his experiences on the Mississippi.

1876	*The Adventures of Tom Sawyer.*
1880	Begins work on *The Adventures of Huckleberry Finn* but makes little progress.
1883	*Life on the Mississippi* published. Resumes work on *The Adventures of Huckleberry Finn.*
1885	*The Adventures of Huckleberry Finn.*
1892	*Pudd'nhead Wilson* published, the fourth and last of his "Mississippi writings."
1904	Olivia dies during a stay in Italy.
1910	Dies at home of heart disease.

The preface to Noah Webster's *American Dictionary of the English Language,* published in 1828, compares American English to the Mississippi River, a powerful medium shaped by the land. In *Huck Finn* the river is a physical, spiritual, and linguistic journey as well, a passage through varieties of speech. In a note titled "Explanatory," Twain anticipated objections to his characters' speech: "In this book a number of dialects are used," he wrote, and he claimed they were re-created "painstakingly." He concluded, "I make this explanation for the reason that without it many readers would suppose that all these characters were trying to talk alike and not succeeding."

Although Twain's Mississippi novels are nostalgic, he took a stance critical of nostalgia, claiming that it was a manifestation of Romanticism, which he felt had contributed to the South's intransigence and thus helped bring about the Civil War. The problem with Romanticism, in Twain's eyes, was that it blinded southerners to reality. Throughout *Huckleberry Finn* he satirizes those whose vision is clouded by false expectations; he believed the South, corrupted by Romantic literature, was blind to the evil of slavery and to the futility of a war to preserve it. His 1895 essay "Fenimore Cooper's Literary Offenses" was written to demonstrate that James Fenimore Cooper, lauded as the "American Sir Walter Scott," was incapable of accurate observation. In *Huckle-berry Finn* he chooses the name Walter Scott for a riverboat that has run aground. The grounded boat symbolizes the ruin that such literature—or the sloppy thinking it encouraged—brought down upon his childhood home.

THE VOYAGE OF HUCK AND JIM

Following the title page of *The Adventures of Huckleberry Finn,* Mark Twain inserted a "Notice" in which he warned that "persons attempting to find a motive in this narrative will be prosecuted; persons attempting to find a moral in it will be banished; persons attempting to find a plot in it will be shot." His warning notwithstanding, Twain's motive is to reveal the ignorance and corruption of the Old South.

The novel begins with Huck Finn introducing himself and explaining his circumstances. In *The Adventures of Tom Sawyer,* Huck and Tom found a stolen treasure that made them rich; invested, it brought them each a dollar a day in interest, at a time when few workers earned four hundred dollars a year. Huck has been informally adopted by the Widow Douglas, who intends to "sivilize" him. Living with the Widow Douglas is Miss Watson. The two women represent, respectively, the gentle and the coercive faces of middle-class life and religiosity. As Huck observes early in chapter 3, the widow's version of "Providence" is attractive; Miss Watson's is oppressive. Their views of heaven are reflections of their earthly lives.

Religion plays an important part in Huck's story. Twain loathed a rationalizing religion that allowed southerners to believe themselves moral while countenancing slavery. In chapter 1 Huck tells readers that Miss Watson equates manners with morality. For Huck, respectability is so burdensome that he would prefer to go to hell, where he would be far from Miss Watson: "Well, I couldn't see no advantage in going where she was going, so I made up my mind I wouldn't try for it." (The scene is comic, but a similar resolution is deadly serious in chapter 31, when Huck cannot bring himself to turn in Jim, the runaway slave, even though the morality of the South says that helping Jim is a sin. Declaring, "All right, then, I'll *go* to hell!" Huck rejects false morality.)

Huck declares his concern with telling the truth, but he is often slow to get at the truth of his own feelings because he has been taught not to trust his own perceptions; the society in which he lives, committed as it is to falsehood, indoctrinates its people into a callous indifference to reality, including the reality of their own hearts. When the widow tells him the story of Moses, for example, Huck is eager to learn what became of the baby set adrift in a basket among the "Bulrushers," as he puts it. After she reveals that "Moses had been dead a considerable long time," he claims he no longer cares "because I don't take no stock in dead people." Yet the next few pages reveal that Huck does indeed take stock in dead people: he imagines he hears ghosts in the sounds of night and that distant lights indicate death watches over the sick. Moreover, throughout most of the novel, as a result of the sham murder that he orchestrates, Huck is believed to be dead; twice he will be mistaken for a ghost. Whenever he has to fabricate a past he includes dead relatives and friends. Floating down the river with so many dead behind him—and, not incidentally, leading a slave to freedom—he is the child Moses set adrift among the "Bulrushers." Yet as long as he is under the direct influence of those he considers more cultivated or knowledgeable, Huck cannot consciously recognize either his parallel with the biblical emancipator or his deep fascination with death.

The second chapter introduces Tom Sawyer, another force for respectability. Huck admires Tom's knowledge of Romance literature, and he goes along with Tom's plan to form a gang of robbers according to the books. Tom challenges one reluctant boy by asking, "Don't you reckon the people that made the books knows what's the correct thing to do?" Huck never doubts it.

When he is away from Tom Sawyer and other voices of civilization, Huck is an empiricist. He tests ideas against facts, and if the facts do not support the idea, he revises the idea, a process of thought entirely beyond the abilities of most other characters in the novel, indeed, of the entire culture. After Tom tells him the story of Aladdin and the magic lamp, for example, Huck finds a lamp and tries the magic for himself, with no satisfactory result: "So then I judged that all that stuff was only just one of Tom Sawyer's lies. I reckoned he believed in the Arabs and the elephants, but as for me I think different. It had all the marks of a Sunday school." "Sunday school"—religion—is another lie. He tests Miss Watson's claims about the efficacy of prayer, for example, by praying for fishhooks; when the effort fails, he concludes that "there ain't nothing in it." Throughout the novel Huck is deceived by others' false views of the world but rediscovers the truth when he escapes the pernicious influence of civilization and tests the view against the facts.

The second chapter also introduces Jim, Miss Watson's slave, who will later be Huck's companion, friend, and surrogate father. At this point, however, Jim is a comic character. Tom and Huck play a trick that makes him believe he has been bewitched, and Jim revels in the fame it brings him among other superstitious blacks. Huck, the empiricist, will need to get to know Jim better—that is, to see the facts about Jim that contradict the racist thinking in which Huck has been raised—before he recognizes his own culpability in playing such jokes.

Huck's moral code is the product of a world that rationalizes slavery, and that values manners more than honest feeling. His heart, however, leads him right—when he can hear it over the mendacious voice of civilization. When he returns to the widow's after a night of playing bandit with Tom Sawyer, he gets "a good going-over . . . from old Miss Watson" and accepts it as the price of his fun. However, the widow looks "so sorry that I thought I would behave a while if I could." To inflict suffering, Huck feels, is truly wrong, and his reluctance to hurt another person will influence him many times in his adventures to come.

After several months at the widow's, during which time he goes to school, where he learns to read and write, he discovers that his father is looking for him—or, rather, for the money he now possesses. When Pap sneaks into Huck's room, Huck applies his empirical method to his own feelings: he had been afraid of his father, who made a habit of beating him, but now he realizes that, aside from being startled, "I warn't scared of him worth bothering about." This seemingly minor moment is an early example of Huck's ability throughout the book to reconsider even his deepest feelings in light of new facts. It is an ability, Twain seems to be saying, that the entire South would have to develop if it were ever to emerge from its cruel past.

Pap berates Huck for wearing clean clothes and sleeping in a bed, and he swears vengeance on those who have elevated him. "I'll learn people to bring up a boy to put on airs over his own father and let on to be better'n what *he* is," Pap says. Paradoxically, although Pap is an outcast, he is also the voice of convention: one must know one's place. Similarly, when Tom Sawyer plays outlaw, he does so in thoroughly conventional ways; even then he embodies the distorted morality of his culture.

In another passage pointing up the South's sentimentality and distorted morality, the widow attempts to gain legal authority over Huck only to have a new judge, who does not know Pap's history, rule that it would be wrong to "take a child away from its father." The judge attempts to reform Pap, and Pap plays the repentant drunk, swearing that he has "started in on a new life, and 'll die before he'll go back." He knows what note will play on the sympathy of his audience. Then, while staying at the judge's house, he sneaks out, gets drunk, and

returns to wreak havoc on his bedroom. Even the most deeply rooted sentimentality, it seems, must sometimes yield to facts: "The judge he felt kind of sore. He said he reckoned a body could reform the ole man with a shot-gun, maybe, but he didn't know any other way." Later, Huck, no sentimentalist to begin with, will come close to doing exactly that.

Pap takes Huck to live in a squalid cabin in the woods across the river. At first Huck wants to escape, but soon he finds that life with his pap, who not only tolerates but encourages his smoking and cursing, is rather pleasant. When Pap's beatings grow intolerable, however, Huck saws a secret escape route, and one day while checking some fishing lines he finds an abandoned canoe and hides it near the cabin.

Meanwhile, in one of his drunken ravings, Pap tells of having seen a black man from Ohio, a college professor who can vote in his home state. Pap speaks as a mouthpiece for his entire culture in his assessment of this phenomenon: "When they told me there was a State in this country where they'd let that nigger vote, I drawed out. I says I'll never vote agin." he accepts, even relishes, the hierarchy that assures him superiority to blacks solely by virtue of his white skin.

Pap drinks until he passes out, then awakens with the hallucination that Huck is the Angel of Death. He takes a knife and chases the boy around the inside of the cabin before once again falling into a stupor. Huck trains a shotgun on him, prepared to kill him if need be, but when Pap awakes the delusion has passed. It is striking that Pap imagines Huck is the Angel of Death, because Huck will soon fake his own death and later will invent more stories about death; he will also witness real death, sometimes brought about through his actions, albeit unintentionally. Huck's obsession with death reflects the sentimentality of his culture, which romanticizes death, but it also, for him, is synonymous with escape.

In chapter 7 Huck makes it appear that thieves have broken in, murdered him, and plundered the cabin. He kills a wild pig and smears its blood and some of his own hair on an ax. The plan is perfect, but Huck feels his lack of sophistication keeps him from adding the "fancy touches" that Tom Sawyer would provide. In the novel's concluding episode, however, Tom Sawyer helps free Jim from a cabin in which he has been imprisoned, and Tom's "fancy touches" not only doom the effort but nearly get Tom himself killed. These episodes contrast Huck's practicality, his attention to facts, with Tom's romanticism.

Huck escapes to Jackson's Island and watches a riverboat firing a canon over the water in search of his remains (the searchers believe the concussion will cause a submerged corpse to surface). The searchers have also set loaves of bread adrift on the water, believing they will seek the corpse, and when one drifts close to Huck he salvages it and eats it. He ponders the possibility that "the widow or the parson or somebody prayed" that the bread would find him, and its having done so shows that "there ain't no doubt but there is something in that thing [prayer]." This, however, contradicts his earlier conclusion that "there ain't nothing" in prayer. Like any good empiricist, he revises his hypothesis in light of new facts, deciding that the "something" works "only for just the right kind [of person]," but not for a person like him. He believes himself to be an outsider not only in society's eyes, but in God's eyes as well.

This belief prepares him for the new relationship into which he is about to enter. On the island he meets Jim, Miss Watson's slave. Jim thinks Huck is a ghost, and his comical fear seems to play on the stereotype of the superstitious black; however, in chapter 33, when Huck and Tom are reunited, Tom reacts the same way. Neither the black man nor the white boy is able to let go of his preconceived notions even in the face of physical evidence to the contrary. The satire is on the superstition that permeated the culture, not on the superstition of any particular race.

Jim makes Huck promise to keep his secret, and then admits that he has run off. Huck is shocked but declares he will stick to his promise. "People would call me a low down Abolitionist and despise me for keeping mum—but that don't make no difference," he says. In his world "Abolitionist" is the worst epithet imaginable. Huck believes that not only society but God himself despises him, yet he follows a code of honor that includes keeping his promises, no matter to whom they are made.

Jim and Huck find a corpse inside a house carried along on the flood. Jim covers the dead man's face and tells Huck not to look. Much later Jim will reveal that the dead man was Huck's father. Here, Jim takes on a father's role, shielding the boy as Huck's real father never did. The reader can ponder which man is the more authentic father, the one who has the legal title through an accident of biology, or the one who enacts the duties and emotional commitments of fatherhood.

Huck disguises himself as a girl and goes to town to try to learn if anyone is looking for either of them. The episode is a contest between two clever souls: Huck, in his makeshift disguise, and a woman who is almost as much an empiricist as he is. The woman, noting flaws in Huck's performance, challenges him. Huck is flustered but does not lose his wits, and he changes his story when the woman inadvertently signals what new lie she will believe: "You see," she says, "you're a runaway 'prentice . . . You've been treated bad, and you made up your mind to cut." Flattering her for her supposed perspicacity, Huck creates a story that appeals even more strongly to her sympathies, telling her that his mother and father are dead. (His mother has been dead since before Huck can remember, but in claiming that his father is dead Huck unwittingly tells the truth.) Even this sharp-eyed woman is susceptible to a sentimental lie.

Huck learns that a group of men have seen the light of a campfire on the island and surmise that Jim, for whom there is a reward, is hiding there; he also learns that Jim is suspected of having murdered him (Huck). Jim and Huck flee downriver on a raft. After several days they come upon the wreck of a riverboat (named the *Walter Scott,* symbolizing the "wreck" of Romanticism), and as they investigate they overhear two thieves planning the murder of an accomplice. This murderous gang contrasts with Tom Sawyer's pretend gang. Like many of Huck's adventures along the river, this experience demolishes a Romantic fantasy.

Huck and Jim steal the gang's boat, leaving them stranded and at risk of drowning as the wreck breaks up. "I begun to think how dreadful it was, even for murderers, to be in such a fix," Huck tells us; "I says to myself, there ain't no telling but I might come to be a murderer myself, yet, and then how would *I* like it?" He contrives a scheme to get a boatman to go rescue them, making up a story about the deaths of several of his own family members in the wreck. No matter what society says about the value of these men's lives, Huck examines his own feelings and finds that he cannot let them die.

A conversation between Jim and Huck marks one of many steps Jim takes toward full humanity in Huck's (and the reader's) eyes. Huck has been reading to Jim about the lives of French royalty, and now has to explain that people in France speak a different language. Jim is baffled. "Dey ain't no sense in it," he says. Huck tries to explain the "sense in it" by asking if cats and cows speak the language and if either can speak as a human being does, and Jim responds by pointing out that different kinds of animals do indeed speak differently but that each animal speaks the same way as all the others of its kind; a man, therefore, should "*talk* like a man," as Jim puts it. Huck says in exasperation, "I see it warn't no use wasting words—you can't learn a nigger to argue." Huck's protest notwithstanding, Jim's point is irrefutable, at least in terms of Huck's original argument. Jim's conclusion squares with the observable facts better than Huck's does: because Jim talks like a man he is

in fact a man, something that Huck cannot yet reconcile with his status as a "nigger."

Chapter 15 marks several turning points. Jim and Huck are drifting down the Mississippi River, deeper into slave territory. Jim's path to freedom lies up the Ohio River, which joins the Mississippi at Cairo, Illinois. However, for Huck to move onto the Ohio, into free territory, would remove him from the environment in which his moral emancipation has to take place, and so Twain was faced with the need to send Huck and Jim deeper into regions to which they had no logical reason to go. This is a turning point because Huck and Jim *do not* turn, but rather allow themselves to drift with the river, in a way not so different from Huck's own moral drifting.

Another turning point is in the composition of the novel: this is the point where Twain set the manuscript aside for more than three years, from the summer of 1876 to late summer or early fall of 1879. These were crucial years, marking the end of Reconstruction and the resurgence of legal racism in the South. When Twain returned to his manuscript, it was with a renewed sense of moral outrage.

The contrivance Twain chose to get Huck and Jim past the mouth of the Ohio River leads to an emotional breakthrough for Huck. Beset with fog, Huck gets into the canoe to try to tie the raft to some trees at the river's edge, but the current tears the raft loose. Hours later, Huck finds the raft, with Jim fast asleep, and decides to play a joke, waking him and telling him that they were never separated and that he (Jim) dreamed the episode. Jim is fooled, and as he recounts his "dream" he embellishes it and interprets it. Up to this point the scene replays the joke that Huck and Tom played on Jim back at the widow's. This time, however, Huck reveals the ruse, and Jim looks straight into Huck's eye (a serious offense for a slave in the Old South), and says, "Trash is what people is dat puts dirt on de head er dey fren's and makes 'em ashamed." Huck has to face the fact that he has hurt someone who considers himself his "fren":

It made me feel so mean I could almost kissed *his* foot to get him to take it back.

It was fifteen minutes before I could work myself up to go and humble myself to a nigger—but I done it, and I warn't ever sorry for it afterwards, neither. I didn't do him no more mean tricks, and I wouldn't done that one if I'd a knowed it would make him feel that way.

As often happens, Twain charges colloquial speech with unexpected power, having Huck say that he had to work himself *up* in order to *humble* himself. Ironically, it is his act of humility that raises him.

Huck's new attitude is soon tested. Continuing down the river, they believe they are approaching Cairo, and every time a settlement appears Jim shouts with joy at the prospect of freedom. Huck's conscience—still corrupted by his racist upbringing—troubles him for stealing Miss Watson's property. To make it worse, Jim says that when he is free he will save money to buy his wife out of slavery and then, if necessary, hire an "Ab'litionist" to steal his children.

Huck takes the canoe, ostensibly to investigate a nearby town but in reality to turn Jim in. As Huck leaves, Jim says, "You's de bes' fren' Jim's ever had; and you's de *only* fren' ole Jim's got now." Suddenly Huck is caught between his conscience and his emotions: He accepts racism in principle, but when he turns his empiricist's eye on his feelings he finds himself torn. On the river he meets two men in a boat who are in search of five escaped slaves and demand to know if the man in the wigwam on the raft is white or black. Huck knows what he should answer but, suddenly facing the prospect of actually betraying Jim, claims the man is white. The slave trackers decide to see for themselves. Huck says, "I wish you would . . . because it's pap that's there, and maybe you'd help me tow the raft to shore where the light is. He's sick—and so is mam and Mary Ann." It is significant that Huck identifies Jim as his father, a role Jim has been gradually taking on, but to the men Huck's story suggests smallpox. Afraid to

approach the raft, they give him forty dollars—a salve for their own consciences—and tell him to move on. Huck feels guilty but also knows he would have regretted betraying Jim. He concludes that the conventional morality provides no useful guidance:

Well, then, says I, what's the use you learning to do right, when it's troublesome to do right and ain't no trouble to do wrong, and the wages is just the same? I was stuck. I couldn't answer that. So I reckoned I wouldn't bother no more about it, but after this always do whichever come handiest at the time.

This is empirical thinking. Huck, like a true pragmatist, asks himself what *works*, what are the consequences of any particular action, rather than what corresponds to received wisdom or conventional morality.

After they learn they have missed the Ohio, as Huck and Jim continue south, they collide with a riverboat and are separated. Huck stumbles ashore into the midst of a feud between two families, the Grangerfords and the Shepherdsons. Huck claims to have fallen off a riverboat, and the Grangerfords take him in. He invents a new identity, telling a story involving a sister who "run off and got married and never was heard of no more" and several brothers who died. The episode will conclude with an elopement, between a Grangerford girl and a Shepherdson boy, that leads to renewed bloodshed. Huck's story about elopement and death turns out to be more a prophecy than a lie. It is as if he has so completely absorbed the foibles of southern thinking that even his fabrications accurately predict the course of events.

This section satirizes the middle class, but in ways that further the novel's themes. Huck describes the Grangerford house, emphasizing (even while being unaware of) its garishness and artificiality; Huck also notices that by his standards they are wealthy, with a big house and plentiful food. Implicit in this is that their moral depravity, dramatized by the feud, is not the product of any material deprivation. Rather, their feud and their bad taste are of a piece. The killing goes on because of a false sense of honor, bred into them by a corrupt culture; in the same way, their house is a monument to bad taste because of a false sense of elegance, bred into them by a shallow, superficial culture that values appearance over substance. A similar weakness is evident in Miss Watson's moral code, which allowed her to own other human beings but that also required that she teach her human chattel to pray, not so much acknowledging their souls as putting on a show of piety, equating manners for morals.

The parallel between the Shepherdsons' feud and their bad taste is made more explicit by the character of Emmeline Grangerford. The girl died long before Huck's arrival, but her bedroom, decorated with her morbid crayon drawings, is preserved as a shrine. Also preserved is her morbid poetry. Buck, a Grangerford boy who becomes Huck's surrogate brother, tells him that Emmeline "could write about anything you choose to give her to write about, just so it was sadful." The commonality between bad taste and the blind pursuit of the feud is sentimentality: heightened, unthinking, socially instilled feeling in place of authentic emotion.

Huck unwittingly serves as a go-between for the eloping couple. When the feud flares up as a result of the elopement, several Grangerfords die, including Buck, and Huck pulls their bodies from where they have fallen into the river, then covers their faces: "I cried a little when I was covering up Buck's face, for he was mighty good to me." Huck's sorrow is genuine, unlike the sentimentality that animated Emmeline Grangerford's drawings and poems, and also unlike the habitual hatred that perpetuates the feud.

Huck has learned from a Grangerford slave that Jim is hiding nearby with the raft. Huck joins him and they set off down the river again: "We said there warn't no home like a raft, after all. Other places do seem so cramped up and smothery, but a raft don't. You feel mighty free and easy and comfortable on a raft." "Home" is an important word here; "free" is crucial: on the raft Jim is free, and Huck is free as well, free of the corrupting influence of civilization.

Their freedom is curtailed by the arrival of two con men who take up residence on the raft as if it were their birthright. One, perhaps thirty years old, claims to be the Duke of Bridgewater. The other, about seventy, claims to be "the pore disappeared Dauphin, Looy the Seventeen, son of Looy the Sixteen and Marry Antonette," therefore the rightful king of France. The con men exploit the gullibility of southern culture when they hire a hall and put on a "Shaksperean Revival!!!" that consists of garbled excerpts from *Hamlet* and *Romeo and Juliet*. When it fails to draw an audience, they change it to "The Royal Nonesuch," with advertising that warns "Ladies and Children Not Admitted"; the duke says, "There . . . if that line don't fetch them, I don't know Arkansaw!" The duke knows that scandal always sells, especially in a world where true moral values are suppressed.

In another scene, recalling Pap's sentimental conversion, the king participates in a revival meeting, claiming to be a reformed pirate and taking up a collection ostensibly to convert his former fellow pirates. Like Pap's hollow pieties, the king's transparent fakery persuades people who will believe any lies that make them feel good.

Huck, unlike supposedly more sophisticated people, recognizes the phonies from the beginning. He plays along, however, because "it's the best way; then you don't have no quarrels, and don't get into no trouble." Huck, though, seems to suspect that they are not harmless: "If I never learnt nothing else out of pap, I learnt that the best way to get along with his kind of people is to let them have their own way." His ability to see through phoniness empowers him to recognize the king and the duke as "his [Pap's] kind of people," that is, as scoundrels who can be as destructive as they need to be to get what they want.

While Jim hides on the raft, Huck goes with the king and the duke and sees another degraded face of southern life. In the little town where they will stage their "Shaksperean Revival" he witnesses the shooting of a man named Boggs, an obstreperous but harmless drunk, by a haughty gentleman named Colonel Sherburn. Boggs has vowed revenge against Sherburn for some imagined slight and has verbally abused him, but everyone knows that Boggs is harmless. Yet Sherburn avenges his own injured pride by shooting the unarmed man. Like the Grangerfords and the Shepherdsons, Sherburn is willing to kill to preserve his pride, no matter how insubstantial the slight.

The town's people declare that Sherburn should be lynched, and Huck runs with the crowd to Sherburn's house. Sherburn confronts them and makes a speech that indicts all of southern culture:

> You didn't want to come. The average man don't like trouble and danger. *You* don't like trouble and danger. But if only *half* a man—like Buck Harkness, there—shouts "Lynch him, lynch him!" you're afraid to back down—afraid you'll be found out to be what you are—*cowards*—and so you raise a yell, and hang yourselves onto that half-a-man's coat tail, and come raging up here, swearing what big things you're going to do. The pitifulest thing out is a mob; that's what an army is—a mob; they don't fight with courage that's born in them, but with courage that's borrowed from their mass, and from their officers.

Like the Grangerfords, with their ersatz elegance and their sentimentality, these people are motivated by what they fear others will think, not by their own authentic feelings; even apparent bravery is motivated by fear of appearing weak. It is ironic that Sherburn, who has committed murder to preserve his pride, should be the mouthpiece for such an accurate assessment.

From the interrupted lynching Huck goes to a circus, as if from one spectacle to another. This one, however, is benign—an equestrian per-formance that displays skill and showmanship. It is based upon deception, but a kind of honest deception: a performer disguised as a drunken audience member mounts a horse and, after some clumsy pratfalls, shows himself to be a magnificent rider. The audience (including Huck) is delighted by the deception; it has no note of cruelty or exploitation.

From the circus, the narrative moves to the show that the king and the duke are planning. The elegance of the circus is a foil for the tawdry Shakespeare performance and, later, "The Royal Nonesuch," in which "the king come a-prancing out on all fours, naked; and he was painted all over, ring-streaked-and-striped, all sorts of colors, as splendid as a rainbow." The audience is amused until they learn that these few minutes of low farce are all their admission buys them. Unlike the circus, which delivered value for their admission fee, this show amounts to theft.

Yet the king and the duke are able to pull off the deception twice more over the ensuing days. The duke knows that pride will keep their victims from revealing to their neighbors that they have been cheated; he knows, in fact, that they will recommend the show and that there will be larger audiences each night. He also knows how far he can carry the fraud, for on the night of the final performance, when the audience comes armed with rotten vegetables, the king, the duke, and Huck flee. The audience that is cheated seems here no more admirable than those who cheat them.

One morning Huck wakes to find that Jim has let him sleep rather than wake him to stand his watch, and now Jim has dozed off and is "moaning and mourning to himself." Huck says, "I knowed what it was about. He was thinking about his wife and his children, away up yonder, and he was low and homesick." Despite his affection for Jim, Huck has not cast off the influence of the slave culture; he cannot yet reconcile what he has been taught to believe and what his senses tell him: "I do believe he cared just as much for his people as white folks does for their'n. It don't seem natural, but I reckon it's so." Jim tells Huck about a time when his four-year-old daughter, who had recently recovered from "sk'yarlet-fever," ignored his command to shut the cabin door. In his anger Jim struck her, only to find that the fever had left her deaf. He remembers crying, "Oh, de po' little thing! de Lord God amighty fogive po' ole Jim, kaze he never gwyne to fogive hisself as long's he live!" Jim contrasts with Huck's pap, who showed no regret for far worse abuse. Huck recognizes Jim's qualities, albeit still in racist terms: "He was a mighty good nigger, Jim was."

The larcenous but essentially harmless antics of the king and the duke take a sinister turn (as Huck's recognition of them as his pap's "kind of people" had predicted) when an unsuspecting young man tells them about a family of orphaned sisters who are awaiting the arrival of their deceased father's two brothers. The con men learn the details of the family and of the two brothers, from England, and then pose as the uncles, with Huck as their servant. This episode satirizes human gullibility, as the imposters put on a show that only the most credulous could believe. However, Huck realizes they are doing grievous harm to the orphaned girls. The king and the duke plan to liquidate all the family's assets and abscond with the money. They even sell off the slaves, breaking up families in the process.

Only one man, a doctor, presumably trained in close observation and therefore akin to Huck, despite their vastly different social levels, sees through the ruse. He warns the young women and the other townsfolk, but their emotions overrule their senses. The dismissal of the doctor's warning is another example of indifference to palpable facts. When the duke expresses concern that the doctor will somehow foil their plan, the king responds, "Cuss the doctor! What do we k'yer for *him*? Hain't we got all the fools in town on our side? and ain't that a big enough majority in any town?"

Hoping to find a way to return a bag of inherited money to the girls without implicating himself, Huck steals it from the king and duke, but as he creeps through the parlor where the dead man lies on display he is nearly caught and has to hide it inside the coffin. When the con men discover it is missing, Huck plays along in confirmation of their suspicions that the house slaves have taken it, a lie they are prepared to believe because of their prejudices, just as the people of the town have been prepared to believe the lies of the king and the duke. The duke has said, "Do you reckon a nigger can run across money and not borrow some of it?" attributing his own criminality to the entire black race. Like Huck's pap, the king and the duke project their own moral defects onto blacks.

Soon Huck's sympathy goads him to act. He overhears Mary Jane, with whom he has become infatuated, crying over the breaking up of the slave family. Although Huck saw the auction, his earlier insight that Jim "cared just as much for his people as white folks does for their'n" was limited to *Jim*—it did not extend to black people in general. His view is still distorted by his indoctrination in southern prejudice. It is his concern for Mary Jane that drives him to intervene, not any empathy with the plight of the slaves.

"Oh, dear, dear," Mary Jane cries, "to think they ain't *ever* going to see each other any more!" Huck, knowing the sale will be invalidated when the con is exposed, says, "But they *will*—and inside of two weeks—and I *know* it!" Then, startled by his own spasm of honesty, he thinks, "Laws it was out before I could think!" He gets at the truth, ironically, by *not* thinking, for thinking draws him into the mendacity of his surroundings. Confused, he has to ask Mary Jane (who naturally wants to know *how* he knows) to be quiet:

> I says to myself, I reckon a body that ups and tells the truth when he is in a tight place is taking considerable many resks, though I ain't had no experience, and can't say for certain; but it looks so to me, anyway; and yet here's a case where I'm blest if it don't look to me like the truth is better, and actually *safer*, than a lie. I must lay it by in my

mind, and think it over some time or other, it's so kind of strange and unregular. I never see nothing like it. Well, I says to myself at last, I'm agoing to chance it; I'll up and tell the truth this time, though it does seem most like setting down on a keg of powder and touching it off just to see where you'll go.

This passage complements the novel's opening lines, in which Huck talks about the difficulty of being honest. The earlier passage was part rationalization, part acknowledgement of human fallibility; this one, using the same pattern of modifiers ("though," "but," "anyway," "and yet"), voices Huck's realization that there are truths that must be acknowledged but that are incendiary. For Twain, the long-suppressed truth about slavery was "a keg of powder" that exploded into the Civil War.

Huck makes Mary Jane promise to leave town for a few hours, until he can engineer the apprehension of the king and the duke and make his own escape. He tells her she must leave because, once she knows the facts, she will be unable to dissemble: "I don't want no better book than what your face is. A body can set down and read it off like coarse print." It takes someone incapable of lying to provoke Huck to tell the truth. Without going into detail, he even acknowledges Jim, telling her that if the plot is revealed immediately "there'd be another person that you don't know about who'd be in big trouble."

It turns out that Huck need only wait. The unmistakably real brothers arrive, but the townspeople, too vain to admit their error, cling to their sentimental illusion. One of the real brothers, however, claims that the deceased man had a distinctive tattoo, and it is decided that the body will be exhumed to check. The tattoo is at last a fact that cannot be shirked. Not only are the king and the duke revealed as frauds, but the gold is found as well—and in the confusion (abetted by a lightning storm) Huck escapes back to the raft, where Jim has been waiting.

The king and the duke catch up with them, having also escaped. Huck, quick as ever with a plausible lie, convinces them that he knew nothing about the gold and that he and Jim were heartbroken to think that the king and the duke had been caught. Like Pap, the con men turn to alcohol "for comfort," and Huck knows he is safe as long as they are drunk.

In the next town Huck escapes when the king and the duke quarrel with one another, but back at the raft he finds that Jim is gone. "I set up a shout—and then another—and then another one; and run this way and that in the woods, whooping and screeching; but it warn't no use— old Jim was gone. Then I set down and cried; I couldn't help it." Huck has seen murder, brutality, and robbery, but losing Jim plunges him into his deepest distress to this point in the story. Although he may not be ready to acknowledge it, his actions here reveal the depth of his feeling for Jim.

He is even more upset to learn that the king and the duke have turned Jim in as a runaway, having printed up a false handbill that offers a two hundred dollar reward and then selling out their interest in the reward for, as Huck puts it, "forty dirty dollars." Now Huck has a crisis. He knows Jim would be better off being returned to Miss Watson than being sold "down the river," where conditions are worse, and he considers writing to Tom Sawyer to ask him to tell Miss Watson where Jim is. Yet he fears that Miss Watson, angry at Jim for running away, would sell him down the river anyway, and that even if she did not sell him Jim's life would be miserable because (as Huck puts it, voicing the racism of his environment) "everybody naturally despises an ungrateful nigger." In addition, like so many of the people he has encountered, Huck is fearful of what others will think: "It would get all around, that Huck Finn had helped a nigger to get his freedom; and if I ever was to see anybody from that town again, I'd be ready to get down and lick his boots for shame":

And at last, when it hit me all of a sudden that this here was the plain hand of Providence slapping me in the face and letting me know my wickedness was being watched all the time from up there in heaven, whilst I was stealing a poor old woman's nigger that hadn't ever done me no harm, and now was showing me there's One that's always on the lookout, and ain't agoing to allow no such miserable doings to go only just so fur and no further, I most dropped in my tracks I was so scared.

The Christianity of the Old South rationalized slavery as a moral institution; Huck accepts his own guilt. This passage is his recitation of received truth, not an expression of his own heart, so the turns ("though," "but," "anyway," "and yet") that characterize his speech when he gropes his way toward deeply felt truth are missing. He is so sure of what he should believe, in fact, that he constructs a subordinate clause of more than eighty words ("when it hit me . . . and no further") that leads seamlessly to his main clause ("I most dropped in my tracks")—none of his usual verbal uncertainty. Yet even here a misplaced modifier suggests more than he realizes: "that hadn't ever done me no harm." Superficially, he means that Miss Watson had never done him any harm, but his syntax betrays him, making *Jim* the person "what hadn't ever done me no harm."

He resolves to pray for forgiveness but finds that he cannot because he has not truly given up his "sin": "Away inside of me I was holding on to the biggest one of all"—his intention to free Jim. Believing he must confess before he can repent, he composes a note to Miss Watson, telling her where Jim is. "I felt good and all washed clean of sin for the first time I ever felt so in my life," Huck says. But before praying he thinks about how Jim and he have talked, sung, and laughed together, how Jim stood Huck's watch for him, and how Jim told Huck he was his best and only friend. Huck finds, "I couldn't seem to strike no places to harden me against him, but only the other kind." He has turned from the generalities of racism, which he accepts, to the specifics of this man for whom he cares deeply; he is caught between corrupt principles and the undeniable facts of his own experience. He must decide "forever, betwixt two things," that is,

between good and evil. He does not realize that his code of good and evil is inverted.

Huck tears up the note, saying, "All right, then, I'll *go* to hell." He decides he will not only rescue Jim but will also do anything worse that he can think of: "As long as I was in, and in for good, I might as well go the whole hog." Huck's colloquial speech again reveals more than he realizes. Superficially meaning only *permanently,* the phrase "in for good" is literally true, though he does not know that.

The concluding episode, which takes up almost a quarter of the novel, follows Huck's effort to free Jim from where he is imprisoned on the farm of a man named Silas Phelps. This part of the story involves unlikely coincidences and implausible farce. The theme, though, is consistent with what has already occurred: Huck has begun to see through the falsehood around him, but he is still easily influenced by the conventional mendacity of those he considers his betters—especially Tom Sawyer.

At the beginning of chapter 33, Huck reaches the Phelps farm, and he returns to his preoccupation with death. The place is quiet, and Huck describes it first as "Sunday-like" and then as

> lonesome and like everybody's dead and gone; and if a breeze fans along and quivers the leaves, it makes you feel mournful, because you feel like it's spirits whispering—spirits that's been dead ever so many years—and you always think they're talking about *you.* As a general thing it makes a body wish *he* was dead, too, and done with it all.

These impressions echo those of the first chapter, when Huck was alone in his room, but they add a note of desperation in the phrase "and done with it all," suggesting that Huck views death as an escape from the cruelty and falsehood around him. Earlier, Huck's preoccupation with death foreshadowed his own feigned death and figurative rebirth as a later-day Moses leading Jim to freedom. Here, it signals the death of the freedom he had on the river, and a rebirth into an unexpected identity.

With no plan, and despite having accepted his own damnation, he trusts "to Providence to put the right words in my mouth when the time come; for I'd noticed that Providence always did put the right words in my mouth, if I left it alone." He believes himself alienated from God, but at another level he is confident in God's guidance because, after all, he has come this far. His received principles tell him he is an outcast from God's grace, but his experience has demonstrated otherwise.

To Huck's surprise, a woman greets him as if he is expected and introduces him to her children as their cousin Tom. Huck, with no idea who she thinks he is, plays along, picking up information as they talk and supplementing it with guesses. He knows how a boy of this time and place would speak: when he claims that the boat on which he was supposedly a passenger blew out a cylinder head, Aunt Sally (as she has instructed him to call her) asks if anyone was injured; Huck replies, "No'm. Killed a nigger." She concludes, "It's lucky; because sometimes people do get hurt," as if the death of a black person does not rise to the level of anyone's being "hurt."

Silas Phelps, the woman's husband, returns from town. Aunt Sally introduces Huck to him as Tom Sawyer, whom Mr. Phelps had gone to pick up. The Phelpses, Huck learns, are Tom Sawyer's aunt and uncle, and they have been awaiting Tom, whom they have not seen recently enough to recognize. Huck states, "It was like being born again, I was so glad to find out who I was."

Huck contrives an excuse to borrow the buckboard to go to town alone, and he intercepts Tom. Just as Jim did when they met on Jackson's Island, Tom takes Huck for a ghost: "I hain't ever done you no harm. You know that. So then, what you want to come back and ha'nt *me* for?" After convincing Tom that he is not a ghost, Huck confesses that he intends to free Jim, expecting that Tom will be repulsed by such a

"dirty low-down business," but Tom, after beginning to say something about Jim and then stopping himself midsentence, instead offers to help. Huck is dumbfounded: "It was the most astonishing speech I ever heard—and I'm bound to say Tom Sawyer fell, considerable, in my estimation. Only I couldn't believe it. Tom Sawyer a *nigger stealer!*" Tom's vow to help, which should raise him in Huck's "estimation," will turn out to be selfishly motivated: he had begun to say that Miss Watson is dead and that her will frees Jim, but keeps it a secret so that he could enjoy the "adventure" of an elaborate escape. The boys will work together, but with very different motives, much as the abolitionist movement brought together activists with widely divergent attitudes toward black people.

Huck returns in far too little time to have made the round trip, but he exploits the gullibility characteristic of Twain's southerners. Uncle Silas is persuaded that his little horse indeed ran fast enough to make the trip, Huck tells readers, because "he warn't only just a farmer, he was a preacher, too." Religion, Twain implies, predisposes these people to accept even patent absurdities, slavery not least among them. It is also easy for the boys to convince the Phelpses that Tom is actually Sid, Tom's brother.

The king and the duke make a final appearance. Huck hears that they are playing their "Royal Nonesuch" scam nearby and that the locals have been alerted. Despite the misery the two fakes have caused him and Jim, Huck wants to warn them, but he is too late, and he sees them tarred and feathered. The sight sickens Huck: "I couldn't ever feel any hardness against them any more in the world . . . It was a dreadful thing to see. Human beings *can* be awful cruel to one another." He felt the same pity for the murderers drowned in the wreck. Huck's native empathy extends even to those the rest of society condemns; in fact, he feels guilty for failing to help them. He is beginning to understand that the demands of his heart cannot be reconciled with the prevailing moral code, here called "conscience": "It don't make no difference whether you do right or wrong, a person's conscience ain't got no sense, and just goes for him *anyway*. If I had a yaller dog that didn't know no more than a person's conscience does, I would pison him." He does not recognize his empathy as a virtue, does not realize that his ability to see human beings *as* human beings, no matter their color or social status, elevates him above those who delight in inflicting misery on those they consider their inferiors. He is, however, learning to place intuition above tuition.

The boys learn that Jim is imprisoned in a shed. Huck proposes that they steal the key to the shed, release Jim, and "shove off down the river on the raft, with Jim, hiding day-times and running nights, the way me and Jim used to do before." Huck, having planned more than one successful escape, including his own from Pap's cabin, should be the authority in this situation. He is practical. But practicality, as already seen many times, counts for nothing in Twain's South.

In Tom's sophisticated view, Huck's plan is embarrassingly simple. Tom invents an elaborate, absurd plan that draws on his knowledge of romance novels. Huck concedes that "I see in a minute it was worth fifteen of mine, for style, and would make Jim just as free a man as mine would, and maybe get us all killed besides. So I was satisfied, and said we would waltz in on it." Huck cannot resist the force of authority, no matter how specious, even though he now recognizes Jim as "a man."

They will pretend that Jim is an imprisoned nobleman who must dig his way out of a dungeon. To add danger, Tom writes anonymous letters telling the Phelpses that something is afoot. Despite a group of volunteer farmers standing guard, Tom and Huck get Jim to the raft, but Tom is shot in the leg. The plan unravels, but not before Huck's inability to hurt another person again gets the better of him. Aunt Sally believes that "Sid" is lost after trying to prevent Jim's escape, although he is in reality ly-ing wounded on the raft while a local doctor ministers to him; Huck, back at the farm, has told Tom he will sneak out that night and rejoin him, but Aunt Sally is distraught and makes him promise that he will not sneak out anymore. Huck recounts, "Laws knows I *wanted* to go, bad enough, to see about Tom, and was all intending to go; but after that, I wouldn't a went, not for kingdoms." This passage mirrors his tenderness toward the Widow Douglas early in the book. Even when it would be in his own best interest to do something that would cause sorrow to another person, he cannot do it—once again, he displays innate virtue that sets him apart from numerous other characters in the novel.

Tom is brought back by the doctor and the group of men who have found them and have recaptured Jim. Some of them want to hang Jim "for an example to all the other niggers around there," but they are dissuaded when someone points out that his owner would make them pay for him. Huck observes, "The people that's always the most anxious for to hang a nigger that hain't done just right, is always the very ones that ain't the most anxious to pay for him when they've got their satisfaction out of him." Mercy for a black man is motivated by economics, not humanity.

The doctor (like the other doctor, who saw through the masquerade of the king and the duke) is capable of seeing beyond the simplistic divisions of race—to a point. He explains that Jim risked his freedom to help Tom: "I liked the nigger for that; I tell you, gentlemen, a nigger like that is worth a thousand dollars—and kind treatment, too." Again, the Old South measures a black man's worth only in dollars, whereas those who would lynch him are, because they are white, "gentlemen."

Tom's Aunt Polly arrives, and Tom reveals what he has known all along: Jim is free. Jim reveals that Huck is also free, in a sense, because the dead man they saw in the derelict house was Huck's pap. Huck need not fear his father's greed and cruelty, just as Jim—at least in principle—need not fear the greed and cruelty of a master.

After their adventure, Tom wants to pursue "howling adventures amongst the Injuns, over in the Territory"—Oklahoma, still Indian Territory. Huck resolves to set out ahead of Tom "because Aunt Sally she's going to adopt me and sivilize me and I can't stand it. I been there before." He knows that savagery is preferable to a civilization based on lies.

INFLUENCE AND CONTROVERSY

The Adventures of Huckleberry Finn is familiar to almost any literate American. Even those who have not read it know the story through countless film, television, and even comic book versions. Moreover, the novel's influence has been so great that any familiarity with American literature from 1885 onward confers an awareness of *Huck Finn;* indeed, Ernest Hemingway claimed that all subsequent American literature grows out of this novel. Many characters in subsequent American fiction bore a resemblance to Huck, with Holden Caulfield, the protagonist of J. D. Salinger's *The Catcher in the Rye,* perhaps the most familiar.

Huck's innocent but discerning heart is both attractive and threatening. Even his anarchic way of speaking is endearing but also an affront to genteel society. The book has always been controversial and often banned, originally because Huck was seen as a bad influence: He smokes, swears, makes fun of pious grownups, and flouts the rules of grammar. Huck's rebellion against slavery is also a rebellion against hypocrisy. Slavery is the proximate problem, but the greater problem is the social tissue of lies that repress honesty, spontaneity, and love.

Since the mid-twentieth century, objections to the book have focused on the use of the word "nigger" (which appears more than two hundred times) and on the portrayal of Jim and other black characters. The novel is widely assigned in high schools and colleges, and many students and parents object that the language degrades students of color. The counterargument is that without the word that was ubiquitous in the antebellum South, the story cannot be told honestly. Any other term would amount to a misrepresentation much like the falsehoods that Huck confronts.

One of the most intense attacks, by John H. Wallace, holds that the use of the word "nigger" violates the Fourteenth Amendment (the Equal Protection Amendment), and that Jim is portrayed as dishonest and stupid. Jane Smiley compares the book unfavorably to Harriet Beecher Stowe's 1852 best-seller *Uncle Tom's Cabin,* claiming that Stowe's picture of slavery is more authentic. The book's ability to stir such controversy, even after more than a century, is the clearest sign of its continuing influence.

Select Bibliography

EDITION

Mississippi Writings: The Adventures of Tom Sawyer, Life on the Mississippi, Adventures of Huckleberry Finn, Pudd'nhead Wilson. New York: Library of America, 1982. (This edition is cited in this essay.)

OTHER WORKS BY TWAIN

Collected Tales, Sketches, Speeches, and Essays. Edited by Louis J. Budd. New York: Library of America, 1992.

The Oxford Mark Twain. 29 vols. Edited by Shelley Fisher Fishkin. New York: Oxford University Press, 1997.

SECONDARY WORKS

Budd, Louis J., ed. *New Essays on "Adventures of Huckleberry Finn."* New York: Cambridge University Press, 1985.

Davis, Thadious M., ed. *Black Writers on "Adventures of Huckleberry Finn": A Hundred Years Later. Mark Twain Journal* 22, no. 2 (fall 1984). (Special edition.)

Emerson, Everett H. *The Authentic Mark Twain: A Literary Biography of Samuel L. Clemens.* Philadelphia: University of Pennsylvania Press, 1984.

Fishkin, Shelley Fisher. *Was Huck Black? Mark Twain and African-American Voices.* New York: Oxford University Press, 1993.

Hoffman, Andrew Jay. *Twain's Heroes, Twain's Worlds: Mark Twain's "Adventures of Huckleberry Finn," "A Connecticut Yankee in King Arthur's Court," and "Pudd'nhead Wilson."* Philadelphia: University of Pennsylvania Press, 1988.

Inge, M. Thomas, ed. *Huck Finn among the Critics: A Centennial Selection.* Frederick, Md.: University Publications of America, 1985.

Kaplan, Justin. *Mr. Clemens and Mark Twain: A Biography.* New York: Simon & Schuster, 1966.

Simpson, Claude M., ed. *Twentieth Century Interpretations of "Adventures of Huckleberry Finn": A Collection of Critical Essays.* Englewood Cliffs, N.J.: Prentice-Hall, 1968.

Smith, Henry Nash. *Mark Twain: The Development of a Writer.* Cambridge, Mass.: Harvard University Press, 1962.

Toni Morrison's
Beloved

PAULS HARIJS TOUTONGHI

BY THE END of the 1990s, Toni Morrison was one of the world's most celebrated authors. Her work had been translated into numerous languages worldwide, and she was venerated and sought after in the academic world as a lecturer and professor. The territory that Morrison delineates in her fiction is a dramatic, far-reaching space, one that includes a broad range of characters, fictional techniques, and settings. She works to illuminate violent history and to provide a voice for the otherwise voiceless. Many of her characters are strong-willed African American women who struggle within cultural traditions of gender inequality, negotiating the intricacies of environments that seek to deny them any sense of their own identity.

The text of *Beloved* moves between two dates, 1855 and 1873, before and after the Civil War era. The part of the novel that occurs around the first date—1855—concentrates on detailing the privations of slavery in its most vile, legally sanctioned form. The Fugitive Slave Act of 1850 had legalized the capture and return of slaves who had escaped to freedom in the North, and the landmark proslavery decision of 1857, *Dred Scott v. Sanford,* had given judicial endorsement to the view that slaves remained their owner's property regardless of whether they were on free soil. The section of the book that takes place in this era brims over with brutal images, a hallmark of Morrison's writing. The chapters set twenty years later also have brutality—yet this brutality becomes internalized, as the site of slavery's legacy has moved from the external to the space of individual memory.

Morrison's broader fiction is characterized by its relationship with intricate narrative structures, and *Beloved* is among the most intricate of her books. *Beloved* is also a work of anticipation, as Morrison reworks the traditional components of a suspenseful gothic plot. The heroine has been recast and altered, and her tormentor is now her own memory, but the claustrophobic environment is quintessentially gothic—the house in which much of the action occurs is haunted—and indeed the gothic flavors nearly every scene. The narrative, however, moves solidly on contemporary footing. It is unexpected and self-questioning, and it moves from internal monologue to a third-person omniscient perspective to a punctuation-freedrift.

Critical response to Morrison's work has been remarkably laudatory: only after the publication of her 2001 novel, *Paradise,* did critics begin to react negatively to her fiction. Yet her earlier books have solidly established her reputation, and her nonfiction—in the form of essays and edited volumes—leaves behind a legacy of academic dedication to the ideals of the liberal arts. As a professor, Morrison has been engaged in a lifelong relationship with teaching. She has held seminars and taught courses at several universities, and she has spoken at countless colleges in America and abroad. As an editor with Random House for nearly sixteen years, Morrison nurtured the careers of many writers, and as a critic, she has penned reviews of a variety of works in the genres of fiction and nonfiction.

Morrison was born to working-class parents in 1931 in Lorain, Ohio. Her father toiled as a welder at the American Shipbuilding Company on the shores of Lake Michigan. Her mother worked in the home. By all accounts, her father was a hard- working, diligent man, who held three jobs simultaneously in order to support his family.

BEGINNINGS

The plot of *Beloved* evolves in a nonlinear, branching way. The setting moves between several moments in time, leaping between what can be termed as "past" and "present." The "present" is located on the outskirts of Cincinnati, Ohio, in 1873, where Sethe, a former slave, lives with her daughter Denver. The "past" occurs approximately eighteen years earlier, in the plantations of eastern Kentucky, the plantations from which Sethe escapes, fleeing slavery and bringing her four children with her.

"124 was spiteful. Full of a baby's venom," the novel begins, and it becomes evident that 124 Bluestone—the house in which Sethe and her daughter Denver live—will animate the text,

CHRONOLOGY

1931	Toni Morrison (Chloe Anthony Wofford) born on February 18 to working-class parents in Lorain, Ohio.
1949	Graduates from Lorain High School with honors.
1953	Graduates from Howard University with a degree in English.
1955	Receives her master's degree in English from Cornell University.
1957	Returns to Howard University to join the faculty in English.
1958	Marries Harold Morrison.
1964	Divorces Harold Morrison.
1967	The book publisher Random House hires Morrison as an editor in its textbook division in Syracuse, New York.
1970	Moves to Random House in New York City, where she becomes a senior editor. *The Bluest Eye,* Morrison's first novel, is published.
1971	The State University of New York at Purchase makes Morrison an associate professor of English.
1973	*Sula* (novel).
1976	Becomes a visiting lecturer at Yale University.
1977	*Song of Solomon* (novel). It wins the National Book Critics Circle Award.
1981	*Tar Baby* (novel).
1983	Morrison leaves her editorial job at Random House.
1984	SUNY Albany names Morrison the Albert Schweitzer Professor of the Humanities.
1986	*Dreaming Emmett* (play) premieres.
1987	*Beloved* (novel). Princeton University names Morrison the Robert F. Goheen Professor in the Humanities.
1988	Wins the Pulitzer Prize in fiction for *Beloved.*
1992	*Jazz* (novel). *Playing in the Dark: Whiteness and the Literary Imagination* (nonfiction).

1993	Becomes the first African American woman to win the Nobel Prize in literature.
1998	A film version of *Beloved* appears in theaters.
1999	Becomes a visiting professor at Cornell University.
2001	*Paradise* (novel).

give it much of its energy. The house serves as the locus for much of the book's action. It is in this house that Baby Suggs, Sethe's mother-in-law, dies. It is also this house that will chase away Sethe's two sons, Howard and Buglar. One will flee when a mirror cracks as he looks into it, and the other when two small handprints appear, ghostly apparitions, in his birthday cake. The house will envelop and animate all of the characters; it will serve as the battleground for their conflicts; it will be the site in which *Beloved*'s complex psychological subwork unfolds, deepens, and seeks resolution.

The story of *Beloved* commences with the appearance of Paul D, a man who lived and labored in slavery with Sethe and whose brothers, all five of them, were murdered by their slaveholders. Sethe was the wife of Paul D's brother Halle, and Paul D has come to Cincinnati to find her, to tell her of his brother's death. Upon Paul D's arrival, he and Sethe begin an unlikely love affair. His closeness to Sethe initiates a rivalry between Paul D and Beloved—the ghost of Sethe's other daughter, who has, until this point in the text, been satisfied with her life in spectral form, haunting the house at 124 Bluestone.

Upon Paul D's arrival, Beloved takes physical form and appears in a tangible body, walking toward the house, appearing to be a traveler in need of shelter and medical care. Beloved's physical manifestation can be read as her attempt to assert dominion over her mother, to achieve an amount of importance and primacy in her mother's life that—because she died in infancy—she could never attain. Paul D's ap-

pearance threatens Beloved's grasp on her mother, a grasp that she has maintained by filling 124 with her spirit.

Throughout the book, Beloved occupies various guises. At first, she moves unseen through the house, creaking boards and knocking pictures from walls. These are archetypal behaviors for ghosts, who frequently perpetrate minor acts of violence in fiction, drawing attention, though noise, to themselves and their entrapped condition. In this suspended state, Beloved can be said to "feel" as if she has a certain amount of control over her mother. Sethe does not have any friends or acquaintances, and people avoid her house because they know that it is haunted. Eventually, however, threatened by Paul D's appearance in Sethe's life, threatened by the love and support that he seems willing to give to her, Beloved takes the form of a young woman. "A fully dressed woman walked out of the water," Morrison writes. The text implies that Beloved has endured a process very similar to the process of birth, and she behaves in a way that suggests a newly birthed baby taking the form of an adult, the form of a woman who has lived roughly the same number of years that have elapsed from the time of her death as an infant to 1873. "Everything hurt but her lungs most of all. Sopping wet and breathing shallow she spent those hours trying to negotiate the weight of her eyelids." She walks from the river and into the lives of the book's central characters.

The reader gradually realizes, with the unfolding of the plot in 1855, that Beloved is the ghost of a murdered child, and that Sethe is the one who killed her, in a windowless shed, with a hand saw. This act of violence is the center of the book; it is the axis around which the plot revolves. Sethe's motivations in the act of murder are clear: Soon after she has escaped the violence-steeped environment of slavery and fled to freedom, her former owner appears, wanting to reclaim her and her four children as his lost property, recoverable under the Fugitive Slave Act of 1850. Sethe sees the slave catcher coming, and she bolts to the woodshed in back of the house. Once there, Sethe tries to kill her children, rather than see them captured and forced into a life of slavery. Though all the children are wounded, only one dies. Confronted by the carnage, her former owner decides that he does not wish to claim her, after all, and Baby Suggs is left to tend to Sethe and try to restore her remaining three children to health. They bury the murdered daughter in a small grave, marking her tombstone with the single word "Beloved."

By guiding Paul D to knowledge of this event, Beloved attempts to undermine his relationship with Sethe, to convince him that Sethe is an unstable woman, unworthy of his love. Though he first denies to himself that Sethe could have committed the murder, she eventually admits it to him, and he leaves her, going to sleep in the basement of a local church. In Paul D's absence, the now-corporeal ghost develops a parasitic relationship with Sethe. Denver, Sethe's daughter, becomes concerned for her mother's well being: "Denver thought she understood the connection between her mother and Beloved: Sethe was trying to make up for the handsaw; Beloved was making her pay for it. But there would never be an end to that, and seeing her mother diminished and shamed infuriated her."

Denver leaves 124 for the first time in twelve years and seeks help from a local teacher, Lady Jones. Together with thirty local women, Lady Jones marches on 124, hoping to rid Sethe and her family of the ghost. Their arrival coincides with the arrival of Edward Bodwin, a Cincinnati abolitionist, who has come to take Denver to her new job, a paid position in his household staff. When Sethe sights Bodwin, in her confused state she perceives him as her former owner and remembers the day when he came to reclaim her, the day on which she murdered Beloved. This time, however, she chooses to rush at Bodwin with an ice pick, and she is barely restrained by

the gathered crowd. In the confusion, Beloved disappears, never to be seen again.

From this base, *Beloved* expands into an intricate, fictional consideration of the place of violence within the broader story of the American cultural past. Although trauma lies immediately beneath the surface of the text, the story line itself functions as a palimpsest—as a somewhat transparent membrane that hovers above a series of difficult, and unspoken, social questions. The collective remembrance of slavery, the effects of slavery on the individual psyche, and the description of the specific violent acts committed by slaveholders against men and women of African descent all play a key role in any reading of *Beloved*, and they lead to more specific questions: How has Sethe's will been shattered by violence? What role does memory play in the commemoration, remembrance, or even the survival of a traumatic act?

The novel's ample sense of history includes a basis in an actual event—the January 27, 1856, murder of two-year-old Mary Garner, the daughter of Margaret and Robert Garner. This husband and wife fled from their imprisonment in slavery in Kentucky to what they hoped would be freedom in Cincinnati, Ohio. Instead, they were tracked and surrounded by U.S. marshals at the home of their cousin, and when the marshals broke into the home, Margaret cut her daughter's throat with a butcher knife. *Beloved* can thus be read in part as an attempt to use fiction to fill the interstitial spaces of history, or, as Dana Heller writes in *College Literature*, as a record of "the larger struggle between the white-dominant culture's interpretation of black history and the interpretations that blacks have pieced together from their own wealth of family stories and experiences."

Besides this documentary importance, however, *Beloved* also boils with other large questions: What kind of anguish, the reader must ask, could motivate a mother to kill her own daughter? Are the lingering effects of slavery part of American cultural memory, if such a thing can be said to exist? And what is the broader role of fiction, in its relationship to actual events, especially ones laced with trauma, violence, or the dehumanization of the individual?

MEMORY AND THE SPLINTERING OF TIME

Although it is a convention she began to use in her earliest fiction, Morrison's use of flashback in *Beloved* is not a static, or standard, employment of the device. The portion of the plot that occurs circa 1855 does not stand separate from the events of 1873, serving as a psychological precursor to the relationship between Paul D and Sethe. Rather, the events of the 1855 plot interact in a dynamic way with the events of the later plot. Together, the two filaments create an energetic and variegated circuit, in which the past works to fertilize the present, and the present communes with the past. This sort of organic formulation exemplifies Morrison's singular ability as a technical innovator and a groundbreaker in the nature of the novelistic form.

As the critical figure in the book is the ghost, Beloved, her appearance merits more consideration. Though her appearance is directly tied to time—she takes on the shape of the woman she would be, had she survived Sethe's attack—she is also directly tied to space and the ways in which the idea of space can be understood as malleable or porous. In fact, because of the way that Beloved's appearance brings the orderly progression of both time and space into question, the book as a whole can be interpreted as an early example of hypertext, a computerized format which allows readers to move throughout a work at will by choosing from "links" in the text. What the reader considers as "present" actually develops an active and fertile relationship with what the reader considers "past." Dramatic tension arcs between the two, as the plot unfolds in two times. The reader struggles with the desire to return to previously read text and consider it within the light of new developments that occur later in the book. Converted to electronic form, the narrative of *Beloved* would translate as a quintessential e-text, in the way the novel seemingly abandons any conventional dependence on "centre, margin, hierarchy and linearity and replace[s] them with [ideas] of multilinearity, nodes, links and networks," to borrow a definition from George Landow. The network of time and place that supports *Beloved* is highly unconventional and decentered.

This decentering process begins with the appearance of the ghost, Beloved, who emerges from the river in her clothes. (The trope of water is called into play here: water as the source of birth, water as the source of cleansing.) Morrison describes the specific details of the ghost's material being with some degree of attention. Her neck, Morrison writes, is "no wider than a parlor-service saucer," and she has "new skin, lineless and smooth, including the knuckles of her hands." The matter of having lineless skin—aside from its obvious allusion to an impossibility, to the impossibility of aging without deteriorating physically—will serve later as a marker for identifying Beloved as a ghost, as a spectral being with destructive intentions. But in her nature as a ghost, she stands outside of time and serves as a device for the unification of past and present.

With the intrusion of Beloved into their lives, Denver, Sethe, and Paul D can never be said to truly occupy the present moment. The presence of the ghost breaks down temporality and allows time simply to engulf all the characters of *Beloved,* making it impossible for them to achieve any sense of meaningful or pleasurable living. Consumed by this broken time, they are isolated from their lives in the present and can never feel truly in possession of themselves, of their lives, of their space.

This sense of alienation even from themselves is a marker, of course, of many characters in modern and postmodern fiction. In modern fiction, the alienation from the self can be said to cause a sense of extreme dislocation and even despair. In postmodern fiction, the alienation from the self is not a source of despair, as the self is so buried that there can be no memory of its existence. By these guidelines, *Beloved* is not a postmodern text. The loss of self and the realization that the self has been lost are the twin brutalities of *Beloved*. The novel could best be described as straddling the line between modern and postmodern: it is modern in its sense of character development, in its sense of alienation and brutalized despair, but postmodern in its form and in the breaking, splintering sense of its structure.

In her well-received article published in the *Arizona Quarterly* in 1998, Robin Blyn states that:

> If the distinguishing features of what is known as "high modernism" or "utopian modernism" are its preoccupation with the theme of temporality and its faith in the restorative powers of human memory, then the problem of imagining narrative fiction within the context of postmodern thought is a difficult task indeed. What is narrative, if not a representation of time?

Throughout this significant piece, Blyn stresses both the problems and benefits of Morrison's approach to matters of form. Because any consideration of time, as well as the way the past intrudes into the present—as Morrison undertakes in *Beloved*—must inevitably dwell on the matter of memory. The reconstruction of memory is a crucial element within the course of the novel. This reconstruction is a painful process. It also cannot be a linear process; any book that considers memory as its main theme must inevitably take the detours and often-painful diversions to which the process is prone.

When Sethe makes her escape from slavery, she has been whipped and raped, denigrated and debased and abused. She encounters a young woman named Amy in the wilderness, and she receives the first aid she will have in her quest for freedom. Amy massages Sethe's feet, which have been pummeled by their travels. Sethe complains when pain ripples through her legs as the girl's hands knead her tired muscles, but Amy rebukes her: "Anything dead coming back to life hurts," she says. This statement echoes through the rest of the book and illuminates the importance of pain, the relationship of pain to the traumatic event. If the novel's characters are to be reborn into any sort of new life, they must suffer through the pain of this regeneration.

Within her form, the ghost Beloved is the embodiment, literally, of memory. She also splits the narrative of the present with the cudgel of the past. What, exactly, Beloved *is*, matters less than what she *represents*, how she threatens to intrude upon and destroy the lives of the inhabitants of 124 Bluestone. When Paul D first arrives, he is immediately enveloped in the tension caused by the ghost—which has not yet taken on material form but which nonetheless creates turmoil (represented as light) and haunts the house in which Sethe is living:

> Paul D tied his shoes together, hung them over his shoulder and followed her through the door straight into a pool of red and undulating light that locked him where he stood.
>
> "You got company?" he whispered, frowning.
>
> "Off and on," said Sethe.
>
> "Good God." He backed out the door and onto the porch. "What kind of evil you got in here?"
>
> "It's not evil, just sad. Come on. Just step through."

The instruction that Sethe gives to Paul D—"just step through"—alludes to both a physical and emotional necessity. He must move through the tangible disturbance of the red light, but he must also move through the intangible memory of hardship that is his constant companion. That this movement will be Paul D's goal, however, does not become evident until much later.

Paul D's movement forward, his movement through, must take the form, however unintentionally, of Beloved's destruction. This destruction will not be simple. Beloved must not be exorcised, effaced from the surface of the novel's action, eliminated. As the scholar Cynthia Dobbs has explained, "As a body who stalls, even reverses history, Beloved must be destroyed. But as a body who marks an unacknowledged past—both her own murder and the collective horrors of the Middle Passage—Beloved must first be re-membered." Indeed, Beloved is the embodiment of splintered time; she can *only* be remembered, not seen, as she is incorporeal and not of the present moment. She can be possessed by Sethe; she can fulfill the role of a daughter. But, ultimately, Beloved will isolate and consume Sethe, and this danger cannot be supported within the narrative—even if the narrative strives for some measure of postmodern identity. When the other characters of the novel go about "destroying" Beloved, they must realize that her destruction means that the "rememory" of slavery's troubles—the remembrance and visceral reliving and commemoration of slavery's violence—will also partially be destroyed. Although the characters may not make this choice consciously, it haunts their actions and wearies their minds.

THE NEO–SLAVE NARRATIVE

Critics have argued that if a narrative, in essence, is a representation of time, the postmodern fictive form does not have room for straightforward narrative. But Morrison here is using components of the postmodern form and shaping them to her advantage. The degree to which this narrative borrows from various genres and broad "types" of fiction only becomes evident toward the end of the book when Morrison employs a variety of literary techniques, some of which are quite conventionally emblematic of varying literary styles.

As a fictional creation, *Beloved* moves from a historical fact—Margaret Garner's murder of her child in 1856—and extrapolates outward in order to delineate a larger history. The scholar

Henry Louis Gates Jr. has argued that editors and book publishers have historically altered slave narratives to give them a more predictable arc and to bring the freed slaves safely into the fold of Western, European culture; the novel *Beloved* stands directly in contrast with such Eurocentric interpretations of the experience of slavery. Morrison's novel is in essence a fictional slave narrative, but unlike the books that were published as the true accounts of former slaves throughout the nineteenth and twentieth centuries, this is a narrative that must be pieced together from fragments. As characters remember and retell the events of the past, an uncompromising picture of a violent history only slowly comes into view.

Moreover, as Teresa Heffernan points out in her 1998 study of the novel, "In classic slave narratives, the argument is often made, the slave moves from object to subject through the act of narration. Yet significantly, Sethe never 'writes' her story and the affirmation of herself as subject at the end of the novel is qualified by question marks." The novel *Beloved* is a written form in which the goal, at least partially, is the empowerment of Sethe. It is an attempt to give her story a voice, an expression, even if, in the novel's imagined sense of history, it has had none. Yet, as Heffernan notes, Sethe does not at any point make an effort toward self-expression. At her death, her story remains essentially untold. Furthermore, the mechanisms of learning—white-run schools, traditional education, even books—are treated with disdain and disregard in *Beloved*. Morrison even chooses to make her most violent white character, her most heinous and repugnant slaveholder, a schoolteacher. Schoolteacher is never seen teaching school; in fact, he is never seen teaching anything except hate and disrespect. The implication seems to be that even ostensibly beneficial social institutions such as education or literary instruction are void of meaning in a culture that has embraced "the evil institution" of slavery, and that the story of the slaves themselves can only be told from outside of traditional institutions.

In *Beloved* Morrison achieves a revolutionary way to bear witness to slavery, by telling a story that offers many of the traditional components of a slave narrative but also subverts those components, gives them a gothic twist, and presents them again in a new form that abandons sequential presentation and requires the reader to sift through the traumatic and fragmented repetition that is necessary to yield an authentic account of the experience of slavery.

THE LEGACY OF TRAUMA

Within the scope of its moral panorama, *Beloved* encompasses most of the human components of the traumatic act: the amoral transgressor, the innocent victim, the bystander who refuses involvement in the entire process. The enforcers and regulators of slavery are numerous. Morrison provides the reader with a panoply of white slave owners or bounty hunters, all of whom view slaves as subhuman and as property. The extension of this belief into violent action, actually, serves as the underlying theme of *Beloved*'s "past" narrative. Whereas the present of the book struggles with the ways in which black Americans are trying to recover and reconstruct their lives in the wake of the Civil War, the past of the book struggles with another set of questions: What were the parameters of slavery's moral void? What were the specifics of its genocide? What kinds of actions did those who enforced slavery undertake? What are the depths of human brutality?

In the culmination of the novel's "past" plot, Morrison tells the story of the attempted escape of the Garner slaves, an episode that epitomizes the slave owners' belief in the inhumanity of the men and women that they own. The escape attempt is mostly unsuccessful. A white mob—inhabitants of the Kentucky town in which the Garner plantation is located—hunts down four fleeing brothers. They kill one of them invisibly; the murder does not take place within the purview of the narrative. But they capture two

others, Paul D and the gentle, otherworldly Sixo, and because Sixo acts in a defiant manner, they try to roast him alive in a fire as punishment for his rebellion. Sixo is the epitome of the massacred innocent, the martyr who dies for nothing other than the color of his skin. Even the fire rebels at the notion of consuming the innocent man—it smokes and fizzles and refuses to take: "The fire keeps failing and the whitemen are put out with themselves at not being prepared for this emergency. . . . What they can manage is only enough for cooking hominy. Dry faggots are scarce and the grass is slick with dew."

The word "whitemen" identifies the race and gender of the members of this mob, men who themselves are willing to exclude and kill based on race and gender. Morrison uses an aloof and mocking tone to isolate the whitemen and detail their callous, merciless treatment of the black slaves they have captured. That they regard Sixo, because he is black, as something to be roasted, not as a human being, becomes clearly evident through terms such as "put out" and even "emergency," ironic language that displays the contempt that the whitemen have for Sixo's life. Both the action and the language of interior monologue in this pivotal scene reveal that the men are not emotionally involved in their crimes; indeed that they do not even regard their actions as criminal.

Sixo's language, by contrast, is literally song and laughter—but this "vocabulary" gets him killed. The long, rebellious melody he sings while he is being captured and bound convinces Sixo's owner, referred to only as "schoolteacher," that Sixo will never be "suitable" for slavery. The very fact that his mind remains autonomous—able to conceive of itself as a singing entity—means that he is not sufficiently debased for Schoolteacher's type of slavery. He will not allow himself to be dominated:

Sixo turns and grabs the mouth of the nearest pointing rifle. He begins to sing. Two others shove Paul D and tie him to a tree. . . . Sixo swings and cracks the ribs of one, but with bound hands cannot get the weapon in position to use it in any other way. All the whitemen have to do is wait. For his song, perhaps, to end?

Sixo's impossible song, sung at impossible odds and the only self-actualization that Sixo can possibly hope for, is perhaps a way of looking at the novel's statement on trauma and the results of slavery. Sixo's song has importance only to himself, and, in the mirror of fiction, it becomes strangely important for each individual reader, in the closed world of the artistic exchange. The reader, newly exposed to Sixo's song, actualizes the text by reading it, by giving the self fully over to the hearing of the song. Furthermore, the song occupies a border space; its full nature is somewhat inaccessible; it cannot fully be realized by any critic or critical reading. The essence of it lies somewhere else, perhaps beneath historical accounts, beneath the page, beyond the standard mechanisms of fiction. The passage continues: "Smoky, stubborn fire. They shoot him to shut him up. Have to." Having finished his song, Sixo dies laughing. "What a laugh. So rippling and full of glee that it put out the fire." His lover is pregnant and has escaped to the north. Thus, his self will live on, in some form, and he has triumphed over mortality.

In the escape scene, Paul D's life is spared because he chooses not to sing. He clings to living even at the cost of slavery, but from this point forward he will feel that he has made a poor compromise. Paul D is shocked and disgusted by hearing the exact price, nine hundred dollars, that Schoolteacher says his body will garner on the open market. Schoolteacher, fearing the way that Paul D has been "spoiled," sells him to a man named Brandywine after leading him away from the site of his capture with a bit in his mouth.

After he tries to kill Brandywine ("He didn't know exactly what prompted him to try"), Paul D is sent to Alfred, Georgia, a penal colony of sorts. In a chain gang with forty-five other men, he is forced to work the feldspar, laboring with a sledgehammer until his hands bleed and his legs

threaten to give out. The rest of the time Paul D and the other men live in five-by-five-foot wooden boxes set in a deep dirt trench. The men begin their days with symbolic violence—"All forty-six awoke to a rifle shot. All forty-six. Three whitemen walked along the trench unlocking the doors one by one"—and then are subject to nauseating debasement, as when the white captors force their starving prisoners to give them oral sex by offering nothing but their semen as "breakfast."

Eventually, as the ditch where they are caged collapses in the midst of a rainstorm, the forty-six men manage to escape by swimming through the mud to get out from under the cages, pulling each other along by the chain that connects their shackled legs. This scene is one of the most dramatic in the whole of literature and contains the essence of desperation, of the desperate struggle of an oppressed people to obtain freedom:

> One by one, from Hi Man back on down the line, they dove. Down through the mud under the bars, blind, groping. Some had sense enough to wrap their heads in their shirts, cover their faces with rags, put on their shoes. Others just plunged, simply ducked down and pushed out, fighting up, reaching for air. Some lost direction and their neighbors, feeling the confused pull of the chain, snatched them around. For one lost, all lost.

This labor through the thick, enveloping mud is one of the numerous moments in the novel in which the trope of birth comes into play. The moment at which Paul D and the other forty-five slaves surge from this mud is the moment at which they are delivered into freedom, the moment at which their rebirth occurs. Their escape becomes secure, however, only after a group of Cherokee Indians helps free them from their shackles and gives them a place to recuperate before each of the men departs to start a new life.

The narrative of Paul D's escape and his travels until he meets again with Sethe comes in glimpses; it is spread through the whole of

Beloved and does not emerge chronologically. As an entirety it would be a riveting but ultimately quite short section of the book. However, because it is spread out over nearly two hundred pages, its physical breadth adds to its dramatic stature. Within the broader text of *Beloved*, this pattern occurs repeatedly. Whenever a character seems to be reaching toward self-definition, toward a sense of stable identity, toward progress within their lives, their progress is corrupted. The violence, like the ghost, haunts the text:

> It was some time before he could put Alfred, Georgia, Sixo, schoolteacher, Halle, his brothers, Sethe, Mister, the taste of iron, the sight of butter, the smell of hickory, notebook paper, one by one, into the tobacco tin lodged in his chest. By the time he got to 124 nothing in this world could pry it open.

The process that Paul D must undergo—the difficult struggle he must endure—simply to forget is, of course, the direct opposite of the process that is occurring on the part of the reader. The characters of the novel—Sethe, Denver, Beloved—mainly struggle to remember. That Paul D is trying, by contrast, to *forget* serves further to mark his struggle and isolate his character.

The image of the tobacco tin will resurface at other points within the text. Paul D will refer to his heart as "rusted" and abused, signifying that he feels as if he is unable to function in the way that a compassionate individual should. This, then, is the legacy of trauma. He must deny his memory, close it up in a part of his psyche that he perceives as free from the wanderings of conscious thought. The memories of his trauma are so horrifying that he cannot even conceive of returning to them, revisiting them, giving in to the demands of "rememory." The "tobacco tin" is also an enigmatic item to choose as an object of personal significance for Paul D; because it has no readily approachable meanings it is a tremendously fertile image, giving rise to numerous interpretations.

The final sentence of the paragraph that establishes the image of Paul D's "tobacco tin" also contains a significant pun: this section is followed by a section concerning Paul D's relationship with the women of 124 Bluestone, and especially his complicated and convoluted relationship with Beloved—and Beloved, of course, is not "of this world." Morrison seems to be implying that Beloved, not Sethe, will pry open the lid of Paul D's tobacco tin of a heart. How will Paul D heal? The tobacco tin does open. Its opening is significant: it means that Paul D is now willing to accept the awful burden of remembering his hardships and sorrows. Within a few pages, he dreams of Beloved, who comes to his room and demands that he sleep with her and call her by her name, by the word "Beloved." He complies, and then:

> he didn't hear the whisper that the flakes of rust made either as they fell away from the seams of his tobacco tin. So when the lid gave he didn't know it. What he knew was that . . . he was saying, "Red heart. Red heart," over and over again. Softly and then so loud it woke Denver, then Paul D himself. "Red heart. Red heart. Red heart."

Although Paul D can only open his "tobacco tin" heart for Beloved, and not Sethe, his response to the women of 124 Bluestone points to the question of trauma and forgetting that is at stake in the novel, of the loss of individual identity that occurs when identity is confronted by the violent past, whether this past is memories of abuse (as for Paul D) or memories of infanticide (as it is with Sethe). Sethe must forget the memory of Beloved's death. Paul D must forget the memory of his imprisonment. Beloved is the bridge between them. As a ghost, she has the same temporal and physical status as a memory. Yet in the course of this particular text, she has a particularly important role. As Katy Ryan writes, "Sethe allows herself to be consumed by Beloved, unwilling to be an accomplice (again) in her death. Both [Sethe and Paul D] have faced death, personally and through another, and their refusal to forget constitutes revolutionary suicide. They risk safety and life, knowing the alternative means an intolerable existence." Sethe and Paul D, then, will both achieve a "red heart," a self that is vital and full of the benefits of remembering. "Red heart" is here synonymous with mental and emotional health. Paul D awakes saying these two words because he palpably longs for stability, for the certainty that his memories will be reliable, that the specter of the suffering that he has endured will not threaten to arise—in an image—at any moment.

The novel *Beloved* has invited numerous lucid accounts of the ways in which trauma and memory—in which Beloved and Sethe, Sethe and Paul D, Paul D and Beloved—intersect. In the present, the past can surface as a ghost. It lingers as a private trauma, yes, but the past can also be a collective suffering, such as the legacy of slavery, which causes societal unrest and demands remembrance and commemoration.

BELOVED AND BELOVED

Although Sixo's death and Paul D's imprisonment precede Sethe's infanticide in a strictly chronological view of the narrative of *Beloved*, Sethe's murder of her child can be considered as the inaugural brutality of the novel because of its primacy with regard to the book's central personality. Also, *Beloved*, as a book, delves deeply into the psyche of the ghost, Beloved. This is a privilege that the reader is not afforded with Paul D. The revelations about his thought processes come in the form of images and actions; the reader does not witness the interior, free-form workings of his mind. With Beloved, however, Morrison provides several pages of her interior monologue.

Using a style reminiscent of certain passages from James Joyce's *Ulysses*, Morrison eschews traditional punctuation in the relation of Beloved's thoughts, choosing instead to use breaks in the text as punctuation of a sort. She also chooses to avoid contractions, using formal verb constructions throughout the chapter.

I am falling like the rain is I watch him eat inside I am crouching to keep from falling with the rain I am going to be in pieces he hurts where I sleep he puts his finger there I drop the food and break into pieces she took my face away . . .

The perspective moves from Beloved to Sethe throughout this chapter, but that fluidity is precisely what serves to illustrate the importance of the ghost to Sethe, the way in which the mother's personality becomes invaded, displaced, consumed.

Finally, when Beloved does disappear again, it is into absence. There is no violence, no eradication of her presence through a brutal act. Instead, the fact that she has vanished is indicated by the presence of the whimsically named dog, Here Boy, who had refused to come near the house when the ghost was present. "Here Boy, feeble and shedding his coat in patches, is asleep by the pump, so Paul D knows Beloved is truly gone. Disappeared, some say." Beloved's soft leaving is a dramatic contrast against the struggles of the preceding chapters. The ultimate resolution of this part of the plot offers some amount of peace, but it is a peace that is elusive and somewhat compromised by the conclusion of the entire novel.

WOUNDS AND WORDS

The ghost, Beloved, does not leave behind a valence of brutality. But throughout the text of the novel, *Beloved*, the brutal image serves two primary purposes. In the "present" plot, the brutal image appears chiefly as a memory, and in this remembered form it interposes itself upon the present moment. The effects of brutality are very real. When Paul D wishes to tell Sethe about the suffering that he has endured at the hands of his various owners and tormentors, he cannot do it. He is silenced: "Paul D had only begun, what he was telling her was only the beginning when her fingers on his knee, soft and reassuring, stopped him. Just as well. Just as well. Saying more might push them both to a place they couldn't come back from." It would seem that the physical touch, the physical re-assurance, of Sethe's hand would steady Paul D, allow him to betray more of his brutal past. The effect, however, is quite the opposite.

Standing in front of Sethe, Paul D cannot begin to vocalize his despair at the way that he was brutalized. The fact that he cannot vocalize this illuminates what it is perhaps the novel's central paradox—that it seeks to express inexpressible things, inexpressible images of violence, inexpressible emotions, through text. An expressive medium, writing fails somewhat when confronted with nearly unimaginable brutality. Writing can only begin to imply these two elements—the memory of the brutal image and the relation of the story of brutality—and place them before the reader in a loose constella-tion. As Nancy Jesser illustrates:

> The master narrative which threatens to cast you in the role of property, or victim, or prisoner can be disrupted by other competing narratives—nar-ratives of escape, of clearing, of generosity. . . . But the stories must be shared and joined, or they become dangerous, self-exhausting, domestic soliloquies in which there are no realizations, no connections, no movement toward a better home.

The stories are not joined. They remain separate, and they cannot connect, be realized, or move in a positive way. They are isolated. In this way, the structure of brutality and physical violence can be said to mirror the trope of the ghost. The ghost, Beloved, causes anomie and alienation in the novel's principal characters; memories of violence endured have the same impact. Paul D is isolated from the opportunity to make a profound connection with Sethe, simply because he cannot make the emotional expenditure that this would entail.

Of all the traumatic images within this traumatic book, none is more potent than that of Sethe's whipped back. The whipping comes in the past of the book, immediately before Sethe's escape. Schoolteacher has whipped her despite the fact that she is pregnant, and the

wounds have become infected. When Amy, the "whitegirl" who finds Sethe in the wilderness, unfastens the back of Sethe's dress and sees the festering, unhealed wounds on her back, the talkative girl is rendered uncharacteristically speechless:

> Sethe guessed it must be bad because after that call to Jesus Amy didn't speak for a while. . . . "It's a tree, Lu. A chokecherry tree. See, here's the trunk—it's red and split wide open, full of sap, and this here's the parting for the branches. You got a mighty lot of branches. . . . Tiny little cherry blos-soms, just as white. . . ."

The chokecherry is—as is evident by its name—a tree with sour and poisonous fruit. This is a tree of the American south, occasionally referred to as "black chokecherry" because of the dark color of its offerings. Despite the allusive nature of this example from the natural world, the chief power of the image comes from the language that Morrison selects. It is the body, and not the intellect, which speaks the most powerful wit-ness to the brutality of slavery. Sethe's wounds have a complete disclosure—in their image—that she and Paul D cannot achieve through their words.

THE ELOQUENCE OF IMAGES AND THE OTHER

Morrison, then, achieves an eloquence with words that words would not have if left to the standard devices of contemporary fiction. She takes an exceedingly traditional language—the traditional language of written literature—and alters it to make it more powerful. Like writers such as Richard Wright and Hubert Selby Jr., who have explored the nature of violence in an urban setting, in situations that are charged by the voltage of racial tension, Morrison is a master of the brutal image. Among American writers who have catalogued the grotesque, and the ways in which images can overwhelm the individual, Flannery O'Connor and William

Faulkner can also be seen as antecedents—both stylistically and with regard to subject matter—for Morrison.

Morrison's achievements in *Beloved* break from traditional forms and genres that would hope to contain the novel. As Cynthia Hamilton writes in the *Journal of American Studies*:

> The "master formula" for the gothic—with its plot which features the threat of physical, spiritual or psychological violation; its settings of claustrophobic isolation; its twin themes of the burden of past guilt and the power of irrational forces, whether preternatural or psychological; and its configuration of characters arranged to explore unequal power dynamics and the psychology of "otherness"—is easily tailored to suit Morrison's needs.

"Otherness" animates much of the text of *Beloved*. The characters are displaced, rootless, homeless in the present; they are rejected by traditional society, based on either their race or on their past history of violence. Within the standard form of the gothic novel, the characters are stock figures. And, much like the ghost, Beloved, who they are matters less than what they represent. But although *Beloved* begins from this foundation, Morrison's work with dramatically new language and stylistic innovation makes her character evolve into an unexpected—an intriguingly fresh—possibility. The burden of the past, in all of its guilt-based, reverberating memory, becomes something to be reinvented, reconsidered, revealed in a language of significance and weight.

The final chapter of *Beloved,* though it is not labeled as an epilogue, takes on many of the tonal and formal aspects of that form. This chapter has the tone of summation, with lengthier paragraphs written in a sort of millennial grandeur: "Everybody knew what she was called, but nobody anywhere knew her name. Disremembered and unaccounted for, she cannot be lost because no one is looking for her." The chief difficulty of Beloved's sorrow, Morrison asserts for one last time, is that the memory of her life and her suffering is too much to bear. In this way, she slips through the grate of memory, disappears into the unremembered, the shapeless and nameless. Included along with these longer paragraphs are several, repetitive one-sentence exclamations—warnings of a sort—that form a backbone for the text. The visual aspect of this section is important:

> It was not a story to pass on.
> . . . .
> It was not a story to pass on.
> . . . .
> This is not a story to pass on . . .

Morrison has created a story that, by its very nature, will be passed on, moving from reader to reader, from hand to hand. Yet she chooses to include a warning in the text, a warning that—if the standard processes of reading and writing fulfill themselves—will be a useless paragraph. Even at the level of the author's most straightforward communication with her public, the text issues an impossible request. The paradox of expressing the inexpressible has saturated the whole of the writing process, at all of its levels of syntax.

IMPORTANCE AND INFLUENCE

Critical approaches to *Beloved* have varied dramatically: the novel has been deconstructed and reconstructed, Leninized, lionized, and even excoriated. A helpful sketch of some major themes in the criticism appears in Mary Paniccia Carden's article in the winter 1999 issue of the academic periodical *Twentieth-Century Literature*: "Most of the voluminous commentary produced on *Beloved* since its publication in 1987," she writes, "approaches the novel as a meditation on the enduring repercussions of slavery as personified in the character Beloved, with a substantial portion of the criticism focused on the text's negotiations of female identity, subjectivity, and embodiment and on its treatment of mother-daughter bonds." The enduring repercussions of slavery, of slavery's brutal image—as well as the book's intricate cultural negotiations—these have fueled the engine of cultural criticism.

Beyond this critical heritage, *Beloved* has accumulated an impressive roster of prizes and awards. In 1988 it was selected for the Pulitzer Prize and also garnered the Robert F. Kennedy Prize for the Novel. In 1993 Toni Morrison became the first African American woman to receive the foremost honor in all of literature, the Nobel Prize. The Nobel Prize was a fitting culmination to over twenty years of published work in the genre.

Morrison published her first novel, *The Bluest Eye,* in 1970, when she was thirty-nine years old. The novel was warmly received by critics, as was her second novel, *Sula* (1973). Her work over the next two decades was solidly prosperous, achieving a rare blend of commercial popularity and critical respect, but the success of *Beloved*—fueled in part by its widespread exposure as the inaugural volume of Oprah Winfrey's daytime television talk show book club—had a watershed impact on Morrison's fame and popularity. Morrison inspires emotional devotion among her readers, and one of the reasons for this loyal following is perhaps the intense, inward-focused tenor of her fiction. *Beloved* is a stretch of writing that allows a significant amount of identification and empathy on the part of the individual witnessing, through the process of observing the text, the brutal image, the traumatic event. (Indeed, Morrison has focused some amount of attention on the relationship between writer and reader; her 1993 book, *Playing in the Dark: Whiteness and the Literary Imagination,* is a learned and carefully built argument about the nature of the expectations and burdens that white audiences can place on books by nonwhite writers.)

In 1998 a remarkably faithful film adaptation of *Beloved* arrived in theaters, starring Danny Glover, Thandie Newton, and Oprah Winfrey (who attempted to give life, onscreen, to a character from the novel that she did so much to promote). The movie was only moderately successful, but numerous aspects of the novel translated well to the conventions of the cinema; the brutal image, so powerfully presented in text, attained a new level of visual impact through the camera's lens.

Select Bibliography

EDITIONS

Beloved. New York: Knopf, 1987. (First edition.)

Beloved. New York: Plume, 1988. (Edition cited.)

SECONDARY WORKS

Armstrong, Nancy. "Why Daughters Die: The Racial Logic of American Sentimentalism." *Yale Journal of Criticism* 7, no. 2 (fall 1994): 1–24.

Blyn, Robin. "Memory under Reconstruction: *Beloved* and the Fugitive Past." *Arizona Quarterly* 54, no. 4 (winter 1998): 111–140.

Bowers, Maggie Ann. "Acknowledging Ambivalence: The Creation of Communal Memory in the Writing of Toni Morrison." *Wasafiri* 19, no. 23 (spring 1998): 19–23.

Carden, Mary Paniccia. "Models of Memory and Romance: The Dual Endings of Toni Morrison's *Beloved.*" *Twentieth-Century Literature* 45, no. 4 (winter 1999): 401–427.

Dobbs, Cynthia. "Toni Morrison's *Beloved:* Bodies Returned, Modernism Revisited." *African American Review* 32, no. 4 (winter 1998): 563–578.

Gates, Henry Louis, Jr., ed. *The Classic Slave Narratives.* New York: New American Library, 1987.

Hamilton, Cynthia. "Revisions, Rememories and Exorcisms: Toni Morrison and the Slave Narrative." *Journal of American Studies* 30, no. 3 (December 1996): 429–445.

Harting, Heike. "Chokecherry Tree(s): Operative Modes of Metaphor in Toni Morrison's *Beloved.*" *Ariel* 29, no. 4 (October 1998): 23–29.

Heffernan, Teresa. "*Beloved* and the Problem of Mourning." *Studies in the Novel* 30, no. 4 (1998): 559–595.

Heller, Dana. "Reconstructing Kin: Family, History, and Narrative in Toni Morrison's *Beloved.*" *College Literature* 21, no. 2 (June 1994): 105–117.

Jesser, Nancy. "Violence, Home, and Community in Toni Morrison's *Beloved.*" *African American Review* 33, no. 2 (summer 1999): 322–345.

Landow, George P., and Paul Delaney, eds. *Hypermedia and Literary Studies.* Cambridge, Mass.: MIT Press, 1991.

Luckhurst, Roger. "'Impossible Mourning' in Toni Morrison's *Beloved* and Michele Roberts's *Daughters of the House.*" *Critique* 37, no. 4 (summer 1996): 243–260.

Morgenstern, Naomi. "Mother's Milk and Sister's Blood: Trauma and the Neoslave Narrative." *Differences* 8, no. 2 (summer 1996): 101–154.

Parrish, Timothy. "Imagining Slavery: Toni Morrison and Charles Johnson." *Studies in American Fiction* 25, no. 1 (spring 1997): 81–100.

Rand, Naomi. "Surviving What Haunts You: The Art of Invisibility in *Ceremony, The Ghost Writer,* and *Beloved.*" *MELUS* 20, no. 3 (fall 1995): 21–32.

Redding, Arthur. "Haints: American Ghosts, Ethnic Memory, and Contemporary Fiction." *Mosaic* 34, no. 4 (December 2001): 163–182.

Rimmon-Kenan, Shlomith. "Narration, Doubt, Retrieval: Toni Morrison's *Beloved.*" *Narrative* 4, no. 2 (May 1996): 109–123.

Ryan, Katy. "Revolutionary Suicide in Toni Morrison's Fiction." *African American Review* 34, no. 3 (fall 2000): 389–412.

J. D. Salinger's
The Catcher in the Rye

TED WEESNER JR.

F EW IF ANY American novels have reached as many hands as J. D. Salinger's *The Catcher in the Rye*, published in 1951. Still required reading in high schools, the book has assumed a cult status that has endured for fifty years. It is unlikely that Salinger foresaw the degree to which his creation would become a cultural document and primer to adolescence, but a mythic turn of the kind would not be beyond the imagination of the book's hero, Holden Caulfield. Salinger's own withdrawal from society into the woods of New Hampshire is in some part responsible for *The Catcher in the Rye*'s mystique, but the novel can be regarded as a masterfully composed piece of art.

Aspects of Jerome David Salinger's life point to a close kinship with his best-known character. Salinger was raised and spent his early years in New York City. Like Holden, Salinger was a mediocre student who attended a Pennsylvania private school. Mirroring Holden's difficulties with school, Salinger dropped out of Ursinus College after a semester. Certainly Salinger's experience is put to use in his novel. Joyce Maynard, whose 1998 memoir describes a year she spent with Salinger when she was eighteen and he was fifty-three, believes that Salinger largely

is Holden. The reading public would seem to have reached a similar opinion. Still, as every fiction writer knows, the creation of a novel involves far more than literal autobiography. For instance, Salinger, unlike Holden with his two brothers and sister, has but one sibling, a sister eight years his senior.

After leaving Ursinus, Salinger attended a writing workshop at Columbia University, and the teacher of that class, Whit Burnett, also the editor of *Story* magazine, published Salinger's first fiction. The stories Salinger wrote before the war are not particularly memorable, but in 1941, the year before getting drafted into the army, he sold his first story to *The New Yorker* featuring a character named Holden Caulfield. Publication was delayed by World War II, and a revised version appeared in 1946. Through the years stories remained Salinger's focus—his three published collections include *Nine Stories, Franny and Zooey,* and *Raise High the Roof Beam, Carpenters and Seymour: An Introduction*—making *The Catcher in the Rye* his only published novel.

Salinger is rarely thought of as a "war writer," yet some have remarked that his experience in World War II informs his work. He was trained in counterintelligence and was close to some of the worst fighting of the war, including the D day invasion, Hürtgen Forest, and the Battle of the Bulge. Letters from the time allude to the trauma he suffered, and it is widely held that he suffered a nervous breakdown that required hospitalization. Though *The Catcher in the Rye* barely mentions the war (Holden's brother is a veteran of the D day invasion), Holden is gripped by a daunting malaise that has him also heading for a nervous breakdown. Henry James believed that an artist's experience is always sublimated into his art, and Holden's grief over his dead brother, Allie, may well be a conduit for Salinger's own wartime pain.

Like any defining work, this novel can be interpreted in several ways. One can register the novel as Salinger/Holden's critique of postwar society; a tone-perfect evocation of adolescent unhappiness; a valentine to childhood and the inextricable bonds of siblings; or even as a guidebook to artistic expression. At an immediate level, the novel charts an adolescent's picaresque excursion through the city. Animating this narrative is a highly sensitive sixteen-year-old boy who is grief-stricken and trying to resolve his universal suffering.

The novel falls into four parts: Holden's last day at Pencey Prep is followed by his journey through the night in Manhattan, which is followed by his wandering throughout the next day and night. The journey concludes with his first genuine human connection of the overall experience, a new bonding with his beloved little sister, Phoebe. Having hit bottom, healing for Holden finally begins. According to the old saw of hitting bottom being ultimately creative, Holden, and Salinger too, "creates" this insightful account of survival.

SCHOOLED IN DISTRESS

The opening paragraph of *The Catcher in the Rye* compresses a great deal into limited space. The dramatic terms of the novel are established,

CHRONOLOGY

1919	Jerome David Salinger born in New York City on January 1.
1936	Graduates from Valley Forge Military Academy.
1938	Attends Ursinus College, Collegetown, Pennsylvania, dropping out after a semester.
1939	Attends Whit Burnett's writing workshop at Columbia University.
1940	Publishes his first story, "The Young Folks," in Whit Burnett's *Story* magazine.
1941	Sells story about Holden Caulfield to *The New Yorker;* publication delayed by World War II.
1942	Drafted into U.S. Army; continues to publish stories in a variety of widely circulated magazines.
1944	Lands on Utah Beach, Normandy, on D day.
1945	Discharged from army.
1948	Begins to publish stories primarily with *The New Yorker*, until 1965.
1951	*The Catcher in the Rye.*
1953	Moves to Cornish, New Hampshire; *Nine Stories.*
1961	*Franny and Zooey.*
1963	*Raise High the Roof Beam, Carpenters and Seymour: An Introduction.*
1965	"Hapworth 16, 1924," published in *The New Yorker.*

namely that Holden Caulfield is going tell a story about "this madman stuff that happened to me around last Christmas," told from a West Coast hospital where he is currently convalescing under the care of his older brother, D. B. Also immediately evident is that this novel *is* Holden Caulfield, his voice, his journey seen via a peculiar and penetrating vision. The first sentence provides a strong dose of Holden's attitude and operating philosophy:

If you really want to hear about it, the first thing you'll probably want to know is where I was born, and what my lousy childhood was like, and how my parents were occupied and all before they had me, and all that David Copperfield kind of crap, but I don't feel like going into it, if you want to know the truth.

The first seven chapters, roughly the first quarter of *The Catcher in the Rye*, document Holden's last day at Pencey Prep: he has been kicked out for failing four classes and not applying himself. In countless ways Salinger strikes chords that resonate with adolescents across time and space. Who does not relish a character with withering opinions and attitude? And what kid—or adult—has not worried that his or her own strain of laziness may, unchecked, turn to failure? Though it might appear by Holden's biting and sarcastic running commentary that he takes his latest scholastic disaster lightly, his actions point to more serious psychic trouble, a trouble that perhaps all readers can identify with.

Holden begins his story on a hilltop overlooking a Pencey Prep football game on the Saturday afternoon before Christmas break. Holden on a hilltop: this image promptly and viscerally suggests his psychological state, one borne out as the story unfolds. Readers come to see he has an overarching view not only of the football game but more compellingly of most of the people and situations that cross his path. This is someone you want to hang around, this sixteen year old with radar vision. Yet this is also the first glimpse of a boy who is disconnected, lonely, confused. Rather than sitting in the stadium with a date on his arm, he is by himself and without a clear idea of whether he could, or wants to, fit in.

Holden avoids the game for several reasons. Earlier in the day, as the manager of the school's fencing team, he left the team's equipment on the subway, causing the meet to be canceled. If every human being can painfully recall points of teenage cruelty, Holden's reaction to his resulting ostracism seems almost blasé and expected. "It was pretty funny, in a way," he says, though in the Holden Caulfield vernacular the qualifier "in a way" seems not quite believable, rather a psychological tic that allows him to contend with his emotions, emotions with which every kid must deal. These qualifiers crop up regularly in his bantering and despairing narration, often to great comic effect. Underneath, readers *feel* his discomfort. Another reason he stands next to a cannon on the hill—his own figurative cannon is trained on most everyone but his siblings—is because he must visit Spencer, the history teacher who has asked him to stop by.

There is yet another reason Holden lurks at the top of the hill. Lodged like a precious stone amid the many rough jags of his attitude, Holden's precarious emotional state flashes briefly and searingly. Throughout the novel Salinger seeks to maintain this artful balance: enough pathos to keep readers emotionally engaged, not so much that sentimentality overwhelms. As Holden says, he was "trying to feel some kind of a good-by," a good-bye he has missed in the past. This is the first hint—a slight one—of the grief Holden feels and is attempting to face. He may be only sixteen, but as everyone eventually experiences, he's suffering the pain that comes with loss. Holden says, "When I leave a place I like to *know* I'm leaving it." Here is a character's humanity helplessly on display; via Salinger's subtle touch, readers feel for (and with) Holden. In a brief but haunting flashback Holden remembers something that seals the good-bye he is looking for: back in October he and two friends had tossed a football as night approached. This is a vintage Salinger moment, the author providing an image that taps into a universal, even primal childhood experience, one which he lets speak for itself. Holden recalls that they "didn't want to stop doing what we were doing." Is there a person alive without a similar childhood memory? As will be revealed throughout the novel, this sentiment speaks for Holden's hunger for the purity and play that vivifies childhood, set against the darker encroachments of adulthood.

From the hilltop Holden runs down to visit old Spencer. Why is Holden running? Certainly it is not to get to Spencer any sooner. If readers have already sensed in this first chapter that Holden is in some psychological trouble, the end of the chapter inches closer to saying it. Holden runs to see if he can locate some sign of his own vitality, some sign that he is alive. He says, "I don't even know what I was running for. . . . I felt like I was sort of disappearing." Beyond Holden's qualifiers in the face of mounting emotion is this explicit eruption of his more profound malaise. The confusing crisis overtaking him verges on the existential and marks the introduction of a universal (and primal) fear.

The visit to Spencer is only the first in a series of disappointments that Holden suffers around adults. One of the main concerns of the novel is the quest of this young man to find a genuine human connection, better yet if it floats on the innocence of childhood. In the biting sea of Holden's ongoing banter, which unto itself serves as a radical critique of postwar capitalist society, he repeatedly (if subtly and bashfully) reaches out, desperate for someone who will understand him. Despite his efforts, his old history teacher is only interested in justifying himself. This meeting with Spencer is wickedly funny in the disjunction between the two characters' wants, and it is a disjunction that recurs throughout the novel. As Holden later mentions, "What I like best is a book that's at least funny once in a while," and surely this is one of Salinger's own aesthetic axioms, whether in the quirky phrasing he employs or in his consistent and crafty use of irreverence and repetition. But there is more going on in this exchange than an opportunity for a laugh. This is the first adult with whom readers see Holden interact, and the subtext of their interaction is wrenching to behold. This is also a significant appearance of a key *Catcher* word: "phony." When Spencer calls his parents "grand," Holden thinks, "There's a word I really hate. It's a phony." Again and again Holden is sensitive to the falsehoods of adults, something every high

school reader has begun to register for himself or herself and an immediate bonding point with Holden.

Holden finds not only disappointment in the old man who is not really listening but also a sharper disillusionment that is already an aspect of Holden's unhappiness. Spencer reminds Holden that life is a game that must be played by strict rules, and Holden politely agrees. His thoughts run the opposite: "Game, my ass. Some game. If you get on the side where all the hot-shots are, then it's a game, all right—I'll admit that. But if you get on the *other* side, where there aren't any hot-shots, then what's a game about it? Nothing. No game." In Holden's recollection of the pleasure of chucking a football with his pals at dusk, a teacher leans out the window to say they must get ready for dinner. Natural impulses of childhood are forestalled by a game with arbitrary, even cruel rules. As Spencer rattles on, Holden thinks of the ducks in his hometown of Manhattan's Central Park, ducks that will reappear in the book as a motif and that have become one of the mythic symbols of Salinger's classic novel. These ducks and Holden's concern for their livelihood, as in his running or ball playing, point again to the purer, more immediate experience of a child.

Back in the dorm—one named after a "big phony bastard" alumnus who made his money in the undertaking business—Holden puts on a red hunting hat he bought in New York, swinging it around backward. This offbeat, trusty cover is another sustained motif, one that gathers emotional resonance that may leave readers weeping in the end. Meanwhile, Holden sets to rereading the novel *Out of Africa* by Isak Dinesen. Another of his ongoing concerns is his view of art, and this is the first glimpse of that impulse, describing his favorite books, as mentioned above, as ones that are at least sometimes humorous. It is difficult to read these passages and not think they mirror something close to Salinger's own notions. In fact, carefully considered, *Catcher* can be read as a sort of Salinger writing guide. Holden likes books in which you wish the author were "a terrific friend" and you could call him anytime. Of course, Salinger has created this precise impulse in many of his own readers. Published in 2002 is a collection of letters written to the author, straining for such contact.

Two of Holden's classmates, Ackley, his insecure neighbor, and Stradlater, his roommate, are introduced. As with Spencer, Holden locates multiple faults in these boys, but still he feels distinct sympathy for them. This secret sympathy is another reason readers pull for Holden: he does not advertise his acute feelings. The sympathy is alluring in its hidden-ness though threatened by the sexual jealousy that Stradlater provokes in him—another example of the darker incursions of adulthood of which Holden wants no part. At first Holden is friendly, even playful with Stradlater, agreeing to write his English composition as Stradlater goes on a date. But when Holden hears his date is with Jane Gallagher, he "nearly dropped *dead.*" There is no mistaking Holden's agitation: "It made me so nervous I nearly went crazy." Jane is a summer home neighbor of Holden's, someone he likes and with whom he wants to communicate throughout the novel, though he never succeeds. When Holden tells Stradlater about the checkers he and Jane used to play and asks him to ask Jane if "she still keeps all her kings in the back row," Stradlater scoffs at this childishness. Stradlater may be right about the childishness, but to Holden his roommate represents the manipulative, even malicious nature of adults and sex. Later Holden recalls Stradlater "snowing" his date in "this Abraham Lincoln, sincere voice" even as Holden heard her say, "No—*please.* Please, don't. *Please.*"

It is interesting to note that as Stradlater is out with Jane, Holden occupies himself by "very childish[ly]" playing in the snow, going to the movies with a couple of other loners, finally writing Stradlater's composition. The subject of his composition, and the act of writing it, show Holden in a rare state of equilibrium. Late in the novel, Holden's sister, Phoebe, asks Holden if

there is *anything* he likes, and he can only come up with his dead brother, Allie. Here, early on, it is clear that Holden likes writing. Readers also learn about Allie's death from leukemia and Holden's deep attachment to him, a terrible loss that can be seen to underpin Holden and his desperate actions. Holden remembers, "I slept in the garage the night he died, and I broke all the goddam windows with my fist, just for the hell of it." Holden's grief again surfaces, provoked by the description he writes of Allie's old baseball glove covered with green-inked poems. On the surface it is surprising to hear Holden say he liked writing this composition for someone else, but in the face of his raging emotions he locates solace in remembering and writing about his dead brother.

Trauma and pain are difficult to remember. Whereas Holden can recollect his brother in sharp detail, the particulars of what happens when Stradlater returns from his date elude him. Stradlater is angry that Holden has written about a baseball glove, and so Holden shreds the composition. When he asks Stradlater if Jane "still keeps all her kings in the back row," Stradlater replies, "What the hell ya think we did all night—play checkers, for Chrissake?" This infuriates Holden—just the hint of sexual activity—provoking a rich stream of hatred, then an outright attack on Stradlater. Holden effectively forces his roommate to beat him. Self-loathing is bubbling inside this bloodied boy; this is punishment he must feel he deserves. Afterward he puts on his hunting hat and looks "at my stupid face in the mirror. You never saw such gore in your life." Holden's alienation from everyone, *everything,* has spiked, still before fleeing Pencey he makes one last stab at connection. The unlikely candidate is Ackley, who like everyone else does not see Holden's desperation. Readers feel it and become equally desperate to see him understood. At this point Holden's distress increases perilously, prompting a suicidal impulse that will recur. "I felt so lonesome, all of a sudden," Holden thinks. "I almost wished I was dead."

Holden leaves Ackley's room and walks the hallway thinking, "All of a sudden, I decided what I'd really do, I'd get the hell out of Pencey—right that same night and all." His plan is to take a room in a cheap New York hotel and hide away for a few days until his parents receive his expulsion letter. In a telling note of his despair, after packing his bags, Holden sells his typewriter, an object associated with the one "grown-up" activity he is seen taking any pleasure in, the act of composing. Crying, he looks down the hallway—a subtle intimation of his looking for a last good-bye—puts on his trusty red hat, and yells, *"Sleep tight, ya morons!"*

HOLDEN IN THE DARK

The second quarter of *The Catcher in the Rye*, another seven chapters, traces Holden's journey through the night. He palpably holds back his own darkness, a steady undercurrent of malaise that he refuses to face, fending it off with a counterstream of real and remembered human contacts. Even when the sun has risen, Holden's day feels like night.

An entire dissertation could explore Holden's encounters with various modes of transportation, whether subway, cab, train, bus, or on foot. Late at night when he leaves Pencey, he walks to the train station. During the ten minutes he waits for the train, he washes his face with snow, a reminder of the recent violence. This will be a different train ride from those he is used to, as he is distraught over what has happened. One in a series of clues hints at his deepeningly depressive nature, summed up in his phrase, "I just didn't feel like it." In his darkest moments, the suicidal fantasy resurfaces, and another point of contact is made with younger readers beginning to face their own shades of sadness. Holden is a universal carrier of this bewildering onset, playing back feelings that have likely been experienced only privately.

When a good-looking, middle-aged woman sits next to him on the train, readers encounter Holden's uneasy desire, a hunger that hovers between the sexual and the maternal. Responding to this hunger could be a solution, though one with a price. "Women kill me," he says: witness the ongoing skirmish between Holden's body and intellect. It turns out that the woman is the mother of one of his classmates, whom Holden thinks is "doubtless the biggest bastard that ever went to Pencey, in the whole crumby history of the school." And so Holden, as he will at various points when he faces emotional discomfort, invents a vivid alter-persona.

This "chucking the old crap around" can be interpreted from several angles. At one level Holden "kids" people who he believes are floating in some degree of phony unreality, people who deserve his malicious embellishments. After he is done, he thinks, "I'm glad I shot it for a while, though. You take a guy like Morrow that's always snapping their towel at people's asses—really trying to *hurt* somebody with it—they don't just stay a rat while they're a kid. They stay a rat their whole life." At the same time the story he embroiders makes the disliked classmate look *good* to his mother. Holden desires, even likes this woman, and as repeatedly shown, he feels a fundamental sympathy for people he identifies as in some way good-hearted, guileless, genuine. At other levels of lying the tension between playful malice and deeper sympathy is never fully resolved. Beyond these impulses Holden takes simple pleasure in making up stories, in using his imagination, as both his living siblings do. In the face of so much unhappiness, readers can feel Holden's exhilaration in these creative outbursts.

Holden's ongoing hunger to connect flows through these chapters, either by his constant attraction to the telephone or in his needy interactions with Manhattan cabbies, elevator operators, and waiters. In these many moments, Holden longs for *any* sort of connection. After twenty minutes in a phone booth, contemplating a list of people he might call, his brother and sister at the top of the list, Holden hops a cab. Returning to one of Salinger's skillfully woven motifs, Holden asks the cabbie about the well-being of Central Park's ducks. Despite the hostility in their conversation, Holden asks the man to join him for a cocktail, as he asked the woman on the train, as he will ask most anyone.

Checked into the "very crumby" Edmont Hotel, Holden is "too depressed to care whether I had a good view or not." He gets even more depressed at the sight of the old bellboy. As with Spencer, Holden is uncomfortable around people in decline. They are the farthest from kids and seem to ring the bell of mortality. Looking out his hotel window, he spots another sort of decline: a "distinguished-looking guy" getting dressed in a "very tight black evening dress" in one window, and in another a couple squirting liquid at each other. This leads Holden into a disquisition on the "*very* crumby" aspects of sex. Again, the tension surfaces in him between light and dark, childhood and adulthood, sex and play. As he says, "I don't *like* the idea," but then a little later, "It's really too bad that so much crumby stuff is a lot of fun sometimes." His body wants it; his mind does not. This tension continues in his phone call to a retired stripper. He is looking for a liaison, but it is late, and again he gets turned down.

Before continuing deeper into the night, Holden thinks of Phoebe, his kid sister, the most significant character outside of the protagonist himself, whom Holden loves most in his life and who will figure prominently in the end. Here is a moment where Salinger inches close to sentimentality but retains balance by the idiosyncratic bravura of his prose. Phoebe is described as "roller-skate skinny" and wildly precocious. In a beguiling density of detail readers see her a step ahead of the actors in the movies she likes, writing her own books, tagging after her brothers. "I'm the only dumb one in the family," Holden says, and he asks his readers to join his affection, swearing to God "you'd like her." It's a relief to see Holden care so dearly for someone, and with the care returned, and Salinger's own love for these characters is af-

fectionately captured in the self-deprecation and particularity of their voices.

In the hotel's Lavender Room, Holden tries to hook up with "these three girls around thirty or so." Even if they are not attractive, he finds himself giving the blonde one "the old eye." As with the cabbie and the ex-stripper, his conversation is disconnected and hilarious. When he tries to talk to the blonde as they dance, she says, "Wudga say?" Though she is not pretty, seemingly stupid, and not of his class, Holden remains interested. She gets angry when he kisses her on the head and even angrier when he curses. Despite this, Holden is dazzled by her dancing and observes the disjunction between physical talent and ignorance. At a more profound level, he is bewildered and intimidated by women. To his mind (or body), he

> was about half in love with her by the time we sat down. That's the thing about girls. Every time they do something pretty, even if they're not much to look at, or even if they're sort of stupid, you fall half in love with them, and then you never know *where* the hell you are.

The competing signals are impossible to sort out. Holden is less depressed by the bar tab the three women leave him than by their "sad, fancy hats." His hypersensitivity, again *hidden,* surely touches a feeling so many readers privately, even frighteningly, thought was theirs alone.

Before Holden lands in another cab and nightclub, he sits in the hotel lobby and reminisces about Jane Gallagher. As with Phoebe, Holden holds great affection for Jane. Their relationship is ambiguous—no wonder, considering Holden's state of confusion—illustrated in the description of their one physical encounter, the closest they came to kissing: After being mistreated by her stepfather, Jane got upset, and the next thing Holden knew, "I was kissing her all over—*any*where—her eyes, her *nose,* her forehead, her eyebrows and all, her *ears*—her whole face except her mouth and all. She sort of wouldn't let me get to her mouth." It is shocking to see Holden so emotionally explicit. Yet he later describes the wonderful countervailing sensation of holding hands with her, and in this more childlike manifestation of desire, he thinks, "All you knew was, you were happy." Salinger is delving here into a most awkward and common adolescent stress point, sexual need rising in one's body as the concomitant complications present themselves.

The night stretches on. Holden's quest to ease his pain, to locate something or someone who might help in the easing, goes on until dawn. In another cab, on his way to a nightclub in Greenwich Village, Holden's loneliness is sharply felt. "New York's terrible when somebody laughs on the street very late at night," he thinks. But he is not going to pass up possible salvation from a hardened cabbie, nor is Salinger going to miss an opportunity to make his readers howl with laughter. Humor rests on a prickly, subterranean foundation of pathos. Holden is still worried about the ducks freezing in Central Park, while the cabbie turns out to be worried about the fish in the park's frozen pond. "It's tougher for the *fish,* the winter and all, than it is for the ducks, for Chrissake. Use your head, for Chrissake." The man is impatient and not pleasurable to talk with, yet Holden asks him to get a drink, calling him "a pretty good guy."

In the nightclub where the pianist Ernie is performing, Holden advances more aesthetic ideas to his readers. Again his concerns regarding art would seem to mirror Salinger's. Holden thinks Ernie is a talented pianist, but "he's so good he's almost corny, in fact." And later: "It was supposed to be something *holy,* for God's sake, when he sat down at the piano. Nobody's *that* good." Ernie sits in front of a big mirror and under a spotlight playing "these dumb, show-offy ripples in the high notes, and a lot of other very tricky stuff that gives me a pain in the ass," and yet the crowd loves it. Here his phony-detector is whirring—Ernie gives "this very phony, *humble* bow"—and Holden believes that he alone is able to detect what is authentic. Readers can only agree and feel knitted to Holden.

Still and perhaps inevitably, Holden feels sorry for Ernie, and tension surfaces between his derision and his helpless sympathy: "I don't even think he *knows* any more when he's playing right or not. It isn't all his fault. I partly blame all those dopes that clap their heads off—they'd foul up *any*body, if you gave them a chance." Perhaps it is not surprising that Salinger himself fled to the woods. Also, it is no surprise that Holden invites the pianist to join him for a drink, loneliness again superseding conviction.

In a nightclub frequented by "prep school jerks and college jerks," Salinger zeroes in on a preoccupation: "all those Ivy League bastards [who] look alike." Their conversations, overheard by Holden, are vapid, with one "Joe Yale–looking guy" trying to touch his date under the table. "Don't, darling," she says, and readers are reminded of Stradlater. When Holden runs into an ex-girlfriend of his brother's, he cannot believe she blocks "the *whole goddam traffic* in the aisle. . . . It was funny. You could tell the waiter didn't like her much, you could tell even the Navy guy didn't like her much, even though he was dating her. And *I* didn't like her much. Nobody did." And still Holden thinks, "You had to sort of feel sorry for her, in a way." Holden extends a fake good-bye and considers his own phoniness: "If you want to stay alive, you have to say that stuff." In seeing Holden not hesitate to turn his critical eye on himself, our sympathy for him only deepens. His self-reproach and downward emotional spiral continues as he walks back to the hotel, declaring himself "one of these very yellow guys." The through-line of bracing honesty helps leaven a character so often dark and derisive. How can one not warm to someone who says, "Maybe I'm not *all* yellow. . . . I think maybe I'm just partly yellow." But self-contempt is always nearby, fueling his fantasies of suicide. Back in the hotel lobby that smells "like fifty million dead cigars," Holden thinks, "I was feeling sort of lousy. Depressed and all. I almost wished I was dead."

In this time of need Holden is approached by the elevator operator, Maurice, who offers him a prostitute. He accepts, then thinks, "It was against my principles and all, but I was feeling so depressed I didn't even *think*. That's the whole trouble. When you're feeling very depressed, you can't even think." Frightened by sex, Holden gets nervous, revealing to readers that he's still a virgin. He attributes this condition to his always stopping when a girl says to stop: "The trouble is, I get to feeling sorry for them." In each of his occasions of "feeling sorry" he seems to be hoping for the sympathy to be returned. Though readers' sympathy may be threatened when Holden confides that "most girls are so dumb"—is this a streak of misogyny?—he clearly envies their ability to get lost in the *feeling* of sex. More precisely he seems to project his frustrations onto the unknown. "After you neck them for a while, you can really *watch* them losing their brains." If he could only let down his defenses long enough to enjoy where his body leans. . . .

It is no shock, perhaps, that when the prostitute appears, Holden has second thoughts. His sexual impulse, like most of his impulses, seems to have dimmed with the weight of not caring (or depression). He thinks, "I sort of just wanted to get it over with," and later, "Sexy was about the *last* thing I was feeling. I felt much more depressed than sexy." He proposes just talking, and then he gets melancholic hanging up her green dress, thinking of her "going in a store and buying it, and nobody in the store knowing she was a prostitute and all." In another moment of stress, Holden makes up a story about himself, telling the prostitute that he is recovering from an operation on his "clavichord." When she presses herself on him, he gets angry at her crude talk. It may seem remarkable that Holden could react this way, his narration laced with obscenities, and yet this appears to be another stricture in his overarching philosophy, at least when it comes to sex. She gets mad after they disagree over price, calling him a "crumb-bum" as she leaves.

If Holden sometimes resorts to an alternative persona in times of stress, he turns to the memory of his dead brother when depression pushes him close to spiritual extinction. In the wake of the prostitute, "very depressed" by what has happened, he recalls a time when he would not let Allie come along on a bicycle ride. Holden carries on a conversation with a phantom Allie, correcting his actions, *remaking* a past he regrets. A religious impulse surfaces when he gets into bed: "I felt like praying or something." Though Holden recalls the phoniness of organized religion—ministers with "these Holy Joe voices"—he has the *feeling*, even if at this moment he cannot make himself successfully pray (as he could not successfully pull off the sex act, impotence threatening from every direction). Body, mind, now spirit present a relief he cannot contain.

Another indignity occurs when the elevator operator and the prostitute return for more money. Maurice unbuttons his uniform coat, revealing a fake collar and nothing but a hairy stomach. As he threatens Holden, the prostitute grabs his wallet. Holden, to readers' surprise, begins to cry; he has been rendered a little boy in over his head. Maurice snaps his finger against Holden's crotch, and after Holden calls him a "dirty moron," seeming to *ask* for violence as with Stradlater, Maurice punches him in the stomach. Holden does not "even try to get out of the way or duck or anything." He intuits once more that harsh punishment is his due, a physical manifestation that perhaps thankfully matches his interior state. Holden thinks he might be dying, which provokes a movie-style revenge fantasy of being shot, chasing down Maurice, pumping him full of bullets, finally getting tended to by Jane. In characteristic Caulfield sarcasm, he thinks, "The goddam movies. They can ruin you. I'm not kidding." His more frightening fantasy erupts: "What I really felt like, though, was committing suicide. I felt like jumping out the window." At this low halfway point of *The Catcher in the Rye,*

Holden once more prevails by being Holden, anxious about "a bunch of stupid rubbernecks looking at me when I was all gory."

NOBODY AROUND ANYWHERE

In the third quarter of *The Catcher in the Rye*, chapters 15 through 20, Holden confronts a series of obstacles that suggest an implicit Salinger critique. Holden reaches out longingly, yet each obstacle precludes true connection or resolution. The telephone is a steady temptation, particularly a call to Jane. Instead, before leaving the hotel, he calls Sally Hayes, someone who first impressed him with her patter about Manhattan cultural life. Holden says, "My big trouble is, I always sort of think whoever I'm necking is a pretty intelligent person." Beauty and attraction override clear thinking. As with the dumb girl who can dance, or the boring guy who can whistle, here is another case of Holden bewildered by the interference between body and mind.

After leaving his bags in a Grand Central Station locker, Holden runs into two nuns. They carry inexpensive suitcases, which launches him into a flashback about an old roommate with similarly cheap suitcases. Salinger is always subtly tuned to class, yet here he pointedly delves into its intricacies as he demonstrates how people gravitate sadly to their own. In Holden's formulation,

> You think if they're intelligent and all, the other person, and have a good sense of humor, that they don't give a damn whose suitcases are better, but they do. They really do. It's one of the reasons why I roomed with a stupid bastard like Stradlater. At least his suitcases were as good as mine.

Later in the same chapter, Holden makes a similar observation about people of like religion cleaving to one another. He describes a friend who "was enjoying the conversation . . . but you could tell he would've enjoyed it *more* if I was a Catholic and all." But Holden relishes these nuns because they put on no airs; he is refreshed by their flouting of the conformist, cliquish, consumerist, capitalist lives of his set. They are content to not participate in the class superstructure, wearing iron glasses and eating sparsely. Holden searches for this sort of clean contentment. He insists on giving them ten dollars, then tells them about the literature he likes, specifically *Romeo and Juliet*. His remarks sound a faint but sure echo of Holden's grief over his dead brother. He says to them, "It drives me crazy if somebody gets killed—especially somebody very smart and entertaining and all." After these women of charity depart, Holden considers the phony charity of his peers. About Sally Hayes's mother, he thinks, "The only way *she* could go around with a basket collecting dough would be if everybody kissed her ass for her when they made a contribution."

Ideas about artistic expression spark again. Holden is on the hunt for an old record for Phoebe, sung by Estelle Fletcher, who "doesn't sound at all mushy. If a white girl was singing it, she'd make it sound *cute* as hell." Later in the same chapter, Holden continues his diatribe against actors and the movies: "In the first place," he thinks, "I hate actors. They never act like people. They just think they do. . . . If any actor's really good, you can always tell he *knows* he's good, and that spoils it." About Hamlet played by Sir Laurence Olivier (whom Salinger is known awkwardly to have met after he wrote these words) Holden says, "He was too much like a goddam general, instead of a sad, screwed-up type guy." The acted moments that Holden does like, along with Phoebe, are those unsung and innocent: Ophelia "horsing around with her brother," Hamlet patting a dog on the head. Holden worries "about whether [an actor] is going to do something phony every minute," and he is so sensitive to falseness that *every* artistic medium would seem hard to enjoy.

The mysterious title of the novel finally surfaces when Holden spots a "sort of poor" family out walking, in particular a little kid walking alongside the curb. In a vintage Salinger moment, one clearly dear to him and his protagonist, the kid "was making out like he was walking a very straight line, the way kids do, and the whole time he kept singing and humming." The lyric goes: "If a body catch a body coming through the rye." "He had a pretty little voice, too," Holden says. "He was just singing for the hell of it, you could tell." The author has his own radar vision for images that impart quintessential *kidness:* the boy's contented self-enclosure, unawarely real and *in* the moment, in contrast to adults always *playing* the crowd. This makes Holden feel "not so depressed any more."

Back by cab to Central Park, Holden wants to find Phoebe and give her the record. He does not locate her, but he does come across one of her classmates, whom he asks to join him for hot chocolate. She declines, however, saying she has to meet her friend. Surely there is no soul in Manhattan whom Holden would not ask for a drink. At the Museum of Natural History, Holden recalls past experiences there. In one of Salinger's loveliest passages, readers experience the range of Holden's despair and the pangs of loss that have prompted it:

> The best thing . . . in that museum was that everything always stayed right where it was. Nobody'd move. You could go there a hundred thousand times, and that Eskimo would still be just finished catching those two fish, the birds would still be on their way south, the deers would still be drinking out of that water hole, with their pretty antlers and their pretty, skinny legs, and that squaw with the naked bosom would still be weaving that same blanket. Nobody'd be different. The only thing that would be different would be *you.*

As usual, Salinger snaps his readers out of anything treading near sentimentality. Holden meets Sally to go to the theater, and expressing his yearning, he thinks, "The funny part is, I felt like marrying her the minute I saw her. I'm crazy. I didn't even *like* her much, and yet all of a sudden I felt like I was in love with her and

wanted to marry her." The battle between body and mind persists as they fool around in a cab, prompting Holden to tell Sally he loves her. "It was lie, of course, but the thing is, I *meant* it when I said it." At the show, before Holden loses even more control of his emotions, he does not miss the chance to digress about art-making: "If you do something *too* good, then, after a while, if you don't watch it, you start showing off. And then you're not as good any more." At the show's intermission, the unraveling begins when Sally runs into an old Ivy League friend. Holden's jealousy is unleashed near to the Stradlater incident, his diction spiked with furious sarcasm, including words like: "nauseating," "slobbering," "snobby," "phoniest," "bastard." In an odd juxtaposition Holden thinks, "He sounded just like a girl. He didn't *hes*itate to horn in on my date."

The two go skating and Holden's misanthropy (maybe clarity) surges as he considers Sally's vanity, certain she wants to show off her body in a little skating skirt. Holden wants to drink, not skate, and finally he gets her off the ice to a bar where he articulates—in a stream of self-loathing and longing—feelings that he has not previously vocalized. Upper-middle-class civility is stripped away when he asks, "Did you ever get fed up? . . . I mean did you ever get scared that everything was going to go lousy unless you did something?" Soon Holden is listing what he hates about his and Sally's demographic. In a stunning piece of dialogue foreshadowing Salinger's own break with society, Holden says, "If you weren't around, I'd probably be someplace way the hell off. In the woods or some goddam place." Sally wants to change the subject, but Holden presses closer to his private precipice. "I'm in bad shape," he says. "I'm in *lousy* shape." In his agitated, almost grandiose state, he gets an idea, an escape fantasy similar to Salinger's own. They could drive north, he proposes, and "we could live somewhere with a brook and all and, later on, we could get married or something. I could chop all our own wood in the wintertime and all." Sally, sensing his alienation, rings the clanging note of conformity, "You can't just *do* something like that." Readers think, but *yes* he can! Animosity between them escalates, Holden continuing his seething critique of their parents' way of life, Sally disbelieving. "We both hated each other's guts by that time," Holden says. When she cries, he laughs helplessly and then flees.

Post-trauma, Holden again repairs to the phone booth with Jane on his mind. Again he does not reach her, but he does set up a drinking date with Carl Luce, an old classmate whom he dislikes. Holden kills time (or seeks distraction from his suffering) thinking of girls, drinking, now going to the movies. He professes to hate movies for the manifold phoniness in which they helplessly traffic. If he cannot passively enjoy his distractions, he goes on the offensive. Holden lacerates war movies, Ernest Hemingway's "phony" war novel *A Farewell to Arms*, then war itself. Holden's feelings about the war are intriguing to examine, as his brother D. B.'s experiences in World War II closely match Salinger's own. This period of Salinger's life is not fully known. He did land on D day like D. B., and it is thought that Salinger suffered a nervous breakdown late in the war. When D. B. was home on furlough, Holden says, "all he did was lie on his bed," telling Holden "the Army was practically as full of bastards as the Nazis were." The thought of being in the army is intolerable for Holden, and so "they better just take me out and stick me in front of a firing squad." Experience surely informs this passionate attack.

Just before Luce shows up at the bar, Holden excoriates not only the usual suspects— "phonies are coming in the window"—but also homosexuals, "flits," as he calls them. This is a rare moment that dates the novel. He questions to himself Luce's sexuality—he was "sort of flitty himself"—and Holden's first words to Luce when he appears are "Hey, I got a flit for you. . . . At the end of the bar. Don't look now. I've been saving him for ya." The meeting between these two verges on the hostile. At first

Holden baits Luce, then he turns serious, angling for help. "You're one of these intellectual guys," he says to Luce. "I need your advice. I'm in a terrific—" and it seems Holden is about to spill the depths of his pain, but Luce cuts him off. There is a recurrence here of Salinger's disdain for fake Ivy League intellectuals, Luce unwilling to talk heart-to-heart with Holden while calling his own ex-girlfriend a whore. Holden cannot believe Luce would say this after she was "decent enough to let you get sexy with her all the time." Luce is clearly accustomed to Holden's moral stands, denouncing this as "a typical Caulfield conversation," and readers comprehend that Holden's highly evolved morality is not a new discovery. Even though he does not like Luce, Holden wants to bare the impossible confusion coursing through him, praying this "intellectual" will have the answers. Holden says to him, "I know [sex is] is supposed to be physical and spiritual, and artistic and all. But what I mean is, you can't do it with *everybody*—every girl you neck with and all— and make it come out that way. Can you?" Luce's solution to Holden's problems? Psychoanalysis. Holden presses him about what this would mean, and Luce says, "I couldn't care less, frankly." There could not be a better headline for Holden's experiences with most fellow human beings. Still, Holden prostrates himself, asking Luce to stay for one more drink. "Please," he says. "I'm lonesome as hell. No kidding," tears just beneath his words.

Holden spirals further downward in the bar, getting increasingly drunk, his pleas for companionship mounting. Fantasies overtake him, first of having a bullet in his gut, then of his own funeral. After a number of drunken exchanges, now really crying, Holden decides to go to Central Park to "see what the hell the ducks were doing." The untarnished image of waddling ducks—further the untarnished motivations of animals— has a better chance of saving Holden than any adult. In a possible death wish, his despair close to bottoming out, Holden walks all around the frozen pond and almost falls in. Sitting on a bench, wearing his talismanic hunting hat, Holden gets lost thinking of his own funeral, and of Allie's actual one. When Holden's grasp on his own life spirit feels most threatened, he summons his lost brother. He reveals that he was not at Allie's funeral but in the hospital because of his hand, which he injured punching out windows. It is the "goddam cemetery" that most rattles Holden, with "people coming and putting a bunch of flowers on your stomach on Sunday." He hopes that when he dies "somebody has sense enough to just dump me in the river or something." He describes a visit to Allie's grave when it started to rain at the cemetery and everybody ran to get in their cars—"everybody except Allie." In a final action reflecting the gravity of his surrender, Holden throws his money into the lagoon. Phoebe, the person he loves most, comes to the rescue in his mind. He cannot imagine inflicting more loss on her. "I figured I'd better sneak home and see her, in case I died and all." And so, in what feels like the first heartening action in the novel, Holden starts home.

LOOKING FOR PHOEBE

Only in the final quarter of *Catcher* does Salinger devote three chapters to a single scene. The space is warranted, however, as it implies the scene's importance. Holden at home with his little sister, Phoebe—their attendant love finally dramatized—may be what keeps him from going to pieces. It is likely not an overstatement to say that she keeps Holden alive.

Once he has tricked the elevator boy and made his way into his family's apartment, Holden finds his sister in D. B.'s old bedroom. For a while he watches her sleep. Salinger's fascination with the innocence and unmediated beauty of childhood is on full display here, while at the same time the author is characteristically careful to offset sentiment with Holden's cutting attitude. It is clear that underneath he is impossibly sensitive. Watching her he thinks, "You

take adults, they look lousy when they're asleep and they have their mouths way open, but kids don't. Kids look all right. They can even have spit all over the pillow and they still look all right." In her presence he "felt swell, for a change," and this is no small revelation.

The objects of Phoebe's life are spread around her sleeping body, and Holden communes with them as if they have a religious shimmer, his feeling for her rising from the page. When he finally wakes her, she says, "*Hold*en!" and puts her arms around his neck. She reminds him about her school production and wants to know if he will attend, but then she asks why he is home early. Even if she gets sidetracked—chattering about movies, parents, the broken record he has given her, a boy who likes her—she is *on* to him. No preceding character has cared so much about him or known him so well. When she asks if he has been kicked out, he claims they have been let out early. She interrupts with "You did get kicked out! You did!" Upset, she starts to hit him, repeating "Daddy'll *kill* you!" then hiding her head under her pillow. In trying to placate her, Holden recounts the bad things about Pencey, recapitulating a number of Salinger targets: cliques, adolescent malice, phony teachers and phony advice, even aging. Yet Phoebe recognizes his diversionary tactic, leveling a devastating indictment, one Holden has a hard time answering. "You don't like *any*thing that's happening," she says. In his mind he scrambles for something, first the nuns, then the memory of a boy named James Castle. In this late-arriving flashback, a significant event that *must* motivate Holden's hardest feelings about adolescent behavior, he describes the James Castle incident. When James refused to take back calling one of his classmates conceited, a gang of boys "started in on him." Holden refuses to tell his readers what this means: "it's too repulsive." A sexual assault may be intimated here. Unwilling to back down, Castle jumps out the window to his death. At the time, he was wearing a sweater that Holden had lent him, which sealed Holden's psychic link to him.

Yet Phoebe continues, pressing Holden to name one thing he likes. He comes up with their brother Allie. "Allie's *dead*—" she shoots back. "You always say that!" When he says he likes it *now,* sitting there talking and joking with her, she replies, "That isn't anything *real*ly!" In a funny but piercing retort Holden thinks, "People never think anything is anything *really.* I'm getting goddam sick of it." After Holden depicts the unavoidable phoniness of their father's work as a corporate lawyer—"How would you know you weren't being a phony? The trouble is, you *wouldn't*"—the title of the novel comes once more into play. Holden tells his sister that he wants to be "the catcher in the rye" of the song lyric. Again, the impossible allure and beauty of childhood is vivified:

> I keep picturing all these little kids playing some game in this big field of rye and all. Thousands of little kids, and nobody's around—nobody big, I mean—except me. And I'm standing on the edge of some crazy cliff. What I have to do, I have to catch everybody if they start to go over the cliff—I mean if they're running and they don't look where they're going I have to come out from somewhere and *catch* them. That's all I'd do all day. I'd just be the catcher in the rye and all. I know it's crazy, but that's the only thing I'd really like to be.

Yes, it may be crazy, but in the moment's intensity and strangeness there is a glimpse of astonishing depth of feeling, regret, nostalgia.

After calling to find out if he can crash with his old teacher Mr. Antolini, the man who carried the dead James Castle to the infirmary not caring if his coat was bloodied, Holden dances with Phoebe. Hearing their parents enter the apartment, Holden hides in the closet, and Phoebe covers for him. When he comes out, there is a searing glimpse of Phoebe's underlying fear. "If you go away, you won't see me in the play," she says, and "her voice sounded funny when she said it." Before he leaves, Phoebe lends him her Christmas money, and this gets Holden crying for quite a while. "I couldn't help it," he tells readers. "I did it so nobody could hear me,

but I did it. It scared hell out of old Phoebe when I started doing it, and she came over and tried to make me stop, but once you get started, you can't just stop on a goddam *dime.*" In a moving, parting gesture, Holden gives Phoebe his hunting hat. In this entire scene, in every action and thought and capped by the handing over of this treasured talisman, Holden's depth of feeling for his sister is felt by the reader.

Though Salinger provides a generally negative portrait of school and schoolteachers, Holden's old teacher Mr. Antolini would appear to be an exception. The man has looked after Holden in his turmoil, and Holden believes his home is a safe haven. Antolini is described as "witty," "sophisticated," a "heavy drinker," with an older, wealthy wife. In his "swanky" Sutton Place apartment, an "oiled" Antolini questions Holden about his latest failure as his wife fixes coffee. Holden defends his F in Oral Expression—students yelled "Digression!" if a speaker strayed off subject—and he says, "The trouble with me is, I *like* it when somebody digresses. It's more *in*teresting and all." Antolini gives Holden this kindly advice: "I have a feeling that you're riding for some kind of a terrible, terrible fall." Antolini advances Phoebe's challenge in less subtle fashion, proposing that a sort of misanthropy will set in for Holden if he does not reverse direction. As Holden defends himself—"I don't hate too many guys. What I may do, I may hate them for a *little* while . . . but it doesn't last too long," and after some time, "I sort of missed them"—readers witness his humanity swirling just beneath the surface. Yet Antolini pushes his dire prediction: "This fall I think you're riding for—it's a special kind of fall, a horrible kind. The man falling isn't permitted to feel or hear himself hit bottom. He just keeps falling and falling." Antolini does not see that Holden is *in* such a state and that his words are hardly comforting. Yet when he tells Holden he is a student at heart and "not the first person who was ever confused and frightened and even sickened by human behavior," some of whom have "happily . . . kept records of their troubles," there is the explicit call to *make* something of his suffering, to create! One recalls the Stradlater composition with which Holden was so consumed.

Antolini makes up the couch for him, but a shocking thing occurs, at least in Holden's mind. He wakes up to find Antolini stroking his forehead. Holden interprets this as "something perverty." He leaps up and insists on leaving, Antolini trying to convince him to stay, "trying to act very goddam casual and cool and all, but he wasn't any too goddam cool." He calls Holden "a very, very strange boy" as he leaves. Holden tells his readers that "that kind of stuff's happened to me about twenty times since I was a kid," leaving them to consider possible sexual trauma he has not shared. But then after sleeping in Grand Central, "more depressed than I ever was in my whole life," Holden begins to wonder if he was wrong to question Antolini's motives. "I mean how can you tell about that stuff for sure?" Holden asks, and readers are left in this same ambiguous place.

After leaving Grand Central and failing to eat the doughnuts he has ordered in a cheap restaurant because it is hard to swallow when he is so depressed, Holden finds himself walking up Fifth Avenue when "something very spooky started happening." Holden becomes convinced that at every block he will not get to the other side of the street: "I'd just go down, down, down, and nobody'd ever see me again." His psychological remedy for this terrifying existential threat is to speak to Allie, repeating, "Allie, don't let me disappear. Please, Allie," and each time he does not disappear, he thanks him. Another sibling to the rescue! At this point Holden decides he must leave the city. The escape fantasy he launches into is akin to the earlier one, except this time he imagines he's a "deaf-mute." Again there is a little cabin, this time with lots of sun, on the edge of the woods with "this beautiful girl that was also a deaf-mute." This closely resembles the life Salinger made for himself upon fleeing Manhattan—his ruthless self-enclosure akin to "deaf-mute-

ness"—so that Holden and Salinger can seem to have merged.

Before he leaves the city, Holden wants to say good-bye to Phoebe, and so he walks up to her school to leave her a note to meet him at the art museum. Holden is deteriorating: sweating profusely, about to puke, almost fainting, suffering diarrhea. On the way to the principal's office, Holden spots the words "fuck you" on the wall, and the violence he wants to inflict upon whomever has written it—"smash his head on the stone steps till he was good and goddam dead and bloody"—is shocking. He rubs out the obscenity worried that Phoebe and the other kids will see it, yet as he leaves the school he sees the words again, this time scratched into the wall. Holden realizes the hopelessness of this enterprise: "If you had a million years to do it in, you couldn't rub out even *half* the 'Fuck you' signs in the world." Even in one of Holden's favorite refuges, the museum, he sees the obscenity written underneath a tomb wall. Again, the adult world incurs. There is no rest for Holden: "You can't ever find a place that's nice and peaceful, because there isn't any." He pictures the obscenity on his own tombstone.

Finally Phoebe appears, a heartrending sight wearing Holden's hunting hat and dragging a big suitcase. Phoebe pleads to run away with Holden. It may not be surprising that he gets dizzy, but it is jolting when he tells Phoebe to shut up. She pleads desperately to come along and starts to cry. Holden further surprises readers when he says he almost hates her, yet since it is mostly because she is following him and disregarding her school play, his hate seems the near flip side of love. He takes her suitcase and checks it at the museum. Phoebe is angry when he returns. She throws his hat in his face and tells *him* to shut up, the first time she has ever said that to him. Holden proposes the zoo, and though Phoebe will not answer him, there is the poignant image of her following him on the other side of the street. Here is another occurrence of one of Salinger's motifs, the innocent and playful action of kids walking, a seemingly unremarkable image that embodies the pure candor of their hearts.

The final location and image of *The Catcher in the Rye* is similarly evocative: the carousel in Central Park. Holden knows Phoebe loves the carousel and so he convinces her to take a ride. She wants him to ride, too, but Holden, on the fault line of adulthood, can only watch. Phoebe tracks down her favorite beat-up horse, and when it begins to circle, she grabs for the gold ring with the rest of the kids. Despite Holden's unerring hunger to be a "catcher in the rye," he does not "say anything or do anything." Salinger is delivering here his hardest-fought, most wrenching piece of wisdom: "The thing with kids is, if they want to grab for the gold ring, you have to let them do it, and not say anything. If they fall off, they fall off, but it's bad if you say anything to them." Of course, Holden is learning the same difficult thing for himself. He cannot be a catcher in the rye. Both he and the kids must find their own way.

In the final pages of the chapter, Phoebe reassures Holden that she is not mad anymore, gives him a kiss, and returns the red hunting hat to his head like a hallowed piece of armor. She wants to know if he will come home, and he says yes; to readers he says, "I wasn't lying to her." Wearing his hat in the rain, watching his beloved sister on the carousel, he says, "I felt so damn happy all of a sudden, the way old Phoebe kept going around and around. I was damn near bawling, I felt so damn happy." Readers feel a similar relief—an understanding has palpably been reached—and it is no surprise that Holden tells us, "God, I wish you could've been there." Of course, in this act of retelling, of setting down, we *have* been there.

In the final, three-paragraph chapter of *The Catcher in the Rye,* Holden continues speaking to his readers, and as in the opening chapter, we return to the West Coast where he is convalescing. Despite all he has said, he remains ambivalent about his story and about the telling of his story. Yet in his final words there is a hint

to his true feelings within another of his disclaimers. "About all I know is, I sort of *miss* everybody I told about," he says, and this includes Stradlater, Ackley, even horrible Maurice. "It's funny," Holden concludes. "Don't ever tell anybody anything. If you do, you start missing everybody." Or, in other words, to the end, Salinger envisions sympathy, even love, at the heart of remembrance and creation.

A CHARACTER WITH LEGS

Can it be possible that a novel over fifty years old, one that features an upper-class white boy who wanders a once-safe Manhattan in the middle of the night, has relevance to today's readers? Can one still take something from this novel?

If a posting on the website http://www.jdsalinger.com is any indication, the answer is yes. Expressing a typical sentiment, a twelve-year-old girl writes to Salinger: "It really fascinates me how you are able to recognize many teenagers' feelings and thoughts precisely. Today, many teenagers feel just like Holden."

Not surprisingly, this student was encouraged to read the novel in school. And it is largely this phenomenon that has kept the book alive—despite occasional efforts to censor the novel for its profanity—as adults have passed the book on to kids, generation after generation. The critic Louis Menand suggests that *The Catcher in the Rye*'s durability can be attributed *not* to kids discovering it for themselves, but to adults wanting to pass along a piece of their own nostalgia, a nostalgia to which kids are susceptible in an increasingly threatening world. As Menand remarks about *Catcher* and other novels influenced by Salinger that capture generational unhappiness, "It is the romantic certainty, which all these books seduce you with, that somehow, somewhere, something was taken away from you, and you cannot get it back. Once, you did ride a carousel. It seemed as though it would last forever." The other novels to which Menand ascribes this addictive quality include Sylvia Plath's *The Bell Jar* (1963), Hunter S. Thompson's *Fear and Loathing in Las Vegas* (1971), Jay McInerney's *Bright Lights, Big City* (1984), and, most recently, Dave Eggers' *A Heartbreaking Work of Staggering Genius* (2000).

The sixty million copies of *The Catcher in the Rye* that have been sold in the last fifty years stand as a testament to the ongoing appeal of Holden Caulfield. Salinger captured an adolescent fragility and bewilderment that has crossed the boundaries of time, race, gender, class. He gave Holden staying power beyond the novel by, in essence, *becoming* his character. Holden's fantasies about escaping to the woods—"I'd build me a little cabin somewhere with the dough I made and live there for the rest of my life"—eerily (for some, exhilaratingly) predict Salinger's own path. Salinger living out Holden's philosophy has given the novel an unearthly glow that has not dimmed.

Salinger's influence lives on: witness the number of voice-rich, coming-of-age novels published each year; a recent collection of essays by young writers delving into his influence, *With Love and Squalor;* a collection of letters written unrequitedly to the author, *Letters to J. D. Salinger;* even a rock 'n' roll band named the Jaded Salingers. Though Holden Caulfield will at least endure on the page, considering his sustained cultural presence, it is easy to picture him still walking the streets, wearing his red hunting hat and wishing "you could've been there."

Select Bibliography

EDITIONS

The Catcher in the Rye. Boston: Little, Brown, 1951. (The novel is widely available in mass market and quality paperback. The 2001 Back Bay paperback edition is cited in this essay.)

OTHER WORKS BY SALINGER

Nine Stories. Boston: Little, Brown, 1953.

Franny and Zooey. Boston: Little, Brown, 1961.

Raise High the Roof Beam, Carpenters and Seymour: An Introduction. Boston: Little, Brown, 1963.

SECONDARY WORKS

Bawer, Bruce. "Salinger's Arrested Development." *New Criterion* 5 (September 1986): 34–47.

Bloom, Harold, ed. *J. D. Salinger.* New York: Chelsea House, 1987. (In the Modern Critical Views series.)

Castronovo, David. "Holden Caulfield's Legacy." *New England Review* 22 (spring 2001): 180–186.

Coles, Robert. "Anna Freud and J. D. Salinger's Holden Caulfield." *Virginia Quarterly Review* 76 (spring 2000): 214–224.

French, Warren G. *J. D. Salinger, Revisited.* Boston: Twayne, 1988.

Grunwald, Henry Anatole, ed. *Salinger: A Critical and Personal Portrait.* New York: Harper & Row, 1962.

Hamilton, Ian. *In Search of J. D. Salinger.* New York: Random House, 1988.

Kotzen, Kip, and Thomas Beller, eds. *With Love and Squalor: 14 Writers Respond to the Work of J. D. Salinger.* New York: Broadway, 2001.

Kubica, Chris, and Will Hochman, eds. *Letters to J. D. Salinger.* Madison: University of Wisconsin Press, 2002.

Lundquist, James. *J. D. Salinger.* New York: Ungar, 1979.

McSweeney, Kerry. "Salinger Revisited." *Critical Quarterly* 20 (spring 1978): 61–68.

Maynard, Joyce. *At Home in the World: A Memoir.* New York: Picador, 1998.

Menand, Louis. "Holden at Fifty." *The New Yorker,* October 1, 2001, pp. 82–87.

Ohmann, Carol, and Richard Ohmann. "Reviewers, Critics, and *The Catcher in the Rye.*" *Critical Inquiry* 3 (autumn 1976): 15–37.

Pinsker, Sanford. "*The Catcher in the Rye* and All: Is the Age of the Formative Book Over?" *Georgia Review* 40 (winter 1986): 953–967.

————. The Catcher in the Rye: *Innocence under Pressure.* New York: Twayne, 1993.

Rachels, David. "Holden Caulfield: A Hero for All the Ages." *Chronicle of Higher Education,* March 30, 2001, p. B5.

Rosen, Gerald. "A Retrospective Look at *The Catcher in the Rye.*" *American Quarterly* 29 (winter 1977): 547–562.

Salinger, Margaret A. *Dream Catcher: A Memoir.* New York: Washington Square Press, 2000.

Salzberg, Joel, ed. *Critical Essays on Salinger's* The Catcher in the Rye. Boston: G. K. Hall, 1990.

Salzman, Jack, ed. *New Essays on* The Catcher in the Rye. Cambridge: Cambridge University Press, 1991.

Steinle, Pamela Hunt. *In Cold Fear:* The Catcher in the Rye *Censorship Controversies and Postwar American Character.* Columbus: Ohio State University Press, 2000.

Sublette, Jack R. *J. D. Salinger: An Annotated Bibliography: 1938–1981.* New York: Garland, 1984.

Arthur Miller's
Death of a Salesman

DOMINIC OLIVER

EATH OF A Salesman was an instant hit on its opening in New York. Reviewers were rhapsodic in their praise. Audiences wept and came to see the play in vast numbers: it ran for 742 perfomances on Broadway. While the New York production continued its run, a touring company took the play to virtually every major city in the United States. The play won not only the Pulitzer Prize and the Drama Critics' Circle Award but the Donaldson Award and Tony Awards for best play, best direction, best scene design, and best supporting actor. The published script was a roaring success, and it is the only play ever to be a Book-of-the-Month Club selection. By February 1950, productions had already been mounted in Great Britain, Denmark, Sweden, Switzerland, Argentina, Italy, France, Austria, Greece, Germany, and Israel. *Death of a Salesman* had found an internationally wide and appreciative audience and was immediately acknowledged as a contemporary classic. On *Salesman's* transfer to London the *Daily Express* said, "This play seems to lay the soul of America bare, throws across the footlights, flat in your face, all the hopes, fears, frustration, inhibitions and terrible yearnings of a nation." Still performed, read, and studied all over the world, the play retains both its popularity and its power.

BEGINNINGS—*THE INSIDE OF HIS HEAD*

Biff speaks these words at the very close of the play, in the "Requiem" section, and the statements are part of his rejection of Willy's dreaming of being "number-one man."

> There were a lot of nice days. When he'd come home from a trip; or on Sundays, making the stoop; finishing the cellar; putting on the new porch; when he built the extra bathroom; and put up the garage. You know something, Charley, there's more of him in that front stoop than in all the sales he ever made.

Linda finally owns the house, having that day made the last payment on their bank loan. Willy's death seems pointless, and they leave the stage to Linda's plaintive and repeated cries of "We're free . . . We're Free." The nullity and despair here are given a neatly ironic force when we become aware of the circumstances of Miller's writing of *Death of a Salesman*. In April of 1948 Miller drove up to the Connecticut farm he had bought the previous summer and built a ten-by-twelve-foot studio to work in. In a self-constructed haven in New England, Miller created a New England salesman who has no sense of comfort even in the home for and on which he has worked so hard. Miller and his creation share craftsmanship, but while the author's studio is a creative space, the happiness of Willy's do-it-yourself work is long gone by the time that the play takes place, and the house is a burden that he can only relieve through his death and a life-insurance payment.

Miller came to write *Death of a Salesman* in the aftermath of the success of *All My Sons* (1947). *All My Sons* is a play in some ways similar to *Salesman* in its dealings with a family in meltdown, but in other ways, particularly in its conventional structure, it is a very different work: as Joe Keller's crime is laid bare, the past is recalled and is the source of the action, but it is not enacted before the audience. Miller has acknowledged the numerous sparks of memory and inspiration that prompted him to write *Salesman*. His autobiography, *Timebends: A Life* (1987), picks out a number of figures and family stories that seem closely allied to the Lomans. Chief among these was his uncle Manny Newman, a traveling salesman who shared with Willy a tendency to self-important fantasy and a relentless competitiveness with regard to his two sons. Elsewhere, Miller has hinted that his relationship with his own father was akin to that between Bernard and Charley. Most specifically, Miller talks in *Timebends* of a chance meeting with Manny outside the Boston theater showing *All My Sons*. Despite his success, Miller felt that he was somehow being subjected to the same belittling competitiveness that had marked adolescent comparisons between him and his cousins. This encounter "cut through time like a knife through a layer cake," and although at this point he was not thinking of writing a play about a salesman, he thought that it would be wonderful "to do a play without any transitions at all, dialogue that would simply leap from bone to bone of a skeleton that would not for an instant

CHRONOLOGY

1915	Arthur Asher Miller born on October 17 in New York City to Isidore and Augusta Miller.
1933	Graduates from high school. Writes his first short story, "In Memoriam," depicting an aging salesman.
1934	Studies journalism at University of Michigan, where he becomes night editor of *Michigan Daily.* Studies playwriting under Professor Kenneth T. Rowe.
1939–1942	Writes radio plays, some of which are broadcast by CBS and NBC.
1940	Marries Mary Grace Slattery.
1944	First Broadway production, *The Man Who Had All the Luck,* closes after four performances but wins Theatre Guild National Award.
1945	Publishes first novel, *Focus,* on anti-Semitism.
1947	*All My Sons* opens on Broadway and wins New York Drama Critics' Circle Award.
1949	*Death of a Salesman* (originally entitled *The Inside of His Head*) opens in New York.
1953	*The Crucible* opens in New York to mixed reviews.
1954	Denied passport by State Department to attend opening of *The Crucible* in Brussels because of his alleged support of the Communist movement.
1956	Testifies before the House Un-American Activities Committee. Divorces Slattery and marries Marilyn Monroe.
1957	Indicted on charges of contempt of Congress, which are later reversed, for refusing to name suspected Communists.
1959	Awarded Gold Medal for Drama by National Institute of Arts and Letters.
1961	*The Misfits* released. Divorces Monroe.
1962	Marries Ingeborg Morath, an Austrian-born photographer.

1964	*After the Fall* and *Incident at Vichy* open in New York.
1965	Elected president of PEN (Poets, Essayists and Novelists), an international literary association.
1969	Publishes *In Russia* (travel journal) with photographs by Morath. In response, the Soviet Union bans all of Miller's works (1970).
1978	*The Theater Essays of Arthur Miller* published. Visits China. Publishes *Chinese Encounters* (travel journal) with photographs by Morath (1979).
1983	Directs *Death of a Salesman* in Beijing with Chinese cast.
1984	Publishes *Salesman in Beijing* with photographs by Morath. *Death of a Salesman* is revived on Broadway with Dustin Hoffman in lead role.
1987	*Timebends: A Life* (Miller's autobiography) published.
1993	*The Last Yankee* opens in New York.
1994	*Broken Glass* opens in New York and London.
1996	Film version of *The Crucible* released.

cease being added to, an organism as strictly economic as a leaf, as trim as an ant."

In *Timebends* Miller explains his wish to write in a way that showed that the past:

> is a formality, merely a dimmer present, for everything we are is at every moment alive in us. How fantastic a play would be that did not still the mind's simultaneity, did not allow a man to "forget" and turned him to see present through past and past through present, a form that in itself, quite apart from its content and meaning, would be inescapable as a psychological process and as a collecting point for all that his life in society had poured into him.

Although the play's plot, originally in three acts, had been worked out fairly carefully in his notes, Miller remembers that as he sat down to write, "all I had was the first two lines and a death." What he needed was a form that would allow

for the simultaneity of past and present and for the tragic trajectory of events to proceed from the fragmented logic of Willy's subjective experience. When he finally sat down to write, he worked all day and most of the night, skipping the parts that he knew would be easy to write. In one sitting he drafted the whole first act of the now two-act play. In six weeks he had a draft of the play in its entirety.

Miller has spoken often of the initial image of the play that was called at one early point in its development *The Inside of His Head.* In his introduction to the *Collected Plays* (1957; reprinted in *The Theater Essays of Arthur Miller,* 1978), Miller says the image "was of an enormous face the height of the proscenium arch which would appear and then open up, and we would see the inside of a man's head. . . . It was conceived half in laughter, for the inside of his head was a mass of contradictions." The image is a clear visual representation of expressionism, the dramatization of subjective reality, in direct opposition to the realistic mode in which Miller had composed *All My Sons.* Miller did not want, however, to represent Willy's experience as a subjective nightmare, detached from the reality around him, which is the usual method of expressionism. Miller said in a 1966 interview (reprinted in *The Theater Essays of Arthur Miller*) that, although he had been moved by expressionist plays, he found the traditional expressionist aesthetic perverse: "there are no people in it any more . . . it's the bitter end of the world where man is a voice of his class function, and that's it."

In *Salesman* Miller was after a more complex representation. He wanted the audience to see reality as Willy saw it, but also to recognize it as objectively real. Onstage there would be three epistemological levels: Willy's fantasies of the past, Willy's perception of the present, and the audience's perception of present stage reality. Miller needed a dramatic form that would combine the subjectivity of expressionism with the illusion of objectivity afforded by realism.

One important step in the development of his form was going with director Elia Kazan to see Tennessee Williams' *A Streetcar Named Desire* during its New Haven preview in November of 1947. In *Timebends* Miller wrote that *Streetcar* "opened one specific door for me . . . the words and their liberation, the joy of the writer in writing them, the radiant eloquence of its composition." This new freedom in the use of language was clearly important to the poetry of the mundane that infuses *Salesman,* but Kazan has suggested an even more important contribution. After seeing the performance, Kazan wrote in his autobiography that Miller "appeared to be full of wonder at the theatre's expressive possibilities. He told me he was amazed at how simply and successfully the non-realistic elements in the play . . . blended with the realistic ones." *Streetcar*'s style of subjective realism, which Kazan and Williams had created with designer Jo Mielziner, went a long way toward solving Miller's dramatic and theatrical problems. Kazan and Mielziner formed the direction and design team that was integral to the success of the first production of *Salesman.*

Subjective realism provides an anchor in reality—a series of events that are accepted by the audience as the objective reality of the play—but presents them through the mediating consciousness of a single character, a Blanche DuBois or a Willy Loman, whose mind is often in the process of breaking down. While the audience can share the nightmare experience of the protagonist, it never quite loses touch with the "real" events that the character is interpreting in what is perceived to be a distorted way. As Miller puts it in his introduction to the *Collected Plays,* Willy "is literally at that terrible moment when the voice of the past is no longer distant but quite as loud as the voice of the present . . . the form, therefore, *is* this process, instead of being a once-removed summation or indication of it." From this dual perspective, the audience can both empathize with the character's ordeal and judge it objectively. This mode of drama combines the strengths of expressionism with those of real-

ism. Miller explained to Christopher Bigsby in *Arthur Miller and Company,* "*Death of a Salesman* was conceived literally on two dimensions at the same time. On one level there are autonomous characters while on another there are characters who exist as symbols for Willy Loman."

Miller put his effort into the play's narrative, the telling of the tale, the juxtaposition of incidents from Willy's internal and external experience that would bring the audience to a sympathetic understanding of his inevitable fate. In his introduction to the *Collected Plays,* he wrote that "the structure of events and the nature of its form are also the direct reflection of Willy Loman's way of thinking at this moment of his life. . . . The way of telling the tale, in this sense, is as mad as Willy and as abrupt and as suddenly lyrical." In order to represent reality as Willy experienced it, Miller juxtaposed the scenes of the play's present with what he called from the beginning not "flashbacks" but "daydreams," reminding himself in his notebook that daydreams black out when they become threatening. Miller continues to explain that "there are no flashbacks in this play but only a mobile concurrency of past and present . . . because in his desperation to justify his life Willy Loman has destroyed the boundaries between now and then." In the early versions, the line between past and present was much clearer than it was to become. The daydreams were more sharply defined against the scenes in the present, but the line of the narrative was clear from the beginning. The events of the play are the events of twenty-four hours in Willy's life as Willy experiences them. To stage this Miller had originally envisioned a set that would be a direct reflection of the *Inside of His Head* idea, a space that, as he told Matthew Roudané in *Conversations with Arthur Miller,* was "the inside of his skull in which he would be crawling around, playing these scenes inside of himself." Such a space would have been an echo of the house/skull setting so often commentated upon by observers of Samuel Beckett's *Endgame.* As the play took shape however, Miller dropped this notion in favor of a minimal set that would make transitions between different times and spaces as smooth as possible; as he wrote in *Timebends,* he visualized "three bare platforms and only the minimum necessary furniture for a kitchen and two bedrooms, with the Boston hotel room as well as Howard's office to be played in open space."

FLUID THEATRICAL SPACE

Death of a Salesman makes constantly fluid use of this theatrical space as a reflection of Willy's increasing agitation and despair. Willy's unexpected return home at the opening of the play comes from his realization that as he is driving, looking at the scenery, "all of a sudden" he starts "goin' off the road! I'm tellin' ya, I absolutely forgot I was driving. If I'd've gone the other way over the white line I might've killed somebody. So I went on again—and five minutes later I'm dreamin' again, and I nearly—." The lack of control Willy describes here is soon manifested for us on stage. The boys are in the midst of a conversation in their bedroom (Biff is talking up the unlikely idea that his old boss, Bill Oliver, will give him funds for a ranch) when Willy starts talking aloud downstairs in the parlor. His conversation is a replay of a time long gone, when the boys are "simonizing" the car and excited at the prospect of a surprise he has brought for them. At first Willy talks to himself as if the boys are replying and upstairs, outside the daydream, the boys are irritated and embarrassed. As the present-day Happy and Biff drift off to sleep, however, the lighting changes, the built-up surroundings of the house fade out to be replaced by a covering of leaves, and we are placed so concretely in a physical rendering of Willy's memory that the younger Happy and Biff materialize to take their part in the scene. From here we move to an encounter with the young neighbor Bernard, a discussion with Linda of Willy's commission earnings, and a shift to a post-coital flirtation

with "The Woman" in Boston. There is another change of time and scene as we return to the house, but this time to argument and stress, where Willy's anger, guilt, and hurt pride that Linda is forced to mend her stockings blends into an anxious row with Bernard, who says that if Biff "doesn't buckle down he'll flunk math." Only at this point do we return to the Loman household in "real" time, as Willy's explosive shouting prompts Happy to come down and try to calm him. This collapse of recapitulated and present action into one staged moment is the seamless movement of the entire play, as worries and failures in the present blend with shames and disappointments in the past, and lead to the moment when Willy drives off to kill himself. But how have we got here?

CHEAP TALK AND FALSE COMFORT

CHARLEY, *an arm on Bernard's shoulder:* How do you like this kid? Gonna argue a case in front of the Supreme Court.

BERNARD, *protesting:* Pop!

WILLY, *genuinely shocked, pained, and happy:* No! The Supreme Court!

BERNARD: I gotta run. Bye, Dad!

CHARLEY: Knock 'em dead, Bernard!

Bernard goes off.

WILLY: The Supreme Court! And he didn't even mention it!

CHARLEY: He don't have to—he's gonna do it.

The boy who Willy called "a worm" has grown up to be a successful lawyer, while his sons of "spirit, personality" are nondescript ne'er-do-wells. Willy constantly talks up the possibilities of the future for himself and the boys while his neighbor and his neighbor's son are quietly but concretely making theirs. There are outright dishonesties in Willy's life—for example, the affair with "The Woman" so catastrophically discovered by Biff being the most obvious—but it is on a heap of trivial exaggerations and winked-at deceits that the mess of the Loman family life is built. It is never clear how much Willy earned at his most successful, but he inflates the sum without thinking when talking to Linda, and like a child caught out he is forced to reduce his claims:

WILLY: I did five hundred gross in Providence and seven hundred gross in Boston.
LINDA: No! Wait a minute, I've got a pencil. *She pulls pencil and paper out of her apron pocket.* That makes your commission . . . Two hundred—my God! Two hundred and twelve dollars!
WILLY: Well, I didn't figure it yet, but . . .
LINDA: How much did you do?
WILLY: Well I—I did—about a hundred and eighty gross in Providence. Well, no—it came to—roughly two hundred gross on the whole trip.
LINDA, *without hesitation:* Two hundred gross. That's . . . *She figures.*
WILLY: The trouble was that three of the stores were half closed for inventory in Boston. Otherwise I woulda broke records.
LINDA: Well, it makes seventy dollars and some pennies. That's very good.

The ease of the exaggeration, the unconvincing excuse, and the way Linda readily accommodates the climb-down gives this the air of an oft-told story, and while insignificant in itself, it is indicative of a pattern of deluded self-aggrandizement that Willy generates and at which Linda connives. Willy himself might characterize this as a positive outlook on life, a sort of "making the most" of what he has, but puffed-up verbiage and slight dishonesties are the rule in the Loman household. Willy is "idolized" by his sons, and in his need for their worship, everything they do, even Biff's theft of a ball from the locker room at school, is turned into a beguiling sign of their special status: "Coach'll probably congratulate you on your initiative!"

In the retrospect allowed us as the audience, we know this act of stealing to be part of a pattern. It is the theft of a box of basketballs that loses Biff his job with Oliver, and a decade later he "can't explain it" but takes Oliver's fountain pen from his office. While encouraging the boys in petty larceny from a building site, Willy has a moment of disquiet: "sometimes I'm afraid that I'm not teaching them the right kind of—. . ." In answer, Ben, who is a half-remembered projection in this recollected moment of the boys' childhood, says, "when I walked into the jungle, I was seventeen. When I walked out I was twenty-one. And by God I was rich!" Willy echoes him, "was rich! That's just the spirit I want to imbue them with! To walk into a jungle! I was right! I was right! I was right!" Willy's repetitions are spoken as the scene flows back into the here and now of his abortive sales trip, but the "right" he claims is a hollow justification for a laissez-faire lack of morality. The scenes that collapse past and present are after all the manifestations of an exhausted man driven to the edge of suicide, but the very fact that this particular scene is edged with regret and uneasiness betrays an awareness in Willy that his indulgent encouragement of the boys' every act was ill-judged.

For all his talk, Willy does not understand the "jungle" of the world in which he invests so much hope, and he certainly does not profit from it. Although happy to give the commercial world a label that connotes unfettered wildness, even viciousness, Willy actually lives and propounds a working creed of sentiment. It is not achievement but appearance that will breed success:

WILLY: Bernard is not well liked, is he?
BIFF: He's liked, but he's not well liked.
HAPPY: That's right, Pop.
WILLY: That's just what I mean. Bernard can get the best marks in school, y'understand, but when he gets out in the business world, y'understand, you are going to be five times ahead of him. That's why I thank almighty God you're both built like Adonises. Because the man who makes an appearance in the business world, the man who creates personal interest, is the man who gets ahead. Be liked and you will never want.

Later, in helping to construct Biff's plan of borrowing money from Bill Oliver, he restates this position: "It's not what you say, it's how you say it—because personality always wins the day." This faith in outward show and in being liked is utterly misplaced, and we know this from the start of the play if only because such hopeful statements are overheard by us in the doomed half-light of recollection and tired anger that make up Willy's last twenty-four hours. Before he fires him, Howard Wagner comes out with the banal but crushing phrases that "everybody's gotta pull his own weight," and "you gotta admit, business is business." It is no matter that Willy has spent thirty-four years working for the firm: he has outlived his usefulness and will be discarded. Willy's response is one of noncomprehension. He worked for the firm before Howard was born and even named him, but cannot see that this means nothing. Charley puts it bluntly:

> . . . when're you gonna realize that them things don't mean anything? You named him Howard, but you can't sell that. The only thing you got in this world is what you can sell . . .
> WILLY: I've always tried to think otherwise, I guess. I always felt that if a man was impressive, and well liked, that nothing—
> CHARLEY: Why must everybody like you? Who liked J. P. Morgan? Was he impressive? In a Turkish bath he'd look like a butcher. But with his pockets on he was very well liked.

Ironically, and despite the insults offered by Willy, Charley offers him work for the sake of friendship, not commerce. However, pride stops Willy from taking the job: it is far too late to reconsider the philosophy on which he has tried to build his life, and he is jealous of a success he does not comprehend. Furthermore, Willy's belief in success-through-admiration is held not just in the face of practical experience but while he is doubtful of whether he is liked himself. For all his bluster with the boys, he reveals to Linda that his appearance is laughed at, that, "people

don't seem to take to me. . . . they just pass me by. I'm not noticed." This doubt is hidden, but it is present and is the spur not for confrontation but retreat. Willy works hard, but in the face of his struggles and an inability to change his circumstances he is left with little choice but withdrawal into the comfort of a dream world he knows, at root, to be false. This is a world in which the future holds boundless opportunities for success and moneymaking, and in which he invests all the rhetorical and imaginative force he can muster. This false comfort kills him, and it destroys his family.

SHARED PERFORMANCES

The false comfort of performative fantasy is a cushion upon which the whole family comes to rely and a drama in which they all participate. As Linda and the boys discuss Willy's disturbed behavior there are moments of clarity, when she can criticize Biff for failing to settle down and call Happy a "philandering bum," but these moments of truthful assessment are rare and, by the time of the play's enaction of Willy's last hours, far too late. Far more typical is the strategy wherby unease and disappointment is talked away in a group effort at constructing a golden future of opportunity. In the midst of a confrontation between Biff and Willy, Happy diverts the tension:

> Wait a minute! I got an idea. I got a feasible idea. Come here, Biff, let's talk this over now, let's talk some sense here. When I was down in Florida last time, I thought of a great idea to sell sporting goods. It just came back to me. You and I, Biff—we have a line, the Loman Line. We train a couple of weeks, and put on a couple of exhibitions, see?
> WILLY: That's an idea!
> HAPPY: Wait! We form two basketball teams, see? Two water-polo teams. We play each other. It's a million dollars' worth of publicity. Two brothers, see? The Loman Brothers. Displays in the Royal Palms—all the hotels. And ban-

ners over the ring and the basketball court: "Loman Brothers." Baby, we could sell sporting goods!

WILLY: That is a one-million-dollar idea!

LINDA: Marvelous!

BIFF: I'm in great shape as far as that's concerned.

Happy takes the lead here in a fantasy that forcefully combines familial memories of Biff's sporting prowess with a commercial vision of wealth and pleasure. The rest of the family follows his lead without prompting: this is an established, almost programmed, pattern. Happy remains the propounder of the Loman behavioral line to the last, saying even at Willy's graveside that he is "gonna show . . . everybody . . . that Willy Loman did not die in vain. He had a good dream. It's the only dream you can have—to come out number-one man." Even Biff, who tries to break out of the pattern, is at a loss for other means with which to cope with his distraught father. At one moment he tries to tell Willy of his failure at Oliver's office, but when Willy starts to behave wildly—he is in the restaurant but simultaneously reliving the moments of Biff's arrival in the Boston hotel room—Biff attempts a half-baked story about Oliver's favorable reaction. This has a calming effect, but when he feels unable to sustain the falsehood and his father once again becomes agitated, Biff's only recourse is to hurry out from the restaurant, a small-scale replaying of the running away that has characterized the whole of his adult life. Biff's escape in the face of the failure of his imaginative coping mechanism is also a mirror of Willy's behavior until unavoidably confronted with the material actualité. In comments that reveal both Willy's persistent optimism and the unbridgeable fissure between father and son, Linda says that Willy likes "to know that there's still a possibility for better things. . . . When you write you're coming, he's all smiles, and talks about the future, and—he's just wonderful. And then the closer you seem to come, the more shaky he gets, and then, by the time you get here, he's arguing, and he seems angry at you."

Even as the play opens we are privy to what is clearly the end of a story, not the beginning. Willy is "tired to the death," and Biff's visit is not in prospect but happening in the here-and-now. The man before us is one for whom the shades of fantasy have become so complexly wrought and thoroughly imbued in his life that they have impinged upon his waking thoughts in a way he cannot control. As his life collapses, the dreams of yet-to-be realized success are all that keep him alive, but he is also tormented in a part-conscious awareness of their insufficiency and, fundamentally, falsity. His last desires for fulfillment, expressed in the midnight planting of seeds in the garden, are a feeble echo of the mythic territory of fecundity, freedom, and wealth into which his brother Ben disappeared. Of course, he does not even live to see his carrots, beets, and lettuce come to fruition, for he is convinced that his insurance policy is the buried "diamond, shining in the dark, hard and rough," which will somehow be his salvation. To believe that his death can somehow be a "shining" resolution to his unfulfilled dreams shows the depth of his disarray. He sees the failure of his life in commerce as somehow soluble through a final commodifying process in which he exchanges his life for twenty thousand dollars. Part of him knows that this contract might not be honored; Ben, conjured from Willy's mind and standing before him in the garden reminds him, "They might not honor the policy." It seems possible (even likely, given Linda's comments early in the play that the insurance firm suspects Willy's previous car wrecks were not all accidents) that his dying-as-financial-exchange will be a final, postmortem failure. His final action is thus as misplacedly optimistic as so much that has gone before.

THE SALESMAN'S SANITY

"Misplaced optimism," "distress," "fantasy": Do these terms add up to a kind of insanity on Willy's part? Miller has often commented negatively on the 1951 Columbia Pictures production of *Salesman*, not least because he saw the film as reducing Willy, played by Fredric March to, as he says in *Timebends*, "a psycho, all but completely out of control, with next to no grip on reality." Laslo Benedek, the director, tried to work out a way in which the film could mimic the play's merging of the past with the present, opting to film as much as possible from Willy's perspective so that there was no easy distinction between Willy's subjective experience and his experience in objective reality. In a scene that was shot in a subway tunnel, according to Benedek, "there were extras walking along with him as long as Willy would be aware of them—when he became submerged in the fantasy about his dead brother, he was alone with him in the endless tunnel." Yet there are crucial moments in the film when the convention of staying with Willy's perception is left behind. When Willy starts talking to himself while sitting in a subway train, for example, the camera frames him with other passengers who react to his strange behavior. The woman passenger sitting next to him edges further and further away, until she finally gets up and changes seats. Lost in his daydream, Willy is aware of none of this, and the effect is to invite the audience to share the perspective of the passengers rather than of Willy, objectively judging him to be crazy. Empathy is lost too. This is forced mis-reading, for in making Willy mad, and thus gaining a kind of melodramatic force, there are two concomitant losses. The first loss is of Willy's responsibility for what happens to him, and the second is of society's share in the blame for his fate. As Miller puts it in *Timebends*, "as a psychotic, he was predictable in the extreme; more than that, the misconception melted the tension between a man and his society, drawing the teeth of the play's social contemporaneity, obliterating its very context." *Death of a Salesman* is not a direct political parable in the manner of *The Crucible*, or a piece of historical-moral documentary like *Incident at Vichy*. Neither, however, is it an examination of individual, or even familial, isolation: Miller does

not write plays of that kind. The Lomans and their fate are embedded in society. Miller is explicit about this in his essay "The Shadow of the Gods" (collected in *The Theater Essays of Arthur Miller*):

> I hope I have made one thing clear—and it is that society is inside of man and man is inside society, and you cannot even create a truthfully drawn psychological entity on the stage until you understand his social relations and their power to make him what he is and to prevent him from being what he is not. The fish is in the water and the water is in the fish.

The vitality and truth of this statement with regard to *Salesman* is illustrated by further consideration of the circumstances in which the 1951 movie was produced. This was the period in which McCarthyite paranoia was reaching a peak in Hollywood, and indeed in the United States as a whole. Stage productions were being picketed by the American Legion because of Miller's (and by extension the play's) leftist sympathies. Even with the film's emphasis on psychological breakdown, its producers knew it to paint a recognizable picture of an Everyman cog in the wheel of commerce, and were fearful that in making a movie that was not an outright affirmation of the virtues of American capitalism, they would be subject to a popular outcry. Their solution was to make a short film that was meant to accompany *Salesman* when it was released into cinemas. Shot at the City College of New York Business School, the film, according to Miller in *Timebends*, consisted of "interviews with professors who blithely explained that Willy Loman was entirely atypical, a throwback to the past when salesmen did indeed have some hard problems. But nowadays selling was a fine profession with limitless spiritual compensations as well as financial ones. In fact, they all sounded like Willy Loman with a diploma." Miller threatened to sue Columbia, and *Salesman* was released without an apologetic preface, but the perceived need for the short film serves to emphasize not just contemporary paranoia but *Salesman*'s undoubted sociological punch.

THE MACHINE STOPS

Willy is not exceptional: the sadness of the situation is that he is typical. At the close of the play, Charley locates Willy's fate firmly in his role as a salesman: "Nobody dast blame this man. . . . A salesman is got to dream, boy. It comes with the territory." Earlier we have seen Linda's despairing attempt to assert Willy's value even as he is "exhausted" by a grind of work that brings no reward but penury:

> I don't say he's a great man. Willy Loman never made a lot of money. His name was never in the paper. He's not the finest character that ever lived. But he's a human being, and a terrible thing is happening to him. So attention must be paid. He's not to be allowed to fall into his grave like an old dog. Attention, attention must be finally paid to such a person.

The callousness of a system that does indeed discard its servants without thought is further underscored by the trivial rewards it offers. In the Loman household we could not be further from the gleaming consumer dream as cars, washing machines, and refrigerators are in a perpetually broken-down state, even when "brand new." Willy exclaims that he "would like to own something outright before it's broken," and that he is "always in a race with the junkyard!" He is, of course himself "junked" as a useless commodity when worn out and unable to sell for Howard's firm. In addition, even these shoddy goods can only be enjoyed in an environment of increasingly claustrophobic urban sprawl. Willy reminisces about elm trees in the garden, lilacs, wisteria, peonies, and daffodils. In his exchanges with Ben we can hear the longing for pastoral, open space. In the opening stage directions however, we see a "*solid vault of apartment houses,*" dwarfing a "*small,*

fragile-seeming home." "*Towering angular shapes*" surround the house, with only a small patch of "*the blue light of the sky*" falling on the property, the dominant light being a threatening and "*angry glow of orange.*" When Willy cries out, "They boxed in the whole goddam neighborhood!" it is a plaint that might easily stand as his epitaph.

An emissary of kindness and caring has remained in the neighborhood: Charley. He lends Willy money in the knowledge that there is little likelihood that it will be repaid, and even offers him a job. His presence in the play demonstrates that successful commerce need not be sterile and indifferent to the plight of those in need, but Charley is the exception, not the rule. As Willy says, "Charley, you're the only friend I got. Isn't that a remarkable thing?" Miller's introductory essay to *A View from the Bridge*, "On Social Plays" (collected in *The Theater Essays of Arthur Miller*), makes the subjected position of men such as Willy explicit:

> the absolute value of the individual human being is believed in only as a secondary value; it stands well below the needs of efficient production. We have finally come to serve the machine. The machine must not be stopped, marred, left dirty, or outmoded. Only man can be left marred, stopped, dirty and alone. . . . So long as modern man conceives of himself as valuable only because he fits into some niche in the machine-tending pattern, he will never know anything more than a pathetic doom.

Death of a Salesman should not be reduced to its sociological or political implications. As Miller asserts in the introduction to his *Collected Plays*, "a play cannot be equated with a political philosophy." However, in the same piece he makes it clear that "Willy Loman has broken a law without whose protection life is insupportable if not incomprehensible to him and to many others; it is the law which says that a failure in society and in business has no right to live." This law "is by no means a wholly agreeable one even as it is slavishly obeyed, for to fail is no longer to belong to society. . . . Therefore, the path is opened for those who wish to call Willy merely a foolish man even as they themselves are living in obedience to the same law that killed him."

A CONTEMPORARY TRAGEDY?

Salesman's status as a tragedy received early and sustained attention. To the opening-night newspaper critics, there was no question that what they were seeing was, in the words of Howard Banes of the *New York Tribune*, a "soaring tragedy" in the traditional mold. Robert Coleman of the *Daily Mirror* asserted that *Salesman* "is composed of essentially the same materials used by the Greek tragedians of the Golden Age." William Hawkins of the *New York World-Telegram* wrote that "*Death of a Salesman* is a play written along the lines of the finest classical tragedy. It is the revelation of a man's downfall . . . whose roots are entirely in his own soul."

These claims to the play's fitting the ancient, Aristotelian principles of tragedy were by no means uncontroversial. Willy, the punningly named low man, is self-evidently not the important figure whose actions shake the state around him. How well does the play fulfill other conventional tragic expectations of *peripeteia* (reversal), *hamartia* ("tragic flaw" or, more accurately, "error of judgment"), and *catharsis* (purification or purgation)? In her exalted position as a former First Lady and popular cultural commentator, Eleanor Roosevelt stated that the play left her

untouched and somewhat critically aloof. One does not hear voices at one moment and talk sensibly to the son of one's old employer a little later on. Surely, there are dreamers and there are totally untruthful people in the world, people who are untruthful with themselves, with their families and with the world as a whole. They fail everyone, including themselves, but I don't know whether

anyone needs a whole evening of gloom to impress that truth upon one.

To someone who was entirely unmoved by the play, a sensation at the mystic heights of tragic catharsis was obviously out of the question. Such an extremely negative reaction was, and remains, uncommon, but more sympathetic approaches to the question of the play's tragic status had to make some sophisticated intellectual maneuvers. In an analysis of *Salesman* written a few days after the New York opening, John Beaufort wrote:

In *Death of a Salesman* Mr. Miller is writing once more about moral responsibility and the misconception of what constitutes moral responsibility. He is writing about the conflict in people and between people. It remains for Biff, who alone perceives the significance of the conflict, to claim his ultimate freedom. Therein lies the catharsis of the play, the journey through "pity and fear" to a heightened sense of what the individual must mean to himself and to others, a repudiation of the false measurements of success. This is not the whole answer. But it is more than Willy Loman perceived.

Beaufort was raising here what was to become one of the central issues in the critical debate over the play. Could *Death of a Salesman* be a tragedy if its hero underwent no "recognition," in the Aristotelian sense, no fundamental process of learning and transcendence as a result of his experience? In offering Biff's new perception as a substitute for Willy's, Beaufort was raising a critical issue that has never been resolved conclusively. In subsequent decades critics have attempted to divine whether Miller's writing in general and *Salesman* in particular is suspended "between pathos and tragedy"; whether the play has the moral grandeur appropriate to tragedy; and whether a play that has such a quotidian center should be discussed in the same breath as the exotic and majestic lyricism of *Hamlet* or *Othello*. However, such discussions seem to miss the point: in *Salesman* and his other work, Miller is trying to reconfigure our notions of what tragedy can be. Discussions as to whether or not the play fits the ancient or Shakespearean tragic mold are irrelevant. It is not that Miller does not recognize the claims of well-established tragedies but that he is attempting something different. In the *Saturday Review* of February 26, 1949, John Mason Brown wrote, "Miller's play is a tragedy modern and personal, not classic and heroic. . . . its central figure is a little man sentenced to discover his smallness rather than a big man undone by his greatness." Miller himself addressed the issue on the following day in the *New York Times*. In a much-reprinted article entitled "Tragedy and the Common Man," Miller preemptively defended the notion of modern tragedy:

> In this age few tragedies are written. It has often been held that the lack is due to a paucity of heroes among us. . . . we are often held to be below tragedy—or tragedy above us. The inevitable conclusion is, of course, that the tragic mode is archaic, fit only for the very highly placed, the kings or the kingly, and where this admission is not made in so many words it is most often implied.

As a challenge to this point of view, Miller asserted, "I believe that the common man is as apt a subject for tragedy in its highest sense as kings were," and in the short space of his newspaper article he proceeded to outline a description of modern tragedy that reversed some of the central assumptions about the genre that had been in force since Aristotle had described it more than two thousand years earlier. Unlike classical descriptions of tragedy, which hold that the hero is punished for his challenge to the gods, a rebellion impelled by overweening pride and followed inevitably by guilt, Miller's held that tragedy "is the consequence of a man's total compulsion to evaluate himself justly." Where the classical theory located evil in the hero's violation of a transcendent order and found him justly punished for it, Miller located evil outside the hero: "if it is true that tragedy is the consequence of a man's total compulsion to

evaluate himself justly, his destruction in the attempt posits a wrong or an evil in his environment." The traditional notion of tragedy affirms a transcendent order through the hero's submission to his punishment for violating that order, but Miller asserts:

> The tragic right is a condition of life, a condition in which the human personality is able to flower and realize itself. The wrong is the condition which suppresses man, perverts the flowing out of his love and creative instinct. Tragedy enlightens—and it must, in that it points the heroic finger at the enemy of man's freedom. The thrust for freedom is the quality in tragedy which exalts. The revolutionary questioning of the stable environment is what terrifies. In no way is the common man debarred from such thoughts or such actions.

While the emphasis in earlier tragic theory had been on the individual's guilt for his violation of a higher order, whether supernatural or social, and the subsequent expulsion of the hero so that order could be restored, Miller's was on the individual's right to self-actualization and to personal freedom, rights that he assumed were inherently human. Miller's notions of good and evil and of the individual's relation to society are thus entirely at odds with the prevailing notions of classical tragedy.

In an essay that appeared in 1945, W. H. Auden remarked that at the end of a Greek play we say, "What a pity it had to be this way," while at the end of a Christian tragedy we say, "What a pity it had to be this way when it might have been otherwise." In Greek drama the situation is given, fixed, and the dramatist concentrates on the way in which his characters respond to the grip events have on them. In Christian tragedy the situation is not given so much as created, and destiny is not known beforehand. In both models there is a fixed system of moral imperatives resting on divine authority, there is an established order, and the tragedy works itself out largely in terms of the hero's conscious or accidental violation of that order. Miller combines the Greek and Christian tragic modes.

As in Christian models, Willy has—or appears to have—agency, the ability to shape his situation, but, as in Greek drama, the forces making for tragedy are outside his control. Willy is by no means faultless, but he is caught in a structure not of his own making. His idle and impractical dreaming; the false expectations and delusion he generates for himself and his sons; his cheating on Linda and subsequent alienation from Biff: all these are accelerating elements to his downfall, but he cannot be blamed for being worn out and unrewarded for his lifetime's work. As he says to Howard as he is being fired, "I put thirty-four years into this firm. . . . You can't eat the orange and throw the peel away—a man is not a piece of fruit!" Willy *has* been commodified and consumed, but somehow the play is not entirely deterministic. Willy is both part of society and apart from it. He is able to dream, able to resist his environment or fate and seek to change it. He does not succeed in generating change, but he *is* more than the forces that shape him. Willy is a subjected failure, but his striving shows that this need not have been his fate: society and its structures are not immutable. Miller wrote, "no tragedy can . . . come about when its author fears to question absolutely everything, when he regards any institution, habit or custom as being either everlasting, immutable or inevitable. In the tragic view the need of man to wholly realize himself is the only fixed star." Furthermore, it is "from this total questioning of what has previously been unquestioned" that "we learn." *Death of a Salesman* is not a tragedy because a hero has been brought low by fault, fate, and the violation of the absolute but because it interrogates a society that challenges its members to dream, and then punishes an old man who dreams and works to no end but suicide.

IMPORTANCE AND INFLUENCE

Some mention has already been made of the first theatrical production and film version of *Death of a Salesman,* but these and subsequent productions deserve further attention. The first Broadway production not only won plaudits from the critics but provoked powerful reactions from an unexpected source—the business community. In *Timebends,* Miller tells with pride the story of Bernard Gimbel, head of one of New York's largest department stores, giving orders on the night he saw *Salesman* that none of his employees were to be fired for being overage. A. Howard Fuller, president of the Fuller Brush Company from 1943 to 1959, was prompted by the play to write an article for *Fortune* magazine (reprinted in *Death of a Salesman: Text and Criticism,* 1967) in which he claimed "A salesman is everybody" and praised Miller for having shown that "in peacetime the professional salesman is the real hero of American Society."

The unalloyed praise of first-night critics was tempered by some negative reactions later on. Some, like Eleanor Roosevelt, focused on what hey perceived as the play's dominant note of gloom. Others criticized Miller's politics as much as the play. Eleanor Clark found in *Salesman* an "intellectual muddle and a lack of candor that regardless of Mr. Miller's conscious intent are the main earmark of contemporary fellow-travelling." Perhaps the most violent attack was that of Frederick Morgan in the *Hudson Review,* who summarized his reaction by calling the play a "sustained snivel." These negative reactions were and remain by far the minority view, however, as the play's enduring popularity attests: since its premiere there has never been a time when *Death of a Salesman* was not being performed somewhere in the world.

The first London production shared Kazan and Mielziner as the back-stage creative team. Paul Muni, a well-established and Oscar-winning star, was chosen to play Willy. Kazan was politely complimentary about Muni's performance, but for Miller, talking in an interview with Ronald Hayman (reprinted in *Conversations with Arthur Miller,* 1987), "The style was too studied, too technical. There was too little real inner life in his performance." Muni was plagued with illness throughout the run, and his decision to leave the show after six months forced it to close. Lee Cobb, too, had left the New York production early, pleading exhaustion, and even the comparatively youthful Dustin Hoffman insisted on cutting his performances back from eight shows a week to seven, and finally six, when he played Willy in 1984: the role is one of the longest and most demanding in the twentieth-century repertoire.

In 1951, in addition to the release of the Columbia movie, *Salesman* was produced in Ireland and South Africa. The Dublin production was picketed on the grounds of Miller's "Communist sympathies," and critical comment both positive and negative focused on the play as moral lesson. Despite technical difficulties on opening, the South African production was a triumph, with its run extended from an initial three weeks to eight in order to cope with demand.

Although Miller did not allow any further professional productions of *Salesman* within one hundred miles of Broadway until 1974, the play held the stage all over America in a range of community, university, and professional theaters. One notable production, in a Yiddish version, provoked a debate over the language of the play, with the critic George Ross contending that "what one feels most strikingly is that this Yiddish play is really the original, and the Broadway production was merely—Arthur Miller's translation into English." In 1972 the Center Stage theater in Baltimore produced an all-black *Salesman*, which provoked mixed reactions for its inevitable foregrounding of race but which was apparently more successful than George C. Scott's 1975 racially mixed cast. For Miller, Scott's casting of himself as Willy against the black actor Dotts Johnson suggested a quality of daring in Willy in having a black man for his best friend during the thirties, a rebelling against accepted social values and prejudices that was antithetical to his character. While praising

Scott's performance, reviewers generally felt the production to be mediocre and ill thought out.

Of productions in the late twentieth century two stand out. The first was in 1979, in London's National Theatre, and the second was Dustin Hoffman's Broadway revival in 1984, subsequently televised by CBS in 1985. According to Miller's interview with Bigsby, Warren Mitchell, the Willy Loman of the London production, Dustin Hoffman, and Lee J. Cobb have been "the three chief players" as far as Miller himself is concerned. Miller continues that, in contrast to Cobb's brooding stage presence, Mitchell and Hoffman exploited their diminutive size:

> They are both small men, feisty fellows. They've got a large world that's trying to kill them and a small man reacts with a kind of nervosity. That's in the part. It is obvious that Willy is leaping from one contradictory attitude to another very rapidly, sometimes with hardly a line in between, and to me that also was the characteristic of a little man, a physically small man. And I wrote it for a small man, if I wrote if for anybody.

Productions in translation have taken place all over the world in the decades since *Salesman*'s 1949 premiere. But perhaps most famously Miller himself directed the play in Beijing, China, in 1983. He details the experience in a revealing and entertaining memoir, *Salesman in Beijing* (1983). Productions outside America have always had to cope with the problem of the play's location: Is this a tale of anthropology, or even cultural archeology, to overseas producers and viewers? Is *Death of a Salesman* a specifically American story? Cold war productions in Soviet Russia (*Salesman* was one of very few American plays to be performed in the eastern bloc) were used to mount an overdetermined critique of bourgeois capitalism in general and America in particular. Miller persuaded his Chinese actors to give up the masking of thick white make-up and heavy light-colored wigs traditionally required in Chinese theater to connote performance as westerners. In *Salesman in*

Beijing Miller states that he came to believe that "by some unplanned magic we may end up creating something not quite American *or* Chinese but a pure style springing from the heart of the play itself—the play as nonnational event, that is, a human circumstance." As Miller said in 1999 in his "*Salesman* at Fifty" (reprinted in *Echoes Down the Corridor,* 2000), what they were thinking in China

turned out to be more or less what they were thinking in New York or London or Paris, namely that being human—a father, mother, son—is something most of us fail at most of the time, and a little mercy is eminently in order given the soci -eties we live in, which purport to be stable and sound as mountains when in fact they are all trembling in a fast wind blowing mindlessly around the earth.

These words are an echo of *Salesman*'s Requiem, where Charley talks of Willy as being at the heart of an "earthquake." Failure in the face of such monstrous forces deserves our pity and even our respect: "attention must be paid."

Select Bibliography

EDITIONS

Death of a Salesman: Certain Private Conversations in Two Acts and a Requiem. New York: Viking, 1949.

Death of a Salesman: A Play in Two Acts. New York: Dramatists Play Service, 1952. Reprinted, 1979.

Theatre Arts 35 (October 1953): 49–91.

Collected Plays. New York: Viking, 1957; Harmondsworth, Eng.: Penguin, 1961.

Plays: One. London: Methuen World Classics, 1988, 2000. (All references in this chapter are to the 2000 edition of Methuen World Classics.)

OTHER WORKS BY MILLER

The Theater Essays of Arthur Miller. Edited by Robert A. Martin. New York: Viking, 1978. (Includes "Tragedy and the Common Man," "On Social Plays," "Introduction to the *Collected Plays,*" and "The Shadow of the Gods.")

Salesman in Beijing. New York: Viking, 1983.

Timebends: A Life. New York: Grove, 1987.

Plays: Two. London: Methuen World Classics, 1988.

Echoes Down the Corridor: Collected Essays, 1944–2000. Edited by Steven R. Centola. New York: Viking, 2000.

SECONDARY WORKS

Aarnes, William. "Tragic Form and the Possibility of Meaning in *Death of a Salesman.*" *Furman Studies* 29 (1983): 57–80.

Auden, W. H. "The Christian Tragic Hero." *New York Times,* December 16, 1945, section 7, pp. 1, 21.

Beaufort, John. "Arthur Miller's Play an Absorbing Experience." *Christian Science Monitor,* February 19, 1949, p. 12.

Becker, Benjamin J. "*Death of a Salesman*: Arthur Miller's Play in the Light of Psychoanalysis." *American Journal of Psychoanalysis* 47 (fall 1987): 195–209.

Benedek, Laslo. "Play into Picture." *Sight and Sound* 22 (October–December 1952): 82–84, 96.

Bigsby, Christopher, ed. *Arthur Miller and Company.* London: Methuen, 1990.

————, ed. *The Cambridge Companion to Arthur Miller.* Cambridge: Cambridge University Press, 1997.

Bliquez, Guerin. "Linda's Role in *Death of a Salesman.*" *Modern Drama* 10 (February 1968): 383–386.

Bloom, Harold, ed. *Arthur Miller.* New York: Chelsea House, 1987.

————. *Arthur Miller's Death of a Salesman.* New York: Chelsea House, 1988.

————. *Willy Loman.* New York: Chelsea House, 1991.

Centola, Steve R. *Arthur Miller in Conversation.* Dallas: Northhouse & Northhouse, 1993.

————. "Family Values in *Death of a Salesman.*" *College Language Association Journal* 37, no. 1 (1993): 29–41.

————, ed. *The Achievement of Arthur Miller: New Essays.* Dallas: Northhouse & Northhouse, 1995.

Clark, Eleanor. "Old Glamour, New Gloom." *Partisan Review* 16, no. 6 (1949): 631–636.

Coffin, Rachel W., ed. "*Death of a Salesman.*" *New York Theatre Critics' Reviews* 10 (1949): 358–361. (Contains reviews by Howard Barnes, Robert Coleman, and William Hawkins).

Corrigan, Robert W., ed. *Arthur Miller: A Collection of Critical Essays.* Englewood Cliffs, N.J.: Prentice-Hall, 1969.

Freedman, Morris. "The Jewishness of Arthur Miller: His Family Epic." In his *American Drama in Social Context.* Carbondale: Southern Illinois University Press, 1971.

Hayashi, Tetsumaro. *Arthur Miller Criticism, 1930–1967.* Metuchen, N.J.: Scarecrow, 1969.

Hayman, Ronald. *Arthur Miller.* New York: Frederick Ungar, 1972, 1983.

Hume, Beverly. "Linda Loman as 'The Woman' in Miller's *Death of a Salesman.*" *Notes on Modern American Literature* 9, no. 3 (winter 1985): item 14.

Hurrell, John D., ed. *Two Modern American Tragedies: Reviews and Criticism of* Death of a Salesman *and* A Streetcar Named Desire. New York: Scribners, 1961.

Kazan, Elia. *A Theatre in Your Head.* Edited by Kenneth Thorpe Rowe. New York: Funk and Wagnalls, 1960.

————. *Elia Kazan: A Life.* New York: Knopf, 1988.

Koon, Hélène Wickam, ed. *Twentieth Century Interpretations of Death of a Salesman.* Englewood Cliffs, N.J.: Prentice-Hall, 1983.

Martin, Robert A., ed. *Arthur Miller: New Perspectives.* Englewood Cliffs, N.J.: Prentice-Hall, 1982.

Meserve, Walter J., ed. *The Merrill Studies in* Death of a Salesman. Columbus, Ohio: Merrill, 1972.

Mielziner, Jo. "Designing a Play: *Death of a Salesman.*" In his *Designing for the Theatre.* New York: Atheneum, 1965.

Morgan, Frederick. "Notes on the Theatre." *Hudson Review* 2, no. 2 (1949): 269–276.

Roosevelt, Eleanor. "Gloomy Hit Show Fails to Depict Average Man." *New York World Telegram,* April 28, 1949.

Ross, George. "*Death of a Salesman* in the Original." *Commentary* 11 (February 1951).

Roudané, Matthew C., ed. *Conversations with Arthur Miller.* Jackson: University Press of Mississippi, 1987. (Includes interview by Ronald Hayman.)

———. *Approaches to Teaching Miller's* Death of a Salesman. New York: Modern Language Association, 1995.

Schleuter, June, ed. *Feminist Re-readings of Modern American Drama.* Rutherford, N.J.: Fairleigh Dickinson University Press, 1989.

Schleuter, June, and James K. Flanagan. *Arthur Miller.* New York: Ungar, 1987.

Shatzky, Joel. "Arthur Miller's 'Jewish' Salesman." *Studies in American Jewish Literature* 2, no. 1 (1976): 1–9.

Spindler, Michael. "Consumer Man in Crisis: Arthur Miller's *Death of a Salesman.*" In his *American Literature and Social Change: William Dean Howells to Arthur Miller.* Bloomington: Indiana University Press, 1983.

Vogel, Dan. "From Milkman to Salesman: Glimpses of the Galut." *Studies in American Jewish Literature* 10 (fall 1991): 172–178.

Weales, Gerald. *Arthur Miller:* Death of a Salesman, *Text and Criticism.* New York: Viking Press, 1967; Harmondsworth, Eng.: Penguin, 1977. (Includes article by A. Howard Fuller.)

Williams, Raymond. "The Realism of Arthur Miller." *Critical Quarterly* 1 (1959): 140–149.

Allen Ginsberg's
"Howl"

SHARON BRYAN

ALLEN GINSBERG'S POEM "Howl," first published in 1956, is one of the most widely read and translated poems of the twentieth century. Many critics consider it a breakthrough in contemporary poetry and a literary masterpiece. Donald Allen, in his introduction to the landmark volume *New American Poetry*, published in 1960, described it as "The *Waste Land* for our age." The poem was also the subject of an obscenity trial when it was first published, based on some of its language and imagery, but after testimony from numerous literary scholars it was deemed "an important work of art" and not obscene. The trial received a great deal of publicity and made "Howl" and Ginsberg famous. Although the poem includes many personal references, it is also an indictment of social attitudes and strictures. It is this intersection of public and private that resonated with readers at the time and continues to do so. The poem's account of down-and-out mad geniuses in New York City's Harlem, including drug taking, graphic sexual encounters, visions, insanity, ecstasy and desperation, poverty, and violent death, tore through the decade's placid, proper veneer in the same way that rock and roll was erupting on the music scene and that—more quietly, but no less

forcefully—Martin Luther King Jr. was emerging as a civil rights leader. Response to the poem in literary circles ranged from praise and admiration to bafflement to contempt, but "Howl" opened up a wide new range of possibilities in poetry for both form and content, including the "confessional" poetry of the 1960s.

When Allen Ginsberg read "Howl" in public for the first time, at the Six Gallery in San Francisco on October 13, 1955, Dwight D. Eisenhower was the president of the United States and Nikita Khrushchev led the Soviet Union. Just a year earlier, Senator Joseph R. McCarthy's vendetta against those he believed to be communists had finally been brought to a halt and censured by the U.S. Senate. For the most part, American society was still shaped by World War II and its aftermath. Following the war's four years of disruption and anxiety, Americans had been eager to get on with their daily lives: they wanted steady jobs, marriage and family, a home in the new suburbs, peace and quiet. Ginsberg's "Howl" erupted into a world that at least on the surface was tidy, well mannered, and well behaved. Men and women wore hats, and women wore white gloves and stockings with straight seams down the back.

When Lucille Ball was pregnant, the writers of her television show could not use the word "pregnant" to describe her "condition."

Much of the poetry of the 1950s shared in this placid propriety. These poets were writing in the daunting shadow of the great modernists—T. S. Eliot, Ezra Pound, Wallace Stevens, and Marianne Moore—who began publishing in the 1910s and 1920s. The modernists had had large ambitions for poetry—their subject matter included mythology, history, art, culture, economics, philosophy, and other related topics, rather than the details of ordinary life. They rejected the Romanticism of Percy Bysshe Shelley, John Keats, Lord Byron, Samuel Taylor Coleridge, and William Wordsworth, which focused on the individual personality. Instead of shaping the poem as the speech of one person, presumably the poet, modernists used personae, or masks, and techniques from collage, cubism, and drama. Poetry of the 1940s and 1950s retained some of the dense allusiveness of modernist poetry, but it contented itself with smaller ambitions. The poems often seemed tightly controlled, dry, and lacking in any genuine emotion, let alone passion. The poetry is sometimes described as "academic" because much of it was produced and read on university campuses and was often written more to lend itself to literary analysis than to express feelings or explore open-ended questions.

Because *Howl and Other Poems* was Ginsberg's first book to be published, many people assume it was his earliest writing. But by the time he finished "Howl," Ginsberg had already been writing poetry for more than ten years and had written two volumes of poetry that were still unpublished. He had enrolled at Columbia University in New York City in 1943, when he was just seventeen, planning to become a labor lawyer. But he soon met and fell in with a loose group of people who saw themselves as thinkers and experimenters far from the mainstream of American life. One such thinker was Jack Kerouac, who was trying to develop a fiction writing style that would capture on the page

CHRONOLOGY

1926	Irwin Allen Ginsberg born June 3 in Newark, New Jersey, to Louis and Naomi Livergant Ginsberg.
1943	Enrolls as a freshman at Columbia University in New York; meets Lucien Carr, William Burroughs.
1948	Has a vision of William Blake that haunts his imagination for the next fifteen years.
1949	Car accident leads to Ginsberg's suspension from college and his sentence to the Columbia Presbyterian Psychiatric Institute.
1953	Arrives in San Francisco.
1955	First public reading of "Howl" on October 13 at the Six Gallery.
1956	Publication of *Howl and Other Poems* by City Lights Press in San Francisco.
1957	Obscenity trial makes Ginsberg and "Howl" famous.
1961	*Kaddish and Other Poems.*
1963	*Reality Sandwiches.*
1968	*Planet News.*
1970	With poet Ann Waldman, founds Jack Kerouac Institute of Disembodied Poetics at Naropa Institute in Boulder, Colorado.
1973	*The Fall of America, Poems of These States.*
1974	National Book Award for *The Fall of America.*
1982	*Plutonian Ode, and Other Poems.*
1984	*Collected Poems, 1947–1980.*
1986	*White Shroud.* Annotated version of "Howl" published.
1996	*Selected Poems, 1947–1995.*
1997	Allen Ginsberg dies April 5 in New York City at age seventy.

something of the speed and spontaneity of impressions as they run through the mind. Kerouac was four years older than Ginsberg, intelligent, hard working, and devoted to his writing; Ginsberg looked to him as a friend and a model and began to apply Kerouac's theories about writing fiction to his own poetry. A few years later Ginsberg met Neal Cassady when he came to New York, and the three formed the heart of what came to be known as the Beat Generation. The group also included John Clellon Holmes (whose novel *Go,* 1951, was based on some of the same people and events Kerouac wrote about in *On the Road,* 1957), and William Burroughs (later the author of *Naked Lunch,* 1959, and other books), who was fascinated by drugs and crime in addition to philosophy and literature.

Ginsberg, Kerouac, and Holmes pursued what they referred to as the New Vision in their writing, as they tried to create a style that would help them reveal their view of a world forever changed by the events of World War II, especially the Holocaust and the dropping of atom bombs on Hiroshima and Nagasaki. They believed that if society and governments could act so inhumanely—even insanely—then they were to be distrusted rather than blindly followed, and that true wisdom was more likely to be found among individuals. Kerouac, who published his novel *On the Road* a year after Ginsberg published *Howl,* first used the word "beat" to describe those in the postwar generation who were weary of the pressures to conform. He later associated it with "beatific," or blessed, following in the Romantic tradition of considering outsiders, the poor, and the suffering to be recipients of grace and sources of wisdom. Holmes first used the phrase Beat Generation in a *New York Times* article: "A man is beat whenever he goes for broke and wages the sum of his resources on a single number."

Ginsberg was drawn to these friends and others in part because he had identified from early on with those on the fringe and because their emotional intensity reflected something of his own mother's mental illness. Ginsberg was born on June 3, 1926, five years after his brother Eugene, to Louis and Naomi Livergant Ginsberg, both from Russian Jewish backgrounds. Louis' grandfather had immigrated to the United States, and Naomi's family had come to this country when she was a child, bringing with them beliefs in communism and social activism. Louis became a teacher and a lyric poet whose work appeared in the *New York Times* and other publications. Naomi took care of the household and her two sons until she was gradually disabled by psychiatric problems that had first appeared before her marriage. She was in and out of mental hospitals, subjected to a variety of treatments for paranoid schizophrenia, and in later years given a lobotomy. From his childhood on, Ginsberg was drawn to literature, social causes, and the wisdom of those outside the mainstream.

When Ginsberg began studying poetry his favorites included William Blake, Shelley, and Keats, some of the same Romantics the modernists had rejected, and his own early efforts, written in meter and rhyme, were heavily influenced by their techniques. His professors at Columbia University included the literary critic Lionel Trilling and the poet and critic Mark Van Doren, both of whom encouraged his early efforts. He wrote steadily but struggled to mesh the forms he was using with his own emotions and his longing to express the visionary. Ginsberg and others in his group distrusted appearances and longed for visions that would reveal what was otherwise hidden or invisible. To this end they drank, used various drugs, went days without sleeping, wandered the city, and immersed themselves in visionary writers. One of the central experiences in Ginsberg's life was a vision in which he heard what he took to be the voice of Blake himself reciting his poems. Ginsberg had been studying intensely and was alone in his apartment when it began. As he listened to Blake's voice, he said later, he suddenly understood that poetry was eternal and that poets separated by centuries could share the same consciousness. He spent the next fifteen years trying—mostly by taking hallucinogenic drugs—to return to that state.

After a series of small clashes with university officials that culminated when Ginsberg and several acquaintances were arrested for possession of stolen property following a car crash, Ginsberg was suspended from Columbia before his senior year. He was sentenced to psychiatric treatment and spent several months in the Columbia Presbyterian Psychiatric Institute, where he met and immediately hit it off with Carl Solomon, the man to whom "Howl" is dedicated. Solomon introduced Ginsberg to the work of the French poet Antonin Artaud, who had lamented the fate of those driven to suicide by society's failure to understand their search for the visionary. Ginsberg also continued to correspond with Trilling and Van Doren during this suspension and returned to the university after he was released. Following his graduation, he began a friendship with William Carlos Williams, who had recently published the first parts of a long poem called *Paterson,* set in the New Jersey town in which they had both grown up, and who was a poet Ginsberg saw as following in the footsteps of Blake and Walt Whitman.

He also continued to steep himself in the local art scene that included the painters Willem de Kooning and Jackson Pollock, dancer Merce Cunningham and composer John Cage, experimental theater, and jazz musicians Miles Davis, Dizzy Gillespie, Coleman Hawkins, and many others. Ginsberg looked constantly for techniques of bridging the modern and the traditional that he could draw on for his own poems. He and his friends often gathered at a Greenwich Village bar, the San Remo, to share their latest breakthroughs and discoveries. Ginsberg finally left New York in 1953 to travel in the United States and Mexico, visiting Burroughs and other friends. He spent several months living in Mexico before he made his way to San Francisco, where he soon met Kenneth Rexroth, Lawrence Ferlinghetti, and others who were part of a lively literary and arts scene known as the San Francisco Renaissance.

Several months after he arrived in San Francisco, Ginsberg met and fell in love with Peter Orlovsky, the man who would be his companion for the next thirty years. Not long

after that he quit his job and lived on unemployment so that he could devote himself full-time to his writing. He was experimenting with form, trying to find something that would combine the consciousness he had achieved in his Blake vision with details of everyday life. He had steeped himself in the work of Whitman, Pound, Williams, Louis-Ferdinand Céline, Arthur Rimbaud, Charles Baudelaire, W. B. Yeats, James Joyce, Hart Crane, and many others who seemed to share his determination to "make it new." He was especially interested in techniques of spontaneity, including surrealism's automatic writing, that allow artists to capture uncensored thoughts and feelings. At Williams' suggestion, Ginsberg began to turn some of his journal entries into poems, and to his surprise discovered that they were often effective, and had the spontaneity and detail he had been unable to incorporate in his poems. He continued to work on this project, poems that would eventually be collected into his book *Empty Mirror* (1961), and to work at the same time on the poems in a more traditional vein that would become *The Gates of Wrath* (1972). (When Ginsberg published his *Collected Poems 1947–1980* in 1984, he put the poems in chronological—or as he said, autobiographical—order, to make clear he had been working in both styles at the same time.)

Then Ginsberg received word that Carl Solomon, who had been working as an editor in New York, needed to return to the psychiatric hospital. He said later that "Howl" was "occasioned by unexpected news of Carl Solomon's removal to Pilgrim State." The news served as a catalyst, as a lightning bolt that brought together and fused what had been many disparate elements. Not long afterward, Ginsberg wrote the first draft of what became parts I and III of "Howl" in a single sitting. He sat down at his typewriter not to work on a formal poem, he said, but to state his "imaginative sympathies." The fact that he did not think of what he was writing as something for publication left him freer to say whatever came to him without censoring it, and he tried to capture the spontaneity of Kerouac's fiction writing technique. He was not attempting to capture speech, as Wordsworth and Williams had, but "the melody of actual thought." When he stopped, he had six single-spaced pages of what was to become part I of the poem (it would go through extensive revisions over the next several months) and all of part III. Soon thereafter a peyote-induced vision in which he saw the Sir Francis Drake hotel as the face of a robotic monster triggered the poem's famous second, or "Moloch" section. Later still, Ginsberg began the fourth, or "Holy" section as he pondered the poem while he was riding a bus.

Ginsberg sent early versions of his new poem to Kerouac and Burroughs, who both praised it—though Kerouac urged him not to revise, to remember that the first thought is the best thought—and to Lawrence Ferlinghetti, who said he would publish it as a chapbook. The poem's public debut came at a now famous reading at the Six Gallery in San Francisco in October 1955. Others on the program that night included Philip Lamantia, Michael McClure, Philip Whalen, and Gary Snyder. Kenneth Rexroth provided the introductions. Jack Kerouac declined to read his work in public, but he supplied wine for the readers and the audience and urged Ginsberg on with rhythmic clapping. The entire event was a great success, and the next day Ferlinghetti sent Ginsberg a telegram that borrowed Ralph Waldo Emerson's words to Whitman: "I greet you at the beginning of a great career," and went on to ask, "When do I get the manuscript?"

THE POEM: PART I

Though "Howl" became famous—and notorious—for its subject matter, its attacks on the establishment, and its obscenities, much of Ginsberg's focus as he wrote and rewrote it was on finding the form that would enable that content to emerge as powerfully as possible. He

began by using Williams' three-part line or three-line stanza:

> I saw the best lines of my generation
> generation destroyed by madness
> starving, mystical, naked . . .

But he found in the midst of a particularly long phrase that the form broke down. He then turned to a longer line similar to the one used by Whitman, and by the eighteenth-century English poet Christopher Smart, which had the necessary muscularity to let the poem's true prophetic voice emerge fully:

> I saw the best minds of my generation destroyed
>   by madness, starving hysterical naked,
> dragging themselves through the negro streets at
>   dawn looking for an angry fix, . . .

But they are looking for more than that; for these "angelheaded hipsters" the fix is a means to a much larger end. They are "burning for the ancient heavenly connection to the starry dynamo in the machinery of night," a spiritual, mystical tie between themselves and the universe. They are looking, as the poem says several lines later, for "the motionless world of Time between" Canada and Paterson, or any two poles on actual earth, they are looking for "kind king light of mind" to reveal eternal truths that cannot be seen in the "drear light of [the Bronx] Zoo."

Ginsberg's opening line echoes the beginning of William Carlos Williams' poem "To Elsie": "The pure products of America / go crazy," but Ginsberg's poem goes on to reveal depths Williams had not imagined. As Williams puts it in concluding his introduction to the first edition of *Howl and Other Poems,* "Hold back the edges of your gown, Ladies, we are going through hell." This trip through hell differs from the best known literary version, the one in Dante's *Inferno,* in a number of ways beyond the specifics. For one thing, Dante had the earlier poet Virgil as guide and protector; Ginsberg acts as the reader's guide, but he has no protector, and means to shock rather than protect those who hear what he says. For another, Dante's vision of hell was hierarchical and systematic, with punishments specifically designed to fit alleged sins, while Ginsberg's hell is chaotic and the sufferings result from society's failure to value its "best minds" rather than from any conscious, deliberate punishment. Yet another difference is that all of the souls Dante encounters are those of people who have already died, and though some of those whose lives are recounted in "Howl" were dead by the time Ginsberg wrote the poem, the miseries he describes all belong to the living—or living dead, those so at odds with the society they live in they cannot function as part of it.

The first draft had read "starving mystical naked," and Ginsberg considered the change to "hysterical" an important one for setting the tone he wanted, one that was hard-edged and unsentimental. He also switched the two adjectives in the second sentence from their first pairings: "angry streets" and "negro fix." The revised noun-adjective pairings reflect Ginsberg's wish to capture the effect of Paul Cézanne's surprising juxtapositions of blocks of color, which he had come to refer to as "eyeball kicks," a technique designed to jolt viewers out of their usual ways of seeing the world that is used throughout the poem. These phrases appear thoroughout: "angelheaded hipsters," "hydrogen jukebox," "bop kabbalah," "nitroglycerin shrieks," "hotrod Golgotha jail-solitude watch."

The final version of this section is one sentence, seventy-eight lines—or verses, as Ginsberg referred to the variable length phrases—long. All of its details come from the lives of people Ginsberg knew—friends, acquaintances, his mother—but have been revised and rearranged as necessary for the poem's rhythm and power. Though he says "I" only twice in this section, it is clear that the speaker's sympathies lie with those he describes, that he is not looking at them from a cool

distance. The poem is at least as much a howl of sorrow for their suffering as it is of anger at the society that fails to understand and support them.

By the fourth line, a phrasing emerges that will anchor most of the lines throughout this section:

> who poverty and tatters and hollow-eyed and
>   high sat up smoking in the supernatural dark-
>   ness of cold-water flats floating across the tops
>   of cities contemplating jazz,
> who bared their brains to Heaven under the El
>   and saw Mohammedan angels staggering on
>   tenement roofs illuminated,
> who passed through universities with radiant cool
>   eyes hallucinating Arkansas and Blake-light
>   tragedy among the scholars of war,
> who were expelled from the academies for crazy
>   & publishing obscene odes on the windows of
>   the skull, . . .

This technique of repeating the opening word of a line, or anaphora, was one Whitman, Smart, and others had used extensively, and of course it can also be found in the King James version of the Bible. It is often used to structure poetry without relying on meter and rhyme. These lines could describe a number of the people Ginsberg knew in New York, living in cheap apartments with no hot water, rattled by the noise of subway trains passing on their elevated tracks. The person with "radiant cool eyes" is Ginsberg himself; "Arkansas" was originally "anarchy," which Ginsberg decided was too abstract. The next lines refer to what he considered the most ridiculous of the reasons cited for his suspension from Columbia, that he had written obscenities in the steam on his dorm room window.

Ginsberg was finally able to accomplish something he had been trying to do for years in his poems, and that was to intermingle the visionary with daily—or nightly—life: "who ate fire in paint hotels or drank turpentine in Paradise Alley" (an apartment house in Harlem), and "incomparable blind streets of shuddering cloud and lightning in the mind." These "angel-headed hipsters" are trying in any way they can think of, from peyote to marijuana to Benzedrine to booze to nonstop talking, to experience the visionary. They are looking for the news not found in newspapers, the news Williams had said men were dying every day for the lack of. But they are also living in abysmal conditions because the rest of the society does not value what they are looking for, has no use for it or for them. They spend their nights in cafeterias like Bickfords or jazz clubs like Fugazzi's, or walking from mental hospitals to museums to bridges. They soldier on, but as "a lost battalion" society fails to sympathize with, let alone honor. When they leave New York and go "on the road" in search of their visions, they take their torments with them to Paterson, Tangiers, China, Kansas, Idaho, Oklahoma, Chicago, the west coast. This is followed by a blizzard of images that seem to be glimpsed from a speeding train: "platonic conversationalists jumping down the stoops off fire escapes off windowsills off Empire State out of the moon / yacketayak-king . . . whole intellects disgorged in total recall for seven days and seven nights," "meat for the Synagogue cast on the pavement," "nowhere Zen New Jersey," "Eastern sweats and Tangerian bone-grindings and migraines of China"—and then the train appears: "boxcars boxcars boxcars racketing through snow toward lonesome farms in grandfather night." The frantic travelers are studying mysticism in any form they can think of, desperately looking for something that will reveal the order of the universe to them. They are hungry for jazz, for soup, for sex, but also for visions, for something they cannot find in daily life.

Specific enemies begin to appear: the FBI, capitalism, the atomic scientists at Los Alamos, the police. At this point the poem begins an extended riff on sex and sexuality, which includes some of the passages cited at the obscenity trial. Sex represented a number of things to Ginsberg: the body, which he considered the home of the soul, and which therefore needed to be brought into poetry (though he struggled for years to accept this truth himself); a potential doorway to altered consciousness; and a source of intense emotions ranging from pleasure to power to shame. The passage begins with a slight ironic distance, and with a sense of the ridiculous, of how absurd the struggles he and his friends were engaged in might look to the world: "who howled on their knees in the subway and were dragged off the roof waving genitals and manuscripts." Ginsberg cited Charlie Chaplin's movies as an important influence on his work, and made the humor in his poems audible in his live readings. He saw himself as a Trickster figure, a jester, a sacred fool who could get away with telling the truth if he made people laugh. But the next line could not be more direct: "who let themselves be fucked in the ass by saintly motorcyclists and screamed with joy." The most important word in this line for Ginsberg was "joy," he said, because he thought most people would assume that the person was screaming in pain. Ginsberg had recognized his homosexual impulses since childhood, and had had affairs with a number of men, but he also went through a period when he slept and lived with women and hoped he could live a heterosexual life. By the time he wrote "Howl," he had accepted his homosexuality, but had not spoken to his father about it and certainly had not written about it in anything he expected to publish. He said later that writing this passage completely freed him from any expectation of publishing the poem and made it possible to say whatever seemed true and necessary. Only after he became aware of the poem's power did he begin to revise it for publication.

The passage continues in a mixture of joy intermixed with sadness, as loves are lost to "the three old shrews of fate the one eyed shrew of the heterosexual dollar the one eyed shrew that winks out of the womb and the one eyed shrew that does nothing but sit on her ass and snip the intellectual golden threads." But the sex continues, an orgiastic flood of images and a figure who ends "fainting on the wall with a vision of ultimate cunt and come eluding the last gyzym of consciousness," and then with references to Neal Cassady, "secret hero of these poems, cocksman and Adonis of Denver—joy to the memory of his innumerable lays of girls in empty lots & diner backyards." The poem's music and pacing are distinctly audible here, controlled by the length of the verse-lines and by the images. The frenetic activity subsides, apparently into the harsh light of day, to the reality of stumbling from "basements hungover with heartless Tokay" to "unemployment offices." Then a surreal reality intrudes, a vision of those "who walked all night with their shoes full of blood on the snowbank docks waiting for a door in the East River to open." They are waiting not for a door that will open and swallow them in death, but for one that will "open to a room full of steamheat and opium." The image is based on Herbert Huncke, a sometime writer, junkie, and petty thief Ginsberg had befriended, who showed up at Ginsberg's apartment one night when he had nowhere else to stay. The image, one of the most memorable in the poem, is a perfect example of Ginsberg's wish to fuse the ordinary with the visionary. It also makes clear that while the speaker walks through the same hell as the others, he is someone who can—as least sometimes, at least temporarily—rescue them from it. The speaker is deeply sympathetic to those whose minds have been destroyed by madness, but he is not one of them—if he were, he would not be capable of writing the poem.

Some of the characters in the poem are so poor they live in boxes under bridges or walk the streets with pushcarts, eating the "lamb stew of the imagination," "the crab at the muddy bottom of the rivers of Bowery," or "rotten animals lung heart feet tail borsht & tortillas dreaming of the pure vegetable kingdom." It is absurd that people are living this way who are capable of building harpsichords, studying theology, "scribbling all night." It is both absurd that they do it, and absurd that society fails to care about them and their talents, and what follows is the poem's most Chaplinesque passage:

> who plunged themselves under meat trucks looking for an egg,
> who threw their watches off the roof to cast their ballot for Eternity outside of Time, & alarm clocks fell on their heads every day for the next decade,
> who cut their wrists three times successively unsuccessfully, gave up and were forced to open antique stores where they thought they were growing old and cried,
> who were burned alive in their innocent flannel suits on Madison Avenue amid blasts of leaden verse . . . or were run down by the drunken taxicabs of Absolute Reality, . . .

Even here, some details are based on specific incidents Ginsberg remembered or had heard about, including the poet Louis Simpson asking for a friend's watch, throwing it out the window, then commenting, "We don't need time when we're already in eternity." In the next line the speaker earnestly insists, in describing someone who jumped from the Brooklyn Bridge and lived to tell about it, "this actually happened," as if this story might be too outrageous to be true. But indeed it did happen, to Tuli Kupferberg, founder of the 1960s band the Fugs. When someone fails at a suicide attempt, it becomes a funny, bitter story of one more failure. The reference in the very next line to someone who "fell out of the subway window" is not funny, but it does describe an absurdly silly death: another friend, William Cannastra, was killed when he tried to leap out a train window as it left the station. This rapid shift between emotional extremes mimic the state of mind of most of the characters who appear in the poem, and makes clear what fine lines separate those emotions from each other, life from death, the saved from the damned. The beautiful "European 1930s German jazz" is inevitably entangled with the ugly: those who smashed the phonograph records that held that music, who "finished the whiskey and threw up groaning into the bloody toilet, moans in their ears."

Despite their intense internal worlds, these are characters for whom connection to others like them is—literally—a driving force:

> who barreled down the highways of the past journeying to each other's hotrod-Golgotha jail-solitude watch or Birmingham jazz incarnation,
> who drove crosscountry seventytwo hours to find out if I had a vision or you had a vision or he had a vision to find out Eternity

The friends are never entirely apart, even when they are in different places, because as they travel they pray for each other and in that gesture achieve the state they are all searching for: "the soul illuminated its hair for a second." At least as often, what they find is the darker side of that ecstatic experience: "who crashed through their minds in jail." The group disperses—physically, at least—to drugs, religion, blue-collar jobs, school, self-absorption, the cemetery, the madhouse. Those who take themselves or are taken to mental hospitals ask to be given a lobotomy exactly because they cannot bear the tormenting hallucinations that are the dark twin of visionary illumination. They are refused lobotomies, but given other treatments that presumably fail, and eventually released into the Reality they find it so difficult to cope with. Not surprisingly, they may return to the hospital "years later truly bald except for a wig of blood," to a place where people's bodies and minds are turned to stone (one real life hospital was Grey-stone, another Rockland).

This section of the poem climaxes in the next verse, the poem's longest, when life has failed, treatments have failed, and there is no place left to go:

> with mother finally ******, and the last fantastic book flung out of the tenement window, and the last door closed at 4 A.M. and the last

telephone slammed at the wall in reply and the last furnished room emptied down to the last piece of mental furniture, a yellow paper rose twisted on a wire hanger in the closet, and even that imaginary, nothing but a hopeful little bit of hallucination—

The asterisks are Ginsberg's, not an editor's, and though he said later they were there to introduce an "appropriate element of uncertainty," the first draft of the poem reads "with mother finally fucked." The last taboo has been broken, all communication has failed, the room is almost bare, and so is the mind—except for this paper rose, made more vivid by the darkness and emptiness around it—and even the rose exists only in the mind. There is a tremendous sense of exhaustion after all the breathless listmaking and activity, after the quests and the visions, after the waves of anger, sorrow, giddy pleasure, ecstasy: it can all come to nothing.

Or almost nothing. The yellow rose gleams in the mind like a little flame, something "hope-ful," the possibility of beginning again. This is what Ginsberg wants to say to anyone in this state, but in this case he is addressing a particular other. After seventy-one lines the poem finally reveals what occasioned this great outpouring, this urgent, passionate, lapel-grabbing, private and public keening: "ah, Carl, while you are not safe I am not safe, and now you're really in / the total animal soup of time—." Carl Solomon's readmittance to a psychiatric hospital might have been the immediate catalyst for the poem, but Ginsberg's mother's illness, and his own ambivalence about it, were obviously driving forces, and a primary source of the intense emo-tions. Ginsberg is a survivor, and wants to rescue those who have been less fortunate. What is it that has saved him, and might save them? The answer turns out to be Art, in its various forms. When the speaker heard about Solomon, he

> . . . therefore ran through the icy streets obsessed with a sudden flash of the alchemy of the use of the ellipsis catalog a variable measure and the vibrating plane, . . .

"Ellipsis" refers to the punctuation mark for something omitted, the series of dots, and Ginsberg has in mind the space between those dots. It is another way to describe "eyeball kicks," or the juxtaposition of images—setting them side by side without explanatory linking phrases between them. He took the term from Céline's use of dots to signal the jump-cuts in his prose, a marker of "the space between thoughts." "Catalog" is the listing technique used by Blake, Whitman, and other Ginsberg favorites to structure their poems. "Variable foot" is a phrase William Carlos Williams used to describe the rhythm he was striving for in his free verse lines, and Ginsberg built on Williams and then Whitman to arrive at his own long "breath" lines. The "vibrating planes" are Cézanne's blocks of color. Ginsberg is after "incarnate gaps" across which sparks will leap in the reader's mind, and this act of creating something out of nothing—the gap, the abyss—makes him feel like a kind of god (Cézanne used the phrase Ginsberg quotes here, Pater Omnipotens Aeterna Deus, all-powerful and eternal god, in a letter describing his own feelings about painting). Here the voice rises to a great crescendo as the speaker describes what he hopes to do:

> to recreate the syntax and measure of poor human
>   prose and stand before you speechless and
>   intelligent and shaking with shame, rejected
>   yet confessing out the soul to conform to the
>   rhythm of thought in his naked and endless
>   head,
> the madman bum and angel beat in Time,
>   unknown, yet putting down here what might
>   be left to say in time come after death,
> and rose reincarnate in the ghostly clothes of jazz
>   in the goldenhorn shadow of the band and
>   blew the suffering of America's naked mind for
>   love into an eli eli lamma lamma sabacthani
>   saxophone cry that shivered the cities down to
>   the last radio
> with the absolute heart of the poem of life
>   butchered out of their own bodies good to eat
>   a thousand years.

The poet is searching for the form that will make it possible for him to "confess out the soul to conform to the rhythm of thought in his naked and endless head," for the alchemy that will transform the lead of daily life into a "goldenhorn . . . saxophone cry" that will shiver the cities "down to the last radio." The poet rises reborn, revitalized, reincarnate (new-blooded) to play this jazz made out of "the suffering of America's naked mind for love," out of the ultimate loneliness of those who feel forsaken even by god, as Jesus did on Golgotha. The visionary is a sacrificial redeemer, and the poem is made out of the flesh and blood of these sufferers: "with the absolute heart of the poem of life butchered out of their own bodies good to eat a thousand years." In this way, if in no other, their suffering is redeemed, comes to mean something, is not forgotten. The transformative power of art saves their lives by putting them in writing. The poet saves his own life by performing this ritual of creation and transformation. Out of flesh and blood and bone, he makes harrowing music.

PART II

Having described at length how the best minds of his generation were destroyed, Ginsberg turns next to the question of what it is that destroyed them. This section is much shorter than the first, and apparently much simpler, but it went through at least eighteen drafts (compared to five for the first section) before Ginsberg was satisfied with it. "What sphinx of cement and aluminum bashed open their skulls and ate up / their brains and imagination? . . ." For his answer he takes the name of a biblical god, Moloch (or Molech), the god of abominations, to whom mothers sacrificed their children—reaching through flames to put their infants in his arms. The Old Testament repeatedly warns against him. "Moloch" plays the same anchoring function in this section that "who" did in the first:

Moloch, whose mind is pure machinery! Moloch
whose blood is running money! Moloch whose
fingers are ten armies! Moloch whose breast is
a cannibal dynamo! Moloch whose ear is a
smoking tomb!

The image itself came to Ginsberg on a night
when he had taken peyote and suddenly saw the
Sir Frances Drake Hotel in San Francisco as a
smoking, thousand-eyed monster, a "vegetable
horror," "dark tower," "impassive robot," "cannibal dynamo." This vision was overlayered
with scenes from Blake's "London," Fritz Lang's
movie *Metropolis*, the "unreal city" of Eliot's
Waste Land, and other images of cities as
mechanical, inhuman, uncaring. Moloch
encompasses everything in human society that
beats down and defeats whatever is individual:
armies, war, "stunned governments," skyscrapers, factories, the love of money and its evil
twin, poverty, "robot apartments," "invisible
suburbs," "demonic industries." A society built
on uniformity and conformity has no use for
individual visions, or indeed anything that
represents the life of the soul—dreams, illumina-
tions, epiphanies. Society ignores those who
have them, tries to silence them or drive them
out, lets the real treasures slip through its fingers.

Some critics have attacked this section of the
poem for taking the easy way out by proposing
an external villain as the answer to the implied
question of part I: How did this happen, who or
what is to blame for all this suffering? But in fact
Ginsberg makes clear throughout the section
that Moloch is ultimately interior: "Mental
Moloch!" "Moloch whose name is the Mind!"
The societal face of Moloch emerges from the
potential Moloch in each person, including the
poet:

Moloch in whom I sit lonely! . . . Crazy in
   Moloch! Cocksucker in Moloch! Lacklove and
   manless in Moloch!
Moloch who entered my soul early! Moloch in
   whom I am a consciousness without a body!
   Moloch who frightened me out of my natural

ecstasy! Moloch whom I abandon! Wake up in
Moloch! Light streaming out of the sky!

Even if society cannot be changed, the individual
can change his own attitudes, behavior, and
relationship to it. He can go crazy, or find a way
to live in the world, he can let society make him
fearful and repressed, or he can stay true to his
own visions. He can wake up and take
responsibility for his own life, without being
deterred by society's response. He can abandon
Moloch—as the speaker has by writing the
poem.

Even as the speaker laments all the valuable
possibilities that have been lost, his sense of
humor flashes through: "Dreams! adorations! il-
luminations! religions! the whole boatload of
sensitive bullshit!" Some critics have turned the
poem's own words against it, saying that "the
whole load of sensitive bullshit" is an apt
description of the poem itself. But for Ginsberg
this attitude, this ability to stand outside oneself,
to see how ridiculous the whole enterprise must
look from the outside—and to respond with
humor, not bitterness—is central to waking up
in Moloch, to freeing himself from the monster.
When he does that the light streams in, and he
sees the lost lives as something to celebrate, not
just to mourn. When he says "Mad generation!
down on the rocks of Time!" the tone is almost
triumphant, as is the section's conclusion:

Real holy laughter in the river! They saw it all!
   the wild eyes! the holy yells! They bade
   farewell! They jumped off the roof! to
   solitude! waving! carrying flowers! Down to
   the river! into the street!

They are choosing their fates, and they seem
ecstatic rather than dismayed. This time they are
not waving "genitals and manuscripts," but
simply waving farewell. Ginsberg has escaped
Moloch by blowing their pain out the saxophone
notes of his poetry, and in doing so he has
transformed his own vision of the world as well.
He has had a great insight: their laughter is holy,

their yells are holy. But while he lets this sink in, Ginsberg turns to address Carl Solomon directly.

PART III

The real-life Carl Solomon was never comfortable with his fame as the dedicatee of "Howl," and took issue with a number of the poem's details that seem to refer to his experiences. But the Carl Solomon in the poem is a created character, shaped by the poem's needs as a work of art, even if he is based on the man Ginsberg had remained friends with since they met as fellow psychiatric patients. Solomon was a fellow intellectual, widely read, passionate, and opinionated. Both hoped to become writers, and they shared the same typewriter in the hospital. Solomon had returned to his work as an editor after his release, and Ginsberg went back to his classes at Columbia, graduated, lived at home in New Jersey, traveled cross country and lived in Mexico, and finally settled on the west coast. He had quit his job to write poetry full time, had finally accepted his homosexuality, and had met and fallen in love with Peter Orlovsky: he had a new life, far from the turmoil of his younger days in New York.

When Ginsberg heard that Carl Solomon had returned to a psychiatric hospital, Solomon became a sort of doppelgänger for Ginsberg, an alter ego, an image of what his own fate might easily have been. Ginsberg begins to ask himself why he has survived when so many others did not. How was he able to wake up in Moloch and abandon Moloch when they could not? The speaker echoes Coleridge's ancient mariner, Melville's Ishmael, even Odysseus—all of whom returned alone to tell of what they had seen. In the post–World War II context, he also evokes images of Holocaust survivors describing their time in concentration camps. The poem's first words bear witness: "I saw. . . ." And he is the only one left to tell it (along with Kerouac, telling it in fiction). He has told, in past tense, what he saw, and he has created the figure of Moloch

to stand for the source of suffering. Now he uses present tense to bridge the gap between himself and Solomon, even to deny that there is any gap:

> Carl Solomon! I'm with you in Rockland
>   where you're madder than I am . . .
> I'm with you in Rockland
>   where you imitate the shade of my mother . . .

"I'm with you" is the refrain here, as "who" was in the first section and "Moloch" in the second. Now the speaker bears witness by bringing the past to life in the present, by insisting that he has not abandoned those he has apparently left behind. Ginsberg is with Solomon in his paranoid fantasies, his sense of the absurd, in the madness that traps him in his mind, cuts off from his own senses, with him playing Ping-Pong and hammering an out-of-tune piano, with him as he gets electroshock therapy. The details are drawn from Ginsberg's own time in the hospital, from stories Solomon told him, and from Ginsberg's lifelong experiences with his mother's paranoid schizophrenia. Ginsberg himself never received any treatments beyond psychiatric therapy. The section peaks with a burst of boyish giddiness and humor:

> . . . we wake up electrified out of the coma by our own souls' airplanes roaring over the roof they've come to drop angelic bombs the hospital illuminates itself imaginary walls collapse O skinny legions run outside O starry-spangled shock of mercy the eternal war is here O victory forget your underwear we're free . . .

It concludes with a sadder but hopeful image reminiscent of Huncke appearing at Ginsberg's apartment door in New York City years earlier: "in my dreams you walk dripping from a sea-journey on the highway / across America in tears to the door of my cottage in the Western night."

"FOOTNOTE TO HOWL"

The poem's fourth section, or "Footnote to Howl," was written a few months later, and

Ginsberg saw it as balancing the second section. It returns to the insight at the end of the second section: "Real holy laughter in the river! They saw it all! the wild eyes! the holy yells!" This is the speaker's great revelation: the antidote to Moloch's poison is the realization that everything in the universe is holy. After opening with fifteen repetitions of that key word, the speaker lists specifics, including things some might consider unholy: the world, the soul, the skin, the tongue and cock and hand and asshole. "Everyman's an angel! the bum's as holy as the seraphim! the madman is holy as you my soul are holy." He goes on to name names: Peter, Allen, Solomon, Lucien, Kerouac, Huncke, Burroughs, Cassady, his mother: all holy. Things remote from the poet are holy: "the cocks of the grandfathers of Kansas," "the vast lamb of the middle-class!" These realizations free him from "Moloch the heavy judger of men!" The world is not inevitably divided into degrees of good and evil: Moloch creates those categories, and people can abandon Moloch. Nothing that exists is despicable; everything is holy, and therefore worthy of love. "Holy the bop apocalypse," the jazz version of the end of the world. From the mundane to the mysterious, "the cafeterias filled with the millions" to "rivers of tears under the streets": all holy. Those who love Los Angeles are what they behold: the angels. All of time and space are holy. The eye, and the abyss it sees, are holy. Traditional religious virtues are holy: forgiveness, mercy, charity, faith, generosity. And what, at the end of this great vision quest, is most holy of all?

> Holy forgiveness! mercy! charity! faith! Holy!
> Ours! bodies! suffering! magnanimity!
> Holy the supernatural extra brilliant intelligent
>   kindness of the soul!

Hard-won kindness, informed kindness, kindness in-spite-of-itself, in spite of everything, kindness in the face of Moloch. Ginsberg began the poem with a lament and an implied question: "I saw the best minds of my generation destroyed by madness"; how and why did that

happen? The second section rages at Moloch, everything in society that is to blame for the loss of those minds—but it also, in the midst of its anger, acknowledges that Moloch is a state of mind. The speaker abandons Moloch and turns instead to his friend—with kindness, empathy, and love. In making that turn he accepts his own past, his own body, his failings and feelings. If the universe is holy, he too must be holy, and worthy of love. And if he is worthy of love, everything else in the world must be too. Ginsberg later offered the following summaries of the first three parts of "Howl": "1. a lament for the Lamb in America with instances of remarkable lamblike youths; 2. the monster of mental consciousness that preys on the Lamb; 3. a litany of affirmation of the Lamb in its glory." Most of the images in "Howl" come from the Judeo-Christian tradition, but there are also suggestions of the Buddhism Kerouac had introduced him to, and to which Ginsberg would later turn more fully.

IMPACT AND AFTERMATH

When *Howl and Other Poems* was published in 1956, Ginsberg quoted Whitman in an epigraph on the title page: "Unscrew the locks from the doors! / Unscrew the doors themselves from the jambs!" He dedicated the book to Jack Kerouac, Lucien Carr (who was dropped in later editions at his own request), William Burroughs, and Neal Cassady, listing books each had written and concluding, "All these books are published in Heaven." William Carlos Williams says, in the introduction, "he proves to us . . . the spirit of love survives to ennoble our lives if we have the wit and the courage and the faith—and the art! to persist." In another poem in the volume, "A Supermarket in California," the poet imagines wandering the store with his predecessor: "Where are we going, Walt Whitman? The doors close in an hour. Which way does your beard point tonight?" In "Sunflower Sutra" he sits with Jack Kerouac in the railroad yards and talks to a dust-covered sunflower, which eventually becomes an image of the soul. It is the entire country he addresses in "America," speaking as if it were a person. He asks it questions: "America when will you be angelic? When will you take off your clothes?" "why are your libraries full of tears"; and confesses to it: "America I used to be a communist when I was a kid I'm not sorry. I smoke marijuana every chance I get . . . I have mystical visions and cosmic vibrations." The poem is good-humored in its criticisms, and the speaker is serious both about his love and about wanting to make changes: "It's true I don't want to join the Army or turn lathes in precison parts factories, I'm nearsighted and psychopathic anyway. / America I'm putting my queer shoulder to the wheel."

Immediate responses to the book ranged from the seizure of its second printing by the San Francisco police to its successful defense as an important work of art at the subsequent obscenity trial. Literary reviews varied as widely, some describing it as "repugnant," and "adolescent maunderings," while others lauded it for "blasting open closed sexual and artistic doors." The poet Richard Eberhart, praising "Howl" in the *New York Times*, described the poem as "a howl against everything in our mechanistic civilization which kills the spirit, lays bare the nerves of suffering and spiritual struggle." John Hollander attacked the work in *Partisan Review*: "It is only fair to Allen Ginsberg to remark on the utter lack of decorum of any kind in his dreadful little volume." Ginsberg's father Louis, to whom he had sent the poem before it was published, expressed a fellow poet's great admiration for the craftsmanship, but was also troubled by the graphic images and wished the poem included more "glad affirmations." To those who decried its violence, Kenneth Rexroth, the central figure in the San Francisco Renaissance, responded that the violence in the poem is society's, not the poem's or the author's. The poem that Ginsberg had begun as a private mediation immediately took on a large and complex public identity. It became one of the defining works of the Beat Generation and, based on its Moloch section, a touchstone for tens of thousands of disaffected young men and women during the 1960s. "Howl" is the best known of Ginsberg's poems, and has become a cultural icon that stands for an entire generation's alienation, for its rage against the Establishment and conventional, mainstream mores.

Ginsberg himself became as large and symbolic a figure as his book, and he and Jack Kerouac came to embody the Beat Generation. Ginsberg was an articulate spokesman for his beliefs in numerous interviews and panel discussions, but Kerouac found the publicity and fame depressing and distracting. He felt that most people paid more attention to the sensationalism and social aspects of the movement than to its works of art, which they failed to understand. Neal Cassady, who had served as an inspiration to Ginsberg and Kerouac, and who was the basis for the Dean Moriarty character in *On the Road*, later served a prison term for drug possession, and eventually drove the bus for Ken Kesey and his band of Merry Pranksters. He died in Mexico in 1968, apparently of alcohol combined with barbiturates. Kerouac, who had by then withdrawn into bitterness and alcoholism, died in 1969 of cirrhosis. The popularity of the Beat movement itself, badly distorted by mainstream media with references to "beatniks" and bongo drums, lasted less than a decade. But Ginsberg, who was the most driven and disciplined of the group, and who thrived in the spotlight, continued his prolific writing and publishing, including poetry, journals, prose, and interviews, for the rest of his life. He was also a tireless supporter of the work of his friends, including Kerouac and Burroughs, and worked hard to see that it got into print and to defend it against censorship.

Many critics consider *Kaddish* (1961), Ginsberg's next book after *Howl*, his greatest work. It is a powerful, moving lament for his mother Naomi, based on the mourning ritual usually performed at Jewish funerals. Not enough people had been present when his mother was buried to hold it, so Ginsberg created his own version in poetry. It is a poem that seems to leave nothing out, from his mother's intelligence and humor to her attempts, in the depths of her madness, to seduce him. In Ginsberg's best poems, the intensity of the content is balanced and barely contained by the poem's formal elements. In those that are less successful, the form fails and what results is a kind of shapeless sprawl.

Ginsberg's openness paved the way for the so-called confessional poets, including Robert Lowell, Sylvia Plath, John Berryman, and many others. His work gave other poets a kind of permission to put the self at the center of the work as Whitman and the Romantics had—something the Modernists had gone to great lengths to avoid, since they considered it egotistical and believed it favored emotion at the expense of intelligence. Following in the Romantic tradition, Ginsberg argued that the self is the center from which true knowledge originates. Critics of the work charge that this approach represents a kind of narcissism and adolescent self-absorption, "navel-gazing" at the expense of the rest of the world. Ginsberg's work was also misread by many critics and young writers, who failed to realize how much study and hard work he had devoted to developing his technique of capturing the inner workings of the mind on the page. A number of critics did come to realize the prodigious extent of Ginsberg's reading and work habits as they read his interviews, essays, and poems over the years, and reconsidered some of their earlier negative opinions of his poetry. Others have held to the position that his work fails to merit the acclaim it has received. In recent years the Beat movement has also been attacked for its treatment of women, and it is true, and perhaps ironic, that while "Howl" condemns a long list of society's failings, it seems entirely a part of its time and place in its obliviousness to the second-class status of women. Some writers have attributed this to the homosexuality of many of the group's members, but the complaint applies equally well to the heterosexual gender roles of sixties protest groups, where for the most part men spoke in public and made the decisions while women made the coffee.

It is difficult to separate Ginsberg's stature as a poet from his status as cult figure, cultural icon, and social activist. His celebrity following the publication of *Howl* gave him access to the media and to public figures, and he used that attention to become a vocal advocate for various political causes. He participated in endless social protests, including those against the Vietnam War, nuclear power, censorship, and many others. His interest in popular culture—and its interest in him—also led to his touring with Bob Dylan as part of Rolling Thunder Review and performing with the British band the Clash. He was a powerful reader of his own poems, and one of the best ways to encounter "Howl" for the first time is to listen to a recording of Ginsberg reading it. He also recorded Blake's *Songs of Innocence and Experience* set to music. In later years Ginsberg and his father Louis gave a number of joint readings in which they read their very different poems to large audiences.

Ginsberg became increasingly interested in and involved with Buddhism, and that interest, combined with a trip to Japan, led to his renunciation of drug taking as a means to experience visions, a shift described in his poem "The Change." In 1970 Ginsberg and the poet Anne Waldman founded the Jack Kerouac School of Disembodied Poetics at the Naropa Institute in Boulder, Colorado, and Ginsberg taught there and at Brooklyn College in New York. He received the National Book Award in 1974 for his collection *The Fall of America*, published his *Collected Poems* in 1984 and his *Selected Poems* in 1996. He also published numerous volumes of interviews, essays, and journal entries.

Although most critics acknowledge Ginsberg's poetic mastery, some lament what they consider his permissiveness, sloppiness, and refusal to edit, especially in later work—his refusal to "separate the wheat from the chaff." Critic Norman Podhoretz and others attacked him repeatedly over the years for being a "self-promoter," but though Ginsberg did like the spotlight, he always used his celebrity to bring attention to the work of others and to causes he considered important. He spent his entire life promoting free speech, for example, and fighting against censorship, but almost fifty years after "Howl" was officially ruled to be "not obscene," it is still banned from some libraries and classrooms, and cannot be read in its entirety on most radio stations.

Though many other countries have a long tradition of honoring their artists and writers, it is extremely rare for an American poet to achieve the level of fame that Ginsberg did. Fewer than two thousand copies are sold of most poetry books published in this country, yet 250,000 copies of *Howl* had been sold by the end of the 1960s. Over the next decades, Ginsberg brought far more people than that into contact with poetry through his readings, recordings, lectures, and interviews. He was also unusual in being an extremely willing and articulate commentator on his own work, and was generous in discussing it with his readers. He continued his travels, teaching, studies, and writing until his death at age seventy on April 5, 1997, at his apartment in New York City.

Select Bibliography

EDITIONS

Howl and Other Poems. San Francisco: City Lights Books, 1956. (The Pocket Poets Series Number 4; introduction by William Carlos Williams.)

Howl: Original draft facsimile, transcript & variant versions, fully annotated by author, with contemporaneous correspondence, account of first public reading, legal skirmishes, precursor texts & bibliography. Edited by Barry Miles. New York: HarperPerennial, 1986. (An invaluable edition that includes drafts of all four sections of "Howl," the author's extensive notes, comments by Carl Solomon, and texts of the works Ginsberg said were in his mind as he worked on the poem.)

OTHER WORKS BY GINSBERG

Kaddish and Other Poems. San Francisco: City Lights Books, 1961.

The Fall of America, Poems of these States, 1965–1971. San Francisco: City Lights Books, 1973.

Collected Poems 1947–1980. New York: Harper & Row, 1984.

Selected Poems 1947–1995. New York: HarperCollins, 1996.

SECONDARY WORKS

Allen, Donald, and Warren Tallman. *The Poetics of the New American Poetry.* New York: Grove, 1973.

Breslin, James. *From Modern to Contemporary: American Poetry, 1945–1965.* Chicago: University of Chicago Press, 1984.

Carroll, Paul. *The Poem in Its Skin.* Chicago: Follett, 1968.

Caveney, Graham. *Screaming with Joy: The Life of Allen Ginsberg.* New York: Broadway Books (a division of Random House), 1999.

Charters, Ann. *The Beats: Literary Bohemians in Postwar America.* Detroit: Gale, 1983.

————, ed. *The Portable Beat Reader.* New York: Viking, 1992.

Charters, Samuel. *Some Poems/Poets: Studies in American Underground Poetry Since 1945.* Berkeley, Calif.: Oyez, 1971.

Doty, Mark. "The 'Forbidden Planet' of Character: The Revolutions of the 1950s." In *A Profile of Twentieth-Century American Poetry.* Edited by Jack Myers and David Wojahn. Carbondale: Southern Illinois University Press, 1991. Pp. 131–157. (See pages 143–144 for the discussion on "Howl.")

Eberhart, Richard. "West Coast Rhythms." *New York Times Book Review,* September 1, 1956, pp. 7–18. (This positive review of "Howl" established Ginsberg's crediblity among many serious readers and writers of poetry.)

Géfin, Laszlo. *Ideogram, History of a Poetic Method.* Austin: University of Texas Press, 1982. (Includes a discussion of how this method applies to the writing of "Howl.")

Gertmenian, Donald. "Remembering and Rereading 'Howl.'" *Ploughshares* 2 (fall 1975): 151–164.

Ginsberg, Allen. Interview in *Writers at Work: The Paris Review Interviews, Third Series.* New York: Viking, 1967. Pp. 291–297. (Discusses the application of Cézanne's ideas to "Howl.")

Hollander, John. Review of *Howl and Other Poems. Partisan Review* 24 (spring 1957): 296–304. (One of the harshest early reviews.)

Holmes, John Clellon. *Go.* New York: New American Library, 1980. (The characters in Kerouac's *On the Road* as seen by another member of the group.)

Howard, Richard. "Allen Ginsberg." In his *Alone with America: Essays on the Art of Poetry in the United States Since 1950.* New York: Atheneum, 1980. Pp. 145–152.

Huncke, Herbert. *Huncke's Journal.* New York: Poets Press, 1965.

Hyde, Lewis, ed. *Under Discussion: On the Poetry of Allen Ginsberg.* Ann Arbor: University of Michigan Press, 1984.

Kerouac, Jack. *On the Road.* New York: Viking, 1957.

————. *The Dharma Bums.* New York: Viking, 1958.

Kramer, Jane. *Allen Ginsberg in America.* New York: Random House, 1969.

Martin, Robert K. *The Homosexual Tradition in American Poetry.* Austin: University of Texas Press, 1979.

McClure, Michael. *Scratching the Beat Surface.* San Francisco: North Point, 1982.

Merrill, Thomas. *Allen Ginsberg.* Boston: Twayne, 1988.

Miles, Barry. *Ginsberg: A Biography.* New York: HarperPerennial, 1989.

Podhoretz, Norman. *Making It.* New York: Random House, 1967. (The case against Ginsberg and other Beats, by one of Ginsberg's most prominent critics.)

Portugés, Paul. *The Visionary Poetics of Allen Ginsberg.* Santa Barbara: Ross-Erikson, 1978.

Schumacher, Michael. *Dharma Lion: A Critical Biography of Allen Ginsberg.* New York: St. Martin's, 1992.

Simpson, Louis. "The Eye Altering Alters All." In his *A Revolution in Taste: Studies of Dylan Thomas, Allen Ginsberg, Sylvia Plath, and Robert Lowell.* New York: Macmillan, 1978. Pp. 45–82.

Stepanchev, Stephen. *American Poetry Since 1945.* New York: Harper & Row, 1965.

Vladimir Nabokov's
Lolita

LYDIA RAINFORD

Lolita, light of my life, fire of my loins. My sin, my soul. Lo-lee-ta: the tip of the tongue taking a trip of three steps down the palate to tap, at three, on the teeth. Lo. Lee. Ta.

(Vladimir Nabokov, *Lolita*)

LOLITA, VLADIMIR NABOKOV'S most provocative novel, seemed to explode out of nowhere in the late 1950s in much the same way as its narrator's first lines explode into life on the page and the teeth. At the time of its publication, Nabokov was an obscure Russian émigré living in America, a university lecturer in literature, and a part-time lepidopterist. *Lolita* was far from being his first literary production. He had already published eleven novels, an autobiographical memoir, poems, short stories, and a number of scholarly pieces on Russian authors; but as nine of the novels had been written in Russian and published in Europe, much of Nabokov's oeuvre was unknown by the American reading public. All of this changed when word spread about his story of a middle-aged man's love affair with a twelve-year-old girl. Once it was published, *Lolita* became a best-seller, an instant "classic," and Nabokov was marked as one of America's most feted and scandalous modern writers.

Nabokov was born into a wealthy, cultured, and aristocratic family in Russia, but the family lost all of its privilege during the Communist Revolution and were forced to flee the country. Nabokov went to university in England, scratched a living teaching and writing in Germany and France, and was forced into exile for a second time in 1940, when the Nazi invasion of France became a threat to Nabokov's Jewish-born wife. The Nabokovs immigrated to America in 1940 and lived in several different university towns until 1959, when Nabokov retired and they once again settled in Europe.

Lolita was Nabokov's first "American" novel. Two previous novels—*The Real Life of Sebastian Knight* and *Bend Sinister*—had been written in English, but this was the first time that Nabokov turned his attention to the culture and landscape of his adopted country. However, the novel's main theme was not a completely new one. As Nabokov said in his afterword, "On a Book Entitled *Lolita*," the "first little throb" of the book went through him "late in 1939 or early in 1940" and resulted in a novella, written in Russian, called *Volshebnik*. Nabokov retrieved this story from obscurity after the publication of *Lolita,* and it was eventually translated and published in English under the title *The Enchanter.* The original story treats the same theme as *Lolita.* A middle-aged man who suffers from "nympholepsy" falls for a girl, marries her sick mother in order to be near her, and when the mother dies, attempts, unsuccessfully, to take advantage of the girl. The girl struggles and screams, and the man flees the scene and throws himself under a passing truck. While *The Enchanter* is typically Nabokovian in its precise and merciless prose, its style is a long way from that of its diabolically funny and multidimensional reincarnation. Apart from a few moments of free indirect speech, the story is narrated in the third person, and this automatically distances readers from the perverse protagonist. The story runs few of the risks that *Lolita* does in handing over most of the narrational responsibility to the criminal wordsmith Humbert Humbert.

Nabokov began writing *Lolita* in 1949, a decade after writing *The Enchanter* and nine years after moving to America. The book took a long time to develop—mainly, Nabokov claimed, because he had to "invent" his new country as he had invented Russia and Western Europe in the past—and on several occasions he considered destroying the manuscript. Yet he managed to finish the novel in 1954 and began to seek suitable publishers. Realizing the controversial nature of *Lolita*'s theme, he initially stipulated that it should be published anonymously. This did not help his chances in America, and when all "respectable" publishers refused the manuscript—in many cases in spite of the editors' admiration for the novel—Nabokov sent it to Maurice Girodias, the owner of Olympia Press in Paris. Olympia Press prided itself on publishing any book that had been ostracized by the mainstream and held in its listings a peculiar mixture of the avant-garde (Samuel Beckett, William Burroughs, Jean Genet) and the straightforwardly pornographic. In 1955 Nabokov agreed to sign his novel over

CHRONOLOGY

1899	Vladimir Vladimirovich Nabokov born in St. Petersburg, Russia, on April 22 (April 10 Julian calendar).
1916	Private publication of a volume of Nabokov's poems.
1919	The Nabokov family flees Russia and settles in Germany. Nabokov goes to Trinity College, Cambridge, to study Slavonic and Romance languages. Subsequently lives in Berlin and Paris.
1925	Marries Véra Evseevna Slonim.
1926	*Mashen'ka (Mary)* published in Berlin.
1928	*Korol', dama, valet (King, Queen, Knave).*
1929–1930	*Zashchita Luzhina (The Defense)* published in serial form in Paris.
1930	*Soglyadatay (The Eye)* serialized in Paris.
1931–1932	*Podvig (Glory)* serialized in Paris.
1932	*Kamera Obscura (Laughter in the Dark)* serialized in Paris.
1934	Son, Dmitri Nabokov, born. *Otchayanie (Despair)* serialized in Paris.
1935–1936	*Priglashenie na kazn' (Invitation to a Beheading)* serialized in Paris.
1937–1938	*Dar (The Gift)* serialized in Paris.
1940	The Nabokovs move to the United States.
1941	*The Real Life of Sebastian Knight.*
1944	*Nikolai Gogol.*
1945	Nabokov becomes a U.S. citizen.
1947	*Bend Sinister.*
1951	*Conclusive Evidence.* (Revised version published as *Speak, Memory* in 1966.)
1955	*Lolita* published in Paris.
1957	*Pnin.* Extract from *Lolita* published in the *Anchor Review.*
1958	*Lolita* published in New York. *Nabokov's Dozen* (short stories).
1962	*Pale Fire.*
1964	Nabokov's translation of *Eugene Onegin.*
1969	*Ada.*
1971	*Poems and Problems.*

| 1974 | *Look at the Harlequins! Lolita: A Screenplay.* |
| 1977 | Nabokov dies on July 2 in Montreux, Switzerland. |

to Girodias, a decision he came to regret. The association of *Lolita* with some of the press's banal erotic titles led at first to complete critical neglect, and then, when the book slowly began to gather admiration from liberal-minded critics (the author Graham Greene was one of the first to recognize its brilliance), it attracted attention over its "scandalous" theme and was consequently banned in several countries, including France and England. The outrage of artists and writers at the bans, however, combined with the fact that Girodias was flooding Western markets with illegal copies, meant that censorship was ineffective and fairly short-lived. In 1956 Doubleday expressed interest in publishing an American edition of *Lolita;* substantial extracts appeared in 1957 in the *Anchor Review;* and after delays caused by Girodias' demand of high royalties, the book was finally published in America by Putnam in 1958.

Even when not suffering outright bans, *Lolita* has always provoked extreme responses in its readers. On its publication in America, Elizabeth Janeway wrote in the *New York Times* that it was both "one of the funniest" and "one of the saddest" novels she had ever read. Writing in the same paper, Orville Prescott countered this view, declaring it "florid," "archly fatuous," "high-brow pornography" (both reviews quoted in *Vladimir Nabokov: The American Years*, 1992). Such disagreements have remained typical because critics are either delighted and seduced by Nabokov's stylistic skills or horrified that he should indulge in such playful prose when portraying such a sordid subject. Aesthetics and ethics seem to clash uncomfortably in Humbert's outlandish narrative, and since Nabokov-the-author refuses to interject with definite guidance or commentary, no one quite

knows how resolve this discomfort, how to judge the narrative, and whether to laugh, cry, or frown.

THE ETHICS OF READING

So why did Nabokov approach his tale of pedophilia from such an oblique angle? Why did he make his main protagonist a masterful aesthete as well as a moral outcast and give him license to narrate his own crime? Was Nabokov simply being provocative—testing the boundaries of taste—or did he have some other, better purpose?

"Purpose" is a controversial word in the context of any discussion about Nabokov, as he was always adamant that art could have no "purpose," especially a social or moral one. In his afterword to *Lolita,* he describes himself as "the kind of author who in starting to work on a book has no other purpose than to get rid of that book," and rejecting what he calls the "Literature of Ideas," he declares, "For me a work of fiction exists only insofar as it affords me what I shall bluntly call aesthetic bliss, that is a sense of being somehow, somewhere, connected with other states of being where art (curiosity, tenderness, kindness, ecstasy) is the norm." In an interview with Alvin Toffler published in *Playboy* in 1964 (reprinted in Nabokov's *Strong Opinions,* 1973), he states:

> A work of art has no importance whatever to society. It is only important to the individual, and only the individual reader is important to me. I don't give a damn for the group, the community, the masses, and so forth. Although I do not care for the slogan "art for art's sake"—because unfortunately such promoters of it as, for instance, Oscar Wilde and various dainty poets, were in reality rank moralists and didacticists—there can be no question that what makes a work of fiction safe from larvae and rust is not its social importance but its art, only its art.

Nabokov is clearly problematizing the distinctions habitually made by scholars in their definitions of art. He rejects outright the realist definition of art as a reflection and mediation of the "real" world, and in dismissing "the community," he denies its social, political, and moral relevance. Nevertheless, he is also evidently wary of reducing art to some hermetically sealed ritual opposed to "reality," which, it seems, is what provokes his labeling of the "dainty poets" as "rank moralists and didacticists." The tendency of the aesthetic movement simply to invert the logic of realist modes of art and to regard literature as a purely sensual form which transcends or refutes nature is as programmatic and limiting as only ever seeking social or moral import.

Nabokov's suspicion of the absolute is key here. There is no doubt that as an artist he has more in common with Wilde than with Balzac, but the moment the sense of "aesthetic bliss" becomes slogan and dogma—"art for art's sake," a kind of secular religion—Nabokov rejects it. Indeed, when he speaks of art, Nabokov seems to be referring to "artistry," a continual process of perceiving and molding "experience" which illuminates and inspires but which never claims to reach a final truth:

> You can get nearer and nearer, so to speak, to reality; but you never get near enough because reality is an infinite succession of steps, levels of perception, false bottoms, and hence unquenchable, unattainable. You can know more and more about one thing but you can never know everything about one thing: it's hopeless. So that we live surrounded by more or less ghostly objects.

In other words, the sleights of hand for which Nabokov's fiction is famous are not simply attributable to him. They are what constitute our perception and knowledge of reality. In fact, they are not even the preserve of human "art" because we can find their parallel in the natural world: "Deception is practiced even more beautifully by that other V. N., Visible Nature," he says in a 1969 *Vogue* interview (reprinted in *Strong Opinions*). "A useful purpose is assigned by science to animal mimicry, protective pat-

terns and shapes, yet their refinement transcends the crude purpose of mere survival." And if the artistry of art is most accurately characterized as a naturally occurring mirage, it fits comfortably with neither realist nor aesthetic definitions. The necessity of evoking the mystery, of preserving the "unquenchable, unattainable" nature of reality, is for Nabokov the main responsibility of the writer, and it is as close as he comes to having an artistic "purpose." Concomitantly, the responsibility of Nabokov's readers must be to accept the vertiginous experience of following "an infinite succession of steps, levels of perception, false bottoms," and not try to force it into some overgeneralized, overweening interpretation.

This is easier said than done, of course, particularly in the case of *Lolita*, which is more loaded with narrative traps and layers than any of Nabokov's other novels. But by reading closely and remaining vigilant readers can see how Nabokov manages to be neither a moralist nor an aesthete while retaining the possibility of both ethical and artistic interrogation and judgment. The most striking moments of the novel do, indeed, follow Walter Pater's aesthetic aspiration, and burn with a "hard, gemlike flame"; but the narrative also wavers, fades, and fails, farcically, to live up to expectations. It is in these other moments of collapse that the novel asks its most important questions about artistic, perceptual, and moral authority. As becomes increasingly apparent, the "fixing" of beauty or ecstasy in words is not only a task fraught with difficulties but is also not necessarily as noble an enterprise as the conventional aesthete would have one believe.

THE DECEPTIVE TEXT

The biggest inhibitor of conclusive interpretations of *Lolita* is its multiple levels of narration. Even as the novel begins, readers are confronted with a number of "false bottoms" which make initial judgments about the nature of the text, and its determining voice, impossible. The foreword is written by one John Ray Jr., Ph.D., who claims to have edited the text for his friend, who is the lawyer of the text's late author, Humbert Humbert. "Humbert Humbert" is not the author's real name—although the events he narrates *are* real—but a "bizarre cognomen" of "his own invention." The author has also changed the names of all the protagonists in his history, but the editor refers readers to the newspapers for a nonfictionalized account of "H. H.'s" true crime. He also gives details of "the destinies of the 'real' people beyond the 'true' story." Indeed, John Ray Jr. seems happy to present the narrative as both a psychiatric case history and "a work of art" which "transcends its expiatory aspects." He declares it a "poignant personal study" but stresses that it provides a "general lesson" to "parents, social workers, [and] educators" by warning of "dangerous trends" in society.

Thus readers do not know if they are reading truth or fiction, science or literature, legal testament or private confession. The supposed author is not only pseudonymous but already dead. These uncertainties are compounded by the first chapter of the narrative proper, which addresses itself to the "ladies and gentlemen of the jury" but whose excessively poetic prose ("Lolita, light of my life, fire of my loins") and darkly ironic asides ("You can always count on a murderer for a fancy prose style") sweep away the po-faced moralizing of John Ray Jr. We are suddenly in the realm of artistic fabrication where heavy-handed notions of "ethical impact" collapse in the face of the virtuosity of style. Humbert Humbert—moral leper, murderer, and the last person one would think of trusting as a guide to this tricky tale of pedophilia—seemingly assumes authorial control.

And yet, in another sense, he does not. If the definition of the "author" is he whose voice dominates, who presents events through is own eyes, and who crafts the narrative, then Humbert is indeed the master narrator. But if the definition of the "author" is he who determines

plot and has a fuller knowledge of events than any character, then Humbert is almost as ignorant as his readers and is a greater fool than they for believing that the narrative is his. For while Humbert's presence and opinions are ubiquitous in the novel, he is certainly not the story's sole dictator. A recurring trope of Humbert's narrative is the "dazzling coincidences" which surround and determine crucial events in the story: the fire at the McCoo house in Ramsdale, which makes Humbert a lodger at the Haze house; Miss Phalen, the spinster who was meant to monitor Dolly, breaking her hip on the day Humbert arrives; Dolly's friend Mary Rose Hamilton "running a temperature" on the day of a planned picnic, which leads to Humbert being left alone with, and able to "solipsize" (secretly masturbate beside), Lolita; the car accident which kills Charlotte Haze at the most opportune moment; the room number of The Enchanted Hunters hotel, where Humbert first has intercourse with Lolita, being the same as the house number in Ramsdale. The list is endless. Humbert thinks of these coincidences as being dictated by fate, or "Aubrey McFate," as he dubs it, taking the name from the list of Dolly's classmates (another useful "coincidence").

As the narrative progresses, however, fewer and fewer of these coincidences seem to be the work of fate, and more and more seem to be the work of Humbert's rival, Clare Quilty. The summer camp Dolly attends (where she loses her virginity) happens to be called "Camp Q" ("Cue" is Quilty's nickname), and Quilty, by chance (or not) is living nearby; he also just happens to be staying at The Enchanted Hunters when Humbert and Lo are there, and he teasingly quizzes Humbert about his "daughter"; he is the coauthor of the play Dolly rehearses in Beardsley, and of the one she and Humbert watch on their second road trip—a road trip which is mapped out in advance by Quilty and Dolly to ensure he can steal her away from Elphinstone to Duk Duk Ranch. As readers we realize the pre-plotted nature of these "coincidences" as slowly as Humbert does—he fails to piece together the Quilty puzzle until Dolly reveals his name in the penultimate episode of the book—and once we have, a degree of unease enters about the coincidences which *did* seem genuine earlier in the book. Charlotte's death, for example, is prefigured by several glancing references to the dog who causes the accident, but when they occur in the text, they seem to have little significance.

Of course, Humbert is narrating these events in the past tense, which means that he now knows more than at the time of the narrative. The dog references could be his way of taunting us with clues about the "bad accident" that "is to happen quite soon." Yet the strange feature of his narration is that even though he is recollecting what has happened, he never quite catches up with the plot in which he is so embroiled. Charlotte's death, when it happens, comes as a tremendous surprise to Humbert, and he certainly does not seem to piece together all the clues left by Quilty during his cat-and-mouse chase of Humbert and Lolita, which would explain why the clues remain for the most part subtextual. Moreover, Humbert *never* knows the one crucial fact regarding the destiny of events and the publication of his narrative—the death of Dolly in childbirth—and while readers may well miss it, because John Ray Jr. calls her by her married name and buries the information in the listed fates of minor characters, this fact has been "known" by the framing narrative from the very beginning of the novel.

This sense of belatedness in Humbert's narrative constantly provokes us to look elsewhere, beyond the current narrative, to question who or what *is* determining the play of coincidences. "McFate" turns out, in part, to have been Quilty in disguise, but only in part. John Ray Jr. is obviously no more than a philistine editor, as he does not recognize that the fate of Lolita is of more significance than that of Mona Dahl. The only other figure that could be considered "authorial" in the text is the very shadowy one of Vivian Darkbloom. Darkbloom is Quilty's

"collaborator" and the author of his biography, *My Cue.* She never appears in person but is acknowledged in print several times, most tellingly in the entry from *Who's Who in the Limelight,* which, in the process of listing Quilty's dramatic career, provides a coded summary of the plot of *Lolita.* In addition to these metatextual clues, "Vivian Darkbloom" is an anagram of "Vladimir Nabokov." Her presence in the text seems to act as a kind of trace signature of the otherwise absent "true" author, a reminder of the fictionality of all the read events, of the unreliability of the book's narrators (Humbert in particular). But equally, insofar as she is *not* Nabokov but a reflection, she is a reminder that there is no final authority over what happens, that the book's fictive events, like "coincidences," can be endlessly reinterpreted. Nabokov thwarts the possibility of omniscient narration and authorial didacticism by denying that his novel carries a "pure" motive. The book's directions, opinions, perspectives, and judgments are multiple and deeply embedded in the specific context of each described event, just like the "tricks" of "visible nature."

ALLEGORIES AND ALLUSIONS

Faced with the uncertainties of its narrative and the unreliability of its narrator, critics have often been tempted to construct a unified interpretation of *Lolita* from the undercurrents of allusion in the text, for the novel is saturated with a collective memory of cultural associations. In his afterword to *Lolita,* Nabokov claims that initial readers of his manuscript declared it to represent "Old Europe debauching young America" or even "Young America debauching old Europe." John Hollander's 1956 piece in the *Partisan Review* (reprinted in *Nabokov: The Critical Heritage,* 1982) picks up on the allusions to Poe's "Annabel Lee" and on the Swinburnian name of the novel's heroine ("Dolores" means sorrow or pain, and Algernon Charles Swinburne wrote several amoral, aesthetic poems to the "Lady of Pain"). He theorizes that "*Lolita,* if it is anything *really,* is the record of Mr. Nabokov's love affair with the romantic novel, a today-unattainable literary object as short-lived of beauty as it is long of memory." Lionel Trilling also emphasizes the romance tradition, receiving the novel as both a satire "upon the peculiar sexual hypocrisy of American life" and a story about "passion-love," the amorous fixation which has been at the heart of literature throughout the ages until our sterile modern times. Nabokov once answered a question about his resistance to being taken as a "moral satirist" by stating "satire is a lesson, parody is a game" (quoted in *Strong Opinions*), and critics such as Alfred Appel have tended to use the "gaming" metaphor in order to explain the novel's allusive texture and its refusal to impart certain morals or conclusions. *Lolita,* then, becomes a narrative about narrative, literature's endless openness to embellishment and reinterpretation.

There is, no doubt, validity in all of these interpretations in relation to particular sections of the book. Humbert's relish for recording Dolly's teenage slang and the names and advertising slogans of motel America must owe something to Nabokov's fascination with his adopted-but-alien homeland. Humbert also clearly shares his author's well-documented disdain for contemporary psychiatry, steeped as it is in Freudian theories of sexual development. Readers may be suspicious of Humbert's claims to have preempted and outwitted the psychiatric diagnoses of various sanatoriums he has visited, but his interview with Miss Pratt in Beardsley School, where she insists, in complete ignorance of Humbert's treatment of his ward, that Dolly is "still shuttling . . . between the anal and genital zones" is too wildly and impeccably satirical to be a Humbertian ruse alone. Nevertheless, to read the rest of the novel through the lens of such satirical moments is clearly too simplistic an approach to the multilayered narrative, and even trusting whole-heartedly in the "game" of parody rather than the "lesson" of satire risks underplaying the importance of *Lolita*'s subtle shiftings of interpretative responsibility.

These critical difficulties are underscored by the half-poetic, half-parodic allusions to other literary texts and genres within the novel. In spite of the ubiquity of references to other renowned stories of lost love, *Lolita* never quite becomes a tribute to the "romantic novel": Humbert is too flawed, too self-serving an appropriator of the form for that. Equally, the "romance" of the book's structure (with its elements of quest, attainment, loss, pursuit, and revenge) never falls away completely and so cannot be figured parodically as a debased "modern" imitation of the form like the scorned "feminine novels" penned by "lady writers" or like the pornographic amorous "confessions" to which Nabokov refers in his afterword.

The allusions in *Lolita* thus refuse to create an allegorical structure on which to hang the wayward pieces of the narrative puzzle. One of Humbert's musings on "McFate" even serves as a warning to pedantic readers who may be busily forging an interpretation through scholarly footnotes:

> It is easy for him and me to decipher *now* a past destiny; but a destiny in the making is, believe me, not one of those honest mystery stories where all you have to do is keep an eye on the clues. In my youth I once read a French detective tale where the clues were actually in italics; but that is not McFate's way—even if one does learn to recognize certain obscure indications.

The double irony here is that Humbert is referring to his failure to recognize Quilty's pursuing presence, which is indeed indicated throughout the narrative as a set of clues that Humbert and readers must "detect"; but the more "obscure indications" of outcome and significance, such as the literary allusions, are not always as "honest." In certain very specific contexts they may function to wake us from our comfortable assumptions about the particular worldview that is being presented: just as we suspend our disbelief and submerge ourselves in the texture and action of the prose, some sneaky allusion suddenly raises its head and makes us conscious of the artifice of the story and its narrator. At the climax of the first part of the novel, when Humbert recalls *"le grand moment"* of his planned seduction of Lolita to the imagined "gentlewomen of the jury," he casually refers to himself as "Jean-Jacques Humbert." This allusion to Jean-Jacques Rousseau, author of the famous autobiographical *Les Confessions,* alerts us to the confessional mode of Humbert's narrative at this point, and it raises the suspicion that Humbert is consciously assuming a role rather than genuinely, spontaneously admitting his guilt. There is an additional irony in play here, as Rousseau is also remembered for his Romantic idealization of the innocence of childhood. Humbert mimes these notions in relation to Lolita, whose purity he already realizes has been "slightly damaged through some juvenile erotic experience" at camp. He uses his "old-fashioned, old-world" views of childhood to claim some kind of nobility in his plan to spare "her purity" by interfering with her "only in the stealth of night," when she has been "completely anesthetized" by his sleeping pills. Of course, his "restraint and reverence" are merely a cover for his fear of being discovered, which is underscored by the distance between the original Jean-Jacques's notions of childhood and Jean-Jacques Humbert's.

When they are sustained, however, the allusions behave less as singular warnings of possible duplicity than as part of the seductive and deceitful fabric of Humbert's tale and the counterplots beyond it. The persistent references to Prosper Mérimée's *Carmen* throughout the novel seem to lead toward an end game where Humbert will kill his deceitful lover Lolita, but when it finally arrives, the denouement is very different. Unlike the original Carmen, Lolita does not leave with Humbert, and rather than murdering her, Humbert murders his own double, Quilty. In this instance the revelation of the allusion's significance is deferred and readers remain oblivious until the last moment in the story. As with the questions posed about authorship and authority, the complications of the metanarrative are not consistent or unidirectional: they *may* alert readers to ironies within the text, they *may* signal generic undercurrents (confessional autobiography, romance, detective story) and metaphorical echoes which help to situate and mold a coherent structure of meaning, but they may equally distract and divert, alerting readers to nothing except the play of textual possibility. Indeed, this is precisely how the most prevalent literary allusions—to *Carmen,* to Poe's "Annabel Lee" and to a whole library of fairy tales—behave. Alfred Appel's footnotes in *The Annotated Lolita* remark upon the Latin etymology of "carmen" as "song, poetry, and charm": "My charmin', my carmen" sings Humbert in the solipsizing scene. The *Carmen* allusions can thus be seen to "charm" readers into a state of confusion. Like Humbert and Quilty, who are mesmerized by their desire for nymphets, we are perpetually "enchanted hunters" of significance.

THE SEDUCTIVE TEXT

To wallow in discussions of metanarrative, however, risks avoiding the central issue and the glaring danger of the novel: the seductiveness of Humbert's tale of seduction. The constant, anxious question which *Lolita* poses is the relation of its charming "language" to its subject, or the relation of form to content, and this question is embedded in the reader's experience of following Humbert's narrative.

Nabokov was adamant in his afterword that *Lolita* is not an erotic confession along the lines of *"Memoirs of a Woman of Pleasure* or *Les Amours de Milord Grosvit,"* but this does not mean that he resists playing with the promises of the genre. The title ascribed to Humbert's "strange pages" in the foreword is "Lolita, or the Confession of a White Widowed Male," which maps comfortably onto a great tradition of titillating literature. And while the narrative never descends into the "simple sexual stimulation" of the "pornographer," the slow journey of the first part of the narrative toward the point of consummation does raise readerly expectations of salacious revelations. Humbert does not simply seduce Lolita; he seduces his audience. He tiptoes carefully between different modes and genres of confession—the anonymous erotic telltale, the testimony of the learned advocate, the reflections of the sophisticated aesthete—appropriating their rhetoric and euphemisms so readers can never grow accustomed to one register or habituated to its manipulative powers.

Humbert's description of his condition of "nympholepsy" is a prime example. He begins with the cool, technical prose of a scholar or lawyer, describing the inarguable phenomenon of maidens "between the age limits of nine and fourteen," whose "true nature . . . is not human, but nymphic (that is, demoniac)," whom he proposes "to designate as 'nymphets.'" In the next paragraph he slips into the shimmering lyricism of the artistic "lone voyager": I would have the reader see "nine" and "fourteen" as the boundaries—the mirrory beaches and rosy rocks—of an enchanted island haunted by those nymphets of mine and surrounded by a vast, misty sea." This voice survives until, describing the nymphic features which provoke the "hot poison" of his lust, he slides into a more suggestive register: "the slightly feline outline of a cheekbone, the slenderness of a downy limb, and other indices which despair and shame and tears of tenderness forbid me to tabulate." The alternation of legal, aesthetic and erotic language continues throughout the chapter until the three modes conflate:

> But how his heart beat when, among the innocent throng, he espied a demon child, *"enfant charmante et fourbe,"* dim eyes, bright lips, ten years in jail if you only show her you are looking at her. So life went. Humbert was perfectly capable of intercourse with Eve, but it was Lilith he longed for. The bud-stage of breast development appears early (10.7 years) in the sequence of somatic changes accompanying pubescence. And the next maturational item available is the first appearance of pigmented pubic hair (11.2 years). My little cup brims with tiddles.

Ostensibly, the last sentence is simply referring to the thoughts he has been collecting (like tiddles in the game of tiddledywinks), but there is an unmistakable sexual innuendo here as well. It becomes a familiar pattern in Humbert's narration. He distracts readers with high thoughts or high prose before slipping in a true signifier of his brute lust, and even this is usually in the guise of an innuendo or euphemism. Not only does this blind unwary readers to the obscenity of what Humbert is talking about, but it potentially makes them complicit in his seductive manipulations: the playfulness of language and the teasing shifts of tone deliver an aesthetic pleasure in themselves, and in failing ever quite to "deliver" a simple statement, they lead readers on in anticipation of what may be revealed. Humbert, like his creator, has a frightening understanding of the erotics of reading, and he throws us into a mire of anxious enjoyment and uncertain moral judgment. It is not surprising that one of his possible pseudonyms was "Mesmer Mesmer," for he is an accomplished hypnotist.

In spite of his linguistic versatility, the register Humbert most relishes and manipulates is his gourmand aestheticism. From the counterpointed rhythms and overripe alliteration of his first, infamous lines to his final invocation of the immortality of his love-in-art, Humbert's constant preoccupation is with the textures and shades of words. He tastes and savors their pleasures as if they were things themselves: "Lo-lee-ta: the tip of the tongue taking a trip of three steps down the palate to tap, at three, on the teeth. Lo. Lee. Ta." The merging of the narrative's sensuous language with its sensuous theme is at once the most seductive and the most suspicious aspect of Humbert's prose. His constant claim is that his interest in writing is purely aesthetic. Even as he completes the description of his first act of intercourse with Dolly, he denies that there is any sexual focus to his narration: "I am not concerned with so-called 'sex' at all. Anybody can imagine those elements of animality. A greater endeavor lures me on: to fix once and for all the perilous magic of nymphets." We have to believe this assertion to an extent because Humbert does indeed continually conjure the blunt physicality of his lust and his treatment of Lo into a poetic existence. The passages of the greatest linguistic play frequently coincide with the moments of Humbert's greatest sexual excitement. Assonance and alliteration abound in the scene where he "solipsizes" Lolita, particularly as he heads toward orgasm: "The implied sun pulsated in the supplied poplars. . . . The corpuscles of Krause were entering the phase of frenzy. The least pressure would suffice to set all paradise loose." And afterward, everything is magically metaphorical: "I had stolen the honey of a spasm without impairing the morals of a minor. Absolutely no harm done. The conjurer had poured milk, molasses, foaming champagne into a young lady's new white purse; and lo, the purse was intact."

His motivation for such tonal displacements, however, is distinctly murky. It cannot simply be coyness because there is far too much relish for, and humor in, the language. And if he is seeking to steer readers away from imagining the base "animality" of coitus, it must have as much to do with his need to evade responsibility for his actions as his having a high-minded sense of artistic significance. The difficulty for readers is to judge where one motivation shades into another and, indeed, whether these motivations are as separable as Humbert's aestheticism would have us believe. Even Humbert has moments where he wonders whether his fantasies about nymphets have had some effect on the real little girls: "Had I not somehow tampered with her fate by involving her image in my voluptas?" This, along with our sense of being complicit in the erotics of reading Humbert's prose, would suggest that stark reality and ideal fiction, truth and lying, are more embroiled and confused than we, and Humbert, may imagine.

Nothing highlights this issue more startlingly than the way in which Humbert's narrative figures the pursuit and seduction of Lolita. Until Humbert "possesses" her, Lo seems to be caught in a game of suggestion and flirtation which in many ways mirrors Humbert's relation to his readers. She allows him to lick a mote out of her eye, sits on his lap, is happy to play physical cat-and-mouse games, and interrupts her mother's attempts to impress the lodger. Lo is not "innocent" in the sense of being ignorant of the language of attraction and seduction. Quite apart from her modern American education, her mother is a notable, if somewhat clumsy, example to her in learning the game of sexual play. Yet none of her actions ever go beyond the perfect equipoise of flirtation: they signal neither a definite "yes" nor a definite "no" and thus remain safe. But all these actions are filtered through Humbert's vision, and while the words he uses to describe her behavior remain true to the spirit of girlish flirtation, it also translates this language into something that makes Lo seem actively complicit—even consenting—in his pursuit of her. He has already sown a suggestive seed in his narrative by claiming that he resembles "some crooner or actor chap on whom Lo has a crush" (this is, in fact, one of the embedded Quilty references), and so when Lo kisses him before leaving for camp, it somehow seems justified that he uses the language of romantic fiction to describe it: "Lolita arrived, in her Sunday frock, stamping, panting, and then she was in my arms, her innocent mouth melting under the ferocious pressure of dark male jaws, my palpitating darling!" This prose hovers uncertainly between the world of distant teenage crushes and the world of actual sexual relations. Description is similarly slippery when she sits on his lap in his study: "All at once I knew I could kiss her throat or the wick of her mouth with perfect impunity. I knew she would let me do so, and even close her eyes as Hollywood teaches. A double vanilla with hot fudge—hardly more unusual than that." The terms he uses here perfectly evoke the consumerist obsessions of the preteen object he is trying to "fix" in art, but it also serves to collapse the distance between his and Lolita's levels of sexual knowledge and power.

Thus when Humbert the Wounded Spider's plot finally comes to fruition in the hotel, all he need do is continue to translate her unknowing and wholly uninvolved juvenile "game" of copulation into his own adult lust: "My life was handled by little Lo in an energetic, matter-of-fact manner as if it were an insensate gadget unconnected with me. While eager to impress me with the world of tough kids, she was not quite prepared for certain discrepancies between a kid's life and mine." The casual nature of this remark elides the discrepancies of understanding between the childish and adult world, as well as the difference of anatomical size, so that what has happened seems "hardly more unusual" than what she did in the bushes at Camp Q. It is a shocking moment, but it is less shocking than it could be because Lo's language and perspective have gradually been appropriated and swallowed up by Humbert. Indeed, she has been so thoroughly "solipsized" by his prose that her (somewhat stereotyped) everyday activities and the very real pain of her abused body are simply and equally absorbed into the vibrant images of Humbert's verbal painting:

> There would have been those luminous globules of gonadal glow that travel up the opalescent sides of juke boxes. There would have been all kinds of camp activities on the part of the intermediate group, Canoeing, Coranting, Combing Curls in the lakeside sun. There would have been poplars, apples, a suburban Sunday. There would have been a fire opal dissolving within a ripple-ringed pool, a last throb, a last dab of color, stinging red, smarting pink, a sigh, a wincing child.

THE TRAPS OF MEMORY

Just as the narrative is pitched uncertainly between public and private confessions, so its position in relation to the unfolding of events is ambiguous. Its frame as a public, published *archive* indicates that the time of its events to be over and in the past (the deaths of all the central protagonists is the surest marker of this), yet since it is also a private *memoir*, the narrative also functions as Humbert's process of discovering connections and significances in relation to these events for the first time—or as if for the first time. Its temporal perspective is both a journeying back and a journeying forward.

The nature of memory was one of Nabokov's enduring preoccupations. His most remarkable exploration of the subject is in *Speak, Memory* (1969), his "Autobiography Revisited," where he weaves together a sequence of luminous recollections of his Russian childhood, adolescence, and young adulthood in exile without conscribing them in the usual chronological order of the autobiographical genre. While utterly different from *Lolita* in texture and tone, *Speak, Memory* is also poised between two depictions of memory: as a power which defeats the "impersonal darkness" of "the walls of time," and as a blind stumbling between randomly illuminated perceptions which ends in the discovery that "the prison of time is spherical and without exits." Nabokov seems to inscribe a hierarchy of memorial quality where the earliest perceptions to be laid down by the mind are the most vivid, faithful, and enduring. He writes that to probe one's childhood recollections "is the next best to probing one's eternity," and in an interview in 1962 he describes his childhood memories as being "absolutely permanent, immortal . . . a permanent possession" (quoted in *Strong Opinions*). This suggests a Proustian undercurrent to his notion of memory. Marcel Proust was influenced by the philosopher Henri Bergson's division of memory into two types—one mechanistic and habitual, the other spontaneous, involuntary, and more faithful in its recollection—and his great work *A la recherche du temps perdu (Remembrance of Things Past)* was structured around the artist's attempt to maintain a brilliant involuntary memory of childhood and mold it in art. The process by which the memory is captured and its aesthetic significance is fathomed is the process by which lost time is regained.

This somewhat crude summary underestimates the complexity and difficulty of Proust's artistic efforts (which, after all, run to several volumes of writing before they are fulfilled), but it is still possible to see the similarities between his and Nabokov's notions of recollection and to see the way *Lolita's* memorial art follows Proust in using a mnemonic image as the singular prompt for a flood of imaginative associations and refigurations. Humbert opens chapter 3 with a description of the "two kinds of visual memory": the voluntary kind where "you skillfully recreate an image in the laboratory of your mind"; and the involuntary kind "when you instantly evoke, with shut eyes, on the dark innerside of your eyelids, the objective, absolutely optical replica of a beloved face." Lolita is remembered in these spontaneous terms, and Humbert's whole narrative functions as an attempt to replicate in words the photographic clarity and immediacy of his vision of her. His lust before he seduces Lolita blinds him so that he can only visualize "an immobilized fraction of her, a cinematographic still"; his description of her approaching his box of gifts at The Enchanted Hunters, runs like a "slow-motion" film, to match her walk; and when he loses her, he longs for a "real" film of her to accompany his memories "in the projection room of [his] pain and despair." Given the filmic graftings of his recollection, it seems no coincidence that Humbert's dead mother, the original lost object of affection, should have been "very photogenic," or that the "redolent remnants" of his childhood should persist in his mind's eye as a play of light, dark, and "summer dusk."

This very question of the "first" vision or "first" perception, however, is even trickier in *Lolita* than the Proustian resonances would imply, for Humbert stakes his claims both to truthful confession and to authentic aesthetic journeying on an idea of primary memory which seems not to have a discernible origin. His first love, Annabel Leigh, is cited as the precursor to Dolores Haze—and thus the original prompt of his nympholepsy—which means his first sight of Lolita as she sunbathes in the garden is not in actual fact a vision of *her,* but of his "Riviera love" "incarnated" in Dolores. This seems to be confirmed by the involuntary nature of his memory at this crucial moment, as Dolores' dark glasses recall, in Proustian fashion, the sunglasses that were witness to Humbert's and Annabel's failed attempt at lovemaking. Nevertheless, we have already been told that it is Lolita who is remembered spontaneously, as "absolutely optical replica," whereas Annabel's image has to be "skillfully recreated," suggesting that Dolores has supplanted rather than merely incorporated Annabel's status as loved, lost object and "first" memorial prompt. Even the passing reference to Humbert's dead mother—dropped into the first few hundred words of his testimony like a Freudian red herring—complicates the picture, for her image recurs in residual form in Quilty's play *The Lady Who Loved Lightning,* listed in *Who's Who in the Limelight,* and in Lo's later, unprompted assertion, "I am not a lady and do not like lightning." Is, then, Lolita the last version of a series of doomed dead muses—and imago of lost childish bliss—or is she the "true" object of Humbert's vision, and the others merely filters? In either case, "Lolita" bears little resemblance to the "real" Dolores Haze. The processes of imaginative association seem to work not so much to illuminate as to obscure Humbert's recollections, which in turn muddies his claim of fidelity to a singular vision. There is, it seems, no authentic version of the memory on which he founds his narrative of artistic discovery.

To some extent this memorial blurring is another example of Humbert–Mesmer Mesmer's hypnotic plotting. At times he plays with the tricks of memory as another way to achieve aesthetic mastery over "real" events. When he reproduces Charlotte Haze's love letter to him, apparently "verbatim," he admits that "there is just a chance" that her idea that he will tear it up and throw it "in the vortex of the toilet" is his "own matter-of-fact contribution" to the memory. His mnemonic technique here is one of deliberate embellishment, as he satirizes Charlotte's histrionic style of writing. Humbert recasts misremembering as aesthetic virtuosity again later in the book when, having mixed up two recollected events, he declares pompously that "such suffusions of swimming colors are not to be disdained by the artist in recollection." Yet in spite of Humbert's cynical manipulation of associative memory, he does seem to hold a genuine faith in its capacity to re-create and re-imagine what has passed, been lost, or has never been possessed. This represents a more profound and pathetic failure of vision because it leads Humbert further and further into a realm of invention and embellishment that ceases to have any connection with the actual "thing" or "moment" he is trying to capture. By the time "Dolorès Disparue" does return to his sight in the form of a letter in his mailbox, his personal myth of time and memory has been so composed that he does not recognize that the very thing he has longed for—the reappearance of "her lovely, loopy, childish scrawl"—has materialized. Thus his "fancy" is both "Proustianized and Procrusteanized," for the (Proustian) moment of "regained" time is forced through the rigid frame of his aestheticized perceptions, just as Procrustes broke the legs of his victims to ensure they fit his bed. What should be a moment of triumph thus becomes a moment of disillusionment.

Significantly, and ironically, the pure Proustian realization does not arrive until Lo, now Dolly Schiller, disabuses Humbert of his final scraps of romantic fixation and reveals the name of her other corrupter. The word "waterproof" flashes through Humbert's mind, an involuntary memory of his swim at Hourglass Lake where Quilty had been mentioned. Only now does memory speak the truth and the memoir's "pattern of branches" allow "the ripe fruit [to] fall at the right moment." With the advantage of hindsight, Humbert tries to claim responsibility for this tying up of loose ends, but it is a laughable gesture of pride, for when it came, the moment of revelation was completely beyond the bounds of his imagination.

MIRRORS AND DOUBLES

Through the reflected layers of authorship and allusion, the projected images of memory, and the duplicity of Humbert's confessional art, we are confronted by a series of mirrors which never quite surrender the true object or true speech. At the same time, when viewed at oblique angles, these mirrors afford readers occasional glimpses of a perspective which defies that of the master narrator. These glimpses increase in frequency, and in irony, once Dolly has deserted Humbert and he begins to realize that he is not the only one capable of creating plots and embellishing experience. As he traces the trail of deception and invention that Quilty has left behind him, it becomes increasingly apparent that his whole affair with Lolita has been neither a glorious artistic endeavor nor a sensational moral transgression, but a hopeless, sordid sham. Rita, the bewildered alcoholic, and "Jack Humbertson," the anonymous amnesiac, are fitting companions for Humbert because, like them, he has become an exile from the main plot and permanently "isolated from his personal past." In parallel with the dawning of this realization, his powers of verbal crafting seem to fade. The two poems he composes between Lo's disappearance and reappearance, one echoing his search for Dolores Haze, the other commemorating The Enchanted Hunters, are full of forced rhythms and desperate rhymes.

Humbert's artistic mirror becomes tarnished, and develops cracks that are revealed in the two very different scenes which are instrumental in bringing about his final downfall and the end of the novel: the episode in Coalmont, when he finds the ruined Dolly Schiller, and his subsequent encounter with and murder of Quilty. The first scene is tragic and lyrical in tone, the second comic and theatrical, but both serve to deliver devastating blows to Humbert's fabricated reflections.

The first blow is a moral one. For Humbert, his urgent journey to Coalmont represents the climactic episode in the story of his "grand péché radieux," when he will gun down his rival in a fit of remorseless passion and reclaim his lost love. Yet when he is confronted with the seventeen-year-old embodiment of the treasured mirage, his plans crumble. Humbert's projection of her as "nymphet" no longer fits his perception. The revenge plot references to Carmen, which have reached a peak, fall away, as do the idealized identifications of her as the "Riviera love," Annabel Leigh. She is now plain Dolly Schiller, "frankly and hugely pregnant" with "rope-veined narrow hands . . . goose-flesh white arms" and "unkempt armpits," "hopelessly worn at seventeen." The contrast to the "folded colt" with "limpid lovely limbs" is startling. For the first time Humbert faces the consequences of his actions, and his narrative vibrates with the shock. On the one hand, he cannot relinquish his obsessive fixation or the language which conveys it, and he still clings to "the faint violet whiff and dead leaf echo of the nymphet" which remains in the dowdy Dolly. On the other hand, the raw disjunction between his poetic version of events and the version which would be commensurate with Dolly's ruination provokes a sequence of alternative visions—"smothered memories"—which testify to what the "poor, bruised child" really suffered:

> There was the day when having withdrawn the functional promise I had made her on the eve . . . I happened to glimpse from the bathroom, through a chance combination of mirror aslant and door ajar, a look on her face . . . that look I cannot exactly describe . . . an expression of helplessness so perfect that it seemed to grade into one of rather comfortable inanity just because this was the very limit of injustice and frustration—and every limit

presupposes something beyond it—hence the neutral illumination.

The simple, certain picture of the effacement and obliteration of Dolly's childish hopes is more devastating and more ethically disturbing than any of Humbert's rhetorical, and somewhat self-pitying, self-accusations of being a "pentapod monster."

Following this scene of moral seriousness, Quilty's murder scene may seem strangely off-kilter, as it marks a return and peculiar escalation of the narrative's fabulous irony. However, if Dolly Schiller in Coalmont is the "real" reflection of Lolita who exposes Humbert's moral failings, then Quilty is the surreal double of Humbert who exposes his aesthetic failings. And since Humbert regards "articulate art" as the only "palliative" left for his misery, the encounter with Quilty really is the final straw.

Until his grubby appearance in Pavor Manor, Quilty is only really present on the level of metanarrative: before Humbert is properly aware of his existence, he is cast as one of the faces of "Aubrey McFate." Readers may or may not recognize his complicity with Vivian Darkbloom, Nabokov's shadowy reflection, but Humbert is entirely blind to it. Quilty's significance remains slippery even when he is physically identifiable as the pursuer of Humbert and Lolita on their road trips across the country. He seemingly becomes a projection of Humbert's guilty psyche, the archetypal doppelgänger of gothic fiction. Yet he is also a more literal double—resembling Humbert's "brother," Humbert's cousin Gustave Trapp, and the playwright's own uncle, the dentist Ivor Quilty—and Humbert is the (lesser) double of Quilty insofar as "Cue" was always Lo's real pinup: the exotic "fellow in the Dromes ad" who kissed her when she was ten. Humbert only *resembled* the "conquering hero" in the advertisement on her wall, was at best a stepfather figure to her, and did not pursue her until she was twelve.

Quilty is never quite contained by any of these symbolic manifestations, and consequently he functions as the principle of contingency and chaos which exceeds Humbert's efforts to possess and "fix" his magical nymphic vision in art. Where Humbert the Wounded Spider carefully weaves his textual web, anatomizing Lolita, American culture, and the country's altering landscapes, Quilty outweaves him in plot, perversity, puns, and in riding and manipulating the threads of "coincidence." And where Humbert always falls back into his faith in beauty and in art's aspiration to make it "immortal," Quilty's artfulness is sheer, pointless exuberance. This is most apparent in the "cryptogrammatic paper chase" he forges for Humbert when he steals Lolita, which combines sophisticated wordplay and crude innuendoes haphazardly. Quilty makes high and low cultural allusions with equal relish and embraces, without apparent purpose, the roles of clown in "Jutting Chin" mask, ringmaster of an erotic freak show, a "mad Nijinski," and, in death, a hammy film noir villain in the vein of Sydney Greenstreet: "Ah, that hurts, sir, enough! Ah, that hurts atrociously, my dear fellow. I pray you, desist." Humbert's meticulous mind, forever savoring strict aesthetic hierarchies, cannot accommodate the sheer lunacy of the "crazy quilt" woven for him, and for us, by his rival, "even now when [he] know[s] what to seek in the past," so that even after Quilty's identity has been revealed and we share in Humbert's hindsight, the hidden references to Quilty scattered through the narrative still have a deranged quality which does not tie up into a "logical pattern." They still resemble a "madman's fancy" or "hallucinations," and Quilty's pathological "logomancy" invades Humbert's syllables like a maniacal subconscious guerrilla: "Queer! I who was jealous of every male we met—queer, how I misinterpreted the designations of doom"; "ah, if I could visualize him as a blond-bearded scholar with rosy lips sucking *la pomme de sa canne* as

he quaffs my manuscript!"; "Wine, wine, wine, quipped the author of *Dark Age* who refused to be photographed"; "Where is he? Quick!"; "Quietly the fusion took place, and everything fell into order."

Thus when the rivals meet, the tone of their interaction is necessarily fanciful and farcical. They are equal in their degeneracy and hypocrisy— "two large dummies, stuffed with dirty cotton and rags"—but where Humbert has the edge physically, and thus kills Quilty, Quilty has the edge inventively. What has enabled him to unravel Humbert's mastery of Lolita and of the narrative is his ability to improvise and extemporize. This talent does not desert him now, as he refers to his pursuit of Humbert and Lolita as a "stunt" and a "joy ride," undercutting the sense of its glorious, fatalistic plottedness. His parodic commentary of the death sentence Humbert hands him mocks its careful composition: the echo of T. S. Eliot's *Ash Wednesday,* the counterpointing of "advantage" with "disadvantage," the lyrical alliteration, and the crescendo of repetitions. The deliberate high-mindedness of Humbert's "poetical justice" is derailed by Quilty's reckless theatricality so that at the very moment of effecting his revenge Humbert realizes that it is, in fact, "the end of the ingenious play staged for me by Quilty." It is thus appropriate that having left the murder scene Humbert should veer off into the reckless abandon of his own miserable "joy ride," adding traffic offenses to his crimes of passion and perversion.

TROUBLESOME ENDINGS

As Humbert's car comes to a "rocking stop," the threads of narrative seem to head toward conclusion. Humbert is captured, and he completes his confession while awaiting trial, half-conscious of his impending death. The revelations of the preceding chapters bring a denouement of sorts regarding narrative authority as well as plot. His rediscovery of Lolita and his confrontation with his double-crossing counterplotter finally dispel the high romance of his narrative and the technical virtuosity of his self-defense. Following the shocks of these two scenes, "the rest is a little flattish and faded." Humbert cannot see and savor as he wants to, and he can no longer dictate the pace, the where and when, of what is revealed to his readers. But this does not mean that it is any easier for readers to know where they are in terms of sympathy and judgment. Even in the last throes of the narrative, the risk of overinterpreting the moral and aesthetic traces looms. As Humbert sits in the car, another "smothered memory" returns which seems to indicate a moment of genuine confession and repentance. He recalls a day after Lolita left him when, having pulled his car onto the side of the highway to throw up, he was suddenly struck by his awareness of "a melodious unity of sounds rising like vapor from a small mining town that lay at [his] feet, in a fold of the valley." He confides in his reader directly:

> Reader! What I heard was but the melody of children at play, nothing but that, and so limpid was the air that within this vapor of blended voices, majestic and minute, remote and magically near, frank and divinely enigmatic—one could hear now and then, as if released, an almost articulate spurt of vivid laughter, or the crack of a bat, or the clatter of a toy wagon, but it was all really too far for the eye to distinguish any movement in the lightly etched streets. I stood listening to that musical vibration from my lofty slope, to those flashes of separate cries with a kind of demure murmur for background, and then I knew that the hopelessly poignant thing was not Lolita's absence from my side, but the absence of her voice from that concord.

This is an uneasy passage because while Humbert's moral insight is (finally) true, the perfectly balanced, sensuous, lyrical prose seems to indicate that he has not actually woken from his aestheticizing dream. Like the "beautiful bright-green flies" which he says stick to his

story, the passage evokes the brutality of his crime—the "bits of marrow" and "blood"—yet distorts it for poetically pleasing ends. The persistent duplicity here could easily be construed as evidence that Humbert's "new" moral insight is insincere: Christina Tekiner has even gone so far as to suggest that the whole last section of the novel, including Coalmont and Quilty's murder, is a further Humbertian fiction so that the ruined Dolly Schiller who provokes his remorse is just another "solipsized" figment. This seems a heavy-handed and overly literal linking of aestheticism and mendacity. We are quite right to continue to distrust Humbert's "slippery self," but this does not mean that there is no real pathos or tragedy in his situation or that his regret for his "nastiness" is purely a pose.

Humbert's tragedy—and it is a genuine tragedy—is that the lost object of his love is irretrievable because his art did not transcend and recuperate time in the way he believed it would. The metaphorical resonance to this failure points to the dangers of singular fiction, of perceiving, reading, and writing without acknowledging the difference, or the unknowability, of the fictive object *in its own terms*. It takes us back to Nabokov's comments about being able to know "more and more about one thing" but never knowing "everything about one thing" or ever getting "near enough" to reality. We must realize and acknowledge that "we live surrounded by . . . ghostly objects," and Humbert's monomaniacal attempt to possess and "fix" his "nymphet" blatantly refuses to do this. And yet the cause of Humbert's tragedy is not simply artistic solipsism—Dante's poetic appropriation of a long-dead Beatrice—but a gross abuse of the other's identity which cost her an ordinary childhood. Now that Quilty has overwritten Humbert's composition, and now that brutish lust can no longer override Dolly's autonomy, Humbert can realize both of these solipsisms individually. But, crucially, he still cannot see how the two are linked, how one leads to the other. Thus his fabrication still seems harmless to him, immune to the contamination of the real, and he still figures it as heroic in its aspiration and failure. His idealized, sentimentalized "Lolita" still shimmers alongside Dolly Schiller and is the last word on his lips. He cannot see that it is deeply inappropriate to persist in writing of "aurochs and angels" and "durable pigments" when the evidence of his very mundane, very mortal error floats like a bad smell through his prose.

It is also laughable—as are all the tragic, pathetic moments in Nabokov's radically undecidable text—and Humbert's continued blindness to his own foolishness allows the cruel comedy of the book to return for its final smirk. Even as he clings to his heightened register and asserts, with his last breath, that he and Lolita will share "immortality" through his prose, Humbert's "refuge of art" is blown apart by the dramatic irony of what *did* happen and how he did not predict and control the fate of his protagonists, right down to getting the sex of Lo's stillborn baby wrong. Humbert's fatal misrecognition is all that will persist for "the minds of later generations," recorded for the sake of posterity in John Ray Jr.'s foreword. This, paradoxically, is the only afterlife he finds.

IMPORTANCE AND INFLUENCE

The extratextual afterlife of *Lolita* has been as fraught with difficult questions and inadequate responses as the book itself. Bans on the book continued in several countries—Australia, New Zealand, South Africa, Belgium, Burma—for some time after its first publication, but elsewhere the book's notoriety ensured that it sold well. The proceeds enabled Nabokov to retire from his teaching job at Cornell in 1959, and by the 1980s *Lolita* had sold fourteen million copies.

The novel is widely accepted as being Nabokov's greatest work, and its status as an American classic has become increasingly assured as the culture of the country has caught up with the book's insights. *Lolita* was probably the first novel to see and fulfill the potential for creating "high art" from "middlebrow" America, and the novel's fond satire of mass consumerism and small-town life remains as illuminating, and just as funny, as it was in the mid-1950s. Moreover, in these days of beauty pageants for under-ten-year-old girls, the moral complexity surrounding Humbert's attraction to "nymphets" seems strangely prophetic. Contemporary culture is obsessed with youth and beauty and uses both to sell its products, but it is ever reluctant to face the unwholesome implications of its objectifying eye. At the same time, a small but vociferous sub-section of the media is always swift to claim the moral high ground and call for censorship when art tackles sexually difficult material, no matter how careful or insightful its treatment. Nabokov's novel can still teach us much about the oblique relation of "reality" and "fiction," the necessarily complex and anxious nature of forming moral judgments, and the facile comforts of hypocrisy.

That *Lolita* remains difficult, controversial, and susceptible to misinterpretation is demonstrated by subsequent adaptations of the novel into different media and by the reactions these adaptations have provoked. The book has been adapted into both a (flop) musical and a play, but in keeping with the visual bias of Nabokov's prose, it has found its most successful translation in film. Stanley Kubrick made the first attempt in 1962, while the scandal of the novel's theme was still fresh—so fresh, in fact, that the film studio played on its notoriety in the advertising tag line, "How did they ever make a movie of *Lolita*?" Yet in spite of this provocation, Kubrick was inhibited by American censorship laws relating to cinema and by the need to appease the film's financial backers. When he first approached Nabokov in 1959 with the request that the author write the screenplay, the suggestion was to avoid trouble by implying in the film that Humbert had been secretly married to Lolita all along. Nabokov balked at this idea and initially refused to adapt the novel, but after several months' contemplation and a promise from Kubrick that he would be given a freer hand, Nabokov changed his mind. He worked on the screenplay for six months and produced an ingenious but too-verbal filmic translation. While Kubrick praised the result, Nabokov, in his foreword to *Lolita: A Screenplay* (1974), said that he used "only ragged odds and ends" of the script in filming, and the writer's reaction when he saw the unfaithful film was "a mixture of aggravation, regret, and reluctant pleasure."

Fidelity to the original text is always a tricky feat with adaptations, and it is even trickier with a work as complex as *Lolita*. While the novel's rich description and dramatic set pieces cry out for translation into film, the layers of narration and embedded ironies do not translate into visual terms. Nabokov's screenplay clearly struggled with this problem and in consequence became cluttered with different voice-overs and interjections. Kubrick cleared the clutter but in the process lost much of the novel's subtlety. In concentrating on the elements which satirize modern American culture, the film too frequently appears to "side" with Humbert's perspective: beside the brash Charlotte (played by Shelley Winters) and Ramsdale cronies, Humbert (played by the debonair James Mason) often appears as the embodiment of restraint and decorum (which is exactly how the original Humbert would have liked things to be!). The phantom figure of Quilty is all too material on-screen, and in the hands of Peter Sellers the comic part loses its sinister edge. While Kubrick does manage to uphold much of the black comedy of the novel, the audience's moral vexations are smothered because the censor would never pass a film that centered on a real "nymphet." The film's Lolita, played by the fourteen-year-old Sue Lyon, was, conspicuously, a sexually mature teenager rather than a twelve year old of four feet and ten inches.

Few people would suggest that a filmmaker should cast a real preteen as Lolita, but the discrepancy between novel and film highlights the crucial distinction between imagined visions and literal ones. The power of the novel's narration lies in its capacity to take readers just far enough down the path of identification with Humbert that they can sense the seductiveness of his visions without losing sight of his depravity and foolishness. Once his visions are projected on-screen, rather than on the "mind's eye," they gain an authority which overrides any perspectival duplicity. Kubrick tries to retrieve this duplicity by using a singularly ironic tone throughout his film, but the tone is always Humbert's.

Adrian Lyne's 1997 remake of *Lolita*, however, did not even attempt to recreate Humbert's tone. While the film was more faithful to the letter of the novel than Kubrick's, it captured none of its dark fluctuations of sympathy and disgust. In Lyne's version, Humbert *is* reliving his original doomed romance with Annabel Leigh, he *is* a tragic hero overcome with loss and regret, and Lolita *is* an abnormal mixture of siren and child (she looks eighteen but wears a retainer, and far from being the book's "Frigid Princess," she gains sexual pleasure from intercourse with Humbert). This overliteral reading of Humbert's narrative made the negative critical responses to it more comprehensible than they would otherwise have been, for the film does seem to romanticize and eroticize sex with underage girls. Nevertheless, newspaper headlines such as "Perverts will flock to this travesty" (quoted in Nick James's article in *Sight and Sound*), and the failure of the film to find distribution in mainstream American cinema, foreclosed intelligent debate about the subject. *Lolita* was cast simply as a smutty film adapted from a naughty book, and once again its transgressive theme obscured and betrayed the complex play ofaesthetics and ethics in Nabokov's original prose.

Select Bibliography

EDITIONS

Lolita. Paris: Olympia Press, 1955; New York: Putnam, 1958.

The Annotated Lolita. Edited with a preface, introduction, and notes by Alfred Appel Jr. London: Weidenfeld & Nicolson, 1971.

Lolita: A Screenplay. New York: McGraw-Hill, 1974.

OTHER WORKS BY NABOKOV

The Real Life of Sebastian Knight. Norfolk, Conn.: New Directions, 1941.

Bend Sinister. New York: Time, 1947; reprinted with a new introduction by Nabokov, 1964.

Speak, Memory: An Autobiography Revisited. New York: Putnam, 1966; London: Weidenfeld & Nicolson, 1967.

Strong Opinions. New York: McGraw-Hill, 1973.

The Enchanter. Translated by Dmitri Nabokov. New York: Putnam, 1986; London: Pan Books, 1986.

SECONDARY WORKS

Andrews, David. *Aestheticism, Nabokov, and* Lolita. Lewiston, N.Y.: Edwin Mellen Press, 1999.

Appel, Alfred, Jr. "*Lolita:* The Springboard of Parody." *Wisconsin Studies in Contemporary Literature* 8, no. 2 (spring 1967): 204–241. Reprinted in L. S. Dembo, *Nabokov: The Man and His Work.* Madison: University of Wisconsin Press, 1967.

Boyd, Brian. *Vladimir Nabokov: The Russian Years.* Princeton, N.J.: Princeton University Press, 1990; London: Chatto & Windus, 1990.

———. *Vladimir Nabokov: The American Years.* Princeton, N.J.: Princeton University Press, 1991; London: Chatto & Windus, 1992. (This is the most recent and comprehensive of the biographies on Nabokov.)

Dembo, L. S., ed. *Nabokov: The Man and His Work.* Madison: University of Wisconsin Press, 1967.

Corliss, Richard. *Lolita.* London: British Film Institute, 1994.

James, Nick. "Humbert's Humbert." *Sight and Sound* 8, no. 5 (May 1998): 20–23.

Jenkins, Greg. *Stanley Kubrick and the Art of Adaptation: Three Novels, Three Films.* Jefferson, N.C.: McFarland, 1997.

Page, Norman, ed. *Nabokov: The Critical Heritage.* London: Routledge & Kegan Paul, 1982.

Rampton, David. *Vladimir Nabokov: A Critical Study of the Novels.* Cambridge: Cambridge University Press, 1984.

———. *Vladimir Nabokov.* London: Macmillan, 1993.

Sharpe, Tony. *Vladimir Nabokov.* London: Edward Arnold, 1991.

Tekiner, Christina. "Time in *Lolita.*" *Modern Fiction Studies* 25, no. 3 (autumn 1979): 463–469.

Toker, Leona. *Nabokov: The Mystery of Literary Structures.* Ithaca, N.Y.: Cornell University Press, 1989.

Wood, Michael. *The Magician's Doubts: Nabokov and the Risks of Fiction.* London: Chatto & Windus, 1994.

———. "Revisiting Lolita." *New York Review of Books,* March 26, 1998, pp. 9–10, 12–13.

Eugene O'Neill's
Long Day's Journey into Night

JASON GRAY

LONG DAY'S JOURNEY into Night is Eugene O'Neill's Pulitzer Prize–winning masterpiece, a work of autobiographical content that seethed within him all his life. It is the story of the Tyrone family, James Sr. (here referred to as "Tyrone," as the play indicates), an actor; Mary, his wife, suffering from a morphine addiction ever since the birth of their youngest son, Edmund; and James Jr., called Jamie, the eldest. A second child, Eugene, died as a baby. Beginning in the clear morning after a night of fog and foghorns and proceeding through the day as the fog returns, the play pits each character against the others in their struggle against fate and their own humanity.

O'Neill began *Long Day's Journey* after a relative dry spell while endeavoring to write his multiplay cycle, "A Tale of Possessors, Self-Dispossessed," a monumental opus that was to be based on autobiography and American history. While that cycle was never finished, excepting two plays within the cycle, he did complete *Journey* in 1941. After one of the most productive ten-year periods (the 1920s) that any writer has experienced—which earned him three Pulitzer Prizes followed by a Nobel Prize—O'Neill finally found both the "interest" and

the "nerve" he needed to confront his past and write a play about it. That it is highly autobiographical is beyond dispute, but whether in writing it he was serving factual details or artistic interests is not clear. O'Neill's father was an actor, made famous by his role of the Count of Monte Cristo; his mother did develop a drug habit after his birth; and he did have an older brother, Edmund, who died as a baby. At the time the play is set (1912), however, O'Neill had been married and divorced to Kathleen Jenkins, a point that he left out of the play (though she is noticeably present via the servant, Cathleen). And he began to suffer from tuberculosis in the fall, not in the summer time setting of *Journey*.

O'Neill's play is full of autobiographical bits, elements of his painful life at home and abroad. There are points in *Journey* where one can feel O'Neill crying out, as when Edmund tells his mother, "Please, Mama! I'm trying to help. Because it's bad for you to forget. The right way is to remember." O'Neill struggled all his life with his past, forcing himself to remember what he desperately must have wanted to forget, because it was the only way to achieve peace. As he noted at the front of this play, in a dedication to his wife, Carlotta: "I mean it as a tribute to your love and tenderness which gave me the faith in love that enabled me to face my dead at last and write this play—write it with deep pity and understanding and forgiveness for *all* the four haunted Tyrones."

This sentiment of Jean Chothia's is echoed by many critics:

> With hindsight, the whole career can be read as a clearing of the ground, a sifting of events, a honing of language and structure in preparation for the extraordinary dramatic control and self-exploration of the final three plays. . . . As Michael Manheim has put it, "O'Neill has been writing versions of *Long Day's Journey into Night* throughout his entire career."

In *Journey,* O'Neill finally was able to strip away all the artifice that went into earlier plays to let realism ring true. He needed only his actors for this play, along with a few chairs, a table, whiskey, and glasses. By simplifying the structure of the play, one scene from morning to night, he reserved a unity that allowed more room for the ramifications of his characters' lives. He is at his most Aristotelian, confining himself to a twenty-four-hour period the Greek philosopher mandated for tragedy in his *Poetics.* Everything he learned from previous experimentation was the ladder he climbed to get here, and he got to the play just in time. Only two years after its completion, Parkinson's disease made his hands shake too violently to write anymore. But he had said everything he needed to say. Whatever O'Neill's decisions were regarding fact and fiction, the play stands as a great achievement in theater on its own artistic merits, and that is what concerns us here.

ACT 1

The play opens in the living room of James Tyrone's summer home. There is a barrage of stage directions, and the first thing the audience sees is a bookcase filled with the likes of "Balzac, Zola, Stendhal, . . . Schopenhauer, Nietzsche,

CHRONOLOGY

1888	Eugene Gladstone O'Neill is born on October 16 in New York City.
1906	O'Neill enters Princeton University (leaves 1907).
1909–1910	Marries Kathleen Jenkins and then leaves for Honduras to prospect for gold. Later sails to Buenos Aires as a member of a ship's crew.
1912	Divorces Kathleen Jenkins and returns to parental home in New London, Connecticut, the scene of *Long Day's Journey into Night.* Works as a reporter for the New London *Telegraph.* Enters Gaylord Farm, a tuberculosis sanatorium, for a six-month stay.
1914	Attends George Pierce Baker's class in playwriting at Harvard University. Publishes *Thirst, and Other One Act Plays.*
1918	Marries Agnes Boulton.
1920	*Beyond the Horizon* is produced and wins the Pulitzer Prize.
1921–1922	*Anna Christie* is produced and wins O'Neill a second Pulitzer Prize.
1928	*Strange Interlude* is produced and wins third Pulitzer Prize.
1929	Divorces Agnes Boulton. Marries Carlotta Monterey.
1936	O'Neill is awarded the Nobel Prize.
1940	Writes *Long Day's Journey into Night.*
1953	O'Neill dies on November 27 in Boston.
1956–1957	*Long Day's Journey into Night* is produced and wins O'Neill a fourth Pulitzer Prize.

Marx, Engels, Kropotkin, Max Stirner, . . . Ibsen, Shaw, Strindberg, . . . Swinburne, Rossetti, Wilde, Ernest Dowson, Kipling." Above these is a portrait of Shakespeare. Note, however, that these authors are known from *reading* the play. It would be extremely difficult for an audience to tell just which books are on the shelves; only the portrait of Shakespeare would be clearly visible. Is this, then, a play to be *read* rather than *seen*? For O'Neill, it was necessary for these details to be recorded for the atmospheric purposes of his writing. Because he could control what readers of the play see, there was at least one possibility of getting the full scope of the drama across.

Then come lengthy descriptions of Mary and James Tyrone as they enter from the dining room. Mary, it is told, will strike us by her "extreme nervousness." She is said to have "pure white hair," which seems even more striking for a woman who is only middle-aged and has a healthful figure. She looks as if she has suffered a horrible shock, and indeed she has. Tyrone is robust, looking ten years younger than his age, and has "never been really sick a day in his life." O'Neill has a novelist's sensibility for description. His directions (which are copious) propel the emotional content of the scenes as much as the dialogue: Mary comes in "excited and self-conscious. . . glanc[ing] everywhere except at any of their faces." O'Neill has seen this all happen in front of him and has to make certain it goes right. Before the play has even started, he is shaping our way of looking at it, leaving little for a director's or an actor's interpretation.

It is a cheerful enough beginning. The fog has lifted, and Tyrone and Mary are bantering back and forth after breakfast, discussing her weight and the conspiratorial laugh at the old man's expense of their boys, who are still in the kitchen. The two enter together, his arm around her waist, in a picture of domestic concord. She counters his kidding about her weight affectionately with "I've gotten too fat, you mean, dear. I really ought to reduce." He will have none of that nonsense, and she says that she could not possibly eat as much as he would like. "I hope I'm not as big a glutton as that sounds." Tyrone is still in a playful mood here, but the word "glutton" is signaling the exposure of subtext.

As in any well-wrought play, O'Neill is laying down the battle lines. Tyrone is hoping that he does not seem a glutton—and he is a glutton in the way that he consumes whiskey, bad real estate, and his need for his family's obeisance. At the same time, he is not a glutton—a money hoarder, he reluctantly spends a dime for anything. Mary is trying to fend off the spying. She hates to be watched—not because of her weight, but because of her past. They are laughing, but even in the midst of their initial conversation, O'Neill shows the fault lines in his stage directions. He marks the pair's dialogue with tags such as *"Jokingly but with an undercurrent of resentment"* or *"A trifle acidly."* The mood shifts when they hear their boys laughing in the kitchen. The shift is reflected in the directions. The dialogue tags evolve from *"with hearty satisfaction"* to *"Huffily"* to *"Forcing a smile."*

The subject of their conversation moves to Tyrone's faulty real estate ventures and Edmund's health. Edmund is suffering from consumption, or, as it is called today, tuberculosis. Mary insists here and throughout that it is just a cold, and until the third act it is only the tone of voice in the male characters that tells the audience this is not so. The same is true of Mary's illness, which plays out slowly throughout the play as she unravels. Mary is constantly fretting with her hands, which become the outward sign of trouble, and touches her white hair.

Very early O'Neill gives us our first clue as to the dramatic subject of the play, with a return to the play's first discussion—Mary's weight:

MARY: . . . What makes you think I'm upset?
TYRONE: Why, nothing, except you've seemed a bit high-strung the past few days.
MARY, *Forcing a smile:* I have? Nonsense, dear. It's your imagination. *With sudden tenseness.* You really must not watch me all the time, James. I mean, it makes me self-conscious.
TYRONE, *Putting a hand over one of her nervously playing ones:* Now, now, Mary. That's your imagination. If I've watched you it was to admire how fat and beautiful you looked. *His voice is suddenly moved by deep feeling.* I can't tell you the deep happiness it gives me, darling,

to see you as you've been since you came back to us, your dear old self again. *He leans over and kisses her cheek impulsively—then turning back adds with a constrained air.* So keep up the good work, Mary.

It is now apparent that something is wrong with Mary. Something is causing this extreme nervousness. But Tyrone's pat words "So keep up the good work, Mary" are so dismissive that it is no wonder she cannot abide him. Mary tries to lighten the conversation by joking about his snoring, but he refuses to pull out of his grumpiness.

As the stage directions indicate, the dialogue of the characters constantly swerves back and forth from adoration to abhorrence. They cannot say one bad thing without qualifying it with a good thing. The den of mixed messages in which they live keeps everyone on edge. There is no relaxing, no comfort from a family member when you cannot be certain what vitriolic thing will spew forth in the next sentence. This will happen throughout the play, as with Jamie's double back: "*Stung into sneering jealousy.* [Edmund]'s always come home broke finally, hasn't he? And what did his going away get him? Look at him now! *He is suddenly shamefaced.* Christ! That's a lousy thing to say. I don't mean that." There's doubling even without premeditation: in reply to a smart comment of Edmund's, Tyrone speaks "*with appreciation, before he thinks.*" After his answer, "*he growls.*" He is appreciative of his son's ideas, but only before he "thinks." And then he catches himself and growls, in order to prepare a tongue-lashing for his son.

When the boys finally enter the scene, it is another round of placating Mama. She is the engine they all work around, trying desperately not to do anything to cause a breakdown. She is constantly nervous, ready to fall to pieces. Mary's hands are always busy, usually with her hair, but it is also her glasses she cannot find. She is continually searching for them. It seems that if she just had her glasses, she could see. But vision

does no one any good in this play. The men do nothing but stare at her and can do nothing to stop her from turning back toward her addiction.

Edmund is introduced in his role of storyteller. He tells of Shaughnessy's pigs, which have caught pneumonia by wallowing in the neighboring ice pond belonging to Harker, the Standard Oil millionaire. Harker has accused Shaughnessy of breaking the fence so that his pigs could get through, but Shaughnessy counters, accusing Harker of breaking the fence so that the pigs would get sick and die. This story serves a good effect in the play. It performs the work of a dumb show, a traditional theatrical device that mimes the play's plot, which is about to be told at length. Harker and Shaughnessy are the two sides of Tyrone, rich like Harker but behaving as if he were poor like Shaughnessy. And Edmund, Mary, and Jamie are the pigs caught breaking free and catching their death for it. Without witnesses, no one will know whether Harker or Shaughnessy is in the right, and the debate could go on forever. Though the audience is witness to this play, the family's dilemma is that there is no single person to blame for everything, and so a solution cannot be rendered.

The news of Edmund's sickness comes out after he leaves. The stage directions have told us that he does not look well, but Mary brings it into the conversation, swearing that it is just a summer cold. The other two know better. The family argument over the nature of Edmund's illness typifies the family dynamics. Instead of doing anything about it, they argue over what it could be instead of what to do. When they discuss doctors, Mary becomes extremely irritated: "I know what doctors are. They're all alike. Anything, they don't care what, to keep you coming to them. . . . What is it? What are you looking at? Is it my hair—?" she continues. That's exactly what they are looking at, her white hair—gone white after her terrible bout with morphine. Still, she does not understand what it is about her hair that is so offensive to them. Just a short time later she starts describing her hair as it was:

> It was a rare shade of reddish brown and so long it came down below my knees. You ought to remember it, too, Jamie. It wasn't until after Edmund was born that I had a single grey hair. Then it began to turn white. *The girlishness fades from her face.*

Another piece of the puzzle is handed to us—Edmund's entrance into the world set off Mary's decline.

The two family illnesses are used as a means for them to attack one another. Tyrone and Jamie tear at each other over who is more responsible for Edmund's sickness—Tyrone for failing to spend the money for a worthy doctor or Jamie for encouraging Edmund to live wildly with his weak constitution and his mother's nerves. In his defense of starting Edmund down the path to hell, Jamie says, "All right. I did put Edmund wise to things, but not until I saw he'd started to raise hell, and knew he'd laugh at me if I tried the good advice, older brother stuff." He gives his father the motto that he passed on to Edmund: "If you can't be good you can at least be careful." He chastises his father: "That's a rotten accusation, Papa. You know how much the Kid means to me." His father replies, "*Impressed—mollifyingly.* I know you may have thought it was for the best, Jamie. I didn't say you did it deliberately to harm him." Tyrone backpedals to save face and the situation, but Jamie refuses to take the respite offered. "Besides it's damned rot! I'd like to see anyone influence Edmund more than he wants to be." Jamie is not content to be blamed for unconscious things; he wants to unshoulder completely the burden of blame. Of course, this is one of the rare moments when responsibility is rightly located. Edmund is responsible for his own choices.

There are other illnesses in the play besides the obvious ones: Jamie's (and Tyrone's) alcoholism and Tyrone's miserliness. Not much is made of the drinking, except when Tyrone and Jamie

contrastingly tell Edmund not to drink because of his health and to drink because of it. Yet their drinking helps spur on their attitudes toward each other. Tyrone and Jamie drown themselves in drink, and both refuse and allow Edmund to do the same. The men are like Mary; they, too, have an addiction problem. And Mary's constant back and forth over Edmund's health—saying, on the one hand, that he should take care of himself and, on the other, that really it is just a cold and he is being a baby—is much like the men's alternately offering and refusing him a drink.

A conversation between Edmund and Mary ends the first act, and her paranoia starts to blossom. She suspects everyone of spying on her, and rightly so. They argue until the spite comes out of her: "It would serve all of you right if it was true!" It is Edmund's suspicion that pushes her over the line. She is hurt that it should come from him of all people—Edmund whose birth began it all, Edmund who is sick, too. It is true that Mary needs to be watched, but the watching alienates her further, thus pushing her toward the morphine. She has not gone to it yet, and there is still the possibility that this day could be like any other. In early drafts, O'Neill had considered having Mary use drugs on the previous night, but he pulled back from the idea because there would have been nowhere for the play to go, and the audience would have no sense of the "normalcy" of the family. It is a tenuous normalcy at best, but it is the border the Tyrones live on every day.

ACT 2

Already in the second act there is no sun coming into the room through the windows; it is sultry out. O'Neill complements the mood with a bottle of whiskey. At the end of the act Mary's drug habit is revealed, so the element of surprise is not an issue for the remainder of the play. The viewer might hope that Edmund does not have consumption, but there is no reason for such hope. By now, it is a foregone conclusion, like Mary's return to her addiction. The rest of the play is a stripping away of emotional layers. Each character slowly confronts his or her rage toward the others for their horrible lives and, even more slowly, faces his or her own fault in the issue. Edmund blames his and his mother's conditions on Tyrone's miserliness; he knows that Tyrone will not send him to anything but a state sanatorium and hates him for that. Mary blames Tyrone for the quack doctor who gave her the drugs and her son for being born. Jamie hates Edmund for having the talent that he himself never had. The problems seem less to do with the dark hand of fate than with mundane human issues.

Cathleen makes her first appearance in the first scene. For such an intensely localized family drama, O'Neill's choice to have an unrelated servant appear is strange. Is her character necessary? The whiskey could have been on stage at the opening of the curtain. Moreover, Mary already has spent time talking to herself, so Cathleen is not absolutely necessary as a means for Mary to reveal things she would not say to her family. Cathleen, then, provides the play with an antithesis to the four main characters. The girl speaks her mind "garrulously"; she is free with her opinions, negative or otherwise, but is not cruel with them. The Tyrones have a difficult time with their feelings for one another, which is not to say that they do not admit their feelings. They spit their anger out at one another, in ill-thought-out bursts of rage that are chased by regret for having kept it veiled for too long. And Cathleen bears the stamp of the old country on her face. (Note, too, that her name, "Cathleen," is the name often given to Mother Ireland.) She is Irish; the Tyrones are American, and they suffer an American tragedy.

Mary has doped up while "resting" upstairs. She comes down bright-eyed and chipper but detached. She begins to make remarks that seem out of place: "Yes, the only way is to make yourself not care," she says with respect to Jamie's worrying over being seen working by the front hedge. And yet one knows that she is talking about removing herself from the trouble of her son's illness and her lack of a home life. Just shortly thereafter, Mary utters one of the most telling bits of dialogue in the play, after attacking Jamie for sneering at his father and being unappreciative:

> MARY, *Bitterly:* Because he's always sneering at someone else, always looking for the worst weakness in everyone. *Then with a strange, abrupt change to a detached, impersonal tone.* But I suppose life has made him like that, and he can't help it. None of us can help the things life has done to us. They're done before you realize it, and once they're done they make you do other things until at last everything comes between you and what you'd like to be, and you've lost your true self forever.

Mary's comment about Jamie seeking out everyone's "worst weakness" is apt, because he does seek them out, feeling more shorn of good qualities than everyone else. But the philosophy espoused afterward is a kind of fatalism that traps the family. Of course, Mary cannot help but succumb to her addiction; and, of course, Jamie cannot help being a jerk; and, of course, Tyrone cannot help being a miser because he grew up poor. The family has no sense of the possibility of change.

Tyrone finds out about Mary when he comes in from the yard and sees her. He knows immediately, when she attacks him straightaway for living in second-rate hotels and never having a proper home, saying that he should have stayed on his own so that "nothing would ever have happened." One of the points of contention—this one between Tyrone and Mary—is the "home" that they live in. Mary has never felt at home in their summer place or on the road during touring season. But Tyrone early on says, "It's been heaven to me," referring to having Mary well and back at home from rehab. "This home has been a home again." She answers this later to Edmund: "I've never felt it was my home. It was wrong from the start." She feels "cut off from everyone."

The idea gets built upon in the next scene of the act, after lunch. With the cat out of the bag, all that is left is to uncover pieces of the past. Mary continues her conversation with herself on their lack of a "proper home" and says, "In a real home one is never lonely. You forget I know from experience what a home is like. I gave up one to marry you—my father's home." This is the first intimation of what lies behind Mary's sickness, though it will not be picked up again until much later in the play. It is easy to understand Mary's addiction through this lens. She is the character who has been pulled from her roots. Tyrone has lived as an actor for his adult life and, as a child, lived in whatever tenement his family could afford. The boys grew up in this situation. Mary is afloat in an unknown sea—she is the only woman in the family. Her religious temperament has not been satisfied or replaced with anything. The drugs, ironically, divide her from her faith by presenting her with the pleasant memory of her youth in the nunnery in which to wallow.

After lunch Mary retreats upstairs, and Jamie puts it bluntly: "Another shot in the arm!" This is exactly what Mary is going to do, but whether the other characters think it or not, everyone is taking another shot in the arm. Edmund and Jamie's quarrel over philosophy leads Tyrone to chastise them both for straying from the Catholic Church:

EDMUND: That's the bunk, Papa!
JAMIE: We don't pretend, at any rate. *Caustically.* I don't notice you've worn any holes in the knees of your pants going to Mass.
TYRONE: It's true I'm a bad Catholic in the observance, God forgive me. But I believe! *Angrily.* And you're a liar! I may not go to church but every night and morning of my life I get on my knees and pray!

Here again is a character who changes attitude midstride. Tyrone is confessional, asking for forgiveness, and then quickly turns to anger and calls Jamie a liar, throwing onto Jamie the negative feelings for which he was asking forgiveness and removing blame from himself:

EDMUND, *Bitingly:* Did you pray for Mama?
TYRONE: I did. I've prayed to God these many years for her.
EDMUND: Then Nietzsche must be right. *He quotes from Thus Spake Zarathustra.* "God is dead: of His pity for man hath God died."
TYRONE, *Ignores this:* If your mother had prayed, too— She hasn't denied her faith, but she's forgotten it, until now there's no strength of the spirit left in her to fight against the curse.

Edmund declares that he will still hold out hope for his mother, while the other two say that they will not. When Edmund calls Jamie a liar for insinuating that his mother has returned to the needle, he is holding out hope to the last that she has not. He is like his mother—both want to deny the other's illness to the point of ridiculousness, Mary more so. But Edmund at least wants his mother to see *his* illness for what it is, even if he will not do the same for her, regardless of whether she wants him to. Edmund is the last to hang on to his hope; his own illness and his guilt at causing, however inadvertently, his mother's addiction are at the root of this hope.

The question of Mary's faith is left hanging here, but it is at the crux of the play. Her faith is what she gave up for James Tyrone, and it has caused her suffering ever since. She wanted a home, a permanent home at the convent in the House of God, and instead she took Tyrone as her husband and never had any home at all, just cheap hotels and a poorly kept summer cottage on what might have been their own tiny island. Mary connects her loss of faith with the development of her habit. She says to her husband, when he is contemplating what Dr. Hardy, the family physician, has had to say about Edmund's illness, "I wouldn't believe him [Dr. Hardy] if he swore on a stack of Bibles." Here she expresses both her lack of faith in the medical profession and her former religion's powerlessness to impart trust in the family's would-be caretaker.

There seems to be a chance of escape toward the end of the second act, when Tyrone pleads with Mary, "Won't you stop now?" O'Neill says that Mary "stammers in guilty confusion for a second," and says, "I—James! Please! . . . We've loved each other! We always will! Let's remember only that, and not try to understand what we cannot understand, or help things that cannot be helped—the things life has done to us we cannot excuse or explain." Mary just as quickly loses this moment of clarity and changes the subject to the afternoon drive Tyrone wants her to take, alone. One gets the feeling that this kind of thinking is what got the Tyrones into this mess, the remembering "only that" and not confronting the issues that are poisoning their existence. Here is where Mary first mentions the convent, complaining that when she was there she

had so many friends. . . . But, naturally, after I married an actor . . . a lot of them gave me the cold shoulder. And then, right after we were married, there was the scandal of that woman who had been your mistress, suing you. From then on, all my old friends either pitied me or cut me dead. I hated the ones who cut me much less than the pitiers

Tyrone's response here is not to "dig up what's long forgotten." This is his chance to save his wife, but his own shame keeps him from dealing with the issue.

What follows is a string of revelations that lay the groundwork for the second half of the play: Mary was healthy before Edmund was born. She had had another child before him, Eugene, who had died after contracting measles, which Jamie was sick with at the time. She blames Jamie for spreading the disease to Eugene on purpose, even though he was only seven. Edmund spends

his last saving of hope and asks his mother to stop taking the drugs, telling her that she has only just begun. Hope is exhausted when she tells him that she is going to town to visit the drugstore. O'Neill has written his reply as "*Brokenly.* Mama! Don't!" This is the turning point in the middle of the play. There is no going back. The curtain falls with Mary, again, alone on stage.

> MARY: It's so lonely here. *Then her face hardens into bitter self-contempt.* You're lying to yourself again. You wanted to get rid of them. Their contempt and disgust aren't pleasant company. You're glad they're gone. *She gives a little despairing laugh.* Then Mother of God, why do I feel so lonely?

ACT 3

As O'Neill opens act 3 with a round of novelistic detail in his stage directions, readers learn that Mary's eyes "shine with unnatural brilliance." He goes on to say that she "has hidden deeper within herself and found refuge and release in a dream where present reality is but an appearance to be accepted and dismissed unfeelingly—even with a hard cynicism—or entirely ignored." These are not stage directions; they are an omniscient narrator's exploration of a character's psyche and a son's explanation for his mother's behavior. The fog has descended again, despite Tyrone's predictions; the foghorn, too, has returned, sounding like "a mournful whale in labor," reminiscent of Mary's birth pains with Edmund.

In conversation with Cathleen, Mary tells her about her dream, her two dreams, to be either a nun, "the more beautiful" dream, or a concert pianist. She forgot these dreams when she met Tyrone and promptly only dreamt about being his wife. In an odd moment, Mary snaps out of her stupor and chastises herself for her romanticism over James Tyrone. Throughout the conversation she has seemed to be talking to herself regardless of Cathleen's presence in the room.

Now that she *is* alone, it is so much starker when she says: "You were much happier before you knew he existed, in the Convent when you used to pray to the Blessed Virgin." Mary tries to utter a Hail Mary but cuts herself off: "You expect the Blessed Virgin to be fooled by a lying dope fiend reciting words! You can't hide from her!" So she goes upstairs to take another dose of morphine, because, she says to herself in an oddly rational moment, "when you start again you never know exactly how much you need." This is the creepiest moment of the play. Mary is in complete control of herself; she knows that she is taking the drugs, and she is trying to calculate the right amount for her escape. She sounds as if she is trying to remember her mother's recipe for chocolate chip cookies. Later she remarks, "I hope, sometime, without meaning it, I will take an overdose." This is a clarity that comes to her only when she is alone. Mary is fully aware of her problem but cannot apply the clarity to solving the issue nor remain clear when her family is around. She retreats into her fog of pretense when they are onstage. Mary does not make it upstairs before Edmund and Tyrone come back.

They see how far she has gone right away; she bears the stamp of it on her. It is her wedding dress she has hidden and of how her father spoiled her that now becomes clear. She quotes her own mother, "You've spoiled that girl so, I pity her husband if she ever marries. She'll expect him to give her the moon. She'll never make a good wife." Edmund tells his mother that he has to go away to a sanatorium to recover from his tuberculosis. She will not believe it; what is worse for Edmund, she did not ask him about it—he had to tell her. His mother's addiction is finally affecting him. He sees her now as not acting like his mother, as not caring for him, and he storms off. Tyrone and Jamie already had resigned themselves to drinking their way through the nightmare, but Edmund has not entirely had that option. He has not gone through this situation before. His eyes are open now to his mother, and he says to her, despair-

ingly, "It's pretty hard to take at times, having a dope fiend for a mother!" There is no more veil before Edmund's eyes as far as his mother is concerned; now it is time to go get drunk and provide a new veil, at least temporarily. But this night, for all the men, not even whiskey will be strong enough.

ACT 4

When act 4 begins, it is the father who is alone, in semidarkness, playing solitaire, drunk. Edmund stomps in after an evening of drinking and bangs his knee in the darkness. They argue over keeping a bulb burning—"I've proved by figures if you left the light bulb on all night it wouldn't be as much as one drink!" Edmund comments. They go on:

> TYRONE: To hell with your figures! The proof is in the bills I have to pay!
> EDMUND: . . . Yes, facts don't mean a thing, do they? What you want to believe, that's the only truth! *Derisively.* Shakespeare was an Irish Catholic, for example.
> TYRONE, *Stubbornly:* So he was. The proof is in his plays.
> EDMUND: Well he wasn't, and there's no proof of it in his plays, except to you! *Jeeringly.* The Duke of Wellington, there was another good Irish Catholic!
> TYRONE: I never said he was a good one. He was a renegade but a Catholic just the same.

One cannot help but feel that there is a little of Tyrone in his own opinion of Wellington, a renegade but a Catholic just the same. Tyrone is not a good Catholic, but he has not departed from it as the backdrop to his life. Their argument over money sets off the ensuing discussion and revelation about Tyrone's childhood, and the Irishness he clings to is the cause of his problems. Despite the torturous upbringing, he is proud of his heritage and would not have it any other way. His boys do not understand this, hence the gap in their communication.

Each of the Tyrones has a dream unfulfilled, a dream they all try to hide from one another but cannot seem to do it. Mary wanted to be a nun or a pianist, Tyrone wanted to be the great actor he had promised to be, and Edmund yearned to be a poet. The characters' failed dreams are symptoms of a psychological disease spreading through the play, a disease that is a counterpoint to Mary's addiction and Edmund's consumption. These players are disaffected in their own ways, and that contributes to the drowning of the family. Now it is the men's turn to face their dreams. Edmund and Tyrone engage in the most heartfelt dialogue of the play, each in turn revealing to the other what has mattered most to him in his life. Edmund speaks of taking a walk in the fog:

> That's what I wanted—to be alone with myself in another world where truth is untrue and life can hide from itself. Out beyond the harbor, where the road runs along the beach, I even lost the feeling of being on land. The fog and the sea seemed part of each other. It was like walking on the bottom of the sea. As if I had drowned long ago. As if I was a ghost belonging to the fog, and the fog was the ghost of the sea. It felt damned peaceful to be nothing more than a ghost within a ghost.

His admiration of it is eerily like that of his mother's words in act 3. Recall that earlier Mary speaks of the fog: "It hides you from the world and the world from you. You feel that everything has changed, and nothing is what it seemed to be. No one can find or touch you any more." Also, Tyrone calls Mary a "mad ghost." Mary and her youngest son are linked by more than just illness. Even Edmund says it outright during the brouhaha that erupts between him and his father during their game of casino: "I'm like Mama, I can't help liking you, in spite of everything."

Edmund's speech provokes actual admiration from his father; he says Edmund has a poet in him, albeit a "damned morbid one." Their different tastes in literature, as reflected as the play opened with their bookcases, comes into play.

For Tyrone, it is Shakespeare or nothing—the good Irish Catholic Shakespeare, who is not one of these atheist moderns that his son likes. "When you deny God, you deny hope," he advises his son, who held on to hope longer than Tyrone did. Their argument is about money. Tyrone has always cried "poorhouse" so doctors would never recommend the best and most expensive treatments, for Mary or for Edmund. Edmund outright blames his father during this debate for his mother's addiction. Then Edmund turns to his own situation:

> God, Papa, ever since I went to sea and was on my own, and found out what hard work for little pay was, and what it felt like to be broke, and starve, and camp on park benches because I had no place to sleep, I've tried to be fair to you because I knew what you'd been up against as a kid. I've tried to make allowances. Christ, you have to make allowances in this damned family or go nuts! . . . But to think when it's a question of your own son having consumption, you can show yourself up before the whole town as such a stinking old tightwad! Don't you know Hardy [the doctor] will talk and the whole damned town will know! Jesus, Papa, haven't you any pride or shame?

Edmund ends his speech with a fit of coughing. This speech finally shakes Tyrone. He gives in: "You can go anywhere you like. I don't give a damn what it costs." He gives his son a "bracer" shot of whiskey to control the coughing.

Tyrone grows angry and counters his son: "You said you realized what I'd been up against as a boy. The hell you do! . . . Oh, I know you had a fling of hard work. . . . But it was a game or romance and adventure to you." They continue:

> EDMUND, *Dully sarcastic:* Yes, particularly the time I tried to commit suicide at Jimmie the Priest's, and almost did.
> TYRONE: You weren't in your right mind. No son of mine would ever—You were drunk.
> EDMUND: I was stone cold sober.

Tyrone tries to explain his tight purse strings to his son in an eloquent speech:

> There was no damned romance in our poverty. Twice we were evicted from the miserable hovel we called home, . . . with my mother and sisters crying. I cried, too, though I tried hard not to, because I was the man of the family. At ten years old! There was no more school for me. I worked twelve hours a day in a machine shop.

It is his description of his mother that actually moves Edmund. Tyrone repeats his offer to send Edmund "any place you like" but, he adds, within reason. Cheapness is ingrained into his being; Edmund knows it and does not comment again. Tyrone is talking now and will not stop. He tells Edmund the grand tragedy of his life, that of giving up his great acting talent for the rights to a sure moneymaker:

> TYRONE, *Sadly:* . . . I've never admitted this to anyone before, lad, but tonight I'm so heartsick I feel at the end of everything, and what's the use of fake pride and pretense. That God-damned play I bought for a song and made such a great success in—a great money success—it ruined me with its promise of easy fortune. I didn't want to do anything else, and by the time I woke up to the fact I'd become a slave to the damned thing and did try other plays, it was too late. They had identified me with that one part, and didn't want me in anything else. They were right too. I'd lost the great talent I once had through years of easy repetition. . . . Yet before I bought the damned thing I was considered one of the three of four young actors with the greatest artistic promise in America.

He speaks of playing Shakespeare alongside Edwin Booth, who said of him, "That young man is playing Othello better than I ever did!" Tyrone has this written down on a piece of paper by the stage manager and has kept it in his wallet, but he can no longer find it. Edmund makes the sad but astute observation that "it might be in an old trunk in the attic, along with Mama's wedding dress."

They certainly are together in whatever repository of lost dreams exists. Tyrone had the paper to cling to once, as if it were his ticket back to artistic greatness. But now it is gone. "I'd be willing to have no home but the poorhouse in my old age if I could look back now on having been the fine artist I might have been." Imagine how the family's lives would have been different if he had been able to—Edmund must be imagining it there at the table. He might have managed his dream, too, which he is moved to relate after his father's tale of woe:

> EDMUND: . . . on the American Line, when I was lookout on the crow's nest in the dawn watch. A calm sea, that time. Only a lazy ground swell and a slow drowsy roll of the ship. The passengers asleep and none of the crew in sight. No sound of man. Black smoke pouring from the funnels behind and beneath me. Dreaming, not keeping lookout, feeling alone, and above, and apart, watching the dawn creep like a painted dream over the sky and sea which slept together. Then the moment of ecstatic freedom came. . . . [I] became the sun, the hot sand, green seaweed anchored to a rock, swaying in the tide. Like a saint's vision of beatitude. Like the veil of things as they seem drawn back by an unseen hand. . . . For a second there is meaning!

Edmund adds to this beautiful passage: "It was a great mistake, my being born a man. I would have been much more successful as a sea gull or a fish. As it is, I will always be a stranger who never feels at home."

> TYRONE, *Stares at him—impressed:* Yes, there's the makings of a poet in you all right.
> EDMUND, *Sardonically:* The *makings* of a poet. No, I'm afraid I'm like the guy who is always panhandling for a smoke. He hasn't even got the makings. He's got only the habit. I couldn't touch what I tried to tell you just now. I just stammered. . . . Stammering is the native eloquence of us fog people.

This is a double revelation, for as Edmund is confessing to his father his feelings of failure and doubt, so O'Neill is telling us about his own failure to get it right, to try to tell us the nature of his life as a fog person, then and now. Edmund's dream is left hanging in the balance. He is not positive about his ability, but the play does not indicate that he absolutely will fail at becoming a writer. He is the only one of the Tyrones who has the possibility of achieving his dream and following through, unlike his brother, who will admit his own failings when he comes home from drinking. His entrance prompts Tyrone to go on the porch to avoid his adder tongue. He announces that he is drunk. "Thanks for telling me your great secret," Edmund replies. What is Jamie's great secret? We have seen Edmund's and Tyrone's, and a little of Mary's. Tyrone's thoughts on this are simple: "If he's ever had a loftier dream than whores and whiskey, he's never shown it."

Jamie reveals his true self to Edmund in the last significant dialogue of the play. They are the closest of any pair in the play, having to help each other out with money and support. It is Jamie who has taught Edmund about the world, for better or worse. Jamie even claims to have put him on to being a writer, saying he wanted to be a writer once, too. He even calls Edmund his "Frankenstein." It is fitting that this encounter is the last between two characters. Edmund has looked up to his brother, and what Jamie has to say to him destroys whatever illusions of his family remained. The emotional charge of the play reaches its climax here. Edmund hits Jamie for calling their mother a "hophead." It is only a glancing blow, but it sobers Jamie up:

> JAMIE: Want to warn you—against me. Mama and Papa are right. I've been rotten bad influence. And worst of it is, I did it on purpose.
> EDMUND, *Uneasily:* Shut up! I don't want to hear—
> JAMIE: Nix, Kid! You listen! Did it on purpose to make a bum of you. Or part of me did. A big part. The part that's been dead so long. That hates life. My putting you wise so you'd learn from my mistakes. . . . Made my mistakes look

good. Made getting drunk romantic. Made whores fascinating vampires instead of poor, stupid, diseased slobs they really are. Made fun of work as sucker's game. Never wanted you to succeed and make me look even worse by comparison. Wanted you to fail. Always jealous of you. Mama's baby, Papa's pet! *He stares at Edmund with increasing enmity.* And it was your being born that started Mama on dope. I know that's not your fault, but all the same, God damn you, I can't help hating your guts—!
> EDMUND, *Almost frightenedly:* Jamie! Cut it out! You're crazy!
> JAMIE: But don't get the wrong idea, Kid. I love you more than I hate you. My saying what I'm telling you now proves it. I run the risk you'll hate me—and you're all I've got left.

Jamie's failed dream is that he really never had one. He borrowed others' dreams and tried them on, but he never felt at home. He is mostly the big dead part of himself now, the one that wants Edmund to stay sick, and he is glad that his mother is back on dope, so that he will not "be the only corpse around the house!"

The play ends as it must. Throughout the last act, the men have heard Mary rumbling about upstairs. As Tyrone and Jamie are drunkenly falling asleep, she comes down, sets the house ablaze with light and begins playing badly, like a child, a Chopin waltz. They wake, and she enters, carrying her wedding gown. When Mary speaks, she is back in her childhood. The sisters of the convent are in the present, and she claims to need to see Sister Martha about her swollen knuckles. "She has things in her medicine chest that'll cure anything." One wonders if Sister Martha did, or if Mary is superimposing her morphine cure for rheumatism on top of this. She has come down to find something, but she cannot remember what. During the whole play she has been looking for her glasses, the vision to see through the fog that has kept her from her faith. When Tyrone takes the gown from Mary, she says, "I found it in the attic hidden in a trunk. But I don't know what I wanted it for."

This is just like Tyrone speaking of trading his talent for money, "What the hell was it I wanted to buy, I wonder."

Mary takes us to the curtain with the story of what led her to marry Tyrone when all she wanted was to be a nun. "I had a talk with Mother Elizabeth," she says, who advises Mary to leave the convent after graduation to live as other girls live for a time, to make sure.

> I never dreamed Holy Mother would give me such advice! I was really shocked. I said, of course, I would do anything she suggested, but I knew it was simply a waste of time. After I left her, I felt all mixed up, so I went to the shrine and prayed to the Blessed Virgin and found peace again because I knew she heard my prayer and would always love me and see no harm ever came to me so long as I never lost my faith in her.

Mary *has* lost it. There would be a temptation to blame Mother Elizabeth for this. If she had said, "Yes, join us," maybe none of this would have happened. But Mary finishes: "That was in the winter of senior year. Then in the spring something happened to me. Yes, I remember. I fell in love with James Tyrone and was so happy for a time." Mary met James Tyrone before she even left the convent.

"She stares before her in a sad dream. Tyrone stirs in his chair. Edmund and Jamie remain motionless." Tyrone stirs; he knows this, but the boys are in shock, the graphic nature of their mother's history has never before been so upfront to them. They cannot move as Tyrone does; they are frozen by her revelation. What she could not remember was that she fell in love with Tyrone and thereby put an end to her dreams of sisterhood and of playing the piano. The Tyrones are victims of negotiating with their dreams. The tragedy is that what they gave up they gave up for what they thought was a good thing. Mary was in love with Tyrone; it was natural that she should want to marry him. Tyrone wanted a stable life for himself and his family; it was natural for him to seek out a steady monetary income. Jamie gave in to the overbearing shadow of his father and never tried to excel in the theater. Edmund is the last holdout. O'Neill became a talented writer, but will Edmund do the same? His last words on the subject would not lead us to believe so, but the answer is beyond the scope of the play. The family is done for. All that's left to them is their various ways of narcotizing life until it ends. Ironically, it is Edmund's need to go to the sanatorium that seems to be his only way out. By getting away from his family, he might break free of the weight of his past.

This is O'Neill's American tragedy. It is not Greek or Shakespearean. As in the story of Oedipus, tragedy ensues from one man's birth, but unlike the tale of Oedipus, the tragedy is not Edmund's fault. Oedipus had control over his actions, or at least they were his actions, whether or not he could choose them. But Edmund's birth was not his action, and the morphine was administered by the doctor. If it is anyone's tragedy, it is Mary's; she fails to overcome her addiction, and the fallout affects her family. This fallout, however, is only one in a series, as each haunted Tyrone's confession in the play makes clear. O'Neill's idea is to expose the several faults so that the tragedy belongs to the entire family. In the land where anyone can lift himself up by the bootstraps (as Tyrone does as a young man), one can fall from that dream or never achieve it. One can never even have a dream but live like a vampire in the glow of other's dreams. Tyrone's and his sons' failure, or possible failure, to succeed is the corruption of the American dream—that Mary should have been stricken with morphine addiction while they were touring in Tyrone's great American success story—financial success anyway—is the ironic center of the family's destruction.

PRODUCTION HISTORY AND INFLUENCE

The story of *Long Day's Journey into Night*'s initial production is long and sordid, involving even the era's secretary-general of the United Nations, Dag Hammarskjöld. O'Neill had placed a twenty-five-year moratorium on publishing and producing the play before he died, and yet the play was made before the end of the decade in which he died. The play's first production occurred in Stockholm, which may seem strange at first, but O'Neill very much admired the Royal Dramatic Theater's productions of his earlier plays and was grateful for his award of the Nobel Prize in 1936. Random House had the play locked in its vault and would not publish it, according to O'Neill's wishes. Carlotta O'Neill gave them permission to do so, but rather than break their word, they relinquished the rights, which subsequently were sold to Yale University Press, the royalties going to fund the Eugene O'Neill Collection at Yale and scholarships for students in the school of drama. After much haggling, the play landed in the hands of José Quintero, whose earlier revival of *The Iceman Cometh*, a play whose initial production flopped, was a much-heralded success. Quintero cast Fredric March and Florence Eldredge as the elder Tyrones and Jason Robards Jr., then starring in *The Iceman Cometh* and who would play Tyrone Sr. thirty years later, as Jamie. Carlotta had approval of the part of Edmund—which went to Bradford Dillman. Quintero brought him to see her, and in an interview (quoted by Brenda Murphy) she said of the meeting, "I said something to amuse him [Dillman], so that he smiled, and his smile was like Gene's. I made him angry for a moment and his scowl was like my husband's."

The play opened in Boston on October 15, 1956, at the Wilbur Theater and then premiered in New York on November 7 at the Helen Hayes Theater. In a vivid review of the first American performance of the play, Walter Kerr wrote:

> *Long Day's Journey into Night* is not a play. It is a lacerating round-robin of recrimination, self-dramatization, lies that deceive no one, confessions that never expiate the crime. Around the whiskey bottles and the tattered leather chairs and

the dangling light-cords that infest the decaying summer home of the Tyrones (read O'Neills), a family of ghosts sit in a perpetual game of four-handed solitaire.

Long Day's Journey into Night was a great success; it ran for 390 performances and earned Eugene O'Neill a posthumous Pulitzer Prize, his fourth. The play has gone into production many times all over the world and has been made into several cinematic adaptations as well.

O'Neill has come to sit atop the American theatrical Parnassus. Curiously enough, as Harold Bloom points out in his introduction to the newest edition of *Journey*, he seemed to have no American influences, relying instead on the Swedish dramatist August Strindberg and the Norwegian playwright Henrik Ibsen. O'Neill, however, has been the influence of many American dramatists who followed him, among them, Arthur Miller, Tennessee Williams, Edward Albee, and, more contemporarily, David Mamet and Sam Shepard. Miller wrote of seeing *Journey* in 1956,

> I can hardly end this ramble without mentioning the most enthralling dramatic experience I have had since I first read Ibsen. It is Eugene O'Neill's recently published play, *Long Day's Journey into Night*. I think it is his most moving work. It is as true as an oak board, a remorselessly just play, a drama from which all his other plays seem to have sprung.

The desolation of the American family in *Journey* is an image that filtered through into future dramas, like Albee's *Who's Afraid of Virginia Woolf?* and Shepard's *Buried Child*.

This is not to say that O'Neill is without his critics. There are two main criticisms of O'Neill. The first is that his use of language is mediocre. The other is that his plays, up until his last, great ones, were not all that good, despite having netted him three Pulitzer Prizes in a decade. (The response to this is, of course, that he had little competition among contemporary American playwrights at the time.) If O'Neill's language is not superior, what, then, is to be made of him? Is he great? After all, plays, like poems and novels, are made up of words. Except that they do not entirely consist of words. O'Neill's genius was in his vision. What he lacked in linguistic capability he made up in dramatic structure and strength of character. In this play O'Neill often has everything at the surface; there is not much covering the subtext. For instance, Mary says quite frankly to Tyrone in act 3,

> I'm sorry if I sounded bitter, James. I'm not. It's all so far away. But I did feel a little hurt when you wished you hadn't come home. I was so relieved and happy when you came, and grateful to you. It's very dreary and sad to be here alone in the fog with night falling.

Things *are* spelled out quite clearly, but the fact is that there is so much to uncover, so much buried wreckage, that there is no time for hiding in this play. In this case, Mary's speech is not the subtext; there is still more beneath.

O'Neill sometimes is faulted as a melodramatist. Considering that the two main revelations of *Journey*—Mary's addiction and Edmund's illness—are revealed in the second and third acts, there is not much melodrama at all, however, beyond the flamboyance of the characters themselves. Remember that two of these characters are actors, and another is a poet. As Mary says to Edmund, "You're so like your father, dear. You love to make a scene out of nothing so you can be dramatic and tragic."

Whether one thinks that O'Neill's language is strong, the stories in his plays are powerful. The scope of human emotion held within them has resonated since they first echoed through the halls of the world's theaters. While O'Neill may have laid to rest his personal demons, the demons of the twentieth-century American family life that haunted the Tyrones have not died quietly and continue to haunt the theater of today.

Select Bibliography

EDITIONS

Long Day's Journey into Night. New Haven, Conn.: Yale University Press, 1989. (This edition features corrections to typescript errors made by Carlotta O'Neill that appeared in the first edition, of 1956. It was reprinted in 2002 with an introduction by Harold Bloom. The second edition is cited in this essay.)

"Long Day's Journey into Night." In *Complete Plays*, vol. 3. Edited by Travis Bogard. New York: Library of America, 1988.

SECONDARY WORKS

Barlow, Judith E. *Final Acts: The Creation of Three Late O'Neill Plays.* Athens: University of Georgia Press, 1985.

Black, Stephen A. *Eugene O'Neill: Beyond Mourning and Tragedy.* New Haven, Conn.: Yale University Press, 1999.

Bloom, Harold, ed. *Eugene O'Neill's "Long Day's Journey into Night."* New York: Chelsea House, 1987.

Bogard, Travis. *Contour in Time: The Plays of Eugene O'Neill.* New York: Oxford University Press, 1987.

Chothia, Jean. "Trying to Write the Family Plays: Autobiography and the Dramatic

Imagination." In *The Cambridge Companion to Eugene O'Neill*. Edited by Michael Manheim. Cambridge: Cambridge University Press, 1998.

Eisen, Kurt. *The Inner Strength of Opposites: O'Neill's Novelistic Drama and the Melodramatic Imagination*. Athens: University of Georgia Press, 1994.

Estrin, Mark W. *Conversations with Eugene O'Neill*. Jackson: University Press of Mississippi, 1990.

Falk, Doris V. *Eugene O'Neill and the Tragic Tension: An Interpretive Study of the Plays*. New Brunswick, N.J.: Rutgers University Press, 1958.

Gelb, Arthur, and Barbara Gelb. *O'Neill*. 2d ed. New York: Harper & Row, 1962, 1987.

———. *O'Neill: Life with Monte Cristo*. New York: Applause, 2000.

Hinden, Michael. *"Long Day's Journey into Night": Native Eloquence*. Boston: Twayne, 1990.

Houchin, John H. *The Critical Response to Eugene O'Neill*. Westport, Conn.: Greenwood, 1993.

Kerr, Walter. *"Long Day's Journey into Night." New York Herald Tribune*, November 8, 1956.

Manheim, Michael, ed. *The Cambridge Companion to Eugene O'Neill*. Cambridge: Cambridge University Press, 1998.

Miller, Arthur. *Echoes down the Corridor*. New York: Viking Penguin, 2000.

Miller, Jordan Y. *Eugene O'Neill and the American Critic*. Hamden, Conn.: Archon Books, 1973.

Murphy, Brenda, ed. *O'Neill: Long Day's Journey into Night*. Cambridge: Cambridge University Press, 2001.

Prasad, Hari M. *The Dramatic Art of Eugene O'Neill*. New Delhi: Associated Publishing House, 1987.

Raleigh, John Henry. *The Plays of Eugene O'Neill*. Carbondale: Southern Illinois University Press, 1965.

Sheaffer, Louis. *O'Neill: Son and Playwright*. Boston: Little, Brown, 1968.

———. *O'Neill: Son and Artist*. Boston: Little, Brown, 1973.

Smith, Madeline, and Richard Eaton. *Eugene O'Neill: An Annotated Bibliography: 1973 through 1999*. Jefferson, N.C.: McFarland, 2001.

Stroupe, John, ed. *Critical Approaches to O'Neill*. New York: AMS, 1988.

Tornqvist, Per Egil. *A Drama of Souls: Studies in O'Neill's Super-naturalistic Technique*. New Haven, Conn.: Yale University Press, 1969.

Sinclair Lewis'
Main Street

TED SUTTON

This is America—a town of a few thousand, in a region of wheat and corn and dairies and little groves.

The town is, in our tale, called "Gopher Prairie, Minnesota." But its Main Street is the continuation of Main Streets everywhere. The story would be the same in Ohio or Montana, in Kansas or Kentucky or Illinois, and not very differently would it be told Up York State or in the Carolina hills.

(Sinclair Lewis, *Main Street*)

IN HIS PROLOGUE to *Main Street*, Sinclair Lewis speaks in the authoritative, self-possessed deadpan voice of an American news announcer, a rich basso profundo. Then, he changes his tone. "Main Street is the climax of civilization," he continues archly, with just barely a straight face, wearing his bombast on his sleeve: "That this Ford car might stand in front of the Bon Ton Store, Hannibal invaded Rome and Erasmus wrote in Oxford cloisters." The noble strivings of civilization have been replaced by vulgarity and banality, Lewis is telling readers, and for his frustrated protagonist, Carol Kennicott, this existence offers no way out.

The title *Main Street*, of course, was already part of the American vernacular before Lewis took it for his own, but once he did, it never remained the same. Now it stood for a smug, provincial, and narrow avenue tracing a path through a bland American landscape: a road full of promise but offering neither diversion nor pleasure, leading ultimately to a dead end. The novel's characters he did not so much create as snatch up, as they made their way up and down the street. He described how they struggled to find a place for themselves there and where they ended up. Sinclair Lewis took a street, a woman, and a small American town, held them up to his exquisite scrutiny, then flung them back in the face of a smug, complacent nation, almost daring it to respond.

Published on October 23, 1920, *Main Street* was a sensation, the most popular book produced in the United States since Harriet Beecher Stowe's *Uncle Tom's Cabin* in 1852. The book sold more than two million copies in two years, making Lewis a household name and earning him the Pulitzer Prize. Literary critics, however, treated the book more like it was pulp fiction than literature. Ignored by most critics in the decades that followed, Lewis' reputation suffered. *Main Street* is rarely taught; it has almost faded from sight. Sauk Centre, Minnesota, however, where Lewis was born and grew up, and the inspiration for Gopher Prairie, is still prospering. In the middle of town, two blocks down Sinclair Lewis Avenue to the right of Main Street, is the cemetery where Lewis' gravestone simply reads: "Sinclair Lewis, Author of *Main Street*, 1885–1951."

In 1885 Sauk Centre was a small town with a population of 2,807, surrounded by prairies and farms and thirty of Minnesota's famous ten thousand lakes. Lewis was an awkward loner who never felt part of the landscape. His mother died of tuberculosis when he was six, and his father, a physician, remarried a year later. Harry, as he was called, felt like an outsider. By age sixteen, he was almost six feet tall and weighed only a hundred and twenty pounds. He had bright red hair and a gawky look, with protruding blue eyes and serious acne, a condition that plagued him all his life. Girls laughed at him, and he had only one real friend. By the end of eighth grade, he was seventeenth in a class of eighteen, but he read constantly.

He began a diary at age fifteen, which he continued for eight years, taking it with him to Oberlin Academy, where he prepared for college, and then on to Yale. In it, he confided his feelings: despair when a poem is rejected from a magazine at sixteen, longing for a classmate named Myra, observations of the dull routine around him. In 1905, back in Sauk Centre on vacation from college, and bored, he made a first attempt at writing the fictional narrative that became *Main Street*, penning a story that is more of a study, calling it "The Village Virus."

At Yale, although he was the editor of *Literary Magazine*, he continued to feel isolated. He dropped out and took odd jobs for a year before graduating in 1908, and for the next twelve years he worked as an editor, reporter, manuscript reader, advertising manager, and book reviewer. His first novel, *Hike and the Aeroplane*, a

CHRONOLOGY

1885	(Harry) Sinclair Lewis is born on February 7 in the prairie village of Sauk Centre, Minnesota.
1902–1908	Attends Oberlin Academy and Yale University, serves as editor of *Yale Literary Magazine*, works at temporary jobs (including hiring on to a transatlantic cattle boat in the summer and serving as a handyman for a month at Upton Sinclair's utopian community, Helicon Hall). Receives master's degree from Yale in 1908.
1908–1915	Travels throughout the United States; works in New York publishing houses.
1912	*Hike and the Aeroplane* published (first book, an adventure story for boys) under the pseudonym Tom Graham.
1914	Marries Grace Hegger. *Our Mr. Wren*.
1917	*The Job* and *The Innocents*. Son, Wells, born. Lewis quits his job at George H. Doran publishing company and devotes himself entirely to writing.
1919	*Free Air*.
1920	*Main Street*.
1922	*Babbitt*.
1925	*Arrowsmith* and *Mantrap*. Lewis is awarded the Pulitzer Prize, which he refuses to accept.
1927	*Elmer Gantry*.
1928	*The Man Who Knew Coolidge*. Divorces Grace Hegger; marries journalist and foreign correspondent Dorothy Thompson.
1929	*Dodsworth*.
1930	Son Michael is born. First American awarded Nobel Prize for literature.
1933	*Ann Vickers*.
1935	*It Can't Happen Here* (last major work).
1936–1951	Lives between America and Europe; continues to publish novels.
1942	Divorces Dorothy Thompson; son Wells is killed by a sniper in World War II in France.

| 1951 | Dies in Rome on January 10 of heart disease caused by alcoholism. Ashes are buried in Sauk Centre. *World So Wide* published posthumously. |

children's book, was published in 1912, and four other relatively obscure novels followed before *Main Street.*

Henry Canby, reflecting on the novel's success, wrote that *Main Street* "might have been written in any time after, say, 1900 but would not have found more than ten thousand readers. By 1920 the restless minds of the writers of new books were getting a response from restless men and women who had been figuratively or literally grabbed out of their Main Streets." Millions of Americans left their hometowns during the war; many never returned. In 1920 most Americans still came from small towns, however, and many were ambivalent about them. It had only been fifty-five years since the Civil War, and America was being transformed by urbanization, industrialization, mass production and marketing, and the cultural changes wrought by automobile. A new American cynicism had evolved, in part as a reaction to the betrayal of Wilsonian ideals following World War I and the brutal political suppression in America following the Red Scare.

Until *Main Street,* American village life had usually been treated by writers as simple and virtuous, the middle class as friendly and hard-working, and America itself as the hope of the world. After *Main Street,* these stereotypes were never the same, and Lewis—who was now rich and famous and who could write whatever he wanted—spent the next thirty years writing novels (seventeen more, in all) that were each, in one way or another, descendents of *Main Street.* Lewis' fiction sought to expose the reality of American culture by mocking and attacking America's sacred institutions and professions and exposing the hypocrisy of the American middle class. His reputation reached its height in the 1920s and culminated in 1930 when he became the first American to be awarded the Nobel Prize for literature.

Over the next decades, Lewis never rested on his laurels and he never stopped writing. There was just too much that needed exposing. But fewer people read his books, and his reputation languished. It was *Main Street,* paradoxically, that had allowed him the freedom to take on the world, and it was Main Street, ironically, where he (like his protagonist Carol Kennicott) remained utterly and tragically trapped.

"SLANG PHRASES AND FLARES OF POETRY"

Three voices dominate the narrative of *Main Street:* that of the protagonist, Carol; that of her husband, Will Kennicott; and that of the narrator. Other characters come but always go, and although readers hear them, and although they may appear distinct, eventually they become shrill, flat, and grating, and all but a few grow repetitious and eventually blend into each other. Chapter 1 begins with Lewis' announcer proclaiming "On a hill by the Mississippi where Chippewas camped two generations ago, a girl stood in relief against the cornflower blue of Northern sky. She saw no Indians now; she saw flour-mills and the blinking windows of skyscrapers in Minneapolis and St. Paul." Carol Milford, the main character of the novel, is not a woman yet, but a girl: "A girl on a hilltop; credulous, plastic, young; drinking the air as she longed to drink life." Carol is full of contradictions, even here, "fleeing for an hour from Blodgett College . . . meditating upon walnut fudge, the plays of Brieux, the reasons why heels run over, and the fact that the chemistry instructor had stared at the new coiffure which concealed her ears." Right from the start, Lewis is letting readers in on Carol's secret: although passionate and idealistic, she is also prosaic, vain, pretentious, flirtatious, and contemplating a snack. At the conclusion of this section, Lewis sweeps his gaze back, positioning her as he did at the beginning, in a historical context, and laying to rest a sacred American myth: "The days of pioneering, of lassies in sunbonnets, and bears killed with axes in piney clearings, are deader now than Camelot; and a rebellious girl is the spirit of that bewildered empire called the American Middlewest."

Carol is the spirit of that "bewildered empire," and for better and worse this will be a story of her dreams as well as her limitations, a story of how she comes to terms with her town, her husband, and herself. Eventually she will blame Main Street and her husband for holding her back from fulfillment, but ultimately she is held accountable for her own life, even while Lewis qualifies her culpability, suggesting that, until the end, she never really knows what she is getting into when she marries Kennicott and moves to a small midwestern town. In the chapter's second section readers learn all they are to know about Carol's childhood and learn much about the young woman she has become. Even here, as a college student taking an hour off from class, she appears fickle. "She was not in love—that is, not often, nor ever long at a time," and "at various times during Senior year Carol finally decided upon studying law, writing motion-picture scenarios, professional nursing, and marrying an unidentified hero."

She may be fickle, but she is likable. Although she does not know exactly what she wants, she wants to do something, something big, with her life. Her sociology teacher, who "had lived among poets and socialists and Jews" and "had a beautiful white strong neck," takes her "giggling class" through "the prisons, the charity bureaus, the employment agencies of Minneapolis and St. Paul. Trailing at the end of the line Carol was indignant at the prodding curiosity of the others, their manner of staring at the poor as at a Zoo." But before one can admire her for her sensitivity, she confides to a classmate, "I just love common workmen."

Carol comes out swinging, in a sympathetic, refreshing manner; then the rug is pulled out from under her, or she pulls it out herself. But Carol is never merely the buffoon—Main Street has too many buffoons, and she would be just one. Despite her contradictions and naïveté, she appears sympathetic, someone for whom to root even when it is apparent she can never win. Lewis never kicks Carol when she is down, rather, it is when she is at her lowest that readers feel most drawn to her. But when she is first introduced, before she is off to get married and take on Main Street, readers gain a portrait that provides a genuine understanding of her psychology. And because, for this once, she is resting in place, not darting about from one vain attempt upon another to shake up her marriage, her town, and her life, she takes on a depth many critics find lacking in the rest of the book. Indeed, much of the criticism leveled at *Main Street*, that the novel is as flat as the terrain it depicts, that it is too episodic, that it never really builds on itself, does not stand up in the first few chapters.

Carol is an orphan, and her only close relative is "a vanilla-flavored sister married to an optician in St. Paul." She appears distant to her classmates; even when "most ardently singing hymns or planning deviltry she seemed gently aloof and critical." While at school, there is only one person with whom she has a real relationship: Stewart Snyder, "a competent bulky young man." Stewart is no mere yokel. After Carol expresses her love of "common workmen" to him, he admonishes her: "Only you don't want to forget that common workmen don't think they're common." And for a moment, she may actually be falling in love—or if not in love, in something—with Stewart. "'You're right! I apologize.' Carol's brows lifted in the astonishment of emoting, in a glory of abasement."

It is significant that the first time Carol declares her love for common workingmen, Stewart "admonishes" her, yet she seems appreciative. It may not simply be his sensitivity she is responding to but the fact that he has actually listened to her, and reflected on what she had to say, before replying. *Main Street,* after all, is about what people have to say and how they say it. The novel is full of characters who cannot stop themselves from talking, certain they have the final word on every topic. Carol and her husband, Kennicott, however, dominate the novel, and the conversation between the two of them is the heart of the plot. Carol, aside from her maid, Bea, is the only character whose interior thoughts are exposed. The quotation marks that often enclose these thoughts remind the reader that even when silent Carol cannot stop clinging to words.

After graduation from Blodgett College, Carol spends a year in Chicago studying library cataloguing and attending concerts and museums. She dabbles in "Bohemian life" and thinks about giving up library work "to become one of the young women who dance in the cheesecloth in the moonlight." She even attends "a certified Studio Party, with beer, cigarettes, bobbed hair, and a Russian Jewess who sang the Internationale." Ultimately she feels out of place and a bit unnerved by this foreign environment, but as much as her attention wanders, she seems more than a mere dilettante. City planning, which had first captured her interest when she was studying sociology at Blodgett, remains a passion. She imagines herself transforming "a prairie town into Georgian homes and Japanese bungalows," but instead she moves to St. Paul, to a job in the library, where after a while "she slowly confessed that she was not visibly affecting lives. . . . When she was giving out books the principal query was, 'Can you tell me of a good, light exciting love story to read? My husband's going away for a week?'"

Three years pass in Minneapolis and although "several men showed diligent interest" in Carol, none of them make a real impact on her. Carol's life is her books at the library. Then, at a dinner party, she meets Dr. Will Kennicott. It is not love at first sight: "They were biology and mystery; their speech was slang phrases and flares of poetry . . . all the commonplaceness of a well-to-do unmarried man encountering a pretty girl at the time when she is slightly weary of her employment and sees no glory ahead nor any man she is glad to serve."

Carol tries to talk herself into falling for him but never—that evening, during their courtship, or throughout their marriage—entirely succeeds. Who can blame her. Kennicott is a bore: sweet and good-natured and sometimes fun, but a bore. "What aroused her to something more than liking," however, "was his boyishness when they went tramping." It is during one of these hikes that he persuades her to marry him. Seated in the woods, he shows her photographs of his hometown, sings its praises and pleads, "Come on. Come to Gopher Prairie. Show us. Make the town—well—make it artistic." Finally, after showing her a picture of a Swedish farm family, he implores her to look at the baby and confides how he needs her to help him. And she decides, "Oh, it would be sweet to help him—so sweet." And then, "As his arms moved toward her, she answered all her doubts with, 'Sweet, so sweet.'" This phrase, which echoes in the next chapter, is all that Carol can muster, but it is enough to "answer her doubt," at least for the moment. Later, however, Carol becomes consumed with doubt, and her husband's voice, the voices she hears on Main Street, and her own inner voice all grow more and more harping. She never can become entirely sweet-talked again.

After a Colorado mountain honeymoon, Carol braves the long train ride to Gopher Prairie. The grime and weariness of their fellow passengers, the bleakness of the towns they pass, and her new husband's response to her observations—"Why, what's the matter with 'em? Good hustling burgs"—disturb her. Doc Kennicott's diagnosis: "You're kind of played out, after this long trip." His prescription: "You'll feel better when you get home and have a good bath, and put on the blue negligée. That's some vampire costume, you witch." Later, staring out the train window:

Here—she meditated—is the newest empire of the world; the Northern Middlewest; a land of dairy herds and exquisite lakes, of new automobiles and tar-paper shanties and silos like red towers, of clumsy speech and a hope that is boundless . . . What is its future? she wondered. A future of cities and factory smut where now are loping empty fields. Homes universal and secure? Or placid châteaux ringed with sullen huts? Youths free to find knowledge and laughter? Willingness to sift the sanctified lies? Or creamy-skinned fat women, smeared with grease and chalk, gorgeous in the skins of beasts and the bloody feathers of slain birds, playing bridge with puffy pink-nailed jeweled fingers, women who after much expenditure of labor and bad temper still grotesquely resemble their own flatulent lap-dogs? . . .

Carol's head ached with the riddle.

Here in "the newest empire of the world," where hope is boundless, Carol cannot help herself from wondering what is going to happen to the landscape passing before her eyes. Frequently, there are moments, such as this, when one wonders how she is capable of seeing the world as she appears to. For instance, it seems disingenuous for Carol, a young woman fresh from college, to imagine "creamy-skinned fat women, smeared with grease and chalk, gorgeous in the skins of beasts and the bloody feathers of slain birds." Such a sophisticated vision is unmistakably Lewis'. If the reader is aware that Carol, at times like this, cannot possibly be quite so perceptive, as unsparing or smart, as he is depicting her to be, then so be it. Carol wants so much for herself, for her husband, and eventually for Gopher Prairie that readers come to share her aspirations and identify with her. Carol may be fickle and naive, but she cares about the right things, and she wants to change the world. Lewis is convinced, though, that nothing will ever change: Carol's longing to do something meaningful with her life is a hopeless fantasy, and in passages such as this, Lewis is seething at the injustice of it all.

While Carol is the protagonist, one senses that if *Main Street* were simply her story, Lewis

would not find her worthy of our attention and would soon tire of her. *Main Street*, however, is not the simple story of a young idealistic woman looking for love in all the wrong places, but the story of those places and the people who live there: who they are and who they might have become. In the unleashed language of this passage, one catches a glimpse of Lewis the idealist, the patriot, the writer reveling in the nobility of his country, but the moment cannot last. The engineer is slowing down, and nobility is about to receive a pie in the face. The train stops, the Kennicotts step off, and the world crashes down upon Carol as she takes in Gopher Prairie for the first time: "It was unprotected and unprotecting; there was no dignity in it nor any hope of greatness." And "the people—they'd be as drab as their houses, as flat as their fields. She couldn't stay here. She would have to wrench loose from this man, and flee." The honeymoon is definitely over.

Several hours later, trying her best to calm herself after unpacking, she walks up and down Main Street, but "with its two-story brick shops, its story-and-a-half wooden residences, its muddy expanse from concrete walk to walk, its huddle of Fords and lumber-wagons, [it] was too small to absorb her. The broad, straight, unenticing gashes of the streets let in the grasping prairie on every side. She realized the vastness and emptiness of the land." And although Gopher Prairie may have three thousand people, all but a few prove dull. Carol realizes this her first night in town, at a party welcoming her. The conversation among the women, where she is herded, is boring, and when she leaves to talk to the men, and brings up more controversial political topics, she soon realizes she has overstepped the bounds. On the way home, Kennicott delivers his first lecture, telling her she will have to be "more careful about shocking folks."

Over the years, Carol, always the reformer, tries to attack the social order by changing the tenor of the town, but she is unable to make a dent. She organizes a dramatic club but cannot persuade her fellow thespians to try out George Bernard Shaw. Instead, they produce one middling performance of the cliché-ridden *The Girl from Kankakee*. She is invited to join the Jolly Seventeen, a bridge club comprising the best of the "married set," but is bored by, among other things, the conversation. At Gopher Prairie's literary society, the Thanatopsis Club, Carol likewise finds the programs hackneyed, maudlin, and pretentious. She is, however, ever hopeful, especially when she is asked to join the library board and discovers that the other members of the board are as well read as she. As always, she is ultimately disappointed; she finds that her fellow board members are stingy about funding the library and disinterested in purchasing new books or encouraging new readers.

Of the eighty characters Lewis introduces in *Main Street*, only eight seem appealing, and, ultimately, all either disappoint Carol or disappear. She is especially close with Bea Sorenson, her maid, and the man Bea eventually marries, Miles Bjornstam, an anarchist-socialist Swedish handyman. Bea, Miles, and their son, Olaf, become as close to a real family as Carol gets. Both Bea and Olaf die of typhoid fever, however (the family has been drinking water from a well that turns out to have been contaminated), and Miles, who is blamed for their death, leaves for Canada. For a while, Vida Sherwin, the local high school teacher, is Carol's best friend, but after Vida marries Raymie Wutherspoon she becomes more "domestic and conservative" and judgmental toward Carol. In turn, Carol finds that Vida has become dull. Guy Pollock, an unmarried lawyer, at first seems appealing. An aesthete and philosopher, he has views similar to Carol's, but, ultimately, he proves passive, a victim of what he calls "Village Virus."

The last chance for Carol to find a true friend in Gopher Prairie rests with Fern Mullins, a young high school teacher who boards at the home of the Widow Bogart, the Kennicotts' neighbor. But Fern becomes involved in an incident with Cy Bogart, one of her students, after they ride together to a barn dance in the country: Fern fends off Cy's drunken advances at the dance and then only barely manages to repulse his attempt at rape as she drives him home in his wagon. After she deposits him, "retching and wabbling," on the Bogart porch, Cy's mother jumps to the conclusion that Fern tried to seduce her son.

Earlier Mrs. Bogart had been referred to as

> not the acid type of Good Influence. She was the soft, damp, fat, sighing, indigestive, clinging, melancholy, depressingly hopeful kind. There are in every large chicken-yard a number of old and indignant hens who resemble Mrs. Bogart, and when they are served at Sunday noon dinner, as fricasseed chicken with thick dumplings, they keep up the resemblance.

Now she is not seen as merely benign: Mrs. Bogart brings Fern into disgrace with her charges about what has happened; within a day she has so destroyed the schoolteacher's reputation that Fern is left with no choice but to resign her job and flee the town.

Malicious gossip is a staple of the world of *Main Street*. Carol is the only one in Gopher Prairie to come to Fern's defense, and the only one to comfort her, but even as she does, she worries, "When will they have me on the scaffold?" She recognizes that her marriage to a respected citizen of the town is all that keeps the scandalmongers at bay: "Wasn't it because they had been prevented by her caste from bounding on her own trail that they were howling at Fern?" she reflects. Unlike Fern, whose life has been ruined by false rumors, Carol has a very real secret to protect from Main Street's gossips: she has been falling in love with Erik Valborg, a tailor's assistant, five years younger than she, who has recently moved to Gopher Prairie. Their relationship seems more than a mere crush for both of them. They hold hands and confide their dreams of life to each other. As a writer who can occasionally be frank when talking of sex, Lewis seems calculated in his decision not to have Carol and Erik cross a line. He was ambitious for his book and may have felt that allowing his character, a married woman with a baby, to have an affair would be a bit too much for his audience to accept. Also, the hesitation to follow through completely on the romance seems true to Carol's character. While at times she appears bold and unconventional, often she also seems indecisive and fickle. Erik Valborg may just be the kind of man who inspires fickleness, but despite his yearnings and swooning, he is likable. Once, after she implores him to cool his ardor, saying, "Don't spoil everything. Be my friend," he replies, "How many thousands and millions of women must have said that! And now you! And it doesn't spoil everything. It glorifies everything!" Erik, like Stewart Snyder, listens to Carol and uses her own words to present his case, and Carol loves listening to a suitor who has actually heard her.

While Erik and Carol are out walking by moonlight one night, Kennicott, who is innocently driving home, comes upon them. Lewis takes this scene, which could so easily have been a hackneyed and melodramatic cliché—the cuckolded husband discovering his wife with the other man—and presents it to the reader with insight and humor, sympathy for all parties, and, ultimately, great psychological understanding. Here, Lewis emerges as the master of plot development. In four pages, he effortlessly pulls the reader along: characters seem just on the verge of making love; they are caught, not quite in the act; the deceived husband takes the romantic bull by the horns, dispenses with him, elegantly, unexpectedly, and wittily, without having to resort to a macho display; he then confronts his wife with wisdom and empathy, and even something of a feminist sensibility, and none of this seems to come from out of the blue. Carol, Erik, and Kennicott all seem exquisitely in character. And all ultimately reveal themselves through what they have to say to one another and what they think one another will or will not say.

Kennicott arrives on the scene: "From behind the dimness of the windshield a voice, annoyed, sharp: 'Hello there!'" but then, "The irritation in his voice smoothed out. 'Having a walk?' They made schoolboyish sounds of assent." Kennicott does not resort to violence, or threats, or riding back to Main Street in stony silence but confidently uses his facility for banal small talk to take over the situation and break up the tryst:

> "Pretty wet, isn't it? Better ride back. Jump in front here, Valborg."
>
> His manner of swinging open the door was a command. Carol was conscious that Erik was climbing in, that she was apparently to sit in the back, and that she had been left to open the rear door for herself. Instantly the wonder which had flamed to the gusty skies was quenched, and she was Mrs. W. P. Kennicott of Gopher Prairie, riding in a squeaking old car. . . .

What could be more American after commenting on the weather, then suggesting a ride back to town, in a car? His wife, however, still does not have the measure of her man: "She feared what Kennicott would say to Erik. She bent toward them. Kennicott was observing, 'Going to have some rain before the night's over, all right.'"

Lewis plays this scene almost as if it were shtick: Kennicott the straight man, rambling on and on, the first mention of weather surprising, the second funny, now the third, devastating:

> Been funny season this year, anyway. Never saw it with such a cold October and such a nice November. 'Member we had a snow way back on October ninth! But it certainly was nice up to the twenty-first, this month—as I remember it, not a flake of snow in November so far, has there been? But I shouldn't wonder if we'd be having some snow 'most any time now.

As Kennicott continues chatting, moving on to the subject of hunting—"Wish I'd had more time to go after the ducks this fall"—one wonders if, perhaps, he is trying to oh-so-carefully scare Erik—he is after all rather fond of guns—but that worry recedes as he continues on to lament his car: "Gosh, this machine hasn't got the power of a fountain pen. Guess the cylinders are jam-cram-full of carbon again. Don't know but what maybe I'll have to put in another set of piston-rings." The weather, hunting, and cars: how stupid he seems to his wife, and to readers, so blind to what is going on right in front of his face.

> But Kennicott was blustrously cheerful. . . . She sat back, neglected, frozen, unheroic heroine in a drama insanely undramatic. She made a decision resolute and enduring. She would tell Kennicott— What would she tell him? She could not say that she loved Erik. *Did* she love him? But she would have it out. She was not sure whether it was pity for Kennicott's blindness, or irritation at his assumption that he was enough to fill any woman's life, which prompted her, but she knew that she was out of the trap, that she could be frank; and she was exhilarated with the adventure of it. . . .

Kennicott, however, is not blind. Not only does he know what has been going on, he has known it for some time. He seems to realize, however, what Lewis pointed out to Harriet Ford, a Broadway producer: "The real triangle . . . is not Kennicott, Carol & Erik, but Kennicott, Carol and Main Street" (quoted in Richard Lingeman, *Sinclair Lewis: Rebel from Main Street*, 2002). At home, after Erik has been dropped off in town, Carol awaits Kennicott, who is parking the car, sure he will be "opaque as ever. Her task wouldn't be anything so lively as having to endure a scolding." Once again, however, she has underestimated her husband. Before joining her in the living room, he stokes the furnace, winds the clock in the hall, and she thinks she knows him so well that when he begins "You better," she predicts he will continue with "take your coat off, Carrie; looks kind of wet." Instead, he dispenses with weather, hunting, and cars and talks to her in a forthright, no-nonsense manner: "I know all about it. What d' you expect in a town that's as filled with busybodies, that have plenty of time to stick their noses into other folks' business, as this is?" When Kennicott briefly outlines his (very accurate) understanding of Carol's love affair,

and his fears for her reputation in town—even while he takes Carol's wet coat and "twiddled his watch-chain, felt the radiator, peered at the thermometer"—his apparent perceptiveness and steadiness may strike the reader as a welcome antidote to Carol's vagueness and inconsistency. And despite everything, he still is capable of declaring his love for her:

> He leaned forward, thick capable hands on thick sturdy thighs, mature and slow, yet beseeching. "No matter if you are cold, I like you better than anybody in the world. One time I said that you were my soul. And that still goes. You're all the things that I see in a sunset when I'm driving in from the country, the things that I like but can't make poetry of. . . . All I need is to have you here at home to welcome me. I don't expect you to be passionate—not any more I don't—but I do expect you to appreciate my work. I bring babies into the world, and save lives, and make cranky husbands quit being mean to their wives. And then you go and moon over a Swede tailor. . . ."

When Carol protests that Erik is not just a tailor but a sensitive and talented artist, Kennicott asks what he has done to actually prove himself, arguing that Erik seems special only by comparison with the dull shopkeepers of Gopher Prairie. He then goes on to describe the kind of life Carol might have with Erik if, as seems likely, the young man never achieves more than "running a one-man tailor shop in some burg about the size of Schoenstrom." The scene he paints of too much work, too many children, and too little space in a squalid home behind a tailor shop seems all too realistic: Kennicott has vividly made his case. "He bent to kiss her neck. 'I don't want to be unfair. I guess love is a great thing, all right. But think it would stand much of that kind of stuff? Oh, honey, am I so bad? Can't you like me at all? I've—I've been so fond of you!'"

It is all too much for Carol.

> She snatched up his hand, she kissed it. . . . "I won't ever see him again. I can't, now. . . . Even if I were sure of him, sure he was the real thing, I

don't think I could actually leave you. This marriage, it weaves people together. It's not easy to break, even when it ought to be broken."

"And do you want to break it?"

"No!"

He lifted her, carried her up-stairs, laid her on her bed, turned to the door.

"Come kiss me," she whimpered.

Kennicott kisses her "lightly"—and leaves the room. In scenes like this, scattered throughout the book, Kennicott emerges as a fully realized character, surprising us by how keen an observer he is of human nature while always remaining the great American optimist. Unlike Carol, who is constantly getting taken in and views life as one disappointment after another, Kennicott never gets mired down. He sees through Carol, yet he is still smitten with her, even after catching her with another man. Although he has few illusions about her, or about Main Street, he is happy with them both, happy with what he has got. "You're all the things that I see in a sunset when I'm driving in from the country, the things that I like but can't make poetry of." Kennicott is the only character who knows who he is and who he is not. He may not be able to "make poetry," but he realizes this about himself, and he loves his wife because she can.

In an attempt to reach out to Carol, Kennicott takes her on a grand tour of the West. Carol returns home, however, as unhappy as ever. Still restless, she leaves for Washington, D.C., with her son, Hugh. Although World War I is nearing its end, she finds a job in the Bureau of War Risk Insurance. For a year, she revels in her independent life and her first job since being a librarian. Gradually, though, she comes to realize that even Washington contains "a thick streak of Main Street." She runs into her old neighbors the Haydocks and is surprised at how much she enjoys her time with them. Later, as she is about to walk out of an "abysmal" movie, she is "startled, incredulous, then wretched," for

there on the screen is Erik Valborg in a "pale part," as a composer, "which he played neither well nor badly." After Carol, who so loves words, is confronted with her old lover as a mediocre bit actor in a silent movie, she goes home and reads Kennicott's letters. "They had seemed stiff and undetailed, but now there strode from them a personality, a personality unlike that of the languishing young man in the velvet jacket playing a dummy piano in a canvas room."

Kennicott arrives after thirteen months to visit his wife and son. He plays his cards perfectly, never demanding or even asking her to come back home, instead letting her know he wants her to, when she is ready, and that they will build a new home, and she can plan it. For two weeks, they have what he calls "a second wooing" in Charleston, and again, he expresses his love. The second wooing proves successful. Five months later, when Carol returns to Gopher Prairie, she is pregnant, and once home, she realizes that some of her old friends seem to have missed her, something that would not have happened in more transient Washington. In August, she gives birth to a girl.

The book concludes in the fall. Carol and Kennicott are duck hunting with their friends the Clarks, and Carol, for the first time, volunteers to sit in the back seat of the car, like a proper Main Street wife. When Ethel Clark extends an invitation for the two couples to go to the movies the next evening, Carol agrees, even though it means giving up her plan to start a new book the next day. Later that evening, in a conversation with her husband about the planning of a Community Day celebration, Carol gives in again. Then, in a prophetic tone, she envisions a world for her baby daughter in 2000 and reflects upon her own life, proud that she has not surrendered to mediocrity.

She led him to the nursery door, pointed at the fuzzy brown head of her daughter. "Do you see that object on the pillow? Do you know what it is? It's a bomb to blow up smugness. If you Tories were wise, you wouldn't arrest anarchists; you'd arrest all these children while they're asleep in their cribs. Think what that baby will see and meddle with before she dies in the year 2000! . . . I've never excused my failures by sneering at my aspirations, by pretending to have gone beyond them. I do not admit that Main Street is as beautiful as it should be! I do not admit that Gopher Prairie is greater or more generous than Europe! I do not admit that dish-washing is enough to satisfy all women! I may not have fought the good fight, but I have kept the faith."

The novel closes, however, not with Carol's but Kennicott's words: "'Sure. You bet you have,' said Kennicott. 'Well, good night. Sort of feels to me like it might snow tomorrow. Have to be thinking about putting up the storm-windows pretty soon. Say, did you notice whether the girl put the screwdriver back?'"

A NOVEL OF "SHEER DATA"

Critics have complained that the episodic narrative of *Main Street* suffers from a wearying lack of plot development. Lewis' characters, especially Carol, have also been criticized for lacking development, flitting from one cause or person to another and never really evolving. Lewis seems aware of this: "She turned to the Chautauqua as she had turned to the dramatic association, to the library-board." And while Carol suffers as the novel does, by turning from one thing to another to another, she cannot seem to help herself, and neither, so it seems, can Lewis. He is, after all, an enormously ambitious writer, taking on not simply small towns, the relationships between husbands and wives, politics, injustice, and hypocrisy, but also the meaning of life. He has assigned himself a Herculean task, and he has a lot of convincing to do.

F. Scott Fitzgerald, who was already a best-selling author in 1920, wrote to Lewis, "I want to tell you that *Main Street* has displaced *Theron Ware* in my favor as the best American novel. The amount of sheer data in it is amazing!

As a writer and a Minnesotan let me swell the chorus—after a third reading" (quoted in Mark Schorer, *Sinclair Lewis: An American Life*, 1961). Fitzgerald's observation acknowledges how much information is packed into *Main Street*, and what a feat it is, but the allusion to "sheer data" points up the negative side of list-making. Although Sinclair Lewis certainly did not see himself, or want to be seen, as a data collector, his novel comprises hundreds of lists. For instance, in the fourth chapter, on the day when Carol first arrives in town, "beholding not only the heart of a place called Gopher Prairie, but ten thousand towns from Albany to San Diego," she proceeds, store by store, down Main Street. Each building is listed in its own paragraph, even if it contains only a sentence. Twenty-six paragraphs each detail a store, office, or building, ranging from "Dyer's Drug Store, a corner building of regular and unreal blocks of artificial stone" to "The State Bank, stucco masking wood."

Reading this list, and others like it throughout the book, considering item upon item upon item, distances the reader from the conventional paragraph, the character, the narration; one becomes caught up in the mechanics of the list itself. Many lists, like this one detailing the buildings on Main Street, take on a rhythm of their own; by breaking down a street, a parlor, or a conversation into discrete units, the list suggests the commonality of each element among the lot; that one is really no better and no worse than the next. A and B and C and D may look different to the eye, but what they have in common is that they are all ugly, or dull, or second-rate, as in Main Street's landscape of "grease and artificial blocks of stone . . . a feed store, its windows opaque with the dust of bran . . . a raw red-brick Catholic church with a varnished yellow door." By seizing what is taken for granted, leaving nothing out, and reducing it all to a list, Lewis forces us to confront what we see, and never allows us to avert our eyes. Each shop and storefront may speak to a different human need or whim, but twenty-six of them, when stitched together, appear relentless and stultifying, in a way they would not by themselves.

Even when Carol contemplates the possibilities offered by the traveling Chautauqua that comes to Gopher Prairie, the banalities of Main Street surface:

These were the several instructors in the condensed university's seven-day course:

Nine lecturers, four of them ex-ministers, and one an ex-congressman, all of them delivering "inspirational addresses" . . .

Four "entertainers" who told Jewish stories, Irish stories, German stories, Chinese stories, and Tennessee mountaineer stories, most of which Carol had heard.

A "lady elocutionist" who recited Kipling and imitated children.

A lecturer with motion-pictures of an Andean exploration; excellent pictures and a halting narrative.

Three brass-bands, a company of six opera-singers, a Hawaiian sextet, and four youths who played saxophones and guitars disguised as washboards.

Contrasting this list with the one detailing what authors Carol has read makes her stand out as even more isolated from her neighbors: "The authors whom she read were . . . young American sociologists, young English realists, Russian horrorists; Anatole France, Rolland, Nexo, Wells, Shaw, Key, Edgar Lee Masters, Theodore Dreiser, Sherwood Anderson . . . Henry Mencken."

Sometimes a list will sum up a character in a single sentence: "Kennicott had five hobbies: medicine, land-investment, Carol, motoring, and hunting. It is not certain in what order he preferred them." The list that defines Carol stands in stark contrast to her husband's pragmatic interests:

Idling on the porch of their summer cottage at the lake, on afternoons when Kennicott was in town, when the water was glazed and the whole air

languid, she pictured a hundred escapes: Fifth Avenue in a snow-storm, with limousines, golden shops, a cathedral spire. A reed hut on fantastic piles above the mud of a jungle river. A suite in Paris, immense high grave rooms, with lambrequins and a balcony. The Enchanted Mesa. An ancient stone mill in Maryland, at the turn of the road, between rocky brook and abrupt hills. An upland moor of sheep and flitting cool sunlight. A clanging dock where steel cranes unloaded steamers from Buenos Aires and Tsing-tao. A Munich concert-hall, and a famous 'cellist playing—playing to her.

Another list, cast as a single sentence, describes the pleasure that Bea, Carol's former maid, takes when she marries Miles, "When she was busy with the activities her work-hungry muscles found—washing, ironing, mending, baking, dusting, preserving, plucking a chicken, painting the sink; tasks which, because she was Miles' full partner, were exciting and creative— Bea listened to the photograph records with rapture like that of cattle in a warm stable." Bea's pleasure in her work stands in contrast to the way Carol feels about how she spends her day:

In Carol's own twenty-four hours a day she got up, dressed the baby, had breakfast, talked to Oscarina about the day's shopping, put the baby on the porch to play, went to the butcher's to choose between steak and pork chops, bathed the baby, nailed up a shelf, had dinner, put the baby to bed for a nap, paid the iceman, read for an hour, took the baby for a walk, called on Vida, had supper, put the baby to bed, darned socks, listened to Kennicott's yawning comment on what a fool Dr. McGanum was to try to use that cheap X-ray outfit of his on an epithelioma, repaired a frock, drowsily heard Kennicott stoke the furnace, tried to read a page of Thorstein Veblen—and the day was gone.

At the end of the novel, the list takes on a new function: no longer simply an endless indictment, nor damning evidence, now it can lead to an epiphany. Carol reflects upon a list of towns and cities she has heard about from those, like her, who have fled them for Washington—from "New England mill-towns with the hands living in rows of cottages like blocks of lava" to a "Western mining-settlement like a tumor"—and she comes to appreciate that Gopher Prairie may not be the worst of towns after all. After Carol's revelation about the relative merits of Gopher Prairie, Lewis breathtakingly moves beyond lists: "The chart which plots Carol's progress," he tells us, "is not easy to read. The lines are broken and uncertain of direction; often instead of rising they sink in wavering scrawls; and the colors are watery blue and pink and the dim gray of rubbed pencil marks. A few lines are traceable." The narrative seems momentarily to rise above the sureness of lists, suggesting that neither Lewis nor Carol has it all down, all checked off. But then, just before the reader can check lists off his list, three more lists immediately follow:

> Unhappy women are given to protecting their sensitiveness by cynical gossip, by whining, by high-church and new-thought religions, or by a fog of vagueness. Carol had hidden in none of these refuges from reality, but she, who was tender and merry, had been made timorous by Gopher Prairie. Even her flight had been but the temporary courage of panic. The thing she gained in Washington was not information about office-systems and labor unions but renewed courage, that amiable contempt called poise. Her glimpse of tasks involving millions of people and a score of nations reduced Main Street from bloated importance to its actual pettiness. She could never again be quite so awed by the power with which she herself had endowed the Vidas and Blaussers and Bogarts. . . .

> And why, she began to ask, did she rage at individuals? Not individuals but institutions are the enemies, and they most afflict the disciples who the most generously serve them. They insinuate their tyranny under a hundred guises and pompous names, such as Polite Society, the Family, the Church, Sound Business, the Party, the Country, the Superior White Race; and the only defense against them, Carol beheld is unembittered laughter.

Lewis uses lists to make a point, and make it again and again and again, not unlike a judge who slams down a gavel calling for order or an auctioneer who signals the irrevocable final bid. With this list, however, Carol finally realizes the futility of raging at individuals and discovers that the real struggle must be fought against institutions. Lewis spares us their "hundred guises" but cannot resist listing a few, including "Polite Society" and "Sound Business." By capitalizing them, a technique he frequently uses, he is letting readers know, just in case it slipped by before, that these organizations are not really proper nouns, no matter how seriously they and their disciples take themselves. Sound Business, the Superior White Race, the Church: they are all the same, one no better then the next. They are all tyrannies, all out to get us, one by one by one.

"Unembittered laughter" is, of course, a far different kind of response to such daily tyranny than a simple ho-ha. Lewis acknowledges that in order to survive Main Street, one must, in a sense, transcend it; not take it so personally; must not let it bring one down to its own level. And laughter may be the only defense against the superficial realities—those lists of fantasies or chores, or buildings on Main Street, or courses at the Chautauqua—that divert our attention from the loftier possibilities of life, from the superficial realities that can never truly be escape from. All those complacent residents of Gopher Prairie, the ones who smirk and, sometimes, chuckle, will just never get it.

A GREAT NATURAL FORCE

When *Main Street* appeared in 1920 it was a sensation, the most popular book in seventy-five years; two years later the critic Robert Littell commented that "if *Main Street* lives, it will probably be not as a novel but as an incident in American life" (quoted in Lingeman, *Sinclair Lewis*). The gray and blue dust jacket, featuring a silhouette of Carol Kennicott peering across

Main Street, became etched in the American imagination. The journalist William Allen White and the poet Vachel Lindsay organized campaigns to promote it. The publisher, Harcourt, Brace, was forced to ration copies to booksellers. Praise poured in from readers otherwise not accustomed to issuing endorsements: "*Dear Sir* I want to thank you very much for using my name in your wonderful story *Main Street*—every one here who has read the book say it is wonderful. Just now there is none on sale at news stand so I am loaning mine to friends. Again thank you I am very truly yours. *Annie Oakley*" (quoted in Schorer, *Sinclair Lewis*). (Twenty years after Oakley's letter, Irving Berlin composed a song for her, whose title, "They Say It's Wonderful," echoes her praise but with more conventional, if less poetic, grammar.) The critic Malcom Cowley, in Brentano's *Book Chat,* summarized the phenomenon of *Main Street*'s appeal to Americans everywhere (as quoted in Lingeman's *Sinclair Lewis*):

> Our normal book-buying public consists, perhaps, of two or three hundred thousand people. When a novel passes the latter figure, it is being purchased by families in the remoter villages, families which acquire no more than ten books in a generation. In the year 1921, if you visited the parlor of almost any boarding house, you would see a copy of *Main Street:* standing between the Bible and *Ben Hur.*

In 1920, of course, publishers and authors were less sophisticated than their later counterparts about the demographics of their readership, but Lewis had been a short story writer, grinding them out for the *Saturday Evening Post,* and he knew his female audience. In many respects, Carol Kennicott is a feminist, and although there were many other women protagonists in novels, many of them seem, in comparison with *Main Street,* more literary. Carol Kennicott received no inheritance, possessed no operatic gifts, did not fall in love with a lord. She settles for a doctor and remains stuck, for the most part, at home. The story is one that most readers, especially women, could relate to.

H. L. Mencken celebrated *Main Street* as "not only genuinely human but also authentically American." Mark Schorer, in his biography of Lewis, agrees:

> The book seemed, above all, to be American, and that, at a time when most American fiction was imitative of the already faint provincial fiction of Great Britain, was another element in its success. Many of its readers had never been exposed to a novel that was so uncompromisingly American both in its seeming truth to the native scene and in the language that communicated it. In spite of novelists like London, Norris, Dreiser, Cather and Anderson, American fiction until the war still labored under the shadow of England and publishers in New York still treated Georgians like Galsworthy, Bennett and Walpole . . . as superior to even our most impressive American talent in fiction.

Another factor accounting for the popularity of *Main Street* was its emphasis on dialogue. Its characters were not only recognizable, but they also sounded uncannily true to life. Heywood Broun, reviewing *Main Street* in the *New York Tribune,* noted, "He hears even better than he sees. I can't think of anybody who has been so unerringly right in reproducing talk. He is right to a degree that is deeper than phonographic exactness" (quoted in Schorer, *Sinclair Lewis*). (For his later novels, Lewis was so intent on making sure his characters accurately reflected the way people talked that in the 1930s he rented hotel rooms in the Midwest and installed dictaphones in them, then invited local citizens in to talk as they naturally would.)

Main Street's author was himself an entertaining, if compulsive, talker: the novelist Rebecca West recalled of her first meeting with Lewis that "his talk was wonderful, but after five solid hours of it I ceased to look upon him as a human being. I could think of him only as a great natural force, like the aurora borealis" (quoted in Schorer, *Sinclair Lewis*). The journalist William McNally observed, "He cannot travel other than 'on high' and has no brakes."

Eventually misanthropy and a compulsion to have the last word seemed to consume Lewis. Even during an attack of the DTs, while his wife, Dorothy Thompson, was guiding him, strait-jacketed, into an ambulance, Lewis could not resist mimicking her: "You've ruined your life, you're ruining mine! You've ruined your sons, you miserable creature. You're sick, you're sick." As John Updike suggests in a 2002 review for *The New Yorker,* "His personal qualities carry over into the fiction: it tends to be, aside from some of its well-felt domestic moments, loud and blatant, more performance than shared experience. Everything illustrates the point."

Other critics agree: *Main Street* is more about characters talking at one another than with one another; more a story told to readers than one that engages readers; and ultimately, readers grow disengaged. Perhaps Lewis was less interested in creating a work of art and more interested—consumed, perhaps—in showing America what it was, and in 1920 it was all those things critics accuse Lewis of being: loud, blatant, smug, relentless. Lewis, in the tradition of James Fenimore Cooper, Ralph Waldo Emerson, Henry David Thoreau, Walt Whitman, and Mark Twain, wanted to smash the polite tea-table literary sensibility of the day. In a mock obituary, he lamented that he had failed and had "affected but little the work of younger writers of fiction." Schorer argues that despite Lewis' falling out of fashion, "he was an extraordinary influence, the major figure, probably, in what is called the liberation of modern American literature."

Lewis grew up in Middle America, but after escaping Main Street he lived his life moving from one place to another, never really settling down, never really finding another home to set roots in or take comfort from. In a sense he traveled Main Streets all his life and remained stuck in them, unable to discover a richer vision. Despite this, he left an important legacy: as the writer Joseph Wood Krutch has noted, Lewis "recorded a reign of grotesque vulgarity which but for him would have left no record of itself because no one else could have adequately reported it" (quoted in Schorer, *Sinclair Lewis*).

The mocking echo of gifted mimicry can stop us in our tracks: the mimic throws our words back at us, and sometimes hearing how we sound—how silly, how vain, how pretentious, how foolish—can be a transformative experience. A little goes a long way, however, and *Main Street*'s mimicry arguably lapses into the tiresome. Furthermore, despite Lewis' gifts, he seems so much a part of a particular era that critics such as Frederick Crews have asked dismissively, "Why bother oneself further with a man who was so contemptibly understandable as a product of a callow and bumptious age?" (quoted in Lingeman, *Sinclair Lewis*).

Richard Lingeman, whose Lewis biography published in 2002 sought to answer this question, points out that Mark Schorer's biography of Lewis, which for forty years seemed the critical last word on the writer, "was a product of its time, the time of the silent 1950's, the era of the anticommunist culture war in academe, the heyday of the New Critics, who placed text above social context." He also notes that "in more recent years, scholars have succeeded in viewing Lewis' books afresh through different critical lenses, with the result that his books have come back into repute." In fact this claim seems unsupported—*Main Street*'s sales rank is not as high as other classics, and it seldom turns up on reading lists. Occasionally, however, the success of a satirical novel like Jonathan Franzen's *The Corrections* (2001) bears witness to Lewis' legacy.

THE LAST LAUGH

Lewis, like most great comics, had impeccable timing. Although Dean Acheson and other friends warned him that "the American public . . . would not pay to be made fun of," they were wrong. Not only was the American public ready, but it seemed to welcome being mocked by Lewis and willing to share in the laughter at itself. The fun Lewis was intent on, however, was of a subversive nature. He grabbed America by its ear and would not let go. Nothing or no one escaped his attention. With Carol Kennicott as his straight man, he even took on the American comic tradition:

> As she went dragging through the prickly-hot street she reflected that a citizen of Gopher Prairie does not have jests—he has a jest. Every cold morning for five winters Lyman Cass had remarked, "Fair to middlin' chilly—get worse before it gets better." Fifty times had Ezra Stowbody informed the public that Carol had once asked, "Shall I endorse this check on the back?" Fifty times had Sam Clark called to her, "Where'd you steal that hat?" Fifty times had the mention of Barney Cahoon, the town drayman, like a nickel in a slot produced from Kennicott the apocryphal story of Barney's directing a minister, "Come down to the depot and get your case of religious books—they're leaking!"

For Carol Kennicott, who may have learned the solace of "unembittered laughter," there is no one to share that laughter with. She can never let down her defenses, forget herself, relax. She will remain isolated, as did Sinclair Lewis, the author of among other stories, "I'm a Stranger Here Myself" (1916). Lewis and Carol may be able to laugh, but they can take no real pleasure in their world and seem condemned to endure it alone. Alfred Kazin once observed that there is a "more significant terror of a kind in Lewis' novels than in a writer like Faulkner or the hard-boiled novelists, for it is the terror immanent in the commonplace, the terror that arises out of the repression, the meannesses, the hard jokes of the world Lewis had soaked into his pores" (quoted in Schorer, *Sinclair Lewis*).

At the conclusion of *Main Street*, Carol still considers herself a maverick, but to the reader it is clear that she has been broken. For the first time she is content to ride in the back seat of her husband's car; she accepts an invitation to the movies from Ethel Clark, putting aside the new book she had been planning to read. Later, at home, she predicts what life will be like for her daughter in the year 2000, and her husband yawns and replies, "I didn't quite catch what you said, dear." No matter: "She patted his pillows, turned down his sheets." As Kennicott drones on about the weather and the storm windows, Carol has finally made a kind of peace, with herself, with her husband, and with Main Street. But at what price?

And since Carol has brought up the year 2000, it seems only fair to wonder what she and Sinclair Lewis would have made of it if, somehow, they could have been alive in 2000, and taken a right turn off the original Main Street in Sauk Center, Minnesota, then hopped onto Route 494 and made their way to Bloomington, Minnesota, home of the Mall of America. With 17,500 places, they would surely find a spot to park. On their way to the 520 stores, they might forgo the roller coasters but probably be intrigued by the "Chapel of Love," which more than 2,500 couples have chosen for their marriage ceremonies. Then it would be on to "Main Street" at the mall, where Nat Hick's Taylor Shop is Abercrombie and Fitch; Dyers's Drugs, a Bath and Body Works; the Rosebud Movie Palace, a 14-Screen General Cinema; the Bon Ton Store, a Gap; Sam Clark's Hardware Store, a Sharper Image; and Billy's Lunch, Starbucks. One can picture Lewis and Carol staggering out, holding each other up. One can imagine Lewis back in the parking lot, taking notes. No question, he would be amused by the bumper stickers: "Stand up for America," "My Child Is an Honor Student at Eastmoor High," "One Day at a Time."

He would not, however, be surprised. Mall of America would inspire him, just as Main Street had, and it would be no safer from his mockery than Main Street was. He would delight in mimicking what he heard, from a waiter urging his customer to "Enjoy your meal," to a clerk at Banana Republic imploring a patron to "Have a nice day!" He would take it all in: the packs of suburban mall-rats, the husbands and wives shuffling off to the food courts, the clerk at Barnes and Noble suggesting a book to a harried mother.

Lewis taught us to take a hard look at what was becoming ordinary and familiar, the Main Streets devouring America, and to see them for what they were and for what they were not. He knew there was no way out, and laughter, unembittered laughter, was to be our only consolation, even if the echo of that laughter was to ring a little hollow. Unfortunately, for Lewis and for Carol Kennicott, this was to be their only consolation. There would be no other escape.

Select Bibliography

EDITIONS

Main Street. New York: Harcourt, Brace, 1920.

Main Street. Mineola, N.Y.: Dover, 1999. (The novel is widely available in paperback through Dover Publications. The 1999 Dover paperback is cited in this essay.)

SECONDARY WORKS

Acheson, Dean. *Morning and Noon.* Boston: Houghton Mifflin, 1965.

Bloom, Harold, ed. *Sinclair Lewis: Modern Critical Interpretations.* New York: Chelsea House, 1987.

Bucco, Martin. *Main Street: The Revolt of Carol Kennicott.* New York: Twayne, 1993.

Canby, Henry Seidel. *American Memoir.* Boston: Houghton Mifflin, 1947.

Dooley, D. J. *The Art of Sinclair Lewis.* Lincoln: University of Nebraska Press, 1967.

Grebstein, Sheldon. *Sinclair Lewis.* New York: Twayne, 1962.

Hilfer, Anthony. *The Revolt from the Village.* Chapel Hill: University of North Carolina Press, 1969.

Kazin, Alfred. *On Native Grounds: An Interpretation of Modern American Prose Literature.* New York: Harcourt, Brace, 1942.

Lewis, Grace Hegger. *With Love from Gracie: Sinclair Lewis, 1912–1915.* New York: Harcourt, Brace, 1955.

Lewis, Sinclair. *From Main Street to Stockholm: Letters of Sinclair Lewis, 1919–1930.* Edited by Harrison Smith. New York: Harcourt, Brace, 1952.

Light, Martin. *The Quixotic Vision of Sinclair Lewis.* West Lafayette, Ind.: Purdue University Press, 1975.

Lingeman, Richard. *Sinclair Lewis: Rebel from Main Street.* New York: Random House, 2002. (While franker than Mark Schorer's 1961 biography, this work is not as developed, nor does it offer as much from the earlier years of Lewis' life.)

McNally, William J. "Americans We Like: Mr. Babbitt, Meet Sinclair Lewis." *The Nation,* September 21, 1927, pp. 278–281.

Mencken, H. L. "The Story of an American Family." In *H. L. Mencken's Smart Set Criticism.* Edited by William H. Nolte. Ithaca, N.Y.: Cornell University Press, 1968. Pp. 279–281.

Schorer, Mark. *Sinclair Lewis: An American Life.* New York: McGraw Hill, 1961.

————. *Sinclair Lewis: A Collection of Critical Essays.* Englewood Cliffs, N.J.: Prentice-Hall, 1962.

Updike, John. "No Brakes: A New Biography of Sinclair Lewis." *The New Yorker,* February 4, 2002, pp. 76–79.

Willa Cather's
My Ántonia

CLARE MORGAN

WILLA CATHER'S *MY Ántonia* was written out of an America undergoing rapid social and economic change. The novel, commenced in 1916 and published in 1918, reflects its author's concerns with the values and structures of the emergent way of life. Did burgeoning materialism offer more opportunity, or less? Were the freedoms gained from acquiring a formal education alluring enough to counterbalance associated problems of alienation and rootlessness? Above all, what could become of that "dream" of individual possibility that had characterized the growth of American nationhood, now that the geographic frontier, and all its possibilities for individual advancement, had been declared by the historian Frederick Jackson Turner, as far back as 1893, "closed"?

My Ántonia does not, as its dates might suggest, concern itself overtly with the dislocations and exigencies of the First World War. Instead, Cather focuses on an earlier period of dislocation, that of the massive emigration from Europe of those people enduringly characterized by the Jewish playwright Israel Zangwill as comprising "the melting pot." In 1908, when his play of that name opened in Washington, the largest influx of immigrants in the history of the United States was under way. Nineteen hundred and eight, the one date referred to concretely in *My Ántonia* (1908 is the year Jim Burden meets Tiny Soderball in Salt Lake City), was situated statistically at the high point of this immigration: the first decade of the twentieth century saw embark on American soil 8,795,386 Europeans hungry for the opportunities the New World seemed to offer. In the face of the inevitable social upheavals such an influx must generate, *My Ántonia*, through its depiction of the status and role of the immigrant population in the Midwest, can be read as an important cultural document that comes out of and feeds into the continuing debate about the structure of American nationhood.

URBANIZATION AND GENDER

Upheavals other than immigration, however, inform *My Ántonia*'s genesis and composition. The fact that the novel's publication date was two years prior to American women being granted the vote attests to the contemporary fluidity of definitions and distinctions attached to the role of the sexes. Were women to be "pioneers" or "homemakers"? How were the prevailing moral values to accommodate changing patterns of life? These are questions that Cather's portrayals of women—and men—seek to illuminate.

Cather's women and men, so often seen as epitomizing the "frontier" spirit, belong also to the new pioneering world so graphically represented in the lamp-posted but as yet un-built Chicago streets of Theodore Dreiser's *Sister Carrie* (1900). This is the world of rapid urbanization, with its attendant questions of place, status, and the inevitable de-positioning of man's relation to the land. As Cather put it, echoing Frederick Jackson Turner, in her 1923 essay "Nebraska: The End of the First Cycle,"

> we must face the fact that the splendid story of the pioneers is finished, and that no new story worthy to take its place has yet begun. . . . The generation now in the driver's seat hates to make anything, wants to live and die in an automobile, scudding past those acres where the old men used to follow the long corn-rows up and down.

The "owners" of *My Ántonia*'s narrative (Jim and the ambiguous outside narrator) have both been transplanted from their Nebraska background into the urbanized and cosmopolitan wider world. They, in effect, are among those whom Cather characterizes in the same essay as wanting "everything ready-made: clothes, food, education, music, pleasure." One of the questions *My Ántonia* asks, like the essay, is what place can be found for individual fulfillment in an environment that has ties to neither nature nor community.

The First World War, which Cather was not to address directly until *One of Ours* (1922), nevertheless exists in *My Ántonia* as a kind of textual obverse, interweaving its unspoken presence as a continuo of loss and absence that acts as a spur to Jim Burden's attempt to reclaim the past. Burden's narrative is, after all, a sustained effort at just such a reclaiming: the modern-day drifter (Jim is always on the move and admits, in

CHRONOLOGY

1873	Willa (Sibert) Cather born December 7 into an established family on a farm near Winchester, Virginia.
1883	Moves to Nebraska and lives among Bohemians, Scandinavians, Germans and French-Canadians.
1890	Goes to Lincoln University; edits university newspaper and publishes her own poetry, articles, and stories in it; hired by *Nebraska State Journal* to write regular column.
1895	Graduates from university and moves to Pittsburgh to become managing editor of *Woman's Home Monthly*.
1902	First journey to Europe.
1903	*April Twilights* (poems).
1906	Moves to Washington Square, works for *McClure's*.
1912	In the spring, makes first visit to Southwest, whose "big and bright and consuming" landscape inspire her.
1913	*O Pioneers!*
1915	*The Song of the Lark*; returns to Southwest.
1916	Begins writing *My Ántonia*.
1918	*My Ántonia*.
1922	*One of Ours*; confirmation in the Episcopal Church at Red Cloud.
1923	Wins Pulitzer Prize; *A Lost Lady*.
1925	Edits *The Best Short Stories of Sarah Orne Jewett*.
1927	*Death Comes for the Archbishop*.
1931	Receives honorary degree from Princeton.
1933	Awarded the Prix Fémina Américain for *Shadows on the Rock*.
1936	*Not under Forty* (essays).
1940	*Sapphira and the Slave Girl*.
1944	Gold medal, American Academy of Arts and Letters.
1947	Dies on April 24 in New York City.

the "Lena Lingard" section, "All this time, of course, I was drifting") is enacting the possibilities of staking not a terrestrial but an imaginative "claim" on a lost world.

The lost world that Cather addresses transcends, though, even the radical split in contemporary consciousness occasioned by the magnitude of the First World War. Cather explores the realm of cultural metaphor through her depiction of the child-in-nature or, rather, the two children in nature—Jim and Ántonia, walking hand in hand through a Nebraska Eden. The idea of the frontier as a kind of Eden was not new: it had been referred to by Frederick Jackson Turner in his influential essay, "The Significance of the Frontier in American History" (1893). Cather, however, takes up this notion not only in the imagery she employs (Jim's fight with the rattlesnake has connotations other than those of frontier bravery—Jim sees the snake as epitomizing "the ancient, eldest Evil") but also in her interweaving, throughout her tale, of memory and desire, of notions of existence before and after the Fall.

CATHER AS DISLOCATED WRITER

Cather wrote from a world of personal as well as cultural dislocation. Her comfortable Virginia childhood was suddenly cut short by her family's move to a Nebraska farm. Although she later came to admire the pioneering journey of the explorer Coronado into what was to become New Mexico (Jim Burden remembers he learned that Coronado "died in the wilderness, of a broken heart"), nevertheless her attitude to her own enforced pioneering was unenthusiastic. Recalling in 1913 her move to Red Cloud at the age of nine, Cather says:

> I shall never forget my introduction to [Nebraska]. . . . As we drove further and further out into the country, I felt a good deal as if we had come to the end of everything—it was a kind of erasure of personality.

Although she was personally less than ecstatic about this unchosen "immigration," she was generally admiring of the pioneering spirit that prevailed. "Nebraska: The End of the First Cycle" celebrates the powers of strength and survival exhibited by the Nebraska farmers who "came into a wilderness and had to make everything, had to be ingenious as shipwrecked sailors." But long before that, as early as 1900, she had written a strongly positive article on William Jennings Bryan, whose radical advocacy of nationalizing railroad, telephone, and telegraph was part of his involvement in 1890s agrarian populism. Bryan stood against encroaching materialist urbanization and appeared, to Cather, to stand also for the qualities of the Midwest that she admired: "all its newness and vigor, its magnitude and monotony, its richness and lack of variety, its inflammability and volubility, its strength and its crudeness, its high seriousness and self-confidence, its egotism and its nobility" (quoted in Curtin, *The World and the Parish*, 1970).

Her admiration of such paradoxical qualities can be traced to those contradictory pulls of nineteenth- and twentieth-century thinking that she and her contemporaries were necessarily subject to. Just as she was uprooted from Virginia and planted all unprepared in the wide and "steel like" Nebraska spaces, so in some respects she found herself negotiating the perils of a land that existed between the old world of frontier exploration and the new world of urban expansion.

Cather's relation to the land and to nature is colored by the necessity of this negotiation. In acknowledging Ralph Waldo Emerson as her favorite prose writer in 1888 (see Mildred R. Bennett, *The World of Willa Cather*, 1951), she engages herself with the intricacies of the nineteenth-century Romantic sublime. The Romantic transcendence of Emerson's portrayals of human relations with nature, epitomized in his desire to feel "the currents of the Universal being circulate through me" (*Nature*, 1836, chapter 1), are echoed in Cather's early comment (quoted in Bennett's *World of Willa Cather*): "Whenever I crossed the Missouri

River coming into Nebraska the very smell of the soil tore me to pieces. I could not decide which was the real and which the fake me." A main concern of *My Ántonia* is how far this view of the world can be reconciled with the increasingly dominant notion of nature (the land) as something to be tamed to conform to the social and economic demands of a "modern" materialist environment.

Cather applies another aspect of her nineteenth-century literary heritage to her investigation of burgeoning twentieth-century human affairs. Her debt to the European literary tradition has been remarked on by many commentators, and her admiration for George Eliot is an evident influence in *My Ántonia,* in that a central preoccupation of the novel is to what extent "accidents" of "Destiny" determine our lives. Like Eliot in *Middlemarch* (1873), Cather invites readers to consider how far individual aspiration is encumbered by social and economic circumstance. To what extent is Ántonia held back by the combined disadvantages of her poverty and her womanhood? Is there some way in which the intricate web of social and economic relationships dictates Jim's metamorphosis from sensing that "I was something that lay under the sun and felt it, like the pumpkins, and I did not want to be anything more" to "drifting" toward Harvard, and a life spent endlessly, it seems, "crossing Iowa on a train"?

In terms of religion, too, Cather's allegiance is complex. From a Baptist background she was confirmed, in 1922, into the Episcopalian Church in Red Cloud. Although this growing allegiance is not overtly present in her fiction until *Death Comes for the Archbishop* (1927), nevertheless the formation of her own belief in a world of increasing skepticism and secularization reverberates through the examination of competing religions put forward in her earlier work, and forms one of the culminating moments of *My Ántonia,* when Mr. Shimerda and Jim's grandfather both bring to the Christmas tree in the Burdens' farmhouse the combined

benefit of their diverse but complementary nonconformist pragmatism and Roman Catholic awe. The role of competing religions in the emergent social framework is exemplified in Mr. Shimerda's burial at the crossroads. This burial symbolizes both doubt and possibility, Shimerda's inability to survive in the new order culminating, through his suicide and resultant burial in unconsecrated ground, in his being effectively excluded from the symbolic consolations of the old. The figure of the gentle and cultivated Shimerda (with its connotations of "chimera," in the sense of passing or illusory) stands or lies at a symbolic as well as an actual crossroads—the crossroads of a particular historical and cultural moment where materialism and the quest for advancement were already ousting considerations of morality and spiritual need.

MY ÁNTONIA AND THE EUROPEAN INFLUENCE

As well as existing in that creative powerhouse where nineteenth and twentieth century meet and blur into each other, Cather's imaginative energy gathers its force from the playoff between the distinct traditions of Europe and those of her American past. The acknowledged debt to Leo Tolstoy's *Kreutzer Sonata* (1891) for *My Ántonia*'s layered narration could as easily be laid at the door of Joseph Conrad's "Heart of Darkness" (1901). Indeed, a 1918 review in the New York *Sun* likens Cather's method to that of Conrad's story "Youth," comparing the two writers' "special genius of Memory."

The intersection of Cather's sensibility with the traditions of Europe is evident in other ways. Mildred R. Bennett quotes Cather ecstatically writing of France, on her first visit in 1902:

The purple chalk cliffs were dazzling white now, and our eyes ... ached with the glare of the sun on the white stone and yellow sand. A little boy on the stone terrace was flying a red and green kite, quite the most magnificent kite I have ever seen, and it went up famously, up and up until his string ran short, and of a truth one's heart went just as high.

On a rather different note, on tracking down her idol A. E. Housman in "some rather drab London suburb," she was made to feel "a raw stupid savage in the face of the old world."

Her European connection follows through in her literary debt to Henry James, whom, she states in an interview in the *Nebraska State Journal* of April 25, 1925, she imitated "laboriously" in her early writing. Cather, in *My Ántonia,* adopts and subverts James's preoccupation with the relation between European and American culture, emphasizing, unlike James, the role of European culture in emergent American identity at a vernacular level. Jamesian moral indeterminacy, evident in such works as *The Ambassadors* (1903) in terms of old and new world cultural intersection, becomes in Cather's hands a tool for investigating the point where the symbolic intersects with the quotidian to produce an epic realm of transcendence. Numerous commentators have identified this realm as the single most distinguishing feature of Cather's work.

Cather's "between-ness" is important in understanding her literary method. As early reviewers of *My Ántonia* perceived, Cather achieved in her prose a telling amalgamation of the particular and the general, to develop a method that was neither realist nor modernist but negotiated the strictures and possibilities of both. Cather's fellow countryman and poet T. S. Eliot believed, together with other modernist artists, that only through what came to be called "the mythic method" could the fragmentary nature of the modern age be adequately reflected. Cather, like Eliot, sought to encompass the actual and the symbolic, to accommodate progress and the stasis of a world extracted from time.

In this mythic method Cather's creative path intersects simultaneously with her American forbears and her European influences. As critics

such as Susie Thomas and Hermione Lee have noted, Cather is indebted for her method to the Virgilian pastoral. On a trip to Europe in 1908 she saw scenes from Virgil's *Georgics* reenacted on the slopes of the Apennines and utilized the form and feel of this "hard" pastoral of labor and endurance (distinct in emphasis from the "soft" pastoral of romantic celebration and nostalgia) to carve out her own literary route through her modernizing homeland. The pastoral had been adopted by the nineteenth-century American literary imagination by writers such as Nathaniel Hawthorne and Henry David Thoreau. Cather's pastoral creates a delicate balance between change and stasis, time and the timeless, reality and myth by combining the changeable "realist" detail of everyday life with the long perspectives of stability offered by the mythic mode. As Eudora Welty says of *My Ántonia:* "There is the foreground, with the living present, its human figures in action; and there is the horizon of infinite distance . . . but there is no intervening ground. . . . There is no recent past. There is no middle-distance."

THE IMPORTANCE OF THE "ANGEL IN THE HOUSE"

In early writings Willa Cather rejected the "feminine" and sought to utilize, via the pastoral, a male tradition of writing modeled on classical forms. Railing against the standards of female fiction of the time, she says in "The Literary Situation in 1895":

> I have not much faith in women in fiction. They have a sort of sex consciousness that is abominable. . . . Women are so horribly subjective and they have such scorn for the healthy commonplace. When a woman writes a story of adventure . . . anything without wine, women and love, then I will begin to hope for something great from them, not before.

Cather particularly abhorred, as did contemporaries such as Frank Norris, the "safe," bourgeois quality of those fictions that "do not call a blush to the cheek of the young" and thus negatively, as Norris put it in "The Decline of the Magazine Short Story" (1897), "determine the standard of the American short story."

Ántonia Shimerda is given little opportunity to be "feminine." The poverty of her family (her thin cotton dress blown up against her legs by the biting Nebraska winter wind makes an indelible impression) renders the necessary upkeep of "femininity" almost impossible. After her father's death Ántonia takes on the male responsibility of working the land, and prides herself that she now "works like mans," a condition Jim's grandmother fears will "spoil that girl. She'll lose all her nice ways and get rough ones." The heroic spirit of this "brown-eyed" and "pretty" young girl is brought out by the exigencies of her situation. If she does not set to with a will, it is likely the Shimerda family will not survive. Her querulous and inept mother, her dependent younger sister, and the always-to-be-directed "crazy boy" Marek are of little use. Ántonia must join forces with, and work like, her exploitative older brother Ambrosch if the family is to survive.

Critics have suggested that Ántonia has no "voice" in the novel, that all her feelings and utterances are mediated through the narration of Jim. This has generally led to the assertion that the novel is concerned with how American society conspires to silence women. And, the argument goes, Ántonia is doubly silenced, as a woman and as a non-English-speaking immigrant.

But if readers look closely at the text they find that Jim's narration does *not* silence Ántonia. On the issue of working in the fields, Jim's negative view of her "shouting to her beasts, sunburned, sweaty, her dress open at the neck, and her throat and chest dust-plastered" is not one the reader ultimately identifies with. Working against Jim's evaluation is a view of Ántonia that seems almost to permeate the text despite Jim's narration, rather than because of it. When,

the first summer after Mr. Shimerda's death, Jim goes to ask Ántonia whether she can join him at the school the following season, she answers, "I ain't got time to learn. . . . School is all right for little boys. I help make this land one good farm." Jim is "vexed" and wonders whether she is "going to grow up boastful like her mother." Later, he notices that she "ate so noisily now, like a man" and begins "to wish [he] had not stayed for supper" because "everything was disagreeable" to him now. Cather, however, has shown to the reader something quite opposed to Jim's view, which profoundly affects how the novel and Ántonia's (and Jim's) respective roles within it can be read. Just after she has made her defiant declaration of helping "make this land one good farm," Ántonia is perceived by Jim to be "crying. She turned her face from me and looked off at the red streak of dying light, over the dark prairie." Jim makes no comment about it, in terms of either Ántonia or his own feelings, just as he refrains from elaborating Ántonia's wish, expressed "with a sudden rush of feeling in her voice" as they are walking back to the house, that Jim will "tell . . . all those nice things you learn at the school, won't you, Jimmy?" In the gap between Jim's narration and the wider narration of the novel lies room for alternative interpretations that give the text much of its power to elucidate and surprise—and give Ántonia a voice in some ways stronger than Jim's because it says so much from the relatively small space it is allowed for such expression. Rather than taking Jim's view of Ántonia, the text invites readers to *judge* that view and—in measuring the difference between the view and the alternative—to arrive at their own interpretation, and in doing so to question the validity of Jim's stance.

The idea that Jim may be an unreliable narrator, although seen as "perverse" by Hermione Lee, is implicit in *My Ántonia*'s genesis. In the 1918 publication, the Introduction was framed in such a way that it appeared "Cather" herself was the frame-narrator who accepts Jim's story to read over, and also to modify. This follows her original plan of presenting in the novel two opposing stories—Cather's and Jim's. In the 1926 publication, the Introduction is shortened, "Cather" becomes a more ambiguous, ungendered figure, and Jim's story stands unmodified. The two opposing stories, however, have been amalgamated not only through Jim's silence or ignorance/innocence about what he is recounting but also through other people's comments or responses to his own actions or observations. A main motivating factor of the novel is this fruitful tension set up between Jim's narration and the host of other possibilities that exist within it yet covertly defy its authority to expound "the truth."

A central question *My Ántonia* addresses is not Sigmund Freud's famous "what does a woman want?" but the pressing "what should a woman be?" The nineteenth-century model of womanhood, fashioned along the lines of the British poet Coventry Patmore's famous "Angel in the House," was based on notions of propriety and moral rectitude. A woman was, essentially, an antidote to men's low (sexual) impulses and the guardian of family morals. The requirement was that a woman's sexuality should, if evident at all, be muted; that her sphere of action (because she was constitutionally unsuited to vigor of any kind) should be limited; and that, in order to remain unsullied by male greed and needs made evident in contemporary terms in the cut and thrust of materialist competitiveness, she should confine her attention to the private and domestic sphere.

These assumptions had of course been questioned throughout nineteenth-century literature in texts as different as Hawthorne's *The Scarlet Letter* (1850), Charlotte Brontë's *Jane Eyre* (1847), and Louisa May Alcott's *Little Women* (1868), with its memorable image of the shorn head of the redoubtable daughter Jo, who has cut and sold her hair, her crowning glory, to earn money. Cather's exploration of the angel in the house is more complex than a mere undercutting of stereotypical expectations of women's behavior. Jim's narration of "My" Ántonia draws attention not only to the role of subjectivity in the construction of character but to the relativity of perception inherent in the definition of gender roles. Jim's view of what a woman should be is shown, by Cather's narration, to be questionable. More than that, it is shown to be highly dependent on his own sense of what a man should be; far from being a feminist polemic, as some critics would read it, *My Ántonia* thus presents, through the complex delicacies of its narrational method, a world where the emergent new woman is considered alongside the possibilities of an equally evolving "New Man."

MURDER AND MALE RESPONSIBILITY

There are two murders of women in *My Ántonia;* the impact of each seeps down through the texture of the tale and colors how the novel presents not only domestic relations but also the complex issues of what is an appropriate role for men in the modern world. The first incident is the throwing to the wolves of the Bohemian bride during the sleigh ride home from the wedding. Pavel recounts this horrific tale as a deathbed confession: it is as if he needs to absolve himself and is using Mr. Shimerda as a priest at the last confessional. Mr. Shimerda "uncovered one of his long bony legs and rubbed it rhythmically," after which "relief came to all of us. . . . the worst was over. Mr. Shimerda signed to us that Pavel was asleep."

The tale is recounted through Ántonia to Jim, and through Jim to the reader; it is recounted in a tone of breathless horror and occupies Jim's and Ántonia's imaginations long afterward. Its setting and mode of narration (Bohemia, the woods, the snow, the past)—and the casting out of Peter and Pavel when the deed is discovered—all conspire to turn the tale into the stuff of legend. The bride could be any bride, "clinging to her husband"; the merrymaking and the snowbound journey on the sleigh the material of many an Eastern European folktale. The realm the story exists in is "other," but what it results in—Peter and Pavel, the immigrant new breed of pioneers—exists in the tangible, physical present of Cather's Nebraska.

What is the message of this story within the story? What is its function in particular for the investigation of men and women that is a central theme of *My Ántonia*? The way in which the bride incident is recounted gives it a cosmic quality—the actions depicted are the actions of all men and all women, the tale is a cautionary one, archetypal and living in imagination as a kind of warning. Marriage within it is associated with community and protection; family and friends are gathered, the future—a short sleigh ride away in the precincts of the next town, its church bell welcoming—looks secure. But the basis of the tragedy lies in a careless misjudgment: the revelers should not have set off, it is too late, the threat of the wolves is ignored or underestimated. As the sleighs one by one fall away and the people are lost, it comes down to a question (in Pavel's mind) of throwing out not the groom but the *bride*—it is she who is expendable, useless, an encumbrance. Men, the notion seems to be, must unite together in order to survive. The groom, in his new mindset as family man (chivalrous protector or sexual possessor), resists his new wife's expulsion and is himself thrown along with her to the wolves.

Two conflicting models of what a man should be are presented through this tale, both of them found to be inadequate in different ways. The central issue the conflict addresses is the validity of naked self-interest and aggression. These qualities had necessarily been fundamental to what might be called the frontier psyche. The necessity to tame the frontier psyche in the face of the domesticating circumstance of settlement is evident in the novel through the behavior of Jake and Otto, the farmhand and cowboy who tries not to "forget himself" and swear before Mrs. Burden, and who turns images of naked women into "angels" for the benefit of the prepubescent and innocent Jim. The fate of Jake and Otto, driven back, by the Burdens' move off the land and into the town (a further step away from the frontier and toward civilization), to the shrinking pioneer environment of the Crazy Girl mine, and thence into oblivion, is illustrative of the need to adapt and indicative of what happens to those who can find no ultimate place in the adaptation.

This necessity to tame what is in effect a Darwinian survival of the fittest instinct is shown to be complex. Pavel's instinct to survive at all costs, a necessary aspect of frontier living, is inappropriate in a world of domestication and community (one important aspect of the Bohemian parable is that it happens between societies, in a no man's land where, the implication is, the force of the usual social and interpersonal rules is weakened). But what of the groom's behavior? He, in acting appropriately for a civilized society, putting altruism before survival, must perish. His model, though, that of domestication and mutuality, is taken on by the "batching" couple, Peter and Pavel. This quasi domesticity, however, linen on the table, pumpkins stewed in milk for supper, and everything clean and tidy with its own particular place, is shown to be equally unsuited to emerging circumstance. If a modification of bare-knuckled Darwinian self-interest is overdue, Peter and Pavel's is not the way forward. Self-interest and survival take on different appearances in the settlement world. Here the batching couple has no defenses. Their adaptation is insufficient; the domestication they espouse will not suffice in this newly fashioned frontier. The last view readers have of Peter is one in which he is devouring his remaining melons, the residue of his failed domesticity, in an impotent gesture against the newly risen Darwinian forces of capitalist competition: Peter must sell up, to the enrichment of the entrepreneurial Wick Cutter, and move out.

ECONOMICS AND THE NEW WOMAN

The second murder takes place at the heart of the very economic forces Peter and Pavel are overcome by. Wick Cutter, the philandering money-lender, organizes his wife's death in a way that denies her the rights of economic inheritance the law has recently granted. Cutter is, in effect, defying the forces that seek to enshrine certain changes in the relations between women and men. Mrs. Cutter is hardly portrayed as the clinging bride of the Pavel and Peter tale. Indeed, Jim's narration paints her as something of a harridan. There is nonetheless in Cather's method enough room to see beyond Jim's narration to Mrs. Cutter's despair and the tragedy of frustration of a woman "sometimes founding new religions," who needs, according to Jim's (male) assessment, to be "tamed." She can be read as a woman attempting to find fulfillment, painting china, "smiling" at babies (unable to have her own) and, through her ugliness, making them cry; engaged in a perpetual war against her husband's obvious infidelity, trying to fulfill that policing of morals demanded of the angel in the house. The impossibility of such a role is made manifest by Cutter's elaborate evasion of her efforts. He gives her the slip in a realm (like the sleigh ride) "between" worlds— but the realm is no longer imaginative, there is no folktale here, but the metal reality of that contemporary world of speed and steam, the railway. It is through the modern agency of train timetables that Cutter evades his wife's moral policing, by deliberately putting her on the wrong train so that he can return to Black Hawk and force his sexual attentions on Ántonia. He has thrown his wife, so to speak, out of his own railway carriage to the (moral) wolves.

Wick Cutter is introduced as a figure trying out extremes of a new kind of survival. The "hundred thousand dollars" he ultimately amasses (obviously dismissed by Jim as a paltry sum, just as clearly a huge amount to Ántonia, Cuzak, and their family) endorses his position as economic frontiersman, one of the emergent breed of refined and respectable townspeople. Cutter's lack of real refinement or respectability (despite his factory teeth and well-brushed whiskers) attests to a central dilemma the novel

is addressing: how social change can be not only accommodated but harnessed for the good of the community. Wick Cutter demonstrates social change out of control; as Jim puts it, "Wick Cutter was different from any other rascal I have ever known." The "difference" lies in a peculiar amalgamation of frontiersman and emergent bourgeois capitalist: a deep aversion to any moral or social control, an extreme desire to assert his will at all costs, and, ultimately, an inability to fit any of the male roles open to him. Cutter's version of frontiersman self-assertion is ultimately no more efficacious than Peter and Pavel's new domesticity. This is partly because what he seeks to ensure is not his own survival but that of his property. He ensures that his wife's family cannot inherit; he has protected, in other words, his masculine economic power, but at the expense of two lives.

Cather's presentation of this tale in burlesque mode is significant. It fits with her own angry sense that the Wick Cutters of the world (note the significance of the name, in its relation to the prevention of light—the "cut wick") were set to be the modern inheritors. Cather's extreme dislike of materialism is made evident in her famous 1922 essay "The Novel Démeublé." Wick Cutter, who is reincarnated as Ivy Peters in *A Lost Lady*, stands, as Hermione Lee puts it, "for the debased American currency Cather saw buying out the pioneers." He acts as an interruption to Jim's Arcadian vision of the Cuzaks' family life, and Jim's recounting as comedy of this grotesque incident almost, but not quite, serves to mask its importance in the novel. The very materialism that lies at the heart of Cutter's behavior is shown as integral to the life the Cuzaks are leading: after all, the Cuzaks will only get "a parlour carpet if they got ninety cents for their wheat." Arcadia is inescapably infused with the materialism Cather abhors.

ÁNTONIA AND MATERIALISM

Ántonia's ill-fated liaison with Larry Donovan invites comparison with the fate of the unfortunate Bohemian sleigh bride. That young woman's trousseau lying forever untouched in its tissue wrapping of legend can be paralleled to the symbolic un-usage of Ántonia's carefully prepared bride clothes—unused because she never becomes her so-called train-crew aristocrat's official wife and is therefore denied the opportunity of fulfilling the traditional female homemaker role.

It is no accident that this failed husband inhabits the same realm Wick Cutter employs to defeat his wife's vigilance—the world of urgent movement, change, expansion, noise, steam, bustle that not only opens the former pioneer land to the ordinary citizen but encourages a life in motion, where the horizon is always changing and being perpetually in transit blurs the necessity for established roots. This modern realm is the one Ántonia hopes to marry into. Although she is troubled she will not "be able to manage so well for him in a city," the marriage is her one opportunity to join the modern world, to become part, that is, of a society whose values focus on material gain.

Although material gain is not, according to Jim's narration, a central feature of Ántonia's aspirations, nevertheless the detail of Widow Steavens' story demonstrates that Ántonia is not immune to the lure of materialism. She wants "to have everything" for her marriage, in particular a set of plated cutlery. Ambrosch does "the right thing" and provides her with three hundred dollars. In other ways, too, Ántonia hungers for the world Larry Donovan symbolizes: when she is hired out in Black Hawk to the Cutters she "seemed to care about nothing but picnics and parties and having a good time." She leaves the Harlings because she refuses to give up the taste of the wider life she has access to through the Vannis' dancing tent. As she puts it to Mrs. Harling: "A girl like me has got to take her good times when she can. Maybe there won't be any tent next year. I guess I want to have my fling, like the other girls." That the "good time" she desires involves material advancement is evident: "Tony wore gloves now, and high-

heeled shoes and feathered bonnets"; she "copied Mrs. Gardener's new party dress and Mrs. Smith's street costume . . . in cheap materials." It is out of this desire to belong to the world of appearances, in particular the appearance of material prosperity and the recreations associated with town life, that Ántonia meets Larry Donovan, one of those "accidents of fortune" that effectively, through her subsequent status of mother without a husband, ensures her confinement to a life of poverty.

Despite her aspiration, her very approach shows how unsuited Ántonia is to the Larry Donovan way of being. All the old-fashioned methods and values attend her wedding preparation. Her "betrayal" occurs because she carries old world values into a new world situation: as she tells Widow Steavens, "I thought if he saw how well I could do for him, he'd want to stay with me." She depends on the protection of Donovan just as the sleigh bride does on her husband; but like the sleigh husband, though for very different reasons, such protection from Larry Donovan is not forthcoming. Ántonia has attached her aspirations to an unsafe vehicle. Donovan deserts her for Old Mexico and "collecting half-fares off the natives and robbing the company," a life dedicated to illicit material gain, and as much "between worlds" as the doomed sleigh riders traversing the wastes of snow.

Marrying into the modern world is one of the models the novel provides to test the possibilities of what a woman should be. The model fails Ántonia because her values and expectations do not equip her to adapt to it. The paradox is that such values and expectations are precisely those shown to be of decisive importance in relation to the earlier model provided for Ántonia—that of fighting the pioneer battle of hard-working immigrant life.

PIONEERING VERSUS THE NEW WOMAN

Ántonia's readiness to adapt to the dire situation her father's death has created is presented, on the one hand, as heroic and admirable. Ántonia sacrifices traditional female roles for the sake of her family's survival, plowing the land, braving the weather, doing the heavy jobs—taking up, in effect, her father's mantle of provider (or at least sharing it with her brother) but with rather more energy and commitment than the displaced Mr. Shimerda ever showed. But in the changing world this altruism, like Peter and Pavel's survival instinct, is outdated. And the way Ántonia enacts it (by "working like mans"), seen as laudable or vital in the days when the frontier was "open," is, in these days, when the new community is seeking to establish itself as civilized, open to criticism. Jim's grandmother, for example, laments "what a life she's led, out in the fields with those rough threshers! Things would have been very different with poor Ántonia if her father had lived"; whereas Jim's adverse comments about the effect of the work on Ántonia's femininity have already been noted.

What the emerging world requires is a new kind of altruism, one equivocally enacted by the figure of Lena Lingard, who contributes to her family's fortunes not by the sweat of her brow but by the dollar bill. Lena eschews the heroic model of physical endeavor and substitutes that of the modern businesswoman who, in the words of Widow Steavens, "turned out so well . . . and [was] doing so much for her mother." Is the novel suggesting, then, that Lena's model is the one that should be followed by women? It has been argued that Jim's ultimate loss of interest in Lena once she has become successful is an indictment on the part of the novel of this mode in the world. But Cather's treatment of Lena is more complex than such a suggestion would allow. Lena is a woman who apparently achieves for herself an independent life while supporting the weaker members of her family. She achieves independence, a degree of sophistication, and a not inconsiderable material prosperity. Why are readers left, then, with a not wholly positive impression of Lena? Jim's loss of interest, his judgment of her "usual complacency," is not a sufficient answer; indeed, it should probably

raise the readers' view of Lena, in that Cather's method invites one (just as with Ántonia) to judge Jim's judgments of Lena, and be privy to the questionableness of his rather traditional male view (even as a young boy, Jim believes that Ántonia, as a girl, should "defer" to him). Rather than convincing the reader of Lena's negative value, Jim's loss of interest in her shows, far more importantly, his inability to allow a modern, successful woman to exert a hold over his imagination. The true significance of Lena in this respect lies in what is implied in Jim's dismissal of her to the outer edges of the (male) imaginative world.

Of the possible models of behavior open to women, the route Lena chooses is presented by the novel as deeply unsatisfactory not because Jim presents it as such but because the behavior that secures it—a judicious and calculated withholding of self and emotions—is judged by *Ántonia* as wrong. When Jim tells Ántonia that Lena allows him to kiss her, Ántonia is outraged: "'Lena does?' Tony gasped. 'If she's up to any of her nonsense with you, I'll scratch her eyes out. . . . if I see you hanging round with Lena much, I'll go to your grandmother.'"

It is quite possible to read the combined ultimate fates of Lena and Tiny Soderball, still together, "after so many years," much to Jim's interest, as one with undeniably Sapphic connotations. Cather's own decided preference for emotional (and perhaps sexual) bonds with women has led contemporary commentators to frame it in this way. Of greater significance to the present argument, however, is the ultimate lack of futurity in the women's situation. If the mythic method is a way of negotiating a timelessness that incorporates both future and past, then Lena and Tiny are shown as mere flotsam, so to speak, spun out by the cosmic wheel. They have no stake in a realm that transcends the material. For Cather, whose hatred of the material became ever more focused (and led to charges of conservatism and old-fashionedness), the businesswoman model, playing for material gain at the expense of genuine feeling, is no more ultimately viable than working "like mans."

EDUCATION AND POSSIBILITY

Ántonia's "work like mans" heroism may save her family from ruin, but it does her no good in Jim's eyes or in the eyes of the Black Hawk world. Indeed, more than anything else it dictates her ultimate position in the world and in the novel. It is one of those "accidents of fortune" that Jim Burden cites at the end of the novel as having divided him from Ántonia. Working "like mans" denies the intelligent girl all opportunity of "bettering herself" by acquiring an education. Her swiftness, her potential for learning, her engagement are all clearly there. But the necessity of working "like mans" divides her from educational possibility and from the delicate checks and balances of childhood equality. Ántonia herself acknowledges the potential effects of her situation, not long after her father's death. When Jim asks her, "Why do you all the time try to be like Ambrosch?" she replies: "If I live here, like you, that is different. Things will be easy for you. But they will be hard for us."

Ántonia and Jim are "equal" out in the prairie, but the differences between them grow as Jim's education grows. The move of Jim and his grandparents to town entrenches and widens the gap between the two children. Early in the novel, Ántonia's natural intelligence and aptitude for learning are demonstrated: "While we snuggled down there out of the wind, she learned a score of words. She was quick, and very eager. . . . It was wonderfully pleasant." But when her father dies and she "ain't got time to learn" and begs Jim (just as her father had) to "tell me all those nice things you learn at the school," her chances of intellectual and educational fulfilment swiftly diminish. As is clear later, "The Bohemian and Scandinavian girls could not get positions as teachers, because they had had no opportunity to learn the language."

As Jim moves further into the future, entering Black Hawk and a world of books and possibili-

ties (although he feels that they enclose him, and he is deeply impatient with the "repressive" nature of small town society), his lens on Ántonia lengthens. She becomes one of the "hired girls" rather than the one human being he is perhaps closest to. It is as if Jim has embarked on a journey of intellect and experience that not only takes him away from his roots but offers a lens—the lens of modern America—that recontextualizes the standards against which things are judged. Through this method, Willa Cather invites readers to assess Ántonia's "progress" as well as the assessment, and therefore evaluate the various models available to Ántonia through a double apprehension of the lengthening subjectivity of Jim's view.

JIM'S UNRELIABLE NARRATION

Just how trustworthy is Jim Burden's narration? The framing narrator of the novel says, in the Introduction, that Jim has a "romantic disposition"; but, as legal counsel for one of the Great Western railways, he must also have a significantly cool analytical brain. Indeed, he has "played an important part in [the railway's] development," his interest and influence fueled, according to the narrator, by the "personal passion" he feels for "the great country through which his railway runs and branches." On the one hand, this is admirable, but, as is clear from Jim's experience, the railroad not only opens up the country and possibility but facilitates the taking up and transplanting of people away from their homes, away from the roots that give them a sense of identity. The railroad is part of the modern world, where improvement in transport goes hand in hand with fragmenting communities. Ántonia's daughter Martha has moved away with her new husband, a move that has made Ántonia cry "like I was putting her into her coffin"; they still see little of each other despite the acquisition by the young couple of a "Ford car."

Jim is thus associated with a way of living Cather ultimately found alien: in a 1924 interview with Rose C. Feld she stated her belief that "restlessness such as ours, striving such as ours, do not make for beauty. Other things must come first: good cookery; cottages that are home, not playthings; gardens; repose." Yet though Jim is a part of the restlessness that Cather did not find beautiful, this alone cannot indict him. Surely, as Hermione Lee has suggested, it is "perverse" to characterize him as "unreliable" in any thoroughgoing and significant way. At worst he is no more than a rather sentimental raconteur who seeks to construct through memorialization what he sees as his now long past and golden time.

A close reading of the final section of the novel reveals some disturbing traits in Jim-as-character. He recounts with a certain relish how Cuzak is "disappointed" when he sees how much bigger Jim's gift of candy for the children is than his own. It is difficult, also, to acquit Jim of a certain unattractive "points scoring" when in response to Ántonia's assertion that, having become a mother she "don't like to kill anything," he tells her "the young Queen of Italy said the same thing once, to a friend of mine." There is a similar covert but chilling assertion of superiority in Jim's description of the "companionable fellow" Cuzak (he has called Jake and Otto "good fellows," recalling how they "served the family to the end"), whom he characterizes as looking "at people sidewise, as a work-horse does at its yoke mate. . . . This trick did not suggest duplicity or secretiveness, but merely long habit, as with the horse."

The patronizing undertow takes on a more subtly pejorative aspect in Jim's description of Leo Cuzak. Jim implicitly compares Leo to Blind d'Arnault, the "Negro pianist" who comes to Black Hawk in Jim's teenage years. Blind d'Arnault has "the Negro head . . . almost no head at all; nothing behind the ears but folds of neck under close-clipped wool." Leo too "hadn't much head behind his ears, and his tawny fleece grew down thick to the back of his neck." Wool, fleece, the pianist's knowledge of musical passages lying "under the bone of his

pinched, conical little skull, definite as animal desires," Leo's "faun-like" appearance, all suggest some way in which the Cuzak family is underlyingly seen by Jim as "other," related to some realm quite distant from the civilized sophistications of "the Queen of Italy." What realm that is might be suggested in a further comparison: when the Cuzak children burst up out of the fruit cave "big and little, tow heads and gold heads and brown," their "explosion of life" makes Jim "dizzy for a moment." Much earlier, just before the childhood incident with the rattlesnake, Jim had thought that "an orderly and very sociable kind of life was going on" in the dog town. As Jim and Ántonia approached, "the dogs were out . . . dozens of them, sitting up on their hind legs. . . . As we approached, they barked, shook their tails at us, and scurried underground." It is perhaps not too farfetched to suggest that the older Jim sees in the Cuzak horde a kind of undifferentiated life force similar to the dog town whose order he approved of years ago. Indeed, Ántonia's own phrase, that she would have brought up her children "like wild rabbits" if she had not acquired some sophistication at the Harlings, supports this reading.

If Jim as character displays some disturbing ambivalences in his relation to the final reunion with Ántonia that is the culmination of the story, he has shown all along a less than consistent attitude to the woman he "was very much in love with . . . once." When he returns to Black Hawk and finds Ántonia "disgraced" with a new baby, he declares his feeling of closeness to her, that she is "a part of" him, and holds her hands "a long while, over [his] heart," promising ultimately "through the soft, intrusive darkness" that he will "come back." A few lines after this scene of intensity, at the beginning of Book V, Jim quite casually informs the reader, "I told Ántonia I would come back, but life intervened, and it was twenty years before I kept my promise." Perhaps, he muses, his reason for staying away was "cowardice," or not wanting to part with a cherished "early" illusion. Perhaps, the reader may feel, there is an underlying comparison to be made with Larry Donovan, who also promised to come back and, just as Jim does, departs for the wider world on the next train.

When Jim does eventually visit Ántonia he momentarily finds her changed, flat-chested and lacking most of her teeth. Ironically Jim soon recognizes the old Ántonia, whereas she at first sees only a stranger whose obvious status causes her to address him respectfully as "sir." Jim finds that Ántonia's retention of "spirit," or life force, allows him to re-create her, in his mind at least, as she always was. How valuable, though, is this re-creation in deciphering what the culmination of Cather's novel points at? If Jim finds Ántonia "like the founders of early races," how significant is it? Jim describes the farm, although some of the children are barefoot, as being a kind of latter-day Eden:

> There was the deepest peace in that orchard. . . . The hedges were so tall that we could see nothing but the blue sky above them. . . . The afternoon sun poured down through the drying grape leaves. The orchard seemed full of sun, like a cup, and we could smell the ripe apples on the trees. The crabs hung on the branches as thick as beads on a string, purple-red, with a thin silvery glaze over them.

But is this, as some critics have read it, an endorsement on Cather's part of the old ways that the Cuzaks' mode of living upholds?

"THE OLD OAKEN BUCKET"

A reading of the novel as unconditional endorsement of the old ways is inadequate on several fronts. At a fundamental level, Ántonia's separation from "the future" is insecure. Her way of life, and the things that she and Cather hold dear, are threatened on all sides. Despite now saying she has never felt at home in towns, and Jim's "wondering" comment that she should never have gone to Black Hawk, the Ántonia portrayed in the Vannis' dancing tent, with her lust for life and her cheaply made-up finery, had some at least of the makings of a town girl. And as Ántonia herself admits, if she had not moved to the town she would have ended up without "nice ways." So town-ness is lurking at the heart of the country idyll. In addition to this, and despite all obvious appearances, Ántonia has taken the "city" way of life to her; her husband is a "city man," admitting that on first moving to the country he "near go crazy with lonesomeness," returning to his town habits when he can, "off dancing with the girls and forgetting that he was an old fellow," and being "rather surprised" by the size and disposition of his family when he returns. When Jim arrives at the house for his final visit, Cuzak and the oldest son are away in town: the house, and Ántonia's way of living within it, seem an anomaly, a time warp tucked away (but only just) out of the malevolent notice of railroad and progress.

A wider reason for doubting the novel's wholehearted endorsement of the "old" way of life that Ántonia has adopted lies in the fundamental difference of her life from the "old." This difference rests in ideas of community and nationhood. Cather lamented later in her career that the old neighborliness of her childhood had gone, and an early review of *My Ántonia* praised it for portraying "an informal league of nations." However, in the Cuzaks' way of life, all hope of that league of nations, and the neighborliness that goes with it, seems to have been lost. The farm is isolated, Ántonia has practically abandoned her English, the younger children have never learned it, and the family see themselves as Bohemian rather than American: "one of the older boys" instructs his mother to "show [Jim] the spiced plums" on the grounds that "Americans don't have those." Even more significantly, Jim has himself lost the kind of distinctions he saw between people when he was a child: where formerly he had criticized the Black Hawk people who just thought of the Bohemians as all alike, by the end of the novel the capacity to differentiate has been replaced by a homogenizing view of otherness, as when he remembered "Bohemians . . . always planted hollyhocks."

Perhaps the most persuasive reason for identifying Cather's view of the Cuzak way of life as negative lies in an earlier and apparently unrelated incident. While Ántonia is working as a servant for Mrs. Harling, she recounts a tale of a tramp who has thrown himself into a threshing machine. The threshing machine in Thomas Hardy's *Tess of the d'Urbervilles* (1891) stood for the malevolent side of progress, exercising an unnatural tyranny over its operatives, and being associated with the dilution of moral judgment and, in Tess's case, with her ultimate destruction. Cather's tramp, then (who has probably arrived "on a freight"—another example of the pernicious influence of the destabilizing railroad— throws himself into the jaws of modernity. He has in his pocket, though, a symbol of the old ways—a well-read cutting of Samuel T. Woodworth's "The Old Oaken Bucket" (1818). The poem is a highly sentimentalized evocation of old-fashioned living:

> How dear to this heart are the scenes of my
>   childhood,
> When fond recollection presents them to view;
> The orchard, the meadow, the deep tangled wild
>   wood,
> And every loved spot which my infancy knew.

These opening four lines of the poem demonstrate precisely Jim Burden's approach to the past and to Ántonia. It is through such "fond recollection" that Jim constructs the Black Hawk world and presents it to the reader's view. The poem continues: "And now far removed from the loved situation, / The tear of regret will intrusively swell." Perhaps Jim's "tear of regret" similarly intrudes itself between readers and the stuff of the world he is describing: just as Mr. Lockwood in Emily Brontë's *Wuthering Heights* (1847) interposes a sentimental lens between readers and the world of passionate anarchy the novel depicts, so Jim Burden filters

the twists and intersections of tragedy, hardship, desire, and greed that inform the substance of his narrative at every turn. But in *My Ántonia* as in *Wuthering Heights* a tension is set up between the authorized narrative and the voices that it seeks to contain. This tension militates against any singular reading. However, Jim Burden's relation to "The Old Oaken Bucket" can be taken as a significant clue to one aspect at least of the novel's emphasis. For if "The Old Oaken Bucket" sets out the very attitudes and approaches to the old way of living that Jim's narration espouses, and the poem, in the tramp's pocket, is fed unceremoniously into the mechanical jaws of the future, then Willa Cather, irrespective of her narrator's predilections, is strongly putting forward in her novel the inefficacy of the old way. And if it is precisely this old way that Ántonia's life ultimately embraces, then Ántonia not only belongs to the past but is doomed, for all her fecundity, to ultimate irrelevance. In modern America, the novel seems to be saying, there will unfortunately no longer be room for the Ántonia Shimerdas of the world.

JIM BURDEN AND SEXUALITY

Jim's construction of Eden, then, and his placing of Ántonia within it as the essential life force that makes ordinary women pale in comparison and keeps her "at the very bottom of my memory," should be viewed circumspectly, in terms of the frame Cather has set up for it. This frame, which is in effect suggesting that Jim's recreation of Ántonia is suspect in its formation of a sentimentalized past whose value in the emergent world is doubtful, is reflected and reinforced in other aspects of the novel's construction.

During his teenage years at Black Hawk Jim's desire to be with the hired girls rather than mix with the people his grandmother says are more "suited to his status" is characterized, by his own narration, as having to do with the sense that he "knew where the real women were . . .

and . . . would not be afraid of them, either!" In other words, his adherence to the hired girls was part of his construction of his own manhood. But on what was the sense that the hired girls had more life in them based? It seems to have been based on a combination of factors, which include a burgeoning physical awareness set within the "repressive" atmosphere of Black Hawk propriety. The well-behaved Black Hawk girls seem to have "no substance to their bodies," whereas the hired (ex-farm) girls have "white arms and throats bare, their cheeks bright as the brightest wild roses."

There are several contradictory elements here. Firstly, Lena Lingard, who with Ántonia is most in demand at the dances, "danced every dance like a waltz" and makes Jim feel as though he was "coming in with the tide . . . coming home to something." But Jim does not want the sense of "coming home," he wants what he gets with Ántonia, which is a feeling that "you didn't return to anything. You set out every time upon a new adventure." Ántonia's physicality (her "bare, brown arms and legs" and her "bonny complexion") combine with the sense of adventure to make this "good looking girl" a potent sexual force. As Mrs. Harling says, "you're likely to have a fling that you won't get up from in a hurry." Yet Jim, who can have erotic dreams about Lena, cannot, to his chagrin, have the same about Ántonia. Why is this, when he acknowledges her attractiveness and tells of how, after Blind d'Arnault's playing, they walk home together "so excited that we dreaded to go to bed" and "whispering in the cold until the restlessness was slowly chilled out of us"?

Jim's sexual attraction to Ántonia is evident when he kisses her in a way that makes her draw "her face away" and whisper "indignantly, 'Why, Jim! You know you ain't right to kiss me like that. I'll tell your grandmother on you!'" Jim, despite his previous desire to have erotic dreams about her, is pleased rather than disappointed or angry. Ántonia is fulfilling the traditional role of guardian of morals, not only her morals but also his. This guardianship, placed precisely in a

realm of sexuality contained by conventional probity, ensures that Ántonia "was still my Ántonia," with her "warm, sweet face, her kind arms, and the true heart in her." Jim is shown, in other words, as a man who judges women according to the angel in the house formula, seeking in a woman, as in his nostalgic reclamation of the lost world of his childhood, a nineteenth-century model in a twentieth-century world that is rapidly outgrowing it. One of the functions of the novel is to question the validity of this model by examining Jim's attitude to it and at the same time tracing its effect on Ántonia's fate.

THE IMPORTANCE OF *MY ÁNTONIA*

What is to be made of the various strands and themes that constitute the complex novel *My Ántonia*? How do they relate to the diverse interpretations the novel has been subject to since its publication in the early years of another century, a century very different, in many ways, from the twenty-first century?

The early reviews of *My Ántonia* set out a broad framework within which Cather's work has continued to be examined by scholars and critics. The diversity of these reviews is perhaps preparation for the subsequent inconsistency of her critical reputation, in that it is difficult for a writer to continue to be all things to all people. *My Ántonia*, however, admits to no singular or simple interpretation. The contributions of early commentators (many of whom are represented in Margaret Anne O'Connor's *Willa Cather: The Contemporary Reviews*, 2001) demonstrate this. A 1918 *New York Times Book Review* judgment, like many others of the time, perceived Cather's writing as locale-based, reading *My Ántonia* as "a carefully detailed picture of daily existence on a Nebraska farm." The influential critic H. L. Mencken, however, was among those who praised the novel's "heroic" spirit and the way Cather sets about infusing her work with "the eternal tragedy of man." A review in the New York *Sun* in 1918 emphasized

My Ántonia's writerly qualities, concentrating on the ways in which the novel denied readers the comfort of "fiction" by using a variety of authorial methods to destabilize response. In 1919 the novel could be seen by the *Independent* as focusing more on "the fascination of the making of Americans from the foreign born."

Cather herself rather peremptorily suggested that little notice had been taken of *My Ántonia* at the time of publication. Nevertheless, it became in her mind the novel that the public wished her to keep on writing. When her 1922 *One of Ours* was savaged by a variety of critics despite going on to win the Pulitzer Prize, it was perceived as having failed to live up to the kind of promise *My Ántonia* had shown. People wanted, perhaps, to be able to continue to perceive Willa Cather as offering positive possibilities for what it meant to be American. The Nebraska boy-turned-soldier of *One of Ours* undercuts, through the novels depiction of "unheroic" behavior, some of the sought-for stereotypes. The book was seen as being disloyal to its roots, its Nebraskan setting; Ernest Hemingway criticized it in an unpublished letter, and H. L. Mencken spoke out against it in a review. In the U.K. it was criticized for being too American. It seemed, despite other supporting reviews and the coveted Pulitzer, that Cather had lost the acclaim that had formerly been hers.

Indeed, during the 1930s and 1940s Cather's reputation was in decline. The New Critics viewed her as reactionary; she came to be associated with the writing of soft romances, which displayed little of the bite or consummate artistry of her earlier work. When her essays appeared in *Not under Forty* (1936) they were sparsely reviewed, like her poetry and short stories, although her later novel *Sapphira and the Slave Girl* (1940) at last attracted more interest and did receive some rather grudging praise.

From the 1960s onward, interest in her writing has been much revived by academic criticism, and feminist interpretations in particular

have created a new context and a new climate of reception for her works. Contemporary critics place Willa Cather as a writer whose importance permeates several literary traditions. Her output may be seen as a culmination of nineteenth-century "regionalism," a mode that enters and brings to recognition in a variety of ways aspects of life that had not, up to then, occupied significant space on the literary stage. She is also seen as part of the turn-of-the-century "pioneer generation" of women writers determined to invade the (male) precincts of established art. At the same time, her work is viewed as contributing to a narrative of domestic ritual, or of being constructed in terms of particular models of time and space.

Most recently, and certainly since the first extended and overt critical discussion of her lesbian sexuality by Sharon O'Brien in 1987, much analysis of her work has focused on what is "hidden" or masked in the text. As well as alerting readers to previously unconsidered nuancings of gender, such discussions have opened the way to a consideration of Cather's relation with her southern heritage, and to how certain charges of racism and political conservatism that have been leveled against her might be addressed.

MY ÁNTONIA AND THE PARADOX OF THE PASTORAL

Leo Marx in *The Machine in the Garden: Technology and the Pastoral Idea in America* (1964) characterizes literary use of the pastoral as increasingly fraught with irony as the nineteenth century progressed, pointing up its changing function in the American imagination. "Down to the twentieth century," Marx believes, "the imagination of Americans was dominated by the idea of transforming the wild heartland into . . . a new 'Garden of the World.'" The use in literature of the pastoral represented the paradoxes of this imaginative construction.

In a world with "no middle distance," a writer can be inside and outside his or her tale at the same time, occupying extremes of perspective that fruitfully illuminate paradoxical aspects of the created world. Cather, like her narrator Jim Burden, led a life characterized by such duality. Her attitude to Nebraska exemplifies this. The first thing she discovered there was "ugliness," and, writing from Red Cloud shortly before her departure to Pittsburgh, she refers to it as "Siberia." Yet the fear that she will never escape coexists with the sense that in some way she "belongs": Nebraska has been "the happiness and the curse of my life" (as quoted in Bennett). She does, of course, "get away" in that, like Jim Burden she acquires an education, travels widely, and moves in sophisticated cultural and professional worlds. But, through the figure of Jim,

the value of such an escape is scrutinized. The motor of *My Ántonia*'s tale is an examination of the sensibility of a man who has allowed himself to be "colonized" by the future. Jim, as much as the characters in Theodore Dreiser's *Sister Carrie* or *Jennie Gerhardt* (1911), is involved in a re-visioning of the notion of frontier from rural- into urban-expansionist terms. But counter-pointing this motor is another, that of Ántonia's failed attempt to be colonized by the "dream" of an urban life of material success and advancement. Cather's mythic/pastoral method, then, allows her to examine, from two opposed views simultaneously, the possibilities of "belonging," which the American Dream, in its process of change and mutation, may no longer allow.

Select Bibliography

EDITIONS

My Ántonia. Boston and New York: Houghton Mifflin, 1918. (The 1995 edition, with a foreword by Kathleen Norris, is cited in this essay; the Virago Press edition, 1998, has an illuminating preface by A. S. Byatt.)

OTHER WORKS BY CATHER

One of Ours. New York: Knopf, 1922; London: Virago, 1987.

A Lost Lady. New York: Knopf, 1923; London: Virago, 1980.

"Nebraska: The End of the First Cycle." *The Nation,* September 5, 1923, pp. 236–238.

Death Comes for the Archbishop. New York: Knopf, 1927.

Not under Forty. New York: Knopf, 1936. (Essays.)

Sapphira and the Slave Girl. New York: Knopf, 1940; London: Virago, 1986.

The Kingdom of Art: Willa Cather's First Principles and Critical Statements, 1893–1896. Edited by Bernice Slote. Lincoln: University of Nebraska Press, 1967.

The World and the Parish: Willa Cather's Articles and Reviews, 1893–1902. Edited by William M. Curtin. Lincoln: University of Nebraska Press, 1970. (Includes "The Literary Situation in 1895.")

Willa Cather in Person: Interviews, Speeches and Letters. Edited by Brent L. Bohlke. Lincoln: University of Nebraska Press, 1986.

SECONDARY WORKS

Ambrose, Jamie. *Willa Cather: Writing at the Frontier.* Oxford: Berg, 1988.

Bennett, Mildred R. *The World of Willa Cather.* New York: Dodd, Mead & Company,

1951; Lincoln: University of Nebraska Press, 1961, 1995. (An anecdotal account of Cather's Nebraska background and influences.)

Carden, Mary Paniccia. "Creative Fertility and the National Romance in Willa Cather's *O Pioneers!* and *My Ántonia.*" *Modern Fiction Studies* 45, no. 2 (1999): 275–302.

Conlogue, William. "Managing the Farm, Educating the Farmer: *O Pioneers!* and the New Agriculture." *Great Plains Quarterly* 21, no. 1 (2001): 3–15.

Crane, Joan. *Willa Cather: A Bibliography.* Lincoln: University of Nebraska Press, 1982.

Daiches, David. *Willa Cather: A Critical Introduction.* Ithaca, N.Y.: Cornell University Press, 1951.

Feld, Rose C. Interview with Willa Cather. *New York Times Book Review,* December 21, 1924, p. 11.

Geismar, Maxwell David. *The Last of the Provincials: The American Novel, 1915–1925.* Boston: Houghton Mifflin, 1947.

Gelfant, Blanche H. "The Forgotten Reaping-Hook: Sex in *My Ántonia.*" *American Literature* 43 (March 1971): 60–82.

Holmes, Catherine D. "Jim Burden's Lost Worlds: Exile in *My Ántonia.*" *Twentieth Century Literature* 45, no. 3 (1999): 336–346.

Kaye, Frances W. "The Virginian and Ántonia Shimerda: Different Sides of the Western Coin." In *Women and Western American Literature.* Edited by Helen Winter Stauffer and Susan J. Rosowski. Troy, N.J.: Whitson Publishing, 1982.

Kleiman, Ed. "Bipolar Vision in Willa Cather's *My Ántonia.*" *English Studies* 82, no. 2 (April 2001): 146–153.

Lambert, Dorothy. "The Defeat of a Hero: Autonomy and Sexuality in *My Ántonia.*" *American Literature* 53, no. 4 (January 1982): 676.

Lee, Hermione. *Willa Cather: A Life Saved Up.* London: Virago, 1997. (An important scholarly work that is also highly readable and entertaining.)

Lindemann, Marilee. *Willa Cather: Queering America.* New York: Columbia University Press, 1999. (A contemporary approach to questions of Cather's divided sexuality.)

Lucenti, Lisa Marie. "Willa Cather's *My Ántonia:* Haunting the Houses of Memory." *Twentieth Century Literature* 46, no. 2 (2000): 193–213.

Norris, Frank. "The Decline of the Magazine Short Story." *Wave* 16 (January 30, 1897): 3. Reprinted in *The Literary Criticism of Frank Norris.* Edited by Donald Pizer. New York: Russell and Russell, 1964.

O'Brien, Sharon. *Willa Cather: The Emerging Voice, 1873–1912.* Oxford: Oxford University Press, 1987; Cambridge, Mass.: Harvard University Press, 1997. (The 1997 edition contains a new preface, illustrations, facsimiles, and genealogical table. O'Brien was probably the first critic to write openly about Cather's divided sexuality.)

———, ed. *New Essays on* My Ántonia. New York: Cambridge University Press, 1999. (Demonstrates range of contemporary approaches to Cather's work.)

O'Connor, Margaret Anne, ed. *Willa Cather: The Contemporary Reviews.* New York: Cambridge University Press, 2001. (A fascinating account of early twentieth-century reception of Cather's novels.)

Reynolds, Guy. *Willa Cather in Context: Progress, Race, Empire.* Basingstoke, Eng.: Macmillan, 1996.

———. "Willa Cather's Sexual Aesthetics and the Male Homosexual Literary Tradition." *Review of English Studies* 52, no. 206 (May 2001): 301–302.

Rosowski, Susan. *The Voyage Perilous: Willa Cather's Romanticism.* Lincoln: University of Nebraska Press, 1986.

Schroeter, James, ed. *Willa Cather and Her Critics.* Ithaca, N.Y.: Cornell University Press, 1967.

Slote, Bernice, and Virginia Faulkner, eds. *The Art of Willa Cather.* Lincoln: University of Nebraska Press, 1974.

Tellefsen, Blythe. "Blood in the Wheat: Willa Cather's *My Ántonia.*" *Studies in American Fiction* 27, no. 2 (1999): 229–244.

Thomas, Susie. *Willa Cather.* London: Macmillan, 1990.

Van Ghent, Dorothy. *Willa Cather.* Minneapolis: University of Minnesota Press, 1964.

Welty, Eudora. "The House of Willa Cather." In her *The Eye of the Story: Selected Essays and Reviews.* New York: Vintage, 1979. Pp. 41–46.

Woodress, James. *Willa Cather: Her Life and Art.* New York: Pegasus, 1970.

———. *Willa Cather: A Literary Life.* Lincoln: University of Nebraska Press, 1987.

Frederick Douglass'
My Bondage and My Freedom

MARK RICHARDSON

Cotton thread holds the union together.
Patriotism is for holidays & summer evenings
with music and rockets, but cotton thread is the
union.

(Ralph Waldo Emerson, 1844)

RALPH WALDO EMERSON had, in 1844, much warrant for his sour observation that cotton, not patriotism, held the union together, which is of course an observation about slavery. Cotton had been cultivated in South Carolina since 1767. But not until the 1780s and 1790s, when more profitable varieties were imported from the Bahamas, did large-scale planting take hold. Cotton exports from South Carolina rose from 9,840 pounds in 1790 to 8,000,000 pounds in 1800. The introduction of the cotton gin in 1793 made the processing of cotton cheap, and, with the opening of new markets, investment in the crop expanded quickly in the early years of the nineteenth century across the whole of the lower South—territory that had only recently been brought into the union. And with cotton went slavery.

National production rates over the period leading up the Civil War illustrate the growth of the commodity, which, by 1840, came to be known simply as "King Cotton," in a fittingly antirepublican phrase. In 1810, 171,000 bales of cotton were produced; in 1830, 731,000 bales; in 1850, 2,133,000, and in 1859, 5,387,000. During the period 1815–1861 cotton was consistently the top U.S. export. In the years 1836–1840 its value was $321 million, or 43 percent of total U.S. export income. Between 1856 and 1860 these figures had risen to $744.6 million, or 54 percent of total export income. Atop this economic base there arose a body of opinion—theological, political, ethnological, and medical—to support the idea that the South's peculiar institution was not merely profitable for the relatively small class of men who engaged in it on a large scale, but, as John C. Calhoun said, a "positive good" for the nation as a whole, and even for the world. The new means of producing wealth had given rise to certain mores. And these crystallized into a new, and frankly white supremacist, morality, which, as John Jay Chapman—the grandson of Maria Weston Chapman, an associate of William Lloyd Garrison—later pointed out would have shocked Americans of Jefferson's day. Millions of women and men—slaves—had become, as Frederick Douglass put it in 1852, "food for the cotton-field." Emerson, for his part, said simply: "Things are in the

163

saddle and ride men." Subordination of men to things was not what the "New World" was meant to bring about. And against this state of affairs, Douglass would, in *My Bondage and My Freedom*, set his own "Columbian," New World ideal of an America not dedicated to production, profit, and consumption, whatever the human cost, but instead to the proper conquest of all strictly material interests, of all interests that would see in men and women chiefly bodies for the making of hay. It would be an America of men and women, not of markets; and a genuinely "republican" Constitution, not cotton thread, would hold it together.

Several schools of antislavery thought flourished in the years between the Revolution and the Civil War. In two of these schools Frederick Douglass was a major figure. Jefferson's generation looked forward to the gradual abolition of slavery, if by no other means than by the work of Almighty God. Obviously, no coherent program of action necessarily follows from this line of reasoning. But in conjunction with the idea of gradual emancipation there arose various colonization schemes, which sought to repatriate slaves and free persons of color, to Africa or to Haiti or some other Caribbean nation. Colonization enjoyed a vogue in the early decades of the nineteenth century and persisted even into the middle years of the Civil War.

Against both colonization schemes and gradualism arose the Garrisonian school, named for its founder and great animating force, William Lloyd Garrison. After brief flirtations both with gradualism and colonization, for which he publicly (and self-scathingly) repented, Garrison developed the doctrine of "immediate and unconditional emancipation," which he propounded in *The Liberator*, the weekly antislavery paper he published in Boston beginning in 1831. Immediacy was not the only novel element in his abolitionism; he also demanded full citizenship rights for black American men. And with Garrison's appearance, the character of the antislavery movement changed forever.

CHRONOLOGY

1818	Born a slave, Frederick Augustus Washington Bailey, in February, near Tuckahoe Creek, Talbot County, Maryland, the son of Harriet Bailey, a slave, and an unknown white father.
1819–1823	Raised by maternal grandmother.
1824	Sent to the Lloyd plantation on the Wye River, twelve miles distant.
1826	Sent to Baltimore to live with the family of Hugh Auld.
1827–1832	Teaches himself to read; works in the shipyards; obtains used copy of *The Columbian Orator*, a primer.
1833	Sent to live in St. Michaels, Talbot County.
1834	Sent to live with Covey, "the Negro breaker."
1835	Hired out to William Freeland, a Talbot County planter; organizes a secret Sabbath school for slaves.
1836	Conspires, with several other slaves, to escape; is betrayed and arrested on April 2. Sent back to to live with Hugh Auld.
1837	Works in the shipyards; is compelled to turn over all of his pay to his master. Meets Anna Murray, a free black woman working as a housekeeper.
1838	Escapes from slavery. Marries Anna Murray; takes the surname Douglass, after the hero in Scott's poem "The Lady of the Lake"; takes odd jobs loading ships, hauling coal, etc.
1839	Subscribes to *The Liberator*.
1841	In August, takes the stage alongside William Lloyd Garrison at a convention of the Massachusetts Anti-Slavery Society in Nantucket; becomes a paid general agent of the Society; travels around New England speaking.
1844	Publicly endorses Garrison's "disunionist" abolitionism.
1845	Publishes *Narrative of the Life of Frederick Douglass, An American Slave*,

Written By Himself in May. Leaves for Great Britain in August, where for the next two years he travels, speaking and raising $711.66 to buy his freedom.

1847	Returns to Boston in April. Buys printing press and establishes his own paper, *The North Star,* in Rochester, New York.
1848	Family joins him in Rochester. Buys nine-room house on Alexander Street; shelters fugitive slaves en route to Canada. Meets John Brown.
1851	Breaks with the Garrisonians; embraces "political abolitionism"; becomes active in the Liberty Party.
	Changes name of his newspaper to *Frederick Douglass's Paper;* accepts financial backing from Gerrit Smith.
1855	*My Bondage and My Freedom* appears in August.
1858	Begins publishing *Douglass's Monthly.*
1860	Lectures in England, Scotland. *Frederick Douglass's Paper* ceases publication.
1863	Recruits volunteers for the Massachusetts 54th Colored Regiment. Meets Lincoln at the White House in August.
1865	Attends Lincoln's Second Inaugural on March 4. After the assassination, delivers eulogy for Lincoln in Rochester.
1870	Moves to Washington, D.C. Becomes editor in chief of *The New National Era.*
1873	Reveals for the first time the details of his escape from slavery.
1874	Appointed president of the Freedman's Savings and Trust Company. *The New National Era* ceases publication.
1877	President Rutherford B. Hayes appoints Douglass U.S. Marshall for the District of Columbia.
1881	President James A. Garfield appoints Douglass Recorder of Deeds for the District of Columbia. Publishes *The Life and Times of Frederick Douglass* in November.
1882	Wife Anna Murray Douglass dies in August.
1884	Marries Helen Pitts, a white woman, in January.
1886–1887	Resigns as Recorder of Deeds. Travels with Helen to England, Europe, Egypt.
1892	Befriends Ida B. Wells, the young black journalist and activist; campaigns against the outbreak of lynchings in the South. Publishes expanded edition of *The Life and Times.*
1895	Dies at home on February 20.

Garrison refined his doctrine over the course of the 1830s. In August 1831 Nat Turner led an insurrection among slaves in Southampton, Virginia. More than fifty whites died in the fighting and more than a hundred blacks. It did not go unnoticed in Massachusetts that Virginia authorities called on the federal government, under the terms of the Constitution, to assist it in suppressing the rebellion. For this reason, and because the Constitution obliged states where slavery did not exist to return fugitive slaves to their owners, Garrison concluded that the Constitution was, both in theory and in practice, a pro-slavery instrument. "There is much declamation," Garrison said in the pages of *The Liberator,* "about the sacredness of the compact which was formed between the free and the slave States on the adoption of the Constitution. A sacred compact, forsooth! We pronounce it the most bloody and heaven-daring arrangement ever made for the continuance and protection of a system of the most atrocious villainy ever exhibited on earth." "So long as we continue one body," he wrote, "as union—as nation—the compact involves us in the guilt and danger of slavery." It took some years for the new thinking to settle out, but here was the beginning of Garrisonian disunionism: the call for the dissolution of the union and for nonparticipation in electoral politics. (Such participation implied consent to the terms of the U.S. Constitution, the document under whose aegis elections are ultimately conducted.) By 1842 the masthead of each number of *The Liberator* bore this unequivocal banner: "THE UNITED STATES CONSTITUTION IS A COVENANT WITH DEATH AND AN AGREEMENT WITH HELL! NO UNION WITH SLAVEHOLDERS!" With that, Garrisonian doctrine had matured, and here it would remain until war came in April 1861. Garrison and his adherents traveled from Maine to Illinois, and beyond. They held rallies; debated their opponents, both within and without the wider abolition movement; distributed pamphlets, books, and newspapers; raised money; and, on occasion, ritually burned copies of the U.S. Constitution in town squares. Frederick Douglass entered this Garrisonian movement with astonishing force in 1841. Within months he was its most popular orator. His first autobiography, *Narrative of the Life of Frederick Douglass, an American Slave, Written By Himself,* appeared in 1845 with a preface by Garrison. Advertisements for it ran in the pages of *The Liberator.* Douglass' *Narrative* was published out of the same office in Cornhill Street, Boston, that printed Garrison's great weekly, and the closing paragraphs of the book take special pains to extol (rightly so, after all) the newspaper. Douglass' debt to the Garrisonians is evident in the *Narrative* from beginning to end. But he would not long remain with them.

The great rival to Garrisonian doctrine emerged from a movement that came to be known as "political abolitionism." Political abolitionism started in New York State around the small but influential Liberty Party, whose central figure and financial backer was the wealthy landholder Gerrit Smith. Smith and the Liberty Party maintained, against the Garrisonians, that the Constitution was antislavery in spirit, notwithstanding the clauses that provided for the return of fugitives, the qualified protection of the slave trade, and the use of federal power in suppressing insurrection. Smith's position was dubious as a reading of the Constitution. But when put into practice it allowed, as

Garrisonian disunionism did not, for the vigorous pursuit, through the instrument of electoral politics, of a policy of complete and immediate abolition; and it held out the productive promise of perfecting the Constitution, a possibility in harmony with the general tendency of American political development.

Douglass began to drift toward political abolition in the late 1840s. The move was complete in 1851 when he merged his paper, the *North Star,* with the *Liberty Party Paper,* and accepted financial backing from Smith in the new enterprise. When *My Bondage and My Freedom* appeared four years later, published by a firm in western New York State, the stronghold of political abolition, it bore, set in the ornate patchwork of typefaces used for such purposes in those days, a dedication to "Honorable Gerrit Smith as a slight token of esteem for his character, admiration for his genius and benevolence," and in gratitude for his "ranking slavery with piracy and murder," and for "denying it either a legal or constitutional existence." The break with Garrison was irrevocable, and Douglass suffered much for it in the Garrisonian press, where he was castigated, often in tawdry ways, as an apostate who had allowed himself to be "bought out" by Gerrit Smith. The view he now took of the Constitution is epitomized in a speech he later gave in 1863:

> I hold that the Federal Government was never, in its essence, anything but an antislavery government. Abolish slavery tomorrow, and not a sentence or syllable of the Constitution need be altered. It was purposely so framed as to give no claim, no sanction to the claim, of property in man. If in its origin slavery had any relation to the government, it was only as the scaffolding to the magnificent structure, to be removed as soon as the building was completed.

MY BONDAGE AND MY FREEDOM

Douglass' first autobiography, the *Narrative* of 1845, was a notable success. By 1849 it had gone through two editions in the United States and three in Great Britain. Why, then, did Douglass publish a second autobiography in 1855? The question is the more intriguing because only 7 percent of the new book, by word count, covers ground not traversed in the *Narrative*. *My Bondage and My Freedom* is hardly a supplement to the earlier book, and not by any means its mere continuation; it is instead a radical revision. Moreover, in *The Life and Times of Frederick Douglass* (1881), the portion of the book devoted to the period through 1855 remains materially unchanged from *My Bondage and My Freedom.* There can be little doubt that the latter is Douglass' definitive account of himself, although teachers in high schools and universities usually assign the shorter, more Garrisonian, and less politically complex text found in the anthologies.

DOUGLASS' BREAK WITH THE GARRISONIANS:
LITERARY CONSEQUENCES

The reader of *My Bondage and My Freedom* soon enough discovers that Douglass' apprenticeship to the Garrisonians was not entirely to his liking. Compare the following two accounts of his watershed inaugural appearance on the podium in Nantucket in 1841, the first from the *Narrative*, the second from *My Bondage:*

[1845:] I had not long been a reader of the "Liberator," before I got a pretty correct idea of the principles, measures and spirit of the anti-slavery reform. I took right hold of the cause. I could do but little; but what I could, I did with a joyful heart, and never felt happier than when in an anti-slavery meeting. I seldom had much to say at the meetings, because what I wanted to say was said so much better by others. But, while attending an anti-slavery convention at Nantucket, on the 11th of August, 1841, I felt strongly moved to speak, and was at the same time much urged to do so by Mr. William C. Coffin, a gentleman who had heard me speak in the colored people's meeting at New Bedford. It was a severe cross, and I took it up reluctantly. The truth was, I felt myself a slave, and the idea of speaking to white people weighed me

down. I spoke but a few moments, when I felt a degree of freedom, and said what I desired with considerable ease. From that time until now, I have been engaged in pleading the cause of my brethren—with what success, and with what devotion, I leave those acquainted with my labors to decide.

[1855:] My speech on this occasion is about the only one I ever made, of which I do not remember a single connected sentence. It was with the utmost difficulty that I could stand erect, or that I could command and articulate two words without hesitation and stammering. I trembled in every limb. I am not sure that my embarrassment was not the most effective part of my speech, if speech it could be called. At any rate, this is about the only part of my performance that I now distinctly remember. But excited and convulsed as I was, the audience, though remarkably quiet before, became as much excited as myself. Mr. Garrison followed me, taking me as his text; and now, whether I had made an eloquent speech in behalf of freedom or not, his was one never to be forgotten by those who heard it. Those who had heard Mr. Garrison oftenest, and had known him longest, were astonished. It was an effort of unequaled power, sweeping down, like a very tornado, every opposing barrier, whether of sentiment or opinion.

So far, both accounts are friendly to Garrison. In fact, the second, from *My Bondage,* is apparently the friendlier of the two—save for one telling remark, from which the rest of this startling chapter will derive: after Douglass spoke, Garrison took him "as his text," it is written. The metaphor is homiletic. Douglass is the text on which Garrison's sermon is based; he is the matter, Garrison the expositor; he is the body, Garrison the mind; he is the storyteller, Garrison the interpreter; he deals in facts, Garrison in theory. Douglass' metaphor intimates the more patronizing features of Garrison's patronage. It is not surprising that Douglass, as he confesses in the 1845 account, felt ill at ease addressing white people.

John Collins, a confederate of Garrison, accompanied Douglass on his first lecture tour, and, in introducing him, inevitably called him "a graduate from the peculiar institution" with his "*diploma written* on [his] *back.*" Douglass' body was, for the Garrisonians, the originating site of his writing; his scars, and not his words and thoughts, authenticated him. The interest his handlers took in that body was, or so at times it appeared, a bit unseemly. Here arose a problem. Douglass explains:

> Among the first duties assigned me, on entering the ranks, was to travel, in company with Mr. George Foster, to secure subscribers to the "Antislavery Standard" and the "Liberator." . . . I was generally introduced as a *"chattel"*—a *"thing"*—a piece of southern *"property"*— the chairman assuring the audience that *it* could speak. . . . During the first three or four months, my speeches were almost exclusively made up of narrations of my own personal experience as a slave. . . . "Give us the facts," said Collins, "we will take care of the philosophy." Just here arose some embarrassment. It was impossible for me to repeat the same old story month after month, and to keep up my interest in it. It was new to the people, it is true, but it was an old story to me; and to go through with it night after night, was a task altogether too mechanical for my nature. "Tell your story, Frederick," would whisper my then revered friend, William Lloyd Garrison, as I stepped upon the platform. I could not always obey, for I was now reading and thinking. New views of the subject were presented to my mind. It did not entirely satisfy me to *narrate* wrongs; I felt like *denouncing* them. . . . "People won't believe you ever was a slave, Frederick, if you keep on this way," said Friend Foster. "Be yourself," said Collins, "and tell your story." It was said to me, "Better have a *little* of the plantation manner of speech than not; 'tis not best that you seem too learned." These excellent friends were actuated by the best of motives, and were not altogether wrong in their advice; and still I must speak just the word that seemed to *me* the word to be spoken *by* me.

It was not necessarily gratifying, or so Douglass hinted in 1855, to be taken as a text for others to expound on. The lecture platform, as Eric Sundquist points out in *To Wake the Nations* (1993) in connection with this passage, soon came to seem rather like an auction block. Douglass felt he had been pinned down, and also discouraged, at least implicitly, from thinking too much. His office, essentially, was to show himself and to obey. Douglass was on display when he mounted the stage, in a way that neither Collins nor Garrison, nor any of the white abolitionists, ever was: his body was the matter, not his mind. Collins enjoins Douglass to be himself, but this really means, "Put on blackface; be a white man's idea of what a black man truly is. Otherwise [so goes the unstated argument], no white man will recognize you; to a white audience you will be, and in the most literal sense of the word, *incredible.*" The abolitionist lecture hall becomes a theater for the staging of a singularly highbrow sort of minstrel show, with the familiar—and deeply sympathetic, to white hearts and minds— "plantation darky," the sort of black man with whom these white Northerners could most be at ease. Who, then, shall represent the slave? The question has both political and literary implications, and Douglass wrote *My Bondage and My Freedom* to address both. In it he would lay claim to the main and most productive tradition in American politics, thereby breaking out of the confines of Garrisonian doctrine; he would appear, in its pages, not chiefly as a black man, and certainly not as a sentimental "plantation darky" in contemplation of whom white women might weep, but as, in the words of the fine introduction to the first edition of the book, the "Representative American man"—as, in fact, the very "type of his countrymen." This required that any trace of the deference he shows in the *Narrative*, with respect to the Garrisonians, be expunged, the better that he might emerge from behind the mask of white patronage. Instead of including authenticating prefaces and letters from white eminences, *My Bondage* begins with an introduction written by James M'Cune Smith, a black, Edinburgh-trained physician. Smith puts the matter unforgettably: "The same strong self-hood" that led Douglass "to measure strength with Mr. Covey," the Negro breaker whom Douglass challenged and humiliated while still in his teens, led him to "wrench himself from the embrace of the Garrisonians." The implicit analogy must have stung Garrison to the quick. But he and his protégé were at irreconcilable odds—partly for party-political reasons but also owing to the scandal-mongering attacks against Douglass that had been appearing in the Garrisonian press since 1851.

The novelty of Douglass' style, in *My Bondage and My Freedom,* is easily gauged by comparison of its opening sentences to the corresponding passage in the 1845 *Narrative.* The latter begins simply enough with an account of his birth in 1818: "I was born in Tuckahoe, near Hillsborough, and about twelve miles from Easton, in Talbot county, Maryland." In 1855 this is greatly expanded:

In Talbot county, Eastern Shore, Maryland, near Easton, the county town of that county, there is a small district of country, thinly populated, and remarkable for nothing that I know of more than for the worn-out, sandy, desert-like appearance of its soil, the general dilapidation of its farms and fences, the indigent and spiritless character of its inhabitants, and the prevalence of ague and fever.

The name of this singularly unpromising and truly famine stricken district is Tuckahoe, a name well known to all Marylanders, black and white. It was given to this section of country probably, at the first, merely in derision; or it may possibly have been applied to it, as I have heard, because some one of its earlier inhabitants had been guilty of the petty meanness of stealing a hoe—or taking a hoe—that did not belong to him. Eastern Shore men usually pronounce the word *took,* as *tuck; Took-a-hoe,* therefore, is, in Maryland parlance, *Tuckahoe.* But, whatever may have been its origin—and about this I will not be positive—that name has stuck to the district in question; and it is seldom mentioned but with contempt and derision, on account of the barrenness of its soil, and the ignorance, indolence, and poverty of its people. Decay and ruin are everywhere visible, and the thin population of the place would have quitted it long ago, but for the Choptank river, which runs through it, from which they take abundance of shad and herring, and plenty of ague and fever.

It was in this dull, flat, and unthrifty district, or neighborhood, surrounded by a white population of the lowest order, indolent and drunken to a proverb, and among slaves, who seemed to ask, "*Oh! what's the use?*" every time they lifted a hoe, that I—without any fault of mine—was born, and spent the first years of my childhood.

The style, the *address,* of this second passage is arch to the point of satire. One can sense an excess of facility, of power held in reserve, power found only in writers of uncommon self-possession. This is evident even in the structure of the sentences, the first of which turns neatly upon its fourfold parallelism, setting in devastating equation desert soil, dilapidated farm, indigent character, and raging fever. And then there is the syntactic wit of the following sentence, which suggests the droll Augustan manner of Alexander Pope: "Decay and ruin are everywhere visible, and the thin population of the place would have quitted it long ago, but for the Choptank river, which runs through it, from which they take abundance of shad and herring, and plenty of ague and fever." The verb "take" has two objects, grammatically parallel but semantically disjunctive: one does not fish for "ague and fever" unless one is an indigent denizen of a barren land and too shiftless to get up and leave. And consider the playfully spurious etymology of the name "Tuckahoe." Here, surely, is a bit of satire carried over from Douglass' immensely popular lectures. As Douglass no doubt knew, Tuckahoe is a common place-name in the eastern United States. It is derived—though this Douglass might not have known—from the Algonquin name of an edible root. Still, Douglass' intimation that "Tuckahoe" has a comical meaning is not entirely off the mark, and it may well be that the name was derisively applied to the inhabitants of that district of rural Talbot County, though not because they made a habit of stealing hoes. George Stewart's *American Place-Names* (1970) reports that "the word passed into English, probably in the 17th century, and most of the namings would seem to be English rather than Indian, and to be from an acquired meaning, i.e., a backwoods or folksy person, such as might live on wild tubers, but with a humorous more than a derogatory suggestion." However that may be, the leisured expansiveness, the liberty, with which this overture is allowed to unfold, characterizes the prose of *My Bondage and My Freedom*. The reader at once understands that *this* is a narrator who will not limit himself merely to giving the facts. And having dispensed with the notion that Douglass means simply to narrate wrongs, one can consider the outlines of what might indeed be called his philosophy of slavery.

DOUGLASS' PHILOSOPHY OF SLAVERY

Douglass tells us of the time—he was still a mere boy—when it first occurred to him to ask: *"Why are some people slaves, and others masters?"* That this question should have overtaken him at all, when slavery everywhere presented itself as "natural," seems to require some explanation. And Douglass takes the view—authorized, if any authority is needed, by the Declaration of Independence—that the will to be free is in fact "an inborn dream of . . . human nature—a constant menace to slavery—and one which all the powers of slavery [are] unable to silence or extinguish." Slavery, then, can never relax; it is an institution most unnatural, whose price is eternal vigilance. Later Douglass will liken slavery to a temperamental and delicate machine, which requires "conductors or safety valves"—for example, the "holiday" permitted slaves at the turn of the New Year—"to carry off explosive elements inseparable from the human mind, when reduced to the condition of slavery. . . . woe to the slaveholder when he undertakes to hinder or to prevent the operation of these electric conductors." Men and women have to be taught to be slaves and masters. "The equality of nature," Douglass says, "is strongly asserted in childhood, and childhood requires children for associates. *Color* makes no difference with a child. Are you a child with wants, tastes and

pursuits common to children, not put on, but natural? then, were you black as ebony you would be welcome to the child of alabaster whiteness." Young boys, he says, feel a hatred of slavery that "springs from nature, unseared and unperverted." Nature, in fact, does "almost nothing to prepare men and women to be either slaves or slaveholders." At such moments Douglass advances what might be termed a Romantic, or Rousseauian, argument: social institutions—in this case, slavery—deform us, pervert our native inclination to charity and loving-kindness. To the hoary question, "Does 'civilization' distort or complement human 'nature'?" he appears to answer, "The former, not the latter." Dispense with slavery, then, and all will be well, or anyway well enough.

But the cruelty of slavery as it developed in North America and the intractability of racism there seem to require a more worldly explanation of the country's inhumanity—a bleaker, less reassuring one; and this, too, emerges in Douglass' narrative. Inborn to us, as well as a love of freedom, is a will to power that has markedly cruel features. Douglass' master, it is written, "could commit outrages, deep, dark and nameless." These outrages, as is clear from facts soon narrated, are at once erotic and violent; they are nothing less than *sadistic*. But, lest Douglass' master be seen as a monster, Douglass assures us that Captain Anthony "was not by nature worse than other men," any one of whom are therefore quite capable of binding a beautiful young woman to a ceiling joist, stripping her to the waist, and, after "shocking preliminaries," and to the accompaniment of "tantalizing epithets," no doubt lewd in nature, lashing her almost to the point of death, and all the while taking delight in the prospect. Inborn human nature, when it is allowed an uninhibited self-expression, will satisfy its darker appetites. This view of humankind is rather more Freudian—or Calvinistic, for that matter—than Rousseauian. Human beings are by nature savage—even depraved—in this view. They need, desperately, the complement of discipline, of some sort of curb against their freedom to act. This discipline may be, to adopt a secular vocabulary, civilization, notwithstanding its inevitable discontents (to paraphrase Freud), which are simply the price to pay to become something more than "a nation of savages" (to borrow Douglass' phrase). As Douglass sees it—and the mild paradox with which he expresses the point is nicely Freudian—the great desiderata are "the just *restraints* of *free* society" (emphasis added): Reason and Chastity. These effect a sublimation, into more socially useful channels, of the rapacious will-to-power that is, by all appearances, simply a human birthright. To realize one's humanity, to transcend one's animality, a person must be disciplined—but with the tempering whip of Reason, not with the incendiary lash of Passion. The problem with slavery is not so much that it entails too much "discipline," but that it involves discipline of the wrong kind—a discipline that is in fact an expression of license (and lust) rather than an instrument of control. The slave system everywhere "robs its victims," master and slave alike, "of every earthly incentive to [lead] a holy life." This fact should chasten us all, for, as Douglass says, "Capt. Anthony might have been as humane a man, and every way as respectable, as many who now oppose the slave system; certainly as humane and respectable as are members of society generally." The twofold idea is this: (1) Slavery sets the passions free, when in fact they should be imprisoned; and (2) human passions are everywhere the same.

Essential to slavery is a kind of general-purpose, sensualizing exercise in debauchery. Consider the following account of a typical holiday on the plantation, a holiday which is one of those protective safety valves built into the machinery of slavery.

> When the slave asks for a few hours of virtuous freedom, his cunning master takes advantage of his ignorance, and cheers him with a dose of vicious and revolting dissipation, artfully labeled with the name of LIBERTY. We were induced to drink, I among the rest, and when the holidays were over,

> we all staggered up from our filth and wallowing, took a long breath, and went away to our various fields of work; feeling, upon the whole, rather glad to go from that which our masters artfully deceived us into the belief was freedom, back again to the arms of slavery. It was not what we had taken it to be, nor what it might have been, had it not been abused by us. It was about as well to be a slave to *master*, as to be a slave to *rum* and *whisky*.

"When a slave is drunk," Douglass concludes, "the slaveholder has no fear that he will plan an insurrection; no fear that he will escape to the north. It is the sober, thinking slave who is dangerous, and needs the vigilance of his master, to keep him a slave." This is more than a mere temperance tract to appease the teetotalers among the abolitionists (of whom there were a great many, including Douglass). The point is that the slave system intoxicates the slave with a delusive sort of liberty the better to make liberty seem toxic. This delusive liberty is, of course, libertinism, or license. And it involves the slave in a brutal descent into sensuality, which Douglass always associates with slavery. Slavery, owing to its very laxity, draws humans down into a state of "revolting dissipation," an animalistic "wallowing" in the "filth" of the body—of the senses. Demon rum, it turns out, is a very efficient overseer: as does slavery, it imprisons reason and makes us thrall to the passions. Sobriety is what is called for; and sobriety is but another name for chastity—for a principled resistance to voluptuary indulgence.

Elsewhere, Douglass calls slavery an "unchaste" institution. A sober slave is a thinking slave—a slave who lives life in the mind, not in the body—a slave who is properly self-possessed. Master the body and you master the self; banish libertinism and liberty follows. Freedom, the attaining of a perfect abolition, is a "resurrection from the dark and pestiferous tomb of slavery," from the "blight and mildew" of a stupefying, merely *bodily* existence. To be a slave is to be entombed in the body, buried alive in it—to be bound in altogether by its fate. To be fully emancipated is to transcend the limits of a merely corporeal existence (the idea seems almost Platonic). It is to achieve a chaste, and therefore perfect, "manhood"—to achieve, through reason, a final mastery of passion. This is no easy struggle, and Frederick Douglass is not a prude. Slavery reveals unspeakable things about us; it does not produce them. And true abolition is nothing less than a struggle to overcome an inborn kind of depravity, a vestigial animality, which slavery is peculiarly (though not uniquely) suited to bringing out. Douglass' philosophy of slavery, in its bleaker phases, may explain his willingness to adopt the much more worldly, and much less absolutist, tactic of political abolitionism. And it may explain as well why he could not, at the end of the day, accept the Garrisonian proposal that New England purify itself of slavery by dissolving the union. Men and women being what they naturally are could purify neither them nor any nation they compose simply by cutting the slave states loose. "Abolition" of the most radical sort is an (almost hopeless) effort to conquer what Mr. Kurtz, in Joseph Conrad's "Heart of Darkness" calls the "horror." The "horror" is what slavery brings out into the open; and the events of 1861–1865 did not finish the job of dispatching *that*. Abolition of slavery to instinct, to passion, to intemperance, to the gross sensualism that sees in a man or a woman chiefly a body—this can never be taken for granted as a thing achieved, or so Douglass implies. The "plantation," as Douglass imagines it in *My Bondage and My Freedom*, is not so much a site in Maryland, or Georgia—though it certainly found a genial habitat there—as it is an uncharted region of the mind.

The plantation, Douglass tells us, is "a little nation of its own," where, "wrapped in its own congenial, midnight darkness," slavery develops "all its malign and shocking characteristics." On the plantation men can be "indecent without shame." The plantation, Douglass says, is a "'tabooed' spot," savage and primitive. Call it the great American unconscious, an unspeakable domain of the mind where taboo inclinations to rape and torture and voluptuarian indulgence find their perfect exhilaration. Only by being brought ever more within reach of the benignly repressive instrument of reason will the plantation be redeemed from darkness, and human beings redeemed from bondage to the more animal tendencies of their nature. This is as unanswerable an argument against Garrisonian disunionism as might be offered. It is naive to suppose that slavery would wither away if it were denied the indulgent protection of the federal government. *My Bondage and My Freedom* does not arrive at a systematic answer that might sort out, for good, the relation between natural cruelty, as this is allowed expression by slavery, and natural kindness, as this is distorted or extinguished in slavery. But of course the book need not settle the matter. Its purposes are not merely, or even chiefly, philosophical. And it seems that Douglass, like Conrad, points to something truly unspeakable in the makeup of humanity. It is a problem to which Freud and others would, of course, return, once the church proved unable to address it adequately under the rubric of evil. Anyway, Douglass never quite belonged in Massachusetts, not in the literary-historical sense. The great optimism of *My Bondage and My Freedom* is not the somewhat mystical optimism of Emerson and his disciple Whitman, the sort that says there really is no death in the world, or that evil will bless and ice will burn. It is instead rationalist, secular, and progressive; it is the Enlightenment optimism of such early republican writers as Thomas Paine, Philip Freneau, and Joel Barlow. Notwithstanding its darker implications as to the nature of humanity—in fact, precisely *because* of them—*My Bondage and My Freedom* believes, and simply *must* believe, in the possibility of a genuinely New World of Reason and chastening Liberty, even if that possibility appeared farcical in the 1850s, given the Kansas-Nebraska Act, the Dred Scott decision, and the arrogant entrenchment of the slaveholders. Douglass' worldly optimism quite naturally attended his break with the Garrisonians, and that break, in turn, opened up for his use—for his full practical and imaginative use—the revolutionary tradition of the American founders.

DOUGLASS AND *THE COLUMBIAN ORATOR*

The Columbian Orator figures prominently in *My Bondage and My Freedom*. Had not Douglass immortalized it in his autobiographies, surely this volume, together with its author, Caleb Bingham, would have passed into oblivion. The book was published first in 1797, when opinion in America, even in the South, was generally antislavery. The speeches, poems, and extracts it collects, which were memorized by a generation or two of American schoolboys studying composition and public speaking, celebrate liberty and republican ideals, and incidentally include forthrightly antislavery material. Douglass used the *Columbian Orator* to learn to read and write. Its title and contents are altogether to the point. The book espouses "Columbian" ideals—imagines the New World, in the fashion of Bingham's contemporaries Freneau and Barlow, as the place where human liberty and redemption from the "feudal superstition" of caste at last were to be effected. Over the course of his narrative, Douglass himself emerges as the essential "Columbian orator." He is a self-emancipated man for a self-emancipated nation, and *My Bondage and My Freedom* is his Columbiad—his New World epic. He is the real expositor of the American revolution, the prophet of the New America. And as the instrument of the *Columbian Orator*, a primer in composition, would imply, his means of self-emancipation is literacy: he arrives at self-possession through mastery of the word.

Douglass speaks, as the title to an early chapter has it, of his "Gradual Initiation into the Mysteries of Slavery." It is quite as if slavery were a "secret society," and as if, in *My Bondage and My Freedom*, Douglass were writing an exposé. Certainly, the content of the book is at times erotic and sensational, as was the case with antebellum anti-Catholic exposés of life inside the convent. An anticlerical, at times frankly anti-Catholic, vein runs through Douglass' writing, as it does through the writing of many abolitionists. The ultra-Protestant strain in Douglass' book is easy enough to detect once it is pointed out.

Douglass tells of how three Christian white men forcibly dispersed an informal Sabbath school, convened by Douglass, that was intended to teach his fellow slaves in St. Michael's how to read the Bible.

> These christian class leaders were, to this extent, consistent. They had settled the question, that slavery is *right*, and, by that standard, they determined that Sabbath schools are wrong. To be sure, they were Protestant, and held to the great Protestant right of every man to *"search the scriptures"* for himself; but, then, to all general rules, there are *exceptions*. How convenient!

Slaveholders, then, are not sufficiently reformed; the plantation is a preeminently counter-Reformation sort of institution. Slaveholders constitute a new priesthood here in the New World—a class that would control utterly the meaning and delivery of "the word." As had the Puritan fathers before him, Douglass conceives of his errand in radically Protestant terms: he would purge the New World of "Old World priestcraft"; he would put people in an immediate relation to the book that sets them free. The difference, obviously, is that the Enlightenment word of the *Columbian Orator* concerns Douglass much more than does the sacred word of God.

Douglass then takes up the subject of the "Great House Farm," the home of the Lloyds, who were among the wealthiest families in Maryland in the antebellum period and who were at the very center of its governing class. He presents us with a vision of decadent corruption—a society absolutely inimical to republican institutions and culture. It is an indictment not simply of slavery but of the whole culture of feudalism, with which slavery is inevitably associated in this book. The idea is a Puritan-republican one: wealth is in some sense sensualizing in its effects; it is the sort of thing which laws are written in order to check. And so Douglass alludes, in the opening paragraphs, to the parable of the rich man and the beggar Lazarus in the book of Luke. Like the rich sinner, the Lloyds go arrayed "in purple and fine linen." This is not merely a description, of course; it is an indictment. And most notable in this chapter is the specifically sensual decadence of the Lloyds. Douglass always wants to reveal how promiscuous slavery is in its inclinations. The Lloyds live in "profuse luxury," in "luxurious extravagance," in "gilded splendor." They are "feverish voluptuaries." They are "self-deluded gourmandizers with aches, pains, fierce temper, uncontrolled passions, dyspepsia, rheumatism, lumbago and gout." They are *troubled, like the restless sea.*" This last phrase Douglass takes from Isaiah 57:20: "The wicked are like the troubled sea, when it cannot rest, whose waters cast up mire and dirt. There is no peace, saith my God, to the wicked." And Douglass certainly intends the "mire and dirt." His slaveholders always wallow.

"COVEY THE NEGRO BREAKER" AND SANDY JENKINS

The best-known chapter in *My Bondage and My* Freedom is "Covey the Negro Breaker." The episode described therein, of Douglass' battle with the notorious "Negro breaker" to whom his owner had committed him, has certain generic elements. It is, among other things, a rural comedy of manners. The sophisticated Douglass, lately of Baltimore, recounts the first time he took up work in the "field" of manual labor, as he punningly suggests. Douglass makes the point in an ironic reversal: "I found myself even more awkward than a green country boy may be supposed to be, upon his first entrance into the bewildering scenes of city life." Covey's farm is, of course, nothing cosmopolitan. But it is a strange enough world, with its "in hand" oxen and "off hand" oxen, and with its arcane language of "woa," "gee," and "hither"—a language which is, as Douglass puts it, "*Greek* to me." The peculiar comedy of the scene, as

Douglass sets it up, is quite affecting. Because the sense of his discomfort is so precisely understated—"My life, hitherto, had led me away from horned cattle"—the writing illustrates just how fragile, and how tragic, the slave's situation is.

Douglass' descriptive language makes Covey appear at once ridiculous and terrible. Covey has a "wolfish visage," "greenish eyes," and a "growl, like a dog." When Douglass takes him down, in the great fight scene, he does it on "the *not over* clean ground," as he fastidiously puts it, "for we were now in the cow yard. He had selected the place for the fight, and it was but right that he should have all the advantages of his own selection." Here, Douglass parodies the chivalrous generosity of a gentleman fighting a contest of honor. And his facility, his achieved levity, always suggests the mastery that Douglass will soon achieve over this "Negro breaker." One cannot but smile at how Covey, after two hours' futile effort to get the better of this sixteen-year-old slave, "gave up the contest," and, "puffing and blowing at a great rate," admonished Douglass: "Now, you scoundrel, go to your work; I would not have whipped you half so much as I have had you not resisted." In the weeks to come, Covey would sometimes say that "he did not want to have to get hold of" Douglass again, to which threat the latter drily rejoins, in an aside to the reader, that it was "a declaration which [he] had no difficulty in believing."

Even the intractable oxen have their comic role to play. Douglass, unused to "horned cattle," has a devil of a time managing them; they slip the yoke and damage the wagon; they run headlong into the trees; they get hung up on the gate. They are, in fact, rascals on a spree, who act up when master is absent, and behave themselves when he looks on—all the better, it appears, to embarrass Douglass. It is "break and be broken," Douglass ruefully says; "such is life." Man and ox alike have but the devices of their own good mother wit. The culture (and agriculture) of slavery corrupts the inborn sincerity even of cattle. These comic flourishes, not one of which is present in the 1845 *Narrative*, show how Douglass' achieved self-possession manifests itself at the level of style. He takes his liberties as a writer, appealing not merely to the moral sense of the reader but also to his or her wit and feeling for play. There are the events themselves (terrible and overwhelming), and then there are the events as rendered here (nicely contained and mastered); the distance between the two, affectively speaking, is the distance between dispossession and self-possession. And yet, notwithstanding his levity, his wit, and his extraordinary range of tone, Douglass always holds before the reader the horror of the experience narrated. As he suffers the ordeal with the oxen, as he is worked to the point of heat exhaustion, as he is kicked and cuffed when he collapses in the sun, "the dark night of slavery" closes in on him.

At this point the reader first encounters Sandy Jenkins, a slave to whom Douglass devotes a great deal of attention in *My Bondage*. Sandy finds Douglass in the woods, where he has retreated to hide from Covey (the day before, Covey had beaten him into insensibility when he fell ill and could no longer work). Douglass introduces Sandy as "an old adviser": "He was not only a religious man, but he professed to believe in a system for which I have no name. He was a genuine African, and had inherited some of the so-called magical powers, said to be possessed by African and eastern nations." Sandy, a man locally renowned for his "good nature," takes Douglass in, feeds him, nurses his wounds, and then unfolds the secrets of a special root: "He told me further, that if I would take that root and wear it on my right side, it would be impossible for Covey to strike me a blow; that with this root about my person, no white man could whip me." For proof, Sandy cites his own case: he had, he assures Douglass, "never received a blow from a slaveholder since he carried it." Douglass takes the root, which, he reports, he had "walked over" every time he "entered the woods," but he is skeptical.

The portrait of Sandy is complex. Sandy appears first as a savior of sorts, as "the good Samaritan." He is praised for his "good nature" and "kind heart." The business of the root may be presented as "superstition"—as "very absurd and ridiculous if not positively sinful." But after all, that alone is no real disgrace. No, the reader's suspicion of Sandy is first aroused, possibly, when he or she reads this: "I had," Douglass says,

> a positive aversion to all pretenders to "*divination.*" It was beneath one of my intelligence to countenance such dealings with the devil, as this power implied. But, with all my learning—it was really precious little—Sandy was more than a match for me. "My book learning," he said, "had not kept Covey off me," (a powerful argument just then), and he entreated me, with flashing eyes, to try this [root].

This sets Sandy's "genuine Africanism," his conjuring, over against Douglass' New World "book learning"—the instruction he had imbibed from the pages of the *Columbian Orator.* The contrast is the more telling in the light of certain facts of which readers are apprised only a page or so earlier. Douglass states that he, "the *only* slave *now* in that region who could read and write," is feared by whites and respected by slaves. Literacy is power; the only other slave who could read and write in those parts had just been sold South as a menace. So, when Sandy disparages book learning, he reveals a great weakness. His African superstitions, insofar as they discourage a slave to look toward book learning as a source of power and encourage him to put his faith in his roots, furnish the slaveholder with a useful instrument. This is why slaveholders, as presented in *My Bondage and My Freedom*, indulge such customs as these, seeing in them no threat whatever. And to the extent that Douglass is seduced by Sandy's conjuring, however momentarily, he puts on, again, the mind-forged manacles of slavery.

Clearly, Douglass wants us to assume two things. Sandy's celebrated good nature is not what it appears to be. It is in fact, at least in certain of its aspects, unrespectable, a thing unbecoming a man: his meekness is what protects him from floggings, not his roots. Sandy, it is later revealed, is not free of what Douglass, speaking an anti-Catholic sort of language, calls the "priestcraft of slavery." He remains essentially feudal in outlook. And this weakness, this distrust of book learning, this effort to turn Douglass away from his *Columbian Orator* all ultimately lead Sandy to betray Douglass and the rest of the slaves once they determine to make their escape. Douglass condemns this impotent sort of weakness when he sums up his great victory in the fight over Covey. The "battle with Covey," says Douglass, "undignified . . . as I fear my narration of it is"— here, the literary self-deprecation is merely conventional—"was the turning point in my *'life as a slave.'* It rekindled in my breast the smouldering embers of liberty; it brought up my Baltimore dreams," themselves inspired by the *Columbian Orator*. It also "revived," he adds, "a sense of my own manhood. I was a changed being after that fight. I was *nothing* before; I WAS A MAN NOW. It recalled to life my crushed self-respect and my self-confidence, and inspired me with a renewed determination to be A FREEMAN. A man, without force," Douglass concludes, "is without the essential dignity of humanity. Human nature is so constituted, that it cannot *honor* a helpless man, although it can *pity* him; and even this it cannot do long, if the signs of power do not arise." The "signs of power" do not arise in Sandy Jenkins, sympathetic though he may initially be. Douglass himself finds it hard to pity him: this "genuine African" is an Old World survival, sadly complicit in his own misery. In fact, through his actions Sandy had, Douglass intimates, "branded" himself a slave. "I did not forget to appeal to the pride of my comrades," Douglass tells us in the section recounting the conspiracy to run away:

If after having solemnly promised to go, as they had done, they now failed to make the attempt, they would, in effect, brand themselves with cowardice, and might as well sit down, fold their arms, and acknowledge themselves as fit only to be *slaves*. This detestable character, all were unwilling to assume. Every man except Sandy (he, much to our regret, withdrew) stood firm.

Sandy Jenkins, it would appear, prefers to rely on his roots.

At times, Sandy's speech appears in Douglass' own literary English and at other times in the vernacular. Consider the following passage. It recounts an ominous dream Sandy had, which, it turns out, anticipates his Judas-like betrayal of the conspirators:

I dreamed, last night, that I was roused from sleep, by strange noises, like the voices of a swarm of angry birds, that caused a roar as they passed, which fell upon my ear like a coming gale over the tops of the trees. Looking up to see what it could mean, . . . I saw you, Frederick, in the claws of a huge bird, surrounded by a large number of birds, of all colors and sizes. These were all picking at you, while you, with your arms, seemed to be trying to protect your eyes. Passing over me, the birds flew in a south-westerly direction, and I watched them until they were clean out of sight. Now, I saw this as plainly as I now see you; and furder, honey, watch de Friday night dream; dare is sumpon in it, shose you born; dare is, indeed, honey.

Douglass is a writer of consummate control; his diction is always well modulated. And yet in these last sentences, he somewhat awkwardly blends dialect and standard English. In *My Bondage and My Freedom*, Douglass' own learned language—the very language that conveys his remarkable self-possession as a writer—circumscribes, or quarantines, vernacular culture. His touchiness as to the matter is evident at once in the account he gives of his initial conference with Sandy Jenkins:

He told me that he could help me; that, in those very woods, there was an herb, which in the morning might be found, possessing all the powers required for my protection (I put his thoughts into my own language); and that, if I would take his advice, he would procure me the root of the herb of which he spoke.

Nowhere else does Douglass thus take pains to assure his reader that *his* English differs markedly from that of an interlocutor. It is as if the vernacular *embarrasses* Douglass.

Douglass proposes to make himself master of the culture of the master class; accordingly, he will have nothing to do with a vernacular counterculture whose contours, he believed, were dialectically shaped by the needs of that same master class. He finds his roots not in folk culture so much as in Enlightenment culture, which he sees as unfriendly both to slavery and Old World superstition, to anything that smacks of mystery and irrationality. Ultimately, Douglass chooses the west, which is what makes this book so thoroughly American. When he actually confronts Covey, at the moment of crisis, he "forgets [his] *roots*," as he puts it, with a pun surely deliberate, and instead stands up in violent, but always dignified, rebellion. This severs his tie to the Old World, as it were, with its unrepublican superstitions that nurse feudal feelings in Sandy Jenkins; this is the point of passage into the New World. This is where he first stands before us as the essential Columbian orator. Book-learning had already freed his mind; now he would use it to free his body. "My hands were no longer tied by my religion," he says, no doubt thinking not only of the Christian injunction to "turn the other cheek" but also of the "priestcraft" of slavery.

In his open rebellion against Covey, the Negro breaker, Douglass forsakes Uncle Tom for Nat Turner, Madison Washington, and Denmark Vesey. But he forsakes him also for Patrick Henry, as he makes clear in the chapter called "The Run-Away Plot": "Patrick Henry, to a listening senate, thrilled by his magic eloquence, and ready to stand by him in his boldest flights, could say," Douglass reminds us, "'GIVE ME LIBERTY OR GIVE ME DEATH,' and this saying was a sublime one, even for a freeman; but, incomparably more sublime, is the same sentiment, when *practically* asserted by men accustomed to the lash and chain—men whose sensibilities must have become more or less deadened by their bondage." Clearly, this defiant reply speaks not only to Covey and to Sandy but also to the romantic Christian racialism of a book like Harriet Beecher Stowe's *Uncle Tom's Cabin*, as well as to the Christian nonresistance of the Garrisonians. This is Douglass' Declaration of Independence: "I was resolved to fight," he says, aligning his personal emancipation ultimately with the national "emancipation" the Founding Fathers achieved. And he would, in realizing that aspiration to liberty, remake the American dream of possibility, referring it to higher and "incomparably more sublime" regions Douglass' fight marks his passage into the future and also into manhood. *My Bondage and My Freedom* is ultimately a coming-of-age story of both personal and national dimensions. Like so many other works of the American Renaissance, it heralds the coming of a *real* "Columbia," with the difference that its New American Adam is, of necessity, forged in the crucible of slavery. *My Bondage and My Freedom* is a book dedicated to "unceasing progress," to the ideal of a "republican" Promised Land; dedicated even to the perfection of the Reformation itself. Douglass engages all of the foundationally "American" narratives.

DOUGLASS AND THE AMERICAN ORDEAL OF "AUTOBIOGRAPHY"

We do not often speak of the plot of an autobiography. Instead, we seem to take for granted that lives simply unfold, or happen; they are not thrown into shape by design. But there is something about peculiarly American lives that should give us pause, that might lead us to reconsider the relation between storytelling and living, and between the imagined and the real.

For America is a nation of "confidence men," of self-made men, of Walt Whitman, Mark Twain, Howard Hughes, Norman Mailer, and Jay Gatsby—of men who are also "characters." America is a nation, for good and for ill, where autobiography *can* come first, and the life itself second; or—and perhaps this is the better way of putting it—where a life can be written out even as it is lived.

As intimated above, the book learning that Sandy Jenkins so easily dismisses ultimately secures Douglass his freedom. He writes in the chapter titled "The Run-Away Plot":

> To [my friends], therefore, with a suitable degree of caution, I began to disclose my sentiments and plans; sounding them, the while on the subject of running away, provided a good chance should offer. . . . That (to me) gem of a book, the *Columbian Orator,* with its eloquent orations and spicy dialogues, denouncing oppression and slavery—telling of what had been dared, done and suffered by men, to obtain the inestimable boon of liberty—was still fresh in my memory, and whirled into the ranks of my speech with the aptitude of well trained soldiers, going through the drill.

That last metaphor neatly equates literacy with militancy, the pen with the sword (or, to be strict about it, words with well-trained soldiers). This equation is what Sandy the root man failed to understand, and that failure naturally issues in his treason. It is necessary, really, that Sandy Jenkins should betray the conspiracy, and for two reasons: first, Douglass has to force a choice upon the reader—a choice between New World rationality and Old World folk belief; second, the manifest complicity of that folk culture with slavery must be demonstrated, even in the very arc of the plot. If Sandy Jenkins had not existed, Douglass would have had to invent him, at least if he were to make his argument genuinely *narrative.*

Sandy's betrayal of the conspirators' trust alerts readers to another plot, or organizing principle, in the narrative—the "Christological" plot. Notice, first, that the abjection at Covey's, even to the point of suicidal despair, is shortly followed by what Douglass calls a "resurrection" from the "tomb" of slavery, an ascension to a "heaven of comparative freedom." Second, Douglass takes on the role, with respect to his co-conspirators, of savior: it is to him that they look for salvation because he alone has the power of the word. And he takes on also the role of the man who freely assumes all responsibility for their transgressions: "I am the man," he says. Third, Douglass appears as a Mosaic figure, leading his fellow slaves out of Egypt and into Canaan. And Moses, after all, in the typological reading of the Old Testament favored by Christians, is a prefiguration of the Messiah: he frees Israel from bondage to Pharaoh; Christ frees all mankind from bondage to death and sin. Fourth, the escape is initially scheduled for Easter and thus would mark a second resurrection for Douglass: the first resurrection, at Covey's, was of the spirit; this second shall carry his very flesh away, northward to "Canaan."

Of course, Douglass did not invent Sandy Jenkins, even if he did refashion him as a character. And there is no reason to doubt that the escape was planned for Easter Sunday; it made perfectly good sense to schedule it for a holiday, when slaves were often permitted to visit family on distant plantations. Douglass is not "making these things up," no matter how well the details lend themselves to his narrative and thematic purposes. Nonetheless, the story he tells is peculiarly overdetermined, strikingly well-ordered, in such a way as to suggest that he was writing it up, so to speak, even as he acted it out—back then, in the 1830s. It is quite as if the word sets us free precisely because it organizes our lives *in prospect*, not merely in retrospect, when we pen an autobiography. It is impossible, Douglass intimates, to live outside of the stories we tell about ourselves; the living is the telling.

That is why Sandy Jenkins died in bondage: the Old World story he was telling about his "roots" could end no other way. And this is—as W. E. B. Du Bois might say—not without interest to the Gentle Reader. The Enlightenment-Republican story that Douglass learned how to tell so well, the story that organized his life toward freedom, the story of the *Columbian Orator*—this is the story he wants the nation never to stop telling itself; and that is why Americans have to read *My Bondage and My Freedom.* The year 1776 was a rehearsal for a play that to this day has not been adequately staged, except as a musical on Broadway. (Sometimes Americans rehearse the play simply to keep from acting it out: in campaigns, oratory, movies, pageants and parades, foreign policy.) America is a promise neither fulfilled in history nor yet altogether foreclosed by unreconstructed, "irrational," "Old World" survivals that strut and fret their hour upon its stage. Only with the perfect emancipation of the slave from the master, and of the master from himself, will "Columbia" have been achieved.

One lesson of *My Bondage and My Freedom* is that to be "American" is to fold stories like the one Douglas tells into the accidents of one's life; it is to live "as if" these stories were real or might be made real. That is what Douglass did. That is how he plotted out a life for himself even as he lived it: three autobiographies in thirty-six years (1845, 1855, 1881), three self-inventions and self re-inventions. And of course, all of this may be simply to say: To be American, in *My Bondage and My Freedom,* is to "dwell in possibility," as Emily Dickinson put it. The act of dwelling in possibility can seem quite hollow, once the curtain comes down. But it need not be so. And as for Douglass: Slavery compelled him to forge a life for himself. He was, as he tells us, "without an intelligible beginning in the world," a curious position for an autobiographer to be in. If he was to have a "self," he had to win it, to make it up.

CONCLUSION

This essay mentions Emily Dickinson, Ralph Waldo Emerson, and Walt Whitman in connection with Douglass. These writers, in their several ways, tell a story about bondage and freedom, a story about movement from the one to the other condition; they hold the past in contempt; all would dwell in possibility. Any story that can somehow accommodate such astonishingly varied lives as Dickinson, Whitman, Douglass, and Emerson is in a sense a representative story of the culture, one to which everyone somehow has imaginative access. "How shall a man escape from his ancestors," Emerson asks in "Fate," "or draw off from his veins the black drop which he drew from his father's or his mother's life? . . . When each comes forth from his mother's womb, the gate of gifts closes behind him. Let him value his hands and feet, he has but one pair. So he has but one future, and that is already predetermined in his lobes, and described in that little fatty face, pig-eye, and squat form." Emerson's disgust is expressed physically because bondage to the past, as readers of Douglass know, is like bondage to the body, to mere physicality, as opposed to spirit or soul. The body is fated; the soul becomes. Douglass, in slavery, had been accounted merely a body; he knew well enough about bondage to the past. After all, what had his roots to offer him in this American world? Bitterly he knew how, when he issued from a black mother's womb, "the gate of gifts closed behind him."

Dickinson knew about this too, in her own way—at least insofar as patriarchy, as it hemmed in her soul, saw in women mere bodies, mere biology. That is why she says in poem 661 that she prefers "to ride indefinite / As doth the Meadow Bee . . . With no Police to follow." The language of bondage and slavery is there for her; it is what Americans always speak of when they think about the self. Better to "run away, / With no Police to follow": such is the wish of every fugitive soul in the New World, of every soul yet imprisoned in the feudal "dungeons" of the past—caste, color, sex, and blood.

Self-emancipation, then, is a transgressive ordeal: the "Negro breakers" and their like are always about. Certainly it is transgressive for Douglass, who could create a self only outside the law. And canonical American literature everywhere intimates that the representative condition of the American soul is, in fact, a condition of bondage; it is a literature of men and women who "tight in dungeons are," as Emily Dickinson wrote. To hear its great writers tell the tale, America is all but totalitarian in its textures; Emerson's "gate of gifts" is always already closed. "Demur—you're straightway dangerous and handled with a chain," as Dickinson elsewhere has it.

It is worth emphasizing here what is already plain. Dickinson describes this condition of "dwelling in possibility," this condition of rootlessness, in such a way as to make it altogether appealing. That is necessary ideological equipment for Americans, and Douglass early on fitted himself out with it. Should it be adapted to the purposes to which he put it, this equipment allows us to accept with good grace, even with a certain satisfaction, a society that can be quite unstable: a society of wanderers, drifters, of people on the make; of self-inventors and confidence men; and of slaveholders and slaves. It allows us to ignore the often gossamer insubstantiality of the ties that bind communities together in America.

Douglass might well have asked himself what the meaning of his life had been when, in 1895, he lived out his last hours in the stately but modest house he had bought in 1878 on a hill in Anacostia, in the southeast quarter of the District of Columbia. He called the house Cedar Hill and furnished it with a desk once owned by Charles Sumner, the abolitionist Republican

from Massachusetts who, in 1856, was assaulted on the floor of the Senate by a representative from South Carolina, Preston Brooks. Douglass decorated the desk with portraits of Garrison, Gerrit Smith, Susan B. Anthony, Elizabeth Cady Stanton, and Lincoln (of course, he had no portraits of his Maryland family or of his much loved "revolutionary conspirators" at St. Michael's). Who can say what price Douglass paid for his passage into the New World, into the District of Columbia? Who knows if he thought he ever arrived?

From his chair on the veranda at Cedar Hill, Douglass could look out over Washington and see the capitol dome; he was separated from the green lawns of the mall only by the Anacostia River. But in 1895 that capitol dome had become the seat of what Twain was soon calling "The United States of Lyncherdom." And the Republican Party for which Frederick Douglass had been, some three decades running, a "wheelhorse," was now the party of the industrialist Mark Hanna and William McKinley, not the old-guard radicals Thaddeus Stevens and Sumner. It was again a nation of markets, not of people.

These days, more than a century later, Cedar Hill is maintained by the National Park Service of the Department of the Interior. A Visitors' Center sits at the foot of the long rise leading up to the house. On weekdays the parking lot outside is full of yellow school buses on pilgrimage. Inside the house, Douglass' violin rests atop his old piano; his books are on the shelves; Charles Sumner's desk is there, as are the nineteenth-century portraits. But when visitors from elsewhere in America cross the Pennsylvania Avenue Bridge over the Anacostia River to see these cherished American things, they also cross a line: the Anacostia River separates black Washington from white, and Frederick Douglass' long looked-for Columbia from itself.

Select Bibliography

EDITIONS

Narrative of the Life of Frederick Douglass, an American Slave, Written By Himself. Boston, 1845. (A second American edition appeared in 1849. Two editions, with minor revisions, were issued in Ireland in 1845 and 1846; a third appeared in England, also in 1846.)

My Bondage and My Freedom. New York and Auburn: Miller, Orton, and Mulligan, 1855. (The only edition published during Douglass' lifetime; 18,000 copies had been sold by 1857.)

The Life and Times of Frederick Douglass. Hartford, Conn.: Park Publishing, 1881. (A second, enlarged edition was published in 1893 by the Boston firm of DeWolfe, Fiske & Company.)

The Life and Writings of Frederick Douglass. 4 vols. Edited by Philip S. Foner. New York: International Publishers, 1950. (An indispensable resource. Reprints essays, speeches, articles, and letters spanning the whole of Douglass' long career. Foner's detailed historical introductions are excellent. This edition has lately been issued, abridged, in a single volume: *Frederick Douglass: Selected Speeches and Writings.* Edited by Philip S. Foner. Abridged and adapted by Yuval Taylor. Chicago: Lawrence Hill Books, 1999.)

The Frederick Douglass Papers. Edited by John W. Blassingame. 5 vols. to date. New Haven, Conn.: Yale University Press, 1979– . (An exhaustive, well-documented compilation of Douglass' nonautobiographical writings.)

Autobiographies. Edited by Henry Louis Gates Jr. New York: Library of America, 1994. (The best single-volume edition of the autobiographies, with a detailed chronology and notes. All citations of Douglass' writings in the present essay refer to this edition.)

SECONDARY WORKS

Barlow, Joel. *The Columbiad.* In *American Poetry: The Nineteenth Century.* Vol. 1. Edited by John Hollander. New York: Library of America, 1993.

Brawley, Lisa. "Frederick Douglass's *My Bondage and My Freedom* and the Fugitive Tourist Industry." *The Novel: A Forum on Fiction* 30, no. 1 (fall 1996): 98–128. (An examination of the book in the context of late-antebellum travel writing about the South.)

Fichtelberg, Joseph. *The Complex Image: Faith and Method in American Autobiography.* Philadelphia: University of Pennsylvania Press, 1989. (A study of Douglass' writings in the context of American autobiographical writing generally.)

Fredrickson, George M. *The Black Image in the White Mind: The Debate on Afro-American Character and Destiny, 1817–1914.* 2d ed. Middletown, Conn.: Wesleyan University Press, 1987. (Essential reading for any student of Douglass, or of American literature and culture generally.)

Genovese, Eugene D. *Roll, Jordan, Roll: The World the Slaves Made.* New York: Pantheon, 1974. (An encyclopedic examination of American slavery.)

Giles, Paul. "Narrative Reversals and Power Exchanges: Frederick Douglass and British Culture." *American Literature* 73, no. 4 (December 2001): 779–810. (Critically reviews the tendency to "yoke" Douglass to "an abstract idea of American nationalism.")

Ginsberg, Allen. "A Supermarket in California." In his *Howl.* San Francisco: City Lights, 1957.

Halnon, Mary. "Crossing the River: Race, Geography, and the Federal Government in Anacostia." (http://xroads.virginia.edu/~CAP/ANACOSTIA/cover.html). (A website dedicated to the district of Washington where Douglass lived in the latter decades of his life, and where the Frederick Douglass National Historic Site now stands.)

Leverenz, David. "Frederick Douglass's Self- Refashioning." *Criticism* 29, no. 3 (summer 1987): 341–370.

McFeeley, William S. *Frederick Douglass.* New York: Norton, 1991. (The standard biography.)

Morris, Richard Brandon. *The Encyclopedia of American History.* New York: Harper & Row, 1970. (Source for the statistics on cotton production.)

Preston, Dickson J. *Young Frederick Douglass: The Maryland Years.* Baltimore: Johns Hopkins University Press, 1980. (Documents Douglass' early years.)

Sundquist, Eric J. *Frederick Douglass: New Literary and Historical Essays.* New York: Cambridge University Press, 1990.

———. *To Wake the Nations: Race in the Making of American Literature.* Cambridge, Mass.: Harvard University Press, 1993. (A book of great breadth; includes extensive discussion of *My Bondage and My Freedom.*)

Timrod, Henry. "Ethnogenesis" and "The Cotton Boll." In *American Poetry: The Nineteenth Century.* Vol. 2. Edited by John Hollander. New York: Library of America, 1993.

Jack Kerouac's
On the Road

STEPHEN F. SOITOS

IN THE SUMMER of 1957 Jack Kerouac was thirty-five years old. He had traveled a long way from Lowell, Massachusetts, in the previous fifteen years. Recently, it had been Mexico and Morocco, then back to the United States. He was exhausted, destitute, sick, and depressed. In the span of twelve years he had written nine books and only the first, *The Town and the City* (1950), had been published and then forgotten.

The manuscript Kerouac once titled *The Beat Generation* and now called *On the Road,* had been written in 1951 in Manhattan but shelved by publishers for years. Viking Press promised to publish it, but Kerouac had little faith in their promises. He had been disappointed too often and now he despaired of any success. He was living once again with his mother Gabrielle, who had rescued him many times. His merchant marine vessel had been attacked in World War II. He had hitchhiked and driven back and forth across the United States too many times to count. He had lived like a hobo and written like a king by candlelight under a royal Mexican sky. His books and poems were composed in feverish binges fueled by drugs and nostalgia. He had invented a new way of writing, composing instantly in long flashes of poetic prose. His books were about visions, about romantic adventure, about love of the lost and addicted, all of them driven by a spiritual desire to record the beauty and immortality of life. He had created a new pantheon of saints, heroic Beat figures composed of the lost, the poor, and the damned. But now he was at the end of his rope literally and physically. His masterpieces of American prose would never be read. They would not inspire the social revolution he had prophesied but failed to initiate. His movie-star good looks and his football-star physique were disintegrating under the pressure of self-destruction, the years of abuse, the intense day and night writing binges that had consumed him. There was no longer any hope. Then, out of the blue, lightning struck. On September 7, 1957, Kerouac's novel *On the Road* was finally published by Viking Press with monumental success. The novel ignited a literary and socio-political debate that would alter Jack Kerouac's life and the future of the United States forever.

In all, Kerouac would write twelve published novels, three poetry collections, essays, short stories, and religious works on Buddhism. He recorded three albums of poems with jazz music accompaniment and was renowned for his live extemporaneous poetry performances. He narrated a short underground movie, *Pull My Daisy* (1959), starring Allen Ginsberg and Gregory Corso, that was influential on the independent film movement of the 1960s and 1970s. Kerouac is further credited with helping launch the San Francisco poetry renaissance that began in the late 1950s and the modern ecological debate, as well as interest in alternative religions. His life was driven by a spiritual quest that was never resolved.

On the Road, like most of Kerouac's work, is a roman à clef, or a thinly disguised autobiographical fiction. It has been called one of the most important works of late twentieth-century American fiction. The book caused a literary scandal and helped launch a radical social revolution. *On the Road* popularized Kerouac's life and the key members of the Beat movement. It hit a live nerve in the public consciousness and established an archetypal Beat character in Dean Moriarty. Future cultural superstars such as Bob Dylan, Jim Morrison of the Doors, and any number of poets and writers considered the book instrumental in their development. *On the Road* and the Beat movement led to the hippie movement of the 1960s, which played a large part in the civil rights, anti–Vietnam War, gay, and feminist movements.

On the Road gave the Beat movement its name and many of its themes. Allen Ginsberg's "Howl" (1956) and William Burroughs' *Naked Lunch* (1959) further contributed to the concept of the Beats and their lifestyle. With the coining of the word "beatnik," the images and characters of the Beat world entered into America's consciousness in a disquieting way. There were articles in *Life* magazine featuring lurid photographs of Beat pads, drugs, and chicks (1957). There were volumes of criticism about the Beat lifestyle, its harmful potential, its impractical message. Beat quickly became an attraction to young Americans and in the next generation would become a lifestyle among the dissatisfied.

CHRONOLOGY

1922	Jack Kerouac (Jean Louis Lebris de Kerouac) born on March 12 in Lowell, Massachusetts, to Leo Alcide and Gabrielle Levesque Kerouac.
1940–1941	Attends Columbia University after winning football scholarship and attending Horace Mann prep school in New York City for a year.
1944	Meets Lucien Carr, Allen Ginsberg, and William Burroughs in New York. Marries Edie Parker on August 22.
1945	Marriage annulled. Collaborates with Burroughs on an unpublished detective novel.
1946	Kerouac meets Neal Cassady and begins work on *The Town and the City.*
1947	Makes first cross-country tour to Denver and San Francisco and back to New York.
1948	Completes *The Town and the City* and begins work on earliest version of *On the Road.*
1950	*The Town and the City.* Marries Joan Haverty on November 17.
1951	Writes *On the Road* on a single roll of paper in three weeks. Separates from second wife.
1955	Viking Press accepts *On the Road.* Meets Gary Snyder and attends poetry reading at the Six Gallery in San Francisco at which Allen Ginsberg delivers "Howl" for the first time.
1957	*On the Road* published September 7.
1959	*Doctor Sax, Mexico City Blues, Maggie Cassidy.* Narrates Robert Frank's film *Pull My Daisy,* based on an unpublished play by Kerouac.
1960	Has a nervous breakdown in Bixby Canyon, Big Sur.
1961	*Book of Dreams.*
1962	*Big Sur.*
1963	*Visions of Gerard.*
1965	*Desolation Angels.* Makes trip to France to study family genealogy.

| 1966 | Marries Stella Sampas on November 19. |
| 1969 | Kerouac dies of a hemorrhage in St. Petersburg, Florida, on October 21. |

FROM MILL TOWN TO BIG CITY

Jack Kerouac was born Jean Louis Lebris de Kerouac on March 12, 1922, in Lowell, Massachusetts, a mill town on the Merrimack River thirty miles north of Boston. His parents were of French Canadian descent and working-class. Kerouac was the last of three children. He spoke French as a first language. At age eleven he moved from French-speaking parochial schools to public schools where he began reading extensively and educating himself in public libraries. He was noticed for his remarkable intelligence, playful control of language, and his questioning nature. As he grew he amazed his friends with feats of memory and earned the nickname "Memory Babe." He was also physically gifted and played all sports, particularly football, with great success. Kerouac would later write and publish four novels about Lowell: *The Town and the City, Maggie Cassidy* (1959), *Doctor Sax* (1959), and *Visions of Gerard* (1963). In *Doctor Sax* he claimed he remembered the day he was born. In *Visions of Gerard* he deified his older brother, Gerard, who died at age nine from rheumatic fever. Jack at four years old was deeply affected by his brother's slow death. The French nuns praised Gerard for his saintly qualities, his gentleness to animals, and his spiritual statements. Gerard's tragic death marked Kerouac for the rest of his life.

At age eight Kerouac began writing comic strips, designed a complicated game of baseball, and by eleven had written a first novel about an orphan boy who runs away down a river. Fascinated with popular culture, Kerouac was an avid reader of superhero comics and detective and adventure stories. He was also fascinated with cinema, sometimes seeing four or five films a day. He favored heroic western adventure as well as film noir with its pessimistic undercur-

rents of social critique. He was also influenced by the rough and tumble life of Jack London, a smuggler, sailor, and gold rush hobo who made himself into a writer. By 1935 Kerouac was outgrowing Lowell. He was proud, ambitious, and difficult with a puzzling dual personality. One side was extroverted and loud, physically aggressive and full of bravado. The other side was mysteriously aloof, quick to anger, and racked by ambivalent sexuality. Although later in life Kerouac was not completely forthright about his sexuality, evidence indicates that he had homosexual affairs.

The poverty of his working-class family primed an explosion in his worldview. The great Lowell flood of March 1936 ruined his father's printing shop. The Kerouacs were hounded by debtors and the family moved many times seeking financial stability. Jack wanted to be a writer but he struggled against a class structure designed to suppress dreamers, particularly if they were French Canadians meant to work in factories. Like his father, Jack aspired to succeed on his own terms. But family life was not all doom and gloom. His parents were social and held big, alcohol-inflamed parties. Gabrielle and Jack shared joie de vivre and enjoyed a close camaraderie. Jack did well academically and became a football hero in high school. He found his way out of Lowell when he was awarded a football scholarship to Columbia University.

Jack Kerouac was elated to move to New York City in September 1939. The atmosphere stoked his grandiose ambitions to become a leader, a philosopher who could change society. He spent a year at the exclusive Horace Mann prep school and made friends among a new class of students. He was a football star at Horace Mann and while Hitler blitzed through Europe Jack wrote his first published fiction for the Horace Mann quarterly. "The Brothers" was a spare, realistic mystery story about two policeman brothers, one of whom is killed by the other. The short story "Une Veille de Noel" was more surreal and set in a Greenwich Village bar where a group of drinkers are visited by a saintly apparition who might be Jesus Christ.

In 1940, in his first year at Columbia, Jack broke a leg playing football. It would prove to be the end of his sports career. While recuperating, he took the opportunity to continue his education and read voraciously—Shakespeare, James Joyce's *Portrait of the Artist* (1928) and *Finnegan's Wake* (1939), and all of Thomas Wolfe, whose style greatly influenced the book he started to write called *The Town and the City*. He was making new friends at Columbia and in Times Square and the jazz clubs. These included Allen Ginsberg, Lucien Carr, Edie Parker, his first wife, and other early Beat characters such as Herbert Huncke and William Burroughs. Kerouac quit Columbia in his second year and joined the merchant marines with a berth on the SS *Dorchester,* sailing to Greenland. He witnessed torpedo fire but returned to New York safely. The *Dorchester* was sunk with a heavy loss of men on its next trip. In 1943 Kerouac signed up for the U.S. Navy but soon received a honorable discharge on psychiatric grounds. He returned to hang around Columbia but now there was no college glory as a football star. He was adrift and consuming vast quantities of everything from bebop music to drugs and alcohol and sex. He realized he was fighting for his life and he had only one tool to help him survive—his great creativity. He moved into an apartment with Edie Parker, William Burroughs, Joan Vollmer, and Allen Ginsberg. The famous Beat triumvirate was together for the first time.

On August 8, 1944, Lucien Carr killed an older homosexual paramour named David Kammerer with a knife and threw his body into the Hudson River. Carr implicated Kerouac in the crime and Kerouac was arrested as an accessory after the fact. Carr went to prison but Kerouac's charges were dropped after Edie Parker raised bail money from her parents in Grosse Pointe, Michigan. Parker and Kerouac were married on August 22, 1944, and Kerouac moved to Grosse Pointe to live with his new wife's family. Six

months later Kerouac left Parker and signed on for another merchant marine voyage. This time he jumped ship before it left port and returned to his friends in New York City. Kerouac and William Burroughs began writing a mystery novel, which was never published. In May 1946 Kerouac's father died, and Kerouac devoted most of the year to writing *The Town and the City* in his mother's Ozone Park apartment. Around Christmas 1946 he met a "cowboy" from Denver. Kerouac knocked at the door to a sleazy flat in Harlem and Neal Cassady opened the door, naked, while a beautiful girl groped for clothes on a disheveled bed behind him. Kerouac had finally met his match.

NEAL CASSADY AND THE NEW VISION

It was a meeting of destiny for them and the world. Cassady would become the hero of *On the Road* under the name Dean Moriarty and of *Visions of Cody* (1972) under the name Cody Pomeray. Neal was a handsome, Gene Autry look-alike, muscular, sensual, and spontaneous to the point of insanity. Born in 1926 in Salt Lake City, his parents divorced when he was six and Neal followed his father into Denver wino hotels and flophouses. Between 1940 and 1944 he claimed to have stolen five hundred cars and lived on the Denver streets hustling to survive. He was sent to reform school three times and educated himself in public and prison libraries. In late 1946 Neal married sixteen-year-old Luanne Henderson in Denver. They zoomed to New York together in a beat-up used car. Neal came to the big city to learn how to write. Soon inseparable from Kerouac, Ginsberg, and Burroughs, Neal absorbed their intellectual discussions until he had enough vocabulary to prime his own pump. The philosophical maelstrom of the Beat boys was finally taking shape. The evolution of the "New Vision" had developed from a number of different strains of thought. It was fueled primarily by an apocalyptic fear. The world could be destroyed in an increasingly plausible atomic holocaust. The Beat vision was born on August 6, 1945, the day the first atomic bomb wiped out the large metropolis of Hiroshima, Japan, in a matter of minutes. It was enough to make one question God. And then there was Oswald Spengler's *Decline of the West* (1926, 1928) to add fuel to the fire. The German philosopher's work traced the cycle of destruction of civilizations. According to Spengler, Western civilization, like all previous hierarchal societies, was destined to collapse and a new culture would emerge from the outcasts of society.

Other literary influences on the Beats ranged from Arthur Rimbaud's theory of disordered senses, to William Blake's claim that the road of excess leads to the palace of wisdom, to Fyodor Dostoyevsky's mad, passionate antiheros. The American Romantics Henry David Thoreau, Ralph Waldo Emerson, and Walt Whitman added inspiration with their notions of deified individualism, transcendent eyeballs, and paeans to blades of grass. Kerouac was perhaps most stylistically influenced by the French iconoclast writer Ferdinand Céline, whose picaresque and humorous *Journey to the End of Night* (1932) exploded the myth of civilized institutions with its outrageous satire of World War I and its aftermath. Kerouac liked to quote the line from the book, "We are all going forward in the silence of facts to die."

Then there were bebop musicians such as Charlie Parker and hipster icon Lester Young blowing intense mind and soul saxophone solos that spoke volumes about transcendence, breaking boundaries, finding a new path to redemption—and a new way to communicate. Kerouac mingled with the hipsters, hoboes, and marginalized and began to envision them as doomed saints.

For Kerouac the next few years (1946–1951) were a heady mix of existential metaphysics, writing, drug experiences, sexual transgressions, and traveling. He sped back and forth across America and into Mexico in the company of Neal Cassady or in search of Neal Cassady. The modes of physical transportation were as varied as the methods of mental stimulation. Kerouac was after the essence of life experiences in all its various forms. As he moved he recorded his passage by writing. His vast collections of notebooks are full of observations on American life. He made lists and catalogued the number of times he had sex. He sketched descriptions of cities, people, landscapes, trying to find God in every particle of human existence. He developed a large-scale plan to capture his generation's life in words, with himself playing a starring role. The saga of his life on paper would give it meaning in what he conceived as "The Duluoz Legend." Each book he wrote would be a chapter from his own life. He and his Beat companions were shaping a Utopian vision based on personal liberation. They preached a new democratic promise of spiritual and physical freedom in a rapidly changing American environment. A new age would rise out of the ashes of the first half of the century destroyed by world war. Like most Utopian movements the Beats' "New Vision" was long on personal liberation philosophy and short on a pragmatic plan to change society. Like their Romantic forebears, the Beats separated themselves from the majority viewpoint by perceiving social reality from a different perspective. In Beat philosophy the personal was always political, the political always religious, and writing was a revolutionary act.

THE WRITING OF *ON THE ROAD*

On March 4, 1947, Neal Cassady left New York City with Luanne to return to Denver. In June 1947 Kerouac was living with his mother and was halfway through his 1,000 page manuscript *The Town and the City.* He decided to hitchhike to the West Coast, stopping off in Denver to visit Neal Cassady and Allen Ginsberg. Thus began the events that were chronicled in *On the Road.* By Christmas 1948 Kerouac was back with his mother at his sister Catherine's house in North Carolina. Cassady unexpectedly turned up in another car with Luanne, and events documented in the second part of *On the Road* ensued, including a cross-country trip to New Orleans to visit William Burroughs, known as Old Bull. Kerouac was back in New York in February 1949. In March 1949 Harcourt Brace accepted *The Town and the City* and cut the manuscript from 1,100 pages to four hundred. The book was published on March 2, 1950, to mixed reviews.

In July 1950 Kerouac was off on a third cross-country journey to the West Coast and this time returned with Cassady to New York. This experience formed the third section of *On the Road,* and it was followed by a trip into Mexico with Cassady that provided material for the fourth section. Back in New York in the fall of 1950 Kerouac moved into the New York apartment of Joan Haverty and married her on November 17. Neal arrived alone in New York in February 1951. Cassady now had two children, no job, and harried relationships with a number of women. He still found time to party. He left in March, and his parting provided Kerouac with an idea for an ending to what he was calling his Beat Generation novel.

On April 5, 1951, Kerouac began the famous scroll version of *On the Road,* composed over a period of three weeks in a continuous day and night word attack on one piece of rolled paper inserted in his typewriter. This 120-foot, 125,000-word paragraph with erratic punctuation proved to be the basic version of a continuously reworked manuscript that was finally published in 1957. Kerouac claimed that editors changed his punctuation and content severely but he was altering the text himself, giving it a series of working titles: *Love on the Road, Hit the Road, Lost on the Road.*

On the Road was Kerouac's first attempt at sustained spontaneous prose written in a picaresque or episodic style. The first-person narration is streamlined and immediate, echoing the unprecedented speed of the contemporary world. The evolution of this style was inspired by Neal Cassady himself in his famous Jane Anderson letter, of which only a fragment exists. According to Kerouac the letter was a long, thirty-page rush of language in which Cassady described one crazy, chaotic weekend. The Joan Anderson letter recounted Neal's escape from a bathroom window after being caught making love to a woman and his hospital visit to another girlfriend, Joan Anderson, following her suicide attempt. The letter was apparently tragic and hilarious as Cassady traced his passage through seedy pool halls, flophouses, and jail cells in a soul-baring frenzy. Kerouac explained his writing theories at this time in two published essays, "Essentials of Spontaneous Prose" (1957) and "Belief and Technique for Modern Prose" (1959). He claimed the best way to write was in one continuous stream of thought without interruption or self-critical analysis and revision. This type of restless writing energy typified his approach to life in general.

ON THE ROAD

On the Road is a first-person depiction of an underground subculture of young rebels racing desperately across the United States in pursuit of "kicks" and spiritual salvation. The book's style and content outraged the literary establishment. Truman Capote famously called the book "typing not writing." But the perceived lack of moral message bothered critics even more. The behavior of the characters ran totally counter to the received values of the dominant American culture of the post–World War II decade. In the 1950s American society was based on respect for the institutions of education, the military, religion, and marriage. The nuclear family was the center of a homogenized and growing materialistic society. The two main protagonists of *On the Road*—Sal Paradise and Dean Moriarty—advocate a spontaneous, hedonistic lifestyle that is lived on the move. The book idealizes the disenfranchised or "beat" segments of society. The characters in *On the Road* thrive on chaos and turmoil, refuse to participate in organized society, and seek personal transcendence through feats of physical daring and extended journeys into the unknown.

The characters live on the borders of lawful society. They steal, they hustle, they whore. They continuously question their existence and the meaning of life. The book attacks complacency, propriety, and status. It denies materialism, property values, cohesive communities, and marriage. It condones outlandish behavior for its own sake, and its complaints against parents, police, and politicians supported growing rebellious instincts in a new generation of Americans. It attacked the growing American military-industrial complex that was polluting the globe with violence and toxins and it predicted a grave existential spiritual crisis developing in American society. The book ignited a feeling of brotherhood among large elements of a dissatisfied American public. *On the Road* is a complex and troubling novel that reveals the state of mind of young, midcentury, white American males. Sal and Dean's experiences illustrate a deep schism taking place in the American culture and presage a country about to be torn asunder by social upheaval.

As an American adventure story, *On the Road* is narrated by an Italian American male about twenty-five years old named Sal Paradise. Sal is from New York City, has dropped out of college, is recently divorced, and is bored. "I was a young writer and I wanted to take off. Somewhere along the line I knew there'd be girls, visions, everything; somewhere along the line the pearl would be handed to me." His journeys across the United States are driven by his need to be with his male friends, particularly Dean Moriarty "because the only people for me are the mad ones, the ones who are mad to live, mad to talk, mad to be saved, . . . the ones who . . . burn, burn, burn like fabulous yellow roman candles exploding like spiders across the stars."

The book is a confessional first-person novel told from a male viewpoint. Sal Paradise is a complicated dual personality with one side full of joy, expectation, and ecstasy and the other burdened with sadness and self-doubt. The text is alive with descriptions of wild car rides across the country and drugged, drunken parties fueled by bebop music. But there are underlying currents of unease laced throughout. Sal Paradise's passionate identification with Dean Moriarty forms the center of the novel. Their relationship reveals two troubled individuals trying to find their way in an increasingly complex American landscape.

On the Road is divided into five parts. The first four are roughly the same length and depict hectic journeys across the continent and through the seedy slums of major American cities such as New York, New Orleans, Denver, and San Francisco. In the process readers visit chaotic apartments, view indiscriminate sex, and participate in drugged intellectual all-nighters. Sal's mental state runs through a series of emotional changes from triumphant bravado to self-pitying exhaustion. Digressions from the main action include forays into a Mexican American migrant work camp, numerous black jazz clubs, and Mexico. The fifth and shortest part occurs in New York City and provides an anticlimactic denouement to a virtually plotless narrative. As much as a year passes between the episodes of the book, about which the reader learns nothing. Sal Paradise apparently spends these periods at home with his aunt writing an unnamed book.

On the Road is not simply a road adventure but a psychological journey. It reveals both the positive and negative of a life spent on the move. At one point Sal writes: "Life is holy and every moment precious." Then later in the novel after he is exhausted by his travels he says: "Everything I had ever secretly held . . . was coming out: how ugly I was and what filth I was discovering in the depths of my own impure psychologies."

Dean Moriarty is the central protagonist of the novel. He is in his early twenties, a working-class drifter from Denver abandoned by his mother and father at age six. Dean is a voluble, handsome charmer with a prison past. He comes to New York City to meet with writers and intellectuals he has heard about through friends. Sal and Dean's friendship is as an awakening for Sal Paradise more profound than anything he has ever experienced. It signifies a change in identity, style, and attitude that radically alters Sal's existence. His infatuation with the Western free-spirited Dean quickly turns into a troubling obsession. "I first met Dean not long after my wife and I split up. . . . With the coming of Dean Moriarty began the part of my life you could call my life on the road."

Dean Moriarty assumes mythic stature in Sal's imagination. Dean is a handsome cowboy superhero on an epic quest for truth. Dean is highly sexualized, always on the move, a Western Noble Savage in a beat-up Hudson sedan. Dean is Dionysian in his appetites, needs no sleep, never retreats from a physical challenge. He is a goofy cowboy outlaw who ignores rational behavior. "Dean . . . was a wild yea-saying overburst of American joy; it was Western, the west wind, an ode from the Plains, something new, long prophesied, long a-coming."

Dean is a guide and role model for a way of life that revolts against a conformist and repressed America. Sal admires Dean's cavalier, lunatic style, which urges the pure joy of just having fun. But as the book progresses Dean's manic self-absorption leaves a trail of problems behind him. Although he is energetic, exuberant, and full of wonder at the possibilities that life presents, he cannot accept responsibility for his own actions. He expresses desires to be a writer, but his restless nature makes him dart from one dangerous and chaotic situation to another.

Dean's first priority is freedom from socially imposed rules and expectations. His disarming irresponsibility and his anarchic flow of activity set the tone for the novel. Sal writes that for Dean "sex was the one and only holy and important thing in life." At the same time Dean is indifferent to women other than as objects for his conquest. The demonic aspects of Dean's behavior are explained away by Sal as characteristics of truly free man, a holy primitive, a saintly possessed individual perpetually in motion.

"He leaped out of the car. Furiously he hustled into the railroad station . . . he had become absolutely mad in his movements, he seemed to be doing everything at the same time." Sal describes Dean as a Groucho Marx figure, a sort of comedic goofy madman who cannot be contained by the normal strictures of society. But Dean is unreliable. He deserts Sal in precarious positions and puts other peoples' lives in danger without a thought.

PART ONE

In the first part of the book, where he tries out his hitchhiking and hobo fantasies, Sal pursues Dean Moriarty across the United States. He goes into the Great American West with an idealized vision of what he will find. But the reality of the West in its sad state of tourist cowboy towns, a dying way of life, and drunken mannequin-like Indians disappoints him. "I was amazed, and at the same time I felt it was ridiculous; in my first shot at the West I was seeing to what absurd devices it had fallen to keep its proud tradition."

When Sal arrives in Denver he finds Dean busily involved in three relationships. Dean and the Columbia intellectual Carlo Marx (Allen Ginsberg) are heavily engaged in "fiendish allday- allnight-talk." Dean also has two girlfriends. Dean is charismatic for women and men alike. His raw power entrances Sal, but Dean has little time for Sal. Feeling snubbed, Sal heads to San Francisco where he gets a job as a security guard. On the weekends he takes his gun into San Francisco bars and gets drunk. "When a queer approached me in a bar john I took out the gun and . . . He bolted. I've never understood why I did that." Sal quits his job and meets a female Mexican American migrant worker on a bus to Los Angeles.

Sal's love affair with Terry forms one of the main digressions in the book. Sal immediately runs away with Terry and her young child to live in a tent and work picking cotton. But Sal's romantic idea of farm work proves difficult as he lives in poverty with Terry, and they argue while the child goes hungry. Terry's Mexican American family rejects Sal. They spend fifteen days together dogged by poverty, drinking, and Sal's growing need to flee back to the road. Sal's romantic vision of migrant labor runs counter to reality. He likens himself to an "old Negro." When a group of "Okies" mistake him for a Mexican, he comments, "in a way, I am." He lasts only few days picking cotton before being worn out by the futility. As soon as the poverty and haphazard existence become a personal challenge, Sal runs away. In one of the most startling and surprising statements later in the novel, he blurts out, "All my life I'd had white ambitions, that was why I'd abandoned a good woman like Terry."

Sal is attracted to the exploited for their purity of soul and the simpler aspects of their existence. But his depiction of the life of the underprivileged provides no ideas for social reform. His identification with the downtrodden omits the hopelessness of poverty to emphasize a romantic sense of brotherly community.

PART TWO

Part two of the novel takes place more than a year later and begins when Dean and his young wife Marylou drive across the United States to pick up Sal in Virginia and travel to New Orleans. After a feverish road journey they end up at the house of a mutual friend named Old Bull Lee (William Burroughs). During their madcap ride south, Moriarty assures Sal that intimate knowledge of America is all that is needed for happiness. "God exists without

qualms. As we roll along this way I am positive beyond doubt that everything will be taken care of for us. . . . Furthermore we know America. . . . I know the people, I know what they do."

At Old Bull Lee's house Sal finds Lee's drug-addled wife Jane (Joan Vollmer), who sits in a daze while her kids run around naked and starving. Old Bull spends most of his time in the bathroom shooting up heroin. (William Burroughs would later shoot Joan Vollmer dead in a drunken accident.) Sal glosses over the depravity by attributing it to eccentricity. The South is proving disappointing. Sal's desire to see the Mississippi River in its natural state is blocked by a chain link fence. Dean, Marylou, and Sal leave for San Francisco and get caught in a dark swamp without clearly marked roads. They see an old "Negro" but do not dare approach him. "We were scared too. . . . We wanted to get out of this mansion of the snake, this mireful dropping dark, and zoom back to familiar American ground and cowtowns . . . a manuscript of the night we couldn't read."

In San Francisco Dean deserts Sal and Marylou for his second wife, Camille. Sal is left alone for days on the streets of San Francisco without food. Then he has a vision: "I had reached the point of ecstasy that I always wanted to reach, which was the complete step across chronological time into timeless shadows . . . the potent and inconceivable radiancies hiding in bright Mind Essence. . . . I had died and been reborn numberless times."

When Sal and Dean are reunited in San Francisco they spend their time running away from Camille and partying in the jazz clubs. "I never saw such crazy musicians. Everybody in Frisco blew. It was the end of the continent; they didn't give a damn. Dean and I goofed around San Francisco." The heroes of Sal and Dean's universe are primarily black musicians with a message of liberation in their lifestyle and music. Bebop is a doorway into ecstasy and an example of how to triumph over circumstances through art. The energy in bebop reflects Dean and Sal's state of mind. Sal and Dean haunt jazz places and pursue jazz musicians trying to emulate their style. Sal leaves San Francisco and travels back to New York by bus with ten sandwiches that go rotten in his pack. When he parts from Dean, Sal writes: "We were all thinking we'd never see one another again and we didn't care."

PART THREE

Part three starts with a digression as Sal decides to leave New York again and go to Denver. He works awhile in a wholesale fruit market and at night he walks through the streets. One night he wanders into the black section of town and in a famous and controversial passage accuses himself of being white.

> At lilac evening I walked with every muscle aching among the lights of 27th and Welton in the Denver colored section, wishing I were a Negro, feeling that the best the white world had offered was not enough ecstasy for me, not enough life, joy, kicks, darkness, music, not enough night. . . . I wished I were . . . anything but what I was so drearily, a "white man" disillusioned.

In his desires to escape his "whiteness," Sal continually returns to the essence of his own nature. He cannot change his ethnicity, but through empathy and the writer's descriptive power he succeeds in moving—for a time—in other worlds. One value of the book is that Sal shows that despite the surface differences among the various "outsiders" he knows, deep human affinities endure. As much as anything else, this awareness may be at the core of what Kerouac meant by "beat."

But the passage also shows a dangerous romantic idealization of the "others" Sal so admires but really knows nothing about. In his attempt to castigate the predominately white male culture of the time he envisions a pure pastoral existence of his imagination. He sees America as a land of cosmic immigrants mingling happy together. Yet he ignores the nightmares of racial violence occurring at that very time. His musing on race was in James Baldwin's words "offensive nonsense" and in many ways reinforced the patronizing attitudes of the dominant culture. Sal and Dean's fascination with the "exoticism" of blacks and their lifestyles uncovers the emptiness of their own lives. Sal and Dean's personal liberation and individualistic concepts do not equate with egalitarianism.

The most telling passages of part three occur when Sal finally reaches Dean's house in San Francisco, where he is living with Camille and their daughter. Dean has broken his thumb hitting his first wife Marylou in the face. Camille kicks Dean and Sal out of the house. Sal is elated because he now has Dean to himself. They will cross the United States and then travel to Italy together. Before they leave they want one more night on the town. They go to a female friend's apartment to try to get money. Suddenly Dean hits a roadblock. The apartment is inhabited by three women who have witnessed Dean's irresponsible behavior to women and children. "For years now you haven't had any sense of responsibility for anyone. You've done so many awful things I don't know what to say to you." Dean is abashed into silence and sweating nods.

Sal writes: "I suddenly realized that Dean, by virtue of his enormous series of sins, was becoming the Idiot, the Imbecile, the Saint of the lot." Sal, intent on whisking Dean away to the Jazz bar around the corner, defends and canonizes Dean Moriarty at his goofiest, most irresponsible moment. "He was BEAT—the root, the soul of Beatific." They escape into the pure moment of an all-night drunken spree that ends up in a black musician's apartment in the early hours of the morning where the man's wife is trying to sleep. They drink and talk and when they leave Dean says: "Now you see, man, there's a *real* woman for you. Never a harsh word, never a complaint . . . her old man can come in any hour of the night. . . . This is a man, and that's his castle."

As they head back across the United States in a mad dash for New York, hysteria and desperation rise to a manic point. Dean is rejected by his cousin in Denver. Dean tries and fails to seduce and then rob a homosexual business man. Sal makes Dean cry in a restaurant after Dean makes an innocent remark about Sal's age. Dean starts to unravel like the dirty bandage around his thumb. His wildness is now psychotic and his rambling philosophic monologues on the "itness" of living in the moment for the pure joy of "kicks" is sounding like cryptic nonsense.

> Oh, man! man! man!! . . . And it's not even the beginning of it. . . . Sal, think of it, we'll dig Denver together and see what everybody's doing although that matters little to us, the point being that we know that IT is and we know TIME and we know that everything is really FINE.

An exhausted Sal begins to see Dean as "the angel of Terror" and then as "a burning, frightful Angel, . . . pursuing me like the Shrouded Traveler on the plain." Near the end of the episode, Dean's life-force has become a death principle, a "Mad Ahab at the wheel." Sal is losing faith in the lure of the endless road. "I was beginning to cross and recross towns in America as though I was a traveling salesman . . . rotten beans in the bottom of my bag of tricks, nobody buying."

Part three ends in New York in a three-paragraph finale involving a wild party where Dean falls in love with a strange women, Inez, proposes marriage to her, and insists on divorcing Camille. Sal retreats to his aunt's apartment.

PART FOUR

Part four begins with Dean still in New York, parking cars and living with Inez. Sal sells the book he has been working on and with the coming spring decides to leave for Denver. He is in Denver only a short time when Dean shows up from New York on his way to Mexico to get a divorce. The trip to the "magic south" is underway.

The trip to Mexico forms the third and last digression of Sal's story. Once again Sal is suddenly alive with anticipation of the most fabulous trip of all as they follow the route of "old American outlaws who used to skip over the border." As they enter Mexico Dean enthuses, "Now, Sal, we're leaving everything behind us and entering a new and unknown phase of things. All the years and troubles and kicks—and now *this*!" But "this" turns out to be only more of the same old frustrations and disillusionment. They have a wild party in a whorehouse and Sal fatuously falls in love with one of the prostitutes, whom he abandons. Dean and Sal speed away through the night into the jungle deepness of Mexico. "We had finally found the magic land at the end of the road and we never dreamed the extent of the magic." When they reach Mexico City Sal writes: "All Mexico was one vast Bohemian camp. . . . This was the great and final wild uninhibited Fellahin-childlike city that we knew we would find at the end of the road." The Indians and poor Mexicans possess in Sal's eyes a fundamental, uncultivated naturalness that represents the Eden of lost civilization. Mexico is the place where people live in harmony with nature and themselves. By contrast people in the United States live in ignorance and suffering, out of joint with their times. "For when destruction comes to the world of 'history' and the Apocalypse of the Fellahin returns once more as so many times before, people will stare with the same eyes from the caves of Mexico."

But suddenly Sal comes down with a bad fever. In a few short days Dean deserts Sal in Mexico City. Dean, who has gotten his divorce, says, "Gotta get back to my life." When Sal recovers he realizes "what a rat" Dean was and recognizes the hopeless complexity of Dean's life. Sal seeks the "beat" genuineness he believes nonwhite races possess. In Mexico myth and reality converge in stifling heat and the haze of marijuana smoke. Mexico is a rite of passage, an imaginative journey that crystalizes his understanding of America. But it is an imaginary space romanticized for its primitivist conditions. Sal once again falls into racial exoticizing, imagining his vision of the future based on an unrecoverable past.

PART FIVE

When Sal returns to New York City he finally meets the woman he will marry. They move in together planning to go to California to meet Dean. But Dean suddenly shows up unannounced in New York after another trip across country. This time he is silent and overcome with confusion, and Sal rejects him. Sal's sad disillusionment with Dean is tangible. In the final scene Dean has decided to leave New York and go back to his second wife. In the course of the novel Dean has been married three times and divorced twice. Sal is sitting with his new girlfriend and others in a limousine on his way to a concert at the Metropolitan Opera. Dean asks for a ride to the bus station because of the cold. None of the Sal's new friends want Dean in the car. Sal writes: "So Dean couldn't ride uptown with us and the only thing I could do was sit in the back of the Cadillac and wave at him. . . . Dean . . . walked off alone." The novel ends with confusion and sadness. Sal sits on the end of a broken pier and ponders the random sad senselessness of existence: "Nobody, nobody knows what's going to happen to anybody besides the forlorn rags of growing old, I think of Dean Moriarty."

CONCLUSION

On the Road documented a new generation's state of mind. It helped created a legend in Dean Moriarty and gave a social movement its name and prototypical character. The novel represents the beginning of a new lifestyle and a similar consciousness. Part of the power of the book is in its transgressions and its honesty. Its journeys are chances for change and discovery. The book is exhilarating when read as an adventure. The characters' insanities and indulgences, which formerly were reserved for aristocrats, now can be shared by a general public. The crazy, enlightened ones are now the social outcasts of a democratic system that reneged on its promise of life, liberty, and the pursuit of happiness. *On the Road* is a rallying cry to the Bohemian margins of society.

Kerouac's power to dramatize the spirit of his own life into romantic fantasy forms the basis of the book. He tries to show that life is to be lived in the moment and that repressive sexual and moral strictures are taking away a naturalness that people such as Dean represent. But Dean begins as a cowboy hero and ends up a lonely fool. Nothing is fixed or immutable in a rapidly changing environment. There is no recoverable American past except in the imagination. A complex array of emotions are expressed, and Sal's vulnerability is both comic and tragic. In this way it represents the spirit of a generation about to launch a social revolution. But it also reports on the frightening alien landscape of America and on a confused male identity.

The influence of Jack Kerouac and the Beat Generation continues to be re-evaluated and discussed in a number of new books and revitalized in current social dialogue. Despite harsh attacks by establishment critics, *On the Road* was an immediate success and has remained steadily in print. Kerouac's intensity of vision and his confused life caught the dreams of a generation who felt that at some point something had been together, that there was a special vision of individual and social renewal they all shared.

After the publication of *On the Road* in 1957, Kerouac began a slow withdrawal from the glare of the spotlight, a retreat with his mother to Florida, and a spiral into alcoholism and depression. As Kerouac became known as the "King of the Beat Generation" he backed away from public scrutiny and denied his influence. He became politically conservative and antisocial. Never again did he feel comfortable with the demands of success even though he was still to write some of his best work.

Kerouac, Ginsberg, Burroughs, and Neal Cassady became the Beat culture's most celebrated and controversial representatives. They influenced other poets and writers of the 1950s and 1960s such as the San Francisco Renaissance poets Lawrence Ferlinghetti, Michael McClure, Gary Snyder, and Philip Whalen. Recent scholars have turned their attention to Beat minority and women writers such as Ted Joans, Philip Kaufmann, Joyce Johnson, Hettie Jones, Kay Johnson, known as Kaja, and Diane DePrima.

The Beats influenced American underground cinema and alternative theater. Maya Deren had led a group of independent filmmakers as early as 1953. Shirley Clarke, Albert Maysles, Donn Pennebaker, and others founded the cooperative Filmakers Inc. in 1958. Edward Bland, the African American director of *The Cry of Jazz*, and Stan Brakhage provided early experimental psychodramas. Judith Malina and Julian Beck founded *The Living Theatre.*

The Beats were precursors of the institutional changes that came about during the 1960s. They caused many Americans to re-evaluate their everyday lives and religious orientations. The Beat Generation's philosophy was picked up by the hippies. By 1967 tens of thousands of hippies were practicing a lifestyle based on free love, peace, the use of consciousness and mind-expanding drugs. It marked the beginning of the most explosive decade of cultural experimentation since the turn of the century. The Beats in general showed little interest in women's rights. The Beat world was still a man's world and women suffered abuse and misuse in a typical fashion for the period. It was not until the early feminist movements of the 1960s and 1970s that women would question the Beat agenda.

As the Beats became a permanent fixture in popular culture, the more sensationalist elements of the Beat lifestyle soon became commodities that were marketed on a major scale. The mythic outlook and visionary sensibility of the radical individualistic Beats was distorted. For example, *The Many Loves of Dobie Gillis*, a television situation comedy featuring beatnik Maynard G. Krebs, debuted in 1959 and continued its run through the 1963 season. Krebs was a watered-down version of an indolent and aimless beatnik out for kicks. His ineptitude furthered the negative mainstream opinions of the Beats. This kind of commodification made the Beats an early example of mass media's growing ability to defuse rebellious ideas and behavior by transforming philosophical ideas into fashion statements. The Beats became a complex national commodity in an extremely short time. The lurid sensationalism of sex, drugs, and fast living quickly overshadowed any message of love and understanding the Beats were trying to convey. They became, for better or worse, revolutionary products to be purchased or discarded by the public at large. Beat is now a pop artifact, much like classic rock and roll, used to sell cars and clothes. But the essential core of Beat's contribution to American society is its legacy in transforming the consciousness of succeeding generations. Beat ideas remain a potent force in contemporary culture and imagination. The Beats were a true literary and lifestyle movement with far-reaching implications.

Select Bibliography

EDITIONS

On the Road. New York: Viking, 1957.

The Jack Kerouac Collection. Audio cassettes. Produced by James Austin. Santa Monica, Calif.: Rhino Records, 1990.

OTHER WORKS BY KEROUAC

The Town and the City. New York: Harcourt Brace, 1950.

"Essentials of Spontaneous Prose." *The Black Mountain Review* 7 (autumn 1957): 226–228, 230–237.

"Belief and Technique for Modern Prose." *Evergreen Review* 2, no. 8 (spring 1959): 57.

"Beatific: On the Origins of the Beat Generation." *Playboy,* June 1959, pp. 31–32, 42, 79.

Doctor Sax: Faust Part Three. New York: Grove, 1959.

Maggie Cassidy. New York: Avon, 1959.

Mexico City Blues. New York: Grove, 1959.

Pull My Daisy. New York: Grove, 1961.

Visions of Gerard. New York: Farrar, Straus, 1963.

Visions of Cody. New York: McGraw-Hill, 1972.

SECONDARY WORKS

Charters, Ann. *Jack Kerouac.* New York: St. Martin's, 1983.

Cook, Bruce. "King of the Road." *Washington Post,* August 31, 1997, p. X15.

Dardness, George. "The Delicate Dynamics of Friendship: A Reconsideration of Jack Kerouac's *On the Road.*" *American Literature* 46 (May 1974): 200–206.

Dempsey, David. "In Pursuit of 'Kicks.'" *New York Times Book Review,* September 8, 1957, p. 4.

Donaldson, Scott, ed. *On the Road: Text and Criticism.* New York: Penguin, 1979.

Ehrenreich, Barbara. *The Hearts of Men: American Dreams and the Flight from Commitment.* Garden City, N.Y.: Anchor Press/Doubleday, 1983.

Feied, Frederick. *No Pie in the Sky: The Hobo as American Cultural Hero in the Works of Jack London, John Dos Passos, and Jack Kerouac.* New York: Citadel, 1964.

French, Warren G. *Jack Kerouac.* Boston: Twayne, 1986.

Holmes, John Clellon. "This Is the Beat Generation." *New York Times Magazine,* November 16, 1952, pp. 10–22.

———. "The Philosophy of the Beat Generation." *Esquire,* February 1958, pp. 35–38.

Hunt, Timothy A. *Kerouac's Crooked Road: Development of a Fiction.* Hamden, Conn: Archon, 1981.

Jackson, Carl T. "The Counterculture Looks East: Beat Writers and Asian Religion." *American Studies* 29 (spring 1988): 51–70.

Knight, Brenda, ed. *Women of the Beat Generation: The Writers, Artists, and Muses at the Heart of a Revolution.* Berkeley, Calif.: Conari Press, 1996.

Krim, Seymour. "King of the Beats." *Commonweal,* January 2, 1959, pp. 359–360.

Lardas, John. *The Bop Apocalypse: The Religious Visions of Kerouac, Ginsberg, and Burroughs.* Urbana: University of Illinois Press, 2001.

MacAdams, Lewis. *Birth of the Cool: Beat, Bebop, and the American Avant-Garde.* New York: Free Press, 2001.

Miles, Barry. *The Beat Hotel: Ginsburg, Burroughs and Corso in Paris—1958–1963.* New York: Grove, 2000.

Oates, Joyce Carol. "Down the Road: Jack Kerouac's Highs and Lows, Reconsidered in

Two Collections." *The New Yorker,* March 27, 1995, pp. 96–100.

O'Neill, Paul. "The Only Rebellion Around." *Life,* November 30, 1959, pp. 114–116, 119–120, 123–124, 126, 129–130.

Peabody, Richard, ed. *A Different Beat: Writings by Women of the Beat Generation (1997).* New York: Serpent's Tail, 1997.

Phillips, Rod. *"Forest Beatniks" and "Urban Thoreaus."* New York: Peter Lang, 2002.

Plummer, William. "Jack Kerouac: The Beat Goes On." *New York Times Magazine,* December 30, 1979, pp. 18–23, 39–41, 44.

Podhoretz, Norman. "The Know-Nothing Bohemians." *Partisan Review* 25 (1958): 305–318.

Seelye, John D. "The American Tramp: A Version of the Picaresque." *American Quarterly* 15 (1963): 535–553.

Sisk, John P. "Beatniks and Tradition." *Commonweal,* April 17, 1959, pp. 74–77.

Sterritt, David. *Mad to be Saved. The Beats, the 50's and Film.* Carbondale and Edwardsville: Southern Illinois University Press, 1998.

Swartz, Omar. *The View from* On the Road: *The Rhetorical Vision of Jack Kerouac.* Carbondale: Southern Illinois University Press, 1999.

Tytell, John. "The Beat Generation and the Continuing American Revolution." *American Scholar* 42 (1973): 308–317.

———. *Naked Angels: The Lives & Literature of the Beat Generation.* New York: McGraw- Hill, 1976.

Watson, Steven. *The Birth of the Beat Generation: Visionaries, Rebels, and Hipsters, 1944–1960.* New York: Pantheon, 1995.

Weinreich, Regina. *The Spontaneous Poetics of Jack Kerouac: A Study of the Fiction.* New York: Paragon House, 1990.

Henry James's
The Portrait of a Lady

JONATHAN FREEDMAN

HENRY JAMES IS undeniably one of America's greatest novelists, and *The Portrait of a Lady* is widely considered one of his greatest achievements. It is certainly his most accessible major novel, rich in social detail and closely observed psychological analysis, written with elegance and wit. As such, it is a brilliant example of the prime imaginative form of his era, the form to which he had devoted most of his considerable intelligence and will to mastering—the nineteenth-century novel. But *Portrait* also anticipated the genre that was to follow it: the modern, and perhaps even the postmodern, novel, that form which raises questions about the very possibilities of realistic representation upon which its predecessor depended. James's narrative echoes the achievement of the nineteenth- century novel and anticipates that of the twentieth-century novel by putting front and center the matter of gender. Like the novels of Jane Austen, *Portrait* centers on the courtship of young women; like those of George Eliot, it tracks their experiences after the wedding knot has been tied. But James complicates the marriage plot by yoking it to the question of how the novel, the society, and the self all try to define female identity, how they paint the *portrait* of a lady. In the novel's most audacious moment, its open conclusion, he suggests that these efforts must inevitably fail—and that, in a world without any stable images of gendered and social identity, men and women alike must struggle to shape their own identities through the choices they make, however blindly.

HENRY JAMES BETWEEN ENGLAND AND AMERICA

Henry James was uniquely positioned by his birth, family, and career to perform this act of literary and cultural negotiation. Born in New York City in 1843, James was part of one of the most extraordinary families America has ever seen. His grandfather, William James Sr., arrived penniless in America from Ireland and made a fortune in real estate (he owned, among other things, the land on which Syracuse, New York, was built). His father, Henry James Sr., devoted himself to mystical and utopian writing. His brother William became one of America's greatest philosophers, and his sister, Alice, wrote an extraordinary diary that offers one of the most vivid records of female experience in nineteenth-century America. Along with his four siblings, James was raised according to his father's belief that children should be exposed to as many experiences as possible; he was irregularly educated in America and Europe until attending, briefly, Harvard Law School. James, however, decided from a very early age that he wanted a career as a writer and began publishing short stories, novels, and criticism. He also spent increasing amounts of time in Europe and England, meeting many of the leading intellectuals, writers, and artists of his era.

In 1878 James scored an astonishing success with the publication of the short story *Daisy Miller*, the tale of an American girl innocent of European social conventions whose adventuresomeness culminates in a late-night visit with a disreputable Italian to the disease-ridden Roman Forum—a visit that leads directly to her death from malaria. *Daisy Miller* was a sensation in both England and America but—to its author's chagrin—netted him virtually nothing because of the lack of an international copyright law. Nevertheless, the story introduced James and his characteristic themes to an increasingly sophisticated audience on both sides of the Atlantic. It was a lesson he kept in mind as he sat down, in 1880, to write the novel that was serialized in 1880–1881, published later in 1881 as *The Portrait of a Lady*, and then extensively revised a quarter-century later for the New York edition of his collected works.

Those themes were of direct relevance to his own moment, in which wealthy Americans began to follow the pattern set by the James family and travel in and even immigrate to Europe. *Daisy Miller* brought to the fore—and *Portrait* deepened—the ensuing tragicomic confrontation between the Old and New Worlds. This had been a central concern of much of James's writing up until that point; it is, for example, central to two of his earlier novels, *Roderick Hudson* (1876) and *The American* (1877). But the protagonists of those two works were American men confronting European or Europeanized women with varying degrees of ineffectuality. In *Daisy Miller*, James successfully yoked the plot of cross-cultural confronta-

CHRONOLOGY

1843	Henry James born on April 15 in New York City.
1862–1863	Enters Harvard Law School but leaves to devote himself to writing.
1864–1872	Begins to place stories in the *Atlantic Monthly* and essays, reviews, and travel writing in the *North American Review*, two of the most prestigious periodicals of the era.
1871	First novel, *Watch and Ward*, serialized in *The Atlantic*.
1876	After traveling back and forth for several years, James finally leaves America for Europe, settling in London.
1877	*The American*.
1878	*Daisy Miller* is published in the *Cornhill Magazine* and becomes an international sensation.
1880–1881	*The Portrait of a Lady* is published, again to international acclaim.
1897–1899	James publishes *The Turn of the Screw*, *What Maisie Knew*, *The Spoils of Poynton*, and *The Awkward Age* in rapid succession.
1900–1904	The so-called Major Phase: *The Wings of the Dove*, *The Ambassadors* and *The Golden Bowl* written and published.
1904–1907	James revisits America; writes *The American Scene*. Works on revisions of his major novels for *The New York Edition*.
1915	Takes British citizenship.
1916	Dies on February 28 and is buried in the James family plot in Cambridge, Massachusetts. The expatriate returns home, one last time.

tion with that of another key concern of the time, the changing status of women. F. O. Matthiessen famously dubbed the first of these "the International Theme"; James and his contemporaries took to referring to Daisy, and her successor, as "the American Girl." Uniting the two became for James a way of posing questions about what it is to be an American in a newly globalizing world while registering the transformations of private as well as public life in that world. Indeed, in the collision of cultures and the fate of the American girls who experience them, James found a way of testing the powers and properties of modernity itself.

THE COURTSHIPS OF ISABEL ARCHER

All of these concerns are present from the very first pages of *Portrait,* in which many of its major characters are carefully established in a place and a time specifically rendered. The characters are Ralph Touchett; his father, Daniel; and their friend, the reform-minded Englishman Lord Warburton. The setting is Mr. Touchett's beloved country house in England, Gardencourt, and the time is "the hour dedicated to the ceremony known as afternoon tea." Yet each of these is packed with implications that far transcend the local and that continue to resonate for the rest of the novel. To begin with setting: Gardencourt is not merely an "old English country-house" that provides "an admirable setting to an innocent pastime"; as its name suggests, it is also the very perfection of that form, uniting the pastoral and the social with harmony. As such, Gardencourt is the first of many places of habitation that define the novel's symbolic landscape and testify to the changing destinies of its characters.

It is time, however, that James most insistently renders in the scene. As ideal as the scene may appear, this "perfect middle of a splendid summer afternoon" is haunted by impending nightfall: "the flood of summer light had begun to ebb, the air had grown mellow, the shadows were long upon the smooth dense turf." We are in familiar late Victorian territory here—the same symbolic terrain traced, for example, in Alfred Lord Tennyson's "Ulysses," whose hero, too, evokes the moment of dusk as a symbol of impending mortality: "the long day wanes; the slow moon climbs; the deep / Moans round with many voices." And, as in Tennyson's poem, the image of impending dusk defines the condition of the scene's protagonists. For when we meet them, Ralph Touchett, Daniel Touchett, and Lord Warburton are not described by their physical characteristics, dress, or appearance; rather, it is their "straight and angular" shadows cast by the late-afternoon sun on the "perfect lawn" upon which the urbane narrator focuses. And these shadows literally foreshadow what we soon learn, that all of these characters are shadowy presences in life as well. Daniel sits in a wicker chair, "taking the rest that precedes the great rest." The other two men pacing in front of him are suffering either from a mortal illness (this is Ralph's condition) or a more historical one: for all of his vitality, Lord Warburton is an anachronism, the representative of a dying aristocratic order.

These men are shadowy in another sense as well. They are defined as less than full-blooded males, at least in the terms in which masculinity traditionally has been defined. Almost the first thing we learn about them is that "they were not of the sex which is supposed to furnish" the afternoon tea's participants. A sense of gender confusion continues to hover over the scene: Ralph is described by his father as his "sick-nurse," and Daniel calls his son and himself "two lame ducks." Even Daniel's appearance emphasizes the lack of traditional masculinity: his gout-troubled legs are draped in his wife's shawl. Far from being the imposing pater familias of the idealized Victorian family, Daniel seems lame, impotent, and—at least maritally—bereft. Mrs. Touchett (whose return these characters are anticipating) has been absent from his side for most of their marriage and has abandoned as well the traditional feminine role of nurturer, leaving her sickly son to play the nursemaid.

Before the plot of the novel even begins, the narrative has sketched a social situation marked by marital breach, the breakdown of national and class distinctions, and a pervasive sense of decline and decay. Our responses to these characters are accordingly complex. We note the delicacy with which they treat each other and the fineness of their sensitivity to the civilized refinements of English culture: Gardencourt was initially purchased by Daniel as a bargain, but he has grown to discover a "real aesthetic passion for it." But we still see them as attenuated, sick, dying bachelors or near-bachelors—at least until they glance up to see, framed in a doorway, "a tall girl in a black dress"—Ralph's cousin Isabel. At that moment, things change utterly.

For Isabel is everything these men are not. She is young; she is lively; she is independent. Throughout the first scene, indeed, throughout the first pages of the novel, she shows a spirited freedom of thought and expression that places her in stark contrast to these cultivated, civilized—perhaps overly civilized—men. To be sure, and it is an important attribute of her character, she is profoundly sensitive to the artistic and cultural riches of Gardencourt and the world of leisured ease it represents: "I've never seen anything so lovely as this place," she exclaims as she looks around her. She is also deeply and proudly American, however, and hence both a breath of fresh air and a potential vexation. "Isabel Archer was a young person of many theories," we are told later in the novel; "her imagination was remarkably active." The narrator's tone here is gently, even affectionately, ironic—even though, as we later learn, it is precisely the last of these qualities that her husband complains about. For now, we are asked to see her in the kindest possible light, as a beautiful, if naive counter to the attenuated, dying world in which she finds herself—a new Eve, one who might potentially regenerate the Garden(court) she has entered.

It is certainly in this redemptive light that all of the characters of the novel treat her. The first to do so is Mrs. Touchett, who is responsible for the invitation that brings her to England. Mrs. Touchett, we learn in a flashback in chapter 4, had encountered her niece Isabel in America, following the death of her brother, from whom she had been estranged largely because of his irregular, if affectionate, treatment of his three daughters. At the hands of their spendthrift father, Isabel and her sisters had

> had no education and no permanent home; they had been at once spoiled and neglected; they had lived with nursemaids and governesses (usually very bad ones) or had been sent to superficial schools, kept by the French, from which, at the end of a month, they had been removed in tears.

What this haphazard upbringing—itself much like the one Henry James received—has produced is a woman of lively fantasy and broad interests who is widely but not deeply read, one eager to see what the world offers without knowing much about its perils. And Lydia Touchett, out of sorts with England but in love with Italy, sees in Isabel a vessel to be filled with knowledge—as well as an impecunious relative in need of guidance in the ways of the world.

However—and this is a repeated pattern in the book—the very qualities that draw Mrs. Touchett to Isabel cause Isabel to struggle against her aunt's authority. In a significant moment in the novel, one that like so many in the first chapters is to take on an ironic, if not tragic, resonance later, Mrs. Touchett discovers just how great Isabel's independent-mindedness turns out to be. Mrs. Touchett warns her niece (in an exchange in chapter 7) about the impropriety of staying up late with Ralph and Lord Warburton, adding:

> "I shall always tell you . . . whenever I see you taking what seems to me too much liberty."
>
> "Pray do; but I don't say I shall always think your remonstrance just."
>
> "Very likely not. You are too fond of your own ways."
>
> "Yes, I think I'm very fond of them. But I always want to know the things one shouldn't do."
>
> "So as to do them?" asked her aunt.
>
> "So as to choose," said Isabel.

Isabel's desire to test conventional ideas by her own standards is defined as a quintessentially American one: it is articulated in the classic American terms of liberty and choice. But James's British readers—and perhaps his American ones as well—could not be blamed for thinking, along with Mrs. Touchett, that such choices are dangerously ill-informed, her desire to judge the force of conventions by the light of her own opinions troubling. Seeking to escape from Mrs. Touchett's constructions of her as a ward to be guided to proper conduct, Isabel falls back on her native (and naive) belief in the powers of the self to make choices without possessing the knowledge or experience to make them wisely.

Mrs. Touchett is not the only one to experience Isabel's resistance to her attempt to fix, define, or shape her. Indeed, the first hundred pages of the novel detail the same dynamic as Isabel encounters—and resists the advances of—a stunning variety of men, all of whom mix appreciation and appropriation in their responses. Lord Warburton is the first to succumb to her charms, and much of the action of the first phase of the novel—roughly its first twelve chapters—is devoted to his courtship. Were this a different kind of narrative—were it, for example, Jane Austen's *Pride and Prejudice*—this would comprise its major action. And, indeed, James seems to be setting us up for a replay of Austen's novel. Like Elizabeth Bennett, Isabel is a dazzlingly self-possessed woman with perhaps too many prefabricated opinions for her own good; like Darcy, Lord Warburton is a somewhat overweening aristocrat who seems perfect for her but whom she rejects as a suitor. James invokes this plot, however, to show its inadequacy to the complexity of his principals. For Warburton is, if anything, not proud enough: although he is wealthy beyond measure, he seems to feel a sense of shame at his own class and historical situation. As Daniel Touchett shrewdly observes, he is torn between his understanding that things must change—that

the British class system and political institutions must be reformed—and his affection for his own privileged way of life. And he looks to Isabel to save him from the bad faith that he knows he is exemplifying, from the boredom that his life has brought him. What might in another novel be, on her part, an irrational prejudice against a lord who seeks to marry a beautiful commoner is here instead a sign of her discernment.

A similar dynamic is at work in her relationship with a second suitor, the young man from Boston who courted her in America and who follows her to England: Caspar Goodwood. If Lord Warburton represents a declining English power, Caspar embodies an ascending American one. Like Warburton he has inherited wealth, but Goodwood is no idler. He exercises his "sharp eye for the mystery of mechanics" by inventing an "improvement in the cotton-spinning process." Physically, Goodwood is described in terms that make him the antithesis of Warburton: he is "square and set, and his figure . . . straight and stiff." He is nothing if not determined, if not obsessed, in pursuing Isabel to England, with the encouragement of *another* American who joins the cavalcade, the intrepid reporter Henrietta Stackpole. Isabel resists his attentions as much as she does Warburton's and for many of the same reasons: to exercise her judgment free of other people's ideas of what that judgment should be. As with Warburton, along with the rejection of Caspar, Isabel seems to be rejecting another potential narrative for herself, one like Emily Brontë's *Wuthering Heights,* in which a woman experiences a blind, romantic passion for a hypermasculine man. Although a practical Yankee like Goodwood may make an odd comparison to Heathcliff, he, too, appears primitive, primal, and profoundly out of place in an overly effete civilized world. And even though Isabel is no Cathy, calling to the moors for her beloved, her feelings for Goodwood are clearly robust: led by an "irresistible impulse," she cries bitterly after she sends him away. Nevertheless, Isabel wants to write the narrative of her own destiny, the fiction of her own fate, not have it determined for her by this passionate, if single-minded, lover, even if—or especially because—it means rejecting her own capacities for passion.

Isabel's desire to construct a new narrative for herself and the novel's desire to break out of the conventions of the nineteenth-century novel collide further in the narrative created by Isabel's third, and most important, lover in the early pages of the book, Ralph. To be sure, Ralph disavows any amorous intent, to his father, to his mother, and to himself. He is too awkward, too melancholy, too self-conscious of his own mortality, to offer himself as anything other than a friend, although he ultimately confesses to Isabel (and himself) that he loves her, albeit, predictably, when she is on the verge of marrying another man. Yet it is evident from the first (chapter 7) that his feelings for Isabel are powerful indeed, if complicated:

> He wondered whether he were falling in love with this spontaneous woman from Albany, but he judged that on the whole he was not. . . . If his cousin were to be nothing more than an entertainment to him, Ralph was conscious that she was an entertainment of a high order. "A character like that," he said to himself, "a real passionate force at play, is the finest thing in nature. It is finer than the finest work of art—than a Greek bas-relief, than a great Titian, than a Gothic cathedral. . . . I had never been more blue, more bored, than for a week before she came; I had never expected less that something pleasant would happen. Suddenly, I received a Titian, by the post, to hang on my wall—a Greek bas-relief to stick over my chimney-piece. The key of a beautiful edifice is thrust into my hand, and I am told to walk in and admire. My poor boy, you've been sadly ungrateful, and now you had better keep very quiet and never grumble again."

Ralph's attitudes are not untroubled or untroubling. It is clear from his interior monologue that he is rechanneling his affections for his cousin into a form of distanced appreciation. To a certain extent, this appreciation is admirable; not only does he compare Isabel to great works of art but he also understands that her generous, expansive character is finer than anything art can offer. Just as that claim collapses in this paragraph, however, into the attitude it disavows—just as Isabel is transformed in Ralph's metaphorical imagination into the art objects he has just finished saying that she transcends—Ralph's response to Isabel seems to be touched with a detached connoisseurship that seems dangerously akin to voyeurism. His response is even more disturbing. As Carolyn Porter has reminded us, Ralph does not stop with mere spectatorship; rather, he actively intervenes in Isabel's life. Understanding that the essential question of her life was what "she [was] going to do with herself"—since Isabel, unlike most women, was not content to wait "in attitudes more or less gracefully passive for a man to come that way and furnish them with a destiny"—he undertakes to put "wind in her sails" by prevailing upon his father (who has just asked Ralph to marry Isabel) to leave her half of the money he had intended for Ralph. Ralph's motives in doing so are undeniably generous, his desire to see her freed of material circumstance to become what she will, not what she has to be. But this plan also chimes with his vicarious desires. He asks his father to "put money in her purse" so that she may "meet the requirements" of his own "imagination." Moreover, far from freeing her from culturally scripted narratives, the plan merely places her in a different one. The plot device of an inheritance mysteriously passing to an unsuspecting orphan is a staple of literary romance and its antecedent, fairy-tale. By unwittingly constructing *this* narrative for Isabel, Ralph equally unconsciously plots a tragedy. For as he learns—and, more powerfully, Isabel learns—all too painfully, neither of their imaginations exerts itself in a vacuum; rather, the imagination is exercised in a world of power, desire, and chicanery that is all too real.

THE GULLING OF ISABEL ARCHER: MADAME MERLE AND THE UNDOING OF ROMANCE

About a third of the way through the novel, Isabel walks into the drawing room at Gardencourt to encounter a woman, with her back mysteriously turned to the room, playing Schubert on the piano. Intrigued, she asks Ralph who this fascinating addition to their little social world, one Serena Merle, may be, and Ralph replies, "the cleverest woman I know, not excepting yourself." As Isabel intuits, this is not intended as a compliment to Madame Merle—although (or perhaps because of the fact that) Ralph was once in love with her. Ralph's warning falls on deaf ears: Isabel, so resistant to her aunt, Lord Warburton, Caspar, and Henrietta's attempts to place her in their narrative frames, falls easily into Madame Merle's, although—so great is her cleverness—Isabel never suspects her.

Before proceeding to her plot (in all senses of the word), it is important to give Madame Merle her due. The reasons why Madame Merle so rapidly places Isabel "under an influence" are palpable. She is sophisticated, accomplished, witty; she has traveled far and read widely and, at least with respect to Isabel, she is opinionated without being judgmental, appreciative without being sycophantic (with respect to Ralph and Daniel, she is severe to the point of cattiness). Most important, unlike the rest of the people Isabel encounters, she is never idle. In a world of connoisseurs, we are told in chapter 19, Madame Merle is something of an artist. "When Madame Merle was neither writing, nor painting, nor touching the piano, she was usually employed upon wonderful tasks of rich embroidery, cushions, curtains, decorations for the chimney-piece: an art in which her bold, free invention was as noted as the agility of her needle." All this gives weight to Isabel's pleased amazement

at her company and credibility to her ignoring the warnings offered not only by Ralph but also by Mrs. Touchett, Henrietta Stackpole, and even Madame Merle herself. Madame Merle, with characteristic disingenuousness, tells the truth about herself to Isabel in the act of urbanely comparing herself to a humble teapot:

> I flatter myself that I'm rather stout, but if I must tell you the truth I've been shockingly chipped and cracked. I do very well for service yet, because I've been cleverly mended; and I try to remain in the cupboard . . . as much as I can. But when I've to come out and into a strong light—then, my dear, I'm a horror.

The metaphoric connection this passage suggests between Madame Merle and objects is not fortuitous. Precisely that connection allows James to set up a debate that resonates throughout the novel. In the course of one of the many conversations the two women have as they cement their friendship, Madame Merle expresses to Isabel a philosophy of life that defines the self in terms of things:

> When you've lived as long as I you'll see that every human being has his shell and that you must take the shell into account. . . . There's no such thing as an isolated man or woman; we're each of us made up of some cluster of appurtenances. What shall we call our "self"? Where does it begin? where does it end? It overflows into everything that belongs to us—and then it flows back again. . . . I've a great respect for *things*.

Isabel answers her friend in terms that take precisely the opposite view: "I know that nothing else expresses me. Nothing that belongs to me is any measure of me; everything's on the contrary a limit, a barrier, and a perfectly arbitrary one. Certainly, the clothes which as you say, I choose to wear, don't express me, and heaven forbid that they should." (Madame Merle perhaps gets the best of this particular exchange when she quietly reminds Isabel: "You dress very well.")

The debate between these two visions has been brewing for much of the novel. If "clothes" metaphorically signify social convention, then this is a version of the quarrel between Isabel and Mrs. Touchett. If "things" imply objectification—the treating of human beings as if they were objects—then it is congruent with Ralph's own split image of Isabel as transcending and being equivalent to a work of art. And if the "cluster of appurtenances" represents the art objects, houses, trappings with which culture surround the self, then the debate here is between a European and an American understanding of the relation between history and identity. (Indeed, Isabel's language could have come out of Ralph Waldo Emerson's "Self-Reliance," with its famous injunction "Trust thyself! Every heart vibrates to that iron string!"). Madame Merle puts one side of that debate with lucidity, just as Isabel's ingenuousness and vitality argue powerfully for the other. Each side in that debate ultimately loses, however, and James's novel affirms—if it can be said to be an affirmation—the tragic recognition that neither an objectified vision, no matter how grimly realistic, nor a transcendental one, no matter how thrillingly idealistic, is adequate to a world of human choices and their consequences.

OSMOND: THE AESTHETE AS REALITY INSTRUCTOR

The teacher of this harsh lesson, to both Isabel and, ironically enough, Madame Merle herself, is the one figure in this ostensibly realistic novel who approaches the status of villain, Gilbert Osmond. Yet another expatriate—a widower raising a young daughter in Rome, a connoisseur who seems to be devoted to the study of Renaissance art—Osmond seems the most unlikely possible partner for Isabel. Yet he is the linchpin of Madame Merle's plan for Isabel's future. She begins talking him up early in her acquaintance with Isabel, puts her in contact with him when they visit Rome, and entices Osmond to drop his habitual indolence, indifference, and contempt to woo Isabel. It is not until he learns of her fortune, however, that he rouses

himself to be interested in her and not until he learns that she has rejected so stunning a suitor as Lord Warburton that he decides that she is qualified "to figure in his collection of choice objects."

We learn fairly early on why Madame Merle should be so intent on making this marriage. She and Osmond had been lovers in the distant past, although there seems to be some other business between them that the novel leaves unspecified. What remains surprising is that Isabel should respond to this self-obsessed, snobbish, contemptuous aesthete—a character who, like many indolent gentlemen in the later nineteenth century, devotes his life to art to the point of collapsing the two into each other. ("One ought to make one's life a work of art," Osmond says at one point, implying that he has mastered both. Ralph is doubtless more accurate when he refers to Gilbert contemptuously as a "sterile dilettante.") Here, as in the other courtship plots, there is ample literary precedent. Isabel makes the same mistake that Dorothea Brooke makes when she marries the aged pedant Casaubon in George Eliot's *Middlemarch* (1872), although Osmond resembles more closely the sadistic Grandcourt of Eliot's *Daniel Deronda* (1876). It would not have helped Isabel to consult either of Eliot's novels, for it is Gilbert's seeming uniqueness that captivates her. "He resembled no one she had ever seen," the narrator tells us. "Her mind contained no class offering a natural place to Mr. Osmond—he was a specimen apart." Or so she thinks. But as the language of this passage suggests, she cannot see that her failure to place Osmond is utterly appropriate: that he has no positive characteristics of his own, that he can be defined only in terms of negation. And these are, indeed, the very terms that every character in the book uses to define Gilbert. Madame Merle describes him to Isabel as follows: "No career, no name, no position, no fortune, no past, no future, no anything." After meeting Osmond for the first time, Ralph identifies him to Warburton by name. "What is he besides?" Warburton asks.

"Nothing at all," Ralph replies. Osmond himself uses this language when, proposing to Isabel, he issues a declaration that like all of his statements, is as morally fatuous as it is literally true: "I've neither fortune, nor fame, nor extrinsic advantages of any kind. So I offer nothing."

Isabel commits the error of mistaking Gilbert's passivity for mystery, his fastidiousness for subtlety, his witholdingness for self-possession, his indifference for reserve. She responds to the mystery of his poverty (in chapter 26) in the same way as Ralph does to that of her plentitude, by transforming Gilbert, mentally, into a work of art:

> She had carried away an image from her visit to his hill-top which her subsequent knowledge of him did nothing to efface and which put on for her a particular harmony with other supposed and divined things, histories within histories: the image of a quiet, sensitive, distinguished man, strolling on a moss-grown terrace above the sweet Val d'Arno and holding by the hand a little girl whose bell-like clarity gave a new grace to childhood. The picture had no flourishes, but she liked its lowness of tone, and the atmosphere of summer twilight that pervaded it.

This genre painting is a complete misperception of Osmond and a sentimental evasion of the truth of his relationship to Pansy: Gilbert seeks the same spirit-crushing obedience from his daughter that he is going to ask from Isabel. But far more troubling is the way that she, like Ralph, misuses this perceptual habit. Seeing people as if they were works of art is one thing; it is part and parcel of Isabel's sensitive, idealistic nature, just as it is part of Ralph's. But she, too, makes the mistake of confusing aesthetic and economic motives. Blinded by her own idealism, she cannot see that for all his talk of artistic cultivation and his sensitive demeanor, Osmond is nothing more than an arrogant fortune hunter. The irony here is manifest: it is usually aesthetes like Osmond who are accused of confusing the line between art and life. Sadly, it turns out to be the kindest, and most generous-spirited,

characters in this book who make that mistake—and who must face its consequences.

MRS. OSMOND

It is at this moment in the novel that James begins to experiment most audaciously with literary form. After devoting many chapters to Osmond's courtship and to Isabel's rebuffs of the objections of Caspar (who offers himself to her yet again), Ralph (who has proclaimed his love but remains silent about his role in the making of her fortune), and Mrs. Touchett (who warns her explicitly that Madame Merle has been working overtime to maneuver her into marrying Osmond), the novel leaves the reader suspended in midair, curious about what will happen in this most misconceived of marriages as it skips forward several years. To heighten the suspense, it defers our vision of Isabel for many pages, focusing on a hitherto minor character, a young collector named Ned Rosier, who has fallen in love with Pansy Osmond. We follow Rosier as he enters the door into the Osmonds' grand home in Rome, the Palazzo Roccanera. We witness his encounter with a cold Osmond, who uses the language of collecting to warn Rosier to stay away from Pansy ("I've nothing I wish to match"), and we look through his eyes as he encounters a changed Isabel:

> She was dressed in black velvet; she looked high and splendid, as he had said, and yet oh so radiantly gentle! . . . Like his appreciation of her dear little stepdaughter [his appreciation of her] was based partly on his eye for decorative character, his instinct for authenticity; but also on a sense for uncatalogued values, for that secret of a "lustre" beyond any recorded losing or rediscovering. . . . Mrs. Osmond, at present, might well have gratified such tastes. The years had touched her only to enrich her; the flower of her youth had not faded, it only hung more quietly on its stem. She had lost something of that quick eagerness to which her husband had privately taken exception—she had more the air of being able to wait. Now, at all events, framed in the gilded doorway,

she struck our young man as the picture of a gracious lady.

Here, as in her first appearance in the novel, Isabel is "framed" in a doorway; here, too, she is wearing black. But both of these images have taken a new significance, at least for the reader (Ned is oblivious to it). The black velvet seems to be a form of mourning—perhaps for her previous life of possibility, perhaps for the daughter whom, we learn, she lost in childbirth. And her "framing" of this "picture of a gracious lady" by a doorway suggests not only that she is a subject in a portrait but also that Isabel has been imprisoned in a gilded cage. The novel, then, raises questions not only about Isabel's marriage but also about its own procedures. Ned sees Isabel as Ralph has unwittingly seen her and as Osmond consciously wishes to see her: as a static art object, one to be "appreciated" perhaps, but one who is fettered by that construction. The novel thus implies that its own author has courted the same representational error. For insofar as the novel claims to be a "portrait of a lady"—a detached, realistic, objective account of Isabel's experience—it aligns itself with possibilities that it criticizes. Moreover, insofar as we, the readers of the novel, have been placed in Rosier's position, we, too, are asked to critique our assumptions about the kinds of experiences we have been enjoying—the ways in which we, like Rosier, Isabel, Ralph, and Osmond, have been imagining as objects the characters whose very human struggles we have been witnessing with aesthetic detachment.

In this way, James's fiction turns from the realistic register in which it has been written and becomes something quite different, something more self-conscious and self-critical. It does so, paradoxically, by moving simultaneously in two distinctly different representational directions. On the one hand, the novel dives inward and starts to investigate, at great length, the thought processes and perspectives of its characters—not only Rosier's but first Ralph's and then, most important and at the greatest length, Isabel's. At

the same time, it gives us scenes that are hyperbolic, stagy, even at times out-and-out melodramatic. James thereby creates that form which Peter Brooks has brilliantly called "the melodrama of consciousness"—a form that brings to the reflections and self-understandings of a novel's characters the same intensity, the same overwhelming dramatic force, that melodrama lends to those in the theater.

Thus the narrative begins on the inside, showing us Isabel undergoing a long, painfully slow process of introspection in which she struggles to make sense of how she could have entered such an unhappy marriage. James performs the remarkably delicate act of showing us a character not so much thinking—although, in this, he anticipates the kind of stream-of-consciousness technique that modernists later employed, with much fanfare, after his death—as *rethinking*, puzzling out the exact train of thought that led to a disastrous set of choices. Even as Isabel mulls over her own motives, she faces radically new complications and questions. Many of them center on Pansy. Isabel has come increasingly to favor Ned's suit—largely because his feelings are reciprocated by the girl—while Osmond, predictably, favors Lord Warburton's, for the meanest of reasons and with the vilest of implications. Osmond believes, correctly, that Warburton still carries a torch for Isabel and wants Isabel to use her influence with Lord Warburton to encourage him to ask for Pansy's hand. As Isabel attempts to sort out what her proper role might be in this delicate situation, she finds herself returning over and over again to the figure of Madame Merle—or, more specifically, to Mrs. Touchett's claim that Madame Merle made her marriage.

James's text represents this process with enormous delicacy, switching between Isabel's illusion about her own life (she still naively asserts that "there had been no plot, no snare" leading to her marriage) and her increasing suspicion of her former friend, who goes to great, too great, lengths to press Warburton's case while disavowing any connection to Osmond. (She even goes so far, with rare bad taste, as to boast that she could have had him if she wanted.) The latter leads Isabel, moreover, to a new alertness. Returning home one day, she encounters a scene (in chapter 40) that, previously, she might have thought innocent:

> Madame Merle was there in her bonnet, and Gilbert Osmond was talking to her; for a minute they were unaware she had come in. Isabel had often seen that before, certainly; but what she had not seen, or at least had not noticed, was that their colloquy had for the moment converted itself into a sort of familiar silence, from which she instantly perceived that her entrance would startle them. Madame Merle was standing on the rug, a little way from the fire; Osmond was in a deep chair, leaning back and looking at her. Her head was erect, as usual, but her eyes were bent on his. What struck Isabel first was that he was sitting while Madame Merle stood; there was an anomaly in this that arrested her. Then she perceived that they had arrived at a desultory pause in their exchange of ideas and were musing, face to face, with the freedom of old friends who sometimes exchange ideas without uttering them. There was nothing to shock in this; they were old friends in fact. But the thing made an image, lasting only a moment, like a sudden flicker of light. Their relative positions, their absorbed mutual gaze, struck her as something detected.

In witnessing this tableau, Isabel learns something we have known all along. But the scene also teaches us, along with her, something about their relationship—and about power tactics in the social world they inhabit. Even though Osmond is still and seated, he seems to exert an ocular power over Madame Merle: however mutual their looks, Madame Merle's gaze is "bent" to Osmond's, as if to express her submission to his will. (He is soon to dismiss her as a friend entirely.) Their visual intimacy is something "detected"—something that only gives itself away to her own spectatorship, very like that of an audience in the theater. As such, this scene of Isabel witnessing people silently gazing suggests the means by which she will become a more effective social player. For its

highly dramatic nature indicates the increasing prominence of the theatrical mode in Isabel's life, posing challenges that nothing in her American past prepares her for. In a world of performances by accomplished actors like Osmond and Merle, Isabel is going to have to learn to be more than just a member of the audience. She, too, is going to have to learn to act—in all senses of that word.

THE AWAKENING OF ISABEL OSMOND

Even as Isabel prepares her entrance on the stage of social performances, the novel moves deeper into her consciousness. After Isabel has been pressed first by Madame Merle and then by Osmond to make Warburton and Pansy's marriage, she sits by the fire and muses over her marriage. In what is doubtless the most audacious formal experiment in the book, James gives us a chapter-long account of Isabel's own thoughts. It is a remarkable performance—as a piece of narration in its own right, as a recapitulation of the major image patterns that the book has been employing, and as a radically new take on the questions of representation and gender that the novel has been raising.

To begin with the first: we learn, as she muses over the question, just why she has chosen Osmond. It is as an act of generosity designed to match Mr. Touchett's and a way of dealing with her sense of guilt at having been given her fairy-tale-like gift. "What would lighten her own conscience more effectually," she asks herself, "than to make it over to the man with the best taste in the world?" But Isabel's language suggests that her motives may not have been quite as pure as she intended. "The finest—in the sense of being the subtlest—manly organism she had ever known had become her property, and the recognition of her having but to put out her hands and take it had been originally a sort of act of devotion." However generous-spirited she might have been, Isabel is starting to reckon with the possibility that her own motives may be—or may have become—touched by the acquisitiveness she is forced to discover in Gilbert. To be sure, his remains uncontaminated by any of her benevolence; in his last appearance in the book, true to form, he dismisses Isabel while sketching a gold coin.

In addition to exhibiting this psychological complexity, the chapter demonstrates an artistic one. Just as Isabel revisits the course of her marriage, trying to figure out how it went so disastrously wrong, she employs the image patterns that other characters and the novel itself have used to define her. When, for example, she thinks of Osmond's power to blight any sense of freedom or expansiveness she might bring to the marriage, she thinks: "It was as if he had had the evil eye." The same image recurs as she claims, metaphorically, "they looked at each other with eyes that were on either side a declaration of the deception suffered"—although here, we may note, Isabel sees herself as Osmond's equal in the staring contest, not, as does Madame Merle, his inferior.

Similarly, the imagery of houses that has been so important in the narrative enters her consciousness. "It was not her fault," Isabel assures herself; "she had taken all the first steps in the purest confidence, and then she had suddenly found the infinite vista of a multiplied life to be a dark, narrow alley with a dead wall at the end." Up until now, we may remember, Isabel has been pictured in doorways—the one leading out to Gardencourt, the second leading from one room to the other in her palazzo. But now she images herself in the reverse, a cul-de-sac leading to a blank wall, a windowless prison not unlike the Palazzo Roccanera—literally Blackrock—in which she and Osmond live. And, indeed, this palazzo, so much the opposite of the open, airy Gardencourt, comes to serve as Isabel's image (in chapter 42) for the prison house that is her marriage:

Between [its] four walls she had lived ever since; they were to surround her for the rest of her life. It was the house of darkness, the house of dumbness, the house of suffocation. Osmond's beautiful mind gave it neither light nor air; Osmond's beautiful mind indeed seemed to peep down from a small high window and mock at her.

If Gardencourt has been established by James as an Edenic spot and Osmond is identified with the tempting serpent ("his facility, his knowledge of life, his egotism lay hidden like a serpent in a bank of flowers"), Isabel images her new life as a demonic parody of that in the innocent Garden:

Her mind was to be his—attached to his own like a small garden-plot to a deer-park. He would rake the soil gently and water the flowers; he would weed the beds and gather an occasional nosegay. It would be a pretty piece of property for a proprietor already far-reaching.

It is at this moment that the novel might best be thought of not as a realistic novel but rather as a self-reflexive, modernist one. For Isabel's mind, "assailed by visions," creates metaphors to encompass her own experience that echo the very terms that hitherto have been used to define or construct her, by other characters and by the narrative itself. James's aim in creating this effect, it needs to be stressed, is not to raise questions about representation per se. Rather, it is to advance his account of the relationship between narrative and gender, between the stories a culture tells about women and a woman's desire to tell new stories about herself. Isabel's task is no longer that of Emersonian self-invention ex nihilo; instead, it is one of refashioning the terms that she has been given. Whether she can do so or not is an open question—a question the novel keeps ranging as Isabel faces one choice after another until the very last pages of the novel confront her with the most weighty choice of all. But before Isabel can even get to this point, she must deal with all the people who have attempted to control her: Madame Merle and Osmond, to be sure, but also Lord Warburton, Caspar Goodwood, and Ralph. Most important, she must come to terms with herself—with who she has become and what she is to do with that self-knowledge.

THE MELODRAMA OF FREEDOM

The first negotiations occur with Osmond. Isabel is forbidden by her husband to go to the long-dying Ralph's deathbed, to which she is summoned by Mrs. Touchett. She is thereby forced choose between her loyalty to her most loyal and loving friend and her commitment to a marriage that has ended in spirit but remains, at least to her, a valued and valuable form. Again, the novel seems to be switching genres. Written in the era of Henrik Ibsen's *Doll's House* (1879); or William Dean Howells' *Modern Instance* (1882), *Portrait* seems to be becoming a "problem" novel in the socially conscious mode. It is a novel addressing directly that most curious and fragile of institutions, marriage, as it faces a modern world in which divorce is an increasingly viable option. Osmond's words to Isabel in chapter 51 brings that issue to the fore:

> I've an ideal of what my wife should do and should not do. She should not travel across Europe alone, in defiance of my deepest desire, to sit at the bedside of other men. Your cousin's nothing to you; he's nothing to us. You smile most expressively, when I talk about *us,* but I assure you that *we, we,* Mrs. Osmond, is all I know. I take our marriage seriously; you appear to have found a way of not doing so. I'm not aware that we're divorced or separated; for me, we're indissolubly united.

The stakes for Isabel—and in the novel—are high, and to raise them even higher James, in the very same chapter, turns the dramatic screw one more notch. Osmond's sister, the Countess Gemini, reveals to Isabel that Pansy is not, as everyone has hitherto believed, the daughter of his dead wife. Rather, Pansy is the product of his affair with Madame Merle, and she and Osmond have been engaged in a complicated deception—or perhaps it would be better to say an artfully conducted performance—ever since. As Robert Weisbuch has suggested, Isabel may have imagined Osmond as a kind of a second Satan, but only now does she actually encounter what evil looks like, out and open in the social world.

While her suspicions of Madame Merle have been growing, only now does she fully understand the manipulative nature of her friend. Earlier, she "asked herself, with an almost childlike horror of the supposition, whether to this intimate friend of several years the great historical epithet of *wicked* were to be applied"; now she is in a position to answer that question in the affirmative.

In order to capture that sense of pure malevolence, this most supple of novels has increasingly explicit recourse to the mode it has been exploring: to melodrama—that dramatic form in which good and evil come into definitive and ferocious conflict with each other. The typical subject matter of melodrama—the confrontation of a usually female innocent with adversities often incarnated by pestiferous men (would-be rapists, child abusers, slave masters)—could not be closer to that, increasingly, plotted by *Portrait.* Neither could the heightened form of expression that characterizes the form, in which characters initiate their plots or bemoan their fates with unaffected directness. But James has, as usual, a complex relationship to the genre he invokes. While Isabel may respond to Osmond by constructing metaphors that partake of melodrama, her encounters with Madame Merle move explicitly into this representational terrain. In their first major confrontation, when Madame Merle starts to push Lord Warburton's suit in ways Isabel properly finds disturbing, the quarrel (in chapter 49) between the two ends as follows:

> "What have you to do with me?" Isabel went on.
>
> Madame Merle slowly got up, stroking her muff, but not removing her eyes from Isabel's face.
>
> "Everything!" she answered.
>
> Isabel sat there looking up at her, without rising; her face was almost a prayer to be enlightened. But the light of her visitor's eyes seemed only a darkness.
>
> "Oh, misery!" she murmured at last, and she fell back, covering her face with her hands. . . .

Mrs. Touchett was right. Madame Merle had married her!

We have come a long way indeed from the realistic register and the genteel authorial commentary that marked the opening chapters of the book. Here gestures are dramatic to the point of unnatural intensity, the language heightened to the point of hyperbole not only on the part of the protagonists but also on that of the narrator. Melodramatic as it seems, however, this encounter between two women complicates the gender dynamics of melodrama, at least as established earlier in the novel. For this scene reproduces the power play we have seen in the equally dramatic scene between Osmond and Madame Merle, in which his "evil eye" seems to possess the power to transfix her, except that in this scene, it is a woman who uses this power to dominate another woman. James asks us, in chapter 52, to keep this reversal in mind in the next confrontation between the two, one fraught with even greater intensity, when Isabel meets Madame Merle, whom she now knows to be Pansy's mother, in the convent-school in which the girl is more or less incarcerated:

> Isabel saw it all as distinctly as if it had been reflected in a large clear glass. It might have been a great moment for her, for it might have been a moment of triumph. That Madame Merle had lost her pluck and saw before her the phantom of exposure—this in itself was revenge. . . . And for a moment during which she stood apparently looking out of the window, with her back half turned, Isabel enjoyed that knowledge. On the other side of the window lay the garden of the convent; but this is not what she saw; she saw nothing of the budding plants and the glowing afternoon. She saw, in the crude light of that revelation which had already became a part of experience . . . the dry staring fact that she had been an applied handled hung-up tool, as senseless and convenient as mere shaped wood and iron. All the bitterness of this knowledge surged into her soul again; it was as if she felt on her lips the taste of dishonor. There was a moment during which, if she had turned and spoken, she would have said something that would hiss like a lash. But she closed her eyes, and then

the hideous vision dropped. What remained was the cleverest woman in the world standing there within a few feet of her and knowing as little what to think as the meanest. Isabel's only revenge was to be silent still—to leave Madame Merle in this unprecedented situation. She left her there for a period that must have seemed long to this lady, who at last seated herself with a movement that was itself a confession of helplessness. Then Isabel turned slow eyes, looking down at her. Madame Merle was very pale; her own eyes covered Isabel's face. She might see what she would, but her danger was over. Isabel would never accuse her, never reproach her; perhaps because she would never give her the opportunity to defend herself.

Here, Isabel shows that she has learned much from her husband. Like Osmond, Isabel acts by doing *nothing* and thereby approaches his cruelty, albeit with some justification. Even though Isabel's first response on learning of her relationship to Pansy was to sympathize ("Ah, poor, poor woman!"), in this confrontation scene, her remaining "silent still" denies Madame Merle not only sympathy but identity itself. Withholding from her the chance to explain, to justify, Isabel's silence is tantamount to negating her motives, her point of view, and her subjectivity. And also like Osmond, Isabel signifies her own triumph by silently staring—signifying both her own superior knowledge and the superiority of her refusal to use it. Madame Merle, to be sure, has some cards left to play. Later in the scene, after Isabel has spoken with Pansy and promised to return to her after visiting Ralph's deathbed, Merle makes an appeal to Isabel's generous spirit: "You're very unhappy. I know. But I'm more so." But Isabel will have none of it. "Yes; I can believe that," she responds. "I think I should like never to see you again." Isabel and Osmond may be on the verge of severing their marriage bond, but ironically they are at one in their common rejection of the woman who links them. Madame Merle acknowledges this with what is for this cultured émigré doubtless the ultimate act of self-abnegation: "I shall go to America."

ISABEL'S FATE: "SO AS TO CHOOSE"

The novel's invocation of melodrama, then, suggests that Isabel has learned her lesson well: in a world of dramatic performances where sincerity is suspect and naïveté a species of victimization, she must act a part whether she likes it or not. But she must learn to act in another sense as well: perform actions in that world in such a way as to affirm her own values. In doing so—as she has said, so long ago, to her aunt—she must choose, and the results of that choice are not always obviously apparent. She already has made the first fateful decision—to defy Osmond and visit Ralph at his deathbed. Once there, the novel builds up to another one of its great dramatic scenes, a final encounter between Isabel and Ralph in which, again, a highly charged dramatic language seems to be the only appropriate form of communication. When Isabel tells Ralph of the abomination that her marriage has become and of her pain at Osmond's seeming dislike for her, he responds with a characteristic warmth purged, by the occasion, of any irony or reserve. "Remember this," Ralph tells her, "that if you've been hated you've also been loved. Ah but, Isabel—*adored!*" "Oh, my brother," Isabel cries, "with a movement of still deeper prostration."

If the scenes between Madame Merle, Osmond, and Isabel have been shaped by the conventions of melodrama, these resemble a different, if linked genre: that of the sentimental novel, in which deathbed scenes, complete with tears, gestures of emotional prostration, and emotion-laden final words, are a staple. Here, too, James is playing with convention even as he invokes such scenes. The most affecting sentimental scenes generally involve the death of young women, like that of Little Eva in the novel that was made into the young Henry James's favorite stage melodrama, Harriet Beecher Stowe's *Uncle Tom's Cabin* (1852). To complete the novel's pattern of gender reversal, it is a sickly man whose impending death is greeted with tears. James is not yet done with invoking

these highly artificial forms of representation, for after Ralph dies, the novel takes another step beyond realism and turns into something of a ghost story. Ralph had once told Isabel, banteringly, that if she should suffer, she would see the ghost of Gardencourt, and in some sense she does. Awakening from sleep as Ralph passes away, she is led to his bedside by the spectral image of Ralph himself: "a vague, hovering figure in the vagueness of the room. She stared a moment; she saw his white face—his kind eyes; then she saw there was nothing." In both these scenes, James finds one more use for generic experimentation; he shifts into sentimental melodrama and ghost story to capture and reproduce human emotions at their highest pitch of intensity.

The novel has one more formal trick up its sleeve, one that enacts the theme of choice that we have been seeing addressed throughout, even as it represents Isabel facing the most important choices yet of her life. Soon after Ralph's burial, she encounters the indefatigable Caspar Goodwood, who has heard from Henrietta Stackpole of Isabel's breach with Osmond. Although she has not yet decided to divorce, he proposes again, with characteristic pragmatism:

> Why shouldn't we be happy—why it's here before us, when it's so easy. . . . What have you to care about? You've no children. . . . You must save what you can of your life; you musn't lose it all simply because you have lost a part. You took the great step in coming away; the next is nothing; it's the natural one. . . . The world's all before us—and the world's very big.

"The world's very small," she responds, but James's prose suggests that she feels otherwise:

> the world in truth had never seemed so large; it seemed to open out, all round her, to take the form of a mighty sea, in which she floated in fathomless waters. She had wanted help; and here was help; it had come in a rushing torrent. I know not whether she believed everything that he said; but she believed just then that to let him take her in his arms would be the next best thing to dying. This

belief, for a moment, was a kind of rapture, in which she felt herself sink and sink. . . .

He glared at her a moment through the dusk, and the next instant she felt his arms about her and his lips on her own lips. His kiss was like white lightning, a flash that spread, and spread again, and stayed; and it was extraordinarily as if, while she took it, she felt each thing in his hard manhood that least pleased her, each aggressive fact of his face, his figure, his presence, justified of its intense identity and made one with this act of possession. So she had heard of those wrecked and under water following a train of images before they sink. But when darkness came she was free.

As this passage suggests, the novel has lurched generically one more time, into a perfervid form of expression that would not be out of place in a Harlequin romance. Again, however, James invokes genre so as to complicate it—and our responses. All the cues in the text direct us to believe that she will fall—as a romantic heroine should—into Caspar's strong arms. His arguments are persuasive indeed, and the text more than hints (as it has been doing throughout) that she is sexually attracted to him as she has not been to any of the other men who engage (or encage) her. But this is precisely what does *not* happen. Rather than launch herself into a life with Caspar, Isabel flees his presence and, we learn, decisively decides to returns to Rome ("She had not known where to turn; but she knew now. There was a very straight path.") Poor Caspar is bereft but encouraged by Henrietta Stackpole to follow her as the novel closes.

In so doing, James creates one of the most famous cruxes in American—if not world—literature. Is Isabel's precipitous retreat from Caspar, as many readers have thought, a retreat as well from her own passions? Certainly the imagery of bursting liquids and surging lighting bolts suggests that she is running as fast and as furiously as she can from the power of her own sexuality as well as the "hard manhood" of Caspar Goodwood. But despite this plethora of generic and imagistic cues, other critics argue, is this not precisely the problem? Does Caspar of-

fer her, as he claims, a form of freedom or just another mode of enthrallment? Moreover, the terms he offers her, while undeniably seductive, are rife with problems.

As we have seen, Isabel has been defined by the text as a new Eve, Osmond as a tempting serpent. (Goodwood even refers to him explicitly as "the deadliest of fiends.") In his speech, Goodwood caps this pattern of allusions by quoting from the greatest poem ever written about the Fall, John Milton's *Paradise Lost*. When Adam and Eve leave the Garden of Eden (in chapter 12) to enter the plain of ordinary human history, Milton tells us

The world was all before them, where to choose
. . . .
They, hand in hand, with wandering steps and
    slow,
Through Eden took their solitary way.

Caspar unwittingly reminds Isabel that she lives not in the Edenic world of Gardencourt but in the fallen world of human choices and the responsibilities that flow from them. Her decision to renounce Goodwood and return to Italy is not to be read as an exercise in masochism, these readers argue, but rather as a fulfillment of her promise to Pansy—and a sign that Isabel has fully accepted the price of her own freedom.

But, still other readers wonder, how long will she stay married to Osmond and on what terms, with Osmond's claiming that she has irrevocably breached the marriage bond and Caspar still planning to pursue her? Here, too, possibilities proliferate. In its 1881 version, the novel ends with Henrietta's encouraging words to Caspar, "Look here, Mr. Goodwood, . . . just you wait!" adding simply: "On which he looked up at her." In the New York edition, James adds a paragraph that makes the quest seem futile:

On which he looked up at her—but only to guess, from her face, with a revulsion, that she simply meant he was young. She stood shining at him with that cheap comfort, and it added, on the spot, thirty years to his life. She walked him away with her, however, as if she had given him now the key to patience.

As downbeat as this ending may be, the inveterate optimist might remember the door imagery with which Isabel's career in the novel begins and ends (she is, just to drive the point home, pictured with her hand on the latch of yet another door after she runs away from Caspar). The words with which James chooses to close, "the key to patience," might suggest to such a reader that Caspar may yet unlock the door behind which Isabel has immured herself. Or, to continue to play with the possibilities, "it may be," F. O. Matthiessen has suggested, that, as Isabel herself conjectures, he may finally "'take her money and let her go.' [Or] it may be that once she has found a husband for Pansy, she will feel that she no longer has to remain in Rome." The best we can conclude is that by ending with Caspar learning of Isabel's fate rather than with an account of that fate itself, James leaves these matters thoroughly up to our readerly imagination. In so doing, he suggests one possible solution to the representational problems that the novel has posed. If reading Isabel in such a way as to fix her identity and fate one way or another puts the reader in the same difficult position as virtually all the characters of the novel, then the resonant ambiguity of its end frees us from our readerly error.

More important, especially in terms of James's concern with gender and representation, this open conclusion suggests the difficulty of the choices available to Isabel. It reminds us that all of the available models of closure offered by the representational forms of the nineteenth century—the realistic novel, which usually ends, however unrealistically, in marriage (as does even so worthy an example as *Middlemarch*); the sentimental melodrama, which usually ends in death; or the social problem novel, which usually ends in social degradation—lock women into an all too familiar set of no-win positions. By leaving his own ending open, James asks us to question all of these socially powerful forms of narrative closure, even while, with the utmost

of authorial generosity, granting Isabel her fondest wish: to choose—and to go on choosing, in the reader's imagination, even after the novel is over.

AFTERIMAGES OF A PORTRAIT

Perhaps this is why *Portrait* has continued to elicit such powerful responses from readers, writers, and artists in the many years since it was first published. Some of these responses were immediate: the novel was a huge success, as great in its own way as *Daisy Miller,* and netted James a fame that he spent much of the rest of his career attempting to recapture. Indeed, perhaps the most important response to *Portrait* may have been his later novel, *The Golden Bowl* (1904), in which James reshuffles the deck of cards he dealt in 1881 and lays out an utterly different hand. Maggie Verver is the daughter of an American aesthete; her best friend, Charlotte Stant, has an affair with her husband that destroys her too-great, too-American innocence. Maggie, like Isabel, chooses to reconstruct the marriage and, like Isabel, adopts tactics of negation and silence in order to pack her antagonist off to America. But Maggie turns out to be far more ruthless than Isabel, lying to Charlotte and turning a deaf ear to her silent but palpable cries of pain. The novel ends, in fact, in a moral ambiguity as great in its own way as the narrative ambiguity with which *Portrait* concludes. It posits that cruelty of the sort that Isabel shrinks from may be not only a by-product of but also essential to the making of human intimacy and its social expression, marriage.

During James's life, other fictions subsequently appeared featuring ardent young women searching for their destinies among connoisseurs and aesthetes: Robert Herrick's *Gospel of Freedom* (1898) is an example. After James's death, T. S. Eliot nodded to the importance of James's novel when he titled a poetic sketch of a failed love affair between a passionate woman and a cold aesthete "Portrait of a Lady." Forty years later, James's meta-fictional experiments were on John Fowles's mind when he wrote *The French Lieutenant's Woman* (1969), a novel in which questions of gender and representation are explored by exploding the notion of a novelistic frame. And Jane Campion has turned *Portrait* into a film (1996) that emphasizes the feminist dimensions of James's narrative, substitutes cinematic pyrotechnics for those of James's prose, and makes explicit, in an extraordinarily vivid dream sequence, the sexual implications of Isabel's responses that James leaves a matter of implication and metaphor.

Each of these responses picks up on one aspect of James's multifaceted novel but seems to miss its spirit, its profoundly sympathetic account of a woman struggling to free herself from social forms even as she finds that those forms have been woven into the very way she thinks about herself. This is very much the story told by a number of fictions at the end of the twentieth century, many of which contain no explicit allusion to *Portrait*, although all of them were made possible by James's remarkable fiction. To cite but one excellent example, the contemporary novelist Pearl Abraham's *Giving Up America* (1998) details the experience of a Jewish woman who has moved away from her traditional Hasidic family and holds a job in advertising. She also has married a man who turns out to be as narrow-minded and constricting as Gilbert Osmond (though his meanness of spirit also leads to flirtations, and near-adultery, with gentile women). Abraham uses much of the imagery of *Portrait:* her protagonists, Deena and Daniel, for example, are renovating a Brooklyn brownstone, which, like Palazzo Roccanera,

increasingly becomes the oppressive image of a constricting marriage. This novel, too, ends with the heroine's flight from a lover to an exotic locale—Jerusalem—while facing an uncertain future. All this is perhaps less importantly Jamesian than Abraham's locking us into the consciousness of her heroine. We watch her gradually realize, and come to terms with, her husband's poverty of spirit and her own growing sense of alienation from the marriage. We witness her lurching from a bad to a worse alternative until, like Isabel, she reaches the best that the modern world can offer for traditional wisdom—the quest for self-awareness. "She had gone forth," Abraham's novel concludes, "and she was coming to know herself, and she would continue this knowing." With this compellingly Jamesian note, the novel reminds us that James's melodrama of gendered consciousness speaks to contemporary writers as it did to his own readers.

While the times may be different, the choices Isabel Archer faces—between freedom and responsibility, between the possibilities of self-invention and the power of social conventions—continue to press both men and women as the world shrinks, traditional institutions like marriage are transformed, and people continue to struggle to make sense of their lives under rapidly changing conditions. *The Portrait of a Lady* still compels not because it provides answers but because it represents such choices as precisely that—choices—fit for and available to our constant re- imaginings as we read and reread this magnificently open-ended novel and attempt, in our own way, to finish the picture.

Select Bibliography

EDITIONS

Portrait of a Lady. Vols. 3 and 4 of *The Novels and Tales of Henry James.* New York: Scribners, 1907–1917. (Quotations in this essay are from this revision of a text that argues for the necessity of constantly revising one's attitudes and experiences.)

Novels 1881–1886. New York: Library of America, 1985. (Includes *Washington Square, The Portrait of a Lady, The Bostonians.*)

OTHER WORKS BY JAMES

The Golden Bowl. Vols. 23 and 24 of *The Novels and Tales of Henry James.* New York: Scribners, 1907–1917.

SECONDARY WORKS

Abraham, Pearl. *Giving Up America.* New York: Riverhead Books, 1998.

Agnew, Jean-Christophe. "The Consuming Vision of Henry James." In *The Culture of Consumption: Critical Essays in American History, 1880–1980.* Edited by Richard Wrightman Fox and T. J. Jackson Lears. New York: Pantheon, 1983. Pp. 65–100.

Anderson, Charles Roberts. *Person, Place, and Thing in Henry James's Novels.* Durham, N.C.: Duke University Press, 1977.

Anderson, Quentin. *The American Henry James.* New Brunswick, N.J.: Rutgers University Press, 1957.

Bell, Millicent. *Meaning in Henry James.* Cambridge, Mass.: Harvard University Press, 1991.

Blackmur, R. P. *Studies in Henry James.* New York: New Directions, 1983.

Brodhead, Richard. *The School of Hawthorne.* New York: Oxford University Press, 1986.

Brooks, Peter. *The Melodramatic Imagination: Balzac, Henry James, Melodrama and the Mode of Excess.* New Haven, Conn.: Yale University Press, 1995.

Buitenhuis, Peter, ed. *Twentieth-Century Interpretations of* The Portrait of a Lady: *A Collection of Critical Essays.* Englewood Cliffs, N.J.: Prentice-Hall, 1968.

Cameron, Sharon. *Thinking in Henry James.* Chicago: University of Chicago Press, 1989.

Donadio, Stephen. *Nietzsche, Henry James, and the Artistic Will.* New York: Oxford University Press, 1978.

Edel, Leon. *Henry James.* 5 vols. Philadelphia: Lippincott, 1953–1972.

Edel, Leon, and Lyall Powers, eds. *The Complete Notebooks of Henry James.* New York: Oxford University Press, 1987.

Feidelson, Charles. "The Moment of *The Portrait of a Lady.*" In *The Portrait of a Lady: An Authoritative Text, Henry James and the Novel, Reviews and Criticism,* 2d ed. Edited by Robert D. Bamberg. New York: Norton, 1995. Pp. 711–719.

Freedman, Jonathan. *Professions of Taste: Henry James, British Aestheticism and Commodity Culture.* Stanford, Calif.: Stanford University Press, 1990.

———. *The Cambridge Companion to Henry James.* New York: Cambridge University Press, 1998.

Griffin, Susan, ed. *Henry James Goes to the Movies.* Lexington: University Press of Kentucky, 2002.

Habeggar, Alfred. *Henry James and the "Woman Business."* New York: Cambridge University Press, 1989.

Holland, Laurence Bedwell. *The Expense of Vision: Essays on the Craft of Henry James.* Baltimore: Johns Hopkins University Press, 1982.

Horne, Philip. *Henry James and Revision: The New York Edition.* Cambridge: Cambridge University Press, 1990.

———. *Henry James: A Life in Letters.* New York: Penguin, 2001.

Krook, Dorothea. *The Ordeal of Consciousness in Henry James.* Cambridge: Cambridge University Press, 1962.

Matthiessen, F. O. *Henry James: The Major Phase.* New York: Oxford University Press, 1944.

McWhirter, David, ed. *Henry James's New York Edition: The Construction of Authorship.* Stanford, Calif.: Stanford University Press, 1995.

Pippin, Robert. *Henry James and the Modern Moral Life.* Cambridge: Cambridge University Press, 2000.

Poirier, Richard. *The Comic Sense of Henry James: A Study of the Early Novels.* New York: Oxford University Press, 1960.

Porte, Joel, ed. *New Essays on "The Portrait of a Lady."* Cambridge: Cambridge University Press, 1990.

Porter, Carolyn. *Seeing and Being: The Plight of the Participant-Observer in Emerson, James, Adams, and Faulkner.* Middletown, Conn.: Wesleyan University Press, 1981.

Posnock, Ross. *The Trial of Curiosity: Henry James, William James, and the Challenge of Modernity.* New York: Oxford University Press, 1991.

Powers, Lyall. *"The Portrait of a Lady": Maiden, Woman, and Heroine.* Boston: Twayne Publishers, 1991.

Rowe, John Carlos. *Theoretical Dimensions of Henry James.* Madison: University of Wisconsin Press, 1984.

———. *The Other Henry James.* Durham, N.C.: Duke University Press, 1998.

Seltzer, Mark. *Henry James and the Art of Power.* Ithaca, N.Y.: Cornell University Press, 1984.

Stafford, William, ed. *Perspectives of James's "The Portrait of a Lady": A Collection of Critical Essays.* New York: New York University Press, 1967.

Van Ghent, Dorothy Bendon. "On *The Portrait of a Lady.*" In her *The English Novel: Form and Function.* New York: Holt, Rinehart and Winston, 1953. Pp. 221–228.

Walton, Priscilla L. *The Disruption of the Feminine in Henry James.* Toronto: University of Toronto Press, 1992.

Winner, Viola Hopkins. *Henry James and the Visual Arts.* Charlottesville: University Press of Virginia, 1970.

Weisbuch, Robert. "Henry James and the Idea of Evil." In *The Cambridge Companion to Henry James.* Edited by Jonathan Freedman. Cambridge: Cambridge University Press, 1998. Pp. 102–119.

John Updike's
Rabbit, Run

PATRICIA B. HEAMAN

JOHN UPDIKE, PERHAPS the most widely respected, versatile, and prolific American author of his era, has written more than fifty books, including novels, short story and poetry collections, art and literary criticism, a play, memoirs, children's books, collections of reviews and essays, and other nonfiction prose. Since the publication of his first book in 1958, he has maintained a consistently productive career, publishing on average at least one book and several creative and critical pieces for magazines and journals each year. Best known as a novelist and short story writer, he has received many prestigious literary awards and prizes. More than twenty-five full-length critical studies have been written on his work, which has also been the subject of two special issues of the journal *Modern Fiction Studies*. He is also well known to the public through readings, lectures, film and television adaptations of his writing, documentaries, websites, and coverage in the media; his picture has twice appeared on the cover of *Time*. He has commented extensively on his body of work, his personal life, and his religious, artistic, and political views in interviews, and he has read from his works and lectured in Europe, South America, Asia, and Africa as well as in the United States. Up-

dike has best described the subject matter of his work in an interview for the *Paris Review:* "Domestic fierceness within the middle class, sex and death as riddles for the thinking animal, social existence as sacrifice, unexpected pleasures and rewards, corruption as a kind of evolution— these are some of the themes."

THE RABBIT NOVELS: BACKGROUND AND CONTEXT

With the publication of his second novel, *Rabbit, Run,* in 1960, John Updike introduced his audience to Harry C. (Rabbit) Angstrom, a character who would also figure as the protagonist of three subsequent novels: *Rabbit Redux* (1971), *Rabbit Is Rich* (1981), and *Rabbit at Rest* (1990). The four novels, republished in a single volume in 1995 as *Rabbit Angstrom,* and described by Updike in his introduction as "a mega-novel," record three decades in the life of an average American as he understands and responds to personal and national events in the second half of the American century. In this loosely serialized representation of the adult life of his protagonist at approximately ten-year intervals, Updike achieved a considerable literary feat: he established a strong, enduring relationship with his readers, and he stimulated intense, often controversial, reactions from both popular and critical audiences that have made him a major figure in contemporary American literature. By bringing together his several incarnations of Rabbit Angstrom in a single publication, Updike has underscored the collaboration of author, protagonist, and readers in a chronicle that prompts their mutual acknowledgment of—and judgment on—the influence of contemporary American history and culture on the everyday lives of ordinary people. As the first novel in this series, *Rabbit, Run* established more than the protagonist whose life provides the unifying thread of the "mega-novel"; it also defined the thematic matter, ethical standpoint, and aesthetic principles that have earned both the first novel and the tetralogy acclaim as Updike's major contribution to American literature.

Although *Rabbit, Run,* having sold more than 2.5 million copies at the end of the twentieth century, is Updike's best-known work, and Rabbit his most recognized character (in the March–April 2002 issue of *Book,* Rabbit Angstrom was chosen the fifth best character in twentieth-century fiction in a survey of readers, writers, critics, and literary agents), at the time of its publication, both readers and critics found the novel and its main character problematic. Stanley Edgar Hyman called it a work of a "first-rate intelligence . . . impressive honesty, and a true creative imagination," whereas a review in *Time* called Harry Angstrom a "hollow hero" and a "desperate weakling." Updike had previously earned a modest reputation as a promising young writer, but the book that made him famous shocked many readers because of its language and sexual explicitness, its disturbing catastrophe, its unresolved ending, and, most of all, its author's apparent moral diffidence regarding Rabbit's character and actions.

The issue of sexual content and language, soon put to rest by changing attitudes, nonetheless had an effect on the publication history of

CHRONOLOGY

1932	John Hoyer Updike born in Reading, Pennsylvania, and raised in nearby Shillington.
1950	Graduates covaledictorian from Shillington High School and attends Harvard University on a scholarship.
1953	Marries Mary E. Pennington.
1954	Graduates summa cum laude from Harvard and attends Ruskin School of Drawing and Fine Art, Oxford, England, on a Knox Fellowship.
1955	Becomes a staff writer and reporter for *The New Yorker.*
1957	Moves with family to Ipswich, Massachusetts.
1960	*Rabbit, Run.*
1968	Lives with family in London.
1971	*Rabbit Redux.*
1976	Divorces Pennington.
1977	Marries Martha Ruggles Bernhard.
1981	*Rabbit Is Rich* (American Book Award, Pulitzer Prize, National Book Critics Circle Award). Awarded the Edward MacDowell Medal for literature.
1989	*Self-Consciousness.* Receives National Medal of Arts at White House ceremony.
1990	*Rabbit at Rest* (Pulitzer Prize; National Book Critics Circle Award).
1995	*Rabbit Angstrom: A Tetralogy;* awarded Howells Medal by American Academy of Arts and Letters for *Rabbit at Rest.*

Rabbit, Run. In his introduction to *Rabbit Angstrom,* Updike notes that prior to the novel's publication by Knopf in 1960, he was legally advised and agreed to make excisions that he felt amounted to a "tactful and non-fatal operation." For the Penguin paperback edition of 1964, Updike made restorations and emendations to the Knopf text. This new version provided the text printed by the Modern Library (1975) and subsequent Knopf editions. Updike made a few further corrections and revisions for *Rabbit Angstrom*, the text of which was reproduced for the Ballantine trade paperback edition of 1996. Although the language and sexual descriptiveness that troubled some readers in 1960 have been rendered unobjectionable by time, manners, and legal interpretations, the darkly disturbing and unsettling qualities of the novel and its protagonist noted by early reviewers continue to complicate readers' and critics' moral and aesthetic responses.

Much of this response centers on the character of Harry Angstrom, who is often described harshly by other characters in the novel. His father calls him "the worst kind of Brewer bum"; his wife Janice calls him "You bastard"; his lover Ruth refers to him as "bad news" and "Mr. Death himself"; and Lucy Eccles, the wife of the minister who tries to persuade Harry to return to his family, dismisses him as a "worthless heel." Yet Harry is also described by Ruth as "a Christian gentleman" and by the minister Jack Eccles as a "good man"; he is even taunted by Janice for trying to become "a saint." In spite of the contradictory judgments he evokes within the novel, for many readers, he has come to represent an American Everyman with whom they can identify, albeit not entirely comfortably. Because the action of the novel takes place in a time frame almost simultaneous with the contemporary reader's experience of historical events, readers have tested their own responses to American history against Rabbit's, regarding him as an alter ego to help them understand and make sense of American reality as the conformist 1950s gave way to the unease and dissatisfaction that would erupt in the protest and violence of the rebellious 1960s. Updike has stated more than once that he too came to regard Rabbit as a contemporary who shares many of his own experiences, responses, values, and personal qualities, even if on first consideration their differences seem most significant. In a 1971 interview he said, "Intellectually, I'm not essentially advanced over Harry Angstrom. I went to Harvard, it's

true, and wasn't much good at basketball . . . [but] other than that we're rather similar."

Specific similarities can be uncovered if one considers *Rabbit, Run*, begun early in 1959, as an oddly premature midlife crisis novel written by a twenty-seven-year-old author only a year older than his protagonist. The novel is set in Mount Judge and Brewer, Pennsylvania, fictionalized names for Updike's suburban hometown of Shillington and its urban hub, Reading. Rabbit's situation suggests what Updike's life might have been if the quality that made him "special" had been the athletic talent he admired in his high school peers rather than the artistic and intellectual gifts that earned him first a scholarship to Harvard and then a Knox Fellowship to the Ruskin School of Drawing and Fine Arts in Oxford. Though he moved quickly into the larger world while Rabbit settled into his hometown, Updike, like Rabbit, married early (at twenty-one), and three of his four children had been born by the time *Rabbit, Run* was published. Like Rabbit, who leaves his job at the beginning of the novel, Updike had recently left a fairly secure position on the staff of *The New Yorker* to take a chance on supporting his growing family as a freelance writer by moving, as he said, "abruptly" out of the closely networked literary milieu of Manhattan to the small New England town of Ipswich, Massachusetts.

There he wrote his novel, during what he has described in his 1989 memoir, *Self-Consciousness*, as a period of deep spiritual crisis: "In my memory there is a grayness to that period of my life . . . an oppressive blanket of funk" connected with "the sullen realization that in a few decades we would all be dead," a realization brought home when he was diagnosed in a routine physical examination as having "slightly emphysematous" lungs. A troubled marriage also contributed to his depressed state of mind. Updike dates to this time his reading of existential theologians, particularly Søren Kierkegaard and Karl Barth, reading that has had a pervasive influence on his imaginative vision as well as an immediate influence on the theme of *Rabbit, Run.* "These remembered gray moments, in which my spirit could scarcely breathe, are scattered over a period of years [in Ipswich]; to give myself brightness and air I read Karl Barth and fell in love with other men's wives. Kierkegaard had gotten me through the two years in New York." He concludes his reminiscence of this difficult time tersely: "In brief: I tried to break out of my marriage on behalf of another, and failed . . . but at least for the time being the dread of eventual death was wholly replaced by immediate distress and emotional violence." If in fact Updike projected much of the emotional, marital, and spiritual conflict of this period of his life onto Harry Angstrom, he did so recognizing that the "angst" of his protagonist was a common condition of Americans in the late 1950s. *Rabbit, Run* shows that such existential anxiety is as poignant in ordinary people who feel it deeply but are unable to articulate the sources of the "grayness" that troubles their lives as it is in those who can turn to existential philosophers and theologians to give words to their distress.

RABBIT ANGSTROM: AN AMERICAN HERO AND HIS EXISTENTIAL PLIGHT

The relatively simple plot of *Rabbit, Run* contrasts with its complex protagonist, its ambiguously dialectical theme of flight and return, and its finely modulated narrative voice. The action progresses with direct, economic linearity: Harry Angstrom, a former high school basketball star, having lost the feeling of being "special" in his current unsatisfying life, impulsively leaves his pregnant wife Janice and two-year-old son Nelson and drives south to no particular destination. After a night on the road, he gives up his flight, returns to his hometown, becomes involved with another woman, Ruth, and lives with her until his wife gives birth to their daughter. He then leaves Ruth and returns to his family, resolved to accept his responsibili-

ties, but bolts again soon after his wife and infant daughter come home from the hospital. Janice, distraught by this second abandonment, accidentally drowns their baby while in a drunken haze. Harry returns home again, and at the funeral of the baby, he proclaims to those gathered, "Don't look at *me* . . . I didn't kill her"; he then runs to Ruth, who insists that he choose between her and Janice. As the novel ends Rabbit is running again, as uncertain as the reader of the direction he will take.

The speed with which the plot of the novel moves, unmarked by formal chapter divisions, results largely from the precisely noted and limited time period in which it occurs, from March 20 to June 24 of 1959. The plot is structured by Rabbit's flight and return, presented through what Updike has described as a "zigzaggy" pattern, and by the two women, Janice and Ruth, who represent the poles of the moral dilemma that provides the central theme of the novel.

In a 1978 interview Updike said that his "most Kierkegaardian or Barthian, or whatever, fiction was, I think, that which was written in my twenties and thirties, and a book like *Rabbit, Run* is a fairly deliberate attempt to examine the human predicament from a theological standpoint." Although Rabbit's anxiety grows essentially from a sense that his life lacks meaning and significance, Updike has emphasized that this inner dread is exacerbated by the external circumstances of American culture. He has labeled the first of his Rabbit novels an "Eisenhower" book to suggest its connection to the American cultural environment of the 1950s. In his introduction to *Rabbit Angstrom,* Updike explains, "my impression is that the character of Harry 'Rabbit' Angstrom was for me a way in—a ticket to the America all around me. What I saw through Rabbit's eyes was more worth telling than what I saw through my own, though the difference was often slight; his life, less defended and logocentric than my own, went places mine could not." In Rabbit, Updike discovered a persona through whom he could explore the relationship between the average citizen and the American experience from the late 1950s to the beginning of the 1990s; the Rabbit novels offer "a kind of running report on the state of my hero and his nation, and their ideal reader became a fellow-American who had read and remembered the previous novels about Rabbit Angstrom." Similarly, Updike's American readers found Rabbit—both the "good man" and the "heel"—a way in to understanding the ambivalence many of them felt about their culture and their personal values, desires, intentions, and actions.

Because he is firmly rooted in his American time and place, Harry Angstrom has often been compared to such classic American literary heroes as James Fenimore Cooper's Leatherstocking, Herman Melville's Ishmael, Mark Twain's Huck Finn, Ernest Hemingway's Nick Adams, William Faulkner's Ike McCaslin, and F. Scott Fitzgerald's Jay Gatsby. Critics have also analyzed Rabbit in relation to various interpretations of the modern hero—the antihero, the nonhero, the absurd hero, the Romantic hero, the existential hero—to account for his grip on the American imagination. In an interview for *Life Magazine* in 1966, Updike summed up his view on heroes in the modern world: "The idea of a hero is aristocratic. As aristocracies have faded, so have heroes. . . . Now either nobody is a hero or everyone is. I vote for everyone." Thus Rabbit Angstrom, like Huck, Gatsby, and other characters whose origins make them unlikely prospects for heroism, has found a place in the American tradition as an everyman who grows larger than life through experiences that test his individual identity in the context of the culture that has shaped him.

"Is it just these people I'm outside or is it all America?" Rabbit asks himself in the first part of the novel, which takes him on his first "run" away from a marriage he has come to perceive as a trap that confines him physically and spiritually. Living with his wife and son in the small working-class town in southeastern Pennsylvania where he was born, Harry at twenty-six,

like many other Americans of the postwar generation, finds himself pushing against the barrier separating working-class from white-collar America, a barrier made more permeable by the economic recovery after World War II; but along with offering the possibility of social mobility, the years that hardened into the cold war raised questions about the values on which American economic and social aspirations were based. Supporting his growing family as a demonstrator of a kitchen gadget called the MagiPeel Peeler in local five-and-tens, Harry senses the emptiness of his bid to achieve the middle-class respectability represented by his wife and in-laws. The only attributes that distinguish him from his solidly blue-collar father and most of the preceding generation in the town where he grew up are the business suit he wears to the job he has held for four weeks and his belief, nourished by a culture based on advertising and consumerism, that a combination of personal charm, clean-cut good looks, confidence, and sales know-how can gain him entrée to the life of middle-class prosperity and happiness promised in the Eisenhower era. Nonetheless, in an environment that values conformity, Rabbit clings to the single quality that makes him "special," the athletic talent that made him "famous through the county; in basketball in his junior year he set a B-league scoring record that in his senior year he broke with a record that was not broken until four years later, that is, four years ago." Having achieved excellence as an athlete that brought him a sense of personal worth and even fame in his limited world, Rabbit has a nostalgic longing to distinguish himself from the crowd, to feel "first-rate" and unique again.

Since his glory days on the basketball court, a life of meaningful identity and action has eluded him. His stint in the army during the Korean War was spent in Texas, so he never saw action. On his return home, he married Janice Springer, a former high school classmate whom he began to date when they both worked at a downtown department store. Janice was pregnant when they married, and Rabbit's mother blames her for trapping her son into a marriage that has prevented the unfolding of his special but unspecified abilities. His field of action has become limited to the dull routine of unrewarding work and a claustrophobic domestic life that leaves both him and Janice feeling cheated. He feels his identity fading from the vital, mobile, much-admired Rabbit to the caged, domestic, unappreciated Harry. Fewer people remember him as the record-breaking basketball star who gave them a sense of reflected glory. His body seems to be losing the strength, grace, and agility that made him a hero eight years ago, and the sexual energy that became for him first a measure of, then a substitute for, athletic performance—a means of validating his identity and vitality—is sapped by what he calls a "second-rate" relationship with a wife who not only is "dumb" but also has "stopped being pretty." As he observes the "tiny advances into age" in Janice, the wrinkles that have appeared at the corners of her mouth and her thinning hair, Rabbit "keeps thinking of her skull under it."

The language of this passage describing Rabbit's perception of Janice demonstrates Updike's power to evoke both Rabbit's cruelty toward his wife and the terrifying insight that makes her and their marriage flash before him as a memento mori, an image that creates sympathy for Rabbit by undermining the insensitivity of his ungenerous description of his wife. This double aspect of Rabbit's character—his apparent callousness set in contrast to his deeply felt but unarticulated sense that some abstract meaning underlies the surface appearance of the visible world he is keenly observant of—is emphasized recurrently and is intricately interwoven with the thematic and structural elements of the novel.

In a character as ordinary and unsophisticated as Rabbit, Updike shows how fear arising from observation of everyday reality escalates to existential dread as his protagonist feels the best of his life retreating into a rapidly fading past

and sees nothing in the future but "the skull under it." In the life he faces without intellectual resources, engagement in satisfying work, or deeply felt love and sympathy in his relationship with his wife, Rabbit confronts the fact that he may be past his peak, that life will offer him increasingly fewer and narrower choices, while his body—which he regards as the sole source of his vitality—submits to inevitable decline. And the prospect of life without meaning advancing only toward death fills him with anxiety that spirals into the near hallucinatory fear apparent in his description of Janice. Ultimately, then, Rabbit's running is understandable as an attempt to ward off death by arresting the dissolution of his being through impulsive bursts of energy and motion that reassure him of his vitality.

A large part of Updike's success in engaging readers' sympathy for Rabbit in spite of his behavior results from the finely tuned present-tense narration that shifts fluently between third-person reportage and Rabbit's interior monologue. Updike is able to express the emotional effect of his protagonist's angst so that Rabbit's complexity is located not only in the contrary moral responses he evokes but also in the sharpness of his observations and the depth of his emotional responses. The interplay of Rabbit's colloquial spoken language, his far richer interior language conveying his sensory responses to the physical world, and the authorial language of the third-person narrator with its subtle echoes of contemporary philosophical and theological discourse is seen in the following passage as Harry's anxiety mixes with memory and modulates into compassion:

He feels frightened. When confused, Janice is a frightening person. Her eyes dwindle in their frowning sockets and her little mouth hangs open in a dumb slot. Since her hair has begun to thin back from her shiny forehead, he keeps getting the feeling of her being brittle, and immovable, of her only going one way, toward deeper wrinkles and skimpier hair. He married relatively late, when he was twenty-three and she was two years out of high school, still scarcely adult, with shy small breasts that when she lay down flattened against her chest so that they were only there as a tipped softness. Nelson was born seven months after the Episcopal service, in prolonged labor: Rabbit's fright then mixes with his fright now and turns it tender. "What did you buy?"

Thus Updike's quickly moving plot is motivated by Rabbit's existential anxiety as it is reflected in the "zigzaggy" movements of a character who responds to his angst by fleeing three times from perceived traps that threaten his freedom and mobility—and who twice returns to his previous life beset by guilt and remorse. His running is a manifestation of an instinctive but unarticulated sense that an "unseen world" underlies the surface reality of life. Although he goes about it in an undirected, almost panicky way, Rabbit's quest to discover whether this underlying reality renders life meaningful or meaningless is not essentially unlike Henry David Thoreau's fixed and deliberate experiment at Walden Pond to discover what life "had to teach, and not, when I came to die, to discover that I had not lived." Like Thoreau, Rabbit wants to know what the essential meaning of life is, "and, if it proved mean, why then to get the whole and genuine meanness of it . . . or if it proved sublime, to know it by experience." And like a long line of American heroes before him, Rabbit feels that he can resolve his conflicts and settle his anxiety by shaping his life to accord with whatever inner meaning or lack of meaning the world of material reality may yield.

THE MOTIONS OF GRACE AND THE HARDNESS OF THE HEART

The dilemma that forms the crux of the novel is writ small in the terse epigraph Updike chose for it, Pascal's *pensée* 507: "The motions of Grace, the hardness of the heart; external circumstances." Pascal presents the three terms of his fragmentary thought not as a series, but as one set of dialectically opposed terms that taken together but unresolved are then set against a third term. Updike makes use of Pascal's shifting dialectical structure as well as his ambiguously related terms in working through the moral choice Rabbit faces: pursuing the claims of freedom and self-gratification through his relationship with Ruth Leonard, or accepting the claims of social responsibility represented by his marriage to Janice. These choices are described in the novel respectively as "the good way" and "the right way."

The "zigzag" structure of alternating motion between flight—prompted by the motions of grace and requiring Rabbit to harden his heart against his family—and return—prompted by guilt and requiring him to harden his heart against the discoveries he can make through freedom—is established in the opening sequence of the novel through the events leading to Rabbit's first "run." After a day of demonstrating the MagiPeeler, he removes his suit jacket on his way home and joins a group of boys playing basketball. The fact that he can still play with skill and grace "elates him. He feels liberated from long gloom." After the game, restored by the "motions of Grace," the feeling that he has not entirely squandered his special gift, Rabbit makes his way home past wasteland images of a decaying city in the gloomy atmosphere of "winter's last day": "Up the alley. Past the deserted ice plant with its rotting wooden skids on the fallen loading porch. Ashcans, garage doors, fences of chickenwire caging crisscrossing stalks of dead flowers." Because Rabbit is attuned to an "unseen world" underlying these images, he senses beneath the decay the promise in the change of seasons, the fact that "Things start anew; Rabbit tastes through sour aftersmoke the fresh chance in the air, plucks the pack of cigarettes from his bobbing shirt pocket, and without breaking stride cans it in somebody's open barrel."

His openness to this intimation that he can shed the deadliness of his life and affirm his freedom to "start anew," which links him to earlier American heroes like Huck, Ishmael, Leatherstocking, and Gatsby, is nullified on his arrival at his apartment. The smooth, controlled motion in ordered space he felt on the makeshift basketball court vanishes when he is assaulted by the disorder inside the apartment, with its mess of toys, newspapers, brimming ashtrays, and dirty old-fashioned glasses. He must take care not to trip on the television wire strung across the floor, and the noise of the television itself, which blocks his entrance to the closet where he neatly hangs his jacket, muddles communication between him and Janice. Rabbit's skill and grace on the basketball court are juxtaposed to his confusion and ineptness in handling the cluttered, claustrophobic space of his apartment. His heart hardens against Janice and his domestic life from the accumulated effect of the deadness he feels in his situation: the sameness of his home to all the others in the rows of duplexes in his neighborhood "covered with composition shingling varying in color from bruise to dung"; the unrewarding day of demonstrating the MagiPeeler to sad women expecting a revelation in the five-and-ten; and the hallucinatory vision he has of Janice's skull beneath her aging face. In its opening pages, the novel thus pits the liberating freedom associated with the "motions of Grace" that Rabbit yearns to recover against the confining responsibilities he owes to Janice, his son, and the child soon to be born.

In a move he will often repeat in the novel, Rabbit looks for a guide who can provide the "coaching" he needs to perform effectively. The first in this series of guides is Jimmy, the Mouseketeer of the Mickey Mouse Club, the children's television program that along with her old-fashioneds holds Janice mesmerized. Jimmy is giving a lesson on the value of individualism as he repeats the advice that to "Know Thyself [as] a wise old Greek once said" is a prerequisite to knowing what one is meant to do in life. As Jimmy concludes his lesson with a possibly conspiratorial wink, Rabbit wonders whether to trust the words of this purveyor of wisdom from twentieth-century American mass culture or to heed his ironic wink:

That was good. Rabbit tries it, pinching the mouth together and then the wink, getting the audience out front with you against some enemy behind, Walt Disney or the MagiPeel Peeler Company, admitting that it's all a fraud but, what the hell, making it likeable. We're all in it together. Fraud makes the world go round.

Rabbit's cynically suspicious stream of consciousness in response to Jimmy suggests his uncertainty about what he may find under the surface of appearances and reflects his growing anxiety as he surveys the messy apartment and his depressed wife. His anxiety grows palpable and threatens to immobilize him when he leaves the apartment in a panic to pick up his son, whom Janice has left at Harry's parents' house: he "freezes, standing looking at his faint yellow shadow on the white door that leads to the hall, and senses he is in a trap. It seems certain. He goes out."

Rabbit's fear of becoming "frozen," reduced to a condition of paralysis, consistently triggers an instinctive response of movement—in any direction, so long as it is movement—throughout the novel. He walks to his parents' house, where he looks through the kitchen window to see a scene—experienced as a flashback to his own childhood—in which his family and Nelson are having dinner in harmony and security. Reluctant to remove his son from this scene and take him back to the disorder of his own home, Harry sprints to the Springers' house, where he avoids being "caught" driving away in his own car, and hardening his heart against the responsibilities that threaten to trap him, he leaves "the mess behind him" and runs—from his family, his job, and Mt. Judge.

He takes to the highway with no plan beyond escape. He visualizes the open road leading to somewhere in the "white sun of the South," a place with "orange groves and smoking rivers and barefoot women" where he can "park on a beach take off [his] shoes and fall asleep by the Gulf of Mexico." He fantasizes about having a new love affair—perhaps with a rich du Pont woman. The images through which Rabbit envisions his destination suggest "the good way," the direction of hedonistic freedom, of pure sensual pleasure and escape from consciousness in an idyllic setting free of responsibility—the direction that will lead him eventually to Ruth.

In the vagueness and uncertainty of his flight, Rabbit invokes the aid of several new guides. When he stops for gas, he asks the attendant where the road he is on will take him, and the attendant answers with his own question: "Where do you want to go?" In a grimly sarcastic and macabre echo of the Mouseketeer's precept to "know thyself," the man tells Rabbit, "The only way to get somewhere, you know, is to figure out where you're going before you go there." The attendant's reliability as a guide is compromised in Rabbit's view, however, by the whiff of whiskey on his breath.

The intimation that there is another direction, a way other than the road to the sensuous South, is almost lost in the bombardment of popular songs, news flashes, and commercials blaring from his car radio as Rabbit instinctively chooses roads that he believes should take him "right down the middle, right into the broad soft belly of the land." A news brief reporting that the Dalai Lama has apparently disappeared penetrates Rabbit's consciousness, and he ponders, "Where is the Dalai Lama?" The search for the missing spiritual guide hints at the religious dimension of Rabbit's quest, which will be played out in the middle section of the novel.

Another guide Rabbit turns to, a map—which, in contrast to the missing Dalai Lama, the whiskey-breathed attendant, and the conspiratorial Mouseketeer, is ostensibly an objective, empirical guide to get people where they want to go—also fails him. The road seems to be taking him where he does not want to go, to cities marked on the map by webs of intersecting lines reminding him of traps. At one point he gets lost in a landscape that looks, after all the miles he has traveled, like "the country

around Mt. Judge." Later, he seems to have hopelessly lost his way on a road that narrows until it is almost completely obscured by a surrounding wilderness of weeds and bramble bushes. Rabbit fears that it leads only one way, to "a black core" in dark space "where he fears his probe of light will stir some beast or ghost." The headlights of an oncoming car appear seemingly miraculously to assure him of the possibility of a return from this fearful wilderness. He discovers that "this road of dread" takes him past a lovers' lane of parked cars to an intersection with a broad highway. Rabbit studies his map, which conveys the same duplicity as his previous guides: looking at it, he thinks that "all those red lines and blue lines and stars" have become "a net he is somewhere caught in." He tears it apart and throws it away, and faced with two possible directions, "he instinctively turns right: north" and circles back to his starting point, escaping the dark and terrifying aspects of nature into which the road has led him. With newfound calm, as if the anxiety that prompted his flight from the world of social responsibility has been relieved by abandoning his journey, Rabbit returns to Mt. Judge.

TRUE SPACE: UNDER THE SKIN AND UPWARD SPACE

His run south has released but not resolved the tension between the motions of grace that inspire Rabbit's belief that he can take the "fresh chance" of starting anew and his hardness of heart in pursuing this intimation to the harm of Janice and his son. By completing the circle to return home, Rabbit recognizes that there is no idyllic natural place where he can shed his conflict and pursue freedom unencumbered by the choices he has made in the past and the social expectations and judgment he has incurred because of those choices. Thus the external circumstances to which he returns, set in dialectical relationship to the motions of grace and the hardness of the heart, are defined not only by his culture, but also by the actions of his past.

By dramatizing Rabbit's attempt to break free of constricting circumstances, Updike challenges readers to make a judgment about whether such a choice can be justified in light of the harm it may do to others. In a 1969 interview Updike elaborated on his central theme of choosing between individual freedom and social responsibility: "in all my books, an act is inspected. Take Harry Angstrom in *Rabbit Run:* there is a case to be made for running away from your wife. In the late fifties beatniks were preaching transcontinental traveling as the answer to man's disquiet. And I was just trying to say: 'Yes, there is certainly that, but then there are all these other people who seem to get hurt.' That distinction is meant to be a moral dilemma." By projecting this unresolved "yes . . . but" aspect of his theme through a point of view that gives intimate access to Rabbit's consciousness while at the same time maintaining a detached moral perspective, Updike suspends judgment and invites the reader to "inspect" with him his protagonist's moral dilemma.

Having attempted escape though horizontal space in his flight south, Rabbit now searches for meaning by exploring the vertical space that ranges from his deepest instincts to his intimation of "something out there [that] wants [him] to find it." Updike dramatizes his dilemma through characters whose relationships with Harry reinforce the shifting dialectic of the novel's theme and structure. Janice's role as the wife representing the moral and social obligations of "the right way" is now backed by Jack Eccles, the Episcopalian minister sent by Janice's family on a mission to bring Harry home. Eccles, as a representative of the right way or the "straight road," speaks to Harry of duty and social responsibility. The "good way," the freedom to pursue the desires prompted by his instincts and to test their authenticity, is represented by Ruth, the former prostitute with whom Harry lives during his separation from his family, introduced to him by his old high school coach, Marty Tothero. Through his interactions with these characters, Rabbit opens himself to the possibility of influence from traditional professional guides: a minister, a prostitute, and a coach. Thus Updike's supporting characters, like the realistic details he introduces, which may seem in the economy of the novel to carry only purely referential meaning, assume metaphoric depth to reinforce the zigzag structure and the shifting dialectic of the theme.

The first guide Rabbit seeks out on his return to Mt. Judge is Tothero. Ousted from the high school and separated from his wife as a result of some unspecified "scandal," presumably his infidelity, Tothero is living in a room over the bar at the run-down Sunshine Athletic Association. He is in some ways an extreme projection of what Rabbit may become, a pathetic has-been trying desperately to maintain a semblance of order and cleanliness in his disintegrating life. After defending Janice's claims to Harry's tolerance and help, Tothero proposes rather inconsistently that Rabbit join him for a date in Brewer. "You and I are two of a kind," he tells Harry, "You and I know what the score is, we know—," but his voice trails off. Unable to follow his line of thought, Rabbit "suspects his old coach is addled." Nonetheless, he dresses to accompany Tothero, feeling "deeper instincts [than those that make him miss Janice and Nelson] flood forward, telling him he is right. He feels freedom, like oxygen everywhere around him." Trusting these instincts, Rabbit proclaims to himself in a mirror that "*he* is the Dalai Lama," his own spiritual guide. His confidence is reinforced, if somewhat feebly, by the guidance he gets from Tothero: "'Do what the heart commands. . . . The heart is our only guide." He sounds weary and far away." Tothero's physical deterioration and self-justifying moralizing later in the novel leave Rabbit feeling "depressed and dirtied," emphasizing Tothero's failure as a guide.

Through Ruth, Rabbit tests the space opened to him by the freedom to follow his heart as a guide. Although her interest in Rabbit seems at first purely professional, Ruth, a woman who has learned from experience to be wary of men, is intrigued enough by him on their first date to agree, in spite of her misgivings, to sleep with him in the pure and simple freedom he wants to find in sex—without her makeup, jewelry, or diaphragm. Partially with fear and partially with curiosity she responds to his urgency to recover through sex the feeling of being first-rate that he has lost since high school. His assurance that he is "a lover" and his response of "Yes; let's be" when she asks him "do you think we're married or something the way you boss me around?" put her off guard as he clings to her, "his teeth bared in a silent exclamation, crying out against her smothering throat that it is not her body he wants, not the flesh and bones, but her, her." His need to find beyond her body a "her, her" corresponds to his desire to recover the "winner" he feels still exists beneath the fading athlete he has become. While Ruth urges him, "Don't try to prove you're a lover on me. Just come and go" and to "undress [her] and stop farting around," Rabbit insists on "making love to her as he would to his wife," rubbing her back and massaging her shoulders, telling her "You're supposed to enjoy this. This is our wedding night." And although their lovemaking is first-rate for both from a physical standpoint, when it is over, "He looks in her face and seems to read in its shadows an expression of forgiveness, as if she knows that at the moment of release, the root of love, he betrayed her by feeling despair."

DESPERATE GAIETY

Rabbit's despair at not finding transcendence through sex shifts the direction of his quest to a spiritual level, also prompted by the motions of grace, but bleaker than the hedonistic "good way" he may have preferred. His failure to uncover an essential Ruth beneath the tough-talking prostitute is juxtaposed to his preoccupation with the austere "church across the way, gray, grave, and mute. Lights behind its rose window are left burning, and this circle of

red and purple and gold seems in the city night a hole punched in reality to show the abstract brilliance burning underneath." Like the map he discarded on his trip south, the church and window assume significance in Rabbit's search. He wants to believe that the stained glass window, like Percy Bysshe Shelley's "dome of many-coloured glass" (in the elegy "Adonais"), "stains the white radiance of eternity"—a radiance that it both emblemizes and hides from sight. The suggestion that the abstract brilliance Rabbit seeks may take him through a way that is "gray, grave, and mute" rather than a way marked by southern sun, barefoot women, and untroubled sleep establishes a new tension and depth in Rabbit's search for the meaning underlying material reality.

Despite Rabbit's metaphysical despair, Ruth does make him feel that he has recaptured his ability to perform authentically and meaningfully in a sexual relationship; as he says, "He has scored." At the same time, however, she feeds his fear of meaninglessness by denying that there is a nonphysical dimension to their relationship, indeed to the world. Her Saturday night compliment to Rabbit, "you're a Christian gentleman," is rendered doubly ironic when she tells him on Sunday morning, when he wants her to validate him and his lovemaking as more than just another fifteen-dollar trick in her life, that she "doesn't believe in anything." Rabbit wants reinforcement of his belief that an "unseen world is instinctive," but Ruth remains solidly in her material world, her feelings for Rabbit based on his innocent faith, which she admires but cannot share, on the fact that he has not "given up" by surrendering his idealism to the ways things are.

The despair Rabbit feels with Ruth paves the way for his acceptance of Jack Eccles' interest in him, although his first impression is that Eccles "doesn't seem to know his job." Eccles' summary of the belief of his church, "that we are all responsible beings, responsible for ourselves and for each other," underscores the essentially social appeal he makes to Rabbit's conscience when they meet for a game of golf. To Eccles' suggestion that his behavior is childish and self-ish, Rabbit has a ready response: "If you're telling me I'm not mature, that's one thing I don't cry over since as far as I can make out it's the same thing as being dead." As he tries to explain his reason for abandoning his family, Rabbit can only say "There was this thing that wasn't there" in his marriage, articulating as best he can the absence of an unseen presence in the exterior world that he instinctively feels within himself: "All I know is what's inside *me*. That's all I have." Eccles expresses his skepticism about the existence of the "thing that wasn't there," the "it" that wants Rabbit to find it, in purely empirical terms as he prods him: "What *is* it? Is it hard or soft? Harry. Is it blue? Is it red? Does it have polka dots?" He suggests that Rabbit's appeal to the God within, his feeling that he may be his own Dalai Lama, is heretical: "We're trying to *serve* God, not *be* God. . . . This was all settled centuries ago, in the heresies of the early Church." Rabbit realizes "depressingly, that [Eccles] really wants to be told. Underneath all of this I-know-more-about-it-than-you heresies-of-the-early-Church business he really wants to be told about it, wants to be told that it is there, that he's not lying to all those people every Sunday."

Although Ruth and Eccles, as prostitute and preacher, traditional representatives of the flesh and the spirit, of matter and transcendence, serve as the metaphysical poles between which Rabbit zigzags, neither is able to satisfy Rabbit's needs. Shortly after he meets Eccles, Rabbit takes Ruth to the top of Mt. Judge to view Brewer from the perspective of its height. Rabbit's hope is that the upward ascent and the view from the mountain will confirm his belief in the unseen world:

> His day has been bothered by God: Ruth mocking, Eccles blinking—why did they teach you such things if no one believed them? It seems plain, standing here, that if there is this floor, there is a ceiling, that the true space in which we live is upward space. Someone is dying. . . . He moves his eyes to find the spot; perhaps he can see the cancer-

blackened soul of an old man mount through the blue like a monkey on a string. He strains his ears to hear the pang of release as this ruddy illusion at his feet gives up this reality. Silence blasts him.

With Ruth at his side, the world stretching below him yields no message; it remains mute.

Neither can Eccles—a minister who must ultimately confess, "I don't believe in anything"—address Rabbit's spiritual needs. He envies Rabbit's unquestioning, intuitive belief, the inarticulate faith that neither his heritage as the son and grandson of clergymen nor his theological education has given him, and he defends Harry to Mrs. Springer as "a good man"; he even wonders if he has been converted by Rabbit, if he may have "gone over to the other side." He continues to play golf with Rabbit throughout the spring, fascinated by his contagious cheerfulness: "only Harry gives the game a desperate gaiety, as if they are together engaged in an impossible quest set by a benevolent but absurd lord, a quest whose humiliations sting them almost to tears but one that is renewed at each tee, in a fresh flood of green." On their first day golfing together, Harry, after a series of bad shots, is able to *show* Eccles the "it" he is unable to describe in empirical terms: he makes a perfect shot in which his ball seems momentarily to escape the pull of gravity:

> his ball is hung way out, lunarly pale against the beautiful black blue of storm clouds. . . . It recedes along a line straight as a ruler-edge. Stricken; sphere, star, speck. It hesitates, and Rabbit thinks it will die, but he's fooled, for the ball makes its hesitation the ground of a final leap: with a kind of visible sob takes the last bite of space before vanishing in falling. "That's *it!*" he cries and, turning to Eccles with a grin of aggrandizement, repeats, "That's it."

His perfect shot demonstrates what Rabbit cannot articulate: the evidence of transcendence. "It," the beauty and miracle of the ball's momentary pause between earth and sky, confirms Rabbit's memory of his feeling on the basketball court that he was capable of anything. "It" verifies his belief that he and all that is ordinary and earthbound can become miraculous.

Caught between two forms of unbelief, Ruth's nihilistic version of "nothing" and Eccles' humanism that upholds ethical behavior with no basis in faith, Rabbit, unable to commit to either, retreats to the "locked hollow hutch" of his self in the freedom he tests through his life with Ruth, in his Edenic job as Mrs. Smith's gardener, and in his weekly golf games with Eccles. Paradoxically, the missing guide of this part of the novel, the character who has no direct interaction with Rabbit, is his family's Lutheran minister, the Reverend Fritz Kruppenbach. Kruppenbach rejects Eccles' request that he intervene, refusing to "meddle in these people's lives" and lecturing Eccles for trying to be a doctor, lawyer, or cop, when his real job is to do what Eccles is incapable of: "make yourself an exemplar of faith . . . make your faith powerful." In his implacable sternness, Kruppenbach dismisses the importance of acts and affirms the value of faith: "It's all in the Book—a thief with faith is worth all of the Pharisees. . . . There is nothing but Christ for us. All the rest, all this decency and busyness, is nothing. It's the Devil's work." In refusing to become involved and remaining aloof, Kruppenbach foreshadows the God Rabbit recognizes at the climax of the novel, the remote, detached God who "in all His strength . . . did nothing" while an infant drowned in a bathtub.

OTHER PEOPLE'LL PAY YOUR PRICE

The months of freedom during which Rabbit zigzags between Ruth and Eccles end abruptly at the major turning point in the novel, when Rabbit returns to Janice. Throughout this period, Ruth says, "he just lived in his skin and didn't give a thought to the consequences." Rabbit has arrogantly asserted to Ruth, "I'm a saint.

. . . I give people faith," and he sums up what he has learned by following his heart: "When I ran from Janice I made an interesting discovery. . . . If you have the guts to be yourself, other people'll pay your price." His cocky assumption of the moral infallibility of his instincts is shattered by two events that initiate a chain of cause and effect that Updike constructs with stunning credibility to move the plot inexorably toward its grim climax, the death of Harry's infant daughter.

The first event is his sexual humiliation of Ruth when he insists that she perform oral sex on him, as she puts it, "in cold blood. You just want it," after learning that she had provided such favors for Rabbit's former high school teammate Ron Harrison. Harrison's suggestion that Rabbit's basketball stardom—as the golden boy of Mt. Judge who never fouled—was made possible by the dirty work that he and others on the team did to make him look good has made Rabbit doubt his special gift. He conflates Ruth with Harrison when he tells her "Tonight you turned against me. I need to see you on your knees." Although she has been preparing to tell Rabbit that she is pregnant with his child, Ruth knows at this point that their relationship has taken a turn from which it cannot recover: "After being a wife a whore's skin feels tight."

The second event is the phone call Rabbit gets from Eccles that night, informing him that Janice is about to give birth to their child. Rabbit, who has given what Mrs. Smith calls his "gift of life" to two women, leaves Ruth to go to Janice. When he looks at Ruth lying in bed silent and unresponsive to his explanation, *I've killed her* flashes through his mind, and he leaves her alone, grieving in her humiliation and loss, as he had left Janice a few months ago. He will repeat this pattern of "having the guts to be [himself]" by walking away from situations he has created with Lucy Eccles and again with Janice before the novel ends.

In the final movement of the novel, fear that he will cause harm or death to others replaces the fear of his own death, the fear that precipitated Rabbit's flight from Janice. As he runs to the hospital, "He is certain that as a consequence of his sin Janice or the baby will die." He later wakes in panic from a nightmare in which he dreams that Nelson has died. Fear, guilt, and despair make him imagine his life as a "sequence of grotesque poses assumed to no purpose, a magic dance empty of belief. *There is no God; Janice can die:* the two thoughts come at once, in one slow wave." But despite his terror that Janice's pain will produce "a monster, a monster of his making" because he is "the runner, the fornicator, the monster," he is surprised and relieved to find Janice happy and forgiving and his daughter "great." Feeling blessed to escape the suffering and death he had anticipated, he resolves to return to the "straight road" to atone for his sins. He is even forgiven by Mrs. Springer, who grudgingly accepts his return, and Mr. Springer, who has made the "straight path . . . smooth" by paying the rent on his apartment and arranging a new job for him at one of his used-car lots. Only Harry's mother asks "And what's going to happen to this poor girl you lived with in Brewer?"

Guilt and gratitude keep Rabbit on "the right way" until he is again tempted by the flesh in the person of Lucy Eccles, who responds with sarcastic taunts and suggestive banter that he interprets as flirtation (a flirtation that he in fact had initiated by slapping her on the behind the first time they met) when he tells her of his intention to follow the "straight road." He walks her home from church, where he has gone in a spirit of thanksgiving for all that has been restored to him, and when she invites him in for coffee after the service, he humiliates her by declining as if she had propositioned him: "You're a doll, but I got this wife now."

Harry returns home "cold with lust" because whether "spurned or misunderstood, Eccles' wife has jazzed him up." His cold lust, echoing the "cold blood" Ruth had accused him of, becomes a presence in the apartment that disturbs the family, making baby Becky wail disconsolately, upsetting Nelson, and creating the tense atmosphere that dries up Janice's milk. It also sets off, in a masterfully plotted sequence, the chain of events leading to the tragic climax. Harry persuades Janice to relax by taking a drink, and when she does, he approaches her sexually despite her painful stitches and exhaustion. When he instructs her to "roll over" so that he can relieve his lust, Janice becomes angry at being used impersonally for his sexual gratification and refuses to go along with a "trick your whore taught you." He leaves the apartment in anger and frustration and runs to Ruth's. Finding her apartment dark and apparently empty, he waits for her on the stoop until the lights go out behind the church window across the street. He stays out all night and most of the next day while Janice resumes the drinking he had encouraged so that she would be relaxed into sex.

In a narrative tour de force, Updike uses a free, indirect third-person style that flows in and out of Janice's stream of consciousness to show how Janice comes to believe that, through her fault, Harry has indeed left her for a second time. In her desperation, she continues drinking through the next morning, fumbling her way through getting Nelson's breakfast and changing Becky's dirty clothes. Fearful that her mother will come to discover her, the apartment, and the children in disorder, she makes an effort to set things right by bathing Becky, who slips from her grasp into the bathtub she has overfilled. As she gropes desperately for the infant in the water and retrieves her inert body, she realizes that the "worst thing that has ever happened to any woman in the world has happened to her."

The fear of death that gave rise to Rabbit's initial anxiety has been horribly realized, and Rabbit responds by assuming guilt for the baby's death, for Janice's desperation, for Nelson's traumatic premature exposure to death, for the grief his family and Eccles feel. His guilt makes him believe that "something held him back" from returning home to prevent the death of the baby, and "whatever it was murdered his daughter." He thinks, "What held him back all day was the feeling that somewhere there was something better for him than listening to babies cry and cheating people in used-car lots and it's this feeling he tries to kill." By accepting guilt, Rabbit is in effect accepting the maturity that he had called "the same thing as being dead." Guilt now hardens his heart against the motions of grace, which had given him the gifts of life and hope that made Ruth, Eccles, and Mrs. Smith see him as special. Without the hope that nourished his belief that he and the world had the potential to become miraculous, he "feels like an insect." He succumbs to the paralysis he had dreaded at the beginning of the novel as he meekly takes direction from the Springers: "He feels he will never resist anything again." In effect, Rabbit surrenders to dread and death.

At the funeral service, Harry listens humbly as Eccles reads: "I am the resurrection and the life, saith the Lord: he that believeth in me, though he were dead, yet shall he live." The words move Rabbit like a surge of grace, and he recognizes another face of God: he suddenly understands that forgiveness, which affirms the resurrection, the triumph of life over death, can restore life to him and all who mourn. This revelation prompts him to publicly reject the death-dealing guilt he had assumed, and in a startling passage he tells those gathered at the graveside: "Don't look at *me* . . . I didn't kill her." It seems that he is blaming Janice when he adds, "You all keep acting as if *I* did it. I wasn't anywhere near. *She's* the one." Unable to articulate the "simplicity he feels now in everything" with "forgiveness . . . big in his heart," he tells Janice, "Hey, it's O.K. . . . You didn't mean to." But she is horrified at his gesture, not comprehending that he is inviting her to join him in forgiveness, and she turns away.

At this moment, like the golf ball that made "its hesitation the ground of a final leap," Rabbit runs upward toward a patch of woods above the cemetery to a place where he hopes he will not "see any sign, even a remote cleared landscape,

of civilization." The language and imagery describing this run recall that of his run south at the beginning of the novel. He runs to leave "the people behind" and find escape and solace in a natural space free of "human intrusion into a world of blind life." In this pure place, he hopes to escape the judgment of those he has fled and the torment of his own consciousness. But there is no natural space unmarked by evidence of "human intrusion," and no inner space unmarked by the consciousness that is the gift and price of humanity. He encounters another face of God when "he obscurely feels lit by a great spark, the spark whereby the blind tumble of matter recognized itself, a spark struck in an encounter a terrible God willed"; he knows he must resume the "impossible quest set by a benevolent but absurd lord, a quest whose humiliations sting . . . to tears but one that is renewed . . . in a fresh flood of green." He moves out of the woods at the top of Mount Judge and makes his descent into the fallen world he must live in.

He goes to Ruth, who castigates him for leaving her, accusing him of having "the touch of death." She confirms his hope that she is pregnant but dissipates his joy at this news by threatening to have an abortion unless he leaves Janice to marry her. Rabbit is last seen in the street outside Ruth's apartment "weighing opposites against each other: Janice and Ruth, Eccles and his mother, the right way and the good way, the way to the delicatessen . . . and the other way, down Summer Street to where the city ends. He tries to picture how it will end . . . he doesn't know." He looks across to the church window, but "because of church poverty or the late summer nights or just carelessness" it is "unlit, a dark circle in a limestone façade." Just when the world seems reduced to its meanest and darkest state, Updike performs, in his final sentence, the stylistic equivalent of Rabbit's perfect golf shot in his description of his protagonist's desperate but irrepressible burst of life and motion: "His hands lift of their own and he feels the wind on his ears even before, his heels hitting heavily on the pavement at first but with an effortless gathering out of a kind of sweet panic growing lighter and quicker and quieter, he runs. Ah: runs. Runs."

This open-ended finale leaves the reader in essentially the same position as Rabbit—unsure of which choice he will make, but affirming the vitality of life and energy. Rabbit's moral dilemma is unresolved, in fact has become unresolvable because Ruth's threat has erased the distinction between the right way and the good way. There is no choice for Rabbit that will avoid harm to either Janice or Ruth. Updike's refusal to resolve the dilemma—which has troubled critics such as Ralph C. Wood, who has accused him of "moral passivity" in his "reluctance to find fault and assess blame"— places the reader in the "yes, but" moral position as Rabbit. Ambiguity, however, is Updike's intended ethical and aesthetic outcome. As he explained in an interview for the *Paris Review,* "I have from the start been wary of the fake, the automatic . . . My work is meditation, not pontification . . . I think of my books not as sermons or directives in a war of ideas, but as objects, with different shapes and textures and the mysteriousness of anything that exists." He concludes this statement of aesthetic practice with a thought that sheds light on the pathos of Harry Angstrom, whose inability to articulate his angst will drive his quest through three more decades and novels: "My first thought about art, as a child, was that the artist brings something into the world that didn't exist before, and that he does it without destroying something else." Because he is not an artist, Harry must run the zigzaggy road of difficult and endless choices through which he tries to create himself while enduring the risks and costs of destroying something else—all part of the game of life set by "the benevolent and absurd lord" who remains detached and aloof. Updike, whose special grace enables him to bring "something into the world that didn't exist before . . . without destroying something else," redeems Harry through the gift of art that makes the game endurable.

Although it is premature to assess the influence of Updike's work on future writers, it is not too soon to speculate on the place he has earned in American literature. Critics unsympathetic to his religious and political views or his essentially realistic aesthetic have been chillingly hostile in the past; John Aldridge's devastating summation, "Mr. Updike has nothing to say," and Harold Bloom's dictum blocking his entrance to the canon, "The American Sublime will never touch his pages," have been competently and convincingly countered in the last twenty years by resounding acclaim from critics like Alfred Kazin and George Steiner and tributes from fellow writers like Joyce Carol Oates, Norman Mailer, Ian McEwan, A. S. Byatt, Salman Rushdie, Martin Amis, Anita Brookner, and Margaret Drabble. The publication of *Rabbit Angstrom* as a sparkling gem in an intricate setting of distinguished fiction, criticism, and other writing seems to confirm James Schiff's estimate that "John Updike seems destined to join the company of such grand American authors as Hawthorne, Whitman, Melville, Dickinson, James, Wharton, Faulkner, Fitzgerald, and Nabokov."

Select Bibliography

EDITIONS

Rabbit, Run. New York: Knopf, 1960. (First edition.)

Rabbit Angstrom. New York: Knopf/Everyman's Library, 1995. (The four Rabbit novels, *Rabbit, Run, Rabbit Redux, Rabbit Is Rich, Rabbit at Rest,* published in a single volume. Includes an introduction by the author, a chronology that puts Updike's life in a literary and historical context, and a select bibliography. This edition, incorporating "corrections and improvements" by the author to previous editions, is cited in this essay.)

Rabbit, Run. New York: Ballantine Books, 1996. (The text and pagination of this trade paperback edition are identical to that of *Rabbit Angstrom.*)

OTHER WORKS BY UPDIKE

Self-Consciousness. New York: Knopf, 1989. (This volume of memoirs consisting of six essays is an indispensable biographical source.)

SECONDARY WORKS

Bloom, Harold, ed. *John Updike: Modern Critical Views.* New York: Chelsea House, 1987. (Includes an introduction by Bloom and reprinted essays by John W. Aldridge, Richard H. Rupp, David Lodge, Tony Tanner, Joyce Carol Oates, Cynthia Ozick, and others.)

Boswell, Marshall. *John Updike's Rabbit Tetralogy: Mastered Irony in Motion.* Columbia: University of Missouri Press, 2001. (A reading of the formal structure of the individual novels and the tetralogy as a whole in the context of the existential thought of Kierkegaard and Barth.)

Broer, Lawrence R., ed. *Rabbit Tales: Poetry and Politics in John Updike's Rabbit Novels.* Tuscaloosa: University of Alabama Press, 1998. (A collection of essays on the tetralogy by such major interpreters of Updike's work as Jeff Campbell, Donald Greiner, Dilvo Ristoff, Ralph Wood, and others.)

De Bellis, Jack. *The John Updike Encyclopedia.* Westport, Conn.: Greenwood Press, 2000. (A comprehensive volume with entries on the works, major characters, themes, biographical data.)

Galloway, David. *The Absurd Hero in American Fiction: Updike, Styron, Bellow, Salinger.* 2d rev. ed. Austin: University of Texas Press, 1981. (A reading of the early fiction in the existential context of Albert Camus' notions of the absurd, particularly *The Myth of Sisyphus.*)

Greiner, Donald J. *John Updike's Novels.* Athens: Ohio University Press, 1984. (A close reading of the novels through *Rabbit Is Rich* with particular attention to critical reception.)

————. *Adultery in the American Novel: Updike, James, and Hawthorne.* Columbia: University of South Carolina Press, 1985. (Uses primarily Updike's essays and reviews to establish links between Updike and his predecessors in the canon, focusing on the religious and social treatment of adultery.)

Hamilton, Alice, and Kenneth Hamilton. *The Elements of John Updike.* Grand Rapids, Mich.: Eerdmans, 1970. (An important early study of religious themes in Updike's work.)

Hunt, George. *John Updike and the Three Great Secret Things: Sex, Religion, and Art.* Grand Rapids, Mich.: Eerdmans, 1980. (An analysis of the early work in the context of Kierkegaard, Barth, and Carl Jung.)

Hyman, Stanley Edgar. "The Artist as a Young Man." *New Leader,* March 19, 1962, pp. 22–23.

Macnaughton, William R., ed., *Critical Essays on John Updike.* Boston: G. K. Hall, 1982.

(Includes essays by Alfred Kazin, Tony Tanner, George Hunt, Robert Detweiler, Joyce Carol Oates, Paul Theroux, and others, along with a survey of criticism.)

Modern Fiction Studies 20, no. 1 (spring 1974) and 37, no. 1 (spring 1991). (Both issues devoted entirely to critical essays on Updike's fiction.)

Neary, John. *Something and Nothingness: The Fiction of John Updike and John Fowles.* Carbondale: Southern Illinois University Press, 1992. (A comparative study of religious and philosophical themes in the works of the two authors.)

O'Connell, Mary. *Updike and the Patriarchal Dilemma: Masculinity in the Rabbit Novels.* Carbondale: Southern Illinois University Press, 1988; revised, 1996. (A feminist reading of the Rabbit novels.)

Plath, James, ed. *Conversations with John Updike.* Jackson: University Press of Mississippi, 1994. (A collection of thirty-two interviews, including those for the *Paris Review, Life,* National Public Radio, and the *Harvard Crimson,* arranged in chronological order and intended for a range of audiences.)

Schiff, James A. *John Updike Revisited.* New York: Twayne, 1998. (A comprehensive evaluation of Updike's work that updates earlier critical overviews to demonstrate the growth of his reputation.)

Thorburn, David, and Howard Eiland, eds. *John Updike: A Collection of Critical Essays.* Englewood Cliffs, N.J.: Prentice-Hall, 1979. (Includes essays by Joyce Carol Oates, George Steiner, David Lodge, Joyce Markle, and others.)

Trachtenberg, Stanley, ed. *New Essays on* Rabbit, Run. New York: Cambridge University Press, 1993. (An introduction by Tractenberg and four essays on the novel.)

Wood, Ralph C. *The Comedy of Redemption: Christian Faith and Comic Vision in Four American Novelists.* Notre Dame, Ind.: University of Notre Dame Press, 1988. (A comparative theological study focusing on the Rabbit novels, *Couples,* and *Midpoint.*)

Yerkes, James, ed. *John Updike and Religion: The Sense of the Sacred and the Motions of Grace.* Grand Rapids, Mich.: Eerdmans, 1999. (A collection of essays by theologians as well as literary critics.)

Stephen Crane's
The Red Badge of Courage

MARK RICHARDSON

IN 1983 CONTROVERSY arose over the memorial that sat in a park at the center of the little town of Port Jervis, New York—the boyhood home of Stephen Crane. A group of veterans in Port Jervis successfully persuaded the town's council to change the name of Stephen Crane Memorial Park to Veteran's Memorial Park at Orange Square. *The Red Badge of Courage,* they maintained, was an affront to the dignity of veterans of all wars. What could they have had in mind? And why had the Union's General Alexander McClurg condemned Crane's novel, shortly after its publication, as "a vicious satire upon American soldiers," saying that its hero is "without a spark of...soldierly ambition"? "No thrill of patriotic devotion to cause or country," he claimed, "ever moves his breast."

These are questions well worth considering. The veterans of Port Jervis may have been wrong to object to the existence of Stephen Crane Memorial Park on the ground that *Red Badge* is an antiwar novel. Surely it is not that, or not that *exactly.* But they were right to detect something insidiously jocular, something perhaps even corrosive, in Crane. He is, as Alfred Kazin puts it in *An American Procession* (1985), a writer whose

"scorn for the American gods is awesome." There is serious matter in this for any student of American literature and culture, for with Crane arrives the decisive fall of what used to be called "the American Adam." Crane's repudiation of our faith in "the American gods" is also an implicit repudiation of the American civil religion of inexhaustible "possibility." To understand that, and to inquire into the novel in detail, the broader historical developments that brought the nation to the pass it reached in 1895, when *Red Badge* first appeared, must be taken into account.

In November of 1863, when he appeared at the Gettysburg battlefield to dedicate the cemetery, President Abraham Lincoln could see about him the open graves of thousands of men who had died in battle there; exhumation and reburial had fallen behind schedule. (In July, when the battle was fought, the heat of the day made necessary a hasty and makeshift disposal of the dead.) Here was evidence of a battle that to many seemed as wasteful and indecisive as the one imagined in *Red Badge* would later seem to Crane. As for the battle at Chancellorsville, which took place in May of the same year and on which *Red Badge* is based, Lee Clark

Mitchell's assessment is apt: "Twenty-seven thousand men died in a conflict whose immediate consequences seemed nil at best and at worst senseless; the North lost despite a decided superiority, the South won a merely Pyrrhic victory, and after two days both sides were left almost exactly where they had been." Nonetheless, Lincoln was able to transfigure the scene, the battle, and the larger war with a splendid new conception of the American errand, an enterprise in which Crane had absolutely no interest in terms of his own response to the great conflagration of the war. Lincoln proposed an America whole, at least in imagination. In it Americans looked to gather paradise—"the last best hope of earth," as he put it in the Annual Message to Congress (December 1, 1862), thinking of the promise of democracy. It was the hour of our greatest imaginary expansion and of our most poetical—our most sublime—"union." What followed, over the next few decades, was the assembly of an America united in prosaic fact.

Markets—literary markets included—were for the first time truly nationalized. Postwar amendments to the U.S. Constitution gave the Union a new consistency and integrity from state to state, from region to region. Truly national, even continental, communication and transportation infrastructures were put into place. These were the sort of infrastructures that would allow Scratchy Wilson, Crane's west Texas outlaw in "The Bride Comes to Yellow Sky" (1898), to dress himself in clothes purchased "for purposes of decoration" and made chiefly by "Jewish women on the East Side of New York." Scratchy Wilson's situation is illustrated vividly in the account of Bell County, Texas, found in Ray Ginger's engaging history of this period, *Age of Excess*. Before 1879 farmers in Bell County grew their own wheat, ground it at local mills, and baked their bread at home. They raised feed for their livestock, which, in turn, supplied them with labor power and meat. They sewed their own

CHRONOLOGY

1871	Crane is born on November 1 in Newark, New Jersey.
1890–1891	Attends Lafayette College and Syracuse University but takes a degree from neither school. Begins work for the New York *Tribune*.
1893	Publishes *Maggie: A Girl of the Streets* under the pseudonym Johnston Smith.
1894	Signs an agreement with the Bachellor newspaper syndicate to serialize *The Red Badge of Courage*.
1895	Travels to Nebraska, New Orleans, Texas, and Mexico as a correspondent for the Bachellor syndicate. D. Appleton Company publishes *Red Badge* in October; the book soon becomes a best-seller.
1896	Meets Cora Steward (also known as Cora Taylor) in Jacksonville, Florida; the two live together for the rest of Crane's life (but never marry).
1897	Travels to Greece (with Cora) to cover the Greco-Turkish War; afterward settles in England.
1898	At the outbreak of the Spanish-American War, returns to New York to secure work as a correspondent. Returns to England in December.
1899	*War Is Kind* (poetry) appears in May; *The Monster and Other Stories* follows in December. Suffers first of several tubercular hemorrhages.
1900	Travels to a sanatorium in Badenweiler, Germany, and dies of tuberculosis on June 5.

clothes. Then, during the 1880s, local mills began to shut down. Flour was now milled on an industrial scale for national markets in Minnesota from wheat grown in Nebraska. It was shipped by rail to every quarter of the nation, including Bell County, Texas—and, presumably, Crane's fictional whistle-stop along the southern transcontinental rail line, Yellow Sky. The farmers now wore store-bought pants, perhaps sewn in New York City sweatshops by immigrants from eastern and southern Europe. They ate Columbia River salmon canned in the Pacific Northwest and baked beans canned in Boston. They drank coffee made from beans grown in Brazil. In sum, by the 1890s, the last decade of a century of American expansion, the frontier was closed. It had been fully assimilated into the work-a-day business and continent-wide markets of America.

In addition, the promise of full civil rights for black Americans had by the century's end been well enough foreclosed. The guarantees of the war amendments to the U.S. Constitution, together with the tentative achievements of the Radical Republicans during President Ulysses S. Grant's two administrations, were inexorably made null as southern legislatures rewrote their state constitutions. The latter developments are well illustrated by a single statistic. In 1896 registered black voters in Louisiana numbered 130,334; by the time Americans voted in the national elections of 1904, only 1,342 remained on the rolls. Black voters constituted majorities in twenty-six parishes of that state in 1896; by 1904 they prevailed in none. The efficiency of disenfranchisement and the means used to achieve it varied from state to state, but Louisiana was not unusual. These restrictions on black suffrage inevitably affected white voter registration as well, with the result that the voting- eligible population in general markedly shrank.

Democracy in the South was more or less a dead letter in the 1890s, and union activists, who often faced armed troops and agrarian populists (who thought that big financial interests had hijacked American institutions), were beginning to feel that it was a dead letter everywhere. A paralyzing economic depression, which peaked in the early 1890s, did nothing to improve matters. The post-Reconstruction years were, in short, a period of diminishing possibility: in Stephen Crane's America, geographical "expan-

sion" and political "emancipation" alike seemed to be at an end.

LITERARY NATURALISM AT THE CLOSE OF THE CENTURY

In 1836 Ralph Waldo Emerson—the greatest of the great American Adams—admonished Americans to "build, therefore, [our] own world." He addressed himself to what the poet Walt Whitman later called "simple separate persons." However consistent his thinking may have been with free-market "possessive individualism," it had a genuine, radically democratic tendency. But by the late nineteenth century, in Stephen Crane's America, the temper of the nation—or at least the temper of those who seemed to determine the nation's course—had changed decisively.

Consider the following remarks from the influential sociologist and political scientist William Graham Sumner, in an 1894 tract called "The Absurd Effort to Make the World Over." (The very title mocks cherished utopian American aspirations to dwell in "possibility," in what the American poet Emily Dickinson went on to call a "fairer house than prose.") Sumner writes in defense of developments that concentrated capital in fewer and fewer hands and reports, with no noticeable chagrin, that "democracy never has done anything, either in politics, social affairs, or industry, to prove its power to bless mankind." That makes short work of Lincoln's last best hope, and it was an idea that powerful men were willing to entertain. But even if it were *not* the case that democracy held no blessings, Sumner suggests, still there would be no point in trying to secure them. In those days, resisting the great engine of American capital, or the reassertion of white supremacy, was like lashing at the wind. Sumner naturalizes the business. Ours simply is, he says,

a tough old world. . . . All its wry and crooked gnarls and knobs are therefore stiff and stubborn. If we puny men by our arts can do anything at all to straighten them, it will only be by modifying the tendencies of some of the forces at work, so that, after a sufficient time, their action may be changed a little.

In short, "the tide will not be changed by us. It will swallow up both us and our experiments." And "that is why it is the greatest folly of which a man can be capable, to sit down with a slate and pencil to plan out a new social world." The reforming, and even utopian, spirit of Emerson's generation, and of the abolitionists particularly, had been pretty much extinguished—at least in the circles that really counted.

Crane's species of literary naturalism harmonizes well with Sumner's philosophy in this sense: it is a prescription for resignation. In the sixth section of his story "The Open Boat" (1897), he says,

> When it occurs to a man that nature does not regard him as important, and that she feels she would not maim the universe by disposing of him, he at first wishes to throw bricks at the temple, and he hates deeply the fact that there are no bricks and no temples. Any visible expression of nature would surely be pelleted with his jeers.
>
> Then, if there be no tangible thing to hoot, he feels, perhaps, the desire to confront a personification and indulge in pleas, bowed to one knee, and with hands supplicant, saying: "Yes, but I love myself."
>
> A high cold star on a winter's night is the word he feels that she says to him. Thereafter he knows the pathos of his situation.

And in 1898's "The Blue Hotel" (section 8),

> We picture the world as thick with conquering and elate humanity, but here, with the bugles of the tempest pealing, it was hard to imagine a peopled earth. One viewed the existence of man then as a marvel, and conceded a glamor of wonder to these lice which were caused to cling to a whirling, fire-smitten, ice-locked, disease-stricken, space-lost bulb. The conceit of man was explained by this storm to be the very engine of life. One was a coxcomb not to die in it.

The first of these sardonic passages appears in a story about a gunrunning junket to Cuba that ends in disaster, perhaps (so the rumors went) as a result of Spanish sabotage. The second is from a parable about the introduction into Nebraska of what a hotel owner, speaking the bumpkinish dialect Crane often resorts to, proudly denominates "a line of ilictric streetcars." The cool, chastened, practical, and material temper of these two stories is quite characteristic of the 1890s—the great epoch of imperial capital in the United States, and the great era of dizzying, hyperaccelerated development. Crane's best-known stories and novels resign readers to the vagaries of the "natural" environment, as in his story "The Open Boat." They also resign readers to those of the essentially social environments with which natural ones so often are confused in his fiction, as in *Maggie: A Girl of the Streets* (1893), a novel about New York City slum life. Against the forces of both natural and social environments resistance is simply absurd. That sentiment, in any event, Crane and Sumner have in common. At the end of the day—and *Red Badge* is no exception to the rule—Crane's great theme is futility: the experience of being inadequate to the project of really understanding, let alone managing, the forces that condition one's environment.

These developments hold important "vocational" consequences, at least for an innovative writer such as Crane. Earlier writers than Crane—writers who dwelt in "possibility"—felt themselves to be intimately engaged in the national enterprise. The remarkable styles of the great writers of the American Renaissance of the early to mid- 1800s took heart from the expanding energies of the nation. This sort of energy, let alone this sort of extravagance, is nowhere to be found in Crane. For him style is what might be called a strictly *private* resource, not a "public" one, and it is nothing if not temperate and "cool." The discipline of writing does not carry him away with the nation; the discipline of writing is there to *prevent* his being carried away by the alienating drift of a nation so impersonal in its maneuvers as to admit no vital participation on the part of the "simple separate person."

Representative of Crane's situation in a nation of diminished possibility is the plight of the journalist who goes undercover, in a short sketch titled "An Experiment in Misery" (1894), to see how the other half lives. A night among the abject on the Lower East Side of New York City leaves him changed utterly. Only no terrible beauty is born:

> And in the background a multitude of buildings, of pitiless hues and sternly high, were to him emblematic of a nation forcing its regal head into the clouds, throwing no downward glances, in the sublimity of its aspirations ignoring the wretches who may flounder at its feet. The roar of the city in his ear was to him the confusion of strange tongues, babbling heedlessly; it was the clink of coin, the voice of the city's hopes, which were to him no hopes.
>
> He confessed himself an outcast, and his eyes from under the lowered rim of his hat began to glance guiltily, wearing the criminal expression that comes with certain convictions.

Crane's arrogantly "regal" New York is a far cry from Whitman's vibrant, "adhesive" Manhattan. The figure in Crane's sketch has spent only one night in the American wilderness, but that is enough to put into question every ideal he had cherished. "Confession" is in order because Crane's new American loner—his updating, if you will, of the more buoyant "self-reliant" type—has essentially committed the crime of treason. He has suffered a crisis of faith in the national errand and sees no point in redeeming it. He is an ideological alien on native ground, confused not so much by the "babble" of strange Eastern European tongues on the streets of New York City as by the babble of an old American idiom no longer intelligible to him at all. He no longer dwells in a fairer house than prose. Crane developed this refusal to dwell in possibility— this un-American lack of "faith" and "hope"—

into a stoic new mode of art. And it everywhere colors his antiheroic novel of the American Civil War.

THE RED BADGE OF COURAGE

Much work has been undertaken to unearth Crane's sources for *The Red Badge of Courage*. Charles LaRocca has investigated the likelihood that Crane based much of what he wrote on the experiences of the New York 124th regiment, many of whose veterans he met in Port Jervis as a boy. In the spring of 1893 Crane was absorbed in reading "Battles and Leaders of the Civil War," a series of memoirs of Union and Confederate soldiers that had run in *Century* magazine in the mid-1880s. There he found, among other things, a detailed account of the battle of Chancellorsville. Lydon Upson Pratt has speculated that Crane, in writing *Red Badge*, had in mind the experiences of a colorful teacher of his at Claverack College, General John Bullock Van Petten, who had fought, among his many engagements, at Antietam.

More interesting, from a literary point of view, is Crane's possible debt to a widely read novel of the war published by Wilbur F. Hinman under the title *Corporal Si Klegg and His "Pard"* (1887). H. T. Webster has traced out numerous associations linking *Red Badge* to *Si Klegg* and has suggested as well that Crane drew on the 193 detailed illustrations that accompanied the novel in its first edition. Crane's first biographer, Thomas Beer, reports that Crane undertook *Red Badge* on the dare of a friend that he could not best Émile Zola's account of warfare in *La Débâcle* (1892), which Crane appears to have read in 1893. And, of course, Crane had available to him the great Civil War battlefield photographs of Mathew Brady. But however things stand with regard to the literary sources of the novel, of more significance is the peculiar character of Crane's prose, which is quite distinctive, and the indirect influence on it of his milieu.

One of Crane's best effects depends on a kind of tonal polyphony that oddly harmonizes what would otherwise be discordant moods. The effect usually suggests the complexity, or the ironic objectivity, of Crane's point of view. A fine example occurs in the first chapter of *Red Badge:*

> After complicated journeyings with many pauses, there had come months of monotonous life in a camp. [Henry Fleming] had had the belief that real war was a series of death struggles with small time in between for sleep and meals; but since the regiment had come to the field the army had done little but sit still and try to keep warm.
>
> He was brought then gradually back to his old ideas. Greeklike struggles would be no more. Men were better, or more timid. Secular and religious education had effaced the throat-grappling instinct, or else firm finance held in check the passions.
>
> He had grown to regard himself merely as a part of a vast blue demonstration. His province was to look out, as far as he could, for his personal comfort. For recreation he could twiddle his thumbs and speculate on the thoughts which must agitate the minds of the generals. Also, he was drilled and drilled and reviewed, and drilled and drilled and reviewed.

The point of the first paragraph is uncomplicated: army life and army myth are not the same. The second paragraph is a repetition, almost verbatim, of an earlier passage describing the content of Henry's "ideas." Crane often resorts to repetition of this sort. Here it suggests (somewhat condescendingly) the poverty of Henry's thinking process and its wavering incoherence. Men no longer fight, because they are "better," because they are too "timid," because they have been educated out of the instinct, or because the lords of the land find it unprofitable to allow them to do it. The alternatives in each case exclude each other. Perhaps Henry sees no irony in his "old ideas" and regards the pairs of alternatives as in each case viable. For Crane the second in each pair pretty clearly undercuts the first, with the final irony

being, simply, that timidity, prudence, decency, and altruism are insufficient, even in combination, to moderate an undignified "throat-grappling instinct" in men. The third paragraph revives the uncomplicated mode of the first, with a flourish of repetition in the last sentence registering the tedium of camp life. Readers are getting a fair picture of the alienation of the common infantryman, who learns to regard himself as "part of a vast blue demonstration."

The next two paragraphs of the passage are pure Crane:

> The only foes [Henry] had seen were some pickets along the river bank. They were a sun-tanned, philosophical lot, who sometimes shot reflectively at the blue pickets. When reproached for this afterward, they usually expressed sorrow, and swore by their gods that the guns had exploded without their permission. The youth, on guard duty one night, conversed across the stream with one of them. He was a slightly ragged man, who spat skillfully between his shoes and possessed a great fund of bland and infantile assurance. The youth liked him personally.
>
> "Yank," the other had informed him, "yer a right dum good feller." This sentiment, floating to him upon the still air, had made him temporarily regret war.

Crane bullies his characters a little; he teases them. He narrates at once from inside and outside his hero's sensibility, so to speak. Henry might well see the rebel pickets as "sun-tanned" and perhaps also as "philosophical" in the colloquial sense of "mature" and "steady of nerve." But Henry would not think of their potshots as "reflective"—an adjective motivated by the term "philosophy," but ironically so in that the idle shooting is almost certainly thoughtless and cruel. To say that the offending pickets are "reproached" by their targets is to speak as if their musketry is essentially a show of bad form. It might be regarded as such either by a cavalier Virginia officer or by the grunts in his command, though the two parties would resent the sniping for different reasons: the first as a sin against honorable combat and the second as a sin against the fellowship that ought to bind together in solidarity the poor grunts on both sides of the skirmish against the conceit of the officer corps. Readers understand the impression the rebel picket makes on Henry and that he is a little foolish to be so impressed: "'Yank,' the other had informed him, 'yer a right dum good feller.' This sentiment, floating to him upon the still air, had made him temporarily regret war." Crane, too, may regret war but not because it has no respect for the dignity of encounters like this one. Crane himself allows for no dignity in it.

The vernacular is employed here not for the neutral purpose of verisimilitude but for the purpose of comical stereotype. Consider the point at which Crane first deploys the diminishing epithet "yokel." It comes in chapter 8 in a passage one might have expected would be allowed to work itself out without a punch line. Henry has fallen in with a group of wounded and dying men:

> The youth joined this crowd and marched along with it. The torn bodies expressed the awful machinery in which the men had been entangled.
>
> Orderlies and couriers occasionally broke through the throng in the roadway, scattering wounded men right and left, galloping on, followed by howls. The melancholy march was continually disturbed by the messengers, and sometimes by bustling batteries that came swinging and thumping down upon them, the officers shouting orders to clear the way.
>
> There was a tattered man, fouled with dust, blood and powder stain from hair to shoes, who trudged quietly at the youth's side. He was listening with eagerness and much humility to the lurid descriptions of a bearded sergeant. His lean features wore an expression of awe and admiration. He was like a listener in a country store to wondrous tales told among the sugar barrels. He eyed the story-teller with unspeakable wonder. His mouth was agape in yokel fashion.

This is meant to be funny, as is also the gratuitous observation, during the charge in which Henry ultimately "distinguishes" himself (in chapter 19), that the enlisted men "stare" up at their commanding lieutenant with "blank and yokel-like eyes." "Yokel" is not really a descriptive epithet; it is rather the sort of epithet that relieves a writer of the obligation to describe. This sort of comedy is specific to the 1890s or to the post-Reconstruction period in general: owing to the new mobility, the cosmopolitan center—where Crane was always based—was ever more often venturing out into the provinces. And the long economic depression of the 1890s had done nothing to make the provinces appear any less backward or any more sophisticated to East Coast urbanites like Crane.

Immediately following the passage in which the Confederate picket and Henry have their moment of tenderness occurs the best part of this first chapter of the novel:

> Various veterans had told him tales. Some talked of gray, bewhiskered hordes, who were advancing with relentless curses and chewing tobacco with unspeakable valor; tremendous bodies of fierce soldiery who were sweeping along like the Huns. Others spoke of tattered and eternally hungry men who fired despondent powders. "They'll charge through hell's fire an' brimstone t' git a holt on a haversack, an' sech stomachs ain't a-lastin' long," he was told. From the stories, the youth imagined the red, live bones sticking out through slits in the faded uniforms.

The insertion of the phrase "chewing tobacco" does the deflationary trick. The irony depends on the way the "advance" of the fierce soldiery and the "chewing" they do share the predicate "unspeakable valor." The parallelism is comically false. It is as if Crane chose *precisely* the wrong adjective to modify "valor": "*inexpressible* valor" appears to be the phrase around which Crane allusively orbits. Of course, "unspeakable," his arch substitution, means something more like "reprehensible"—a nuance perhaps motivated by the sense of affronted outrage the green Yankee soldiers feel. As they experience them, the Confederate attacks are a capital rudeness, a breech of good decorum, as much deserving of "reproach" as of counterattack. It is as if Crane's diction slyly evokes, in its parodying way, the gentlemanly cult of good breeding that some still believed, especially in the post-Reconstruction era, had governed the combat at least of the rebels. *Red Badge* is nothing if not a satire of chivalry.

Crane's manner persistently suggests that he regards himself as existing above and outside the situations with which he has to do; his investment is typically cool, ironic, and detached. This is precisely why readers have never been able comfortably to assimilate *The Red Badge of Courage* to conventionally "heroic" modes as well as why readers whose cultural orientation sets them apart from Crane's rather cocky urbanity often find his writing unsettling and vaguely offensive. The tonal complexity (and comedy) of passages like the ones noted here at once can explain and perhaps settle the most important and long-standing controversy surrounding the novel: Is Henry Fleming a "hero"? Does he or does he not "mature" as the novel progresses? Does the conclusion of the novel mark a turn, an upward development, in his character? Or is he, all the way through to the bitter end, regarded with ironic condescension by the narrator (and by Crane)? Related to this is another important controversy: Is there in Crane an acid sort of irony, an inexhaustible impiety? Or, instead of a cynical ironist, is Crane a writer genuinely in search of the providential sense of national and individual purpose that Americans apparently lost in the Gilded Age? In this debate, the former view may be more in harmony with Crane's sense of style, with the work Crane did as a writer.

To be sure, the novel does lend itself inevitably to readings of it as a bildungsroman, a novel about the moral and psychological growth of Henry. As Andrew Delbanco points out in his *Required Reading*, "it has long been an English teacher's favorite, because it has a conveniently interrogatory form: What, it obliges us to ask, does Henry Fleming learn?"

This question has been answered variously by critics. Henry learns to accept mortality as the inevitable fate of the body. Or he learns to become a soldier—to subordinate his merely private interests to the imperatives of the larger social body to which he belongs, the army. Or he learns how to be a "man," that is, he faces his fears, disciplines and manages them, and in the end recognizes that honor (for example) is a higher principle than mere survival. But, ultimately, perhaps the question "What does Henry learn?" is impertinent. Henry, in fact, learns nothing.

To some extent, the interpretive controversies arise from a simple historical fact: the text of *The Red Badge of Courage* has been difficult to establish. The first text to appear was an abridged version, which ran in several newspapers late in 1894. The second was a much longer text published in book form in 1895 by D. Appleton and Company of New York. For decades readers assumed that the latter text was the most authoritative one available, and it was upon the basis of it that the debate as to Henry Fleming's "heroism" arose. But beginning in the 1950s more documentary evidence came to light, and, as the textual scholar Hershel Parker showed in a masterly essay, the Appleton text is not, in fact, reliable—or even, perhaps, quite coherent. Crane's editor at Appleton, Ripley Hitchcock, caused him, however indirectly, to cancel many passages from the novel and, indeed, an entire chapter (which would have been the twelfth chapter in the original, swelling the total to twenty-five chapters). The effect of the excisions—which amount to several thousand words—is to mute, somewhat, the severity of Crane's ironic treatment of Henry, with the result that it becomes possible to see, in the broad outline of the plot, a story of his redemption.

The extreme to which this reading of the novel may be taken is best illustrated by R. W. Stallman's influential interpretation of it as a *Christian* allegory of redemption:

The theme is that man's salvation lies in change, in spiritual growth. . . . Henry Fleming recognizes the necessity for change and development but wars against it. But man must lose his soul in order to save it. The youth develops into a veteran: "So it came to pass . . . his soul changed." Significantly enough, in stating what the book is about Crane intones Biblical phrasing.

In due course Stallman concludes that as he witnesses Jim Conklin's death, Henry figuratively "partakes of the sacramental blood and body of Christ and the process of his spiritual rebirth begins at the moment when the wafer-like sun appears in the sky. It is a symbol of salvation through death." This is a far cry from the usual reading of Crane as a wiseacre rebel against his parents' strict Methodism. It is a reading that finds the father and the mother in the son, and the Son of the Father himself in that most famous "sun" in late-nineteenth-century American literature, the one Crane "pastes" in the sky "like a wafer," a communion wafer, if Stallman is to be believed.

There is a sense in which this reading has integrity, a way in which it holds together. It has been an influential reading owing to the fact that Stallman's detailed biography of Crane, which recapitulates it, remains to this day a standard. But this "redemptive" sort of reading ought to make any reader wary, if only because its solemnity, its gravity, sorts so uncomfortably with Crane's playfully sardonic prose. The network of ecclesiastical metaphors possibly is motivated more by Crane's tendency to follow out the implications of the figurative language available to him. A reference in the third chapter to the "cathedral light of the forest" is nothing other than an extension of what is, after all, a centuries-old figure (the forest as "cathedral"). Readers should not be either surprised or put on guard for deep meaning when the youth stumbles (in chapter 7) into a grove "where the high, arching boughs made a chapel." As chapels tend to do, it also has "portals" and "doors" (in this case, green) and a "carpet" (in this instance, of pine needles). What else would one expect to

find in the "chapel" of a forest "cathedral" than "religious half light"? And why would not the wind-swayed trees be said to "sing a hymn of twilight" in "chorus" and the insects, their own song abating, be said to "bow their beaks" and make a "devotional pause"?

Crane's habit is to follow out even the most commonplace of metaphors in careful, at times ludicrous, detail. His interest is precisely in what critics used to call the "vehicles" of his metaphors more than in what can be called their "tenor," or cargo, which explains the characteristic fastidiousness with which he so often develops them. His prose everywhere has the effect of arresting our movement from vehicle to tenor: the vehicles are, for Crane, simply too much fun to play with; they absorb him. In the chapel passage, for example, his mind is likely on the fact that cathedrals imply chapels, and chapels imply portals and carpets, and on the fact that all of these things imply hymns, bowing, and devotion. Nothing in a religious allegory would require Crane to lay it on so thick. The details of the famous "chapel" scene do not seem to highlight a seriously Christian crisis in the spiritual growth of Henry Fleming. Of course, *Red Badge* does have a plot, and that plot has an arc, which accounts for the illusion of "moral progress," on Henry's part, that the novel can both foster and sustain. *Red Badge* has, in a way, a three-part structure. In its first movement, readers are introduced to the set of dispositions toward war, and beliefs about it, with which Henry and his green comrades are equipped at the outset. These involve sentimental ideas about heroism and battle, partly associated with boyish adolescence and partly arrived at from reading, in secondary school, too many accounts of "Greeklike struggles." Over against this, in a second movement, is set the experience of battle itself. The adolescent sense of integrity these young soldiers had felt is utterly shattered by battle, and it must be reorganized—re-consolidated around some new central ideal. This new ideal, which emerges in a third, or final, movement, goes in the novel by the name of manhood: the "youths" become "men."

But does it very much matter that the battle effecting this transformation is "an episode of the *American* Civil War," as Crane's subtitle reminds us? Would any other battle in any other war have done as well? It is nice question, because the Civil War, as many have suggested, marked America's "coming of age"—its loss of innocence (if it had any to lose) and its long-awaited maturation. The Civil War for the first time made "America" *real*—in promise, in maturity, in responsibility. It is tempting to suggest, with Stallman, that Henry becomes "real" in precisely this serious sense. But if that realization is, in fact, what the war achieved, Henry and his comrades, as Crane portrays them toward the novel's end, can hardly be an index of it. Nothing about them is ever really dignified—not to Crane anyway. The "manhood" and the new integrity into which they emerge are pretenses hardly tenable—no more tenable than the idea that America had, through the war, at last made good its promise of liberty: the 1890s made that idea preposterous, as Crane intuitively understood. So the state of affairs as *Red Badge* concludes is really not so different from the state of affairs with which it began: men, in Crane's assessment, are pretentious, naive, fragile, and "infinitely humorous" in their historical situation, to borrow a phrase from Crane's "The Bride Comes to Yellow Sky."

Consider the famous conclusion to the novel:

And at last his eyes seemed to open to some new ways. He found that he could look back upon the brass and bombast of his earlier gospels and see them truly. He was gleeful when he discovered that he now despised them.

With the conviction came a store of assurance. He felt a quiet manhood, non-assertive but of sturdy and strong blood. He knew that he would no more quail before his guides wherever they should point. He had been to touch the great death, and found that, after all, it was but the great death. He was a man.

So it came to pass that as he trudged from the place of blood and wrath his soul changed. He came from hot plowshares to prospects of clover tranquilly, and it was as if hot plowshares were not. Scars faded as flowers.

It rained. The procession of weary soldiers became a bedraggled train, despondent and muttering, marching with churning effort in a trough of liquid brown mud under a low, wretched sky. Yet the youth smiled, for he saw that the world was a world for him, though many discovered it to be made of oaths and walking sticks. He had rid himself of the red sickness of battle. The sultry nightmare was in the past. He had been an animal blistered and sweating in the heat and pain of war. He turned now with a lover's thirst to images of tranquil skies, fresh meadows, cool brooks—an existence of soft and eternal peace.

Over the river a golden ray of sun came through the hosts of leaden rain clouds.

The world, Crane tells the reader, is now a world "for" Henry Fleming, "though many discovered it to be made of oaths and walking sticks." Any claim of possession, however, is a mere conceit. For what can be the meaning of these oaths and walking sticks? The reader is invited to suppose that Henry is no longer "hobbled" by the world—that on the serene plateau to which he thinks he has ascended, no more vexations will elicit from him "oaths," nor any constitutional weakness send him reaching for his "walking stick." But the reader simply must conclude—Crane's arch tone leaves him little choice—that for Henry the world will always be, as it is for every other character in Crane, made *precisely* of oaths and walking sticks and that he is a coxcomb not to die in it.

The mastery, the sheer *fluency* that Henry here supposes that he has achieved is an illusion. The postcard pastoral of the scene evoked, with its tranquil skies and fresh meadows, is but the emanation of Henry's still naively "youthful" state of mind. He has recovered what Crane calls in chapter 11 an ability "to see himself in a heroic light." He has acquired adequate breathing space, as Crane says (in chapter 21) after the first of the two climactic charges is done, "in which to appreciate himself"—and he does just that, with "much satisfaction." The successful charge against the enemy color guard only leaves him (in chapter 24) "preparing to resent some new monstrosity in the way of dins and smashes." And it would be hard to demonstrate that the following late passage is any less ironic in tone than those toward the beginning of the book, in which Henry's self-knowledge is clearly faulty in the extreme:

> He found that he could look back upon the brass and bombast of his earlier gospels and see them truly. He was gleeful when he discovered that he now despised them.

> With this conviction came a store of assurance. He felt a quiet manhood, non-assertive but of sturdy and strong blood. He knew that he would no more quail before his guides wherever they should point. He had been to touch the great death, and found that, after all, it was but the great death. He was a man.

These are Henry's assessments, not Crane's.

And what of the last sentence in the novel, the one so often quoted? "Over the river a golden ray of sun came through the hosts of leaden rain clouds." Readers who find in *Red Badge* an intricate pattern of contrasts—light/dark, haze/translucence, confusion/insight—regard this conclusion as the capstone to the whole symbolic edifice of the novel. Henry has at last emerged from the tempest of his youthful ordeal into something like a harbor. It is as if the weather of the novel exteriorizes Henry's state of mind. "That Crane plotted the entire novel by images and situations evoking contradictory moods of despair and hope is evidenced not only in this terminal image of the book," writes Stallman, "but in the opening image of chapter one." And yet this terminal image, so integral to the pattern of the book as Stallman understands it, is not present in the surviving manuscript of *Red Badge*, and there is some controversy as to whether it "belongs" in the book at all. As Her-shel Parker sees it—and the evidence is strong—Crane's editor Ripley Hitchcock

> prevailed upon [him] to compose a new and upbeat final paragraph: "Over the river a golden ray of sun came through the hosts of leaden rain clouds." As John T. Winterich said in 1951, this sentence "bears the unmistakable spoor of the editor" and "sounds like a concession to the send-the-audience-home-feeling-good school." With these last changes—maybe the little decisively placed addition was the last of all—Hitchcock had engineered disproportionately great changes in the apparent meaning of crucial passages. In the first stage of expurgation, he had purged the book of passages likely to prove most objectionable, those where Henry Fleming indulged in vaingloriously adolescent ontological heroics; in the second, the mopping-up stage, he had purged it of those where Fleming displayed a heartlessly triumphant egotism.

In short, the passages missing from the published text and present in the manuscripts, or else present in the published text and missing from the manuscripts, strongly suggest that the novel as Crane "really" wrote it is unremitting in its irony. Fleming is a youth who never comes into his majority; he remains perpetually a minor, in what Crane in chapter 6 calls "an ecstasy of self-satisfaction." Never does he attain what Stallman calls his "own bright serenity, his own tranquility of mind"; never is his "conscience reborn and purified." No "education" worthy of the name has taken place, and there has been no profound "development" in Henry's character. The elements of the bildungsroman are certainly there, but the effect is essentially parody.

THE STYLE IS THE MAN

If Crane is not *really* writing about the progress of a boy into manhood or the redemption of a boy from fear or "spiritual" growth or the sacramental blood of Christ or even the making of a veteran soldier, what is the "subject" of the novel, the "theme"? Perhaps the best answer to this question is found in Crane's prose. Crane's fiction is concerned chiefly with, or captivated chiefly by, writing, or style. Style, as Crane developed it, is a way of cutting a figure in the world. Style is charisma, a mode of address, a thing cultivated not for the purpose of realizing any *particular* work of art but for the purpose of creating, of making vividly real a literary personality.

R. G. Vosburgh, with whom Crane shared a room in 1893, published a brief memoir of the writer in 1901. "In revising his work," Vosburgh recalls, Crane "would rewrite a whole sheet when a correction was necessary rather than make an erasure, if only to change one word." So captivated was he by his own turns of phrase and by his metaphors that he "studied them out with much care, and after they had been trimmed and turned to final form he would repeat them aloud and dwell on them lovingly."

A good place to begin an inquiry along these lines is in the first chapter, which opens as follows:

> The cold passed reluctantly from the earth, and the retiring fogs revealed an army stretched out on the hills, resting. As the landscape changed from brown to green, the army awakened, and began to tremble with eagerness at the noise of rumors. It cast its eyes upon the roads, which were growing from long troughs of liquid mud to proper thoroughfares. A river, amber-tinted in the shadow of its banks, purled at the army's feet; and at night, when the stream had become of a sorrowful blackness, one could see across it the red, eyelike gleam of hostile camp fires set in the low brows of distant hills.

Informing these sentences is a simple equation: the army is like a single man; the army *is* in fact a man, which might, as men do, "stretch out on the hills, resting" and which might "awaken" and "cast its eyes upon the roads." Nothing seems out of the ordinary here, and the personification is, in certain respects, conventional—so conventional as not to be strongly

felt as a metaphor. But Crane is doing something new with this familiar metaphor, which is always implicit in military terminology: an army is a "corps," a body. And as the novel unfolds this metaphor becomes oddly literal. If the army is a body, a corps, then the individual soldiers must be its cells or corpuscles. Much later, in the fifth chapter, Crane develops precisely this idea: "A small procession of wounded men were going drearily toward the rear. It was a flow of blood from the torn body of the brigade." The corps is here in danger of becoming a corpse, and at one point on its march the great body divides to clear the way for exactly that, a "corpse," in which it no doubt sees itself mirrored. The metaphoric nature of phrases like "a great body of troops" (chapter 3) has been worn away through their sheer familiarity. Crane's achievement is to make them feel like metaphors again, as he does with another phrase in chapter 2: "At nightfall the column broke into regimental pieces, and the fragments went into the fields to camp." Crane takes what is usually not felt as a metaphor—the column "broke"—and follows it out scrupulously as if it were one; he makes the metaphor live again. Even the most unadorned English comes to seem peculiar and fresh.

More complex is Crane's handling of another conventional metaphor first introduced in the eighteenth chapter of *Red Badge,* in which Henry Fleming overhears two officers discussing tactics. In this passage the officers dismissively call the infantrymen "mule drivers." It is a revelation to Henry:

> New eyes were given to him. And the most startling thing was to learn suddenly that he was very insignificant. The officer spoke of the regiment as if he referred to a broom. Some part of the woods needed sweeping, perhaps, and he merely indicated a broom in a tone properly indifferent to its fate. It was war, no doubt, but it appeared strange.

What startles Henry is the idea, forced upon him many times during the course of the novel, that he is merely an instrument in "a vast blue demonstration"—that he is not a "real" agent at all. He is a broom, or, what is worse (and more accurate), a single straw in the homely regimental brush of a broom. The broom is first brought out of the closet by another soldier, and to another purpose, in a remark made in chapter 17 about the Confederate dead: "Lost a piler men, they did. If an' ol' woman swep' up the woods she'd git a dustpanful." He imagines his and Henry's regiment wreaking havoc and an old woman cleaning up after them. It is a satisfying thought, and "sweeping" or "mopping" up is commonplace military slang. But on hearing the officers confer, Henry reworks the regiment's relation to the "broom" along humiliating lines. He now feels that a broom is no sort of implement to carry into battle, let alone to *be* in battle; brooms are for women's work. It is a double indignity (Henry feels) for a soldier to think of himself as one; it unmans him. And soon after (in chapter 18), a grunt along the line prophesies to Henry, as they contemplate the opposing Confederates: "We'll git swallowed."

The ideas of the broom and of the swallowing coalesce to absurd effect in chapter 20: "As [Henry] noted the vicious, wolflike temper of his comrades he had a sweet thought that if the enemy was about to swallow the regimental broom as a large prisoner, it could at least have the consolation of going down with bristles forward." The thought is "sweet" not least because it redeems the figure of the regimental broom, here oddly imagined as a "prisoner" of war. If the soldiers are but a broom, in the eyes of haughty commanders, they may as well fight dirty. So, the "bristling" gunfire mentioned becomes the porcupine "bristles" of a "broom" reluctant to be "swallowed" by the enemy, as if in some terrible (and terribly undignified) kitchen brawl. It is not clear whether Henry appreciates the ludic quality of the metaphor as much, and in the same way, as does the narrator. Defeating a hostile and tenacious regiment is like swallowing a broom, bristles forward. True,

in what is for him an impressive show of intellection, Henry himself draws together the broom and the swallowing, and readers are given access to his thoughts. But it is doubtful that Crane ascribes to him the full ironic purchase on his commander's disdain that this "sweet," "bristling" thought would allow. Nonetheless, the refreshing thing about the passage is the way it recalls two distinct metaphors from two chapters earlier in the novel—the broom and the swallowing—and adds to them the lucky flourish of "bristles." The facility with which Crane performs the maneuver argues a spirited but leisurely sort of play carried on superfluously above the narrative and hard to associate with the business of war, let alone with the gravitas of much discourse about the Grand Army of the Republic. The effect is entirely characteristic of him.

Earlier in the novel (in chapter 16), in the midst of a passage describing the clamor of battle, one reads that "at last the guns stopped, and among the men in the rifle pits rumors again flew, like birds, but they were now for the most part black creatures who flapped their wings drearily near to the ground and refused to rise on any wings of hope." Here Crane takes up a figure laid down first at the start of chapter 4: "[The soldiers] mouthed rumors that had flown like birds out of the unknown." In this second example, the simile is developed with almost whimsical deliberation, as if Crane's interest, again, were more in the vehicle than in the tenor of the figure. Crane's technique, in passages like this, is to take more seriously than is usual the implications of commonplace figures of speech like "the rumors flew" or "the wings of hope." His writing is forever a commentary on the unexploited possibilities for play that exist in "ordinary" language.

Then there is the queer comedy of this passage from the fourth chapter: "Bullets began to whistle among the branches and nip at the trees. Twigs and leaves came sailing down. It was if a thousand axes, wee and invisible, were being wielded." Bullets as "wee axes"? The technique, here, involves a well-managed incongruity of adjective and noun: "wee" belongs to a rather effete, infantile (or perhaps just quaintly Irish) lexicon; its association with axes is a bit startling. Are readers to imagine, if only for an instant, a welter of tiny elves chipping away at the trees piecemeal? Also to be accounted for are odd flourishes like this one in chapter 4: "They of the reserves had to hold on. They grew pale and firm, and red and quaking." The sense is that some men were pale and firm, whereas others were flushed and trembling. Assimilating the two sorts of men into the undiscriminating pronoun "they"—as if each particular soldier were, by turns and in concert with all the other soldiers, doing these incompatible things— nicely conveys the disarray of the regiment.

A bit later, in chapter 5, the reader is told of a colonel who scolds his troops "like a wet parrot." The addition of "wet" (how *does* a parrot behave when wet?) nudges into novelty what otherwise would be something of a cliché: to scold like a parrot. The reader is left to consider the sheer *parrotness* of the scolding. And then there are such phrases as this from chapter 14: "Strange gods were addressed in condemnation of the early hours necessary to correct war"? Here the verb "to correct" alternately means "to conduct war correctly" or to "put war aright" or "to admonish war," and yet it can be reduced to none of these. Its ambiguity, its suspension, is perfect. Here is a description of Henry, as he readies himself to panic: "His hands," as described in chapter 6, "seemed large and awkward as if he was wearing invisible mittens. And there was a great uncertainty about his knee joints." What, strictly speaking, is the difference between saying "as if he were wearing mittens" and saying "as if he were wearing *invisible* mittens"? The "as if" makes the "invisible" oddly redundant, at least for the purposes of the figure. Fleming is thought of not so much as wearing *mittens* but as wearing *invisible* mittens. Better still is the preposition "about" in "there was a great uncertainty about his knee joints." Crane neatly allows the secondary sense of "about"

("in the vicinity of") to infect the primary sense ("concerning"), quite as if the "great uncertainty" were something Henry might shoo away from his knee joints, as he would a fly.

As a last example, consider what Crane does with the expression "stir the fire," in chapter 13, where the wounded Henry at last returns to his regiment. A soldier is preparing to nurse him and to that end gets the fire going: "He fussed around the fire and stirred the sticks to brilliant exertions." "Exertions" brings out the figurative sense of "stir." The soldier is imagined to inspire the sticks, to move and exhort them, which is, of course, what "stirring" can mean, though it is usually treated in this context as a reference merely to physical movement.

Many more such examples might be given. In the aggregate, as they accumulate page after page, these verbal tricks dislodge readers from their customary habits of attention to words; that dislodging is what Crane's work is somehow always "about." Crane is much more interested in the texture of what he says than in the "weight" of it; he is all about levity, not gravity. This gives a clue as to why he should treat the Civil War as he does in *The Red Badge of Courage*—that is, with no sense at all of the ideological dimensions of the catastrophe. Crane is not really writing about war, certainly not about the American Civil War; he is writing, and writing playfully, in the *vicinity* of war. Crane simply cannot forget that he is writing, and he cannot be persuaded that the writing is not always the main thing after all. *Red Badge* was not written out of, and about, a "crisis of faith" in God and in "God's instrument, the American nation," as Delbanco puts it in his essay on the context of the novel. Crane wrote it out of the more or less tacit assumption that faith, whether in God or in America as God's instrument, was probably the sort of thing about which only a certain sort of politician made "heartfelt" appeals to a certain sort of constituency. In any case, this is what the novel seems to "take for granted"; this is the assumption that grounds its peculiar comedy.

CRANE'S TREATMENT OF THE WAR

Thomas Beer's *Stephen Crane* was the first book-length study of Crane, and it is still among the most provocative responses to him, despite its many inaccuracies as to the details of Crane's life. "As heroic legend," Beer says, the history of the Civil War "has been curious and remains unwritten because of that spiritual censorship which strictly forbids the telling of truth about any American record until the material of such an essay is scattered and gone." He goes on:

> How did the men who scorched their youth and scarred their bodies think of those four years, before the easy sentiment of senility clouded down? One knows that in 1868 General Custer's wife noted: "My husband's troopers seem to have absolutely no unkind feeling toward the Secessionists at all and they never talk about their triumphs and exploits. They are always teasing each other about how badly they fought and how many times they ran away. It is distressing to see and hear how little exalted their views are." And one knows that in 1869 at a banquet of the Grand Army a man lifted his glass and toasted: "Everyone that ran at Shiloh, like I did!"
>
> The distress of Mrs. Custer [supplies] a conjecture.... The common man's attitude toward the myth of a pure, courageous host bent on the Lord's work was truly shocking. The swift cynicism of the American which is the basis of our popular thought rounded promptly on romantic views of the Rebellion. Duval, the leading ballad singer of New York, was hissed from the stage in June of 1865 when he tried to please an audience speckled with soldiers by chanting: *Home Have Come Our Boys in Blue.* The gunbearing animals shouted: "Dry up!" and "Sing something funny!"

The details of Beer's report may or may not be largely invented. But the parable he tells is both suggestive and acute as to the sentiment of the 1890s. Imagine *Red Badge* as a toast proposed to

the nation along precisely these lines: "Everyone that ran at Shiloh, like I did!" It is certainly a book to disconcert loyalty to military service, as General McClurg's oft-cited denunciation of it implies. In Crane's army there is always what he calls, in chapter 5, "a singular absence of heroic poses"—a singular "neglect" of "picturesque attitudes." And in that sense his novel is indeed antiheroic and essentially satirical in its relation to the literature of war.

Still, if one is altogether to explode "The myth of the Lord's good work," that is another matter. It was necessary in the 1890s to repudiate "romantic views" of the Rebellion if the Republican Party, and the businessmen it represented, were to consummate their rapprochement with a New South ready to draw Northern investments into its cheap labor markets. It was "ideologically" necessary to deflate anyone breaking out with "Home Have Come Our Boys in Blue." After 1877 waving the bloody shirt, reviving partisan antipathy, was no longer in good form in the North. This is clear from the decisive defeat in Congress of the 1890 Force Bill, which would have provided for supervision of federal elections in the South, with the constitutionally sound aim of enforcing the 14th and 15th amendments—the so-called war amendments. *Red Badge* perfectly serves the turn: "Dry up!" Crane's novel redescribes the Civil War—or at least a "representative" part of it—in such a way as to make impossible a "heroic" reading of it. Perhaps *Red Badge* is written expressly to make untenable all talk about the glory of the coming of the Lord, as the patriotic tune "Battle Hymn of the Republic" would have it.

Coincident with the demolition of "romantic views" about the Grand Army of the Republic was the cultivation of decidedly romantic views about the Southern ancien régime. Indeed, the 1880s and 1890s saw the perfection of the so-called plantation myth, with its happy darkies, its mammies, and its "paternal" institutions. This is a mythic sort of fiction most unlike Crane's work in character and tone but very like it in at least *one* tendency: in its inclination to consign what Beer archly calls "the Lord's work" to the dustbin of history. It is worth considering whether, in the 1890s, a general deflation of "exalted views" about the war did help facilitate a reconciliation, which, in due course, allowed for a businesslike reinstitution of white supremacy in the southern states and the ascendancy of "big business" as the major player in American politics. The nation, as with one set of eyes, simply looked the other way. To some extent the cynicism of which Beer speaks doubtless was associated with the new order of things in the 1890s, though that was not its only significance. An appreciation of its possible political resonance makes clear both how and why, as Delbanco puts it in his essay, "reading *Red Badge* relieves us of our ideology."

Red Badge is a thoroughly disenchanting devaluation of that problematic word "courage." Crane everywhere suggests that such words, which are used to dignify conduct and beliefs, are always eventually misleading. And he developed, in his prose, a tactically useful engine of rhetorical analysis. His habits of expression, his ironic style, are adverse to all sorts of sentimental talk about "nation," "justice," "responsibility," "self-sacrifice," and so on. His Civil War fiction may do nothing to keep the fires of the great American mission burning. It may, indeed, give up the Lincolnian national errand—to bring about "a new birth of freedom"—with a shrug. It may even have no use for the American religion of "possibility" and "optimism." But at least it refuses, in good conscience, to countenance any hypocrisy about the redemptive legacy of the Civil War— hypocrisy that still often disingenuously colored the sentiments of a nation falling all over itself in the 1890s to abandon its dedication, as Lincoln put it at Gettysburg, to "the proposition" that "all men are created equal." Crane, it might be said, put the whole "American" enterprise in

quotation marks so that it can be seen for what it is and for what it can be made to be.

CONCLUSION

There is at least one illusion beyond which Crane never ventures, because he does not apparently see it as an illusion: the idea that life simply *is* a kind of war—necessarily a brutal, confusing, and probably pointless affair. At the end of the day, this is the experience of war in *The Red Badge of Courage* (despite Stallman's unpromising Christian interpretation of it).

What, then, is missing in Crane's world? "Truth with a big T," as the American philosopher William James, another pragmatist, once put it. There is nowhere any Truth for Crane. There are only ways of seeing. In certain respects, his thinking is what is now called "anti-foundational" or, in American contexts, "pragmatist." But his is the anti-foundationalism, the suave "irony," that many writers on the left now complain about on the grounds that it simply cannot support, let alone offer, a program of practical political reform. The battle described in *The Red Badge of Courage* was, "in real life," many things. It represented an episode in a Democratic-Republican struggle to abolish slavery, an incident in a national-Providential story about the glory of the coming of the Lord, and an event in the extension of politics by other means to settle a question about the nature of federal power and to resolve forever the future of slave labor in the American West. It was also an exercise in military strategy, in which warfare was decisively "modernized," a theater for the staging of an adolescent crisis, and an episode in a centuries-old conflict over the right relations of whites to non-whites everywhere in the world (that is to say, a local occurrence in a global struggle). The battle is undoubtedly all of these things at once. But not one of them, for Crane, is ever allowed "essentially" to characterize it.

He lacks commitment. He had, in fact, *perfected* the art of "lacking commitment." There is, for Crane, no master narrative in terms of which the motives and aims of the men involved in making the Civil War might be understood. This is precisely why Andrew Delbanco, in "The American Stephen Crane," is mistaken to find in Crane some notable vestige of "the appetite for the very idea of divine superintendence that the Civil War had thrown into doubt and, more seriously, into disrepute." On the contrary, Crane resists altogether the priority of the master narrative of "emancipation." Crane is not writing any jeremiads; he is not recalling Americans to their forgotten covenant. (He never seems even to address his readers as Americans.) His ultimate achievement was to discredit the possibility of American jeremiads: for him, there is no chosen people, no Promised Land, no covenant, and no judgment. Crane did not go to his grave believing that Americans can build the New Jerusalem. One really cannot look to his fiction for what Delbanco appears to have found there, that is, "lamentation for a bygone day of moral clarity" or a quest for new reasons "to be pious about America" in the face of so many reasons, in the 1890s, not to be.

For Crane, the Civil War was determined by nothing much at all. And the implication in *Red Badge,* as in Crane's fiction generally, is that Henry Fleming's alienated situation is *representative.* It is pure egotism to think of oneself or of one's nation as having a special claim to make on the sympathies of the on-looking world. The life of each person is, to that person, fraught with significance and interest. People "love" themselves. But to others a person may be merely an anecdote, a part of the scenery—what the Union officer Henry overhears contemptuously refers to as "mule drivers." To know these things as Crane did is to dwell in a nation of diminished possibility, a house of prose.

Select Bibliography

EDITIONS

The Red Badge of Courage. New York: D. Appleton, 1895. (This first book edition is considerably longer than the abridged serialized text published late in 1894. For discussion of important textual problems associated with *Red Badge,* see Hershel Parker.)

The Red Badge of Courage: An Authoritative Text, Background and Sources, Criticism. 2d ed. Edited by Sculley Bradley, Richmond Croom Beatty, and E. Hudson Long. Revised by Donald Pizer. New York: Norton, 1976.

Stephen Crane: An Omnibus. Edited by Robert Wooster Stallman. New York: Knopf, 1952. (The text of *Red Badge* in this volume includes, within brackets, manuscript passages canceled for the 1895 first edition.)

Stephen Crane: Prose and Poetry. Edited by J. C. Levenson. New York: Library of America, 1984. (The best single-volume edition of Crane. Unless otherwise indicated, all citations of Crane's work are from this edition.)

OTHER WORKS BY CRANE

Maggie: A Girl of the Streets. New York: D. Appleton, 1893. (Published under the name Johnston Smith. A revised and bowdlerized text was published in 1896.)

The Open Boat and Other Tales of Adventure. New York: Doubleday & McClure, 1898.

The Works of Stephen Crane, 6 vols. Edited by Fredson Bowers. Charlottesville: University Press of Virginia, 1969–1976. (A comprehensive edition of Crane's works, with extensive textual and bibliographical notes.)

SECONDARY WORKS

Aaron, Daniel. *The Unwritten War: American Writers and the Civil War.* New York: Knopf, 1973. (A fine survey of the field.)

Beer, Thomas. *Stephen Crane: A Study in American Letters.* New York: Octagon Books, 1972. (Reprint of the 1923 edition. The first book-length study of Crane, it is controversial and unreliable as to biographical detail but highly suggestive and very well written.)

Benfey, Christopher. *The Double Life of Stephen Crane.* New York: Knopf, 1992.

Crews, Frederick C. "Crane's Life and Times." In *The Red Badge of Courage: An Authoritative Text, Background and Sources, Criticism,* 2d ed. Edited by Sculley Bradley, Richmond Croom Beatty, and E. Hudson Long. Revised by Donald Pizer. New York: Norton, 1976. Pp. 111–116.

Delbanco, Andrew. "The American Stephen Crane: The Context of *The Red Badge of Courage.*" In *New Essays on* The Red Badge of Courage. Edited by Lee Clark Mitchell. New York: Cambridge University Press, 1986. Pp. 49–76.

————. *Required Reading: Why Our American Classics Matter Now.* New York: Farrar, Straus and Giroux, 1997.

Dooley, Patrick. *The Pluralistic Philosophy of Stephen Crane.* Urbana: University of Illinois Press, 1993.

Emerson, Ralph Waldo. *Essays and Lectures.* Edited by Joel Porte. New York: Library of America, 1983.

Frohock, W. M. "*The Red Badge* and the Limits of Parody." *Southern Review* 6, no. 1 (January 1970): 137–148. (A critical response to Solomon.)

Ginger, Ray. *Age of Excess: The United States from 1877 to 1914.* New York: Macmillan, 1965. (An engaging history of the Gilded Age.)

Gullason, Thomas A., ed. *Stephen Crane's Career: Perspectives and Evaluations.* New York: New York University Press, 1972. (A helpful collection of reviews, reminiscences, and criticism.)

Hofstadter, Richard. *The Age of Reform: From Bryan to F.D.R.* New York: Vintage, 1955. (Hofstadter is among the best and most engaging guides to the political history of Crane's era.)

————. *Social Darwinism in American Thought.* Boston: Beacon, 1955.

James, William. *Writings, 1902–1910.* Edited by Bruce Kuklick. New York: Library of America, 1987.

Kazin, Alfred. Introduction to *The Red Badge of Courage.* New York: Bantam, 1983.

————. *An American Procession.* New York: Vintage, 1985. (The chapter on Crane is among the best short studies of the writer.)

LaRocca, Charles. "Stephen Crane's Inspiration." *American Heritage* (May/June 1991): 108–109. (LaRocca argues that Crane drew on the experiences of the New York 124th Regiment in writing *Red Badge.*)

Lewinson, Paul. *Race, Class, and Party: A History of Negro Suffrage and White Politics in the South.* New York: Grosser & Dunlap, 1965.

Mitchell, Lee Clark, ed. *New Essays on* The Red Badge of Courage. New York: Cambridge University Press, 1986. (An important collection of recent assessments of *Red Badge.*)

Parker, Hershel. "Getting Used to the 'Original Form' of *The Red Badge of Courage.*" In *New Essays on* The Red Badge of Courage. Edited by Lee Clark Mitchell. New York: Cambridge University Press, 1986. Pp. 25–47. (An indispensable study of textual problems in *Red Badge.*)

Pratt, Lydon Upson. "A Possible Source of *The Red Badge of Courage.*" *American Literature* 11 (March 1939): 1–10.

Robertson, Michael. *Stephen Crane, Journalism, and the Making of Modern American Literature.* New York: Columbia University Press, 1997.

Solomon, Eric. *Stephen Crane: From Parody to Realism.* Cambridge, Mass.: Harvard University Press, 1966.

Stallman, R. W. *Stephen Crane: A Biography.* New York: G. Braziller, 1968. (The most extensive biography published to date.)

Sumner, William Graham. "The Absurd Effort to Make the World Over." In *Great Issues in American History,* rev. ed. Vol. 3, *From Reconstruction to the Present Day, 1864–1981.* Edited by Richard Hofstadter and Beatrice Hofstadter. New York: Vintage, 1982. Pp. 84–91.

Vosburgh, R. G. "The Darkest Hour of Stephen Crane." *Book Lover* 2 (summer 1901): 338–339. (A brief memoir, written by a friend of Crane.)

Webster, H. T. "Wilbur F. Hinman's *Corporal Si Klegg* and Stephen Crane's *The Red Badge of Courage.*" *American Literature* 11 (November 1939): 285–293.

Wertheim, Stanley, and Paul Sorrentino. *The Crane Log: A Documentary Life of Stephen Crane, 1871–1900.* New York: G. K. Hall, 1994.

Nathaniel Hawthorne's
The Scarlet Letter

ELLEN WEINAUER

NATHANIEL HAWTHORNE'S BIRTH on July 4, 1804—Independence Day—seems fitting indeed for a writer who went on to play a critical role in making the dream of a "national" literature, a literature that the still new nation could call its own, a reality. Hawthorne published his first collection of stories, *Twice-Told Tales,* in 1837—the same year that Ralph Waldo Emerson delivered and published an address, "The American Scholar," to Harvard's Phi Beta Kappa Society in which he called, famously, for America's literary independence. For Emerson, the nation's democratic promise could never be realized while America remained reliant upon "foreign" cultural production, while its writers merely imitated the writers of the "mother country." "We have listened too long to the courtly muses of Europe," he insisted. Now was the time to reject imitation, to embrace the boundless resources of the "new" world, and to create an "American" art drawn from "American" materials. "Our day of dependence, our long apprenticeship to the learning of other lands, draws to a close," Emerson declared in tones at once triumphant and hopeful.

Although Hawthorne was influenced by his reading in the British and European "high art"

tradition, his writings seemed, in many respects, to anticipate and answer Emerson's call. Hawthorne was a descendent of Puritan immigrants and a member of a family whose history was woven deeply into the social fabric of New England. Indeed, one of his paternal ancestors was a judge in the Salem witchcraft trials, and his grandfather, a member of the fourth generation of his family living in the American colonies, was a Revolutionary War hero. Hawthorne embraced his "Americanness" from his earliest years as an author. Returning to Salem, Massachusetts—his ancestral town—after four years at Bowdoin College in Maine (1821–1825), Hawthorne embarked on an ambitious, self-directed program of reading in the history of colonial New England. Not surprisingly, his writing developed in large part from such reading: his first planned story collection was tellingly entitled "Seven Tales of My Native Land." By the time Hawthorne published *The Scarlet Letter,* typically viewed as his masterpiece, in 1850, he was known throughout New England and down the eastern seaboard as both an editor and a writer of historical, regionally grounded tales for adults and children. By virtue of his interest in the history and culture of the colonies he was deemed to be an important and distinctly

257

American voice. "Our literature has given to the world no truer product of the American soil . . . than Nathaniel Hawthorne," proclaimed the *Literary World* in an early review of *The Scarlet Letter*. Another reviewer, this time for *Peterson's*, offered a more specific version of the same point: "We regard 'The Scarlet Letter' as one of the most valuable contributions yet made to American literature." In Hawthorne and his 1850 novel, in other words, critics found an important answer to Emerson's call: they found a writer writing about and for America.

While there were many reasons for Hawthorne to congratulate himself on his reputation and professional success in his own day, there were also changes afoot in the literary marketplace that clearly made him aware of the precariousness of literary "position." In an 1855 letter to his friend and publisher, William D. Ticknor, Hawthorne commented on such changes in a remark that, especially in recent years, has become one of the most talked about things this often talked about writer ever said or wrote. Writing from Liverpool, England, where he was the U.S. Consul, Hawthorne noted that he hoped to "hold this office two years longer." His writing was going slowly, he said. He went on:

> Besides, America is now wholly given over to a d——d mob of scribbling women, and I should have no chance of success while the public taste is occupied with their trash—and should be ashamed of myself if I did succeed. What is the mystery of these innumerable editions of the *Lamplighter* [a novel published in 1854 by Maria Susanna Cummins], and other books neither better nor worse?—worse they could not be, and better they need not be, when they sell by 100,000.

Although just a few weeks later, in another letter written to Ticknor, Hawthorne praised one such "scribbling woman" (the immensely popular Fanny Fern, whose autobiographical novel *Ruth Hall* was just then making waves), it has been his seemingly wholesale derogation of women writers that has remained foremost in the minds

CHRONOLOGY

1804	Hawthorne is born on July 4 in Salem, Massachusetts.
1825	Hawthorne graduates from Bowdoin College, where he has been the classmate and friend of Henry Wadsworth Longfellow and Franklin Pierce.
1828	Hawthorne publishes, at his own expense, his first novel, *Fanshawe*.
1830	Begins publishing (anonymously) tales and sketches in the Salem *Gazette* and the Boston annual, *The Token*.
1837	March, publishes *Twice-Told Tales* under his own name.
1839	Appointed measurer at the Boston Custom House; continues in post until January of 1841.
1841	Joins Brook Farm, a utopian commune, in April; leaves in November.
1842	Marries Sophia Peabody and moves with her to the Old Manse in Concord, Massachusetts.
1846	Hawthorne takes his second political appointment as surveyor of the Salem Custom House.
1849	After Democrats lose the White House to the Whigs, Hawthorne is dismissed from his Custom House post.
1850	*The Scarlet Letter.*
1851	*The House of the Seven Gables.*
1852	*The Blithedale Romance;* campaign biography of his friend from college days, Franklin Pierce.
1853	As a reward for serving the presidential campaign of Franklin Pierce, Hawthorne is appointed U.S. Consul at Liverpool, England.
1857	Resigns consulship and moves with his family to Italy, where they stay until 1859.
1860	Publishes *The Marble Faun* and returns to the United States.

1864 On May 19, Hawthorne dies in Plymouth, New Hampshire, and is buried in Sleepy Hollow cemetery at Concord.

of critics, particularly those working to expand the list of texts deemed "valuable" to and worthy of study in the American literary tradition. The effort to reconstruct and expand the American "canon" has involved the recovery of voices heretofore lost or neglected in our understanding of American literary history—voices such as those of the "scribbling women" who wrote the "trash" that Hawthorne excoriated in his letter to Ticknor. Not surprisingly, critics immersed in such recovery work have become deeply interested in the literary and gender politics of Hawthorne's remark. What could have motivated him to describe the arena of literary production as a kind of battlefield, where men are pitted against women and where "high" art is associated with the former and "low" art with the latter? A closer look at that arena suggests that the gender politics of Hawthorne's remark were driven specifically by changes in the literary marketplace and more generally by challenges to women's privatized and exclusively "domestic" role. Not surprisingly, such changes also are registered in *The Scarlet Letter*, a text whose meditations on the dynamics of gender roles and relations are profoundly rooted in the literary and social milieu of Hawthorne's own day.

Five years before writing to Ticknor, Hawthorne had published *The Scarlet Letter* to widespread acclaim and popular success. He had been publishing since the late 1820s—first anonymously, in magazines and literary annuals, and then, with the publication of *Twice-Told Tales*, with his name on the title page. But he had never attempted a work of full-length fiction—and, indeed, when he began work on *The Scarlet Letter*, he intended to make it part of another story collection. He was encouraged to expand the long tale for publication as a separate narrative by the Boston publisher James T. Fields, who (from that point on in the writer's career) became Hawthorne's most assiduous promoter. Hawthorne feared that the story's somber hues (not to mention its treatment of adultery—a delicate subject indeed for the middle-class audience that Hawthorne hoped to find), unmitigated by "lighter" surrounding fare, would alienate his reading public. After all, as such literary historians as William Charvat and Jane Tompkins have noted, although audiences today are most familiar with the "darker," sin-obsessed Hawthorne of *The Scarlet Letter* and such widely anthologized short stories as "Young Goodman Brown" and "The Minister's Black Veil," these works do not really reflect the majority of Hawthorne's work. Nor were they the texts that critics singled out for attention in Hawthorne's own day. Indeed, the works likeliest to be reprinted in the nineteenth century were Hawthorne's much lighter, sentimental, and fanciful sketches and tales, such as "A Rill from the Town Pump" and "Little Annie's Ramble." These are texts that rarely, if ever, appear in anthologies today (texts that, incidentally, situate Hawthorne much closer to his "scribbling" contemporaries than the writer himself might care to admit).

Despite Hawthorne's expressed anxieties, his publisher was confident that the darker tale would find an audience, and he thus worked to overcome Hawthorne's reluctance about publishing it on its own. Deploying his considerable skills in marketing and promotion, Fields worked hard in the months before publication to pave the way for the volume's success. Within six months of publication, *The Scarlet Letter* had sold somewhere around six thousand copies—a respectably high number in Hawthorne's day. Although some critics faulted the writer for the subject matter of *The Scarlet Letter* and the alleged "bad feeling" manifested in its introductory sketch, "The Custom-House," Hawthorne's fears that his work would not find readers clearly had not been realized.

Even as Hawthorne took pleasure in having made a critical and popular "hit"—and capitalized on his newfound popularity by publishing, in quick succession, two more novels (*The House of the Seven Gables* in 1851 and *The Blithedale Romance* in 1852)—, he was well aware that his work was not capturing the mass audience that new printing and distribution technologies, along with the middle-class cultivation of "leisure time," had made available. Significantly, the year of *The Scarlet Letter* was also the year of Susan Warner's *The Wide, Wide World*—a best-selling novel that quickly went through fourteen editions. Just two years later, in March of 1852, Harriet Beecher Stowe published *Uncle Tom's Cabin* in book form (the text had been serialized in the antislavery periodical the *National Era* in 1851 and 1852). Within a few months, Stowe's novel was selling an unprecedented ten thousand copies each week; in less than a year, the novel sold about 150,000 copies all told. *The Lamplighter*, the novel Hawthorne lambasted in his letter to Ticknor, was nearly as successful, selling forty thousand copies in just two months. With such runaway best-sellers on the cultural scene, Hawthorne would have had a hard time seeing his "success" in anything other than highly qualified terms.

With this brief history in mind, one cannot help but conclude that in his letter to Ticknor, Hawthorne was suffering from a severe case of sour grapes. Certainly Hawthorne was always frustrated by his inability to provide for his family solely by his writing—a problem that he had anticipated long before 1855. Toying with career choices in a letter to his mother written in 1821, just before he left for college, he queried her: "What do you think of my becoming an Author, and relying for support upon my pen?" Even as Hawthorne pointed early on to authorship as the profession to which he felt most suited (in the same letter he rejected categorically careers in the ministry, law, and medicine), he seemed well aware that "support" would be hard to come by in the practical-minded and materialist world of the antebellum United States. "Authors," he admitted, "are always poor Devils." Hawthorne's early predictions came to pass: as an author, he struggled throughout his life with being a "poor Devil," often looking—as the autobiographical "Custom-House" sketch tells us—to other forms of work, including political appointment, and the financial assistance of friends and relations to make ends meet. In this context, his epistolary complaint about women who write trash and the undiscriminating public that consumes it seems to mask thinly a wish that *he* were the one selling "by 100,000."

In dealing with the fact of his own *comparative* literary invisibility, Hawthorne adopted an important and compelling rhetorical strategy. He marked a distinct line of division between "high" art and "trash," between artful work produced by and for a discriminating few and popular work produced by anyone who chooses to wield a pen for the undiscriminating masses. Within this framework, *lack* of popularity becomes a mark of distinction: "I should have no chance of success while the public taste is occupied with" the "trash" written by the "scribbling women," Hawthorne stated flatly, "—and should be ashamed of myself if I did succeed." His sentiments would be echoed by many, including Hawthorne's sometime friend and literary compatriot Herman Melville, who complained in an 1851 letter to Hawthorne about his own inability to "rely for support upon his pen." "Try to get a living by the Truth—and go to the Soup Societies," he complained. "What I feel most moved to write, that is banned,—it will not pay," he went on. "Yet, altogether, write the *other* way I cannot. So the product is a final hash, and all my books are botches." Like Hawthorne, Melville frets about the choice he must seemingly make between writing for the public and telling the "Truth," between selling books and writing what he is "most moved to write." Blaming the perceived flaws of his published books on the pressure to produce "marketable" work,

Melville, like his more famous and established contemporary, erected a clear dividing line between "high" and "low" art. For each writer, policing that line became vitally important in ensuring that he had a place in a literary market that seemed often indifferent to his endeavors.

Given who was selling books "by 100,000" when both Melville and Hawthorne wrote their letters—white women in particular—such aesthetic divisions encode obvious gender divisions as well. Perhaps not surprisingly, the notion of a high art tradition to which a beleaguered group (under-read, white, and male) of writers devoted itself—in what often is depicted as righteous opposition to a crass reading public—was for many years an accepted "fact" of mid-nineteenth-century American literary history. This reading has complex origins in the effort to establish American literature as a legitimate field of critical and aesthetic concern, an effort that saw its first major gestures in the 1950s and early 1960s. American culture often had been faulted, by critics and authors alike, for failing to provide the writer with the appropriate social and historical materials out of which to create "great" works of fiction. In the preface to his fourth and final novel, *The Marble Faun* (1860), Hawthorne himself noted the "difficulty of writing a romance about a country where there is no shadow, no antiquity, no mystery, no picturesque and gloomy wrong, nor anything but a common-place prosperity, in broad and simple daylight." Strangely setting aside his own use, throughout his long career, of manifestly "American" historical materials and settings, he offers a categorical pronouncement: "Romance and poetry, like ivy, lichens, and wallflowers, need ruin to make them grow."

But nearly 100 years later, as critics worked to establish a "great tradition" in America—one that would hold its own against the British "Great Tradition" celebrated by the influential critic F. R. Leavis—they found themselves arguing that the alleged thinness of the American scene was, in fact, an aesthetic virtue. The nation's literary greatness, critics of the late

1950s suggested, was based precisely on writers' ostensible resistance to engaging the "social" scene, their refusal to write realistic social fiction. As opposed to the novel in the British tradition, Richard Chase, Henry Nash Smith, and many others argued, American writers wrote something called "the romance" (a term, as we will see, that Hawthorne himself uses in the introduction to *The Scarlet Letter*). Liberated by the thinness of the American scene into new worlds "within," Chase suggested, such American romancers as Hawthorne and Melville found themselves roaming dark and complex interior landscapes, seeking not to "assuage and reconcile the contradictions of life" but rather to explore the "aesthetic possibilities" of "radical forms of alienation, contradiction, and disorder." American writers, Chase argued, are interested in investigating and depicting psychic depths, not the political and social world around them.

Within such critical formulations, then, writers like Hawthorne and Melville were celebrated for an ostensible disengagement (and conscious alienation) from their middle-class society—in precisely such disengagement, indeed, did the greatness of American literature consist. By extension, of course, the "scribbling women," such as Maria Susanna Cummins, Fanny Fern, Susan Warner, and Harriet Beecher Stowe, were seen as emissaries of and writers for that society. According to Henry Nash Smith, their works express not noble forms of social alienation but an ignoble "ethos of conformity"; they "soothe the sensibilities" of their readers by "expressing only received ideas" and allowing for the "unimpeded discharge of strong but crude feelings." In this formulation—one that Hawthorne himself doubtless would have found comforting—Hawthorne and other romancers were marked for distinction by their difference from their female contemporaries. This difference was signaled by their refusal to cater to the sensibilities and ideologies of the middle-class reading audience and their comparative inability to sell. By extension and by contrast, of course, the "scribbling women" who could "sell by 100,000," were marked for critical obscurity.

Just as significant for American literary history as the long neglect of popular women writers that this critical approach put in place has been the ways in which its understanding of literary "greatness" has necessarily deflected attention away from what "canonical" American texts say and do socially and politically. In the case of *The Scarlet Letter,* to be more specific, this has meant emphasizing the novel's "universality" rather than its status as a product of its own time and place and addressing its rendering of "timeless" themes, like sin and redemption or love and desire, rather than exploring how such themes might reflect responses to the social turmoil of the antebellum United States. In recent years, scholars have worked to rectify this gap, examining *The Scarlet Letter* in terms of political, social, and cultural issues ranging from slavery to domesticity, from democracy and national identity to citizenship, from masturbation to homoerotics, from mothering to the making of the middle class. Not surprisingly, perhaps, one of the issues in Hawthorne scholarship to which critics turned most frequently at the end of the twentieth century was that of gender. For in *The Scarlet Letter,* Hawthorne not only provides American literature with one of its most compelling and complex female characters, an impassioned, sexually desiring, and socially resistant woman of whom Hawthorne insists (just as critics would later insist about Hawthorne himself) "the world's law was no law for her mind," but he also writes a narrative centered on the very nature of gender identity, the meanings of "manhood" and "womanhood."

To come to terms with Hawthorne's treatment of gender identity—and the novel's engagement of the twin themes of male authority and female insurgency—we need to be aware not only of the complex gender politics of the literary marketplace but also of white, middle-class women's increasing public visibility in the antebellum period. In the 1840s and 1850s,

women were not only making their voices heard in fiction, but they also were speaking out in more "public" and visible forums—in lectures, conventions, and even street demonstrations. Perhaps most important, in 1848, just two years before Hawthorne published *The Scarlet Letter,* Elizabeth Cady Stanton, Lucretia Mott, and others convened the first National Women's Rights Convention, held at Seneca Falls, New York. In the decade or so preceding the Seneca Falls convention, women had begun to extend their designated role as "moral housekeeper" in the domestic sphere into public arenas. In particular, many women (and not a few men) asserted that the piety and innate morality with which antebellum culture endowed them necessitated women's involvement in the most pressing social movements of the day—temperance, education reform, and, chiefly, antislavery work. Women no longer operated exclusively behind the scenes in such reform work. Instead, they mixed it up in public demonstrations and spoke from the lecture platform. On the antislavery lecture circuit, for example, activist women spoke to mixed-sex audiences—a "scandalous" act that fueled the hostility toward the abolitionists expressed by many in the early years of the movement.

Even as women found increasing numbers of ways to participate publicly in the nation's work, they also recognized the limitations placed upon them by the nation's laws and civic codes. Women could not hold elective office or vote—although they could be taxed if they were property owners. Marriage was the designated path for virtually all women. Upon marriage, however, women gave up whatever slim rights they had. Married women could not own property independently, make contracts in their own names, sue for divorce, claim their own wages, or claim custody of their own children. Many women felt frustrated by the ways in which their limited rights constrained their ability to act publicly; Stanton and Mott were reminded of just such constraints when they traveled to London to attend the World's

Antislavery Convention of 1840. There, after a day of deliberation, the members of the convention voted not to seat women delegates, who, instead of participating from the floor, had to sit in a gallery, observing and listening from behind a curtain. Angered by being silenced and excluded, and recognizing the ways in which such treatment posed practical impediments to their antislavery work, Stanton and Mott decided to hold their own convention, devoted exclusively to the cause of women.

Eight years later, they finally acted on their determination, announcing in the July 14, 1848, edition of the *Seneca County Courier* a "Convention to discuss the social, civil and religious condition and rights of woman" to be held just five days later. Despite the late notice, some three hundred people attended the convention. At its end, sixty-eight women and thirty-two men signed the *Declaration of Sentiments and Resolutions*, a manifesto for the fledgling but now "official" women's rights movement. It opened with the following, stunning revision of the Declaration of Independence: "We hold these truths to be self-evident: that all men *and women* are created equal" (emphasis added).

The convention and the calls made by its participants for women's full civic enfranchisement seemed to stun the general public. Bemused, mocking, outraged, or (less frequently) affirming, columns in newspapers throughout New England (quoted in Stanton's *History of Woman Suffrage*) offered commentary on the women and their "insurrection." "This is *bolting* with a vengeance," asserted the *Worcester Telegraph*. "The great effort seemed to be to bring out some new, impracticable, absurd, and ridiculous proposition, and the greater its absurdity the better," grumbled the *Rochester Democrat*. Amid such responses, the *Mechanic's Advocate* offered perhaps the most sober-minded assessment of what the *Declaration of Sentiments* demanded.

Society would have to be radically remodelled in order to accommodate itself to so great a change in the most vital part of the compact of the social relations of life; and the order of things established at the creation of mankind, and continued *six thousand years,* would be completely broken up. . . . In a thousand other ways that might be mentioned, if we had room to make, and our readers had patience to hear them, would this sweeping reform be attended by fundamental changes in the public and private, civil and religious, moral and social relations of the sexes, of life, and of the Government.

It is difficult to read such a remark—pointing to the "sweeping," "fundamental" nature of the changes called for at Seneca Falls—and not think of Hester Prynne, who, in the last chapter of *The Scarlet Letter*, prophecies a time when "a new truth would be revealed, in order to establish the whole relation between man and woman on a surer ground of mutual happiness." Like the women of Seneca Falls, Hester envisions an utterly changed world, one in which the old "relation between man and woman" and the society established on its foundation would be "completely broken up" and then reimagined in terms of *new* roles, *new* gender formations.

It is not only possible but also important to read *The Scarlet Letter* against the backdrop of antebellum debates about gender and changes in designated roles for men and women. Contending with a literary marketplace in which men felt increasingly marginalized, in a society in which the work of the artist was (already) devalued and women were asserting new forms of power and authority, Hawthorne takes up issues of femininity, masculinity, and resistance to patriarchal power that situate his text at the dead center of that society from which earlier critics deemed him to retreat. Ironically, perhaps, Hawthorne seems to want to be the sort of social iconoclast—the slayer of middle-class ideology—described by earlier critics. Like Hester, Hawthorne seems to wish to make "the world's law no law for [his] mind," to work against the pull of his society and ratify his heroine's spirit of resistance and the changes in how men and women are defined to which her "freedom of speculation" correlates. But ultimately, again like Hester, Hawthorne cannot escape the reach of that law. By the end of the novel, Hester's subversive power is largely contained, and the text's investigation of alternative gender identities is brought to an effective close.

UNDERSTANDING "THE CUSTOM-HOUSE"

Just as it is important to understand the general cultural context of *The Scarlet Letter,* so, too, it is necessary to know the immediate history behind the novel's composition. In particular, it is critical to acknowledge that just before embarking on *The Scarlet Letter,* Hawthorne went through a period of personal turmoil that deeply influenced both the novel and its prefatory sketch, "The Custom-House." That the controlled tones of the "Introductory" to *The Scarlet Letter* offer little overt indication of such turmoil suggests that at least superficially Hawthorne has been successful in his effort to write autobiographically even while keeping the "inmost Me behind its veil."

For three years, from 1846 until 1849, Hawthorne had served as surveyor of the Custom House at Salem, a political appointment that had been secured for him through the efforts of well-placed Democratic friends. (One such friend was Franklin Pierce, who was elected president of the United States in 1852; another was the influential editor John L. O'Sullivan, a proponent of American expansionism whose phrase "Manifest Destiny" has continued to influence U.S. political thought down to the present day.) As he had during a previous tenure as a political appointee and a Custom House officer in Boston, Hawthorne felt frustrated by the ways in which his labors in the world of commerce dulled his imagination and his intellect, and he saw his writing slow to a trickle. The income seemed critical, however—just two months after taking the oath as surveyor, Hawthorne's wife, Sophia, gave birth to the couple's second child. Hawthorne was therefore incensed when the fall of the Democrats to the Whigs in the 1848 elections led to his ouster from the Custom House in June of 1849. He embarked on a campaign for reinstatement on the (arguably shaky) ground of what he claimed was his own political neutrality, and he saw his situation taken up on both sides in a noisy and often ugly political fracas in the newspapers. Efforts on his behalf availed him nothing, except perhaps the desire to be well out of political office. The months of fighting, capped by the death of his mother in late July, led to a surfeit of emotion that Hawthorne seemed to channel into his writing. By September he was spending more than nine hours a day at his pen, working feverishly on what would soon become *The Scarlet Letter.*

Hawthorne's complex response to being dismissed from the Custom House—a combination of fury and relief—is transformed by the alembic of Hawthorne's imagination into the deeply significant and highly controlled preface to this novel, "The Custom-House." At first blush, this sketch, with its autobiographical focus on Hawthorne's tenure as a Custom House surveyor and how he came to write *The Scarlet Letter,* seems to function merely as textual "preamble," only indirectly relevant to the narrative itself. A closer examination of the sketch's treatment of governmental authority, masculinity, and imaginative power, however, suggests that it has far more important thematic connections to the narrative that follows, connoting anxieties about gender and authorship that shape the treatment of Hester Prynne along with her male protagonists, Roger Chillingworth and Arthur Dimmesdale.

Above all, of course, "The Custom-House" is about the Salem Custom House, a "spacious edifice of brick" whose pavement "has grass enough growing in its chinks to show that it has not, of late days, been worn by any multitudinous resort of business." From the beginning of the sketch, then, it would appear that as the surveyor of the Custom House, Hawthorne presides over a dying operation. Indeed, images of death and decay circulate throughout the earliest pages of "The Custom-House." While Salem was once a prosperous port, Hawthorne tells us, its "bustling" wharf is "now burdened with decayed wooden warehouses, and exhibits few or no symptoms of commercial life." The grass along the wharf is "unthrifty," the wharf itself "melancholy" and "dilapidated." If the exterior of the Custom House and its environs indicate a commercial industry in decline, so, too, does its interior. The surveyor's office is "cobwebbed, and dingy with old paint; its floor is strewn with gray sand, in a fashion that has elsewhere fallen into long disuse." Also characterized by "long disuse," apparently, are the Custom House's inhabitants. Most often, Hawthorne tells us, upon "ascending the steps" of the "edifice of brick,"

> you would discern . . . a row of venerable figures, sitting in old-fashioned chairs, which were tipped on their hind legs back against the wall. Often-times they were asleep, but occasionally might be heard talking together, in voices between speech and a snore, and with that lack of energy that distinguishes the occupants of alms-houses, and all other human beings who depend for subsistence on charity, on monopolized labor, or any thing else but their own independent exertions. These old gentlemen . . . were Custom-House officers.

A few pages later, significantly, Hawthorne reiterates this same image. Turning again to the "excellent old persons" over whom he had authority, he notes:

> They spent a good deal of time . . . asleep in their accustomed corners, with their chairs tilted back against the wall; awaking, however, once or twice in a forenoon, to bore one another with the several thousandth repetition of old sea-stories, and mouldy jokes, that had grown to be passwords and countersigns among them.

While such depictions of sleepy old men seem at first quaint and picturesque, when they are read against the other images of decay and degenera-

tion that circulate through "The Custom-House," they point to an anxious meditation on the matter of masculine power and authority with which the sketch seems increasingly preoccupied. The text reminds us repeatedly that the space of the Custom House is male. "It is easy to conclude, from the general slovenliness of the place," Hawthorne writes, "that this is a sanctuary into which womankind, with her tools of magic, the broom and mop, has very infrequent access." The aged officers who preside over this male "sanctuary" are described as a "patriarchal body of veterans," a kind of Masonic fraternity, complete with "pass-words and countersigns." The old "Inspector" is the "father of the Custom-House," the "patriarch . . . of this little squad of officials." But the connotations of authority and potency that the notions of fraternity and patriarchy carry are undercut completely by the old men's "lack of energy" and agency, their willingness to rely for support on anything other than "their own independent exertions." The Inspector may be potent in a procreative sense (Hawthorne points out that he was the "husband of three wives" and the "father of twenty children"), but his sphere of influence is profoundly limited. "He possessed no power of thought, no depth of feeling, no troublesome sensibilities; nothing, in short, but a few commonplace instincts . . . in lieu of a heart." He has, Hawthorne reiterates, "no soul, no heart, no mind." Apparently, the "passwords and countersigns" with which the men communicate point to nothing but themselves. At best, patriarchy has lost its power; at worst, such images suggest, it is devoid of all meaning and substance.

Hawthorne takes pains to explore the causes of this attenuation of masculine power, which he locates in the very nature of government employment. The "effect of public office" on men, he notes, is "not very favorable." While a man "leans on the mighty arm of the Republic" for his employment, "his own proper strength departs from him. He loses, in an extent proportioned to the weakness or force of his original nature, the capability of self-support." "Uncle Sam's gold," he goes on, "has, in this respect, a quality of enchantment like that of the Devil's wages." He who takes it compromises "if not his soul, yet many of its better attributes; its sturdy force, its courage and constancy, its truth, its self-reliance, and all that gives the emphasis to manly character." Such reiterations of threats to "manly character" lead to what Hawthorne names as his own fears that he would not be exempt from the effects of taking "Uncle Sam's gold." "I endeavoured to calculate how much longer I could stay in the Custom-House, and yet go forth a man," he declares. "To confess the truth, it was my greatest apprehension . . . that I was likely to grow gray and decrepit in the Surveyorship, and become such another animal as the old Inspector."

The threat to (his own) masculinity posed by such political appointment as Hawthorne himself "enjoyed" as a customs inspector is signaled early in the sketch by the depiction of the Custom House itself. "Over the entrance" of the building, Hawthorne writes,

> hovers an enormous specimen of the American eagle, with outspread wings, a shield before her breast, and, if I recollect aright, a bunch of intermingled thunderbolts and barbed arrows in each claw. With the customary infirmity of temper that characterizes this unhappy fowl, she appears, by the fierceness of her beak and eye and the general truculency of her attitude, to threaten mischief to the inoffensive community; and especially to warn all citizens, careful of their safety, against intruding on the premises which she overshadows with her wings. . . . She has no great tenderness, even in her best of moods, and, sooner or later,—oftener soon than late,—is apt to fling off her nestlings with a scratch of her claw, a dab of her beak, or a rankling wound from her barbed arrows.

To walk into the Custom House, one must walk under this eagle—figuratively subjecting oneself to the "intermingled thunderbolts and barbed arrows" that she is capable of wielding. While the men who inhabit the patriarchal space of the Custom House have lost their power, the federal eagle—notably gendered female—is superpotent. But while she possesses generative power, she uses it to no good end. In imagery that is deeply significant, given its place in an introduction to a text that is about a mother, Hawthorne describes the eagle as a kind of anti-mother: possessed of both female generative capacities and phallic potency (thunderbolts and arrows), she is unnatural and manifestly antimaternal. The eagle cares little about her "nestlings," whom she is "apt to fling off . . . with a scratch," a "dab of her beak," or a "rankling wound from her barbed arrows." Given this gender-bending image—the female eagle possessed of the (male) power that all the "men" in the Custom House can no longer claim—it is no wonder that the text depicts the Custom House as deeply threatening to masculinity and that Hawthorne figures his own "manly character" as under duress.

Hawthorne makes it clear that a long tenure in the Custom House would compromise not only his manhood but also—and at the same time—his art. As a consequence of his long years of service to "Uncle Sam," we might remember, the Inspector has lost all mental capacity: he is "possessed no power of thought, no depth of feeling, no troublesome sensibilities." He lacks, in other words, everything a writer needs in order to write. Significantly, Hawthorne finds himself similarly (if temporarily) affected by his Custom House labors. He has been translated, he suggests, from a "man of thought, fancy, and sensibility" into a "man of affairs." As a result, "Literature, its exertions and objects, were now of little moment in my regard. I cared not, at this period, for books; they were apart from me. . . . A gift, a faculty, if it had not departed, was suspended and inanimate within me." Drawing a line between the work of the writer and the work of commerce (a line similar to the one he draws in his letter about the "scribbling women"), Hawthorne writes that his name, no longer "blazoned abroad on title-pages," "had now another kind of vogue. The Custom-

House marker imprinted it, with a stencil and black paint, on pepper-bags, and baskets of anatto, and cigar-boxes, and bales of all kinds of dutiable merchandise."

Hawthorne repeatedly insists that he is content with this state of things: he "no longer seek[s] nor car[es]" that his name is on bales of merchandise rather than books, trusting that the life he leads is merely "transitory" and that "whenever a new change of custom should be essential to my good, a change would come." But such explicitly stated complacency about his situation's temporary nature is belied by the story he tells of finding the letter itself. Hawthorne gives an account of finding in the attic of the Custom House, amongst some "heaped-up papers" and "worthless scratchings of the pen," a "certain affair of fine red cloth, much worn and faded," with "traces about it of gold embroidery." This "capital letter A" is twisted around a "small roll of dingy paper," a supposed account of the "whole affair" of the letter itself offered by a previous surveyor, Jonathan Pue.

This account of "how a large portion of the following pages came into my possession" is itself a fiction, Hawthorne's nod to nineteenth-century literary conventions by which writers claim that their fictions are based in truth and that they themselves are merely editors. But while the actual story about finding the letter is a patent falsehood, Hawthorne uses it to convey a truth about the perceived effects of his work in the Custom House. In the "found" letter, he tells us, he sees "the groundwork of a tale," and yet it is a tale he cannot write:

> So little adapted is the atmosphere of a Custom-House to the delicate harvest of fancy and sensibility, that, had I remained there through ten Presidencies yet to come, I doubt whether the tale of 'The Scarlet Letter' would ever have been brought before the public eye. My imagination was a tarnished mirror.

Hawthorne provides a much discussed example to make this point about his loss of artistic capacity more concrete. Inspired by the letter

and his desire to tell its story, he describes himself sitting at home "late at night" in his "deserted parlour, lighted only by the glimmering coal-fire and the moon, striving to picture forth imaginary scenes, which, the next day, might flow out on the brightening page in many-hued description." In a passage that critics have long seen as central to a theory of the "romance genre" in American literature, Hawthorne describes why he sees this particular setting as enabling the work of the imagination. Moonlight, he explains, can transform the world of everyday reality into something less familiar, less concrete—and hence more aesthetically generative. In the light of the moon, "the floor of our familiar room has become a neutral territory, somewhere between the real world and fairy-land, where the Actual and the Imaginary may meet, and each imbue itself with the nature of the other." The "dim coal-fire" plays a role in "producing the effect" Hawthorne describes, for its "warmer light mingles itself with the cold spirituality of the moonbeams, and communicates, as it were, a heart and sensibilities of human tenderness to the forms which fancy summons up."

Just as important as what this passage tells us about the developing genre of "romance" is what it points to in terms of Hawthorne's own alleged artistic crisis:

> At such an hour, and with such a scene before him, if a man, sitting all alone, cannot dream strange things, and make them look like truth, he need never try to write romances.
>
> But for myself, during the whole of my Custom-House experience, moonlight and sunshine, and the glow of firelight, were just alike in my regard; and neither of them was of one whit more avail than the twinkle of a tallow-candle. An entire class of susceptibilities, and a gift connected with them,—of no great richness or value, but the best I had,—was gone from me.

Despite Hawthorne's own earlier claims that he is not bothered by his transformation from a published writer to a "man of affairs," such images as these reveal a deeper anxiety—he says he is "haunted" by his fears—about how his work in the Custom House is compromising his very self. Not surprisingly, perhaps, it is at this point in "The Custom-House" that Hawthorne moves into his discussion of how governmental service challenges "manly character," suggesting that, for Hawthorne, *manhood* is equated with his work as an *artist.* It is thus no wonder that Hawthorne describes his ejection from the Custom House—a place repeatedly associated with emasculation, with the loss of masculine power—as a return to both art *and* manhood. Admitting that he finds what he images as his decapitation unsettling ("The moment when a man's head drops off is seldom or never, I am inclined to think, precisely the most agreeable of his life," he notes), he insists that he "had brought himself to the comfortable conclusion, that every thing was for the best." "Making an investment in ink, paper, and steel-pens," he tells us, he "had opened his long-disused writing-desk, and was again a literary man."

If Hawthorne here depicts his departure from the Custom House as a return to "literary manhood"—to a manhood that is affirmed by his work as an artist—there are other details of "The Custom-House" that suggest that things are not so simple. When discussing his own deep roots in his ancestral town of Salem, he contemplates his ancestors, among the first Puritans to arrive in the "new" world colonies. In descriptions that resonate with those of the Puritan men who judge Hester Prynne in the following narrative, Hawthorne notes that his first such ancestor was a "soldier, legislator, judge," and "bitter persecutor." This man's son "inherited the persecuting spirit, and made himself so conspicuous in the martyrdom of the witches, that their blood may fairly be said to have left a stain upon him." Wondering how such men, burdened as they are with sin, have fared in "another state of being," Hawthorne figures himself as requiting their guilt. They "would have thought it quite a sufficient retribution," he notes, "that, after so long

a lapse of years, the old trunk of the family tree . . . should have borne, as its topmost bough, an idler like myself." He goes on:

> No aim, that I have ever cherished, would they recognize as laudable; no success of mine—if my life, beyond its domestic scope, had ever been brightened by success—would they deem otherwise than worthless, if not positively disgraceful. "What is he?" murmurs one gray shadow of my forefathers to the other. "A writer of story-books! What kind of a business in life . . . may that be?"

Given Hawthorne's unambiguously negative depiction of his "persecuting" ancestors, it would seem that he might well reject their judgments of his frivolity, reject the idea that there is an inherent lack of worth in being a "writer of story-books." In a middle-class culture increasingly divided into "separate spheres" for men and women, where men went out into the "public" world of business to earn support for their families, the work of the artist might well be perceived as aberrant, even unmanly. It is "impractical" and immaterial and has no obvious exchange value; furthermore, it emphasizes interior ("feminine") spheres of contemplation rather than the sorts of public interaction that occupied men of "business." Adding to this the fact that in the literary marketplace, works by women were suddenly more financially viable than those by men, and we can see that Hawthorne might well have found plenty of reasons to feel his own worth—indeed, his own manhood—compromised by his chosen profession. As the critic Scott Derrick notes, "In a society which increasingly seemed to feel . . . that writing was a feminine activity, male literature existed in a gender crisis of intense form." Even more flatly, Andrew Scheiber asserts that "Hawthorne might have felt his predilection for authorship . . . as a betrayal of his destiny as an American male." In this light, Hawthorne's triumphant insistence that he has left the (emasculating) realm of the Custom House to claim his manhood and his literariness all at once—that he has become a "literary man"—reads more like wishful thinking than anything else.

As a writer, Hawthorne repeatedly uses the metaphor of the "threshold" to mark a distinction between the preamble to a story and the story itself. In *The House of the Seven Gables,* for example, the narrator describes himself as "loitering faint-heartedly on the threshold of our story." In the first chapter of *The Scarlet Letter,* having set the scene in preparation for Hester's emergence from the prison, the narrator pauses "on the threshold of [his] narrative" to pluck a flower and give it to the reader. A threshold both signals and functions as a mechanism of transition—it simultaneously demarcates space and serves as that which enables us to get from one space to another. So, too, might we think of "The Custom-House": it serves as a kind of "threshold," that which is both different from and prepares us to enter the narrative of *The Scarlet Letter* itself. Having read "The Custom-House," we are ready to read *The Scarlet Letter.* More specifically, having examined "The Custom-House" in terms of its complex treatment of gender, masculine power, and authorship, we are prepared to understand the almost obsessive attention paid to what Karen Kilcup has called, simply, the "problem of gender identity" in *The Scarlet Letter.* Perhaps unwittingly, Hawthorne's preface to the novel establishes Hester's story as one that reflects on Hawthorne's contemporary moment as much as on the seventeenth-century Puritan society that it purports to represent. In particular, it helps us understand the deeply ambivalent attitudes toward its central character that the novel itself manifests. Written at a time when ideas about what men and women should do and be were under challenge and duress, *The Scarlet Letter* provides us with a heroine who, like the Seneca Falls activists of 1848, defies male authority and contests its ability to define and contain her. Alternatively affirming and condemning of Hester Prynne, the text manifests the author's own ambivalence toward the kind of insurgency and gender role contestation she embodies.

HESTER AND THE DEFIANCE OF PATRIARCHAL AUTHORITY

Set in Boston in an early period of colonial settlement, between 1642 and 1649, *The Scarlet Letter* signals its concern with gender and authority from its opening pages, when Hester is led from prison to the scaffold, where she is to receive her public punishment. Situated above Hester, and looking down upon her and the rest of the community, are the "eminent characters" of the colony: "the Governor, and several of his counsellors, a judge, a general, and the ministers of the town." Their spatial location *above* the townspeople points to the positions of privilege and power these men—"fathers and founders"—occupy in the Puritan community. In that community, indeed, fathering and founding go hand in hand. In an image that might be seen to juxtapose that of the diminished potency we encountered in the Salem Custom House, the narrator explains that the Puritan colony owes its "origin and progress" to the "stern and tempered energies of manhood." The stress laid on paternal genesis in the world of Hawthorne's Puritans is emblematized in the "hall of entrance" to the Governor's mansion, where hangs "a row of portraits, representing the forefathers of the Bellingham lineage." The fore*mothers* are conspicuously absent.

In such a male-defined world, Hester's role as a single mother is all the more marked. Evoking in her beauty and her "mien" the "image of Divine Maternity," Hester is symbolically allied with Catholicism, not Puritanism, and with maternity, not paternity. Of course, Hester's opposition to the Puritan men who judge her is more than symbolic: she literally defies the "eminent characters" by refusing to speak the name of Pearl's father: "'I will not speak!'" says Hester when asked to "give [her] child a father." Hester has flouted the sovereign power of the

Puritan patriarchs first by defying their laws and committing adultery. Her refusal to speak her lover's name and to "give her child a father" in the opening scaffold scene merely seals her defiance. By not "giving" Pearl a father, Hester becomes the sole generative force behind and the sole guardian of Pearl. Furthermore, her insistence on *not speaking* even when she is commanded by the ministers and magistrates to do so indicates that Hester is determined to be guided in her actions not by (male) external authority but by a self-generated code of conduct and ethics. Later, when Hester and Dimmesdale meet in the forest, Hester will make her moral autonomy explicit: "'What we did had a consecration of its own,'" she insists, reminding Dimmesdale—a man who seems largely unable to act without external supports—that "'We felt it so! We said so to each other!'"

From the beginning of *The Scarlet Letter*, the narrator situates Hester's insistence on her own power to determine moral action in terms of a real-life Puritan woman who ran afoul of male authorities: Anne Hutchinson, whose defiance of Puritan "laws" precipitated what came to be called the Antinomian Crisis and led to her excommunication and banishment from the Massachusetts Bay Colony in 1638. Hutchinson's views on such theological and doctrinal issues as resurrection, the covenant of grace, and ministerial intermediation—views she promulgated in "meetings" she held with both men and women—were seen as heretical by Puritan leaders, whose spiritual authority over her she repeatedly denied. Her insistence in her civil trial before the General Court in 1637 that "You have power over my body but the Lord Jesus hath power over my body and soul" finds an echo in Hester Prynne's willingness to accept the bodily discipline of the scarlet letter while maintaining her autonomous moral code. (Here we might recall the "elaborate embroidery and fantastic flourishes of gold thread" with which Hester decorates her letter, transforming it from an instrument of punishment into a "fitting decoration" that violates the colony's "sumptuary laws.") Like Hutchinson, who laid claim to what Michael Colacurcio terms "a totally self-sufficient private illumination" that was deeply threatening to the authority of the Puritan fathers, Hester "assumed a freedom of speculation . . . which our forefathers, had they known of it, would have held to be a deadlier crime than that stigmatized by the scarlet letter." In the context of such parallels, it is not surprising that Anne Hutchinson is evoked as a precursor for Hester in the novel's opening paragraphs: it is a flower from a rose-bush alleged to have "sprung up under the footsteps of the sainted Ann Hutchinson, as she entered the prison-door" that the narrator plucks and "present[s] . . . to the reader" at the narrative "threshold."

Later, in chapter 13 ("Another View of Hester"), we are told that had "Pearl never come to her from the spiritual world," Hester

> might have come down to us in history, hand in hand with Ann Hutchinson, as the foundress of a religious sect. She might, in one of her phases, have been a prophetess. She might, and not improbably would, have suffered death from the stern tribunals of the period, for attempting to undermine the foundations of the Puritan establishment. But, in the education of her child, the mother's enthusiasm of thought had something to wreak itself upon.

In this passage, Hawthorne draws attention to Hester's divergence from Hutchinson. Although Hester may not walk "hand in hand" with Hutchinson, her path, in its intellectual and social defiance, certainly parallels Hutchinson's own—as in the case of Anne Hutchinson, in Hester's case "The world's law was no law for her mind." The narrator suggests that Pearl serves as the instrument of Hester's comparative socialization: in Pearl, Hester can find an outlet for her "enthusiasm of thought" and so remain within the pale of the "Puritan establishment." But Pearl's ability to deflect Hester from Hutchinson's more heretical path is qualified by an earlier scene, in which Pearl essentially claims

Hutchinson as her progenitor. Brought to Governor Bellingham's mansion, where Hester hopes to secure guardianship over her daughter, Pearl is catechized by the "grandfatherly" Reverend Wilson: "Canst thou tell me, my child, who made thee?" Having just before this question insisted on her origins in a maternal line—"I am mother's child," she proclaims—Pearl goes on to announce "that she had not been made at all, but had been plucked by her mother off the bush of wild roses, that grew by the prison-door." Pearl's function as a socializing and "civilizing" agent for Hester (she is "the scarlet letter endowed with life," obsessed with touching the "A," inquiring perpetually about its meanings and origins) is undermined by this image. It allies Pearl not with the Puritan "fathers" (or the godly father they ostensibly represent) but rather with other unruly women. Not surprisingly, then, we learn that Pearl is a "being . . . all in disorder," one whose very identity seems to defy the Puritan community. While she is "beautiful and brilliant," the Puritan rulers are "sombre" and "stern"; while she resembles a "wild tropical bird, of rich plumage," they are "sages of rigid aspect"; and while they are associated with the "black flower" of the Puritan prison, she is a "delicate gem" plucked from the "wild rose-bush." And like both of her "mothers" (Hester and Hutchinson), whose actions so defy the edicts of the Puritan fathers, Pearl "could not be made amenable to rules."

JUDGING HESTER

It seems clear that images of and allusions to female insurgency circulate throughout *The Scarlet Letter* in the depictions of both Pearl and Hester. It remains to determine how the text seems to evaluate and assess such insurgency. It is here that the novel becomes almost dizzyingly complex, alternately championing Hester's freedom of thought and condemning it as dangerous, affirming her challenge to conventional gender hierarchies and faulting her for

being "unwomanly." Certainly one has to acknowledge that the opening pages of *The Scarlet Letter* lead us to sympathize with Hester Prynne—rather shockingly, perhaps, given her adulterous act—over and against those who judge her, both women and men. Anne Hutchinson is "sainted," and Hester is an image of "divine" maternity. While the Puritan authorities are "doubtless, good men, just and sage," one could not, the narrator tells us, find a group of people "less capable of sitting in judgment on an erring woman's heart, and disentangling its mesh of good and evil, than the sages of rigid aspect towards whom Hester Prynne now turned her face." If Hester can expect little understanding from the men above her, neither can she look to the women standing below, in the marketplace, for sympathy. While one "young wife" recognizes the pain Hester must be feeling, an "autumnal matron" recommends putting "the brand of a hot iron" on her forehead, and another, depicted as "the ugliest as well as the most pitiless of these self-constituted judges," says she "ought to die."

Given the antipathetic treatment of such "judges," whether "self-constituted" or otherwise, it is hardly surprising that Hawthorne was condemned by some early critics for his harsh treatment of the Puritans as well as for his sympathetic rendition of Hester. Many critics have seen the origins of that rendition in Hawthorne's own imagined experience of Puritan judgment in "The Custom-House." Like Hester, Hawthorne is "condemned" by his Puritan ancestors as "degenerate." Hawthorne himself draws a tangible parallel between Hester's experience and his own: having found the letter in the second story of the Custom House, Hawthorne describes placing it on his breast, and experiencing a "sensation not altogether physical, yet almost so, as of burning heat." Nina Baym points out that with this image, Hawthorne "suggests that the writing of his romance is in some sense" an act analogous to Hester's own, for it "originate[s] as expression of his own feelings of social defiance and discontent, as a reaction to the stifling position of surveyor in the Custom House at Salem." Such details as Hester's artful embroidery of the scarlet letter draw her character even closer to that of the literary artist, to Hawthorne as he appears in "The Custom-House."

Despite—or perhaps even because of—such associations, other details in *The Scarlet Letter* run against the sympathy elsewhere extended to Hester, suggesting that her "freedom of speculation" and "social defiance" are as threatening as they are appealing to her creator. Perhaps most notably, in the chapter that gives us "Another View" into Hester's socially defiant interior life, the narrator explains that the letter has desexualized her:

> All the light and graceful foliage of her character had been withered up by this red-hot brand, and had long ago fallen away, leaving a bare and harsh outline. . . . There seemed to be no longer any thing in Hester's face for Love to dwell upon; nothing in Hester's form . . . that Passion would ever dream of clasping in its embrace; nothing in Hester's bosom, to make it ever again the pillow of Affection. Some attribute had departed from her, the permanence of which had been essential to keep her a woman.

Hester's loss of "womanliness," her defeminization, is associated clearly with her freedom of thought, her embrace of moral autonomy, and her refusal to accede to man- made laws. Her "fierce independence," critic Michael Gilmore has written in "Hawthorne and the Making of the Middle Class," "suggests less Victorian womanhood than the Jacksonian individualist" championed by Ralph Waldo Emerson and other proponents of self-reliant manhood. Hester, in short, is not just "unfeminine," she is masculine—and quite successfully so.

CHILLINGWORTH, DIMMESDALE, AND (NON)FUNCTIONAL MANHOOD

In many respects, one could suggest that Hester is the most fully functional man in the whole of *The Scarlet Letter*—and, further, that her as-

sumption of "masculine" qualities correlates with a concomitant feminization in the two male characters with whom she is most closely associated: Chillingworth, her husband, and Dimmesdale, her lover and the father of her child. With his powerful intellect and ratiocinative skills, Chillingworth might seem to manifest less impotence than a kind of perverse hyper-maleness. Indeed, one might suggest that his ability to "go deep into [Dimmesdale's] bosom," "delving," "prying," and "probing every thing," reaffirms the penetrative, phallic power he lost when Hester gave herself to Dimmesdale. But while the narrative grants Chillingworth such power—power that he demonically deploys—at the same time it casts doubt on his masculinity. As Karen Kilcup notes, the antebellum period in which Hawthorne was writing saw the emergence of new ideals of manhood that laid emphasis on physical health, robustness, and self-control. Read in this context, Chillingworth's physical deformity, coupled with what the narrative depicts as his moral disease, "precludes his ability to fulfill the ideal of vigorous manhood increasingly demanded at midcentury, marking his gender as physically ambiguous." Having been in Indian captivity, Chillingworth, when we first see him, is "clad in a strange disarray of civilized and savage costume," and he proves to be as familiar with native medicinal treatments as he is with western, institutionalized medical practice. Kilcup remarks that Chillingworth's association with Indians and with witchcraft (he is repeatedly described, by Pearl in particular, as the "Black Man") further sets him beyond the pale of conventional (nineteenth-century) manhood and "renders him ambiguously gendered."

Even more obviously "ambiguously gendered" is Arthur Dimmesdale, who, from his earliest appearance in the text, Gilmore notes, is "delineated in terms that typify nineteenth-century femininity more than conventional maleness." His eyes "large, brown, melancholy," his mouth "tremulous," and his voice "tremulously sweet," Dimmesdale is associated with the conventionally feminine sphere of the emotions rather than the conventionally masculine sphere of the intellect (as is Hester). When he speaks in the first scaffold scene, "charging" Hester to "speak out the name of thy fellow-sinner and fellow-sufferer," the "feeling" that his voice "manifested . . . caused it to vibrate within all hearts, and brought the listeners into one accord of sympathy." If Dimmesdale's feminization here seems to be the source of his power, elsewhere it is depicted as an almost unnatural attenuation. Having been weakened progressively by his own failure of moral courage and Chillingworth's obsessive penetration of his conscience, when Dimmesdale meets Hester in the woods in chapter 16 ("A Forest Walk") he is a broken man. Picking his way through the forest, alone and seemingly unobserved, Dimmesdale resembles more the emasculated old men of Salem's Custom House than Boston's most celebrated, admired, and beloved young minister:

> Leaning on a staff. . . . He looked haggard and feeble, and betrayed a nerveless despondency in his air. . . . There was a listlessness in his gait; as if he saw no reason for taking one step farther, nor felt any desire to do so, but would have been glad . . . to fling himself down at the root of the nearest tree, and lie there passive for evermore.

Like the man who accepts Uncle Sam's gold, Dimmesdale has relied on the sociopolitical structure of the Puritan colony to grant him identity and meaning; this reliance, the narrative suggests, has compromised his "sturdy force," his "courage and constancy," and "all that gives the emphasis to manly character." Thus, when Hester tries to persuade him to leave Boston and start a new life with her elsewhere, he is unable to navigate his own moral position. The fact that Dimmesdale and Hester have switched gender positions in this regard is brought home by Dimmesdale's plea to Hester to make a decision for him: "Think for me, Hester!" he begs. "Thou art strong. Resolve for me!"

RESTORING MANHOOD: THE FINAL SCAFFOLD SCENE

If the body of *The Scarlet Letter* stages such gender switches, its final scaffold scene seems to restore the main characters to more ostensibly "natural" gender role positions. Having allowed Hester to "think for him," Dimmesdale leaves the forest with the plan to preach the Election Day sermon and then depart for England with Hester and Pearl—a restored family. In the interval between his meeting with Hester and Election Day, Dimmesdale seems to remember how to think for himself. Rather than adhering to Hester's plan, Dimmesdale, upon conclusion of his sermon, walks to the scaffold and at last is "true" to Pearl's request that he "take my hand, and mother's hand" at "noontide." Still relying upon Hester, Dimmesdale ascends the scaffold "leaning on Hester's shoulder and supported by her arm around him." But if his request that Hester "twine thy strength" about him seems to indicate a still compromised manhood, the quasi-confession that Dimmesdale offers on the scaffold leads to a restoration of patriarchal authority and paternal power. On a basic level, in ascending the scaffold rather than leaving with Hester, Dimmesdale makes plain his allegiance to the moral and civil codes of his fathers and brothers. More subtly, Dimmesdale's act of "confession" effectively socializes Pearl, whose capacities of subversion are thereby brought to an end:

> Pearl kissed his lips. A spell was broken. The great scene of grief, in which the wild infant bore a part, had developed all her sympathies; and as her tears fell upon her father's cheek, they were the pledge that she would grow up amid human joy and sorrow, nor for ever do battle with the world, but be a woman in it.

So, too, are Hester's insurgent tendencies for the most part contained at novel's end. Having lived for some time in some "unknown region" with Pearl, Hester "had returned" to her cottage at the margin of the sea and had "resumed, of her own free will, for not the sternest magistrate of that iron period would have imposed it,—resumed the symbol of which we have related so dark a tale." Once a woman for whom the "world's law" was largely irrelevant, Hester now, "of her own free will," subjects herself to that law. While her cottage was once the site of "dark question[s] . . . with reference to the whole race of womanhood" that Hester posed in isolation, it is now a place where women come for comfort and counsel. Hester's visions of a time when "a new truth would be revealed, in order to establish the whole relation between man and woman on a surer ground of mutual happiness" may seem to partake of the radicalism of the Seneca Falls activists who so unsettled many of Hawthorne's contemporaries. But her gradualist view that such a change must wait for "Heaven's own time" and her belief that she is a woman too "stained with sin, bowed down with shame" to function as the vehicle for such a "mission" suggest that Hester's radicalism has been largely checked. By the end of the novel, Hester, like Pearl, is ready once again to "be a woman" in the world. When recounting Hester's loss of womanly attributes in "Another View of Hester," the narrator notes that "She who has once been woman, and ceased to be so, might at any moment become a woman again, if there were only the magic touch to effect that transfiguration." On the scaffold Dimmesdale offers precisely this "magic touch"; by it, Hester is indeed "transfigured," restored to what Hawthorne's own society would have termed "true womanhood."

Given the text's intriguing treatment of gender role flexibility in general and its interest in powerful, subversive women in particular, we might find such an ending disappointing. But in the context of what "The Custom-House" tells us, and in the context of the literary and social milieu of Hawthorne's own time, we ought not to find it particularly surprising. Like the middle-class reading audience to which he sought to appeal, Hawthorne found himself faced with a complex barrage of unwritten

"laws" that distinguished "man" from "woman," and severely constrained the life options open to each. At the same time, he witnessed challenges to the lines of gender division posed by, among others, women's rights activists, female antislavery workers, and—perhaps most important—women writers. It would seem that this latter group posed the greatest difficulty for Hawthorne, whose status as a literary artist cast some doubt on his claims to vigorous "manhood" and who felt himself to be increasingly marginalized in the literary marketplace. Regardless of where one locates the source of the text's seeming discomfort with Hester's power—regardless, even, of whether one reads the ending of the text as more affirming of that power than the present reading of the novel suggests—it appears that the meanings of manhood and womanhood, masculinity and femininity, are very much on Hawthorne's mind. Certainly, a close examination of *The Scarlet Letter* reveals that, contrary to earlier readings that stressed his social estrangement, Hawthorne is, however unwittingly, very much a writer of his own time.

IMPORTANCE AND INFLUENCE

This essay opened with an explanation of Hawthorne's emergence, in his own day, as a crucial American voice—a writer whose work seemed to affirm the aesthetic potential of the nation and to initiate its move into full cultural independence. What is perhaps most interesting about such claims of the centrality of Hawthorne and *The Scarlet Letter* to a "classic" American tradition is that they have endured into our own day and are likely to endure well beyond it. Critics and cultural commentators from Hawthorne's period down to the contemporary moment have devoted themselves to mapping an "American tradition," to determining the works and writers deemed "valuable" to and worthy of study in that tradition. Not surprisingly, of course, different historical moments yield different maps, since those creating the maps themselves necessarily reflect the values of their times. The literary

historian Richard Brodhead noted in 1986 that while the works of "Melville, Emerson, Whitman, Thoreau, Dickinson, Poe, and Hawthorne" would today be deemed "central to American literature," an earlier map would have placed "Longfellow, not Dickinson, Whittier, not Whitman, Lowell, not Melville, and Holmes, not Poe, in the rank of our literary immortals." By the beginning of the twenty-first century, many scholars would offer their own supplements and replacements to Brodhead's list, deeming it of fundamental importance to add such writers as Frederick Douglass, Harriet Jacobs, Harriet Beecher Stowe, and Elizabeth Stoddard to our vision of what constitutes a notable "American" tradition.

Significantly, no matter how flexible the "canon" and no matter how many changes are worked in and upon it, Hawthorne is never jettisoned. *The Scarlet Letter,* the work for which he is best known, remains one of the most deeply influential, widely available, and widely discussed American novels ever written. The list of writers influenced by Hawthorne and by *The Scarlet Letter* is large and impressive: in the United States alone we can cite Herman Melville, Elizabeth Stoddard, Henry James, William Dean Howells, Stephen Crane, William Faulkner, Flannery O'Connor, and John Irving just for starters. A search of the academic database for the *Modern Language Association* reveals that Hawthorne is a significant critical industry as well: the *MLA Bibliography* turns up more than 500 articles and books that address *The Scarlet Letter;* Hawthorne's name calls up more than 3,000 entries. Adapted for film no fewer than eight times (including several silent versions and Roland Joffé's widely criticized but

very interesting 1995 version starring De[mi] Moore) and still one of the most widely tau[ght] texts, if not *the* most widely taught text, [in] American classrooms, *The Scarlet Letter* cros[ses] some of the very lines between "popularity" a[nd] "high art" that Hawthorne worked so hard [to] elaborate in his own day.

Perhaps most notably, each retelling, ea[ch] interpretation, each adaptation is different— highlighting some elements and putting othe[rs] in the background—a fact that tells us that th[is] is, essentially, a flexible text, elastic an[d] responsive to the times and contexts in which [it] is read. As Jane Tompkins asserts, *The Scarl[et] Letter* is a "great novel in 1850, in 1876, in 190[4,] in 1942, and in 1966"—as well as in 1975, 199[0,] and 2002—"but each time it is great for differe[nt] reasons." The jury remains out concerning wh[y] this novel sustains its appeal at such diverse mo[ments] and for disparate audiences. Some woul[d] argue that *The Scarlet Letter* endures because i[t] is a great work of art, a classic that has passe[d] the test of time. Others would insist that it[s] centrality has a great deal to do with an interes[t] in perpetuating what Tompkins calls "the idea o[f] a classic"—and with the economics and cultural politics of publishing and teaching. Regardless of how one explains *The Scarlet Letter*'s centrality, it remains just that—central. It is a text whose style, thematic suppleness, ideological complexity, and canonical place keep writers, teachers, filmmakers, critics, students, and even cartoonists returning to it again and again. Above all, one might say that Hawthorne's novel is like the "A" from which it takes its title: never fixed in meaning, calling us to inquire and reflect. *The Scarlet Letter* remains an ever unsolvable but always inviting mystery.

Select Bibliography

EDITIONS

The Scarlet Letter. Vol. 1 of *The Centenary Edition of the Works of Nathaniel Hawthorne.* Edited by William Charvat, Roy Harvey Pearce, and Claude M. Simpson.

Columbus: Ohio State University Press, 1962. (*The Centenary Edition*, cited in this essay, is the definitive scholarly edition of Hawthorne's work. See "Introduction to *The Scarlet Letter*" by William Charvat.)

The Scarlet Letter: A Romance. New York: Penguin Books, 1983. (This paperback edition reprints the text of *The Centenary Edition*.)

OTHER WORKS BY HAWTHORNE

The Letters: 1813–1843. Vol. 15 of *The Centenary Edition of the Works of Nathaniel Hawthorne.* Edited by Thomas Woodson, L. Neale Smith, and Norman Holmes Pearson. Columbus: Ohio State University Press, 1984.

The Letters: 1843–1853. Vol. 16 of *The Centenary Edition of the Works of Nathaniel Hawthorne.* Edited by Thomas Woodson, L. Neale Smith, and Norman Holmes Pearson. Columbus: Ohio State University Press, 1985.

The Letters: 1853–1856. Vol. 17 of *The Centenary Edition of the Works of Nathaniel Hawthorne.* Edited by Thomas Woodson, James A. Rubino, L. Neale Smith, and Norman Holmes Pearson. Columbus: Ohio State University Press, 1985.

The Marble Faun; Or, The Romance of Monte Beni. New York: Penguin Books, 1990.

The House of the Seven Gables. New York: Penguin Books, 2001.

SECONDARY WORKS

Arac, Jonathan. "The Politics of *The Scarlet Letter.*" In *Ideology and Classic American Literature.* Edited by Sacvan Bercovitch and Myra Jehlen. Cambridge: Cambridge University Press, 1986. Pp. 247–266.

Baym, Nina. *The Shape of Hawthorne's Career.* Ithaca, N.Y.: Cornell University Press, 1976.

Bell, Michael Davitt. *The Development of American Romance: The Sacrifice of Relation.* Chicago: University of Chicago Press, 1980.

Bell, Millicent. *Hawthorne's View of the Artist.* Albany: State University of New York Press, 1962.

Bercovitch, Sacvan. *The Office of the Scarlet Letter.* Baltimore: Johns Hopkins University Press, 1991.

Berlant, Lauren Gail. *The Anatomy of National Fantasy: Hawthorne, Utopia, and Everyday Life.* Chicago: University of Chicago Press, 1991.

Brodhead, Richard H. *The School of Hawthorne.* New York: Oxford University Press, 1986.

Brown, Gillian. "Hawthorne, Inheritance, and Women's Property." *Studies in the Novel* 23, no. 1 (1991): 107–118.

Chase, Richard. *The American Novel and Its Tradition.* New York: Doubleday, 1957.

Colacurcio, Michael. "Footsteps of Ann Hutchinson: The Context of *The Scarlet Letter.*" *English Literary History*, no. 39 (September 1972): 466–489.

———, ed. *New Essays on* The Scarlet Letter. Cambridge: Cambridge University Press, 1985.

Crews, Frederick C. *The Sins of the Fathers: Hawthorne's Psychological Themes.* New York: Oxford University Press, 1966.

Crowley, Joseph Donald. *Hawthorne: The Critical Heritage.* London: Routledge, 1970. (Includes contemporary reviews of Hawthorne's work.)

Derrick, Scott. "Prometheus Ashamed: *The Scarlet Letter* and the Masculinity of Art." In *Nathaniel Hawthorne's* The Scarlet Letter. Edited by Harold Bloom. New York: Chelsea House, 1986.

Douglas, Ann. "Introduction." In *Uncle Tom's Cabin; or, Life Among the Lowly.* By Harriet Beecher Stowe. New York: Penguin Books, 1981. Pp. 7–34.

Feidelson, Charles. *Symbolism and American Literature.* Chicago: University of Chicago Press, 1953. (Classic "New Critical" study.)

Gerber, John C. *Twentieth Century Interpretations of "The Scarlet Letter": A Collection of Critical Essays.* Englewood Cliffs, N.J.: Prentice-Hall, 1968. (Collection that gathers standard interpretations of the novel from the 1950s and 1960s.)

Gilmore, Michael T. *American Romanticism and the Marketplace.* Chicago: University of Chicago Press, 1985.

———. "Hawthorne and the Making of the Middle Class." In *Rethinking Class: Literary Studies and Social Formations.* Edited by Wai Chee Dimock and Michael T. Gilmore. New York: Columbia University Press, 1994.

Goddu, Teresa A., and Leland Person, eds. *The Scarlet Letter after 150 Years: A Special Issue. Studies in American Fiction* 29, no. 2 (2001). (A fine collection of essays reflecting current critical efforts to situate Hawthorne's novel in terms of nineteenth-century American culture.)

Hall, David D., ed. *The Antinomian Controversy, 1636–1638: A Documentary History.* 2d ed. Durham: Duke University Press, 1990.

Hawthorne, Julian. *Nathaniel Hawthorne and His Wife: A Biography.* 2 vols. Boston: Houghton, Mifflin, 1884. (Still useful and interesting, although more recent, and less subjective, biographers have challenged many of its "facts.")

Herbert, T. Walter. "Nathaniel Hawthorne, Una Hawthorne, and *The Scarlet Letter*: Interactive Selfhood and the Cultural Construction of Gender." *PMLA* 103, no. 3 (1988): 285–297.

———. *Dearest Beloved: The Hawthornes and the Making of the Middle-Class Family.* Berkeley: University of California Press, 1993. (Monumentally useful critical biography that situates Hawthorne's art in the context of nineteenth-century attitudes about domesticity and marriage.)

James, Henry. *Hawthorne.* 1879. Ithaca, N.Y.: Cornell University Press, 1967.

Johnson, Claudia Durst. *Understanding* The Scarlet Letter: *A Student Casebook to Issues, Sources, and Historical Documents.* Westport, Conn.: Greenwood Press, 1995. (Collection of historical and source material and thematic overviews that is especially useful for high school and undergraduate students.)

Kesterton, David B. *Critical Essays on Hawthorne's* The Scarlet Letter. Boston: G. K. Hall, 1988. (Collects nineteenth-century reviews, along with "Criticism to 1950," "Criticism Since 1950," and "New Essays.")

Kilcup, Karen. "'Ourself behind Ourself, Concealed—': The Homoerotics of Reading in *The Scarlet Letter.*" *ESQ* 42, no. 1 (1996): 1–28.

Lang, Amy Schrager. *Prophetic Women: Anne Hutchinson and the Problem of Dissent in the Literature of New England.* Berkeley: University of California Press, 1987.

Leavis, F. R. *The Great Tradition: George Eliot, Henry James, Joseph Conrad.* New York: New York University Press, 1964.

Leverenz, Davis. "Mrs. Hawthorne's Headache: Reading *The Scarlet Letter.*" *Nineteenth- Century Fiction* 37 (March 1983): 552–575.

———. *Manhood and the American Renaissance.* Ithaca, N.Y.: Cornell University Press, 1989.

Martin, Robert K. "Hester Prynne, *C'est Moi:* Nathaniel Hawthorne and the Anxieties of Gender." In *Engendering Men: The Question of Male Feminist Criticism.* Edited by Joseph A. Boone and Michael Cadden. New York: Routledge, 1990. Pp. 122–139.

Matthiessen, F. O. *The American Renaissance: Art and Expression in the Age of Emerson and Whitman.* London: Oxford University Press, 1941. (Classic "New Critical" study.)

Mellow, James R. *Nathaniel Hawthorne in His Times.* Boston: Houghton Mifflin, 1980. (A standard biography.)

Miller, Edwin Haviland. *Salem is My Dwelling Place: A Life of Nathaniel Hawthorne.* Iowa City: Iowa University Press, 1991. (Biography with emphasis on psychosexual issues.)

Mottram, Eric. "Power and Law in Hawthorne's Fictions." In *Nathaniel Hawthorne: New Critical Essays.* Edited by A. Robert Lee. London: Vision Press, 1982. Pp. 187–228.

Newfield, Christopher. "The Politics of Male Suffering: Masochism and Hegemony in the American Renaissance." *Differences: A Journal of Feminist Cultural Studies* 1, no. 3 (1989): 55–87.

Nudelman, Franny. "'Emblem and Product of Sin': The Poisoned Child in *The Scarlet Letter* and Domestic Advice Literature." *Yale Journal of Criticism* 10, no. 1 (1997): 193–213.

Pearce, Roy Harvey, ed. *Hawthorne Centenary Essays.* Columbus: Ohio State University Press, 1964. (Indicative of trends in criticism of the 1950s and 1960s.)

Person, Leland S. *Aesthetic Headaches: Women and Masculine Poetics in Poe, Melville, and Hawthorne.* Athens: University of Georgia Press, 1988.

Reynolds, David S. *Beneath the American Renaissance: The Subversive Imagination in the Age of Emerson and Melville.* New York: Knopf, 1988. (Emphasizes how classic "American Renaissance" writers make use of popular materials.)

Reynolds, Larry J. *European Revolutions and the American Literary Renaissance.* New Haven, Conn.: Yale University Press, 1988.

Scharnhorst, Gary, ed. *The Critical Response to Nathaniel Hawthorne's "The Scarlet Letter."* New York: Greenwood Press, 1992. (Useful collection of critical responses to the novel from Hawthorne's day into our own, including the reviews in *Literary World* and *Peterson's* quoted in the text.)

Scheiber, Andrew J. "Public Force, Private Sentiment: Hawthorne and the Gender of Politics." *American Transcendental Quarterly* 2, no. 4 (1988): 285–299.

Smith, Henry Nash. "The Scribbling Women and the Cosmic Success Story." *Critical Inquiry* 1, no. 1 (1974): 47–70.

Stanton, Elizabeth Cady, Susan B. Anthony, and Matilda Joslyn Gage, eds. *History of Woman Suffrage.* Vol. 1, *1848–1861.* New York: Arno and the New York Times, 1969.

Tompkins, Jane. *Sensational Designs: The Cultural Work of American Fiction, 1790–1860.* New York: Oxford University Press, 1985.

Turner, Arlin. *Nathaniel Hawthorne: A Biography.* New York: Oxford University Press, 1980. (A standard biography.)

Wallace, James D. "Hawthorne and the Scribbling Women Reconsidered." *American Literature* 62, no. 2 (1990): 201–222.

W. E. B. Du Bois's
The Souls of Black Folk

MARK RICHARDSON

IN 1872 ULYSSES S. Grant, a Republican, was elected to his second term as president of the United States. That year marked, perhaps, the height of what came to be called the Radical Reconstruction: the Republican Party controlled state legislatures and statehouses in many of what had been the Confederate states of America. Black voters were registered in the South in numbers never to be seen again until 1965. African Americans there held public office at nearly all levels of government, from city hall to the Senate of the United States. Here, W. E. B. Du Bois would later maintain, were the first steps toward real democracy ever taken in the New World or, for that matter, anyplace in the world where whites and people of color lived side by side. In 1872 in South Carolina, for example, blacks were elected to the statewide posts of Lieutenant Governor and Attorney General; of 155 seats in the legislature, 96 would now be filled by former slaves or by men who shared their complexion. Reactionaries later attributed this to corruption in the Republican "carpetbag" regime. But 60 percent of the South Carolina population was African American in 1872 (the majority was larger still in a number of lowland counties). The Fourteenth and Fifteenth Amendments to the U.S. Constitution had enfranchised them—and they voted.

Resistance to Reconstruction had always been bitter in South Carolina and often violent. By the mid-1870s, white South Carolinians and the state Democratic Party were prepared to "redeem" the state from Republican rule—by any means necessary. The opportunity came in July 1876, as the nation celebrated one hundred years of difficult history. On July 4, a detachment of state militia under the command of a black veteran of the Union Army and Republican Party activist named Dock Adams assembled for a centennial celebration in the town of Hamburg, a largely black settlement just across the Savannah River from Augusta, Georgia. Two young white men found their way blocked by the assembly. Insults were exchanged, and the two white men took the measure of retaining an attorney to press charges against Adams for "blocking the public way." Their attorney was the former Confederate general Matthew C. Butler, a Democratic Party agitator. Butler set out for the courthouse in Hamburg on July 8, accompanied by a band of heavily armed whites. By day's end, seven blacks had been murdered, some thirty more had been summarily imprisoned, and homes and shops belonging to Hamburg's black citizens lay in ruin. The Redemption of South Carolina was under way, as was the Redemption all across the South.

The tactics and tempo of the Redemption varied from state to state, but the result was astonishing. By 1903, when Du Bois published *The Souls of Black Folk,* better than 90 percent of the voting-eligible black population of the South had been disenfranchised, more than a thousand had been murdered, and hundreds of thousands had been returned to a condition of tenant-farming serfdom little better than slavery itself. These events have been well described in two chapters of *Souls,* called "Of the Black Belt" and "Of the Quest of the Golden Fleece." As Du Bois later put it in *Black Reconstruction in America: 1860–1880* (1935), "the Civil War began again—indeed had never ceased": the "black Prometheus" was again "bound to the Rock of Ages by hate, hurt, and humiliation," the better that his "vitals" might be "eaten out as they grew." It was to enter this ongoing civil war, as a sort of literary combatant on all fronts, that the young Harvard-trained sociologist and historian sat down, in his office at Atlanta University, in the heart of the New South, to write of *The Souls of Black Folk.*

This was at the dawn of a century whose problem, as Du Bois therein predicted, would be "the problem of the color-line—the relation of the darker to the lighter races of men in Asia and Africa, in America and the islands of the sea." He saw that this most intractable of American problems was but a "phase" of a genuinely global enterprise, which traced its origin to the slave trade and saw its refinement in a system of colonialism that, as he wrote in 1903, was attaining a kind of bureaucratic perfection. Born in the year Grant was first elected and buried in the year John F. Kennedy was assassinated, Du Bois would see it all. And his many books, his hundreds of essays and

CHRONOLOGY

1868	Du Bois is born in Great Barrington, Massachusetts, of mixed French and African ancestry.
1888	Graduates with a bachelor's degree from Fisk University and is admitted to Harvard as a junior.
1890	Attains a bachelor's degree in philosophy from Harvard.
1891	Attains an master's degree in history from Harvard.
1895	Earns doctorate in history from Harvard, the first black to be awarded the degree.
1897	Takes a position at Atlanta University.
1903	*The Souls of Black Folk* wins Du Bois national recognition.
1910	The National Association for the Advancement of Colored People (NAACP) is organized with Du Bois as director of publications and research; becomes editor of *Crisis.*
1920	*Darkwater: Voices from within the Veil.*
1928	Publishes *Dark Princess: A Romance,* a novel depicting an international alliance of Africans, Asians, and American blacks.
1934	Returns to Atlanta University.
1940	*Dusk of Dawn* (an autobiography).
1944	Retires from Atlanta University and moves to New York to work once more for the NAACP.
1948	Dismissed from the NAACP for harsh criticism of U.S. foreign policy.
1963	Becomes a citizen of Ghana and dies there in Accra.

articles, constitute an indispensable record of the making of the twentieth-century United States.

BACKGROUND

The Souls of Black Folk marks Du Bois's entry into the ranks of the radical civil rights movement. Up to this point Du Bois had lived in scholarly detachment, studying, teaching, working as a research fellow, and writing history and sociology. But events in the 1890s, which Du Bois discusses in his autobiography *Dusk of Dawn* (1940), gradually made this sort of academic life impossible for him. Booker T. Washington's "Tuskegee" philosophy of "industrial training" for blacks, as against traditional "liberal arts" education, had by this time attained its majority. It was underwritten by such men as John D. Rockefeller of the Standard Oil Trust and Andrew Carnegie, steel magnate and author of the Social Darwinist-inflected pamphlet called *The Gospel of Wealth*. These men, and many others like them, sought to reconcile North and South, the better to make Southern labor markets safe for Northern capital, and the better—as Du Bois came to believe—to weaken the working class everywhere. Alongside the great industrialists in this enterprise were all the exponents of the "New South," who believed that traditional liberal arts education for blacks would give rise to needless social tension between the races and, moreover, that black men and women were not really (or not yet) suited for liberal arts education in the first place. A host of anthropologists, eugenicists, and biologists stood ready to support that belief with "scientific" evidence, often arguing from the same Social Darwinist premises that gladdened the "deregulationist" hearts of the great robber barons. The idea, Du Bois charged, was plainly to adjust the education made available to black men and women to the requirements of southern industrialization, which were, in turn, the requirements of industry as a whole—and *only* to those requirements.

In addition, the 1880s and 1890s saw a steady rise in lynchings. The record logs 235 public lynchings in the Deep South in 1892, a rate of more than four per week; a number of these were unspeakably brutal. In *Dusk of Dawn*, Du Bois places the figure for the period between 1885 and 1894 at 1,700. This great tide of reaction, which had deepened in force with every passing year since the Redemption of 1876, compelled Du Bois to leave his academic sanctuary and enter the political fray. He says in *Dusk of Dawn*: "One could not be a calm, cool, and detached scientist while Negroes were lynched, murdered, and starved."

The Souls of Black Folk is one result of this decision. It was written to put to rest for good all the slanders against blacks that seemed to be issuing from every quarter of the country in 1903 and to bring white Americans, generally, to the hard-won insight of a fourteen-year-old character called Huckleberry Finn. As Mark Twain's Huck puts it, "Though it don't seem natural," "Nigger" Jim "cares just as much for his people as white folks does for their'n." "Ignorant it may be, and poverty stricken, black and curious in limb and ways and thought," Du Bois writes in "Of the Quest of the Golden Fleece" of the black peasantry of Georgia, "and yet it loves and hates, it toils and tires, it laughs and weeps its bitter tears, and looks in vague and awful longing at the grim horizon of its life,—all this, even as you and I." David Levering Lewis rightly calls *Souls* an epoch-making book, the sort of book that divides history into a before and after. It is a book of international reach and consequence. Du Bois sets the situation of black Americans in the broader context of the situation of colonized peoples across the globe. The Spanish-American War of 1898, which decisively marked the entry of the United States into the great game of empire, was an important impetus behind Du Bois's book. In 1903 the U.S. Army was fighting Filipino republicans for control of a country they only five years earlier had "liberated" from imperial Spain, and the U.S. Senate was investigating its alleged atrocities.

Nine of the fourteen essays collected in *The Souls of Black Folk* had been published previously in periodicals, some of them professional journals of historical and sociological scholarship, but Du Bois reworked them all for the new book. They range widely in character and subject. Two of the essays combine memoir with a literary blend of philosophy and polemic: "Of Our Spiritual Strivings" and "Of the Meaning of Progress." Several are chiefly historical or sociological in bearing: "Of the Dawn of Freedom" (a revisionist account of the rise and fall of the Freedmen's Bureau), "Of the Quest of the Golden Fleece" (about cotton agriculture and black peonage in the postwar period), "Of the Black Belt" (a study of the largely black counties of southern Georgia), and "Of the Sons of Master and Man." One, "Of Alexander Crummell," is a portrait of a major figure in the history of American education.

Another chapter, "Of the Coming of John," is a paradigmatic short story about the education of one young black man from Georgia. "Of the Passing of the First-Born," an intensely personal elegy for Du Bois's first child, who died in infancy, approaches the intensity of a prose poem. There is an essay on religion in the South, "Of the Faith of the Fathers"; a polemical engagement with Washington in "Of Mr. Booker T. Washington and Others"; a treatise on postwar education in "Of the Training of Black Men"; a suggestive, allegorical treatment of the ideal of a liberal education titled "Of the Wings of Atalanta"; and a concluding chapter, "Of the Sorrow Songs," that constitutes a pioneering inquiry into the meaning of the Negro spiritual, which had only lately begun to attract the attention of musicologists and historians.

Souls is artfully designed. At the head of each essay appears an epigraph, usually from the English poets but always shrewdly chosen, together with several bars of music, without words, from what Du Bois calls the "sorrow songs." Bracketing everything are "The Forethought" and "The Afterthought." The effect is distinctly "literary" and quite different from that produced by Du Bois's first two books, *The Suppression of the African Slave Trade to the United States of America, 1638–1870* (1896; a revision of his Harvard thesis still consulted by historians) and *The Philadelphia Negro: A Special Study* (1899; a sociological study of black life in the Quaker City). With *Souls*, Du Bois broke decisively from the academic tradition of writing into which he had been trained, and thenceforth even his serious contributions to historiography—for example, *Black Reconstruction*—would challenge the limits of academic writing.

The Souls of Black Folk was something of a sensation: twelve printings were exhausted by June of its first year in print, and by October two hundred copies per week were selling—remarkable figures for a book of such uncommon erudition. Five years after it first appeared, more than 9,500 copies had been sold. Southern responses were intemperate and often savage, as might be expected. In his first biography of Du Bois, Lewis quotes the *Nashville American* as declaring the book "dangerous for the Negro to read." A reviewer for the *Houston Chronicle*, in a fit of panic perhaps indicative of his own preoccupations, demanded that authorities arrest Du Bois for "inciting rape." Even the relatively moderate *New York Times* chose a white Southerner to review the book. Although he was not so severe as his compatriots in the South, he expressed grave reservations and speculated that Du Bois, born and reared in Massachusetts, really did not know the South at all.

THE READER IN *SOULS*

There is no better place to begin this inquiry into *Souls* than with the "Forethought" Du Bois affixed to the book by way of preface:

> Herein lie buried many things which if read with patience may show the strange meaning of being black here at the dawning of the Twentieth Century. This meaning is not without interest to you, Gentle Reader; for the problem of the Twentieth Century is the problem of the color line. I pray you, then, receive my little book in all charity, studying my words with me, forgiving mistake and foible for sake of the faith and passion that is in me, and seeking the grain of truth hidden there.

. . . And, finally, need I add that I who speak here am bone of the bone and flesh of the flesh of them that live within the Veil?

There is a deviously mortuary grace to the phrase with which Du Bois opens the book: "Herein lie buried many things." *Souls* will be an exhumation of sorts: after all, Du Bois and his fellows "within the veil" know best where the American bodies are buried. He establishes at once that the "color line" of which he speaks not only separates whites and blacks generally in America and throughout the world but also separates him from his reader—a figure with whom, he intimates, his relations are perhaps to be difficult. "Need I add that I who speak here am bone of the bone and flesh of the flesh of them that live within the Veil?" he asks. Du Bois wonders whether he will be read with "charity" or even with "patience." This lends the word "gentle," in the conventional address to the reader, an ever so slightly bitter tone.

Readers are made aware here of a fact of singular importance: almost always it is simply taken "for granted" that the "American" reader is "white." The effect of this revelation is all the more complicated if, taking the logical next step, one imagines a black reader of the book, who will read therein not so much about "black folk" as about black folk described as if for a (perhaps uncharitable) white reader. A similar effect is achieved much later in *Souls,* in the essay on Georgia's "black belt": "If you wish to ride with me," Du Bois says, inviting his reader to make this (literary) journey south, "you must come into the 'Jim Crow Car.' He goes on:

> There will be no objection,—already four other white men, and a little white girl with her nurse, are in there. Usually the races are mixed in there; but the white coach is all white. Of course this car is not so good as the other, but it is fairly clean and comfortable. The discomfort lies chiefly in the hearts of those four black men yonder—and in mine.

It is evident that in speaking of the *souls* of black folk to white readers, in raising the "Veil" behind which they live, Du Bois lays himself open. The "discomfort" of writing the book, he lets readers see, is precisely the "discomfort" he would feel on being forced to take his white companion with him into the Jim Crow car. He is not writing out of self-satisfaction. His is always, of necessity, the discomfort of an affronted dignity: Why should he so expose himself and his people to the gaze of impatient eyes? But his is also the discomfort of a frustrating and private sorrow: Why should he constantly be compelled to see himself as a "black" man rather than merely as a "man"? Is there nowhere, not even in the sanctuary of his own candid mind, a place where he can be "undisguised," as Walt Whitman hoped people could become in this "New World"? Has he ever really "known" himself?

When Du Bois startles readers into the thought that the "American gaze" is, in the first instance, always a *white* gaze—even when situated (so to speak) in a "black" mind—he hints at an important idea: to read American literature or American history, both of which take for granted a necessarily unscrutinized "white" way of seeing, is, for black folk, to be given an education in self-distrust. *Huckleberry Finn*—Twain's unimpeachable politics notwithstanding—somehow manages to admire a black man, Jim, chiefly by making an innocent, self-sacrificial child of him. American literature is simply constituted, for better or worse, by books like these; even the best of them is always somehow compromised. Black readers who would educate themselves by reading literature must undertake something of a struggle: they must "decolonize" their minds, as the radicals used to say in the 1960s—and Du Bois was well ahead of them.

In *Black Reconstruction* Du Bois wrote:

> An American youth attending college today would learn from the current textbooks of history that the Constitution recognized slavery; that the chance of getting rid of slavery by peaceful methods was ruined by the Abolitionists; that after the period of Andrew Jackson, the two sections of the United States had become fully conscious of

their conflicting interests. Two irreconcilable forms of civilization [arose:] in the North, the democratic . . . in the South, a more stationary and aristocratic civilization.

Black readers would read that "Harriet Beecher Stowe brought on the Civil War . . . and that Negroes were the only people to achieve emancipation with no effort on their part." They would learn further "that Reconstruction was a disgraceful attempt to subject white people to ignorant Negro rule." A similar review of the popular American fiction of the period would yield a similar result. Faced with all of this, black American readers must take pains if they would see themselves "directly"—without refraction through the formulating gaze of "white" eyes. And when Du Bois shocks all readers into this recognition, in the opening pages of *The Souls of Black Folk*, he at the same time introduces one of his most provocative and fertile ideas, the concept of "double consciousness."

Du Bois writes in the first chapter of *Souls*:

After the Egyptian and Indian, the Greek and Roman, the Teuton and Mongolian, the Negro is a sort of seventh son, born with a veil, and gifted with second-sight in this American world,—a world which yields him no true self-consciousness, but only lets him see himself through the revelation of the other world. It is a peculiar sensation, this double-consciousness, this sense of always looking at one's self through the eyes of others, of measuring one's soul by the tape of a world that looks on in amused contempt and pity. One ever feels his twoness,—an American, a Negro; two souls, . . . two thoughts, two unreconciled strivings; two warring ideals in one dark body, whose dogged strength alone keeps it from being torn asunder.

Double consciousness is equivocally a gift and a curse. It is a "gift" insofar as it helps those who have it toward a purchase on the social world that those without the Veil might never achieve: namely, the intuition (later, the conviction) that the social world Americans inhabit is not of a "natural" kind but of an "absurd" kind. It is a

contingent and historical world, a *made* world that can be remade in turn. But double consciousness is at the same time a curse, because it first requires of black folk that they measure their souls by "the tape" of a world that holds them in contempt or regards them, simply, with pity. They can have no "true" self-consciousness. They are, for example, seen to act from passion more than from reason and to be more readily assimilated to nature than to culture. The biological, literary, historiographical, and anthropological writing of the nineteenth century—especially of the period after 1840—is everywhere shaped by precisely these assumptions, such that it becomes difficult ever to think *entirely* beyond the reach of them.

THE BODY IN *SOULS*

Du Bois often speaks a philosophical sort of language. This is no accident, and neither is the somewhat eschatological bearing of the title of the essay in which the passage on double consciousness appears: "Of Our Spiritual Strivings." As a young man, Du Bois had studied at the University of Berlin and had imbibed from his studies there the essentially Hegelian idea that there is a World Spirit struggling upward in time toward a more and more perfect consciousness of itself. People as yet have achieved but an imperfect realization of their "essential" humanity—an imperfect emancipation of "spirit" from its bondage to time, contingency, and error. The "spiritual strivings" toward "true self-consciousness" of which Du Bois speaks in *Souls* have precisely this larger significance, and the decision to speak chiefly of the "souls" of black folk and of the "spiritual world in which they live" involves Du Bois in a Hegelian sort of argument. He wishes above all to emancipate spirit from the fate of the body, from the contingency of being forever reduced to mere body, for that is exactly what chattel slavery had done. It had made bodies of men—*things* of them.

Soul and spirit, then, are the ideals. Over against them Du Bois forever sets the prison house of the flesh. There is in his thinking an abiding idealist notion that self *cannot* be identical with body, and this leads him to speak of the "unmanning" of men by the allure of the flesh, by which Du Bois means, in the farther reaches of his allegory, the allure of *all* things purely material. The peculiar situation of African American men probably made a certain patriarchal drift to the language of *The Souls of Black Folk* inevitable. Some reassertion of masculinity simply had to be poised against the predations of a culture that would assign the prerogatives of manhood to white men only—a culture that insisted, moreover, on articulating its power in more or less gendered (and sexualized) terms. So, the "aspiring self" Du Bois imagines in *Souls* is implicitly gendered masculine; the terms of the debate in which he was engaged—and these he certainly did not set—required it. White supremacy exploits the sheer *givenness* of a black body in order to set an absolute limit on the powers black men can exercise. Every day and in a hundred ways, men are reminded in the culture Du Bois writes about, that their horizons are tightly bounded by the mere *fact* of their flesh. Accordingly, in *Souls*, the flesh is at times figured as a kind of prison to which the "crime" of having a black skin absurdly sentences men without possibility of parole—until the moment of death, when the bond binding black soul to black body is cut.

Du Bois's son, Burghardt, died from dysentery in 1899. When he writes about the event in *Souls*, Du Bois begs the reader's forgiveness. In his heart, "all that day and all that night," had sat "an awful gladness": "Blame me not if I see the world thus darkly through the Veil," he implores, or if "my soul whispers ever to me, saying, 'Not dead, not dead, but escaped; not bond, but free.'" Neither he nor his son will live to see the choking and deforming Veil of "color" lifted for all "souls" *here on earth*—better to be off to heaven or, anyway, off to the grave. This elegy nonetheless occasions a hope: that "fresh young souls" might someday wake in this New World to find men asking "of the workman, not 'Is he white?' but 'Can he work?'" and of "artists, not 'Are they black?' but 'Do they know?'" The summary cruelty of white supremacy is to apply this law asymmetrically: black selves are bound to the bodily realm of the natural, but white selves are not. Bear in mind that in the thinking of the West, this fundamental asymmetry applies also to gender—feminine selves dwell chiefly in the bodily sphere of the natural, whereas masculine selves do not—and it is easy to see why Du Bois should be led to masculinize the souls of black folk. It is easy to see as well that patriarchy and white supremacy, as they have developed in the West, essentially imply each other.

For many in America, and for many in the West generally, blackness came to embody sexuality *as such*, the flesh *as such*: this is the idea Du Bois most wishes to chasten his "Gentle Readers" out of when he speaks of the souls of black folk. This white, imperious association of color and sexuality explains much about *Souls*. It explains, for example, why it so often relies on metaphors of sensualist decadence to figure what had been done to the freedmen and their posterity. It also explains why Booker T. Washington should be so consistently stigmatized in the book as a kind of "feminizing" force, as a seducer who would "unman" African Americans, giving them over entirely to the fate of the body. Moreover, it explains why Du Bois should be at pains to defend black Americans against the charge, urged constantly in those days and often on so-called scientific grounds, of sexual immorality and why he at times sounds rather monkish and otherworldly. For the moment, and to complete the picture, we need only add that, for Du Bois, the black American is a colonized subject, as were people of color almost everywhere on earth in 1903. Colonial subjects are tactically feminine: submissive, dominated, and locked in the immanence and repetition of a merely physical sort of life. They are locked, in fact, in the contingency and fate of the past. They are denied a future.

But there is a gift in this curse of bitter subjection. David Levering Lewis is right to find in Georg W. F. Hegel an important anticipation of Du Bois's theory of the double consciousness of slaves and their posterity. As Lewis says in his first biography of Du Bois,

> Hegel . . . explicated a complex reciprocity of master and slave in which the identities of both could be fully realized only to the extent that the consciousness of one was mediated through that of the other. If the master understood dominance, it was the slave who truly understood the sovereign value of freedom. "Just as lordship showed its essential nature to be the reverse of what it wants to be," Du Bois read in Hegel, "so, too, bondage will, when completed pass into the opposite of what it immediately is: being a consciousness repressed within itself, it will enter into itself, and change round into real and true independence."

Du Bois develops an argument whereby the emancipation of those who live "behind the Veil" will mark the emancipation of humanity as such—for they alone "truly understand the sovereign value of freedom." "There are today," says Du Bois in "Of Our Spiritual Strivings," "no truer exponents of the pure human spirit of the Declaration of Independence than the American Negroes." The emancipation of the American Negro will be the emancipation of America from bondage to itself; only then will America be made real, as the black/white antagonism is resolved in the higher unity of humanity beyond color.

The German socialist philosopher Karl Marx refined this dialectic in his almost messianic account of the "class struggle"—an antagonism that will resolve itself at last only through the emancipation of the most alienated, the most perfectly enslaved, of all classes—the proletariat. Du Bois, working as much from Marx as from Hegel, added to this idea the necessary complement of color: humanity can fully realize its spirit only through self-emancipation from the sensualizing delusion of race. That is why the struggle of colonized peoples for independence

from the great European powers holds, for Du Bois, such epochal significance. In it he sees the struggle not merely of an abject population in what is now called the Third World but also the promise of humanity's emergence, at last, into true self-consciousness. Much of Du Bois's later analysis of the course of European empire in *Darkwater: Voices from within the Veil* (1920) and in *Color and Democracy: Colonies and Peace* (1945) is anticipated in *The Souls of Black Folk*.

THE EXODUS OF *SOULS*

Du Bois writes not simply in a philosophical vocabulary; his is a thoroughly American book, and he adapts to the purposes of this story about the "spiritual strivings" of black folk a foundationally American allegory. Since the early seventeenth century, Americans have been attracted to a typological reading of the Old Testament wherein Europe figures as "Egypt," the New World as "Canaan," the passage across the Atlantic as the "Exodus," and the Puritan settlers themselves as the "New Israelites." The New World, it was believed, had been held in reserve for the Puritans, who were to achieve two things there: the perfect reformation of Christianity, which had fallen into decadence in the Old World under the stewardship of the Roman Catholic Church, and the conversion of the aboriginal peoples. By the end of the eighteenth century, this "errand into the wilderness" had been secularized, reconceived as the errand of building in the New World, on a foundation of reason, an unprecedented sort of republic. This ideal would become a model for all humanity and, in turn, would emancipate an Old World yet groaning under the decadent, irrational institutions of monarchy and feudal serfdom. In the nineteenth century, American slaves transformed the allegory yet again, and to new purposes, in a body of song, poetry, and autobiographical narrative that re-imagined American slavery as Pharonic oppression—the South (and later the Confederacy) became our

Egypt—and emancipation as a crossing of the river Jordan into Canaan.

This is the centuries-old American tradition that Du Bois revives in "Of Our Spiritual Strivings" when he writes: "The Nation has not yet found peace from its sins; the freedman has not yet found freedom in his promised land." He is a Jeremiah, recalling the New Israel to its forsaken covenant, to its essential (and now somewhat Hegelian) errand to emancipate soul from body. The allegory of New Israelites lost in a Sinai wilderness gives force to Du Bois's suggestion that "we black men seem the sole oasis of simple faith and reverence in a dusty desert of dollars and smartness." The idea that America has a "special" role to play in history certainly informs the following claim, also from "Of Our Spiritual Strivings":

> Merely a concrete test of the underlying principles of the great republic is the Negro Problem, and the spiritual striving of the freedmen's sons is the travail of souls whose burden is almost beyond the measure of their strength, but who bear it in the name of an historic race, in the name of this the land of their fathers' fathers, and in the name of human opportunity.

The story of Exodus authorizes as well Du Bois's incriminating challenge to "knightly America" that black men and women be allowed full access to liberal education, as he says in "Of the Training of Black Men": "Are you so afraid lest peering from this high Pisgah, between Philistine and Amalekite, we sight the Promised Land?"

Of unusual interest in this connection is a passage from the Song of Solomon, which Du Bois sets at the head of his essay "Of the Black Belt":

> I am black but comely, O ye daughters of Jerusalem,
> As the tents of Kedar, as the curtains of Solomon.
> Look not upon me, because I am black,
> Because the sun hath looked upon me:
> My mother's children were angry with me;

> They made me the keeper of the vineyards;
> But mine own vineyard have I not kept.

As an implicit address to Du Bois's (white) Gentle Reader, these lines acquire a biting sort of irony. America was to have become the New Jerusalem, but it became instead a second Egypt. The real daughters of Jerusalem, the true Israelites, are the "comely" black "keepers of the vineyards," whom their white siblings had made to suffer in anger. The irony is only compounded, and not in ways flattering to Du Bois, when the daughters of Jerusalem of his epigraph become, in the body of the essay itself, the Jew who, as "heir to the slave barons," now owns much of the land in Georgia's black belt and "squeezes out the blood" of the "debt-cursed tenants." Du Bois allows his reader to suppose that black men and women, perversely, had been made a new "Land of Canaan," ripe for the pillage by carpetbagging Jewish investors.

The long history of the appropriation of the story of the Exodus by black Americans is not without its bitter turns. To his credit, Du Bois removed all of this talk about "the Jew" from the 1953 Jubilee edition of *The Souls of Black Folk*. Certainly, he never dealt in the coarser sort of anti-Semitism that to this day stains a certain element within the black radical tradition. In 1921 Du Bois publicly condemned Henry Ford for publishing the anti-Semitic imposture called *The Protocols of the Elders of Zion*. In any case, the burden of *Souls* is this: the liberation of black Americans will be the liberation of the idea of "America," the decisive crossing of a river, of a color line, that has for so long divided us from the covenanted fate of our greatest national promise. Du Bois's argument could not be clearer: it is simply impossible for Americans *as Americans* not to be vitally interested in the fate of people of color everywhere.

THE GREAT DEBATE

Du Bois's great debate with Booker T. Washington about the souls of black folk reveals that there is still more to this allegorical business of an exodus. In "Of Our Spiritual Strivings," Du Bois sketches out the history of the postwar period for African Americans. There was Emancipation itself, then the granting of citizenship and suffrage, and then what Du Bois bitterly calls "the revolution of 1876." With that, the freedmen and their sons and daughters were left to wander, like forsaken Israelites, in a desert somewhere between Pharaoh and a nation they could rightly call home. In this "wilderness" appeared before the freedmen, like the Biblical "pillar of fire," what Du Bois calls "the ideal of 'book learning'; the curiosity, born of compulsory ignorance, to know and test the power of the cabalistic letters of the white man. . . . Here at last seemed to have been discovered the mountain path to Canaan." The adjective "cabalistic" is carefully chosen: the Cabala is the word of God handed down by Moses in the desert. Du Bois is setting up a rather exact allegory: "ten thousand thousand" black Americans are adrift, and two men would be their Moses—Du Bois with his Cabala (all the "book learning" of the West) and Washington with his Tuskegee program of "industrial training." The one tends to the souls of black folk and the other to their bodies alone.

The chief underwriters of black educational institutions in the South in the post-Reconstruction period were organizations whose funds came for the most part from Northern capitalists. The money was disbursed largely through two organizations: the Southern Education Board and the General Education Board. The directors of these organizations sought reconciliation between North and South and the development of Southern labor and resources by Northern capital; these goals required that they defer to Southern opinion on the "Negro Question." "The rich and dominating North," Du Bois explains in "Of Booker T. Washington and Others," "was not only weary of the race problem, but was investing largely in Southern enterprises, and welcomed any method of peaceful cooperation." Washington perfectly

suited their purposes after his groundbreaking 1895 speech, familiarly known as the "Atlanta Compromise." In it he agreed to put off demands for real political and civil rights in favor of economic development. In *Up from Slavery* (1901), Washington said to his white audience:

> As we have proved our loyalty to you in the past, nursing your children, watching by the sick-bed of your mothers and fathers, and often following them with tear-dimmed eyes to their graves, so in the future, in our humble way, we shall stand by you with a devotion that no foreigner can approach, ready to lay down our lives, if need be, in defence of yours, interlacing our industrial, commercial, civil, and religious life with yours in a way that shall make the interests of both races one. In all things that are purely social we can be as separate as the fingers, yet one as the hand in all things essential to mutual progress.

The studied "humility" of the address struck Du Bois as embarrassing and the concession to social separation as reprehensible.

Washington reports in *Up from Slavery* that "one of the saddest things" he ever saw was a young black man "sitting down in a one-room cabin, with grease on his clothing, filth all around him, and weeds in the yard and garden, engaged in studying a French grammar." The youth, Washington implied, would be much better off, and much happier, if he practiced a trade instead of studying "big books" with "high sounding names." Du Bois dryly retorts in *Souls:* "One wonders what Socrates and St. Francis of Assisi would say to this." What Northern capital had to say to it was plain enough: Washington on the merits of studying French grammar was music to their ears. He soon became a salaried field agent for the Southern Education Board, with the result (among other things) that Du Bois's Atlanta University was ignored by Northern benefactors, while Washington's Tuskegee flourished. Du Bois later remarked of the period in *Dusk of Dawn:* "The control [of the Southern Education Board and the General Education Board] was to be drastic. The Negro intelligentsia was to be suppressed and hammered into conformity." This explains why Du Bois's attack on Washington in *The Souls of Black Folk* is so utterly devastating—despite the fact that Du Bois manages throughout to sustain an essentially temperate, even cordial, tone

The heart of his argument against Washington, in "Of Mr. Booker T. Washington and Others," is this:

> Mr. Washington represents in Negro thought the old attitude of adjustment and submission; but adjustment at such a peculiar time as to make his programme unique. This is an age of unusual economic development, and Mr. Washington's programme naturally takes an economic cast, becoming a gospel of Work and Money to such an extent as apparently almost completely to overshadow the higher aims of life. Moreover, this is an age when the more advanced races are coming in closer contact with the less developed races, and the race-feeling is therefore intensified; and Mr. Washington's programme practically accepts the alleged inferiority of the Negro races. Again, in our own land, the reaction from the sentiment of war time has given impetus to race-prejudice against Negroes, and Mr. Washington withdraws many of the high demands of Negroes as men and American citizens. In other periods of intensified prejudice all the Negro's tendency to self-assertion has been called forth; at this period a policy of submission is advocated. In the history of nearly all other races and peoples the doctrine preached at such crises has been that manly self-respect is worth more than lands and houses, and that a people who voluntarily surrender such respect, or cease striving for it, are not worth civilizing.

Washington becomes, in the story Du Bois tells, an instrument in the hands of white supremacy and of capital. Both institutions—the political and the economic—employ him for the purpose of "re-enslaving" the freedman. Du Bois associates Washington with what might be called the capitalist extremism of the Gilded Age, which, in its "astonishing commercial development," had grown "ashamed of having bestowed so much sentiment on Negroes" and which henceforth would be "concentrating its energies on Dollars." This economic development had come to comprise as well the acquisition and administration of colonies in Hawaii, the West Indies, and the Philippines. The reassertion of white supremacy at home, in the post-Reconstruction period, was but a part of a larger project: the consolidation of white authority over peoples of color everywhere in the world—by the United States, England, France, Germany, Italy, and Belgium.

When he is set in this larger, global context, Washington emerges as a veritable agent of colonial rule—as a figure who would sell out black manhood and who would pander his race to a white ravisher. He had become, Du Bois clearly implies, the Great Emasculator: he had "sapped the manhood" of the race, advocated a "policy of submission," acquiesced in the relegation of Negroes to a "servile caste," and "overlooked certain elements of true manhood." It is exactly as Du Bois would have it in the epigraph he chose for this essay: "From birth to death enslaved; in word, in deed, *unmanned!*" This line from the English Romantic poet Lord Byron comes in a passage often cited in the literature of the more fiery abolitionists of old: "Hereditary bondsmen! Know ye not / Who would be free themselves must strike the blow?" As is evident from these passages, Du Bois's argument against Washington takes on a "gendered" inflection, which is of paramount importance in *The Souls of Black Folk.*

"OF THE WINGS OF ATALANTA"

"Of the Wings of Atalanta" is an essay about the New South, whose unofficial capital was the city of Atlanta, a city that had risen phoenix-like from the ashes of the war, reinventing itself as a center of commerce and industry. It is also an essay about America in the post-Reconstruction Gilded Age, for which Atlanta serves as a kind of epitomizing symbol. And it is an essay about education—about the fate of Du Bois's own Atlanta University in an era when the monies of a madly moneymaking nation were directed ever more exclusively, at least when it came to the education of black Americans, into schools of vocational training. Above all, it is an essay about what sort of nation America should become in the twentieth century.

In the years after Reconstruction ended, writes Du Bois,

> they of Atlanta turned resolutely toward the future; and that future held aloft vistas of purple and gold:—Atlanta, Queen of the cotton kingdom; Atlanta, Gateway to the Land of the Sun; Atlanta, the new Lachesis, spinner of web and woof for the world. So the city crowned her hundred hills with factories, and stored her shops with cunning handiwork, and stretched long iron ways to greet the busy Mercury in his coming. And the Nation talked of her striving.

Mercury is the god of commerce and the market, and Lachesis is one of the Fates (here, she spins, out of Southern cotton, a web of trade and finance that would bind to her the far-flung markets of the world). The question Du Bois puts before his reader is simple. Shall the "fate" of the on-looking nation be to sell out its "soul" for this great promise of wealth and power? Shall it prostitute its Declaration of Independence in market-driven idolatry before the mercurial gods of "greed" and "lust," whose instrument at home is Jim Crow and whose instrument abroad is empire? Du Bois continues:

> Perhaps Atlanta was not christened for the winged maiden of dull Boeotia; you know the tale,—how swarthy Atalanta, tall and wild, would marry only him who out-raced her; and how the wily Hippomenes laid three apples of gold in the way. She fled like a shadow, paused, startled over the first apple, but even as he stretched his hand, fled again; hovered over the second, then, slipping from his hot grasp, flew over river, vale, and hill; but as she lingered over the third, his arms fell round her, and looking on each other, the blazing passion of their love profaned the sanctuary of Love, and they were cursed. If Atlanta be not named for Atalanta, she ought to have been.

Atalanta is not the first or the last maiden whom greed of gold has led to defile the temple of Love; and not maids alone, but men in the race of life, sink from the high and generous ideals of youth to the gambler's code of the Bourse; and in all our Nation's striving is not the Gospel of Work befouled by the Gospel of Pay? So common is this that one-half think it normal; so unquestioned, that we almost fear to question if the end of racing is not gold, if the aim of man is not rightly to be rich. And if this is the fault of America, how dire a danger lies before a new land and a new city, lest Atlanta, stooping for mere gold, shall find that gold accursed!

Atalanta/Atlanta is "swarthy" and "wild." Her great energies, almost libidinal in their intensity, might issue in the downward-looking appetites of a "blazing passion," or else they might be sublimated, through self-discipline and sacrifice, into "high and generous ideals." Greed and lust exist, for Du Bois, in a kind of equation: each is a species of materialism, of sensualism—a species of a tendency always to reduce humanity to "bodiliness," to "defile the Temple of Love," and to befoul the chaste "Gospel of Work." Slavery had done all of these things; it had degraded both slave and master. Now the new slavery of empire and Jim Crow, on which the United States seemed to have embarked, promised to do it all again.

Out of this strange allegory emerges the full force of Du Bois's decision to speak of the *souls* of black folk. For Du Bois, it is as if the white mind forever sexualizes the black body, forever sees in it something swarthy and wild. As he says in "Of Our Spiritual Strivings," what he intimates is a "wanton license of fancy," post-Reconstruction sociologists "gleefully count [the freedmen's] bastards and prostitutes." This lewd sociological imagination, which would reduce black souls to black bodies, is but a refinement of a will to power over black men and women that had itself impressed on those bodies, as a token of their utter domination, what Du Bois calls in the same essay "the red stain of bastardy": "Two centuries of systematic legal defilement of Negro women [under slavery] meant not only the loss of ancient African chastity, but also the hereditary weight of a mass of corruption from white adulterers, threatening almost the obliteration of the Negro home." Atlanta is vulnerable indeed. Her burden is not merely to save herself but to save her tempter as well: she is the last best hope of the nation—the truest exponent of the human spirit of the Declaration of Independence. Her chastity is of great moment in *The Souls of Black Folk.*

"Two figures," Du Bois says in "Of the Dawn of Freedom," " ever stand to typify" the epoch of slavery "to coming ages." He goes on:

> A gray-haired gentleman, whose fathers had quit themselves like men, whose sons lay in nameless graves; who bowed to the evil of slavery because its abolition threatened untold ill to all; who stood at last, in the evening of life, a blighted, ruined form, with hate in his eyes;—and the other, a form hovering dark and mother-like, her awful face black with the mists of centuries, had aforetime quailed at that white master's command, had bent in love over the cradles of his sons and daughters, and closed in death the sunken eyes of his wife;— aye, too, at his behest had laid herself low to his lust, and borne a tawny man- child to the world, only to see her dark boy's limbs scattered to the winds by midnight marauders riding after "damned Niggers."

The formula Du Bois develops in this typifying allegory goes like this: master is to slave as man is to woman and as the ravisher is to the ravished. Bondage had unmanned the slave; it had put him in a feminine position with respect to the master class. The "mother-like" figure in the passage above is representative, of course: in her are comprehended both men and women. And even today, Du Bois says in an apostrophe to the "Southern Gentleman" in "Of the Train- ing of Black Men,"

> the masses of the Negroes see all too clearly the anomalies of their position and the moral crooked- ness of yours. . . . When you cry, Deliver us from

the vision of intermarriage, they answer that legal marriage is infinitely better than systematic concu- binage and prostitution. And if in just fury you ac- cuse their vagabonds of violating women, they also in fury quite as just may reply: The rape which your gentlemen have done against helpless black women in defiance of your own laws is written on the foreheads of two millions of mulattoes, and written in ineffaceable blood.

So much for the decadent legacy of the planter; so much for his peculiar "husbandry" of Southern "institutions." His successor in the New South that emerged after 1876—a succes- sor whose good husbandry even of the body of the land itself is in doubt—must now be ad- dressed.

"The Wizard of the North—the Capitalist— had rushed down in the 1870s to woo this coy dark soil," readers are told in "Of the Black Belt." The land had been "raped" by the old regime of slave agriculture. Now it would be raped again—or at any rate "wooed"—by the abusive system of tenancy that arose in slavery's wake. All of lower Georgia, Du Bois explains, was being "ravished into a red waste." Plainly, the relation of Northern capital to Southern labor was to be abusive in the extreme. Landlord is to land as white man is to black, as man is to woman, and as rapist is to victim: that is the bleak equation arrived at. As Du Bois puts it in "Of the Training of Black Men," the decades- old tendency "born of slavery" had been "quickened to renewed life by the crazy imperialism" of the 1890s, with the result that "human beings" were ranged "among the mate- rial resources of a land to be trained with an eye single to future dividends."

No wonder that when Du Bois takes his Gentle Reader down to what had been the "Egypt of the Confederacy," the black belt of Georgia, he finds there a "pretty blue-eyed quadroon." Thinking of the competition among the European nations for their "place in the sun" and for cheap, colored labor, he writes in "Of the Training of Black Men":

Plain it is to us that what the world seeks through desert and wild we have within our threshold,—a stalwart laboring force, suited to the semi-tropics; if, deaf to the voice of the Zeitgeist, we refuse to use and develop these men, we risk poverty and loss. If, on the other hand, seized by the brutal afterthought, we debauch the race thus caught in our talons, selfishly sucking their blood and brains in the future as in the past, what shall save us from national decadence?

Such is the tendency and the legacy of a culture that "debauches" everything it touches, that everywhere turns souls into bodies. And in the midst of it all Atlanta begins the difficult race of her new American life. As she goes, so will go the nation.

After the brief "democratic" interlude of 1868–1872, Americans set about to reassert "white supremacy" at home through the establishment of the new Jim Crow apartheid and abroad through the suppression of Filipino republicans. As Du Bois saw it, Americans were selling out nothing less than the New World promise of America itself. In the following passage from "Of the Wings of Atalanta," notice the metaphors of sexual encounter and of degeneracy so characteristic of Du Bois's writing in *Souls* and notice as well the quiet reminders of our forsaken American errand:

> In the Black World, the Preacher and Teacher embodied once the ideals of this people,—the strife for another and a juster world, the vague dream of righteousness, . . . but to-day the danger is that these ideals, . . . will suddenly sink to a question of cash and a lust for gold. Here stands this black young Atalanta, girding herself for the race that must be run; and if her eyes be still toward the hills and sky as in the days of old, then we may look for noble running; but what if some ruthless or wily or even thoughtless Hippomenes lay golden apples before her? What if the Negro people be wooed from a strife for righteousness, . . . to regard dollars as the be-all and end-all of life? What if to the Mammonism of America be added the rising Mammonism of the re-born South, and the Mammonism of this South be reinforced by the budding Mammonism of its half-

wakened black millions? Whither, then, is the new-world quest of Goodness and Beauty and Truth gone glimmering? Must this, and that fair flower of Freedom which, despite the jeers of latter-day striplings, sprung from our fathers' blood, must that too degenerate into a dusty quest of gold,— into lawless lust with Hippomenes?

The allegory is crystal clear: Du Bois warns us all lest black Americans—those "truest exponents of the Declaration of Independence"—bed down with white capital. The defilement would in this case be double, for it is a figure for the most rapacious sort of husbandry, both of our natural and of our human resources. It is the sort of husbandry that antebellum white planters, post-1876 absentee landholders, and colonial bureaucrats alike indulged in—even as their demagogic constabulary in the Democratic Party of an un-Reconstructed South seldom let slip an opportunity to get up lynching parties with whispers of fates worse than death visited on the pure white magnolias of the South. And Washington's role in the whole gaudy pageant, at least as scripted in *Souls,* is hardly enviable. Du Bois's careful phrasing does allow for the possibility that Washington might merely be a "thoughtless" Hippomenes rather than a "ruthless" or a "wily" one, but that is thin absolution indeed.

What is to be done? After unwinding this devastating allegory of America in its Gilded Age "debauch," Du Bois suggests that "the hundred hills of Atlanta are not all crowned with factories":

> On one . . . the setting sun throws three buildings in bold relief against the sky. The beauty of the group lies in its simple unity:—a broad lawn of green rising from the red street with mingled roses and peaches; north and south, two plain and stately halls; and in the midst, half hidden in ivy, a larger building, boldly graceful, sparingly decorated, and with one low spire. It is a restful group. . . . There I live, and there I hear from day to day the low hum of restful life. In winter's twilight, . . . I can see the dark figures pass between the halls to the music of

the night-bell. In the morning, . . . the clang of the day-bell brings the hurry and laughter of . . . children all dark and heavy-haired;—to join their clear young voices in the music of the morning sacrifice. In a half-dozen classrooms they gather then. . . . The riddle of existence is the college curriculum that was laid before the Pharaohs, that was taught in the groves by Plato, that formed the *trivium* and *quadrivium,* and is today laid before the freedman's sons by Atlanta University. And this course of study will not change; its methods will grow more deft and effectual, its content richer by toil of scholar and sight of seer; but the true college will ever have one goal,—not to earn meat, but to know the end and aim of that life which meat nourishes. . . . Here, amid a wide desert of caste and proscription, amid the heart-hurting slights and jars and vagaries of a deep race-dislike, lies this green oasis, . . . and here men may lie and listen, and learn of a future fuller than the past, and hear the voice of Time:

"Entbehren sollst du, sollst entbehren."

The very architecture of the place is modest, chaste, and retiring: "plain," "half-hidden in ivy," "simply decorated," and conducive to rites of "morning sacrifice." And students at Atlanta University in 1903 would presumably have recognized that bit of German as a line from Goethe's *Faust,* a poem Du Bois no doubt studied at the University of Berlin and which he here ascribes to "the voice of Time" itself: "Deny yourself, you must deny yourself." True, it is a somewhat monkish ideal—and not the sort of thing marketing offices at most universities now are often heard to say. But its "unworldliness" is precisely the point: bodies are of the world merely; souls, it seems, are not. Du Bois's answer to Washington, then, is essentially this: "Chasten yourself. America—and, in an age of empire, *all* the world—is alive with 'golden apples.' Tend to the souls of black folk more than to their bodies, shun Hippomenes, and you will help this nation realize its errand into the wilderness: to reform a world that white Europe, at its worst, had left reeling and debauched."

In the story Du Bois would tell, black America is Atalanta, the last best hope of the na-

tion; Booker T. Washington is her "thoughtless" Hippomenes; and the golden apple he holds out—his Tuskegee program of "industrial training," social "separation," and "humility"—is the worst poison of a Gilded Age, mere breadwinning in the service of white supremacy. So, Du Bois implies, if Atalanta should turn to whoring and take all of America with her, it will be apparent who pandered her off. Du Bois's assessment of his rival—and, more important, of his rival's capitalist backers, for *they* are the "ruthless" and "wily" ones—is just that unforgiving, no matter how suavely delivered.

But what of the *trivium* and *quadrivium*? What of the course pursued at Du Bois's own Atlanta University, as at the great universities of Old World? This, of course, is but a token of a larger and decidedly political promise, which readers can approach by inference from what Du Bois says. "The Wings of Atalanta," he explains, "are the coming universities of the South":

> They alone can bear the maiden past the temptation of golden fruit. . . . They will not guide her flying feet away from the cotton and gold; for— ah, thoughtful Hippomenes!—do not the apples lie in the very Way of Life? But They will guide her over and beyond them, and leave her kneeling in the Sanctuary of Truth and Freedom and broad Humanity, virgin and undefiled. Sadly did the Old South err in human education, despising the education of the masses, and niggardly in the support of colleges. Her ancient university foundations dwindled and withered under the foul breath of slavery; and even since the war they have fought a failing fight for life in the tainted air of social unrest and commercial selfishness, stunted by the death of criticism, and starving for lack of broadly cultured men. . . . Let us build the Southern university. . . . Why not here, and perhaps elsewhere, plant deeply and for all time centres of learning and living, colleges that yearly would send into the life of the South a few white men and a few black men of broad culture, catholic tolerance, and trained ability, joining their hands to other hands, and giving to this squabble of the Races a decent and dignified peace?

Here, without some committee meeting wrangle, young black men will study German poetry and French grammar, as Du Bois preferred, or accounting and agriculture, as Washington preferred, or some new combination of all these subjects.

At stake for Du Bois is nothing less than the fate of human beings everywhere in the twentieth century. Are men and women of color to be treated as bodies alone? And is the body of the earth to be ravished in an economy of depletion such as had threatened even the forgiving soil of the Deep South? Shall the market's "golden apples" direct *all* the energies of production? Is there no other end to the race? Only in light of these questions can the full force of Du Bois's chastening allegory be understood:

> When night falls on the City of a Hundred Hills, a wind gathers itself from the seas and comes murmuring westward. And at its bidding, the smoke of the drowsy factories sweeps down upon the mighty city and covers it like a pall, while yonder at the University the stars twinkle above Stone Hall. And they say that yon gray mist is the tunic of Atalanta pausing over her golden apples. Fly, my maiden, fly, for yonder comes Hippomenes!

"THE COMING OF JOHN"

In the penultimate chapter of *The Souls of Black Folk*, Du Bois tells an emblematic story of two young men named John. The two boys grow up "playfellows" in the Georgia hamlet of Altamaha: one is white and the son of the local judge; the other is black and poor. In due course white John heads to Princeton to become a "man." Black John goes North—despite dark words of warning from his white townsmen—to work his way through a small Negro college in Pennsylvania. At Wells Institute, black John takes hard-won courses in Du Bois's *trivium* and *quadrivium*, pondering "long over every new Greek word" and wondering "how it must have felt to think all things in Greek."

Meanwhile, at Princeton, white John does what well-bred gentlemen of uncertain aspirations always do in college.

Seven years pass. Then, one afternoon, the two Johns of Altamaha encounter each other in a queue at the box office of a New York City opera house. White John has come with a lady on his arm. Black John has come alone—and he is not at ease in this unfamiliar setting:

> He was pushed toward the ticket-office with the others, and felt in his pocket for the new five-dollar bill he had hoarded. There seemed really no time for hesitation, so he drew it bravely out, passed it to the busy clerk, and received simply a ticket but no change. When at last he realized that he had paid five dollars to enter he knew not what, he stood stockstill amazed. "Be careful," said a low voice behind him; "you must not lynch the colored gentleman simply because he's in your way," and a girl looked up roguishly into the eyes of her fair-haired escort. A shade of annoyance passed over the escort's face. "You *will* not understand us at the South," he said half impatiently, as if continuing an argument. "With all your professions, one never sees in the North so cordial and intimate relations between white and black as are everyday occurrences with us. Why, I remember my closest playfellow in boyhood was a little Negro named after me, and surely no two,—*well*!" The man stopped short and flushed to the roots of his hair, for there directly beside his reserved orchestra chairs sat the negro he had stumbled over in the hallway. He hesitated and grew pale with anger, called the usher and gave him his card, with a few peremptory words, and slowly sat down. . . .

> All this John did not see, for he sat in a half-maze minding the scene about him; the delicate beauty of the hall, the faint perfume, the moving myriad of men, the rich clothing and low hum of talking seemed all a part of a world so different from his, . . . that he sat in dreamland, and started when, after a hush, rose high and clear the music of Lohengrin's swan. The infinite beauty of the wail lingered and swept through every muscle of his frame, and put it all a-tune. He closed his eyes and grasped the elbows of the chair, touching unwittingly the lady's arm. And the lady drew

away. A deep longing swelled in all his heart to rise with that clear music out of the dirt and dust of that low life that held him prisoned and befouled. If he could only live up in the free air where birds sang and setting suns had no touch of blood! Who had called him to be the slave and butt of all? And if he had called, what right had he to call when a world like this lay open before men?

All the post-Reconstruction American elements are here: the genteel hypocrisy of the South ("one never sees in the North so cordial and intimate relations between black and white as are everyday occurrences with us"); the indulgent, "roguish" winking of the North ("Be careful, you must not lynch the colored gentleman simply because he's in your way"); and then the inadvertent touch of the skin ("and the lady drew away"). This last is all it takes to bring black John down again into the "imprisoning" immanence of his body, "befouled" by dirt and dust. He would "rise high and clear," like Lohengrin's swan; he would have a soul as well as a body. But to white eyes he is merely and always the *flesh*—alive with a vivid animality. That is why his accidental jostling of this white lady on the arm of white John, is later reimagined, as it often was in Du Bois's South, as a veritable act of "force." "Oh," white John says, on encountering his black playfellow again back home in Altamaha, "it's the darky that tried to force himself into a seat beside the lady I was escorting."

The half-muted fantasy of rape, the almost religious certainty that in the person of black John, white John simply *must* find something fundamentally sensual, is what *The Souls of Black Folk* tries to make its "Gentle Reader" understand. The animating motive of white supremacy, as Du Bois sees it, is nothing less than a *sensualizing* will to power, everywhere fascinated by what it everywhere also detests, whereby black souls are reduced to black bodies. Under this regime, "whiteness" is to "blackness" as "soul" is to "body." That is why Du Bois simply had to write his book about the *souls* of black folk. And as for Jennie, black

John's younger sister, the girl who cleans the Judge's kitchen, she is mere flesh too. "Why," says white John, "I never noticed before what a trim little body she is. Hello, Jennie! Why, you haven't kissed me since I came home."

In "The Forethought," Du Bois calls "The Coming of John" a "tale twice told but seldom written." The plot has all the weird familiarity of the uncanny. Its logic is inscrutably felt: when a black body lays claim to its soul down south, there simply *must* be bloodshed—any American reader knows it. In due course, white John tackles Jennie in callous erotic sport. Black John hears the cry, comes running, and strikes dead his white doppelgänger "with all the pent-up hatred of his great black arm." All that remains is for black John to take leave of his mother. Telling her a truth that is also not a truth, he says: "Mammy, I'm going away,—I'm going to be free." With his eye not on the North, as she supposes, but on "the North Star pale above the waters," he heads for the breakers, there to await the lynching party. When it arrives, black John hums a strain of a Wagner opera to himself— "Freudig geführt, ziehet dahin" (Joyfully led, pass along to that place) from "Song of the Bride"—and lets "the storm burst round him." "And the world," Du Bois says, "whistled in his ears."

The reader on the other side of the color line is perhaps left thinking about a stanza from the *Rubáiyát of Omar Khayyám*, translated by Edward FitzGerald, which Du Bois places at the head of his essay on "The Training of Black Men":

Why, if the Soul can fling the Dust aside,
And naked on the Air of Heaven ride,
Were't not a Shame—were't not a Shame for him
In this clay carcase crippled to abide?

CONCLUSION

This inquiry began with a discussion of the Hamburg massacre of 1876, an episode representative, in too many ways, of the

Redemption of the South from Reconstruction. That Redemption is what *The Souls of Black Folk* was written to denounce and also to explain. Two months after the Hamburg massacre, a band of armed white men gathered in Edgefield, South Carolina, northeast of Hamburg. At their head was Nathaniel Butler, a Confederate veteran and the brother of the attorney who was to have brought charges against Dock Adams—the black Union Army veteran who headed up the local militia in Hamburg. Butler's mob went looking for Simon Coker, an African American who was, at the time, a Republican state senator and who had embarked on an investigation of white militancy in that part of South Carolina. Butler and his men seized Coker and led him into the brush along a country road; after permitting him to pray, they shot him dead where he knelt. Among the party was a young white farmer named Benjamin Tillman (he had also been a participant in the Hamburg riots). The bloody summer of 1876 marked Tillman's debut in South Carolina politics. He eventually became governor and sat for several terms in the U.S. Senate.

When Tillman died in 1918, Du Bois wrote an obituary for the *Crisis.* "It can hardly be expected that any Negro would regret the death of Benjamin Tillman," Du Bois wrote. He went on:

> And yet it is our duty to understand this man in relation to his time. He represented the rebound of the unlettered white proletariat of the South from the oppression of slavery to new industrial and political freedom. The visible sign of their former degradation was the Negro. They kicked him because he was kickable and stood for what they hated; but they must as they grow in knowledge and power come to realize that the Negro far from being the cause of their former suffering was their co-sufferer with them. Some day a greater than Tillman will rise in the South to lead the white laborers and small farmer, and he will greet the Negro as a friend and helper and build with him and not on him. This leader is not yet come, but the death of Tillman foretells his

coming and the real enfranchisement of the Negro will herald his birth.

The "unlettered white proletariat of the South," the very men Ben Tillman represented, had been "oppressed" by slavery. The insight is characteristic of Du Bois, as is the promise he holds out of a *real* redemption—the vision of an almost revolutionary class solidarity that would eventually resolve the problem of the color line. It may be that only a man burdened by "double consciousness" could have achieved this insight and entertained this promise in the last year of World War I and the first year of the Bolshevik Revolution. It is certainly the case that Du Bois was writing, as he penned his oddly inspiring obituary of a damned Redeemer, about the souls of white folk.

On March 29, 1900, Ben Tillman had stood in the Senate chamber to deliver a speech. In it he acknowledged that the "race question" had "been the cause of more sorrow, more misery, more loss of life, more expenditure of treasure than any and all questions which have confronted the American people from the foundation of the Government to the present day.... The South has this question always with it. . . . It is like Banquo's ghost and will not down." Had he read this, Du Bois might have said: Give the unlettered old boy enough rope and he will hang even himself. Here is an example of a man astonishingly unaware of what his words imply. Here is dramatic irony of a very high order. But it may be better to imagine that Tillman was *somehow* aware that his allusion to *Macbeth* constituted the inadvertent confession of a ruthless politician—a politician who murdered another politician in order to get his start. Surely it is fitting that Tillman should be haunted, as Macbeth was, by the specter of a good man slaughtered along the king's highway in a drive for absolute power and fitting, as well, that he should have been made sleepless by the fear that the good man's sons must someday inherit the kingdom.

A shrewder, more deliberate evocation of the same unquiet banquet in Shakespeare's tragedy comes in *The Souls of Black Folk*. Thinking of Banquo's apparition and quoting Macbeth's horrible importunity, Du Bois says in "Of Our Spiritual Strivings":

And yet the swarthy spectre sits in its accustomed seat at the Nation's feast. In vain do we cry to this our vastest social problem:—

"Take any shape but that, and my firm nerves Shall never tremble!"

The Nation has not yet found peace from its sins; the freedman has not yet found in freedom his promised land.

That Tillman and Du Bois alike should have been enthralled by *Macbeth*—that they should both, in fact, have reimagined our America as Macbeth's bloody Scotland—is a telling irony of American literary history. Terror, as Du Bois understood, was nothing new on American soil when it came to Oklahoma City in a rented van in 1995. The terrorist carried in his pocket a novel by a white supremacist devotee of an early anti-Semitic tract called *The Protocols of the Elders of Zion*. The problem of the twentieth century was the problem of the color line.

Select Bibliography

EDITIONS

The Souls of Black Folk. Chicago: A. C. McClurg and Company, 1903.

The Souls of Black Folk. Fiftieth anniversary Jubilee edition. New York: Blue Heron Press, 1953. (For this edition Du Bois revised a handful of passages that had led some readers of the 1903 text to accuse him of anti-Semitism.)

Writings. Edited by Nathan Huggins. New York: Library of America, 1986. (The best single-volume edition of Du Bois's work. In addition to *Souls*, it includes *The Suppression of the African Slave Trade*, *Dusk of Dawn*, and more than seventy articles and essays originally published in *Crisis* and other periodicals. All citations of Du Bois's writings, except from *Black Reconstruction*, are from this edition.)

OTHER WORKS BY DU BOIS

Black Reconstruction in America: 1860–1880. New York: Atheneum, 1992. (Reprint of the 1935 edition, with an introduction by David Levering Lewis.)

SECONDARY WORKS

Berman, Russell A. "Du Bois and Wagner: Race, Nation, and Culture between the United States and Germany." *German Quarterly* 70, no. 2 (spring 1997): 123–135.

Bone, Robert. *The Negro Novel in America*. Rev. ed. New Haven, Conn.: Yale University Press, 1965. (Still an excellent resource, with much material on Du Bois and his milieu.)

Broderick, Francis L., and August Meier, eds. *Negro Protest Thought in the Twentieth Century*. Indianapolis: Bobbs-Merrill, 1965. (A useful anthology of primary material, including, in a section titled "From Accommodation to Protest," important documents from the history of Du Bois's very public debate with Washington.)

Butterfield, Fox. *All God's Children: The Bosket Family and the American Tradition of Violence*. New York: Alfred Knopf, 1995.

Foner, Eric. *Reconstruction: America's Unfinished Revolution, 1863–1877*. New York: Harper & Row, 1988.

Franklin, John Hope, and Isidore Starr, eds. *The Negro in Twentieth Century America: A Reader on the Struggle for Civil Rights*. New York: Vintage, 1967. (An excellent resource, this reader includes the speech of Benjamin Tillman to the U.S. Senate in March 1900.)

Frederickson, George M. *The Black Image in the White Mind: The Debate on Afro-American Character and Destiny, 1817–1914*. 2d ed. Middletown, Conn.: Wesleyan University Press, 1987. (Essential reading for any student of Du Bois or of American literature and culture.)

Glaude, Eddie S., Jr. "Exodus and the Politics of Nation." In *Race Consciousness: African-American Studies for the New Century*. Edited by Judith Jackson Fossett and Jeffrey A. Tucker. New York: New York University Press, 1997. Pp. 115–135.

Huggins, Nathan. *Harlem Renaissance*. New York: Oxford University Press, 1971. (A finely written history of African American literature and culture in the early decades of the twentieth century.)

————. "W. E. B. Du Bois and Heroes." In his *Revelations: American History, American Myths*. New York: Oxford University Press, 1995.

Lewis, David Levering. *W. E. B. Du Bois: Biography of a Race, 1868–1919*. New York: Holt, 1993. (This and the companion volume constitute the best biography of Du Bois.)

————. *W. E. B. Du Bois: The Fight for Equality and the American Century, 1919–1963*. New York: Holt, 2000.

Lewison, Paul. *Race, Class, and Party: A History of Negro Suffrage and White Politics in the South*. New York: Grosset and Dunlap, 1965. (Meticulously researched and documented.)

Lott, Tommy Lee. "Du Bois and Locke on the Scientific Study of the Negro." *Boundary 2* 27, no. 3 (fall 2000): 135–152.

MacLean, Nancy. *Behind the Mask of Chivalry: The Making of the Second Ku Klux Klan*. New York: Oxford University Press, 1994. (Groundbreaking work—indispensable for understanding the Georgia in which Du Bois lived and worked from 1897 to 1910.)

Miles, Kevin Thomas. "Haunting Music in *The Souls of Black Folk*." *Boundary 2* 27, no. 3 (fall 2000): 199–214.

Morrison, Toni. *Playing in the Dark: Whiteness and the Literary Imagination*. New York: Vintage, 1993.

Mostern, Kenneth. "Postcolonialism after W. E. B. Du Bois." In *Postcolonial Theory and the United States: Race, Ethnicity, and Literature*. Edited by Amritjit Singh and Peter Schmidt. Jackson: University Press of Mississippi, 2000. Pp. 258–276.

Posnock, Ross. "How It Feels to Be a Problem: Du Bois, Fanon, and the 'Impossible Life of the Black Intellectual.'" *Critical Inquiry* 23, no. 2 (winter 1997): 323–349.

Rampersad, Arnold. *The Art and Imagination of W. E. B. Du Bois*. Cambridge, Mass.: Harvard University Press, 1976. (Among the best books on Du Bois.)

————. "Slavery and the Literary Imagination: Du Bois's *The Souls of Black Folk*." In *Slavery and the Literary Imagination*. Edited by Deborah E. McDowell and Arnold Rampersad. Baltimore: Johns Hopkins University Press, 1989. Pp. 104–124.

Reed, Adolph, Jr. *W. E. B. Du Bois and American Political Thought: Fabianism and the Color Line*. New York: Oxford University Press, 1997.

Sundquist, Eric J. *To Wake the Nations: Race in the Making of American Literature*.

Cambridge, Mass.: Harvard University Press, 1993. (A book of great breadth that includes an extensive, nuanced study of Du Bois.)

Velikova, Roumiana. "W. E. B. Du Bois vs. 'the Sons of the Fathers': A Reading of *The Souls of Black Folk* in the Context of American Nationalism." *African American Review* 34, no. 3 (fall 2000): 431–442.

Washington, Booker T. *Up from Slavery.* 1901; New York: Doubleday, 1998.

Woodward, C. Vann. *The Origins of the New South, 1877–1913.* Baton Rouge: Louisiana State University Press, 1971. (A classic study.)

Zamir, Shamoon. *Dark Voices: W. E. B. Du Bois and American Thought, 1888–1903.* Chicago: University of Chicago Press, 1995. (Includes a chapter on Hegelianism in Du Bois and in American thought in the last decades of the nineteenth century.)

Tennessee Williams'
A Streetcar Named Desire

PHILIP PARRY

IN *A STREETCAR Named Desire* (1947) Tennessee Williams holds up many relationships for inspection, but it is the relationship, destructive though not mutually destructive, between Blanche DuBois and her brother-in-law, Stanley Kowalski, that is central to understanding the play. "We've had this date with each other from the beginning!" he tells her in words that echo (though he was not there to hear them) her admission that, the first time she laid eyes on him, "I thought to myself, that man is my executioner!" Their mutual antipathy and rivalry, because it ends in rape and madness, often is interpreted as essentially sexual and sometimes is generalized: a conflict between a man and a woman becomes part of a greater conflict between men and women. But *Streetcar* is a play in which class and social conflicts operate—conflicts between old American families and immigrants, imagination and reality, rural and urban values, past and future. The relationship between Blanche and Stanley reflects all of these conflicts.

Four topics dominate any discussion of *Streetcar*. First there is the relationship between the play and its author's life, especially Williams' emotional life. In which ways and to what extent is *Streetcar* disguised autobiography? A second and contiguous topic, large enough to require separate treatment, is the play's homosexual subject matter. Third, there are those social assumptions that the play takes for granted but which, now that they have changed substantially in modern liberal societies, threaten its contemporary relevance. And, finally, there is the theatrical self-awareness and self-projection that so many of Williams' characters exhibit and that Blanche takes to extremes.

BACKGROUND

Tennessee Williams, born Thomas Lanier Williams III, was a man who was unusually sensitive to the way in which place names and personal names form bridges between past and present. Thomas Lanier Williams II (1849–1908) was his paternal grandfather and Thomas Lanier Williams I (1786–1856) his paternal grandfather's great-uncle. Lanier was a name that attached all three men to a line of poets and musicians, some of whom were early Huguenot immigrants. Through his paternal grandmother Williams claimed kinship with the Seviers, who were also Huguenots. One ancestor in this line was the first governor of Tennessee, and it was the Sevier contribution to the history of that state that Williams acknowledged when, in 1939, he adopted his famous nom de plume. An earlier ancestor was Valentine Sevier (1712–1803), who founded the American line and was a collateral descendant of Saint Francis Xavier. (Val Sevier was a pen name that Williams considered adopting; Val Xavier is the doomed hero of *Orpheus Descending*.) His maternal grandmother ("Grand") was Rosina Maria Francesca von Albertzart-Otte, a name too good to waste. (Franz Albertzart is one of Alexandra del Lago's dead lovers in *Sweet Bird of Youth*, 1959.) Williams, starkly unglamorous by contrast, was a mark of Welsh ancestry and of bardic ambition.

Because the farther back one travels in time, the smaller the ancestral pond becomes, exotic ancestry is deceptive; it is the norm rather than the exception. Certainly Williams' more immediate relatives were thoroughly mundane. His father worked briefly for a telephone company (like Tom Wingfield's father in *The Glass Menagerie*) and then in a shoe factory (like both Tom Wingfield and Tennessee Williams). His mother ("Miss Edwina") felt that she was her husband's social superior: her father, the Reverend Walter Edwin Dakin (1857–1955), was an Episcopal minister who had married Rosina von Albertzart-Otte. He lived long enough to be a major influence on his grandson's life and to witness him at the height of his success. Williams' sister, Rose Isabel ("Miss Rose"), was born in 1909, and his brother, Walter Dakin Williams, in 1919. Rose, who was confined to mental hospitals for most of her adult life, was (apart from "Grand") the only woman toward whom he felt strong and lasting affection. By contrast, his relationships with his parents, Cornelius Coffin Williams and "Miss Edwina" (whom in his *Memoirs* he dubbed "an almost criminally foolish woman"), were strained, cold, and painful, though not entirely unloving. The exact details of Rose Williams' illness and of its cause have never fully emerged. Its consequences, sadly, are not in dispute: in 1943 she underwent

CHRONOLOGY

1911	Tennessee Williams (Thomas Lanier Williams) is born on March 26 in Columbus, Mississippi.
1929–1932	He attends the University of Missouri, Columbia, but does not graduate.
1932–1935	Works for the International Shoe Company.
1935–1937	Williams enters Washington University, St. Louis. Completes his studies at the University of Iowa and graduates.
1940	He gains a Rockefeller Fellowship and also wins a scholarship that enables him to study playwriting at the New School for Social Research in New York.
1944	In December *The Glass Menagerie* opens in Chicago. Transfers to New York City in March 1945.
1947	In December *A Streetcar Named Desire,* directed by Elia Kazan, with Marlon Brando as Stanley Kowalski and Jessica Tandy as Blanche DuBois, opens in New York.
1949	In October *A Streetcar Named Desire,* directed by Laurence Olivier, opens in London.
1951	In September, Elia Kazan's film version of *Streetcar* is released, with Brando as Stanley and Vivien Leigh as Blanche.
1955	*Cat on a Hot Tin Roof,* directed by Elia Kazan, opens in New York in March.
1959	*Sweet Bird of Youth,* perhaps his last major play, opens in New York in March.
1983	In February Williams dies in New York.

a lobotomy, was reduced to a condition of emotional and mental feebleness, and spent the rest of her life in mental hospitals and nursing homes or cared for by companions that her brother hired for her. The incident profoundly affected Williams, who blamed both parents (his mother more than his father).

Writing was the one highly organized activity in an otherwise disorderly life. Nonetheless, despite his regular writing sessions, Williams' career as a major dramatist was short-lived, stretching from *The Glass Menagerie* (1944), which marked his arrival as a successful playwright, to *Sweet Bird of Youth*, perhaps his last unequivocal success. Some critics see even in that play evidence of a falling away of talent; others extend his successes to include *The Night of the Iguana* (1961), but few are prepared to be more generous. After the late 1950s, though he wrote much that is interesting, he produced nothing coherent or extended enough to rival his earlier achievements. Severely damaged by alcohol and drug abuse, though buoyed up financially by lucrative film deals, he wasted the 1960s (his "stoned age") as thoroughly as the sixties wasted him. He never really recovered from the punishments that he inflicted upon himself during these years and died in a New York hotel bedroom on the night of February 24, 1983, having apparently choked on a plastic top from a bottle of eyedrops. He was buried in St. Louis, a city he had never liked, close to his mother but in a separate grave. His *Memoirs* (published in 1975) are, like the man himself at the time that he wrote them, crude and disordered and unreliable and shamingly unashamed. Although they were heavily censored by his publishers' lawyers, they remain an indispensable introduction to his life and work.

ART AND AUTOBIOGRAPHY

Doubtless all art is autobiographical, and every autobiography is a work of fiction. Nevertheless, artists do vary in the degree to which—and in the ways in which—they incorporate themselves into their creations. In Williams' work, self-incorporation is extreme and barely disguised. Tom Wingfield (both character in and narrator of *The Glass Menagerie*) is obviously a self-portrait. Just as obviously, his mother (Amanda Wingfield) is a compassionate *but* not entirely accepting portrayal of "Miss Edwina," and Laura, Tom's sister, is a compassionate *and*

entirely accepting portrayal of "Miss Rose." ("But" and "and"—the one conjunction excluding, the other including—exactly measure the difference in the quality of the love that Williams felt for his mother and his sister.) Even details that are wrong are right in the only way that matters in works of art: Amanda's husband was "a telephone man who fell in love with long distances" and ran away; Williams' father was emotionally absent even when physically present. In *Vieux Carré* (1977) there is another Tennessee Williams/Tom Wingfield narrator-character, known simply as the Writer. He is, Williams notes in his *Memoirs,* "myself those many years ago." In no play, however, is Williams obliged to get all of the details right. (*Vieux Carré* is set in New Orleans in 1938–1939. The Writer, just beginning his career and a long way from any literary success, is mourning the death of his grandmother, whom he calls "Grand." Rosina Dakin, Williams' own "Grand," died in 1944, only eleven months before *The Glass Menagerie* premiered.) Reflecting the greater freedom that advancing years and changes in public outlook had brought him, *Vieux Carré* far exceeds *The Glass Menagerie* in candor though not in art, especially in its graphic exposure of Williams' homosexual lifestyle.

Streetcar's title is a good example of the benign relationship between life and art. Williams lived in the Vieux Carré at a point where two tramlines shared a route. A traveler whose ultimate destination was the city's burial places—the ultimate destination of all travelers—would first take a streetcar headed for Desire and then, like Blanche herself, "transfer to one called Cemeteries." "Death was as close as you are," Blanche tells Stanley's coworker and poker buddy Harold ("Mitch") Mitchell (or perhaps she is speaking to the Mexican flower-seller or to herself) much later in the play, and the opposite of death "is desire." Thus, she journeys through a play whose symbolism is not, as might otherwise be supposed, the product of an overheated imagination (the title would be an unforgivably mawkish one were it simply invented) but was put together from the street names and stopping points of a real city's transport system.

Though Stanley Kowalski and Harold Mitchell were the names of young men that Williams had known at work and in college, respectively, *Streetcar* is much less nakedly autobiographical than either *The Glass Menagerie* or *Vieux Carré*. There is no single character who can be readily identified with Williams, and, more fully dramatized than either of the other two plays, *Streetcar* dispenses with the services of a narrator. Yet many have felt that there is a special kinship between Williams and Blanche, and support for this view can be derived from Williams' own statements. In his *Memoirs* there are curious occasions when he refers to, even defers to, Blanche as though she were a living person rather than one of his creations. This powerful identification with her makes us question whether Williams achieves a distance between himself and her that is sufficient to guarantee his artistic objectivity, for in each of his plays there is an image (sometimes simple, more usually compound) of Williams himself. He was willing to admit that Blanche was one of these visions and versions—"I can identify completely with Blanche DuBois," he said in a *Playboy* interview—even while angrily rejecting as hurtful and obtuse the claim that his heroines are gay men who wear dresses. Williams was oddly sensitive in this matter, but the evidence points in more ways than one. Princess Kosmonopolis (Alexandra del Lago) in *Sweet Bird of Youth* was originally a part written for a man. Moreover, Williams joked that Tallulah Bankhead, in a 1956 revival of *Streetcar*, made Blanche seem like a transvestite in a drag show, but he thought that Candy Darling, a transvestite actor more usually associated with Andy Warhol, was quite brilliant as Violet in *Small Craft Warnings* (1972).

In a 1981 interview with Dotson Rader, Williams insisted that he was able to write from whichever sexual vantage point his characters possessed, and he defended himself from the charge of dishonesty in terms that echo Blanche's defense: "My work is *emotionally* autobiographical. It has no relationship to the actual events of my life, but it reflects the emotional currents of my life." "No relationship" puts the point too strongly, but it remains nonetheless a strong point. Part of what links Blanche and Williams and explains the flow of his sympathy toward her is that both are, in the ancient meaning of the term, *hypocrites* ("actors," from the Greek *hypokrites*). But, Williams would always have wanted to insist, they are hypocrites of impeccable honesty and trustworthiness.

Identifying Blanche with Williams is tempting but should not let us forget that she is also an image of Rose Williams, for in different ways and with differing intensities "Miss Rose" left her mark upon most of her brother's plays. *Streetcar* first formed itself in his mind as an image of a woman, her youth just about to fade, sitting in a chair near a window and realizing that the man she wishes to marry has deserted her. Williams was thinking, Dotson Rader claims in *An Intimate Memoir*, of his sister. Much more controversially, in *Out on Stage*—a study of "lesbian and gay theatre in the twentieth century"—Alan Sinfield applies Rose's history directly and in detail to *Streetcar*, by equating Blanche DuBois with Rose and Stanley Kowalski with Cornelius Williams. Blanche, he says, "is lobotomised in order to protect a dreadful truth about family violence." But is Blanche sent away at the end of the play to be lobotomized? In a March 23, 1945, letter to his agent, in which Williams outlined in remarkable detail an early draft of *Streetcar*, he contemplated three possible endings: Blanche simply leaves, she goes mad, or she throws herself in front of a train. Later, in a joking mood, he said that she would have talked herself out of the asylum within a few weeks, perhaps by marrying a handsome young doctor.

SOMETHING [DIFFERENT] ABOUT THE BOY

In a play constructed in eleven discrete scenes, scene 6 is likely to be significant: so it is with *Streetcar*, which when first staged was punctuated by intervals after its fourth and sixth scenes. The resultant three-act structure suits the play well, because it concentrates attention on scenes 5 and 6, which fit neatly together, and devotes most of the third act to the events of a single evening and night. But in modern productions, where one interval is the more usual fashion, a break after scene 5 is more practical than a break after either scene 4 or scene 6 and makes good sense structurally. On this staging Blanche's date with Mitch takes place in the interval: she is preparing for it in scene 5 (with her not fully serious attempt to seduce the newspaper boy as part of her preparation), and its consequences are apparent immediately after the interval.

Scene 6 is at the play's center, and not just arithmetically. Hints dropped in scenes 1 and 2 develop into the revelation of Blanche's early marriage and of the part that she played in her husband's suicide. It is a scene composed with great skill and clarity, but one that has been persistently mishandled, mangled, and misinterpreted. Its crucial speech is Blanche's long explanation to Mitch, which begins: "He was a boy, just a boy, when I was a very young girl. When I was sixteen." There was, Blanche tells Mitch, "something different about the boy." From Kazan's film the word "different" is omitted: "something about the boy" and "something different about the boy" are not equivalent idioms. This is a minor but significant excision from a scene that in the film is massively truncated, for, ironically, in view of Brando's emergence as a gay icon on the strength of his clinging sweatshirt and provocatively tailored trousers, Kazan worked hard to straighten out Williams' play. He did so to comply with the very strict cinematic censorship that was then current in the United States but also from conviction and preference.

In the stage version commonly performed in the United States, however, the first part of this speech, before Blanche is interrupted by the noise of an approaching locomotive, ends quite explicitly:

Then I found out. In the worst of all possible ways. By coming suddenly into a room that I thought was empty—which wasn't empty, but had two people in it . . . the boy I had married and an older man who had been his friend for years.

What is masterly here is the way in which Blanche's revelation drips out of her, reluctantly but inexorably. Perhaps she is fighting her natural unwillingness to reach a conclusion, or perhaps, being Blanche, she knows how to tell a story well enough to hold her audience's attention. There are at least seven or eight places where Blanche's words could be halted:

Then I found out. [1] In the worst of all possible ways. [2] By coming suddenly into a room [3] that I thought was empty [4]—which wasn't empty, [5] but had two people in it [6] . . . the boy I had married and [7] an older man [8] who had been his friend for years.

The seventh potential halting point assumes that Blanche trails off into silence, unable to proceed. She has still not reached the core of her revelation. The eighth point, once the core has been reached, requires an actress to make a further choice. Perhaps Blanche feels that the last seven words are a final degradation, or perhaps an-older-man-who-had-been-his-friend-for-years should be run together swiftly as a compound description, as though Blanche is trying to take the edge off her revelation. In Kazan's film, however, Vivien Leigh had no choices to make, for this part of the speech, together with almost all of the last part of the scene, is omitted.

Moreover, *Streetcar*'s queerness is being thinned down in even the most recent stage productions, and this suppression of Allan's "difference" has a history. Laurence Olivier's 1949 London production, which also starred

Vivien Leigh, had to be submitted for approval to the Lord Chamberlain's office. (The Lord Chamberlain was a royal official who had wide-ranging powers of censorship over public stage performances in Britain until 1967. The real work of censorship was done in his name by assistants.) Predictably, references to Allan's sexuality had to be removed, and the Lord Chamberlain, in a creative mood, suggested that he should be found with a negress "instead of just another man" (as Philip Kolin tells us in *Williams: "A Streetcar Named Desire,"* 2000). Olivier rejected this absurd proposal and suggested a simple cut instead. The final sixteen words would be removed from the passage cited, and this section of the speech would thus end at the sixth stop. Perhaps piqued that its own emendation had been rejected, the Lord Chamberlain's office would not allow Blanche to get further than the fifth stop. None of this would matter much were it not that Olivier's compromise was taken up into the text of the play published by Penguin, where it remains as an influence on those British productions that, perhaps in simple ignorance, follow this edition. The homosexual revelation was, for example, left out of the Edinburgh Royal Lyceum's production in March 2002.

Scene 6 has troubled and muddled even critics who do not share the presuppositions of Williams' and Kazan's censors. Gregory Black, whose *Catholic Crusade against the Movies* (1998) is an indispensable guide to the history of film censorship in the United States, slips up when he says that in Kazan's film Blanche tells Mitch about having caught her husband Allan in bed with a man. In fact, there is no mention of a bed or a man. And Marjorie Garber in *Vice Versa* (2000), a book devoted to the making of precise discriminations between sexual preferences, points out that most of Williams' plays are expressions of a "guilty secret buried in the past." She argues that this secret is seriously compromised in Kazan's film, which suppresses the fact that Blanche has found her young husband "in bed with a boy." But this is not

what the film suppresses: Allan Grey is quite definitely found in a room with "an older man who had been his friend for years." "In a room with" might be euphemistic, but "older man" is not a term that Williams would use vaguely, nor was he unaware of the resonances of "friend." What Blanche sees is the seduction of a boy by an older mentor: out of tact or shock, she withdraws discreetly. It is the further embarrassment of being forced to acknowledge that he has been seen that she forces on Allan in Moon Lake casino when she tells him: "I saw! I know! You disgust me." (The Penguin text, because it omits the sexual discovery, prints a far weaker reading: "I know! I know! You disgust me.")

Blanche's part in her husband's death is neither gentle nor loving; her insensitivity prompts his suicide and seriously calls into question her claim that she has never been deliberately cruel to anyone. One possible defense of her conduct is to say that she is spontaneously cruel to Allan rather than deliberately so. But it is a defense that Blanche, who is true in the deepest things, rejects. Her resultant guilt damages her woefully and clearly has been doing so long before she moves in with Stanley and her sister, Stella. Allan's suicide is a defining incident in her life, and the age difference between Allan and his lover (emphasized by "older" and "man") and the breach of trust that is implied (underscored by "older" and "friend") set the pattern for her own later assaults on the vulnerable and the inexperienced. Once again, Alan Sinfield's judgment goes beyond what the play offers: Blanche's "sleeping with boys," he says, "was gentle and loving." But this is a flattering judgment that the play neither explicitly makes nor implicitly supports.

What, in the light of these excisions, dilutions, and misreadings, are we to make of those recent interpretations of the play that see homosexuality as *Streetcar*'s "absent presence" and its suppression as the gap where the play's meaning dwells? Or of those gay or gay-friendly critics who think that the play, even in its uncensored form, sacrifices integrity (by killing

Allan and silencing Blanche) to achieve acceptability? What, for example, of Blanche's promiscuity? On a "straight" interpretation she has simply frozen Allan in time and seeks to thaw out his memory by bedding schoolboys, cadets, and young men collecting payment for newspapers. This is the interpretation that Roxana Stuart, an actress who twice appeared in the role, gave when she suggested that Blanche's enthusiasm for very young men was prompted either by a recognition of their innocence or by a desire to meet replicas of her lost young husband. Williams' response, recorded in a contribution that Stuart made to the *Tennessee Williams Newsletter*, was unequivocally homosexual: Blanche, he insisted, was imaginatively identifying herself with her husband and was acting out *her* fantasy of *his* relations with young boys. Williams thus adds himself to the long list of his play's misreaders. If Blanche identifies with Allan on the basis of the one incident that she has seen, she should be imagining affairs with men older than Allan. This, however, would have disrupted the fantasy-weaving Williams' self-identification with the fantasy-weaving Blanche.

Toward the end of his life, in the course of his interview with Dotson Rader, Williams said of homosexuality: "I never found it necessary to deal with it in my work." Now, however, Williams' homosexuality is firmly at the center of critical discussion. Gay and a playwright, with the gayness and the playwriting significantly related, but not a gay playwright: that was Williams' own not at all paradoxical assessment of his status. He had never written and would never wish to write an openly gay play, because he wanted to remain a force in mainstream theater, because an openly gay play would narrow significantly the range of his appeal to audiences, and because he could say all that he really wished to say "through other means" and could do so because sexual orientation—whether his own or that of his characters—was not his principal interest. Here is a coherent account that is not at all evasive,

but some critics disagree. In *Still Acting Gay* (2000), John Clum argues that Williams' sexual preferences are formative of his plays but cannot be given direct expression in them. The "other means" that Williams mentions are dismissed as "fascinating, if sad"; the plays, like so many of their closeted heroes, are damaged by their self-suppressions. (Perhaps that is why, in a wonderfully telling misprint, Williams' most famous work is converted into *A Stretcher Named Desire*.) Moreover, despite Clum's judgment that "*Streetcar* is a gay play in its theatricalization . . . of experience," the selective list of published gay drama that forms such a useful appendix to his book contains no mention of any play by Williams. In its own way, that is as gross an excision as any.

VIOLENCE

Social attitudes change with the passing of time. The principal aspects of *Streetcar* that these changes have called into question are Stella's acceptance of domestic violence and the play's penultimate scene, in which Stanley rapes Blanche. Modern sensitivity toward sexual and other forms of domestic and family abuse has led some recent critics to claim that *Streetcar* displays a double injustice: Blanche, essentially innocent, is punished by Stanley, who is guilty but who escapes punishment. Where does Williams stand in this disputed matter?

"I don't believe in individual guilt," he told Rader in 1981. "I don't think people are responsible for what they do. We are products of circumstances that determine what we do." Casting the twenty-five-year-old Marlon Brando (so that in Kazan's original production Stanley was made to seem conspicuously younger than Mitch and his other drinking companions) helped to reduce, Williams felt, an awareness of Stanley's "black-dyed" villainy. Instead, as Kazan records in his autobiography, it is misunderstanding ("a thing . . . not a person") that destroys Blanche. The stage direction that marks Stanley's entrance for readers sums up the view that his life is to be measured in sexual terms that are not necessarily moral:

Since earliest manhood the center of his life has been pleasure with women, the giving and taking of it, not with weak indulgence, dependently, but with the power and pride of a richly feathered male bird among hens.

Williams was unduly fond of stage directions of this kind, which belong to a play's literary rather than its dramatic life, and the literary influence on this particular example is clearly the English novelist D. H. Lawrence. This influence is scarcely surprising: Williams, who visited Lawrence's widow in New Mexico in 1939 and later wrote a one-act play about him, admired Lawrence for his insight into the sexual life of his characters and for the honesty with which he gave expression to that insight. In the preface to *I Rise in Flame, Cried the Phoenix* (1941) he described him as a man who "felt the mystery and power of sex, as the primal life urge." Nonetheless, Williams' admiration is qualified: he finds Lawrence's work distorted by "his insistence upon the woman's subservience to the male." "Why did I want to *write*?" Lawrence asks himself in Williams' play:

Because I'm an artist.—What is an artist?—A man who loves life too intensely, a man who loves life till he hates her and has to strike out with his fist like I struck at Frieda—to show her he knows her tricks, and he's still the master!

The Lawrentian positives of female subservience and male mastery are insisted upon by Stanley even in financial matters. He does not give Stella a housekeeping allowance, pays bills himself, and treats money as a present "to smooth things over." He also, quite notoriously, hits her. Blanche is shocked by his conduct, and so is Mitch, though it is the effect on Blanche that chiefly bothers him: "It's a shame this had to happen when you just got here," he says, reducing it to a faux pas. What prompts him to minimize its significance is his awareness that

similar things have happened in the past and will recur. Even as he speaks, Stella runs back in to rejoin Stanley for an amorous reunion. Moreover, the fight between Steve and Eunice in scene 5, which is treated humorously (Blanche asks *brightly*, "Did he *kill* her?"), is surely meant to take the edge off Stanley's violence:

STELLA: She and Steve had a row. Has she got the police?
STANLEY: Naw. She's gettin' a drink.
STELLA: That's much more practical!
[*Steve comes down nursing a bruise on his forehead . . .*]

What further places the violence and serves to diminish it is Stella's eloquent defense of her marriage as a relationship from which she does not wish to escape. By telling the story of Stanley's smashing light bulbs with the heel of her slipper on their wedding night, she makes clear her acceptance of the link between his sexual energy and his violent outbursts: "I was—sort of—thrilled by it." In the Vieux Carré of New Orleans, Williams suggests, sex and violence go together like a horse and carriage.

SEX

Not everyone accepts Stella's acceptance. The novelist and playwright Thornton Wilder, on the night when *Streetcar* opened in New Haven, irritated Williams by saying that no one who, like Stella, had ever been a true lady could possibly ever marry someone like Stanley. "I thought, privately," Williams writes, that this comment came from a man who had "never had a good lay." Here is a crude, though inward response to a crass, because outward, comment. But Williams is also laying claim to superior insight into the nature of human emotional bonding: Stella, precisely because she is a lady, is attracted to Stanley, precisely because he is not a gentleman. It is a very Lawrentian relationship.

It is, moreover, a relationship that Williams takes great pains to put into context: every moment in *Streetcar,* every physical action, every shift in conversation is charged with sexual energy. Williams moves swiftly to establish the easygoing, loose-living quality of life in the old quarter of New Orleans. The play begins with the "overlapping" voices of people in the street. (The Penguin text at this point fills out this direction with scripted dialogue between Eunice, a sailor, a black woman, and a street vendor.) Stanley and Mitch enter, Stanley carrying a package of meat, which he throws to Stella. He is going bowling, and Stella is eager to join him. There is bawdy conversation: Eunice implies that she has run out of sexual rations for her husband, and the black woman jokes about Stanley's "package." Into this relaxed atmosphere of sexually charged banter Blanche enters, as though from another world, another time, another play. A stage direction operates chattily: she is dressed as though visiting the fashionable Garden District (where the play *Suddenly Last Summer* is set), she is five years older than Stella, she has the kind of beauty that instinctively avoids a bright light, she is dressed in a frothy white suit, and she looks like a moth. But moths are attracted to bright lights and are trapped and die. As soon as Blanche meets Stella, she asks that a light be switched off: "I won't be looked at in this merciless glare!" Being looked at in terms that she cannot dictate is death to the aging Blanche.

Into this coarse quarter she brings, if first appearances are a reliable guide, primness and propriety, gentility and reticence. Almost immediately, however, we are shown beneath her careful pose. When she sets up her grand scene of revelation about the loss of Belle Reve, the DuBois family estate, she ends it with a jibe, crude enough to have been cut from Kazan's film, about Stella's sexual fulfilment with Stanley: while funeral after funeral dragged the estate from her hands, "Where were *you*! In bed with your—Polack!"

The sexual antagonism, which amounts to rivalry for Stella's favors, between Blanche and Stanley expresses itself territorially right from

the start. When he reminds her that Laurel is "not in my territory," he is effectively accusing her of trespassing. This mixture of sexual rivalry, social distance, and territorial hostility is a very potent one. It flares up in scene 2 in an argument between Stanley and Stella that both grows out of and feeds back into class antagonism: Stella compares the "different notions" of the DuBoises and the Kowalskis; Stanley will not be ordered about in his own house. Their row is exacerbated by Blanche's flirtatious entry wearing a red satin robe, which parallels the red pajamas that Stanley wears for the rape. Blanche is clearly seeking to interest him sexually, not to bed him but rather to show who has the ascendancy. Throughout there is a power struggle expressed in sexual and financial and class terms. This is made very clear when Blanche pauses after saying, "To interest you a woman would have to. . . ." Stanley responds with the single sexually explicit word "Lay" before completing the sentence more or less innocently with "her cards on the table."

In a play that was once to have been entitled, as its third scene still is, "The Poker Night," such symbolism is not accidental and recurs at the end of the play. As Stanley and Stella renew their bond in the way they know best ("his fingers find the opening of her blouse"), Steve calls out: "This game is seven-card stud." In that game of chance which is every human life, Blanche's bluff is called. But she also manages the hand that she has been dealt with little skill. When Stella returns from the errand that she has been sent on to get her out of the house, she is greeted by Blanche's usual trick of owning up to something as though to render it innocuous. She has called Stanley a little boy to his face "and laughed and flirted. Yes, I was flirting with your husband!" It is an admission that will help tip the balance when Stella has to choose whom to believe (or whom to seem to believe) after the rape.

In scene 3, when Blanche and Stella return home, having dined out to avoid the poker players, Blanche's first instinct before even entering the house is to freshen up her makeup. She unbuttons her blouse while speaking to Stella about Mitch: though she is in the process of changing her dress, the combination of conversation ("What does—what does he do?") and action is significant. Similarly, she stands scantily clad with the light falling onto her so that she can be seen by the men in the next room. Then, when Stella goes to the bathroom, Blanche—the stage direction says she does so in a *leisurely* fashion—turns on the radio. This is surely attention-seeking behavior (radio sets both receive and send out signals) that has its effect on Stanley, who exhibits signs of arousal and sexual jealousy when he leaps up and pulls the curtains closed savagely to prevent Mitch from looking at Stella through them.

Scene 4 opens with a typically brilliant contrast between the sexually fulfilled Stella, who has clearly been reconciled to Stanley during the night ("Why, you must have slept with him!"), and the sleeplessly neurotic and sexually unsatisfied Blanche. There is perhaps a hidden sexual symbol when Stella picks up a broom and "*twirls it in her hands.*" "Are you deliberately shaking that thing in my face?" is Blanche's rather strange response. Certainly she is aware that Stanley is a sexual being with whom a woman can have only one relationship: "The only way to live with such a man is to—go to bed with him! And that's your job—not mine!" she tells Stella.

Scene 5 is highly suggestive sexually, whichever version one reads (though, unusually, it is a scene that undergoes strengthening in the Penguin text). There is a good deal of erotic by-play between Stanley and Blanche. She assumes that he is the ram astrologically but feels vindicated when she is told that he is the goat. She is the virgin, which prompts a contemptuous snort from Stanley, and he immediately begins to question her about her guilt-ridden past. When, egged on by the realization of what Stanley must have learned, she seeks to explain herself to Stella, her speech ends with a coarse expression: "I'm fading now! I don't know how

much longer I can turn the trick." This is replaced by a longer, less coarse but more explicit speech in the Penguin text: "Men don't—don't even admit your existence unless they are making love to you." Blanche's own dangerously heightened sexual awareness throughout this scene is shown by the incident in which foaming Coke is spilled over her white dress. Luckily, she says, it has not stained. She then talks about Mitch and his respectful handling of her: the implication is that she is more practiced than he is and that his respect is misplaced. This aspect of the scene ends with Blanche alone (Eunice and Steve, Stanley and Stella having gone off together), at which point the newspaper boy enters.

The danger of exposure in which Blanche knows she stands after Stanley's conversation prompts her risk-taking and potentially self-destructive flirtation with this young man. His entrance is amplified in the Penguin text, where he is seen resisting the overtures of a prostitute, an incident that sets up and morally positions Blanche's attempted seduction. Though there are numerous small differences between the two versions here, in both (but perhaps more strongly in the standard text) there is an obviously suggestive emphasis on the young man's lighter that does not always work but which flares when he uses it to light Blanche's cigarette. And notice, finally, his having stopped for a "cherry" soda: a word that Blanche picks up and which clearly signifies his virginity.

RAPE, CLASS, AND RACE

There is an essential interpretative freedom in the theater that must never be squandered. For as long as *Streetcar* has life left in it, there cannot be a definitive performance or production. In particular, because so much depends upon it, the relationship between Blanche DuBois and Stanley Kowalski is one that actors and directors must renegotiate each time the play is produced. This might seem strange: more than fifty years after its first performance and almost as many years after it was fixed in celluloid, one surely might be forgiven for thinking that here at least is something that has been fully and finally worked out. But the history of a play in performance is always the history of interpretative change. In the play's first production Elia Kazan and Jessica Tandy thought that Blanche had worked as a prostitute before hurriedly moving to New Orleans. It was Tandy's real distinction in the role that, thinking this, she still invested Blanche with so much ladylike dignity. But the dignity was false, supreme evidence of Blanche's ability to fool everyone around her for a short time and herself forever. However, in the play's first British production, Laurence Olivier and Vivien Leigh took a different view. They did not doubt that Blanche had fallen from grace, but her affairs were matters of the heart rather than of the wallet and the purse, and they vigorously protested their right to their own interpretation.

These two productions mapped out territory that every subsequent production with any new life in it must explore afresh. No doubt there are illicit interpretations (ones that are "off the map"), but there is no point on the map at which *Streetcar* is uniquely locatable. So there are uncertainties—uncertainties are interpretative possibilities—over when or whether Blanche goes mad and over whether and how far she is complicit with her attacker in the rape scene.

Williams, when he was arguing that the rape scene should not be cut from the film, identified Stanley, perhaps a little desperately, as a representative of "the savage and brutal resources of modern society" that are victorious over "the sensitive, the tender, the delicate." This at least indicates that Stanley's rape of Blanche is more than a sexual assault and that it expresses frustrations and antagonisms of more than one kind. One significant source of antagonism is established by the stage direction that marks Stella's entrance in scene 1: she is "of a background obviously quite different from her husband's." Stella's embarrassment at this differ-

ence in the presence of her sister is caught beautifully by Williams in the following piece of dialogue:

> BLANCHE: But there's no door between the two rooms, and Stanley—will it be decent?
> STELLA: Stanley is Polish, you know.

Stella's reply is clearly adrift: she has been tricked by a subterranean pun into admitting that Stanley is Polish but unpolished.

This bad, nervous, and quite unintended joke immediately emphasizes Stanley's racial background. In a country where, if one goes back far enough, everyone is an immigrant, dates of immigration can become marks of distinction. Blanche certainly thinks so: "Our first American ancestors were French Huguenots," she tells Mitch as a way to distinguish herself from more recent Italian, Irish, or Polish immigrants. And when, much later, she tells Stanley that she has dismissed Mitch, she uses similar terms: "Our ways of life are too different. Our attitudes and our backgrounds are incompatible. We have to be realistic about such things." "The Kowalskis and the DuBois have different notions," Stanley himself admits when he is quarreling with Stella in scene 2 over the Napoleonic code. Again, difference is the key word, and this difference, unlike Allan Grey's, is not one that censorship has so far sought to remove or dilute. When—as in the scene where Stanley, under cover provided by the noise of railway engines, overhears Blanche's denouncing him as an animal—this difference is linked with other disparagements, it becomes a powerful source of opposition and animosity. Its renewal on Stella's lips in the birthday scene—"Mr. Kowalski is too busy making a pig of himself to think of anything else!"—outrages Stanley because he fears that it shows Blanche's influence over her sister. It is this fear that prompts his furious response as he clears the table violently: "Don't ever talk that way to me! 'Pig—Polack—disgusting—vulgar—greasy!'—them kind of words have been on your tongue and your sister's too much around here!"

Later that same night Blanche revives many of these sensitive issues in her drunken conversation with Stanley in scene 10. "Does that mean we are to be alone in here?" she asks. Shep Huntleigh, a rich married man upon whom she has set her sights, will preserve her privacy, respects her, is a "gentleman":

> BLANCHE: But I have been foolish—casting my pearls before swine!
> STANLEY: Swine, huh!
> BLANCHE: Yes, swine! Swine! And I'm thinking not only of you but of your friend, Mr. Mitchell.

The table violently cleared in the earlier scene is equally violently overturned. Scenes 7 through 10 plot a single action: the outworkings of an explosive mixture of sexual attraction and class and social antagonism.

RURAL AND URBAN VALUES

Belle Reve (inaccurate French for "beautiful dream": perhaps a reminiscence of the Bellerive Country Club in St. Louis where Cornelius Williams was a member) is clearly a rural estate, a point that Williams emphasizes with a rather obvious piece of theatrical sign posting:

> STELLA: Stan, we've—lost Belle Reve!
> STANLEY: The place in the country?
> STELLA: Yes

And, as Blanche tells Mitch, her name means "white woods"; she is an orchard in springtime. By contrast, Mitch and Stanley belong to the city and to its industries: Mitch works "on the precision bench in the spare parts department. At the plant Stanley travels for." Moreover, Stella and Stanley live on a street named Elysian Fields, located between the river and a railway track. The noise of passing locomotives allows Stanley to approach and retreat without being discovered when he overhears Blanche's unflattering description of him, and the noise and lights of an engine punctuate Blanche's recollection of her husband's suicide.

PAST, PRESENT, AND FUTURE

Sweet Bird of Youth, perhaps Williams' last great play, ends with Chance Wayne—his youth behind him and soon to be robbed of his virility—"*rising and advancing to the forestage,*" facing the audience, and pleading for its recognition "of me in you, and the enemy, time, in us all." Time is an undeclared character in every play that Williams wrote. Time is always the villain; and it is time, as much as Stanley, that dominates the last part of *Streetcar*. This last point is very often missed: *Streetcar* begins in May but moves to "late afternoon in mid-September" in scene 7, where Stella (heavily pregnant and about to be taken into hospital) completes her preparations for Blanche's birthday party. Scene 8, where Blanche is dismissed by Stanley during the meal; scene 9, where she loses Mitch; and scene 10, where she is raped, follow rapidly on the same day ("three-quarters of an hour later," "a while later that evening," "a few hours later that night"). The play's final scene, set "some weeks later," combines two images: Blanche is taken away to a mental hospital (replaced by Stella, who is home from the hospital), and Stanley, Stella, and their baby form a group on the stairs in the porch as the curtain falls. The baby, handed to Stella by Eunice to complete the tableau, is a symbol of their life together both now and in the years to come. By contrast, Blanche's future is, as her present has been, no more than the ceaseless reliving of her past. The film's very different ending, in which Stanley's treatment of Blanche ensures that his marriage is over, was imposed upon Kazan by a fiercely moralistic censorship and never met with Williams' approval.

THEATRICALITY

"Chekhov! Chekhov! Chekhov!" was Williams' response when, in his *Paris Review* interview, he was asked to name his favorite playwright. He admired and was influenced by the musical composition of Anton Chekhov's plays: the way in which themes and moods are expressed and re-expressed in major and minor keys, in large actions and in tiny details. Moreover, many of Chekhov's plays are dominated by characters whose self-perception is intrinsically theatrical, whose awareness of their roles in life, and of those around them as the audience before whom they perform, is paramount. (Vanya in *Uncle Vanya*, 1896, is a very clear instance.) Because theater is a self-regarding and introverted art, images *of* the theater abound *in* the theater: self-reflecting images of this kind permeate and dominate Williams' plays. *Out Cry* (1973, known also as *The Two-Character Play*), one of his last and least successful experiments, takes this image to extremes. In the play two actors impersonate two characters who are themselves actors who impersonate characters in a two-character play. Setting his performance within a representation of performance forces an awareness of the play's meta-theatricality. Yet most of Williams' heroes and heroines are caught up in their own performance, though few are professional actors; it is a performance that is at once their refuge and a measure of their weakness.

Theatricality, the universal impulse toward self-dramatization, was a quality that Williams was especially acute at noticing in himself and in others. In "Person-to-Person," a short essay with which he prefaces *Cat on a Hot Tin Roof* (1958), he tells of meeting a group of very small girls, dolled up in cast-off clothing, imitating their elders in an impromptu performance staged on a Mississippi sidewalk. He says that one of the girls (he thinks her an image of the southern artist or of any kind of artist—or of Blanche DuBois, it could be said):

> was not satisfied with the attention paid her enraptured performance by the others, they were too involved in their own performances to suit her, so she stretched out her skinny arms and threw back her skinny neck and shrieked to the deaf heavens and her equally oblivious playmates, "Look at me, look at me, look at me!"

In almost every one of Williams' plays, wherever they are set, there is at least one prominent character. Often, indeed, the play's central character does not so much live life as perform it and attempts (more often than not, unsuccessfully) to transform other characters into feeds or fall-guys, stooges or spectators. A remarkably telling example of this habit occurs in a stage direction in scene 6 that tells us that Blanche, in the middle of a conversation with Mitch in which she has proclaimed her old-fashioned ideals, "rolls her eyes, knowing he cannot see her face." Thus, the real audience watches her appealing to an unreal audience, one that she has imaginatively summoned up to applaud her performance.

Blanche's sense of theater rebounds on her, with the direst consequences, in the second scene of *Streetcar*, when Stanley confronts her about the lavish clothing and jewelry that she has brought with her from Belle Reve. The scene is intensely theatrical, as Stanley hurls Blanche's "solid-gold dress," "genuine fox fur pieces," and "bracelets of solid gold" round the room, but also is an image of the theater itself. The furs are inexpensive, Stella says, the jewelry is paste, and the tiara is set with rhinestones ("next door to glass"). And this assessment is confirmed by a stage direction: Stanley "jerks open [a] small drawer in the trunk and pulls up a fist-full of costume jewelry." But because, in all productions save the most irresponsibly prodigal, costume jewelry substitutes for real jewelry on stage, nothing seen here directly contradicts the possibility that Stanley ignorantly entertains. Williams' stage direction settles for a reader an issue that a spectator must settle by other means. What does settle the matter is growing awareness of Blanche's own staginess. She almost instantly arouses this awareness when, after replying with a catty remark to Stanley's invoking of the Napoleonic code, she tries to turn him into a patsy by spraying him provocatively with her scent: "*She sprays herself with her atomizer;*

then playfully sprays him with it. He seizes the atomizer and slams it down on the dresser. She throws back her head and laughs." "Playfully" means flirtatiously or in jest, but it also means "as in a play" and adds to the theatrical heavy-handedness of a scene that would be merely heavy-handed were we not made aware of it by Blanche's continual overplaying of her role.

One does not have to wait even this short time to experience Blanche's characteristically theatrical way of talking. Her first speech to Stella reveals her habit of deliberately voicing her thoughts under cover of their having accidentally slipped out. (It is an awareness of this habit that fashions one's interpretation of her last words to Allan Grey.) She says: "I thought you would never come back to this horrible place! What am I saying? I didn't mean to say that. I meant to be nice about it and say—Oh, what a convenient location and such." This sets her up as a bit of an actress, graciously taking her audience backstage to reveal how the machinery works. She indicates ("Oh, what a convenient location and such.") those words that conventional politeness has set down for her to speak, but then she "pretends" to depart from her text and then "pretends" to apologize for the departure. The effect is meant to be charming and gracious but comes across as brittle. Her candor is similarly fragile. When she tells Stella not to worry about her ("your sister hasn't turned into a drunkard"), it is clear, not least because her drinking has already been revealed, that what she denies is precisely what is true. The words are doubtless meant to reassure Stella, though they may well alert her suspicions (and a competent actress could easily show this). But their chief and unavailing purpose is self-assurance.

This, too, is one of Blanche's characteristic linguistic habits; she self-destructively alerts suspicion in the act of attempting to allay it. So it is she who raises the issue of her dismissal from school ("You haven't asked me how I happened to get away from the school before the spring term ended"). It is she who excites suspicion by denying it ("You thought I'd been fired?"). And it is she who then pleads nervous delicacy as the real reason for her leaving. The point is that Blanche is not naturally a liar and, like a bad actor, is poor at deceiving others. Perhaps she is the only one gullible enough to be taken in by her embroidering of the truth whenever she is buoyed up by the exhilaration of her performance.

The question of Blanche's honesty or dishonesty is frequently raised throughout the play. When Blanche first meets Mitch, she plays on his (presumed) inexperience by deliberately lying about her age. But she does so with extraordinary clumsiness. What initiates the exchange is Mitch's simple question: "You are Stella's sister, are you not?" But perhaps this is not such a simple question after all: Blanche, rather like Williams himself, has been parading her grand ancestry, and Mitch's question might be interpreted as a slight rebuke. This interpretation explains the nervousness of her response: "Yes, Stella is my precious little sister. I call her little in spite of the fact she's somewhat older than I. Just slightly. Less than a year. Will you do something for me?" Blanche's dishonest qualification of "little" in her second sentence is damaged by the two further qualifications that she adds and by her diversionary question. One would need to be very artless indeed (perhaps that is why Blanche is fond of young men) to be taken in, and the clue lies not merely in her appearance but also in her manner of speaking. If Blanche is to be thought of as an actor, as many critics have suggested she should be, then one ought surely to comment on the poverty of her performance.

Scene 3 (two scenes from the beginning of the play) is echoed in scene 9 (two from its end), in which Blanche's hopes of marrying Mitch are permanently dashed. It is a scene that Williams has constructed with great skill. Blanche is sitting, a stage direction informs us, hunched in a "chair that she has recovered with diagonal green and white stripes," wearing her scarlet satin robe, when Mitch enters, wearing his working clothes. Attention to detail at this level is typical of Williams' imaginative eye: "When I write, everything is visual, as brilliantly as if it were on a lit stage," he told Rader in his 1981 interview. The contrast between their clothes, of course, matters: Mitch is entering, in Blanche's self-obsessed vision of the world, a regal presence; he does so as an inferior, and he bears a request. Blanche's regal self-imaging is more fully developed when she tells Mitch to get his feet off the bed—reasserting her authority where Mitch has been questioning it—and points to the general improvements in the room that she has effected. "Everything here isn't Stan's," the schoolteacher-queen says, muddling her grammar. ("Not everything here is Stan's" is the correct version. But Blanche's version, which logically equates with "Nothing in this room belongs to Stanley," much more aggressively, and a shade desperately, asserts her rights of ownership.) "Some things on the premises are actually mine!"—with its implication that her body is hers and Mitch can have what belongs to her—really serves to set up the rape scene that follows. For Stanley confirms, by taking her, that everything indeed "is Stan's." Ownership (what belongs to Stan and what does not belong to him) is important throughout this scene. When Blanche finds some Southern Comfort and flirtatiously pretends not to know what it is (though she has been drinking it for years), Mitch, upon whom her flirtatiousness is now lost, replies that not recognizing the bottle is proof that it "must belong to Stan."

Alerted to her true age and her predatory and promiscuous past, Mitch says that she is incapable of telling the truth: "Lies, lies, inside and out, all lies." Her response is characteristic: she is like a good actor, though she does not make this image explicit. Actors, whose art is pretence, have from ancient times been accused of lying. But, though reviled as liars, actors also have been revered as truth-bearers: it is this more approving aspect of their work with which Blanche identifies herself when she asserts that she is uncorrupted at the core. ("Never inside," she says, "I didn't lie in my heart.") This is part of her larger defense of the theater of her own life. Goaded by Mitch's insistence that he wants to make a realistic assessment of her, she replies: "I don't want realism. I want magic! . . . I try to give that to people. I misrepresent things to them. I don't tell truth, I tell what *ought* to be truth. And if that is sinful, then let me be damned for it!"

She then implores Mitch to leave her in the protective and carefully controlled semidarkness that she has created, to preserve (as Mitch judges matters) her lies about her age and (as she judges them) the magic that is imaginative truthfulness. Mitch angrily ignores her request, tears down the Chinese shade, and for the first time in the play—freed from the seductive glow of her own lighting plan—sees her as she really is. It is this moment that is cruelly echoed "some weeks later," when Stanley, furious that Blanche will not leave the house meekly, "seizes the paper lantern, tearing it off the light bulb, and extends it toward her." Her self-image violated, she enters the next phase of her mental collapse.

This aspect of Blanche—actor, hypocrite, and fraud—is dwelt on powerfully in the rape scene. By this time, reacting badly to her loss of Mitch, Blanche is well on in drink and wears, appropriately enough, a "soiled and crumpled" satin evening gown (an image of her moral state) and a fake tiara. Stung into reprisal by her renewal of an earlier insult, Stanley accuses her of imagination, a compound of "lies and conceit and tricks." What he describes and dismisses is the magic of the theater: "You come in here and sprinkle the place with powder and spray perfume and cover the light-bulb with a paper lantern, and lo and behold the place has turned into Egypt and you are the Queen of the Nile!" Surely what Stanley has in mind (or, if not Stanley, then Williams) is not merely Cleopatra but specifically Shakespeare's great vision of her in *Antony and Cleopatra*: seated at her dressing-table preparing for her final performance and calling imperiously for her robes, her crown, and her basket of snakes.

The lush Shakespearean ending is not entirely inappropriate. Octavius Caesar announces at the end of *Antony and Cleopatra* that Cleopatra's physician has told him that she has "pursued conclusions infinite / Of easy ways to die." None quite so easy, however, as the one that Blanche imagines for herself: an unwashed grape, an unstoppable fever, a handsome young doctor ("a very young one"), dropping in a pure white wrap into the waters of an ocean "as blue as . . . my first lover's eyes!" But this Cleopatra is virginal:

EUNICE: What a pretty blue jacket.

STELLA: It's lilac colored.

BLANCHE: You're both mistaken. It's Della Robbia blue. The blue of the robe in the old Madonna pictures. Are these grapes washed?

Surely the end of the play suggests that Blanche is going to yet another place where she can fabricate a world out of her imagination or, for those who reject her magic, out of lies and conceit and tricks.

Select Bibliography

EDITIONS

A Streetcar Named Desire: A Play. London: John Lehmann, 1949.

A Streetcar Named Desire. New York: Dramatists Play Service, 1953. (This acting edition records the state of the text that was used in Kazan's 1947 production.)

A Streetcar Named Desire and Other Plays. Edited by E. Martin Browne. Harmondsworth, Eng.: Penguin Books, 1962. (Includes *The Glass Menagerie* and *Sweet Bird of Youth.* This is the text that most British productions follow.)

A Streetcar Named Desire. In *The Theatre of Tennessee Williams.* 8 vols. New York: New Directions, 1971–1992. (Quotations from Williams' plays, unless noted otherwise, are drawn from this volume.)

A Streetcar Named Desire. Edited by Patricia Hern, London: Methuen, 1984. (Reproduces the Penguin text.)

OTHER WORKS BY WILLIAMS

The Theatre of Tennessee Williams. 8 vols. New York: New Directions, 1971–1992. (Includes *The Glass Menagerie, Orpheus Descending, Suddenly Last Summer, Sweet Bird of Youth, The Night of the Iguana, Small Craft Warnings, The Two-Character Play, I Rise in Flame, Cried the Phoenix,* and *Vieux Carré.*)

Memoirs. Garden City, N.Y.: Doubleday, 1975; London: W. H. Allen, 1976; paperback reprint, 1977.

Five O'Clock Angel: Letters of Tennessee Williams to Maria St. Just, 1948–1982. Edited by Maria St. Just. New York: Knopf, 1990.

The Selected Letters of Tennessee Williams, 1920–1945. Edited by Albert J. Devlin and Nancy M. Tischler. New York: New Directions, 2000.

SECONDARY SOURCES

Arnott, Catherine M. *Tennessee Williams on File.* London: Methuen, 1985.

Barranger, Milly S. "New Orleans as Theatrical Image in Plays by Tennessee Williams." *Southern Quarterly* 23 (winter 1985): 38–54.

Behlmer, Rudy. *Behind the Scenes.* New York: Samuel French, 1990.

Berkowitz, Gerald M. *American Drama of the Twentieth Century.* London: Longman, 1992.

Bigsby, C. W. E. *Modern American Drama, 1945–1990.* Cambridge: Cambridge University Press, 1992.

Black, Gregory D. *The Catholic Crusade against the Movies, 1940–1975.* Cambridge: Cambridge University Press, 1998.

Bourne, Bette (with Paul Shaw, Peggy Shaw, and Lois Weaver). *Belle Reprieve.* In *Split Britches: Lesbian Practice/Feminist Performance.* Edited by Sue-Ellen Case. New York: Routledge, 1996. Pp. 149–183. (Originally staged at The Drill Hall Arts Centre in London in January 1991.)

Clum, John M. *Still Acting Gay: Male Homosexuality in Modern Drama.* New York: St. Martin's, 2000.

Devlin, Albert J., ed. *Conversations with Tennessee Williams.* Jackson: University Press of Mississippi, 1986.

Eyre, Richard, and Nicholas Wright. *Changing Stages: A View of British and American Theatre in the Twentieth Century.* New York: Knopf, 2001.

Fleche, Anne. *Mimetic Disillusion: Eugene O'Neill, Tennessee Williams, and U.S. Dramatic Realism.* Tuscaloosa: University of Alabama Press, 1997.

Garber, Marjorie. *Vice Versa: Bisexuality and the Eroticism of Everyday Life.* New York: Routledge, 2000.

Hayman, Ronald. *Tennessee Williams: Everyone Else Is an Audience.* New Haven: Yale University Press, 1993.

Hulley, Kathleen. "The Fate of the Symbolic in *A Streetcar Named Desire.*" In *Themes in Drama.* Vol. 4, *Drama and Symbolism.* Edited by James Redmond. Cambridge: Cambridge University Press, 1982. Pp. 88–99.

Israel, Lee. *Miss Tallulah Bankhead.* New York: Putnam, 1972.

Jennings, Robert C. "Interview with Tennessee Williams." *Playboy,* April 1973, p. 72.

Kazan, Elia. "Notebook for *A Streetcar Named Desire.*" In *Directors on Directing: A Source Book of the Modern Theater.* Edited by Toby Cole and Helen Krich Chinoy. Indianapolis: Bobbs-Merrill, 1963.

———. *Elia Kazan: A Life.* New York: Knopf, 1988.

Kolin, Philip C., ed. *Confronting Tennessee Williams' "A Streetcar Named Desire": Essays in Critical Pluralism.* Westport, Conn.: Greenwood Press, 1993.

———. *Williams:* A Streetcar Named Desire. Cambridge: Cambridge University Press, 2000.

Lant, Kathleen Margaret. "A Streetcar Named Misogyny." In *Themes in Drama.* Vol. 13, *Violence in Drama.* Edited by James Redmond. Cambridge: Cambridge University Press, 1991. Pp. 225–238.

Leverich, Lyle. *Tom: The Unknown Tennessee Williams.* London: Hodder and Stoughton, 1995; New York: Crown, 1995.

Mamet, David. "Epitaph for Tennessee Williams." In his *A Whore's Profession: Notes and Essays.* London: Faber and Faber, 1994.

McDonough, Carla J. *Staging Masculinity: Male Identity in Contemporary American Drama.* Jefferson, N.C.: McFarland, 1997.

Miller, Arthur. "Tennessee Williams' Legacy: An Eloquence and Amplitude of Feeling." In *Echoes Down the Corridor: Collected Essays 1947–1999.* Edited by Steven R. Centola. New York: Viking, 2000.

Murphy, Brenda. *Tennessee Williams and Elia Kazan: A Collaboration in the Theatre.* Cambridge: Cambridge University Press, 1992.

Rader, Dotson. *Tennessee Williams: An Intimate Memoir.* London: Grafton Books, 1986.

———. "Tennessee Williams: The Art of Theater V." *Paris Review* 81 (fall 1981): 145–185. Reprinted in *Playwrights at Work: The Paris Review.* Edited by George Plimpton. New York: Modern Library, 2000.

Rasky, Harry. *Tennessee Williams: A Portrait in Laughter and Lamentation.* New York: Dodd Mead, 1986.

Roudane, Matthew C., ed. *The Cambridge Companion to Tennessee Williams.* Cambridge: Cambridge University Press, 1997.

Savran, David. *Communists, Cowboys and Queers: The Politics of Masculinity in the Work of Arthur Miller and Tennessee Williams.* Minneapolis: University of Minnesota Press, 1992.

Sinfield, Alan. "Reading Tennessee Williams." In his *Out on Stage: Lesbian and Gay Theatre in the Twentieth Century.* New Haven: Yale University Press, 1999. Pp. 186–207.

Spoto, Donald. *The Kindness of Strangers: The Life of Tennessee Williams.* London: Bodley Head, 1985.

Stuart, Roxana. "The Southernmost DESIRE." *Tennessee Williams Newsletter* 1, no. 2 (fall 1979): 3–7, and 2, no. 1 (spring 1980): 5–10.

Tharpe, Jac, ed. *Tennessee Williams: A Tribute.* Jackson: University Press of Mississippi, 1977.

Williams, Dakin, and Shepherd Mead. *Tennessee Williams: An Intimate Biography.* New York: Arbor House, 1983.

Williams, Edwina Dakin, and Lucy Freeman. *Remember Me to Tom.* New York: Putnam, 1963.

Wilmeth, Don B., and Tice L. Miller, eds. *Cambridge Guide to American Theatre.* Cambridge: Cambridge University Press, 1993.

Windham, Donald. *Lost Friendships: A Memoir of Truman Capote, Tennessee Williams, and Others.* New York: Morrow, 1987.

Yacowar, Maurice. *Tennessee Williams and Film.* New York: Frederick Ungar, 1977.

Ernest Hemingway's
The Sun Also Rises

STEPHEN AMIDON

HE SUN ALSO Rises is Ernest Hemingway's first serious novel, written while the author was still in his mid-twenties. It is widely deemed to be his best. Published before Hemingway's lifestyle and literary technique became the stuff of legend, it struck contemporary readers and critics with a directness of voice and subtlety of vision that placed the author at the forefront of his literary generation. Readers coming to the book for the first time continue to be impressed by these qualities. Along with F. Scott Fitzgerald's *Great Gatsby* (1925), Hemingway's novel provides the definitive fictional portrait of the "lost generation" of young people coming of age after the catastrophic events of the World War I. It also represents a watershed in the way Americans write fiction. The author's spare, evocative style was to exert a powerful influence on the evolution of American writing in the twentieth century.

Hemingway's two epigraphs provide the most immediate points of entry into the fictional landscape of *The Sun Also Rises*. The first famously quotes Hemingway's friend and mentor Gertrude Stein in conversation—"You are all a lost generation." Although Hemingway later downplayed the importance of this statement, there is no doubt that as he wrote and published his first novel, he was intent on capturing the malaise and anguish created by the general slaughter of World War I. (In its early stages, the book was actually titled "The Lost Generation.") The story, based upon Hemingway's own summertime journeys to Spain with a group of Paris-based American and English expatriates, strives to capture the chaotic reality of its era. Although the Great War is rarely discussed and never depicted at all in the course of the book, its effects on the generation represented by the novel's characters are acute. From Jake Barnes's battlefield wound, which renders him impotent, to Mike Campbell's alcoholism and Lady Brett Ashley's emotional paralysis, most of the central characters suffer from war traumas that are all the deeper for their initial invisibility. As the prostitute Georgette remarks during her brief appearance in the third chapter, "Everybody's sick." The world Hemingway depicts is one in which the values of patriotism, romantic love, traditional religion, and faith in the future have been swept away by the unimaginable butchery of the trenches. His traveling band of writers, drunks, and dilettantes have no real connection to the communities they fleetingly inhabit, whether it is hectic nighttime Paris or the equally fervid atmosphere of Pamplona during a bullfighting fiesta. They truly are a lost generation.

Hemingway provided a balance to this pessimistic view of his generation in the novel's second epigraph, which is taken from Ecclesiastes and gives the novel its title.

> One generation passeth away, and another generation cometh; but the earth abideth forever . . . The sun also riseth, and the sun goeth down, and hasteth to the place where he arose . . . The wind goeth toward the south, and turneth about unto the north; it whirleth about continually, and the wind returneth again according to his circuits. . . . All the rivers run into the sea; yet the sea is not full; unto the place from whence the rivers come, thither they return again.

While much of *The Sun Also Rises* presents the author's vision of a society in a state of rapid disintegration, Hemingway also suggests with this citation that there are enduring values that will survive this period of decay, a moral order located in the earth itself, in its seasons and immutable laws. The sun, the winds, and the earth's waters will continue their inexorable progress no matter what triumph or disaster befalls the human race, even if it is a catastrophe on the level of world war. This vision is represented most explicitly in the fishing trip Jake and his friend Bill Gorton take to the Spanish town of Burguete and the nearby Irati River in chapters 11 and 12. This location of wild beauty provides a respite from the chaos and nihilism of the novel's two cities, Paris and Pamplona. Here the novel's troubled hero finds an interval of peace, drawing strength and meaning from the earth that is denied him by the fractured human communities he briefly inhabits.

Thus, even before its opening sentence, it is clear that Hemingway's novel is located in two worlds. The first is represented by the modern city, a decadent place of lost men and woman, where drunkenness and promiscuity are frantically indulged as a means to chase away the ter-

CHRONOLOGY

1899	Hemingway is born on July 21 in Oak Park, Illinois.
1917	Graduates from high school and begins work as a reporter for the *Kansas City Star.*
1918	Enlists in the American Red Cross ambulance service in Italy during World War I and is badly wounded.
1921	Marries Elizabeth Hadley Richardson. Returns with her to Europe as a foreign correspondent for the *Toronto Star* and settles in Paris.
1926	*The Sun Also Rises* is published.
1927	Hemingway divorces Hadley and marries Pauline Pfeiffer, a wealthy American heiress.
1928	Leaves Paris to return to the United States. Takes up residence in Key West, Florida.
1929	Publishes *A Farewell to Arms,* the best-selling novel based on his experiences in wartime Italy.
1937	Covers the Spanish Civil War as a journalist.
1939	Hemingway divorces Pauline Pfeiffer.
1940	Publishes *For Whom the Bell Tolls,* based upon his experience during the Spanish Civil War. Moves to Cuba and marries the writer and journalist Martha Gellhorn.
1942–1945	Serves as war correspondent in Europe for a variety of newspapers and magazines.
1945	Divorces Martha Gellhorn to marry Mary Welsh.
1952	*The Old Man and the Sea* published in *Life* magazine. Hemingway is awarded the Pulitzer Prize.
1954	Awarded Nobel Prize for literature.
1961	After a period of intense depression, Hemingway commits suicide in Ketchum, Idaho, on July 2.

rible nothingness left by war. The second is the natural earth, a place of timeless tranquility that cannot be affected by mankind's vicissitudes. It is only when characters escape the former and connect to the latter that there can be peace.

THE CODE

The Sun Also Rises marks the first coherent appearance of Hemingway's famous "code," the loose set of rules he devised to govern proper conduct in a hostile and meaningless world. The code allows Hemingway's characters to live without romantic illusions but still maintain a sense of honor in a world ruled by "nada," or nothingness. Because traditional systems of value no longer hold sway in the author's view, it is up to each individual character to decide how he or she is going to live. Although Hemingway's overriding interest in outdoor sports, rugged contests, and war occasionally is portrayed as a sign of his artistic (and personal) immaturity, he in fact employed these devices in his fiction as a means of dramatically representing his code of heroic conduct. Life is a game, a contest that easily can turn deadly. Winning does not matter, since death makes losers of us all in the end. (Indeed, Hemingway was to name a subsequent book of short stories *Winner Take Nothing.*) But a person can still achieve honor and dignity in the face of his inevitable defeat. It is all in how the game is played, how much authenticity and risk the player brings to the contest.

A hunter who shoots his prey from the safety of a helicopter, for instance, is grossly violating the code. He may succeed in killing his target, but he squanders his dignity in the process. According to Hemingway, a person must place himself in some sort of jeopardy if he is to experience the hunt—or any aspect of life—with authenticity. He must risk something of himself, whether it is bodily harm or emotional exposure. And the code hero also must be careful not to impose any false or romantic ideals on the contest. One does not win salvation, happiness, or eternal life by playing the game well. The only prize is a sense of honor. While some critics are quick to condemn this system as little more than a glorified recasting of the laws of the playground, it is clear that Hemingway intended it to symbolize the proper means of living with dignity and full involvement in a world whose traditions and regulations have been blasted by war and atheism.

In *The Sun Also Rises*, the Hemingway code is best personified by the brilliant young matador Pedro Romero. He is, in fact, Hemingway's first true code hero, prefiguring the stoical bridge blower Robert Jordan in *For Whom the Bell Tolls* (1940) and the aging fisherman Santiago in *The Old Man and the Sea* (1952). Romero comes to epitomize the author's belief that true heroism manifests itself by the quality of "grace under pressure." When facing a charging bull, the novel's narrator Jake Barnes reports in chapter 15,

> Romero never made any contortions, always it was straight and pure and natural in line. . . . Romero's bull-fighting gave real emotion, because he kept the absolute purity of line in his movements and always quietly and calmly let the horns pass him close each time. . . . Romero had the old thing, the holding of his purity of line through the maximum of exposure, while he dominated the bull by making him realize he was unattainable, while he prepared him for the killing.

Romero not only performs with a maximum of skill but also puts himself in a position of utmost danger while in the ring. Although he experiences this extreme stress, he never displays the fear he must certainly be feeling. His bullfighting involves "no tricks and no mystifications." He stands above his aging rival, Belmonte, who introduces an element of the fake into his work by making sure the bulls that he fights are not too large or sharp-horned. Like the hunter who shoots from the helicopter, Belmonte violates the code by removing the element of danger, thereby denying himself full involvement in his contest.

Among the novel's central characters, it is Robert Cohn who stands in the starkest contrast to Romero. Although he is a former collegiate boxing champion who does not hesitate to use his fists to settle what he perceives to be matters of honor, Cohn's code is false because it is fundamentally romantic, based on the illusion that a love affair with the attractive but emotionally crippled Brett is possible. The true code hero accepts the world as it is and tries to live in it with as much dignity as possible; Cohn violates the code and abases himself by trying to live in an idealized, prettified world. This can be seen, in chapter 2, by his enthusiasm for the novel *The Purple Land*, a book that Jake is horrified to discover Cohn takes literally:

> "The Purple Land" is a very sinister book if read too late in life. It recounts splendid imaginary amorous adventures of a perfect English gentleman in an intensely romantic land. . . . For a man to take it at thirty-four as a guide-book to what life holds is about as safe as it would be for a man of the same age to enter Wall Street direct from a French convent.

Another writer, Harvey Stone, refers to Cohn as "a case of arrested development." Cohn does not derive his dignity from the struggles the world presents him but rather strives to achieve an honor that does not exist. While Romero enters into a very real fight against very dangerous animals, Cohn is only "ready to do battle for his lady love," an illusory ideal, since this particular lady has no interest in him after their brief fling in San Sebastian. Even though Cohn is able to pummel Romero in the bedroom fight he provokes to win back Brett's nonexistent love, he ultimately is defeated by Romero, who refuses to give in to his hysterical bullying. Cohn might gain a surface victory over Romero with his fists, but the matador comprehensively vanquishes him by his refusal to surrender, leaving Cohn a blubbering and pitiable wreck. "He ruined Cohn," Mike reports. There is no grace in Cohn's behavior, nor is there any acknowledgement of the reality with which he is faced—

that Brett does not love him. Romero's strength, built upon a sense of self and a purpose that is grounded firmly in reality, ultimately defeats Cohn's self-deluding romanticism.

Jake finds himself caught between the opposing codes represented by these two characters. He spends a considerable portion of the novel in a state of acute confusion about how to act in an incoherent world that has left him mutilated but has not taken away his need for sexual contact. At first (in chapter 4), he finds the pressures of this contradiction almost unbearable:

> This was Brett, that I had felt like crying about. Then I thought of her walking up the street and stepping into the car, as I had last seen her, and of course in a little while I felt like hell again. It is awfully easy to be hard-boiled about everything in the daytime, but at night it is another thing.

He badly needs a code that will teach him how to be "hard-boiled" about his fate. Since this is Hemingway's fictional world, he must develop one of his own. Religion, psychology, and philosophy are not going to provide him with any consolation, as comically demonstrated when an Italian general searches in vain for the right words to comfort Jake on his loss. "What a speech!" Jake remarks. "I would like to have it illuminated to hang in the office. He never laughed." Fine speeches, public honors, and therapeutic sessions have nothing for Jake. He must figure out how to live with his wound in a world that will show him no pity. "All I wanted to know was how to live in it," he explains. "Maybe if you found out how to live in it you learned from that what it was all about." Although he is not able to be a code hero through action like Romero, he is a student of the code and eventually learns how to act by watching the young matador at work. Jake is an aficionado, someone who possesses a passionate appreciation for the "grace under pressure" represented by Romero in the bullring. "Aficion means passion. An aficionado is one who is passionate about the bull-fights." His mentor in this tutelage is the hotel owner Montoya, who recognizes in Jake someone who is on the verge of learning how to conduct himself with dignity.

This passion for bullfighting comes to represent Hemingway's code in the novel. As Jake says early in the narrative: "Nobody ever lives their life all the way up except bull-fighters." It is not courage or success in the ring that counts, nor is it how many bulls one kills or how much fame one accrues in the process. In fact, these things do not really matter. "Montoya could forgive anything of a bull-fighter who had afición. He could forgive attacks of nerves, panic, bad unexplainable actions, all sorts of lapses." The only thing that cannot be forgiven is to deny the afición, the passion for living life all the way, for a less worthy, a less real, goal.

This is precisely what Jake does by helping Brett when she sets her sights on Romero. He forgets his afición by indulging an illusory passion for an unattainable woman. By bringing Brett and Romero together—pimping for them, as Cohn harshly but accurately points out—he introduces an element into the bullfighter's world that threatens to undermine Romero's strength and dignity. Although there has been considerable debate over Jake's motivation for this act of weakness, there can be little doubt that it stems from his frustration over his inability to serve as Brett's lover. Because he does not have the grace and the courage to accept the impotence caused by his meaningless and patently unfair maiming, he tries to please Brett by handing her the man she wants. He also seeks to undermine Romero by introducing him to Brett, who is capable of doing more damage to the naive bullfighter than the most savage animal.

Jake's act is a petty violation of the code, one for which he is punished by Montoya, who will no longer acknowledge Jake as a friend and apprentice after he sees Romero and Brett together. Jake recovers from this violation of the code only when, at the novel's end, he tells Brett that the possibility of an affair with her is nothing more than a "pretty" illusion. He has come to accept his cruel fate with stoical resignation. The student has finally learned how to live by the code. He has become "hard-boiled," an achievement Hemingway acknowledges when he has Jake eat hard-boiled eggs during his fishing trip to Burguete. Unlike Cohn, he accepts the limitations the world has imposed upon him; he understands that many things will now be denied him and that he must learn to appreciate that which remains. At long last, he knows how to live in the world.

LOVE, SEX, AND FRIENDSHIP

The Sun Also Rises provides a darkly pessimistic view of the traditional concept of romantic love. The roster of relationships in the book is one of almost unrelieved unhappiness and loss. Romantic love does not provide solace or tranquility, but rather their opposites, driving each of the main characters into periods of anguish and emotional disruption. Some of the relationships have been ruined by the war. Although there appears to be real affection between Brett and Jake, the love affair both fantasize about is prevented by his impotence and her wayward sexual appetites. Although Brett and Mike Campbell are engaged, there is no optimism or joy in the prospect of their wedding. "He's so damned nice and he's so awful," she claims. "He's my sort of thing." Both are emotional cripples. Brett has been ruined by a disastrous marriage to a war veteran, while Mike's wartime service has left him a bankrupt drunk who has no authority to put an end to Brett's sexual adventures. The best they can hope for is an uneasy, tumultuous alliance.

It is not just the war that has left Hemingway's characters emotionally devastated, however. Robert Cohn's immature romanticism renders him unable to conduct a love affair with Brett, and he also is involved in futile relationship with an older woman, Frances. Although their relationship had at first been one of travel and carefree expatriation, after two years she finds that her "looks were going, and her attitude toward Robert changed from one of careless possession and exploitation to the absolute determination that he should marry her." Cohn escapes her by effectively paying her off with two hundred pounds so that she can go visit friends while he pursues Brett.

Another damaging instance of sexual love in the book is the affair between Brett and Romero. From the outset, the Englishwoman is viewed as potentially ruinous to the young matador. Robert Cohn at one point refers to her as Circe, the mythological enchantress who turns men to swine, and this indeed appears to be her role throughout much of the novel. She torments Mike with her infidelities and tortures Cohn with her refusal to view their affair in San Sebastian as anything more than a brief, meaningless fling. And while she appears to have real affection for Jake, the torment she puts him through is abundantly clear—in Paris he breaks down in tears at the thought of his feelings for her, while in Pamplona he winds up being beaten unconscious by Cohn in a fight over her. But it is with Romero that Brett's sexuality proves most threatening. Romero's supporters, most notably the hotel owner Montoya, clearly see her as being a more menacing prospect than the bulls he must face, a perception that comes true when Romero is badly wounded not by an animal but by Brett's jilted lover. He then runs off to Madrid with her, leaving behind his support network of family and friends and placing his promising career in grave jeopardy. It is only when Brett decides that she is "not going to be one of these bitches that ruins children" and sends Romero away that he is saved from destruction.

Despite the path of erotic devastation she cuts through the novel, Brett Ashley remains a complex and ultimately sympathetic woman. While there is ample evidence of her strong attractiveness to the opposite sex, Hemingway is also at pains to show that there is something unfeminine about her. When demanding a drink, she jokingly refers to herself as one of the guys—"I say, give a chap a brandy and soda." Her "hair was brushed back like a boy's." Running beneath this masculine hardness is a contradictory feminine tenderness. Her very different feelings of affection for Jake, Mike, and even Cohn share a strong streak of maternal pity. She meets Jake while nursing him as he is recuperating from his wounds. Mike claims that "she loves looking after people. That's how we came to go off together. She was looking after me." She sleeps with Cohn, meanwhile, because she thinks it will do him good. It is with Romero that her nurturing female side looks ready to overcome the acquisitive male one. Romero seeks to feminize her, requesting that she grow her hair longer so she will look more "womanly." But she cannot bring herself to do it. "Me, with long hair. I'd look so like hell." Just as the sexually ruined Jake can truly be himself only by giving up the idea of a love affair with Brett, so she cannot escape the fact that she is too damaged to play a role that is beyond her. She knows that if she were to become Romero's passive feminine lover, it would mean ruin for them both. In a novel that takes a thoroughly cynical view of the possibility of healthy romantic love, it is perhaps inevitable that Lady Brett can achieve a measure of dignity and compassion only through an act of renunciation.

Hemingway's cynical view of sexual relationships is balanced at least in part by the possibility of friendship put forward in the novel, especially among men. The shared aficion for bullfighting between Jake and Montoya provides an instance of authentic communion. The novel's most rewarding interval of human contact, however, occurs when Jake and his old friend Bill Gorton flee the sterile urban rancor of Paris and Pamplona on a fishing trip to the Spanish countryside. There, the men are able to fish and drink without the invasive presence of women. Although there is much ironic banter between them, real feeling and compassion are communicated through silence or tersely eloquent phrases such as Bill's "This is country" as the men approach the wild and beautiful Irati River. The sexual obsession and sentimentality that mar the atmosphere in the novel's two cities are replaced by emotions that are simple, true, and deep. When they are joined by the Englishman Harris, the atmosphere only improves, with Harris finding joy and solace in his brief spell of companionship with the other two men. "I say. Really you don't know how much it means. I've not had much fun since the war." It is interesting to note that Harris equates their woman-less idyll with another activity that did not involve the opposite sex—battle. Hemingway was to follow *The Sun Also Rises* with a short-story collection called *Men Without Women*, which also might have served as a fitting title for the single interlude in the novel where human relationships are free of the poison that afflicts them throughout the remainder of the narrative.

VALUE

Running through *The Sun Also Rises* is a complex and subtle examination of the concept of value. From the first, Jake strives to figure out what he truly values and what he must give up to get those objects that are dear to him. He is a man who wants to know the price of things. On a surface level, this means that he is constantly concerned with getting his money's worth. He is forever tallying restaurant bills, balancing his bank account, bargaining with drivers over fares, arguing about who picks up the tab after a night on the town. Of his Parisian gang, he is the only one who appears to be working regularly, a fact he clearly enjoys. "All along people were going to work. It felt pleasant to be going to work." Unlike Mike, the undischarged bankrupt; or Brett, who usually relies on men to foot the bill; or even Cohn, who inherits his money, Jake is clearly a person who likes to pay his own way.

Jake's concern with money and paying one's own way are Hemingway's sly method of introducing the notion of value into his novel.

Indeed, the author constantly uses minor, seemingly meaningless financial exchanges to remind us that this is a book about how people are forced to pay the price for what they want. For instance, the author uses a humorous scene where Bill Gorton drunkenly discourses on the notion of buying a stuffed dog from a Parisian taxidermist to provide a gloss on his theme of value. "Simple exchange of values. You give them money. They give you a stuffed dog." In other words, you get what you pay for, whether it is from a street vendor or a lover. Jake's ironic ruminations on France, in chapter 19, expand on the notion of value:

> It felt comfortable to be in a country where it is so simple to make people happy. You can never tell whether a Spanish waiter will thank you. Everything is on such a clear financial basis in France. It is the simplest country to live in. No one makes things complicated by becoming your friend for any obscure reason. If you want people to like you you have only to spend a little money.

Value also is embodied in the rotund form of Count Mippipopolous, the veteran hedonist who explains to Jake that the key to living well is that "you must get to know the values." The count is a man who does not fool himself about what it takes to get the things he wants. Realizing that Brett is incapable of carrying on a serious relationship, he can offer her ten thousand dollars to go to Biarritz without seeing it as insulting or degrading. He has come to learn that everything in life has its price, whether fiscal or emotional, and the trick is to figure out exactly what that cost is. A man of the world in every sense, he is without illusions about the price of what he wants, from the best champagne to the most beautiful women. Once again, Cohn provides a rather pathetic contrast. He thinks that a brief fling with Brett entitles him to her lasting affection, that serving as her lover for a few nights "buys" her everlasting passion and devotion. Brett is clearly a woman who is valued by many men, but Cohn believes he can pick her up on the cheap. Unlike the count, he is a man who does not know the price of things.

At first, Jake is uncertain about the proper exchange of values within his emotional entanglements, particularly with the woman he loves. As he describes it in chapter 14:

> I had been having Brett for a friend. I had not been thinking about her side of it. I had been getting something for nothing. That only delayed the presentation of the bill. The bill always came. That was one of the swell things you could count on
>
> I thought I had paid for everything. Not like the woman pays and pays and pays. No idea of retribution or punishment. Just exchange of values.

In other words, the impotent Jake has been trying to enjoy the benefits of a love affair with Brett without being able to give her back anything in return. It is not a fair exchange. He is not giving Brett enough of himself that is of value to her to get what he wants. But this does not mean that he is not paying the price in another way. By trying to get something for nothing, Jake instead is paying with the spiritual anguish that leads him first to cry himself to sleep and later to betray his aficion for Romero's bullfighting when he introduces him to Brett. She also comes to understand this notion of exchange. "Don't we pay for all the things we do, though?" she asks Jake at one point. And then: "When I think of the hell I've put chaps through. I'm paying for it all now." Even as she continues to engage in hollow flings with men, she understands that by not investing herself emotionally she is running up a psychic debt that eventually will come due—with a vengeance.

It is once again left for Romero to show the others the proper values. As the man who risks death in the bullring on a regular basis, he proves himself willing to pay the ultimate price to appreciate life. He is willing to trade his life for the chance to experience the excitement, honor, and heroism of the bullfight. This understanding of value spills over into his dealings with others.

When he first meets Brett, their relationship proves to be finely balanced, a fair emotional exchange. This is evidenced in the scene in chapter 18 where the matador performs for her in the bullring:

> Because he did not look up to ask if it pleased he did it all for himself inside, and it strengthened him, and yet he did it for her, too. But he did not do it for her at any loss to himself. He gained by it all through the afternoon.

Unlike Jake, Romero is able to give Brett the thrill of his masculinity without sacrificing anything, while she is able to return her admiration without stealing away his strength. Both gain. It is an exchange that will become skewered later, when Brett and Romero run off together. By pursuing Brett, Romero puts himself in the position of losing his currency—his professional strength. If this happens, he will have nothing to give her. The simple exchange of values evident in the bullring scene will become skewered. To her credit, this is something that Brett senses when she sends him away. She no longer wants to be the sort of woman who ruins men by taking things from them without giving anything back.

Like Brett, Jake also learns his lesson about true value. He comes to realize that he has been trading unfairly with Brett—and himself—over his feelings for her. What he must pay, or give up, is the illusion that he and Brett can ever have a meaningful romantic relationship. This is the price of being with her, as he says in chapter 14:

> You gave up something and got something else. Or you worked for something. You paid some way for everything that was any good. I paid my way into enough things that I liked, so that I had a good time. Either you paid by learning about them, or by experience, or by taking chances, or by money. Enjoying living was learning to get your money's worth and knowing when you had it. You could get your money's worth. The world was a good place to buy in.

After Jake has paid his dues, he is able to achieve a serenity and a dignity that were lacking in his behavior during the festival.

STYLE

The Sun Also Rises is justifiably famous for its style. At the time of the book's initial publication, Hemingway's prose struck many critics as something almost entirely unprecedented. To many of his contemporaries, his style constituted a radical break with immediate predecessors, such as Theodore Dreiser, Sinclair Lewis, and Sherwood Anderson. Hemingway, quite simply, wrote in a way no one before him ever had. As Carlos Baker points out in his definitive biography of Hemingway, "To a considerable extent he would have to create the taste by which his stories would eventually be judged." While the elements of the Hemingway style were expanded and formalized in his later writing, they were never to seem as startling or fresh as they do in the pages of his first serious novel.

Hemingway's prose was honed by his work as a journalist, a career begun while he was still in his teens. In the years leading up to the writing of *The Sun Also Rises,* he was, like Jake Barnes, a hard-working and conscientious foreign correspondent. The terse, succinct requirements of this sort of writing came to be known as "cablese," from the telegraphic cables reporters sent back to their papers. It was a style in which brevity and concision were core virtues, especially when the text was being sent at considerable cost and difficulty across the Atlantic. Simple, declarative sentences, rife with nouns and active verbs, were the bedrock of his style; adverbs, adjectives, and any sort of metaphorical flourish were considered anathema. As Hemingway was to claim in his posthumously published memoir of his Paris years, *A Moveable Feast,* he was forever searching for the "true simple declarative sentence." Indeed, the novel's opening line provides a clear

sense of what is to come, both in *The Sun Also Rises* and Hemingway's subsequent career. "Robert Cohn was once middleweight boxing champion of Princeton." This coolly factual sentence might just as easily have begun a newspaper feature (or an obituary, for that matter). This directness and simplicity continue throughout the book. The description of the scene in chapter 18 where Romero kills a bull in the ring is almost photographic in its exactitude.

> Out in the centre of the ring Romero profiled in front of the bull, drew the sword out from the folds of the muleta, rose on his toes, and sighted along the blade. The bull charged as Romero charged. Romero's left hand dropped the muleta over the bull's muzzle to blind him, his left shoulder went forward between the horns as the sword went in, and for just an instant he and the bull were one, Romero way out over the bull, the right arm extended high up to where the hilt of the sword had gone in between the bull's shoulders. Then the figure was broken. There was a little jolt as Romero came clear, and then he was standing, one hand up, facing the bull, his shirt ripped out from under his sleeve, the white blowing in the wind, and the bull, the red sword hilt tight between his shoulders, his head going down and his legs settling.
>
> "There he goes," Bill said.
>
> Romero was close enough so the bull could see him. His hand still up, he spoke to the bull. The bull gathered himself, then his head went forward and he went over slowly, then all over, suddenly, four feet in the air.

Hemingway's achievement in passages such as this is to make the attentive reader feel as if he is a spectator in the bullring no less than the novel's characters. The author achieves this by employing a prose that is fundamentally dynamic. The bull charges, Romero's shoulder moves forward, the sword goes in, there is a jolt, and, finally, after that moment of almost tender stillness when the matador speaks to his prey, the bull goes over and dies. Writing at a time when the cinema was first beginning to take hold of the public's imagination, Hemingway was able to forge a style that appealed directly to the eye as strongly as any filmed scene. This allowed his fiction to be about more than simple description. At his best, Hemingway could provoke the very emotions and sensations that the reader might experience if he were at the event itself.

Hemingway's prose does not appeal just to the sense of sight. After a hard day's fishing at the Irati River, when Jake and Bill settle down for a well-earned drink, the author is able, in chapter 12, to speak to the other senses as well:

> I walked up the road and got out the two bottles of wine. They were cold. Moisture beaded on the bottles as I walked back to the trees. I spread the lunch on a newspaper, and uncorked one of the bottles and leaned the other against a tree. Bill came up drying his hands, his bag plump with ferns.
>
> "Let's see that bottle," he said. He pulled the cork, and tipped up the bottle and drank. "Whew! That makes my eyes ache."
>
> "Let's try it."
>
> The wine was icy cold and tasted faintly rusty.

The feel of the beaded moisture on the bottles, the smell of the fern branches used to insulate the caught trout, the sound of a popping cork, the faint rusty taste—in nine lines Hemingway provides an almost complete catalogue of the sensual experience of a picnic in rural Spain. The result is a style that appeals directly to the reader's senses with practically no recourse to standard literary techniques such as simile or metaphor. In fact, on those very rare occasions when Hemingway uses figures of speech, he does so in a manner that focuses squarely on the object being described rather than on the author's skill and cleverness. "Brett was damned good- looking. She wore a slipover jersey sweater and a tweed skirt, and her hair was brushed back like a boy's. She started all that. She was built with curves like the hull of a racing yacht, and you missed none of it with that wool jersey." It is easy to miss the two similes in the passage, since one's attention is drawn so unavoidably to the figure of Lady Brett.

The other means by which Hemingway's style conveys a sense of dramatic intensity is through his presentation of the story's action. From start to finish, his narrative comes directly at the reader. Like Romero's bullfighting, "always it was straight and pure and natural in line." There are no flashbacks; the point of view remains Jake's, locked in direct address to the reader. The plot unfolds in a strictly linear manner, with one action following directly upon another. Digressions and asides, such as the story of Mike's bankruptcy or the matador Belmonte's disgrace, are woven seamlessly into the narrative's taut fabric in the space of a few brief paragraphs. Repetition is employed to give the narrative a driving musical momentum—the word "nice," for example, appears constantly throughout the book, three times in the first paragraph of the second chapter. The conjunction "and" is employed in an innovative manner to give the narrative a headlong, almost breathless sense of movement "There were pigeons out in the square, and the houses were a yellow, sun-baked color, and I did not want to leave the café." At times, this radical use of a simple conjunction allows Hemingway's prose to approximate the sequential process of thought itself, such as in the scene in chapter 4 where a drunk and sleepless Jake contemplates the impossibility of his love for Brett:

> I lay awake thinking and my mind jumping around. Then I couldn't keep away from it, and I started to think about Brett and all the rest of it went away. I was thinking about Brett and my mind stopped jumping around and started to go in sort of smooth waves. Then all of a sudden I started to cry. Then after a while it was better and I lay in bed and listened to the heavy trams go by and way down the street, and then I went to sleep.

Hemingway's dialogue is also notable for its naturalness and authenticity. His characters do not explain things to one another; they do not use speech to summarize emotions or conveniently reveal their plans and motivations. Rather, dialogue flows like the cold waters of the Irati, fast and sparkling and largely concealing the life beneath it. It is in his use of dialogue, more than anywhere else, that one can sense Hemingway the reporter at work, recording with phonographic precision the speech and slang of his contemporaries. The scene in chapter 9 in which Brett admits her fling with Robert Cohn to a jealous Jake is characteristic of Hemingway's spare but evocative dialogue:

Brett looked at me. "I say," she said, "is Robert Cohn going on this trip?"

"Yes. Why?"

"Don't you think it will be a bit rough on him?"

"Why should it?

"Who did you think I went down to San Sebastian with?"

"Congratulations," I said.

We walked along.

"What did you say that for?"

"I don't know. What would you like me to say?"

We walked along and turned a corner.

"He behaved rather well, too. He gets a little dull."

"Does he?"

"I rather thought it would be good for him."

"You might take up social service."

"Don't be nasty."

"I won't."

"Didn't you really know?"

Jake never states his feelings; he does not lose his temper or level insults. Brett, for her part, does not try to justify or explain. Passersby would never for a moment suspect that a lover's quarrel is in progress. That said, the author still manages through this brisk exchange to create an intense drama in which deep emotions are conveyed. In fact, the most emotionally dense line in the entire scene is the speechless "We walked along," during which Brett realizes that she has hurt Jake's feelings, yet also understands the impossibility of apologizing to him.

Of course, there is much more at work in Hemingway's style than its directness and simplicity. The author was not just recording reality with a news reporter's concision but was, in fact, using his spare, hyperrealistic style as the concrete basis for his profound meditations on value, heroism, and the lost generation of his peers. As he often stated, he was "inventing from experience." The building blocks of his fiction might be hyperrealistic, but the edifice he was constructing was something of his own imagination. To achieve this effect, he needed to forge a style that not only captured reality but also suggested the truths hidden beneath it. In his bullfighting memoir *Death in the Afternoon* (1932), Hemingway described his prose as being like an iceberg, with the bulk of the story's action and meaning taking place beneath the surface. "The dignity of movement of an iceberg is due to only one-eighth of it being above water." Hemingway believed that what was omitted often could provide more power and resonance than what was explicitly described. His prose was fundamentally suggestive, using surface brilliance and excitement to hint at great depths. What is left unsaid is often more important than what is stated.

Jake and Brett almost never directly discuss his impotence, for example, though it informs nearly every exchange they have. Brett's terrible previous marriage, which involved abuse and death threats, is only hinted at, yet these oblique mentions serve to explain her feckless behavior more effectively than a fully articulated "back story." The fact that Mike's bankruptcy and alcoholism stem from a very difficult time in the trenches is, once again, only suggested. It is interesting to note that Hemingway cut the first thirty pages from the original manuscript of the novel at the suggestion of F. Scott Fitzgerald, a section that included a great deal of description of the histories of Brett, Jake, and Mike Campbell. By submerging these aspects of the story in the natural flow of his narrative, Hemingway was able to give them more power and mystery.

One of the methods Hemingway employs to suggest these hidden depths is irony, which pervades both Jake's narration and the dialogue among the central characters. "Aren't you going to show a little irony and pity?" Bill asks Jake as they prepare for their fishing expedition, and though Jake thumbs his nose at his friend, his basic narrative stance does prove to be an ever deepening irony. Time and again Hemingway—through Jake's narration—uses verbal misdirection to lead the reader to his true meaning. In chapter 3, Jake picks up the prostitute Georgette and takes her to meet his crowd at a restaurant, where he introduces her as his fiancée, an ironic reference to his inability to have a real marital relationship. Later, while he and Bill are fishing, Bill makes a joke about "Henry's bicycle," a sly nod at the legend that the writer Henry James damaged his testicles while riding a tricycle as a boy. Once again, Jake's wound is evoked ironically without being openly discussed.

In the novel's last chapter, after receiving Brett's telegram begging him to come rescue her after her abortive affair with Romero, Jake's self-lacerating thoughts provide the novel's most devastating ironic moment. "That seemed to handle it. That was it. Send a girl off with one man. Introduce her to another to go off with him. Now go and bring her back. And sign the wire with love. That was it all right. I went in to lunch." Finally, when Brett concludes the novel by suggesting that she and Jake "could have had such a damned good time together" if not for his wound, Jake responds with the irony that has been his hallmark throughout the book, although now it is shot through with a hard-earned, wistful self-understanding. "'Yes,' I said. 'Isn't it pretty to think so?'"

Perhaps Hemingway's greatest achievement in *The Sun Also Rises* was to create a style that expresses the fundamental tenets of his "code." His writing is reticent, honest, and free of delusions. It is directly engaged with the physical world, taking delight in the earth, while at the same time adopting an ironic view of human behavior. Like the code hero, it is stoic in its refusal to be showy, to mystify, or to rely on tricks to achieve its ends. Just as Jake Barnes wanted to find a style of life that allowed him to live fully in the world, Hemingway in *The Sun Also Rises* developed a style of writing that allows readers to feel that they are living fully in the world the author has created.

SYMBOLISM

Although Hemingway's language is free of literary affect and ornament, beneath the novel's surface simplicity rests an elaborate web of symbolism. Hemingway's iceberg paradigm is never more apt than in the novel's symbolic dimension. It is a testament to his authorial cunning that he is able to incorporate a wide range of profound and carefully conceived symbols into his novel without disturbing its dramatic flow. Wounds, for instance, play a very concrete role in the narrative while also carrying significant thematic weight. Nearly every character in the book has a wound of some sort, illustrating Hemingway's view that to be human is to suffer the torments of the world's nada. It is the way characters react to this inevitable wounding that determines their dignity and their worth. Jake, of course, was wounded in the groin during the war, an injury that has left him impotent but still possessed by strong sexual urges. "My head started to work. The old grievance. Well, it was a rotten way to be wounded." While this wound initially causes him considerable anguish and leads to his "pimping" for Brett, by novel's end he has come to accept it with a degree of stoic nobility.

Brett is also a wounded character, psychologically damaged by a bad marriage. As Mike explains, her former husband "used to tell her he'd kill her. Always slept with a loaded service revolver. Brett used to take the shells out when he'd gone to sleep. She hasn't had an absolutely happy life, Brett." Her ultimate refusal to "ruin" Romero shows that she, like Jake, ultimately is able to overcome the effects of this emotional damage. Even the seemingly sound Count Mippipopolous bears arrow wounds inflicted during a trip to Abyssinia, "two raised white welts" he gladly shows to Jake, though he laughingly dismisses them as the price of being fully engaged with the world. Brett's response to his display hints at the commonality of suffering Hemingway was establishing among his characters. "I told you he was one of us. Didn't I?" Mike's attraction to Brett is explained in part by the fact that he, too, suffers from traumatic war stress that causes him to drink and spend money irresponsibly. Cohn, of course, with his unrequited love for Brett, conducts himself with a demeanor that can be described only as "wounded." Even the heroic Romero bears the wounds of his fistfight with Cohn, though he is able to ignore the pain and discomfort of his swollen face and bruised ribs to perform nobly in the bullring. Once again, it is left to Romero, the exemplary hero, to show best how to bear the inevitable injuries of a hostile world.

The rituals of bullfighting also give the novel a sturdily symbolic underpinning. In a world where meaning has been stripped away by war and doubt, the rituals of bravery and honor inherent in the bullfight satisfy the natural human craving for order. But there is a dark symbolic side to the bullfight as well. The bloody activities of the picadors and the matadors as they torment and kill the bulls provide the ultimate symbol of Hemingway's conception of a hostile universe. They also contribute a symbolic gloss on the novel's erotic pessimism, most obviously during the ceremonial separation of the herd into bulls and steers, the latter furnishing a memorable image not only for the impotent Jake but also of the braying and pitiful Cohn. Both men are pierced by the novel's most formidable picador, Brett Ashley. This symbolism becomes explicit after the gang of expatriates watches the grizzly scene in chapter 13 where two steers are gored as they are used to help corral the festival's rampaging bulls:

"It's no life being a steer," Robert Cohn said.

"Don't you think so?" Mike said. "I would have thought you'd loved being a steer, Robert."

"What do you mean, Mike?"

"They lead such a quiet life. They never say anything and they're always hanging about so."

The festival of San Fermin itself becomes a symbol for the triumph of paganism over traditional religious values in the lives of Jake, Brett, and their coterie. Time and again, these members of the lost generation are thwarted in their attempts to find solace in Christian ritual and values. While fishing in Burguete, Jake tries to pray at the cathedral but is ultimately unable to take any comfort from it. "I was a little ashamed, and regretted that I was such a rotten Catholic, but realized there was nothing I could do about it, at least for a while, and maybe never." On the train down to Spain, he and Bill are excluded from having lunch by a group of American Catholics making a pilgrimage to Lourdes. "It's a pity you boys ain't Catholics," a fellow passenger tells them. "You could get a meal, then, all right." The fact that Jake is indeed a Catholic (at least in name) makes his exclusion from the ring of traditional belief all the more acute. Brett, too, is frustrated in her attempts to find refuge in the church. When she asks to accompany Jake to confession at a chapel in Pamplona, he tells her not to bother, since "it was not as interesting as it sounded, and, besides, it would be in a language she did not know." Later, during the raucous festival itself, Jake and the others attempt to enter the chapel, "but Brett was stopped just inside the door because she had no hat."

What replaces the vanished comforts of traditional religion in the lives of the expatriates is the brutal pagan ritual represented by the fiesta. The copious amounts of wine consumed in the course of the novel's tumultuous action have nothing to do with Christ's redemptive blood, but are rather a means of achieving a

Dionysian excess that the characters hope will bring about an oblivion sufficient to ease their pain. Even the abstemious Robert Cohn winds up dead drunk during the height of the festivities in a misguided effort to forget his anguish over his love for Brett. In a postwar world stripped of meaning, the festival of San Fermin (chapter 15) symbolizes the lost generation's desperate attempt to achieve some sort of transcendence:

> The fiesta was really started. It kept up day and night for seven days. The dancing kept up, the drinking kept up, the noise went on. The things that happened could only have happened during a fiesta. Everything became quite unreal finally and it seemed as though nothing could have any consequences. It seemed out of place to think of consequences during the fiesta.

This twentieth-century bacchanal even results in a form of human sacrifice, when a local farmer named Vicente Girones is gored to death during the running of the bulls. In keeping with the festival's primal decadence, his corpse is accompanied in procession not by a solemn priest but rather by "all the members of the dancing and drinking societies" attending the festival.

At the center of this week-long bacchanal stands Brett. Time and again, she is imaged as a sort of bitch goddess who inspires lunacy in the men about her. During the traditional riau-riau dance, the Spanish men will not let her take part but rather "wanted her as an image to dance around." She is Circe, turning the men around her to swine, forcing them to fight among themselves. When Romero kills the bull that gored Girones, he slices off its ear and presents it to Brett as an offering. Any sense of meaning in this ritual evaporates when Jake later reports that she wrapped it in Jake's handkerchief, "and left both ear and handkerchief, along with a number of Muratti cigarette-stubs, shoved far back in the drawer of the bed-table that stood beside her bed in the Hotel Montoya, in Pamplona." In the madness of the novel's post-

religious world, noble gestures can quickly become meaningless and forgotten souvenirs.

IMPORTANCE AND INFLUENCE

It is difficult to overstate the importance of *The Sun Also Rises* in the development of American fiction in the twentieth century. Hemingway's novels are easily among the most widely discussed and read of serious American twentieth-century novelists, and *The Sun Also Rises* stands at the forefront of this body of work. Even his harshest critics, like the biographer Jeffrey Meyers, concede that it is a book that will endure any vacillations in the author's reputation.

One reason for this legacy is that *The Sun Also Rises* remains one of the most vital documents of the 1920s. In it, Hemingway perfectly re-created the peculiar blend of excitement and boredom that plagued his postwar generation. Like the work of his contemporary and sometime friend Fitzgerald, it also expresses the restless expatriation that caused so many of that decade's young people to migrate to cities like Paris, abandoning what they saw to be the empty certainties of American life. It was a novel that not only showed us with a reporter's accuracy how things were during that turbulent time but also, like Rudolph Valentino's films, Al Jolson's music, and Babe Ruth's home run swing, has become an important artifact of the era itself.

The groundbreaking style of *The Sun Also Rises* also continues to ensure its place in the top drawer of American fiction. Hemingway's literary economy set an undeniable benchmark for those who followed. Never again would writers be able to employ the sort of wooden prolixity of a Dreiser or Lewis without knowing that they were in danger of being harshly judged against Hemingway's standard. With his first novel, he demonstrated that understatement could convey emotion more powerfully than verbosity and that silence could be as eloquent as speech. From his deadpan opening line to its devastating final encounter between Jake and Brett, Hemingway was an artist in absolute control of his medium. One reads the novel with the sense that it contains not a single word more than absolutely necessary.

Most important, *The Sun Also Rises* provides a memorable tale of wounded souls dealing with what had already become a brutal and unjust century. During Hemingway's lifetime, the world was to transform from the carefree idyll represented by the bourgeois Midwestern serenity of his youth into a place where war and technology decimated the old certainties. The examples of Jake, Romero, and even Brett continue to provide guidance about how to live with a measure of dignity and grace in an impersonal and savage world.

Hemingway's influence on subsequent generations of writers is equally profound. Love him or hate him, Hemingway's achievements as a novelist were something with which those who followed inevitably had to contend. The two-fisted, extroverted public personality—who never met a war or contest he did not like—

influenced later writers such as Norman Mailer, encouraging them to engage more fully with their turbulent times. But it is his craftsmanship that continues to be his lasting influence. And that artistry was never more profound than in *The Sun Also Rises*. The naturalism and the concision—the sense that every word in a piece of fiction must count—are the final legacies of this remarkable novel. The celebrated "dirty realist" short-story writer Raymond Carver, whose tersely eloquent work is difficult to imagine without Hemingway's influence, expressed the feelings of indebtedness shared by countless other authors in his 1985 review of two Hemingway biographies in the *New York Times Book Review*:

> How clear, serene and solid the best work still seems; it's as if there were a physical communion taking place among the fingers turning the page, the eyes taking in the words, the brain imaginatively re-creating what the words stand for and, as Hemingway put it, "making it a part of your own experience." Hemingway did his work, and he'll last.

Select Bibliography

EDITION

The Sun Also Rises. New York: Scribners, 1926. (The Scribner Paperback Fiction edition, reissued 1995, is cited in this essay.)

OTHER WORKS BY HEMINGWAY

Death in the Afternoon. New York: Scribners, 1932.

Winner Take Nothing. New York: Scribners, 1933.

For Whom the Bell Tolls. New York: Scribners, 1940.

The Old Man and the Sea. New York: Scribners, 1952.

A Moveable Feast. New York: Scribners, 1964.

"The Unpublished Opening of *The Sun Also Rises*." *Antaeus* 33 (spring 1979): 7–14.

SECONDARY WORKS

Baker, Carlos, ed. *Hemingway and His Critics: An International Anthology.* New York: Hill & Wang, 1961.

————. *Ernest Hemingway: Critiques of Four Major Novels.* New York: Scribners, 1962.

————. *Ernest Hemingway: A Life Story.* New York: Scribners, 1969. (The standard biography that has been challenged but never surpassed.)

————. *Ernest Hemingway: Selected Letters, 1917–1961.* New York: Scribners, 1981.

Benson, Jackson J. *Hemingway: The Writer's Art of Self Defense.* Minneapolis: University of Minnesota Press, 1969. (An astute examination of the style Hemingway began to forge in *The Sun Also Rises.*)

Bloom, Harold, ed. *Ernest Hemingway's* The Sun Also Rises. New York: Chelsea House Publishers, 1987.

Carver, Raymond. "Coming of Age, Going to Pieces." In his *No Heroics, Please: Uncollected Writings.* New York: Vintage Books, 1992. (An essay that passionately expresses the influence Hemingway had on subsequent generations of writers.)

Donaldson, Scott. *By Force of Will: The Life and Art of Ernest Hemingway.* New York: Viking Press, 1977. (An essential complement to Baker's biography, providing additional insights and balancing Baker's occasionally too-sunny point of view.)

Fussell, Paul. *The Great War and Modern Memory.* New York: Oxford University Press, 1975. (A groundbreaking work that is very helpful in understanding the postwar climate in which *The Sun Also Rises* was written.)

Grebstein, Sheldon Norman. *Hemingway's Craft.* Carbondale: Southern Illinois University Press, 1973.

Griffin, Peter. *Along with Youth: Hemingway, the Early Years.* New York: Oxford University Press, 1985.

Hanneman, Audre. *Ernest Hemingway: A Comprehensive Bibliography.* Princeton, N.J.: Princeton University Press, 1969; with a supplement, 1975.

Hovey, Richard B. *Hemingway: The Inward Terrain.* Seattle: University of Washington Press, 1968.

Meyers, Jeffrey, ed. *Hemingway: The Critical Heritage.* Boston: Routledge & Kegan Paul, 1982.

————. *Hemingway: A Biography.* New York: Harper & Row, 1985. (A highly critical but always fascinating account of the author's tempestuous life.)

Plimpton, George. "Ernest Hemingway: The Art of Fiction XXI." *Paris Review* 18 (spring 1958): 60–89. (The most revealing interview ever conducted with Hemingway.)

Reynolds, Michael S. *The Young Hemingway.* New York: Basil Blackwell, 1986.

Rovit, Earl. *Ernest Hemingway.* Boston: Twayne, 1986.

Sarason, Bertram D. *Hemingway and the Sun Set.* Washington, D.C.: NCR Microcard Editions, 1972. (An insightful historical background to the novel.)

Stein, Gertrude. *The Autobiography of Alice B. Toklas.* New York: Random House, 1933. Pp. 212–220. (Hemingway's onetime friend and mentor provides a not entirely flattering portrait of the author around the time he was writing *The Sun Also Rises.*)

Svoboda, F. J. *Hemingway and* The Sun Also Rises: *The Crafting of a Style.* Lawrence: University Press of Kansas, 1983.

Wagner-Martin, Linda, ed. *New Essays on* The Sun Also Rises. New York: Cambridge University Press, 1987. (A valuable collection of recent criticism of the novel.)

Waldhorn, Arthur. *A Reader's Guide to Ernest Hemingway.* New York: Farrar, Straus and Giroux, 1972.

Weeks, Robert P., ed. *Hemingway: A Collection of Critical Essays.* Englewood Cliffs, N.J.: Prentice-Hall, 1962.

Young, Philip. *Ernest Hemingway: A Reconsideration.* University Park: Pennsylvania State University Press, 1966. (A key study of the motivation and psychological background of Hemingway's writing.)

Edgar Allan Poe's
Tales of the Grotesque and Arabesque

THOMAS WRIGHT

P OE REMARKED THAT two thousand years would have to pass for his works to be appreciated. For once his powers of prophecy failed him, as only one hundred fifty years after his death his popularity and influence are enormous. The stories contained in *Tales of the Grotesque and Arabesque,* along with Poe's other fictions, are often among the first works of literature that adolescents read, and they have been translated into countless languages. They also have a spectacular existence in contemporary popular culture. Rock songs are based on them, and episodes of the television program *The Simpsons* have alluded to them; as a result, Poe himself has become a kind of symbol or icon of literature. This is fitting, because Poe arguably has had a greater influence on world literature than any other American writer. Not only have his stories been of immense importance to authors as diverse as Vladimir Nabokov and Stephen King, but they also inaugurated, or at the very least helped to establish, the genres of science fiction and the detective story. Indeed, as Sir Arthur Conan

Doyle, the creator of Sherlock Holmes, remarked, Poe's tales were so pregnant with suggestion that they each resemble a root from which entire literatures have developed.

Still, in another sense Poe's elevation to the status of a literary god is surprising, because he has always had his doubters and detractors. Immediately after his death, his "friend" Rufus Wilmot Griswold created the so-called Poe legend of a depraved and demonic writer. Griswold's caricature influenced early Poe criticism, much of which dismissed Poe's work as immoral, inhuman, and distinctly un-American. More serious, and more enduring, were the charges of vulgarity and immaturity that came from such writers as Aldous Huxley, T. S. Eliot, and Henry James. Even today, Poe's canonical status is challenged: the few critics, such as Harold Bloom, who are still interested in making aesthetic judgments continue to express reservations about his work. The suspicion remains that Poe is something of a charlatan, and many agree with James Russell Lowell's famous comment that Poe was "three-fifths of him genius, and two-fifths sheer fudge." Generally, however, Poe criticism over the past hundred years has been favorable, and the contents of *Tales of the Grotesque and Arabesque* and Poe's other stories have proved to be wonderfully suggestive and adaptable to various schools of critical thought, among them, New Criticism, New Historicism, and Post-Structuralism. This is a testimony to the variety, richness, and ambiguity of Poe's fictions: the contents of *Tales* remain as enigmatic as ever and do not seem to be in any danger of being explained away.

BACKGROUND

Because Poe's three early volumes of poetry were not commercial successes, he turned his hand early in his career to the short story, a far more popular form of writing. Poe may have written a few tales while he was at university, and it is likely that his first published short story was "A Dream," which appeared over the initial "P" in the *Saturday Evening Post* in August 1831. The first short stories that can be attributed definitely to him are the five that were published in the Philadelphia *Saturday Courier* between January and December 1832: "Metzengerstein," "The Duc De L'Omelette," "The Bargain Lost" (republished in *Tales* as "Bon-Bon"), "A Tale of Jerusalem," and "A Decided Loss" (republished as "Loss of Breath"). All of them were to be included, in revised form, in *Tales of the Grotesque and Arabesque*. With the possible exception of "Why the Little Frenchman Wears His Hand in a Sling," all of the *Tales of the Grotesque and Arabesque* were published in the popular press between 1832 and 1839. Magazine literature boomed in the period: "The whole tendency of the age," Poe wrote (in "Marginalia"), is "Magazine-ward." It is important to remember the original place of the publication of Poe's stories, because it exercised an enormous influence on their form and content.

Four of the five *Courier* tales were witty satires on contemporary topics, a genre then

CHRONOLOGY

1809	Poe is born on January 19 in Boston, the second child of the itinerant actors David and Elizabeth Poe.
1811	After having been deserted by her husband, Elizabeth Poe dies. Poe becomes the foster son of John Allan, a Richmond tobacco merchant.
1826	Poe enters the University of Virginia.
1827	Poe leaves the university after a brief period and joins the U.S. Army. He publishes *Tamerlane and Other Poems,* his first volume of poetry.
1831	Poe is dismissed from the U.S. Army and begins a career as a journalist and short-story writer.
1836	Poe marries Virginia, the thirteen-year-old daughter of his aunt, Maria Clemm.
1838	*The Narrative of Arthur Gordon Pym.*
1839	*Tales of the Grotesque and Arabesque.*
1845	*Tales* and *The Raven and Other Poems.*
1847	Death of Virginia Poe.
1849	Poe dies on October 7 in Baltimore.

very much in vogue. The other tale, "Metzengerstein," was the first of Poe's Gothic productions. From a letter that Poe wrote to Thomas Willis White, editor of the *Southern Literary Messenger,* it is clear that he believed Gothic fiction to be a popular form. The public, he remarked, have a taste for "the fearful coloured into the horrible . . . the singular wrought out into the strange and mystical" (quoted in Kenneth Silverman, *Edgar A. Poe: Mournful and Never-Ending Remembrance*). The sensationalism of the stories in *Tales*, which include accounts of balloon journeys to the moon, premature burials, encounters with the devil, and numerous gruesome deaths, must be understood in the context of the tastes of the magazine-reading public. Poe knew that readers demanded extravagant subjects treated in a flamboyant style, and that is exactly what he gave them.

The diversity of the contents of *Tales* and the variety within individual stories must also be seen in this context, because the audience of magazine readers was extremely heterogeneous. This may help explain why Poe's tales vary in form, atmosphere, length, and style and why, even within the space of a single story, the mood can change quickly from comedy to tragedy and then back again. It also may help us to understand why Poe combines a highly erudite tone that might appeal to more intellectual readers with the whole repertoire of the popular short story writers' techniques and effects. We should remember, too, that unlike subscribers to weightier publications, the attention span of the magazine-reading public was fairly limited; consequently, readers craved novelty and diversity. This may account for Poe's emphasis on the powerful effect of his fiction on the reader as well as for its variety, brevity, and concision. "We need," he wrote in his "Marginalia," in an entry on magazine literature, "the curt, the condensed, the pointed."

From the early 1830s Poe wanted to gather together his short stories and publish them in book form. In May 1833, he offered for publication a collection of stories entitled *Eleven Tales of the Arabesque* that comprised the five *Courier* tales and six others that he had entered for a competition organized by the *Baltimore Saturday Visiter*. Although Poe failed to interest a publisher, he won the *Visiter* competition with the story "MS. Found in a Bottle." Poe devised an elaborate plan for *Eleven Tales*. The stories, he wrote, "are supposed to be read at table, by the eleven members of a literary club, and are followed by the remarks of the company upon each. These remarks are intended as a burlesque upon criticism," as quoted in Eric W. Carlson's *Edgar Allen Poe.* This design, loosely based on Plato's *Symposium*, was later reused by Poe when he offered a larger collection of his stories to various publishers in the mid-1830s under the title *Tales of the Folio Club.*

Although the projected book was never published, all of its contents appeared in *Tales of the Grotesque and Arabesque.* In a surviving manuscript of an introduction to the book, and in his letters to publishers, Poe set out his ideas for the volume. Once again he imagined a gathering of a literary club whose members, over the course of a single evening, would each read out a story, which would be criticized by the company. The author of the tale judged to be the best would become president of the club; the author of the worst had to provide the food and drink at the next meeting. *Tales of the Folio Club* evidently was intended as a satire in the manner of Poe's English contemporary, Thomas Love Peacock. It was, in other words, an elaborate burlesque of popular contemporary modes of fiction and criticism. This is clearly indicated by the names and descriptions of the various club members, which include "Mr. Horribile Dictu, with white eyelashes, who had graduated at Gottingen" and "Mr. Snap, the President, who is a very lank man with a hawk nose." Many of these figures were based upon real characters: the president, for example, was a caricature of John Neal, the editor of the *Yankee.*

When considering *Tales of the Grotesque and Arabesque,* it is important to remember the dramatic and satirical nature of its forerunner. Our knowledge of the Folio Club gathering encourages us to read Poe's stories as the compositions of various personae and to regard Poe as "author of the authors" of the tales. *Tales* can thus be compared to an intellectual opera or a Chaucerian pilgrimage, in which a series of storytellers take the floor. It is impossible to discover in this universe of voices Poe's individual voice or to analyze them from the point of view of his authorial intentions. An understanding of the satirical character of the Folio symposium also makes us sensitive to the burlesque and parodic attributes of Poe's tales.

Having failed to find a publisher, Poe abandoned the idea of the elaborate framing device of the literary club and offered his work as a more conventional collection. By the time that he had persuaded Lea and Blanchard to issue a two-volume edition under the title *Tales of the Grotesque and Arabesque,* he had written twenty-five tales, all of which are included in the book. Only 750 copies were published, and a decade later even this small edition was not exhausted. Although the two volumes, which were bound in purple muslin, are dated 1840, it is likely that they appeared in December 1839.

POE'S THEORY OF THE SHORT STORY

Poe is regarded as one of the fathers of the modern short story not only because of his fictions but also because he was one of the first critics to articulate a theory of the form. And just as his ideas concerning poetical composition help us understand his verse, so do the various theories of the short story he adumbrated in book reviews help us understand his tales. Poe was concerned above all with the "effect" of his tale on the reader. This effect, he thought, should be single and unified. When readers finished the story, they ought to be left with a "totality of impression" (quoted in Satish Kumar's *Edgar Allan Poe*), and every element of the story—character, style, tone, plot, and so forth—should contribute to this effect. Works too long to be read at a single sitting could not, in Poe's view, achieve such powerful and unified effects; hence the brevity of his productions. He also advocated the Aristotelian unities of place, time, and action and placed special emphasis on the opening and conclusion of his stories.

Poe thought that the reader must believe and become caught up in his stories. He was not, however, in any way a realist. There is no place in his tales for psychological realism, for instance, or for the development of character. Instead, as quoted by Kent L. Ljungquist, through the use of "the infinity of arts which give verisimilitude to a narration" (in particular, through minute details) and through inexorable narratives and powerful emotional effects, Poe

sought to beguile the reader into believing that his fantastic stories had a reality of their own. One gets the impression from Poe's theoretical comments that he imagined the reader to resemble the audience at a theater. (One remembers that Poe's parents were actors and that he himself wrote scenes from a play and dramatic criticism.) During the hour or so that the author has the reader's soul under his or her control (as Poe put it), the reader receives powerful emotional effects; at the end of the tale, readers are to applaud the consummate artistry of the writer-performer who has wrought them. Poe thus sought to give his readers emotional and aesthetic pleasure; the aim of his tales, and every other part of his oeuvre, was never a didactic one.

Instead of providing the reader with a transparent upper current of meaning, he wanted to create a "suggestive indefiniteness of meaning" (quoted in Rachel Polonsky) that would bring about a "definiteness of vague and therefore of spiritual effect" (quoted in Edmund Wilson). This would lead the reader to contemplate the ideal of supernal beauty that Poe passionately believed in and craved throughout his life. This emphasis on indefiniteness helps us to understand the enduring fascination of Poe's stories: their vagueness has led to their being interpreted in an endless variety of ways.

TALES OF THE ARABESQUE

Poe revised the content, style, and even the titles of some of his stories as they were published and republished in magazines and collections. For the sake of simplicity, the titles used here are the ones that appear in *Tales.* The final titles Poe gave his stories are also given because these tend to be the titles used by editors of anthologies of Poe's writings. Those interested in the subject of Poe's revisions are referred to Thomas Mabbott's *Collected Works.*

Because of the diversity and variety of Poe's tales, it is extremely difficult to classify them in anything but an arbitrary manner. The arabesque tales contain elements of the comic, his grotesques are at times profoundly Gothic, and his science fictions also can be satirical. For the sake of convenience, however, for the purposes of this essay, the contents of *Tales* are divided into these three groups. The meaning of "arabesque" has been much debated. The word derives from the vocabulary of art, where it refers to a type of surface decoration composed of fancifully intertwined and flowing lines. It would seem, then, to refer to those tales that are intricately constructed. More specifically, the word has been applied to stories that describe and examine extreme psychological states. As used here, however, the word is synonymous with "Gothic."

Gothic literature, which typically aimed to produce effects of mystery and horror, was established in the latter half of the eighteenth century by such writers as Horace Walpole, Ann Radcliffe, and E. T. A. Hoffmann. Gothic tales were usually set in desolate and wild landscapes, environments that reflected the moods of their doomed protagonists and provided the perfect background for bloodcurdling and often supernatural incidents. Dungeons, winding staircases, and secret passages also featured, as did castles and ruined abbeys, which symbolized the continuing presence of a distant and usually medieval past. In Gothic literature the ghost of the Catholic past haunts the post-Reformation, scientific, and rationalistic age. By the beginning of the nineteenth century, the genre had become extremely popular. The craze spread to America, where Isaac Mitchell achieved great success with *The Asylum* (1811) and Charles Brockden Brown produced a series of widely read Gothic romances. German writers such as Hoffmann established the Gothic short story as a distinct genre, and by the 1820s it had become probably the most popular form of magazine literature in England and America. *Blackwood's Edinburgh Magazine*, in particular, was renowned for its Gothic tales; Poe was to parody its productions mercilessly.

It is generally agreed that Poe's particular contribution to Gothic literature was his use of the genre to evoke and explore philosophical ideas and extreme psychological states. Just as in his science fiction stories Poe imagined journeys beyond the known limits of the universe, in his arabesque tales he described the soul of man under appalling and abnormal conditions. Typically, his characters are at the mercy of powers over which they have no control and which their reason cannot comprehend fully. These forces may take the form of a sudden, irrational impulse, as in "The Imp of the Perverse," or, as is the case with the eponymous hero of "William Wilson," a hereditary disease.

"WILLIAM WILSON"

"Let me call myself, for the present, William Wilson." Thus, with customary abruptness and mysteriousness, Poe opens the first arabesque tale of *Tales.* We are immediately drawn into the strange universe of the hero, who, like so many of Poe's narrators, is writing a confessional autobiography. "I have been," Wilson continues, "the slave of circumstances beyond human control. . . . I am the descendent of a race whose imaginative and easily excitable temperament has at all times rendered them remarkable." As the years pass, he grows "self-willed" and dedicates himself to a life of vice. At every stage of his progress down the path of sin he is dogged by a man who is his exact counterpart in almost every respect. This character, who generally is taken to represent Wilson's conscience, relentlessly pursues him throughout his life until one day they confront each other. Wilson stabs his double, but in the process murders his own soul.

"William Wilson" is a classic doppelgänger tale. These tales are common to the mythology and folklore of many cultures, in which an encounter with one's double usually prefigures death. Poe's immediate source of inspiration was an article by the writer Washington Irving, "An Unwritten Drama of Lord Byron"; the double theme was, however, common to Gothic literature. It is also common to Poe's tales, in which we find reincarnations, mirror images, and characters that closely resemble each other. It is fitting that Poe found inspiration in an ancient superstition, because, as his biographer Kenneth Silverman has suggested, the enduring fascination of his own stories lies, in part, in their ability to evoke the Freudian sensation of the "uncanny." They revive, in other words, the ancient and magical forms of thinking that lie dormant within us. In an enlightened age of science and rationality, Poe looked to alternative and archaic ways of understanding the world and was able to embody them in his fictions. There is, of course, something characteristically Romantic about this: the sleep of the age of reason, to adapt a contemporary phrase, bred monsters, many of which can be found in Poe's tales.

"THE FALL OF THE HOUSE OF USHER"

The second arabesque story included in *Tales* is perhaps the most famous of all. Since its appearance in the collection, "The Fall of the House of Usher" has been republished in countless anthologies of Poe's stories; it also has inspired a variety of theatrical and cinematic adaptations. "Usher" exhibits many of the trappings of Gothic fiction: a decaying mansion located in a gloomy setting; a protagonist suffering from madness and a peculiar sensibility of temperament inherited from his ancient family; and a woman, his sister, who is prematurely buried and who rises from her tomb. And yet from such Gothic clichés Poe produced a tale of extraordinary power. In that sense, it is a representative example of his achievement. Part of the tale's power derives from the intimate relationship that exists between Roderick Usher and the house that he and his sister occupy. As the writer of horror stories H. P. Lovecraft noted, the tale hints at the strange life in inanimate things. The house and its inhabitants seem to share a single soul. As an evil and vampiric presence, the house is similar to earlier

buildings in Gothic fiction; it also prefigures later Gothic buildings, such as Overlook Hotel in Stephen King's *The Shining*. Few writers, however, both before and after Poe, have invested a building with such horror or so successfully conveyed the impression that it is alive.

An unbearably heavy air of gloom, decay, and stagnation seems to cling to the pages of the tale, the essence of which lies in its atmosphere and style rather than its plot. A representative example of Poe's weighty and dark baroque prose can be found in the opening words, which set the tone of the tale perfectly. "During the whole of a dull, dark, and soundless day in the autumn of the year," recalls the narrator, "when the clouds hung oppressively low in the heavens, I had been passing alone, on horseback, through a singularly dreary tract of country." The plot is thin and almost incidental; instead of moving forward, it is held up by numerous digressions and repetitions. Usher paints pictures, improvises melodies on his guitar, and composes poems that are microcosms of the story. The structure of the tale thus resembles a vast fractal pattern, such as those we find in computer-generated graphic representations of chaos theory. It comes as no surprise to find the words "arabesque" and "intricacies" on the first few pages of the tale, for these, also, accurately evoke its architecture. And just as one becomes lost in the contemplation of such patterns, so, too, have critics been absorbed in the contemplation of the meaning of the tale. Some have regarded it as a dark oedipal drama; others have seen in it an allegory of Poe's world of the mind, with the three characters representing intellect, taste, and the moral sense. Speculations such as these are encouraged by the symbolic suggestiveness of the tale, which, like the poem Usher composes, appears to have an undercurrent, or mystic current, of meaning.

"MS. FOUND IN A BOTTLE"

This tale—the journal of an unnamed scientist adrift on a ghost ship in the southern seas—

displays certain crudities of style that Poe later bemoaned; it is, however, interesting for several reasons. For instance, it is a characteristic Poe production, insofar as it embodies and dramatizes a philosophical idea. Many of Poe's tales grow out of a specific intellectual concept or speculation, which is usually referred to in its epigraph or opening paragraph. Poe's mind characteristically moved from an idea to an anecdote that exemplified and, as it were, worked out the idea in the context of a human life. In "MS.," we are offered the spectacle of a typical product of the age of reason confronted with events—a shipwreck and a journey on a ghost ship—and sensations that his reason cannot comprehend. "A feeling," the narrator writes, "has taken possession of my soul—a sensation that will admit of no analysis. . . . To a mind constituted like my own [this] is an evil." Here we are in classic Poe territory: a narrator experiences something so utterly novel that he can find no words, and no theory, to describe or account for it. There is more in heaven and earth, the Romantic in Poe always delights in reminding us, than is dreamt of in our scientific and rational philosophy.

"MS." is also noteworthy as one of the first stories in which Poe combines a realistic style with an utterly fantastic subject. The tale is presented as a fragmentary journal, a form frequently used by genuine scientists and geographers. It also is based on a real scientific theory current at the time, which suggested that the earth had an opening at both of the poles. And yet, from the very beginning, the reader is aware that there is something fantastic and distinctly fishy about the narrative. If one considers the design of *Tales of the Folio Club*, this is quite literally the case, since the tale was the composition of one "Mr. Solomon Seadrift, who had every appearance of a fish."

"SHADOW—A PARABLE"

"Shadow" reads like an early version of "The Masque of the Red Death." At the end of Greco-Roman civilization, seven revelers from the Egyptian city Ptolemais take refuge from the pestilence in a hall, where they attempt to cheer themselves with talk, laughter, wine, and song. There is one other member of the party, a young man who lies dead on the floor. The narrator sings loud and long but suddenly falls silent when, from the sable draperies in the room, a dark and undefined shadow steps out and speaks with the mingled voices of the company's departed friends. This brief prose poem, which is written in the style of the King James Bible, has been praised justly as a powerful evocation of an intensely dramatic situation. Drawing upon countless literary sources, baroque painting techniques, and familiar Gothic devices—portents, the presence of the corpse, the entrance of an unwelcome guest, among others—Poe offers the short story equivalent of the last scene in a sensational verse drama. It is a fine piece of Gothic theater: suggestive, terrifying, and also very funny.

The humor derives in part from the elements of parody and self-parody in the fable and from the obvious *staginess* of the writing and the situation. Poe has often been attacked for the theatrical quality of the style, dialogue, and decor of his tales, but, as W. H. Auden has noted, it is an essential quality of his writing. Even when Poe's writing is weak, vague, and verbose, it is, as Auden explained, usually dramatically appropriate for a particular narrator or for the effect he is trying to create. The fact that the story was probably a Folio Club tale encourages us to look for humorous elements. Our laughter, however, is not that of pure comedy or delight; it is, in the circumstances, as hysterical as that of the participants in the fated symposium. Here, too, we might recall the mad hilarity of Usher, which is the natural response to mounting terror. Poe's humor, then, does not detract from the horror of his tales; it intensifies it by setting it in relief. Poe understood (and those who have adapted his tales for the cinema also have realized) that comedy is an essential element in Gothic literature.

"METZENGERSTEIN"

In this tale, Baron Metzengerstein kills his neighbor and ancient enemy Count Berlifitzing, who, in turn, exacts a terrible revenge through the agency of a horse in which his soul is reincarnated. Summarized thus, the tale appears to be utterly preposterous, and many critics, most notably G. R. Thompson, believe it to have been a parody of Gothic literature. First published along with Poe's early satires with the subtitle "A Tale in Imitation of the German" and probably intended, at the Folio Club meeting, as the offering of "Mr. Horribile Dictu [from] Gottingen," it is certainly possible to read it in this way. Such is the power of Poe's conception (the story is based upon the idea of metempsychosis, the passing of a soul at death into another body) and execution, however, that it also can be read as a chilling tale of the arabesque. The concluding image of smoke in the shape of a gigantic horse rising from Metzengerstein's castle is a masterstroke; the description of the magical tapestry in which a horse appears to move is also brilliantly written. In this, and in other Poe stories, the line between life and art becomes blurred as an ancient horse leaps out of a tapestry into the world.

We do not need to take an either/or approach to Poe's tales, however. This is not only because much of Gothic literature contains comic elements but also because the most successful parodists tend to be those who love and reverence the work they mock. We also must remember that Poe's work is characterized by its ambiguity and variety and that, consequently, in the imaginary worlds he created, things can be solemn and ridiculous, comic and somber. He wears by turns the theatrical masks of tragedy and comedy; sometimes he even tries to put them on at the same time.

"THE VISIONARY"

"Venice" is the subtitle of this lyrical and operatic arabesque tale (later revised as "The Assignation"), and it is certainly a wonderful portrait of "that city of dim visions" and "Elysium of the sea." Poe's labyrinthine tale, based upon a Romantic incident from the life of Lord Byron, seems to emerge inevitably out of the city's tortuous canals and streets. Along with the Doctor Watson–like narrator, the reader becomes lost in a mysterious story of adultery, suicide, and revenge. The allusion to the detective story is apposite, because, like Poe's detective C. Auguste Dupin, we are forced to piece together the narrative of the tale from shadowy hints and clues. In tandem with its heavy atmosphere, this makes the story memorable and compelling.

At the end of the tale we are lead into the Byronic hero's Palazzo. There we find "a broad winding staircase of mosaics" and "an apartment whose unparalleled splendour burst through the opening door," where we are dazzled and oppressed by "conflicting perfumes" and "rich draperies" that "trembled to the vibration of low, melancholy music." Again the scene is distinctly baroque and arabesque, and Poe's prose is successful at providing a literary equivalent of these artistic schools. The style of the story has been described as operatic, and as with many operatic productions, the tale borders on the camp and the ridiculous. At the Folio Club gathering it was to be read to the company by "Mr. Convolvulus Gondola," a caricature of Byron's biographer Thomas Moore, a man excessively fond of an elaborate prose style.

"MORELLA"

The beautiful young lover of the Byronic hero in "The Visionary" intends to commit suicide. She is a distant relative of the angelic heroines who die prematurely in "Morella," "Ligeia," and "Berenice," three stories that form the so-called marriage group within Poe's arabesque tales. Poe believed the death of a beautiful woman to be the most poetical topic in the world, and he used it throughout his verse and fictional writings.

The eponymous heroine of "Morella," the first story in the first volume of *Tales,* is an archetypal Gothic figure. Deeply learned in arcane philosophy, with a mysterious air and an ethereal "Pre-Raphaelite" beauty, her character first attracts and then repels the story's hysterical narrator. His love for her wanes, and she pines away in consequence. On her deathbed she leaves him with this prophesy: "Her whom in life thou didst abhor, in death thou shalt adore." As she dies, she gives birth to a girl who is, in every respect, her double. Once again the ancient myths of metempsychosis and the doppelgänger inform a Poe story. The language of Morella's prophesy is typical of the tale, which is written in a lyrical style that at times borders on the melodramatic. It is rich, artificial, and extremely colorful, but its colors are the phosphorescent hues of decay and death. At the denouement the narrator seems to stand, as it were, in front of his reader-audience and deliver an impassioned and rather camp soliloquy: "Years—years," he moans, "may pass away, but the memory of that epoch never!" He goes on to describe how the little girl is struck dead by the mention of her mother's name—one of many examples in a Poe story of the terrible power of words. On carrying the child to the tomb of her mother he discovers that it is empty! The struggle between the narrator and his love is typical of the "marriage group" of tales. It has been interpreted allegorically as a battle of the rational intellect and the poetic imagination, but its power derives from the fact that it is a war between the sexes rather than from any symbolic meaning.

"LIGEIA"

"Ligeia," which Poe regarded as his finest tale, also is written in an intensely lyrical style. The narrator tries to summon up the memory of his love Ligeia through rhythmical and incantatory prose. When he comes to describe her premature departure from the earth, however, his lyricism gives way to hysterical and breathless prose. In this frenzied style he tells us how he retired to a ruined abbey in one of the wildest and least frequented portions of England and marries his second wife, a woman whom he loathes. Inside the abbey we find "gorgeous and fantastic draperies . . . Bedlam patterns [on] the carpets of tufted gold!" There is a "huge censer . . . Saracenic in pattern" and an enormous tapestry "spotted all over, at irregular intervals, with arabesque figures." The patterns of the tapestry seem to move and change shape as the viewer walks toward it. Up close they resemble an "endless succession of . . . ghastly forms" whose "phantasmagoric effect [is] vastly heightened by the artificial introduction of a strong continual current of wind behind the draperies—giving a hideous and uneasy animation to the whole." The pattern of the tapestry once again may serve as an evocative symbol of Poe's own arabesque prose, with its rich artificial colors and intricate repetitions. The narrator, who becomes the slave of opium, contemplates the patterns and the body of his second wife (who is dying) and gradually descends into madness.

It may be insanity that leads him to claim, at the conclusion of the story, that his wife's corpse suddenly has become possessed by the spirit of Ligeia. Rising from its deathbed, the corpse's eyes suddenly open: they are the eyes of Ligeia, whose will to live is, we are led to suppose, so strong that she is resurrected in another body. Critics have for many years debated the question of whether the denouement is "real" or simply one of the many "wild visions, opium-engendered," that flit "shadow-like" before the narrator's eye. The question is itself rather insane, because it attempts to apply the standards of reality to a work of art. Another question frequently asked about "Ligeia," and, indeed, about all of Poe's *Tales,* concerns his relationship to the narrator. Is the narrator, it is asked, a thinly veiled version of Poe? Because of the dramatic nature of Poe's writing, it is perhaps better to think of him as the director of a personal stock company of actors rather than as someone who speaks directly through them.

"BERENICE"

"Berenice" is the intimate dramatic monologue of Egaeus, who, as it were, whispers his gruesome little tale in the reader's ear. "It is mere idleness," he says at one point, "to say that I had not lived before. . . . You deny it?—let us not argue the matter." Egaeus is a typical Poe creation: his disposition is sickly, melancholy, and bookish. (He was born in a library.) He is so idealistic that, to him, visions are realities and realities mere dreams. One of these dreamlike figures is his wife, Berenice, who, like Poe's other heroines, has no independent existence outside the narrator's mind. Egaeus becomes obsessed with Berenice's teeth (which he seems to confuse with the Platonic idea of teeth) and, after her premature burial, he digs up her body and surgically removes them.

In a letter to Thomas Willis White, Poe admitted that the tale approached "the very verge of bad-taste," In self-defense, he said that the story "originated in a bet that I could produce nothing effective on a subject so singular" (quoted in Mabbott's *Collected Works of Edgar Allan Poe*). (Here Poe's attitude to writing as a kind of personal performance is clear.) He also said that countless magazines were full of equally horrific stories. Poe plainly understood the human fascination with the hideous and the gruesome; the fact that the tale has been reproduced frequently in anthologies of his stories proves that that fascination is enduring. Put simply, we enjoy tales that, in the words of Charles Dickens' "Fat Boy," from *The Pickwick Papers*, make our flesh creep even when, as is the case with "Berenice," they come close to making us sick.

TALES OF THE GROTESQUE

Poe's comic tales are rarely reproduced in modern anthologies of his writings, which tend to feature only his arabesque stories. As a result, our appreciation of the variety of his fictions has greatly diminished. This would have horrified Poe, who prided himself on his ability to turn his hand to every type of tale: "Variety" as he remarked in 1844, "has been one of my chief aims" (quoted in Mabbott). Just like his mother, who was renowned for her ability to play a range of tragic and comic roles in the same theatrical season, Poe effortlessly swapped his suit of sables for motley attire.

Tales reminds us of this gift, as over half of its contents are comic or "grotesque." The meaning of this word in relation to Poe has been a matter of much conjecture. Poe himself frequently substituted for "grotesques" words such as "bizarreries," "extravagances," "satires," and "burlesques." One characteristic of Poe's grotesque writing is exaggeration and caricature; another is the introduction of incongruous elements, such as comedy and tragedy. There are also elements of the ludicrous, the absurd, and the surreal about Poe's comic writing: he allows his imagination and his pen the license to wander where they wish. This is what gives them their intense but rather manic energy. And it is this, along with Poe's consistently black brand of humor that makes them rather inhuman and hysterical.

There is a philosophic dimension to Poe's comedy. As we have seen, he seems to have regarded the human condition as inherently grotesque. With only the inadequate tools of language and reason to assist them, his characters are utterly incapable of understanding themselves or the world around them. At times, Poe's attitude appears closer to that of twentieth-century existentialists than it does to many of his contemporaries. There is certainly a sense in which his humor derives from his detachment from the world of nineteenth-century America.

Without wishing to repeat the cliché of Poe as "the other" of American society—with its belief in progress, rationality, democracy, and the inherent goodness of the human being—it is impossible not to see Poe as something of an outsider. And it is, of course, social outsiders who traditionally have been comedians. We think of medieval jesters, such as Poe's own "Hop-Frog," or of eighteenth-century satirists, such as the misanthropic Jonathan Swift, who was the self-appointed conscience of his society. There is certainly a Swiftian quality in Poe's satirical pieces, particularly when he attacks the literary world of nineteenth-century America; it is also at the very heart of his design for the *Tales of the Folio Club.* Poe's comic tales also contain elements of genuine tragedy and horror. Just as we found traces of humor, parody, and self-parody in his arabesque works, so, too, can his grotesques suddenly shift in mood from the ridiculous to the serious and the sublime. G. R. Thompson is surely correct to suggest a similarity between the comic and tragic parts of Poe's oeuvre.

"LIONIZING"

Perhaps to display the variety of his talents and his actorlike ability to play an infinite number of narratorial roles, Poe placed the funny story "Lionizing" straight after "Morella" in the first volume of *Tales.* It opens with the words of the narrator Robert Jones: "I am—that is to say, I *was*—a great man" and goes on to describe his progress in the literary circles of "the city of Fum-Fudge" (London). Jones, who seems to have been based on the writer and politician Benjamin Disraeli, becomes so famous for his pamphlet on Nosology (here defined as the science of Noses), that he is invited to dinner by "that sad little rake, the Prince of Wales." At the dinner he finds a gathering of the intellectual heavyweights of the day, all of whose ideas and pretensions are satirized. The scene, which is worthy of the satirist Thomas Love Peacock, is a Folio Club meeting in little.

Here Poe exhibits his great gifts as a dramatist and mimic. Jones's description of his own speech at the Prince's dinner is reminiscent of Laurence Sterne, who also famously wrote "Of Noses" in *The Life and Opinions of Tristram Shandy.* "I spoke of myself" Jones remarks, "—of myself, of myself, of myself;— of Nosology, of my pamphlet, and of myself. I turned up my nose, and I spoke of myself." The most obvious targets of Poe's satire were the egotistical and mediocre writers who tried to carve their way to literary fame through self-advertisement and the literary establishment and reading public that allowed them to do so. An ironic footnote to the tale is provided by Poe himself, who was to out-Jones Jones when he praised his own story in an anonymous review. Of course, the story is itself a bid for literary celebrity, something he seems to have craved but also despised.

"THE MAN THAT WAS USED UP: A TALE OF THE LATE BUGABOO AND KICKAPOO CAMPAIGN"

This story is a satire of the beliefs and pretensions of Poe's contemporaries. We are told at the beginning that the General John A. B. C. Smith is the paragon of the age—a handsome and altogether *remarkable* man—but discover at the denouement that he is, quite literally, a collection of artificial limbs. The general reels off platitudes of praise for the age he represents: he tells the narrator they narrator that they live "in a wonderful age. Parachutes and rail-roads— man-traps and spring guns! . . . electro magnetics!" The other characters in the story spout similar clichés about progress and the greatness of the age. The obvious point that Poe makes in the surreal conclusion, in which we see the general as he really is, is that beneath all the chatter the age is devoid of substance.

Poe's satire is extremely grotesque. The detachment that is necessary for his wit is also disturbing: he presents humanity in this tale as artificial automata. The Reverend Dr. Drummummup, Mr. Tattle, and Mrs. Pirouette are just a few of the names of his walking, talking caricatures. There is no depth to any of them, and the surfaces are hideous. It is a very dark vision of the world. References to contemporary politicians, generals, and events are scattered throughout the tale, which is one of those whose context must be understood before it is fully appreciated. One aspect of the tale's humor that the modern reader *can* understand is the element of self-parody it contains. It opens with the line, "I cannot just now remember when or where I first made the acquaintance of [the general]," which is direct parody of the beginning of "Ligeia."

"THE DUC DE L'OMELETTE"

This is also a tale that needs a great deal of annotation to make it accessible to the modern reader; even then, however, it is difficult to enjoy. It concerns a Parisian Duc who is so revolted at being served an ortolan in an incorrect manner that he expires on the spot. He wakes up in hell and challenges the devil to a game of cards; if he wins he will be allowed to return to earth. At the Folio Club meeting the tale was almost certainly the offering of the host (and thus the loser of the previous literary contest), "Mr. Rouge-et-Noir, who admired Lady Morgan," a contemporary Irish novelist. Mr. Rouge-et-Noir is a caricature of N. P. Willis, editor of the *American Monthly Magazine*. Unfortunately, because most readers of the tale know little about Willis (whose main claim to fame is that he is the subject of Poe's satire), most of the jokes are lost on us.

Certain aspects of the story, however, can be appreciated. It is a good example of a Poe tale that is close to an essay or article. The tone of the opening line, "Keats fell by a criticism," is that of the book review and thus may demonstrate the influence of Poe's journalism on his fictional writing. The beginning is also characteristic of the method of many of Poe tales—that of bombarding the reader with a great deal of information. After the title and an epigraph, we are given the statement about Keats; this is followed by a literary allusion, a (plagiarized) footnote in French and English, and an invocation to the spirit of Apicius. Here, as elsewhere, Poe immediately immerses the reader in his story: the effect can be disorientating, but it also makes one curious about what is going on.

"BON-BON"

The grotesqueness of this tale lies in its combination of the apparently incompatible disciplines of philosophy and cooking and its comparisons between food and ideas. The hero, Pierre Bon-Bon, is a chef and a metaphysician. In his restaurant "a dish of polemics stood peacefully upon the dresser. . . . Plato reclined at his ease in the frying-pan." He believes that "the powers of the intellect [hold] intimate connection with the capabilities of the stomach." The joke is continued when the devil, who is both an epicure and an Epicurean, arrives on the scene to discuss the nature of the soul. When the devil informs Bon-Bon that he eats souls, the metaphysician offers the devil his soul prepared as stew, soufflé, or fricassee. The tale is still effective, because the target of Poe's caustic wit is very general: it can be read as a satire of philosophers who, while discussing the soul, really think about more earthly matters all the time.

"THE DEVIL IN THE BELFRY"

The devil makes another appearance in this funny burlesque tale that parodies both historical writing and small-town bourgeois life. The narrator relates with "all that rigid impartiality, all that cautious examination into facts . . . which should ever distinguish him who aspires to the title of historian" a purely fictional incident in the Dutch borough of Vondervotteimittiss ("wonder what time it is"—a typically silly Poe name). The borough is a bourgeois utopia. Each house and citizen is alike, nothing out of the ordinary ever occurs, and everyone is united in their love of cabbages and clocks and in their determination to stick by "the good old course of things." The devil, however, has other ideas. On entering the borough in flamboyant attire, he ascends the belfry and, when midday arrives, takes enormous delight in ringing the great town bell not twelve but thirteen times. The citizens' sense of reality is destroyed, and uproar ensues.

As a satire of the bourgeois mentality the story is very effective. In the nineteenth century "time" became an all-powerful god. Greenwich Mean Time, which set global time, was established; punctuality was elevated to the status of one of the seven deadly virtues; and work was measured by the hour. Where previously the seasons, the position of the sun in the sky, or the church bell had set and regulated the rhythm of people's lives, the clock now determined everything. In many of Poe's tales, such as "The Masque of the Red Death," clocks are objects of horror and fear; in "The Devil" they are treated in a lighter manner.

"THE SIGNORA ZENOBIA" AND "THE SCYTHE OF TIME"

These companion pieces (the two were originally published together and later revised as "How to Write a Blackwood's Article" and "A Predicament," respectively) are witty parodies of the kind of sensational stories that were printed in the popular *Blackwood's Edinburgh Magazine*. The silly Signora Zenobia is a seeker of literary fame who travels from America to Edinburgh to consult the editor of *Blackwood's* about fictional writing. Poe mimics her voice to perfection: "I presume everybody has heard of me," she says, by way of introduction. "My name is Signora Psyche Zenobia. This I know to be a fact. Nobody but my enemies ever calls me Suky Snobbs." The editor of the celebrated organ advises her always to give a record of her sensations. "Sensations are the great things after all," he says. "Should you ever be drowned or hung, be sure and make a note of your sensations—they will be worth to you ten guineas a sheet." Along with this he suggests that she adopt the "tone metaphysical" and an air of erudition. Furthermore, she must "above all, study innuendo. Hint everything—assert nothing."

The interview draws to a close with a few specific words of advice concerning the inclusion of certain expressions and quotations. These are incorporated verbatim into "The Scythe of Time," a portentously titled story based on the Signora's experience immediately after the meet-

ing. In the tale, which is a parody of a real *Blackwood's* story, Zenobia ascends the steeple of Edinburgh cathedral and there gets her head stuck in an aperture. To her horror, she finds that the minute hand of the cathedral clock is slowly descending toward her neck; eventually it severs her head from her body. While this is happening she conveys her "sensations" in a marvelously hyperbolic *Blackwood's* style and continues writing long after her head falls down to the street below. The humor here is as grotesque and hysterical as anything that can be found in the works of Charles Dickens.

In these two tales Poe once again proves himself to be a master of parody. He displays a genius for breaking down a typical *Blackwood's* story into a series of clichés and formulas (an aspect of his genius that is also exhibited in his analyses of his own and others' writing); his imitation of silly bluestocking authoresses is also superb. Yet, at the same time, he is parodying his own Gothic productions. As we have seen, his arabesque tales are extremely sensational; they also have an air of indefiniteness and profound erudition. Indeed "The Scythe of Time" has an obvious "double" in Poe's oeuvre: the terrifying tale "The Pit and the Pendulum." Poe's fondness for self-parody reveals an intelligence that is endlessly playful and self-conscious. One source of his self-consciousness, clearly evident in this case, was his ambivalent attitude to magazine writing. Although he excelled at the form, the "aristocratic" artist in him obviously regarded typical magazine stories as nothing more than a collection of hackneyed images and cheap tricks. His genius lay in his ability to use those clichés and tricks to create stories of great power, originality, and, in the case of these two tales, considerable wit.

"VON JUNG"

"Von Jung" ("Mystification") is essentially a character sketch of the eponymous hero, Baron Ritzner Von Jung. One of the many sources of the modern short story was the character sketch, which featured in eighteenth-century publications, such as the *Spectator*. Von Jung is a trickster of genius who dedicates his life to "the science of *mystification*" His hoaxes are designed to expose the ignorance and pretensions of his victims. One evening, at a drinking party at his university that is reminiscent of a similar occasion in "William Wilson," Von Jung elects as his victim Hermann, who is a devotee of chivalry. Poe's tale is an account of this anecdote, related by a Doctor Watson–like narrator, who appears to be the only friend of Von Jung. The tale is indeed not unlike a detective story, except that the master intellectual does not explain a crime but one of his own elaborate hoaxes. Von Jung has been regarded as a self-portrait. A consummate actor and a mischievous prankster, Von Jung mercilessly pokes fun at his contemporaries. In this instance he does so through the device of an arcane text whose meaning can be deciphered only by the initiated. His victim pretends that he understands the text and in doing so reveals his own stupidity and pomposity. When commenting on Poe, there is always the danger that the critic will find himself in a similarly embarrassing position.

"LOSS OF BREATH"

Like "The Scythe of Time," this is a parody of the sensational stories that frequently appeared in *Blackwood's*. The tale, which is by turns ludicrous, terrifying, hilarious, and sickening, is at all times utterly grotesque. It is the first-person narration of a bizarre individual with the Dickensian name of Lackobreath. One morning, while cursing his "hag" of a wife, he literally loses his breath. Going out in search of it, he is caught up in a series of adventures that involves, among other things, his hanging, dismemberment by a surgeon, and premature burial—all of which are carried out by people who believe him to be a corpse. Lackobreath narrates these incidents in a calm and meditative manner; there are many erudite allusions and philosophical asides along the way.

In "Loss of Breath," Poe allows his surreal, absurd, and endlessly inventive imagination to run wild. To read it is to enter a looking-glass world in which everything is turned on its head. It is the brilliantly executed soliloquy of a madman, and, though comic in intent, at times it is as horrific as "Berenice." Sentences such as the following, which remind one of Dickens and look forward to Samuel Beckett and Franz Kafka, are typical: "It was ordered that I should be interred in a public vault. Here, after due interval, I was deposited. . . . A line in Marston's *Malcontent* . . . struck me at that moment as a palpable lie." Elements of self-parody can be found throughout the tale. Indeed, many of Poe's famous themes—the double, premature burial, the imp of the perverse, among them—are brilliantly sent up.

"WHY THE LITTLE FRENCHMAN WEARS HIS HAND IN A SLING"

This is an account of an incident involving the narrator, Sir Pathrick O'Grandison, and a Frenchman, who are competing for the affections of one Mistress Tracle. The story, which is essentially a brief anecdote, gives Poe the opportunity to display his considerable gifts as a mimic, and its comedy lies in the dialects of his protagonists. The Frenchman is fond of such phrases as "Pully woo" and "Wully woo," while the narrator speaks with a thick Irish accent. "'Tip o' the mornin' to ye' says I, 'Mrs. Tracle,' and thin I made sich an illigant obaysance that it wud ha quite althegither bewildered the brain o' ye.'" Like many of Poe's tales, this has to be read aloud, and in character, to be appreciated. Judging from this and other tales, it is a shame that Poe never wrote comedies for the stage. The situation in "The Little Frenchman" could easily have appeared in a contemporary farce. The critic Stephen L. Mooney has suggested that vaudeville and popular comedy were the inspiration for many of Poe's grotesque tales, and that certainly seems to be the case with this story.

"KING PEST"

This grotesque exercise in historical fiction is set in plague-ridden fourteenth-century London. It is an account of two sailors who, fleeing from a pub in which they owe money, take refuge at an undertaker's. There they meet a group of actors dressed up as King Pest and his court, all of whom are disease-ridden, mad, and intoxicated. Poe powerfully invokes this bizarre company with a Dickensian attention to detail. The scene is characteristic of Poe—it recalls, for instance, the group of revelers in "Shadow." Indeed, it might serve as a symbol of his vision of humanity. Like a writer of the Renaissance, Poe never tires of reminding us that life is a play that will soon be over and that, ultimately, it signifies nothing.

Poe's evocation of noisome and labyrinthine fourteenth-century London is superb. "The air was cold and misty. The paving-stones, loosened from their beds, lay in wild disorder amid the tall, rank grass, which sprang up around the feet and ankles." Such is his mastery of the genre that it seems a shame that he did not write other historical fictions. ("Metzengerstein" could be classed as a historical fiction, and "The Devil in the Belfry," "Epimanes," and "A Tale of Jerusalem" can be read as parodies of the genre.) The genre would have suited him, because many of his writings are concerned with the haunting of the living by the dead and of the present by the past. In addition, he would have been able to return to epochs that were far more congenial to his imagination and intellect than his own age. Here, for instance, he can write of pest-spirits, plague-goblins, and other superstitions that the age of reason and science had tried to banish.

"EPIMANES"

The target of Poe's satire in "Epimanes" ("Four Beasts in One—The Homo Cameleopard") was Horace Smith, the style of whose *Tales of the Early Ages* is wittily parodied. The anonymous narrator in Poe's tale conducts an absurd dialogue with the reader and introduces a number of silly anachronisms into his narrative. The tale concerns a Syrian king of the second century B.C. who was famous for cultivating the affection of a mob, which worshipped and then turned on him. The situation affords Poe the opportunity to satirize President Andrew Jackson (who also may have been a satirical target in "King Pest"), whom Poe seems to have regarded as a demagogue. Poe is also able to ridicule "the people" (one of his great bugbears), here described as "a tumultuous mob of idiots and madmen" who worship an animal. The comedy and the satirical bite of the story thus derive from its contemporary associations. Without an understanding of its immediate context, it is difficult to appreciate the tale, except perhaps as an allegory concerning the savageness that lies beneath any society's civilized surface.

"SIOPE—A FABLE"

This marvelous prose poem (later retitled "Silence—A Fable") is written in the style of the King James Bible. "It was night," a demon tells the narrator, "and the rain fell; and, falling, it was rain, but, having fallen, it was blood." The demon goes on to describe a Byronic solitary who sits on a rock somewhere in Africa and who is so disturbed by the desolation of the landscape and by the silence that, suddenly, he runs away. "Siope" is more like a picture or an account of a dream than a "tale." It is a characteristic Poe production in its indefiniteness and suggestiveness, and its ultimate "meaning" has eluded the critics. It has been read as an allegory of Christ's time in the wilderness or of the crisis that the modern human being faces in a godless universe. It also has been regarded as a satire of New England transcendentalists and as a parody of such writers as Edward Bulwer-Lytton. At the Folio Club meeting it is likely that it was to have been the offering of "a very little man in a black coat and with very black eyes." This, along with the numerous echoes of

Poe's poetry that it contains, has led certain critics to suggest that the tale is an exercise in self-parody.

"A TALE OF JERUSALEM"

Like "Epimanes," this tale, an account of an incident that occurred when Pompey the Great besieged the Holy City in 63 B.C., is a parody of the historical fiction of Horace Smith. Introducing phrases from Smith's *Zillah: A Tale of the Holy City* (1828) and mimicking his pretentious and pseudo-scholarly style, Poe mercilessly sends up this popular author. While Poe's purpose is obviously satirical, he also is demonstrating his ability to master yet another prose style. In this respect, the story is a typical Poe performance; as readers, we applaud his genius for mastering a new voice. Again, he can be compared to an actor who wishes to be famous for the range of characters, styles, and effects in his repertoire. The closest nineteenth-century literary parallel that can be drawn is with the poet Robert Browning, who, in his dramatic monologues, also gave eyewitness accounts of historical episodes.

SCIENCE FICTION TALES

The extent to which Poe invented, discovered, or shaped the genre of modern science fiction has been a matter of some controversy. Those who argue that Poe was the founder of the genre point to the futuristic; technological; and, particularly in the detective stories, rationalistic elements of his work. It is suggested that while older precursors of the genre, such as Thomas More, Lucian of Samosata, and Swift, used futuristic and utopian settings to make moral and satirical points, Poe was the first to employ them to examine purely material and scientific issues. It is perhaps better to approach the question through a consideration of Poe's influence. Poe's science fiction stories, two of which appeared in *Tales,* profoundly influenced later

masters of the genre, such as Jules Verne, H. G. Wells, and Isaac Asimov. It is because of Poe's importance for Verne and Wells that critics, at the turn of the last century and later, could define science fiction as the Verne-Wells-Poe "type of story—a charming romance intermingled with scientific fact and prophetic vision" (quoted in John Tresch).

This leads us to an important general point about Poe's writing that may explain the confusion certain critics feel when they attempt to estimate his literary significance. Coming to his works with knowledge of their profound influence, critics expect to find writings that meet their particular criteria of great literature. Inevitably, there are instances where this fails to occur, and they feel baffled and even cheated as a result. T. S. Eliot, who regarded Poe as an enigma for precisely this reason, is a good example of such a critic. Predictably, it is difficult to separate Poe's science fiction tales from his other works. Like the utopian literature from which they descended, his science fiction stories also contain elements of satire, sometimes of science itself. Poe's argument with science, which was rapidly becoming the most important intellectual discipline and belief system in his age, was in some respects typically Romantic. Science and industrialization, it is suggested in "The Colloquy of Monos and Una," have given human beings the false idea that they have dominion over nature; it also has led to the neglect of the poetic intellect.

Yet Poe went further than this conventional Romantic position and challenged both science's claims to objectivity and its emphasis on empiricism. So far as objectivity is concerned, Poe's tales, as David Ketterer put it, "are directed towards the demonstration that reality is a lie." Reading such hoax stories as "Hans Phaall," one is certainly left with the impression that scientific explanations of the world are not unlike stories and that science is a kind of fiction. Regarding the limitations of empiricism, Poe believed that the discovery of "facts" was not enough and that it is what one does with them that is important. It requires, Poe suggests, a visionary rather than a scientist to sort, connect, and shape them into theories. This figure, who is both poet and mathematician, appears throughout Poe's writings. Sometimes he is Dupin, the great detective; at other times he is Poe, the theorist of poetic composition.

"HANS PHAALL"

By far the longest tale in the collection, "Hans Phaall" ("The Unparalleled Adventure of One Hans Pfaall") is the eponymous hero's account of his nineteen-day balloon journey to the moon. His chronicle takes the form of a letter addressed to the President and Vice-President of the States' College of Astronomers in Rotterdam. As a setting for the tale, Rotterdam is not unlike Vondervotteimittiss (the town that features in "The Devil in the Belfry"); it offers Poe the opportunity to mock its sturdy burghers and its idiotic scientists and professors. "Hans Phaall" is one of Poe's most elaborate hoaxes. As well as being a political satire on President Jackson, it is, like Lucian's famous "True History," also a clever burlesque of popular stories concerning voyages to the moon. Yet it is at the same time a brilliant moon-journey story in its own right. As usual, Poe seems to have wanted it both ways, and, as usual, that is exactly how he got it. In an endnote to the tale, first introduced in the *Tales* version of the story, he claims that "Hans Phaall" is original "inasmuch as regards an attempt at *verisimiltude,* in the application of scientific principles . . . to the actual passage between the earth and the moon" (quoted in *Poetry and Tales*). His claim is certainly justified, as his tale is full of convincing Defoe-like detail.

This, of course, makes an either/or approach to the interpretation of the story impossible. If we regard it as a "true" and serious story, we are surely missing the joke; if we dismiss it as a hoax, we are rather like the obtuse burghers of Rotterdam to whom hoax is, as the narrator comments, "a general term for all matters above their comprehension." It is better to regard it as both a serious and comic, satirical and scientific, complex and heterogeneous production.

"THE CONVERSATION OF EIROS AND CHARMION"

The last item in *Tales* provides a perfect epilogue to the volume. In it, two disembodied spirits, sometime in the distant future, calmly discuss the destruction of the earth by a comet. The ignorant multitude, the learned scientists, and the religious are all incapable of understanding or explaining the approaching disaster, and all are consumed by fire. In his poetry and in his fiction, Poe searched for a language that could rival music in its power to evoke the spiritual realm. Here he falls back on the old language and form of the Platonic dialogue: a form then very popular among satirical writers, such as Peacock and the poet William Blake. It also was used by such intellectual pessimists as the Italian lyric poet and philosopher Giacomo Leopardi, who used it in his *Operette morali* (1827) to view humankind, as it were, from a great distance. From this perspective humans are presented as insignificant and idiotic: this is precisely the vision of "The Conversation." Poe later wrote other Platonic dialogues, and it is hardly surprising that he was attracted to the form. It gave him the opportunity to examine issues from multiple perspectives; it is also essentially an oral and a theatrical form.

RECEPTION AND INFLUENCE

Tales of the Grotesque and Arabesque did not sell particularly well, and it received mixed reviews. Certain critics took objection to what they referred to as Poe's "extravagance" and "Germanism," but others looked more favorably on the volume, praising Poe's artistry, variety, originality, and learning. Poe displayed a gift for self-publicity that would have impressed the hero of "Lionizing," by reproducing some of the favorable comments that he had received in the second volume of *Tales*. He was praised by fellow writers, among them Washington Irving and Charles Dickens, who tried, unsuccessfully, to find a publisher for the book in England. These were the first in a long line of authors who understood the nature and the magnitude of Poe's achievement. Later writers would be even more enthusiastic and hail Poe as an original genius and an inspiration.

The influence of *Tales,* and of Poe's stories generally, has indeed been profound. His arabesque tales influenced, among many others, Stephen King, H. P. Lovecraft (who referred to his own tales of horror as "Poe stories"), Kafka, and Fyodor Dostoyevsky. The Argentine writer Jorge Luis Borges, who regarded Poe as the unacknowledged father of twentieth-century literature, remarked that when he composed several of his stories, he had the sensation that it was Poe's ghost that was writing them. The master of cinematic suspense and terror, Alfred Hitchcock, read the *Tales* at the age of sixteen, and the experience was a formative one; he later remarked that they inspired him to make films. More broadly, Poe's tales, with their consummate artistry, self-consciousness, and heavy atmosphere of decay, greatly influenced "decadent" and "symbolist" writers of the nineteenth century. Charles Baudelaire, among whose earliest works were translations of Poe's stories, famously died with a copy of Poe's tales beside his bed; Oscar Wilde worshiped him.

Poe's influence has endured to this day; one recent example of his influence can be mentioned in conclusion. In 1999 the English author Peter Ackroyd published a utopian novel entitled *The Plato Papers,* which in its structure and style is not unlike one of Poe's own futuristic dialogues. In this book, the society of the future discovers a sealed casket that contains a copy of Poe's *Tales.* From the *Tales* they reconstruct the characteristics of American society in the nineteenth century, surmising, for instance, that Americans were aristocrats with pale countenances and large eyes. *The Plato Papers* is both a fitting homage to Poe and a testimony to the fact that he is still haunting writers and artists. Indeed, like one of his own characters, he continues to return, in various guises, to the world of the living and to speak, in different voices, from beyond the grave.

Select Bibliography

EDITIONS

Collected Works of Edgar Allan Poe. Vol. 2, *Tales and Sketches.* Edited by Thomas Ollive Mabbott. Cambridge, Mass.: Belknap Press of Harvard University Press, 1969. (The best edition.)

Edgar Allan Poe: Poetry and Tales. Edited by Patrick F. Quinn. New York: Library of America, 1984.

Edgar Allan Poe: Essays and Reviews. Edited by Gary Richard Thompson. New York: Library of America, 1984. (The two volumes published by Library of America are a cheaper, more accessible, option than the *Collected Works. Essays and Reviews* includes "Marginalia.")

SECONDARY WORKS

Ackroyd, Peter. *The Plato Papers: A Novel.* London: Chatto & Windus, 1999. (Includes a spoof lecture on Poe.)

Auden, Wystan H. Introduction to *The Recognition of Edgar Allan Poe: Selected Criticism Since 1829*. Edited by Eric W. Carlson. Ann Arbor: University of Michigan Press, 1966.

Baudelaire, Charles. *Selected Writings on Art and Artists*. Harmondsworth, Eng.: Penguin, 1972. (Includes the famous essays on Poe.)

Bloom, Harold. "Introduction." In *Edgar Allan Poe. Modern Critial Views*. Edited by Harold Bloom. New York: Chelsea House, 1985.

Carlson, Eric W., ed. *The Recognition of Edgar Allan Poe: Selected Criticism Since 1829*. Ann Arbor: University of Michigan Press, 1966. (Collection of all of the famous essays on Poe, including those by T. S. Eliot, W. H. Auden, Walt Whitman, and others.)

———. "Edgar Allan Poe." In *Dictionary of Literary Biography*. Vol. 74, *American Short Story Writers before 1880*. Edited by Bobby Ellen Kimbel. Detroit: Gale, 1988. Pp. 303–322.

———, ed. *A Companion to Poe Studies*. Westport, Conn.: Greenwood Press, 1996. (A comprehensive, but expensive, collection of modern appraisals of every aspect of Poe's life and work.)

Clarke, Graham. *Edgar Allan Poe: Critical Assessments*. 4 vols. Mountfield, Eng.: Helm Information, 1991.

Hammond, Alexander. "A Reconstruction of Poe's 1833 'Folio Club.'" *Poe Studies* 5, no. 2 (December 1972): 25–32.

Hayes, Kevin J. *The Cambridge Companion to Edgar Allan Poe*. Cambridge: Cambridge University Press, 2002. (Excellent and wide-ranging collection of essays on Poe's work.)

Hoffman, Daniel. *Poe Poe Poe Poe Poe Poe Poe*. Baton Rouge: Louisiana State University Press, 1998. (Eccentric, original, and occasionally illuminating study of Poe's works.)

Hyneman, Esther F. *Edgar Allan Poe: An Annotated Bibliography of Books and Articles in English, 1827–1973*. Boston: G. K. Hall, 1974.

Jungquist, Kent L. "The Poet as Critic." In *The Cambridge Companion to Edgar Allan Poe*. Edited by Kevin J. Hayes. Cambridge: Cambridge University Press, 2002.

Kennedy, J. Gerald, ed. *A Historical Guide to Edgar Allan Poe*. New York: Oxford University Press, 2001. (New Historicist approach to Poe.)

Ketterer, David. *New Worlds for Old: The Apocalyptic Imagination, Science Fiction, and American Literature*. Garden City, N.Y.: Anchor Press, 1974. (Interesting comments on Poe's science fiction.)

Kumar, Satish. *Edgar Allan Poe: Structure and Style of His Short Stories*. New Delhi: Bahr Publications, 1989.

Mooney, Stephen L. "Poe's Gothic Wasteland." In *The Recognition of Edgar Allan Poe: Selected Criticism Since 1829*. Edited by Eric W. Carlson. Ann Arbor: University of Michigan Press, 1966.

Peeples, Scott. *Edgar Allan Poe Revisited*. New York: Twayne, 1998. (Good as an introduction to present-day Poe criticism.)

Polonsky, Rachel. "Poe's Aesthetic Theory." In *The Cambridge Companion to Edgar Allan Poe*. Edited by Kevin J. Hayes. Cambridge: Cambridge University Press, 2002.

Regan, Robert, ed. *Poe: A Collection of Critical Essays*. Englewood Cliffs, N. J.: Prentice-Hall, 1967. (Inexpensive collection of the important older essays on Poe.)

Silverman, Kenneth. *Edgar A. Poe: Mournful and Never-Ending Remembrance.* New York: HarperCollins, 1991. (The best biography to date.)

———, ed. *New Essays on Poe's Major Tales.* New York: Cambridge University Press, 1993.

Thompson, G. R. *Poe's Fiction: Romantic Irony in the Gothic Tales.* Madison: University of Wisconsin Press, 1973. (Excellent analysis of the humorous and satirical elements in Poe's fiction.)

Tresch, John. "Extra! Extra! Poe invents science fiction!" In *The Cambridge Companion to Edgar Allan Poe.* Edited by Kevin J. Hayes. Cambridge: Cambridge University Press, 2002.

Walker, I. M., ed. *Edgar Allan Poe: The Critical Heritage.* New York: Routledge & Kegan Paul, 1986. (Includes several reviews of *Tales.*)

Wilson, Edmund. "Poe at Home and Abroad." In *Edgar Allan Poe: Critical Assessments.* Vol. 4. Edited by Graham Clarke. Mountfield, Eng.: Helm Information, 1991.

T. S. Eliot's
The Waste Land

JAY PARINI

AMERICAN POETRY IN the twentieth century has no more obvious and important landmark than *The Waste Land,* T. S. Eliot's famously difficult and original poem in five parts. It remains one of the founding texts in the movement known as literary modernism. Since its initial publication by Hogarth Press in 1922, the poem has compelled vast critical attention, yet it remains elusive—a masterwork that critics and casual readers alike have failed to comprehend fully. Indeed, its nature is such that no single reading of the poem can exhaust its mystery, which inheres in endlessly suggestive passages that cluster and reverberate in fresh ways on each successive reading.

Though it was written by one of America's great poets, the poem has a decidedly European flavor. This is because Eliot was an expatriate, who spent most of his adult life in London and who read widely in world literature and thought of himself as an international writer. Nevertheless, Eliot's debt to American literature, especially to Walt Whitman—the pioneer of the long poetic sequence—is obvious in the rhythms of the poem, the use of poetic "catalogues," and the mastery of free verse. Eliot himself

acknowledged this debt to Whitman in his later years, as did his friend and fellow poet Ezra Pound in his poem "A Pact," where he addresses Whitman directly as the breaker of "new wood."

The Waste Land was largely composed in 1921 in Lausanne, Switzerland, where Eliot had gone by himself to recover from a nervous breakdown precipitated by overwork and a difficult marriage. It is really a sequence of loosely connected poems that, with help from Pound, were hewn from a much longer manuscript. (The original version, with Pound's editing cuts and comments, has been published and is fascinating to examine.) Pound's influence on Eliot— especially on *The Waste Land*—can hardly be overestimated; his cuts contribute immeasurably to the feeling of radical disjunction that permeates the poem. The logic of the poem as it stands, its argument and structure, defies the usual norms of narrative progression. Eliot allowed himself, and the sense of the poem, to proceed by association, following a kind of dream logic as the subject of the poem leaps from image to image as if irrationally. The usual connective tissue that might have held together a more conventional narrative is missing—on purpose.

Eliot wanted the reader to experience the aura of dislocation, which might be called the principal affect of the poem.

The sequence originally was called "He Do the Police in Different Voices," a line lifted from Charles Dickens' novel *Our Mutual Friend* (1864–1865), where Dickens refers to a character good at impersonating various policemen. Eliot, the grand ventriloquist, becomes the impersonator in his poem, taking on different voices from many segments of society. As always, his ear is astonishing, capturing the cadences and diction of many classes and types, from the aristocratic Marie of the first section, "The Burial of the Dead," to the Cockney women in the pub who make a memorable appearance in the second section, "A Game of Chess." A wide range of characters from high and low, past and present, are summoned in broad strokes, disappearing almost as quickly as they appear in the poem's vivid phantasmagoria of association.

One has to wonder if *The Waste Land* would have made such an impact on readers had it not carried its suggestive title, which so perfectly captures the feeling of alienation and psychic trauma that marked the period immediately following World War I. That war—the first in history where the technological capabilities for destruction matched the human impulse to destroy everything in its wake—seems to have had a particularly brutal impact on Great Britain, which lost a whole generation of talented young men in what seemed to many a senseless cause. The streets of London, where Eliot lived (he had been forced to terminate studies in Germany because of the conflict), were littered with wounded veterans, many of them deeply traumatized by their experience.

THE DISLOCATED AMERICAN

Eliot was born in St. Louis in 1888, the son of well-to-do parents with deep roots in Puritan New England. He was educated in private schools before attending Harvard, from which

CHRONOLOGY

1888	Thomas Stearns Eliot is born in St. Louis, Missouri, on September 26.
1910	Graduates from Harvard with a master's degree.
1911–1914	Studies in France. Returns to Harvard for graduate studies in philosophy and then studies in Germany and England.
1915	Marries Vivienne Haigh-Wood and publishes "The Love Song of J. Alfred Prufrock."
1920	First book of criticism, *The Sacred Wood.*
1922	*The Waste Land.*
1922–1939	Serves as editor of the *Criterion*, an important quarterly review of literature.
1935	First of his many plays, *Murder in the Cathedral,* is performed.
1936–1942	Publishes *Four Quartets* in four installments.
1948	Receives the Nobel Prize for literature.
1965	Dies on January 4.

he graduated in 1910. He migrated to Paris to study philosophy at the Sorbonne and then returned to Harvard to pursue postgraduate study in philosophy. There he completed all the requirements for the doctorate except a dissertation. He went to Germany in the summer of 1914 to study philosophy at Marburg but was driven by the outbreak of war to England, where he continued his studies at Merton College, Oxford. It was England that fired his imagination, and he soon decided to make his home there, transforming himself into a perfect English gentleman, complete with bowler hat and rolled umbrella. He married Vivienne Haigh-Wood, an emotionally unstable Englishwoman, in 1915. Rejecting an academic career, he took a job with a London bank, where he worked in the foreign exchange department. He found this occupation exhausting and ill paid and had to make ends meet by writing countless reviews for a range of English periodicals. This literary journalism forced Eliot to read, and reread, huge quantities of poetry, and he began to form ideas and opinions that would serve him well in years to come, when his profile as a critic grew immensely. Indeed, his critical writing was so distinctive that Eliot quickly became one of the most influential critics of the era.

The sense of extreme personal dislocation that Eliot experienced after the war mirrored the historical moment, and it was captured forcibly in *The Waste Land.* "I can connect / Nothing with nothing," says the narrator in the third section of the poem, "The Fire Sermon." One can fairly assume that this sentiment reflects Eliot's private situation as well as something larger— the condition of a generation picking its way through the mental and physical rubble of the war. Not surprisingly, however, readers responded in various ways to the poem, and many were frustrated by its apparent lack of narrative coherence. *The Waste Land* presents many problems to the reader, but one of the central mysteries of this poem attaches to the simplest of questions: Who is talking? One of the few identified speakers is Tiresias, who announces his presence midway through "The Fire Sermon," referring to himself as an "old man with wrinkled female breasts" who has "seen it all," quite literally. In classical myth, Tiresias is the blind old prophet who foretells the future. He is androgynous: a man with female breasts. Because he contains both man and woman in one body—so the myth suggests—he has acquired the gift of clairvoyance, and that talent seems crucial as it operates here. Eliot is writing a prophetic poem, taking his place in the line of poet-prophets from John Milton and William Blake through (in its American inflection) Ralph Waldo Emerson and Whitman.

Yet Eliot remains highly individual, with no obvious debts to his predecessors. He has been called by Hugh Kenner "the invisible poet," and this characterization makes sense in obvious ways. Eliot, in his highly influential essays, promoted the notion of a poet's "impersonality." That is, the poet ideally disappears behind

the work itself. "The progress of an artist is a continual self-sacrifice, a continual extinction of personality," he maintains in "Tradition and the Individual Talent," which he collected in a volume of essays called *The Sacred Wood: Essays on Poetry and Criticism* (1920). This formulation, coming when it did, could not have seemed more original, seeming to contradict the Romantic idea of poetry as self-expression (from the Latin *ex-pressus,* suggesting that the poet's job was to push something from inside the poet to the outside). Eliot appeared to sweep away received aesthetic opinion in one fell swoop—a daring move designed to create the right conditions for the reception of a poem like *The Waste Land,* which could hardly be regarded as personal expression except in the most deflected manner.

"THE BURIAL OF THE DEAD"

The poet in *The Waste Land* hides behind various masks, or personae. He winks from the corners of the poem, a controlling yet invisible presence, the poet-as-puppet master. Often he appears to hide behind the voices of other poets, whom he quotes literally or imitates in parodic ways, as in the eloquent opening lines of the first section, "The Burial of the Dead" (a rite from the Anglican *Book of Common Prayer*):

> April is the cruelest month, breeding
> Lilacs out of the dead land, mixing
> Memory and desire, stirring
> Dull roots with spring rain.

Eliot here parodies Chaucer in his prologue to the *Canterbury Tales* (ca. 1387–1400), turning the earlier poet on his head. April should be, as it was for Chaucer, a time of fecundity, a prelude to summer's fullness, and the ideal time to go on a pilgrimage:

> Whan that Aprille with his shoures sote
> The droghte of Marche hath perced to the rote

And bathed every veyne in swich licour
Of which vertu engendred is the flour. . . .
Thanne longen folk to goon on pilgrimages.

But Eliot's April seems oddly malevolent, breeding lilacs, the most overpowering of flowers. There is something deeply unpleasant about these lilacs, as if what they summon in the poet—a mixture of memory and desire—is unnerving. Certainly the images culled from memory throughout the poem are mostly painful, and the desires stirred by spring rain are largely unwelcome, a call to appetite—the wish to satisfy sexual and emotional urges—without the controlling discipline of love. In a crucially important line toward the end of the poem's fifth section, "What the Thunder Said," Eliot writes: "These fragments I have shored against my ruins." In a very real sense, this line encapsulates Eliot's method: he culls from the vast chambers of literature, both sacred and profane, dozens and dozens of quotations, giving the term "allusiveness" a whole new meaning. Against the ruins of time and the loss of memory and life, he puts into play these beautiful and moving lines from the literary past.

Eliot's impressive learning was not worn lightly; indeed, he uses his erudition as a means of intimidation, quoting from various ancient and modern languages, invoking a range of mythological figures, assuming familiarity with Eastern and Western religious traditions. No reader can possibly hope to recognize or understand anything but a small percentage of the works quoted or alluded to; there is something exhausting about the range of reference. This remains part of Eliot's plan. He wants to intimidate and exhaust the reader, generating a sense of ennui and alienation that reflects his own. The generous and patient reader who allows the process of alienation to take place without resenting Eliot's method, however, will be rewarded in the end, as pieces of the emotional mosaic fall into place.

The poem begins with an epigraph that stands like a dragon folded at the gate, forbidding entrance to the poem. Modestly dedicating the poem to Ezra Pound, "*il miglior fabbro*," or "the better craftsman," Eliot quotes from the *Satyricon* of Petronius, a fragmentary satirical romance written during the first century A.D. which describes the vices and social mores of imperial Rome during the time of Nero. He refuses to translate either the Latin or the Greek. The speaker in the quotation is Trimalchio, a wealthy and vulgar man who says: "With my own eyes I saw the Sibyl suspended in a glass bottle at Cumae—and when the boys said to her, 'Sibyl, what's the matter?' she would always respond, 'I yearn to die.'" The Sibyl of Cumae, in ancient Greek myth, was a figure of dark prognostications, a prophet—a version of Tiresias. She foretold the future in riddles, understanding that the unvarnished truth would be intolerable, since, as Eliot later wrote in part I of "Burnt Norton," "Human kind cannot bear very much reality." One could take the epigraph as a riddle, encoded doubly in Latin and Greek: a teasing (and annoying) gesture by which Eliot seems to say, "Break my code if you can." Like the Sibyl and like Tiresias, he also holds out to the reader the possibility of illumination, a promise that the rewards of decoding his riddle of a poem will be considerable.

Having suffered a nervous breakdown in 1921, Eliot went to Lausanne, Switzerland, to recuperate, and there he pulled the various pieces of *The Waste Land* together into a single poetic sequence. One can imagine him at the sanatorium as he sat among a crowd of neurotic and bored aristocrats, listening to their idle chatter. One of those voices, summoned brilliantly in "The Burial of the Dead," is Marie, a cousin of an anonymous archduke, who remembers riding a sled at a mountain retreat. Readers hear only a snatch of the archduke's voice as he calls to his presumably younger cousin, Marie, telling her to "hold on tight" as they ride a sled down the hillside. "In the mountains, there you feel free," Marie says, adding: "I read, much of the night, and go south in the winter." Nostalgically, she recalls a lost world of prewar European stability and the pleasures of being a member of the upper class, for whom freedom—at least freedom of movement—was taken for granted. Marie's snobbishness is captured in her ramblings, where she insists on being *"echt deutsch,"* or true German, not some mixed breed—a hint of the passion for racial purity that soon led to the attempt by Adolf Hitler to eradicate the Jews of Europe.

In the second movement of the first section, Eliot himself steps forward, assuming an almost biblical voice: "What are the roots that clutch, what branches grow / Out of this stony rubbish?" he wonders, addressing the Son of man, who is traditionally Christ. (The poet appropriates language from two Old Testament books here, alluding to *Ezekiel* in line 20 and *Ecclesiastes* in line 23.) Although he later became a confirmed member of the Church of England and a devout Anglican Christian, Eliot at this time was still searching for meaning, rooting in the dust, where he found only "a heap of broken images." The Cross of Christ, "the dead tree," offers "no shelter." The wasteland, dry, parched, and barren, emerges literally as the controlling image in this section, with Eliot offering no hope for restitution or recovery. "I will show you fear in a handful of dust," he writes and then quotes Richard Wagner's opera *Tristan und Isolde* in German (translated in English as "Fresh blew the wind to the homeland. My Irish child, where art thou?"). These are lines full of unrequited sexual longing that give way at once to one of the most lyrical moments in the poem, the evocation of the hyacinth girl:

> You gave me hyacinths first a year ago;
> "They called me the hyacinth girl."
> —Yet when we came back, late, from the hyacinth
>   garden,
> Your arms full, and your hair wet, I could not
> Speak, and my eyes failed, I was neither
> Living nor dead, and I knew nothing,
> Looking into the heart of light, the silence.
> *Oed' un leer das Meer.*

Just as the lilacs in the first lines suggest hypersensual experience—a feeling of overload—so the hyacinth floods the senses with meaning. The hyacinth flower is a potent symbol, rooted in the Greek myth of Hyakinthos, one of the most beautiful boys in Greece, who was killed accidentally by Apollo when a discus the god threw hit the boy in the head. He fell to the earth, and his blood drained into the soil, emerging as a painfully beautiful and sensuous flower, the hyacinth—a potent symbol of unrequited love. (Some critics have found concealed homoerotic meaning in these lines, suggesting that Eliot was enamored of Jean Verdenal, a young Frenchman whom he met in Paris and who was killed in the war. This line of thinking remains highly speculative but no less tantalizing.)

With an infallible ear, Eliot manages to segue from the German lyric into English and concludes the section with another quotation from Wagner's opera, which translates: "Waste and empty the sea." The Wagner opera tells the sad story of lovers doomed to suffer more pain than joy from their love. It is a story of separation and anguish, of lack of fulfillment, and Eliot wants the reader to have access to that whole range of powerful feelings—which he attempts to evoke by simply quoting a few poignant lines in German. (Of course, Eliot assumes familiarity with the opera and the story that lies behind it.) This technique of blending languages, of mingling his own verse with quotations (acknowledged and unacknowledged), was and remains highly original. One rarely sees such allusiveness in poetry. Indeed, were Eliot writing now, he might well be accused—unfairly—of plagiarism. But as he himself suggested, great poets do not imitate; they steal. Eliot takes whatever he needs, rifling through major and minor texts for fragments that he shores against his ruins. The crucial point is that he places these quotations in a new context. He boldly makes them his own.

The third major section of "The Burial of the Dead" brings into play another prophet, though perhaps a bogus one: Madame Sosostris, a clairvoyant modeled loosely on Madame Blavatsky, a famous spiritualist who cut a broad swathe through British upper-class society in Eliot's time. (Seances were especially popular in the immediate postwar period and were used by bereaved parents, wives, and children as a means of getting in touch with departed loved ones.) The craze for spiritualism was such that various techniques for telling the future were employed, including the use of Tarot cards. In Eliot's poem, the Tarot figures became convenient symbols linking to other characters and events in the poem. But as the poet carefully points out in his footnotes, he possessed no deep knowledge of the Tarot pack and used the names of various cards to suit his own convenience.

One hears Madame Sosostris talking, as if calling up a vision of the walking dead as she hovers above a crystal ball: "I see crowds of people walking round in a ring." This was the sort of thing a medium at a seance would commonly say, drawing the attention of those around the table. A voice answers, "Thank you. If you see dear Mrs. Equitone, / Tell her I bring the horoscope myself: / One must be so careful these days." Here Eliot summons a contemporary upper-middle-class voice, embodied in the parodic name of Equitone (her voice uniformly false at all moments). Her obsession with bringing her own horoscope suggests that nobody trusts anyone else anymore and that one must control the paraphernalia of spiritualism oneself—a guard against false prophets that is obviously futile, especially in this situation. The card selected from the Tarot pack by Eliot—the drowned Phoenician Sailor, for example—will emerge later in the poem, in other contexts.

As a whole, "The Burial of the Dead" refers specifically to the Anglican burial ceremony, and the final movement of the section constitutes a majestic evocation of the Unreal City, where the dead from all eras walk together in dismal consort. That city is specifically London, but it reaches beyond any geographic locale, standing in contrast to the Eternal City promised to those

who believe in God. Indeed, the poet-prophet (Tiresias again?) looks out over London Bridge at the crowd and says, "I had not thought death had undone so many." Dante utters these very words in the *Inferno,* the first part of the *Divine Comedy* (begun ca. 1307), when he considers the multitude of dead souls. As ever, Eliot conflates his own voice with the Voice—the generalized voice of poetry and prophecy, as embodied by Tiresias, Dante, and so many others.

The final movement of "The Burial of the Dead" ends with a blizzard of quotations, including a reference to the drowned Phoenician Sailor, here given an arbitrary name, Stetson (not very Greek, just to confound any attempt to locate this figure in real time). Stetson was supposedly with the speaker in an ancient naval battle at Mylae. Quotations from the English Elizabethan dramatist John Webster's play *The White Devil* (performed 1612) and from the preface to *Les Fleurs du mal* (Flowers of evil, 1857), a book of poetry by the nineteenth-century French poet Charles Baudelaire, commingle in the final lines as Eliot turns directly toward the reader, whom he addresses as "hypocrite lecteur!" Readers are hypocritical, perhaps, because they mock these dead in their hearts, even though they shall soon enough join them. Indeed, some of the poem's disconcerting effects derive from this sense of complicity between writer and reader.

During the years just before he wrote *The Waste Land,* Eliot was reading widely in a variety of fields, including anthropology. Two crucial books for him, as he suggests in his notes to the poem, were Jessie L. Weston's *From Ritual to Romance* (1920), a study of the themes of medieval romances and legends, and *The Golden Bough* (1890–1915), a comprehensive work on comparative religion and myth by James Frazer—two pioneering works. These books alerted Eliot to certain patterns in world mythology. Primitive people, for example, found coherence and meaning in vegetation myths that followed the cycles of the seasons, from birth in spring through fullness in summer, decay in autumn, death in winter, and return to rebirth in spring. The vegetable kingdom and its cycles informed the religions that arose in agrarian communities; in particular, one found recurring versions of the myth of the dying and reviving god, which in turn often were associated with fertility myths. The connection between Osiris, the creator god of ancient Egypt, and Christ was pointed out. Within Christian myth, the search for the Holy Grail (the actual cup used by Christ during the first Communion) was associated with heroic efforts to redeem the time. Eliot used aspects of these various myths to underpin *The Waste Land,* thus providing structure and coherence to a wildly disparate body of material. The overarching "story" of the poem concerns the Fisher King, who inherited a dry and barren land; fertility and prosperity can be restored only if a hero comes along who can find the Holy Grail. This search for a key to the restoration of his kingdom controls the narrative on many levels, bringing together on one plane so many eras.

In Eliot's poem, the wasteland of postwar London becomes analogous to earlier civilizations and periods of waste and devastation. The name of the battle that involved the mysterious drowned sailor, Stetson, recalls a conflict in which the Carthaginians were defeated, for example, and so Eliot draws the reader's attention to the sameness of all wars. The poet becomes, in effect, the hero in search of the Grail, digging amid the rubble of culture for the lost key. His search is identified with that of other great religious searchers, from the Buddha through John the Baptist and Christ.

Eliot has much in common with James Joyce here, his great counterpart in the world of fiction. In "*Ulysses,* Order, and Myth," an article on Joyce that was published in 1923, Eliot reflects on the Irish writer's use of myth in *Ulysses,* a novel that likens the travels of one man, Leopold Bloom, around Dublin to the journey of Ulysses from the Trojan War to his home on Ithaca. Eliot writes:

In using the myth, in manipulating a continuous parallel between contemporaneity and antiquity, Mr. Joyce is pursuing a method which others must pursue after him. They will not be imitators, any more than the scientist who uses the discoveries of an Einstein in pursuing his own, independent, further investigations. It is simply a way of controlling, of ordering, of giving a shape and a significance to the immense panorama of futility and anarchy which is contemporary history. It is a method already adumbrated by Mr. Yeats, and of the need for which I believe Mr. Yeats to have been the first contemporary to be conscious. . . . It is, I seriously believe, a step toward making the modern world possible for art.

"A GAME OF CHESS"

Eliot narrows the focus of *The Waste Land* considerably in the second section, "A Game of Chess," where he explores the poles of society from high to low, beginning with a section written in formal blank verse that has a classical "feel" to it. In "The Burial of the Dead" Eliot sweeps through history and geography, especially in the last section. He finds vacancy and boredom everywhere. The title of this second section comes from a play by Shakespeare's contemporary, Thomas Middleton, who, in *Women, Beware Women* (ca. 1623), presents a mother absorbed in a game of chess that distracts her from the seduction of her daughter in a room overhead. The consequences of seduction thus run throughout the section as it moves from the society of kings to that of pawns—the range found, of course, on a chessboard.

Like the girl Belinda in Alexander Pope's *The Rape of the Lock* (1714), the queen at the outset sits at her dressing table, and, like Pope, Eliot uses a mock-heroic form, beginning with echoes of Shakespeare's *Antony and Cleopatra.* "The Chair she sat in, like a burnished throne, / Glowed on the marble" directly parodies a famous passage in Shakespeare's play, when

Enobarbus depicts the royal progress of the queen on her river barge in act II, scene 2:

> The barge she sat in, like a burnish'd throne,
> Burnt on the water: the poop was beaten gold;
> Purple the sails, and so perfuméd that
> The winds were love-sick with them: the oars
>   were silver,
> Which to the tune of flutes kept stroke, and made
> The water, which they beat, to follow faster,
> As amorous of their strokes.

By contrast, the atmosphere in Eliot's royal world is sinister, with its "vials of ivory and coloured glass / Unstoppered" in which there "lurked" her strange perfumes. Above the queen's mantel is not a window looking out to a genuinely fresh country scene but a painting of a cruel scene from classical myth: the rape of Philomela (called "Philomel" here), daughter of the king of Attica, by the lascivious king Tereus of Thrace. In this world of forced entry, love and lust are confused. The sound of the nightingale, which enchanted the Romantic poet John Keats in the ode "To a Nightingale," has been crudely transformed into a world where the "inviolable voice" of the bird that Keats described has become "'Jug Jug' to dirty ears." (The word "jug" in Elizabethan English was the equivalent of a rude four-letter word that is not usually printed in dignified essays like this one!) Eliot undoubtedly refers back to the version of the nightingale/Philomela myth preferred by the sixteenth-century poet-playwright John Lyly, who wrote in "Spring's Welcome":

> What bird so sings yet so dos wayle?
> O 'Tis the ravishd Nightingale.
> Jug, Jug, Jug, tereu, shee cryes,
> And still her woes at Midnight rise.

In the myth, the beautiful Philomela is raped by Tereus (called "tereu" by Lyly) and then transformed into a nightingale—the source of poetry thus located in pain and rupture. Eliot has no wish to glorify the myth, reduced here to a painting that, along with others, he calls "withered stumps of time."

The first section bleeds into contemporary dialogue, and the voices of a man and woman are more overheard than heard—a harrowing conversation that might well occur in one of the enigmatic plays of the British playwright Harold Pinter: "My nerves are bad to-night. Yes, bad. Stay with me." There is a strange noise: "The wind under the door." Eliot's voice offers the following bizarre suggestion: "I think we are in rats' alley / Where the dead men lost their bones." The word "nothing" recurs. One does not know who is speaking or to whom; in a sense, there is no such thing as dialogue in this wasted land, where human isolation is taken to the extreme. Voices merely tumble in the void, occasionally glancing off another voice or hard object. "Nothing again nothing" gathers in its hollow paws the empty globe of meaning.

Eliot then repeats a line from Shakespeare's *Tempest*: "Those are pearls that were his eyes." The language segues into an ironic snatch of song from a contemporary pop song: "that Shakespeherian Rag." This passage is quite literally a transit from high to low society, and the final movement finds us in a London pub, where lust is once again a substitute for love: a world of artificial teeth and induced abortions. Eliot plunges into Cockney conversation that suggests that life at the lower end of society is just as barren as life at the top. Lil's husband, Albert, has just been "demobbed," or released from the army, after four years in the war. He will come home wanting "a good time"; if his wife will not give it to him, "there's others will," as Lil's friend tells her. Albert had given her money to buy false teeth—a symbol of artificiality and decay—but she had used it for an abortion. The conversation is punctuated, with a haunting regularity, by the bartender's cry: "HURRY UP PLEASE ITS TIME." (It is time to close the bar, of course, but time as well for the characters in the poem to put their house in order.) This cry is repeated with greater frequency and urgency until, in the final lines, it bleeds into the last words of Ophelia, the betrayed heroine of Shakespeare's *Hamlet:* "Good night, ladies, good night, sweet ladies; good night, good night."

"THE FIRE SERMON"

In the third section, "The Fire Sermon," Eliot brings together a dizzying array of insights that refers back to and expands upon images and references already in play. The title refers to a Buddhist tradition in which the speaker warns of the fires of lust but also posits fire as a form of redemption. Cleverly, Eliot brings both Eastern and Western traditions together here, since fire plays a similar role in Christian theology—especially in the work of Saint Augustine, which Eliot summons toward the end of the section.

Past and present, as before, mingle in the Unreal City, which is the London of Eliot's day as well as some mythical kingdom, where the dead still walk. The river Thames is central to the poem, a symbol of the stream of time that carries in its flow all sorts of bits and pieces from history as well as much irrelevant garbage. Quoting from Edmund Spenser's lovely lyric poem "Prothalamion" (1596)—"Sweet Thames, run softly, till I end my song"—Eliot contrasts the pristine river of the Elizabethan age with the littered banks of London in his day, where one sees "empty bottles, sandwich papers, / Silk handkerchiefs, cardboard boxes, cigarette ends" and other "testimony of summer nights." A horrific vision of the city seems to foreshadow death, as Eliot purposefully misquotes Andrew Marvell's poem "To His Coy Mistress" (1650), distorting the famous lines ("But at my back I always hear / Time's wingéd chariot hurrying near") to suit his needs: "But at my back in a cold blast I hear / The rattle of bones, and chuckle spread from ear to ear."

Here he introduces, for the first time, the character of the Fisher King, pictured obliquely as a man fishing in "the dull canal" while he is "musing upon the king my brother's wreck / And on the king my father's death before him." Eliot never stays in one place long, shifting back to the present with snatches of pop songs ("O the moon shone bright on Mrs. Porter") before the movement culminates in a quotation from the French symbolist poet Paul Verlaine's "Parsifal" (1886), a poem in which the Fisher King has been restored to his throne, the parched land having been saved when Parsifal found the Holy Grail. (Eliot extracted this mythology—and the idea of a mysterious Fisher King, who supposedly goes on a quest to redeem his kingdom—from Jessie L. Weston's popular anthropological study, *From Ritual to Romance.*)

This apparently serene moment of achievement is interrupted, rudely, by the return to Philomel and her rape by Tereus: "Twit twit twit. . . . Tereu." Heterosexual rape is followed by an oblique image of a homosexual proposition; the speaker (unidentified) describes a meeting with an unshaven Smyrna merchant, Mr. Eugenides, who asks him to go away for the weekend to a well-known homosexual retreat, the Metropole. One can hardly get a handle on Mr. Eugenides, a man "with a pocket full of currents." He may be an echo of the "one-eyed merchant" announced by Madame Sosostris in the first section. In any case, lust again figures as a prelude to a primary scene of *The Waste Land,* the seduction of a typist at her appalling flat by a "young man carbuncular." To call this scene memorable is to understate the situation: Eliot portrays bored and lifeless sexuality with a kind of vicious, almost malicious, eye for detail, launching into a verse manner reminiscent of Pope:

> The time is now propitious, as he guesses,
> The meal is ended, she is bored and tired,
> Endeavours to engage her in caresses
> Which still are unreproved, if undesired.
> Flushed and decided, he assaults at once;
> Exploring hands encounter no defence;

His vanity requires no response,
And makes a welcome of indifference.

Tiresias, the perpetual voyeur, reports on this encounter, suggesting that he has "foresuffered all / Enacted on this same divan or bed." That is, this lustful but loveless scene is nothing new, and it has been enacted again and again throughout history. In a real sense, Tiresias absorbs the other narrative voices here, becoming the Voice of the poem. In his important reading of the poem, Hugh Kenner explains that Tiresias has three crucial manifestations in classical literature, and each of them is important to Eliot:

> In *Oedipus Rex,* sitting "by Thebes below the wall" he knew why, and as a consequence of what violent death and what illicit amour, the pestilence had fallen on the unreal city, but declines to tell. In the *Odyssey* he "walked among the lowest of the dead" and evaded predicting Odysseus' death by water; the encounter was somehow necessary to Odysseus' homecoming, and Odysseus was somehow satisfied with it, and did get home, for a while. In the *Metamorphoses* he underwent a change of sex for watching the coupling of snakes: presumably the occasion on which he "foresuffered" what is tonight "enacted on this same divan or bed."

In each of these instances, Tiresias is a prophet who holds a key of some kind, knowledge that he either chooses or is forced to withhold.

The seduction of the secretary, bland and boring, by definition unfulfilling, occurs in the Unreal City, which is a version of Hell or Hades, filled with the walking dead. That city becomes, in the next movement, London: a bar in Lower Thames Street, where "fishmen lounge at noon." Perhaps for the first time, a note of regeneration creeps into the poem. These fishermen are possibly not dead as they listen to "The pleasant whining of a mandoline." The church outside the bar is Magnus Martyr, the great martyr, in whom the possibility of redemption exists, however potential. The walls of this church

"hold / Inexplicable splendour of Ionian white and gold." While this movement hardly reverses the gloom and doom of what has gone before, it begins the process of restoration that is crucial to the meaning of the poem as a whole.

A weird song of three "Thames daughters" follows (as Eliot tells us in his extensive footnotes), a brilliantly lyrical section, contrasting modern and Elizabethan versions of the river. These daughters also seem to suggest the Rhinetöchter, or Rhine maidens, of Wagner's opera *Götterdämmerung* (The twilight of the gods)—a sign that Eliot was clearly interested in, if not obsessed by, Wagner's music, which was extremely controversial at the time and much debated by intellectuals in Britain. In all, Eliot wanted his verse to have as many layers of reference as possible, freighting each line with myriad levels of allusion. The point of all this referentiality seems to be this: Western and Eastern culture, the past and present, intermingle, repeating the same forms of thought and feeling, in different guises.

At the center of the lyric are Queen Elizabeth and her lover, Robert Dudley, the earl of Leicester, who wishes to seduce the famously virgin queen. Again, readers are in "The Fire Sermon," and part of this fire is lust. It overwhelms everything and everyone in this section of *The Waste Land,* which concludes magnificently with evocations of Saint Augustine (who experienced the flames of sexual desire at Carthage, a commercial city on the North African shore that no longer exists):

> To Carthage then I came
> Burning burning burning burning
> O Lord Thou pluckest me out
> O Lord Thou pluckest
> burning

One can hardly imagine a more vivid or memorable closure, as Eliot begins to pull various strands of his sprawling poem together. This is the nadir of the poem, the low point, the pit of hell (although the next section plumbs the depths, under water). Everything from this point on represents a move toward redemption, however tentative. It is not unimportant that the notion of prayer as a redemptive move occurs to the narrator—a cry to God for help: "O Lord Thou pluckest me out."

"DEATH BY WATER"

The haunting fourth section of the poem, "Death by Water," appears next—a brief lyric that recollects the devastation that has gone before and prefigures the redemptive final movement of the poem. The Tarot figure of the drowned sailor is tossed onto the narrative table, a man now "a fortnight dead," buried under the sea, beyond the "cry of gulls, and the deep sea swell / and the profit and loss." (Eliot's job at the bank, of course, was a world controlled by the balance sheet, and escape from it must have seemed sweet.) The currents underwater "Picked his bones in whispers." The reader is warned by the Voice of the poem to "Consider Phlebas, who was once handsome and tall as you." This memento mori, or reminder of our mortality, comes at a critical point in the poem. It also points to liberation—from the fires of lust, from the wheel of life, that Hinduism (and Buddhism after it) posits. Freedom is detachment, liberation from the round of birth, copulation, and death. Water, in this section and in general, both drowns and rejuvenates. The parched land needs water. The lustfully burning Saint Augustine needs something to quench his fire. The human race needs release and refreshment.

"WHAT THE THUNDER SAID"

The fifth section of the poem, "What the Thunder Said," opens in the garden of Gethsemane, where Christ went to pray before the Crucifixion; the setting quickly switches to the hill of Golgotha itself. It segues into a dark journey through hideous dreams, suggesting a world where nothing makes sense anymore, where every symbol or cultural reference point is dislodged from its usual meaning. In this wilderness one hears "dry sterile thunder without rain." There is not even the pleasure of solitude or peace in these mountains, nothing but "red sullen faces" that seem to "sneer and snarl" from their "mudcracked houses." In the aftermath of the Crucifixion, the lost disciples wander without hope. But suddenly, as on the road to Emmaus, a mysterious stranger appears. (It was on this road that two of Christ's disciples were met by a ghostly stranger who, they realized, was the already buried Christ.)

In the footnotes Eliot refers to an Antarctic expedition, where explorers at the end of their mental rope felt the presence of a ghostly person in their midst. One has to wonder if this feeling of a supernatural presence is real or fake. It was real for the Apostles, at least according to Christian tradition; obviously, it was a fantasy for the Antarctic explorers, the result of a stressful situation. How does one separate fact and fantasy? What would it mean for supernatural help to manifest itself? Eliot seems to play with these questions, posing but never answering them. It would, indeed, be a severe mistake to impose a specifically Christian interpretation on this poem because Eliot is careful to undercut this line of thinking in order to keep the questions open.

In one of the great passages of the poem, in the fifth section, Eliot summons a vision of destruction, an image of "hooded hordes swarming / Over endless plains, stumbling in cracked earth / Ringed by the flat horizon only." The nightmare visions found in the biblical Revelation offer nothing worse. Eliot conflates the various cities of the world into one Unreal City: "Falling towers / Jerusalem Athens Alexandria / Vienna London." With an insight that can only be called prophetic, Eliot seems almost to anticipate the worldwide destruction that was to occur in just two decades, with bombs falling on London, Dresden, Berlin, Nagasaki, and Hiroshima. He remembers, of course, the destruction of such great cities of the past as Jerusalem and Athens and Alexandria, all sacked at various points and the latter utterly destroyed. Eliot's nightmare borrows images from the Dutch painter Hieronymus Bosch (1450–1516), who conjured hell in *The Garden of Earthly Delights*, a famous three-paneled allegorical panorama of fantastic creatures and strange events in which a woman fiddles on her stretched-out black hair, and

> bats with baby faces in the violet light
> Whistled, and beat their wings,
> And crawled head downward down a blackened
>   wall
> And upside down in air.

But even this vision of blackness begins to fade, as the narrator realizes that "Dry bones can harm no one." In a decayed hole in the mountains, seemingly in the midst of chaos and evil night, an empty chapel appears. This is the Chapel Perilous discovered by Parsifal. The Holy Grail is there, as perhaps suggested by the highly charged atmosphere outside the cave, a place where even "the grass is singing." In the myth, the quester who finds this chapel is shown many things; he has only to ask their meaning, and it will be given. Thus, in a world where everything seems like "a heap of broken images," the work of imagination involves questioning. The past remains in fragments because nobody bothers to assemble the fragments, to ask real and penetrating questions, to do the hard work of making things whole. This is the work of the artist, of course; implicitly, Eliot is doing this job for us here, assembling the shards of a broken civilization. He interrogates the imagery of the past. He is putting the puzzle together when suddenly a cock crows (as it did when the apostle Peter denied Christ), crying "Co co rico co co rico." The poem pivots dramatically: "In a flash of lightning. Then a damp gust / Bringing rain."

Having been purged by fire and water in the third and fourth sections of the poem and hav-

ing sat in the wilderness and found the chapel and Holy Grail (perhaps) in the early part of the fifth section, the reader is prepared for the final movements of the poem. Here Eliot meditates on the riddle of language, focusing on several related Sanskrit words: *Datta, Dayadhvam,* and *Damyata.* They translate roughly as follows: give, sympathize, control. All have at their roots the primitive syllable *Da.* (This word foreshadows the Latin *dare*—"to give"—and survives in various English words, such as "donation.") In the rubble of the linguistic past, Eliot has found a clue of sorts, something he can use to solve the mystery, to generate new meaning, to bring rain to the parched land. His own extraordinary learning has turned up a key.

Giving is the key. To offer sympathy is to give something of oneself beyond estimate. This form of giving inheres in "The awful daring of a moment's surrender." This phrase suggests, of course, sexual consent; but it goes beyond that, into the realm of love, the ultimate act of giving. One gives one's self over to another wholly, without qualifications. So love begins in an act of generosity that cannot be broken or retracted. Nor will this love be found "in our obituaries / Or in memories draped by the beneficent spider / Or under seals broken by the lean solicitor." That is, what happens after death—obituaries, cobwebbed memories, wills read and property dispersed by lawyers—does not undermine the fact of love, the act of giving.

"*Dayadhvam,*" the next movement of "DA," relates to sympathy, another form of giving. The narrator, not unlike Ugolino, who is found in the ninth circle of hell among the traitors in Dante's *Inferno,* hears the key turn once in the lock, enclosing him forever. The thirteenth-century count of Pisa betrayed his city and was turned on by his ally, Archbishop Ruggiero, who imprisoned him until he starved to death. Ugolino, to Eliot, may represent the lost intellectual, out of touch with his culture, unable to make any contact outside himself. The poem thus far has expressed a profound dissatisfaction with the state of things, calling up a landscape of alienation that mirrors the isolation of the sensitive individual for whom civilization seems to be in shards. Eliot identifies himself here with Shakespeare's Coriolanus, the shattered Roman king, who fails because he thinks he can stand alone, "As if a man were author of himself / And knew no other kin," as Shakespeare says. Being sympathetic to the plight of the adolescent king is, for the narrator, a form of self-sympathy, and Eliot clearly regards this turn as a healthy one, a step on the path toward regeneration and renewal.

The final movement of "DA" is *"Damyata,"* meaning control, an intriguing form of giving. Eliot suggests that one gives one's expertise to control an unruly situation, much as a well-trained sailor controls a vessel in difficult waters by guiding it with a steady hand. The boat in the poem, under such firm and knowledgeable control, was hardly unhappy; indeed, it "responded / Gaily, to the hand expert with sail and oar." Similarly, the poet's heart would respond gaily, too, to the discipline of love and to the various forms of sympathy already intimated.

This leads to the final movement of the poem as a whole, a marvelous all-encompassing passage where so many elements are brought forcefully together. In a triumph of technique, Eliot reaches freely for bits and pieces of past culture, high and low, as the "I" appears, now clearly the Fisher King, who "sat upon the shore / Fishing," with the arid plain behind him. The king realizes that the time for action has come: "Shall I at least set my lands in order?" He is reminded of the vision of destruction already witnessed, which is embodied in a nursery rhyme that dates back to the era of the Great Plague: "London Bridge is falling down, falling down, falling down." But he will not let that pessimistic note stand as the conclusion. Eliot has taken us through the various forms of sympathy and giving. He now can piece together the fragments in his own way, through the use of creative imagination.

A spray of quotations from the past follows. Quotations that suggest renewal are balanced against ones that hint at despair ("Hieronymo's mad againe"). The transition to sanity and wholeness is not accomplished; that would seem false in the context. Wholeness remains an aspiration. Yet the mere fact that Eliot quotes from so many languages suggests that the situation of the biblical Tower of Babel remains in effect: the dream of a common language is only a dream. *The Waste Land* offers a portrait of an age, and it puts before sympathetic and questing readers a key, but the poet himself does not turn the key. He merely points in a direction that can be called vaguely positive. In the last two lines, mimicking the repetitions of liturgy, Eliot repeats the Hindu words: *"Datta. Dyadhvam. Damyata."* Then he concludes, as a liturgy might well conclude, with the blessing of peace, mimicking the Hindu scriptures, the Upanishads, which sometimes end with such a blessing: *"Shantih shantih shantih."*

WHAT DOES IT ALL MEAN?

The final meaning of *The Waste Land* defies easy summary. The poem obviously expressed the anxiety and malaise of postwar Britain. The sense of discontinuity, doubtless felt by many at the time, had never before been embodied in such a brilliant fashion, in a style that paralleled the achievement of modernists in other fields. In painting, one thinks immediately of such artists of the Cubist movement as Picasso, whose images were fractured and rearranged in disconcerting and suggestive ways. In music, one recalls *Le Sacre du printemps* (*Rite of Spring*, 1913) by Igor Stravinsky, a musical work that defied conventions, playing with new forms of tonality and structure. What seems odd, in retrospect, is that Eliot's innovations should remain, after many decades, so modern, so fresh, and so challenging. Later poets have rarely attempted anything as profoundly strange and ambitious as *The Waste Land*.

The poem succeeds on many fronts. It conveys the feeling of the age, but it does so in a way that remains perpetually new and undated. (One recalls Ezra Pound's appealing definition of literature as "news that stays news.") As a sequence, the poem is pioneering; each section relates to every other section in a way that can only be called musical. Eliot, indeed, seems to play with the music of ideas, picking up a theme in one section (the drowned sailor, for example) and playing off it in later parts (as in the fourth section, about Phlebas the Phoenician). The poem also succeeds as a portrait of the sophisticated European mind, one broadly familiar with a wide range of places and, of course, a range of texts. Throughout, Eliot appears to have read everything, blending texts in his own unique way, creating a dense mosaic from myriad fragments and echoes of previous literature, sacred and secular, Eastern and Western. It is a dazzling performance.

The reading public was hardly ready for a five-part, obscure poem of 434 lines. The wrenching juxtapositions and quotations from many languages, including Sanskrit, seemed shocking to an audience used to Alfred Lord Tennyson and Rudyard Kipling. The poem was published first in two parts, in two different magazines. When it was to appear in book form, the editor suggested that Eliot add footnotes to make it longer (otherwise, there would have been too many blank pages because printers worked in folios of specified numbers of pages). Eliot identified a number of his quotations in order to spike the guns of narrow-minded critics, some of whom had accused him of plagiarism in his earlier poems. The notes soon acquired a life of their own, and they must be regarded partly as a satire on academic footnoting—although some of them seem quite serious as well.

Eliot used footnotes to credit several books that influenced his thinking, such as Weston's *From Ritual to Romance* and Frazer's *Golden Bough.* "Anyone who is acquainted with these works will immediately recognize in the poem certain references to vegetation ceremonies," Eliot intones. Rather amusingly, he also says: "I am not familiar with the exact constitution of the Tarot pack of cards, from which I have obviously departed to suit my own convenience." In fact, he departs everywhere from everything, using sources however he pleases. He copies out nineteen lines from Ovid and thirty-three words from Frank M. Chapman's *Handbook of Birds of Eastern North America.* He meditates on the interior of the Church of St. Magnus Martyr (one of the finest of the distinguished architect Sir Christopher Wren's designs), nods toward a great Buddhist scholar, Henry Clarke Warren, and pads the notes with odd, exotic references, some relevant and others not. Eliot later commented in Kenner's *The Invisible Poet:*

> I have sometimes thought of getting rid of these notes; but now they can never be unstuck. They have had almost greater popularity than the poem itself. . . . It was just, no doubt, that I should pay my tribute to the work of Miss Jessie Weston; but I regret having sent so many inquirers off on a wild goose chase after Tarot cards and the Holy Grail.

Well, yes and no. The Tarot pack and the Holy Grail are fairly central as motifs in the poem, although one could probably do without the footnotes.

The Waste Land manages to communicate a great deal, even if the exact references are not quite understood—if, indeed, they can ever be totally understood. The poem conveys a mood, a texture, a sensibility. As Ezra Pound said in an interview, "I saw the poem in typescript, and I did not see the notes till 6 or 8 months afterward; and they have not increased my enjoyment of the poem one atom." The voice of the poem—bored, terrified, detached, knowing—has become part of the voice of modernity, and in this regard Eliot succeeded with *The Waste Land* beyond his wildest dreams. It has become a classic text, one of the great poems of the English language.

Select Bibliography

EDITIONS

The Waste Land. London: Hogarth Press, 1922.

Collected Poems: 1909–1962. New York: Harcourt, Brace, and World, 1963. (This edition is cited from in the essay.)

Complete Poems and Plays. New York: Harcourt, Brace, and World, 1969.

OTHER WORKS BY ELIOT

The Sacred Word: Essays on Poetry and Criticism. London: Methuen, 1920.

"Ulysses, Order, and Myth," *The Dial* 75, no. 5 (November 1923): 480–483. Reprinted in *Selected Prose of T. S. Eliot.* Edited by Frank Kermode. New York: Harcourt Brace Jovanovich, 1975. Pp 175–178. (Review of *Ulysses* by James Joyce.)

SECONDARY WORKS

Ackroyd, Peter. *T. S. Eliot: A Life.* New York: Simon & Schuster, 1984.

Asher, Kenneth. *T. S. Eliot and Ideology.* New York: Cambridge University Press, 1995.

Bolgan, Anne C. *What the Thunder Really Said: A Retrospective Essay on the Making of* The Waste Land. Montreal: McGill-Queen's University Press, 1973.

Brooker, Jewel Spears, and Joseph Bentley. *Reading* The Waste Land: *Modernism and the Limits of Interpretation.* Amherst: University of Massachusetts Press, 1990.

Bush, Ronald. *T. S. Eliot: The Modernist in History.* New York: Cambridge University Press, 1991.

Clarke, Graham, ed. *T. S. Eliot: Critical Assessments.* 4 vols. London: Christopher Helm, 1990.

Cuddy, Lois A., and David Hirsch, eds. *Critical Essays on T. S. Eliot's* The Waste Land. Boston: G. K. Hall, 1991.

Davidson, Harriet. *T. S. Eliot and Hermeneutics: Absence and Interpretation in* The Waste Land. Baton Rouge: Louisiana State University Press, 1985.

Gardner, Helen. *The Art of T. S. Eliot.* New York: Dutton, 1959.

Gordon, Lyndall. *Eliot's Early Years.* New York: Oxford University Press, 1977.

Julius, Anthony. *T. S. Eliot, Anti-Semitism, and Literary Form.* New York: Cambridge University Press, 1995.

Kearns, Cleo McNelly. *T. S. Eliot and Indic Traditions: A Study in Poetry and Belief.* New York: Cambridge University Press, 1987.

Kenner, Hugh *The Invisible Poet: T. S. Eliot.* New York: McDowell, Obolensky, 1959.

Longenbach, James. *Modernist Poetics of History: Pound, Eliot, and the Sense of the Past.* Princeton, N.J.: Princeton University Press, 1987.

Matthiessen, F. O. *The Achievement of T. S. Eliot: An Essay on the Nature of Poetry.* Boston: Houghton Mifflin, 1935.

Mayer, John. *T. S. Eliot's Silent Voices.* New York: Oxford University Press, 1989.

Menand, Louis. *Discovering Modernism: T. S. Eliot and His Context.* New York: Oxford University Press, 1987.

Miller, James E. *T. S. Eliot's Personal Waste Land: Exorcism of the Demons.* University Park: Pennsylvania State University Press, 1977.

Moody, A. Dwight, ed. The Waste Land *in Different Voices.* London: Edward Arnold, 1974. (Revised lectures given at the University of York on the fiftieth anniversary of the publication of *The Waste Land.*)

———, ed. *The Cambridge Companion to T. S. Eliot.* Cambridge: Cambridge University Press, 1994.

Smith, Grover. *T. S. Eliot's Poetry and Plays: A Study in Sources and Meaning.* Chicago: University of Chicago Press, 1950.

Thormählen, Marianne. The Waste Land: *A Fragmentary Wholeness.* Lund: LiberLäromedel/Gleerup, 1978.

Index

Arabic numbers printed in bold-face type refer to extended treatment of a subject.

Abraham, Pearl, **I**: 216
"Absurd Effort to Make the World Over, The" (W. Sumner), **I**: 239
Acheson, Dean, **I**: 139
Ackroyd, Peter, **I**: 356
Ada (Nabokov), **I**: 90
Adams, Dock, **I**: 281, 298
"Adonais" (Shelley), **I**: 229
Adventures of Huckleberry Finn, The (Twain), **I**: **1–17**, 285
Adventures of Tom Sawyer, The (Twain), **I**: 1–2, 3
After the Fall (A. Miller), **I**: 55
"Afterthought, The" (Du Bois), **I**: 284
Age of Excess (Ginger), **I**: 238
A la recherche du temps perdu. See *Remembrance of Things Past* (Proust)
Albee, Edward, **I**: 122
Albertzart-Otte, Rosina Maria Francesca von, **I**: 304
Alcott, Louisa May, **I**: 149
All My Sons (A. Miller), **I**: 54, 55
Ambassadors, The (H. James), **I**: 147, 200
American, The (H. James), **I**: 200
American Dictionary of the English Language (Webster), **I**: 3
American Scene, The (H. James), **I**: 200
"American Scholar, The" (Hawthorne), **I**: 257
Amis, Martin, **I**: 234
Anderson, Joan, **I**: 188
Anderson, Sherwood, **I**: 329
"Angel in the House" (Patmore), **I**: 149
"Annabel Lee" (Poe), **I**: 94, 96
Anna Christie (O'Neill), **I**: 110
Annotated Lolita, The (Nabokov), **I**: 96
Ann Vickers (Lewis), **I**: 126
"Another View of Hester" (Hawthorne), **I**: 272, 274
Anthony, Susan B., **I**: 180
Antony and Cleopatra (Shakespeare), **I**: 317–318, 365–366
Apicius, **I**: 350
April Twilights (Cather), **I**: 144
Aristotle, **I**: 110
Arrowsmith (Lewis), **I**: 126
Artaud, Antonin, **I**: 74
Arthur Miller and Company (Bigsby), **I**: 56
Ash Wednesday (T. S. Eliot), **I**: 103

Asimov, Isaac, **I**: 354
"Assignation, The" (Poe), **I**: 346
Asylum, The (Mitchell), **I**: 343
"Atlanta Compromise" (Washington), **I**: 290
Auden, W. H., **I**: 345
Augustine, Saint, **I**: 367, 368, 369
Austen, Jane, **I**: 199, 203
Autry, Gene, **I**: 186
Awkward Age, The (H. James), **I**: 200
Babbitt (Lewis), **I**: 126
Baldwin, James, **I**: 192
Balzac, Honoré de, **I**: 92, 110
"Bargain Lost, The" (Poe), **I**: 340
Barlow, Joel, **I**: 172, 173
Barth, Karl, **I**: 221, 222
"Battle Hymn of the Republic, The" (song), **I**: 251
"Battles and Leaders of the Civil War" (memoir series), **I**: 241
Baudelaire, Charles, **I**: 74, 356, 364
Beat Generation, The (Kerouac), **I**: 183
Beck, Julian, **I**: 195
Beckett, Samuel, **I**: 56, 90, 352
"Belief and Technique for Modern Prose" (Kerouac), **I**: 188
Bell Jar, The (Plath), **I**: 51
Beloved (Morrison), **I**: **19–33**
Bend Sinister (Nabokov), **I**: 89, 90
Ben Hur (Wallace), **I**: 138
"Berenice" (Poe), **I**: 346, 348, 352
Bergson, Henri, **I**: 99
Berlin, Irving, **I**: 138
Berryman, John, **I**: 85
Best Short Stories of Sarah Orne Jewett, The (Cather, ed.), **I**: 144
Beyond the Horizon (O'Neill), **I**: 110
Bible, **I**: 76, 80–81, 138, 174, 178, 288–290, 322, 345, 353, 363
Bigsby, Christopher, **I**: 56
Big Sur (Kerouac), **I**: 184
Bingham, Caleb, **I**: 173
Black Reconstruction in America: 1860–1880 (Du Bois), **I**: 282, 284–285
Blake, William, **I**: 72, 73, 74, 76, 80, 81, 85, 187, 355, 361
Bland, Edward, **I**: 195
Blavatsky, Madame Helena Petrovna, **I**: 364
Blithedale Romance, The (Hawthorne), **I**: 258, 260
"Blue Hotel, The" (S. Crane), **I**: 240
Bluest Eye, The (Morrison), **I**: 20, 32

"Bon-Bon" (Poe), **I**: 340, 350
Book of Common Prayer (Anglican), **I**: 361
Book of Dreams (Kerouac), **I**: 184
Booth, Edwin, **I**: 119
Borges, Jorge Luis, **I**: 356
Bosch, Hieronymus, **I**: 370
Brady, Mathew, **I**: 241
Brakhage, Stan, **I**: 195
"Bride Comes to Yellow Sky, The" (S. Crane), **I**: 238, 246
Brieux, Eugène, **I**: 127
Bright Lights, Big City (McInerney), **I**: 51
Broken Glass (A. Miller), **I**: 55
Brontë, Charlotte, **I**: 149
Brontë, Emily, **I**: 157, 203
Brookner, Anita, **I**: 234
Brooks, Preston, **I**: 180
"Brothers, The" (Kerouac), **I**: 85
Brown, Charles Brockden, **I**: 343
Brown, John, **I**: 165
Browning, Robert, **I**: 354
Bryan, William Jennings, **I**: 145
Buddha, **I**: 365
Bulwer-Lytton, Edward, **I**: 353
"Burial of the Dead, The" (T. S. Eliot), **I**: 360, 361–365
Buried Child (Shepard), **I**: 122
Burnett, Whit, **I**: 35, 36
"Burnt Norton" (T. S. Eliot), **I**: 362
Burroughs, William, **I**: 72, 73, 74, 75, 83, 84, 90, 184, 186, 188, 191, 195
Butler, Matthew C., **I**: 281
Butler, Nathaniel, **I**: 298
Byatt, A. S., **I**: 234
Byron, George Gordon, Lord, **I**: 72, 291, 343, 346
Cage, John, **I**: 74
Calhoun, John C., **I**: 163
Campion, Jane, **I**: 216
Cannastra, William, **I**: 78
Canterbury Tales (Chaucer), **I**: 361–362
Capote, Truman, **I**: 188
Carmen (Mérimée), **I**: 96
Carnegie, Andrew, **I**: 283
Carr, Lucien, **I**: 72, 83, 184, 186
Carver, Raymond, **I**: 335
Cassady, Neal, **I**: 73, 78, 83, 84, 184, 186, 187–188, 195
Catcher in the Rye, The (Salinger), **I**: 16, **35–52**
Cather, Willa, **I**: 143–162

Cat on a Hot Tin Roof (T. Williams), **I:** 315

Celebrated Jumping Frog of Calaveras County and Other Sketches, The (Twain), **I:** 2

Céline, Louis-Ferdinand, **I:** 74, 80, 187

Cézanne, Paul, **I:** 76, 80

"Change, The" (Ginsberg), **I:** 85

Chaplin, Charlie, **I:** 77

Chapman, Frank M., **I:** 372

Chapman, John Jay, **I:** 163

Chapman, Maria Weston, **I:** 163

Chaucer, Geoffrey, **I:** 361

Chekhov, Anton, **I:** 314–315

Chinese Encounters (A. Miller), **I:** 55

Chopin, Frédéric, **I:** 120

Clarke, Shirley, **I:** 195

Coffin, William C., **I:** 167

Coker, Simon, **I:** 298

Coleridge, Samuel Taylor, **I:** 72, 82

Collected Plays (A. Miller), **I:** 55, 56, 62

Collected Poems, 1947–1980 (Ginsberg), **I:** 72, 74, 85

Collected Works (Poe; Mabbott, ed.), **I:** 342, 348

Collins, John, **I:** 167–168

"Colloquy of Monos and Una, The" (Poe), **I:** 354

Color and Democracy: Colonies and Peace (Du Bois), **I:** 288

Columbian Orator, The (Bingham), **I:** 164, 173, 175, 176, 178, 179

Conclusive Evidence (Nabokov), **I:** 90

Confessions, Les (Rousseau), **I:** 96

Conrad, Joseph, **I:** 146, 172

"Conversation of Eiros and Charmion, The" (Poe), **I:** 355

Conversations with Arthur Miller (Roudané, ed.), **I:** 56

Cooper, James Fenimore, **I:** 3, 139, 223

Corporal Si Klegg and His "Pard" (Hinman), **I:** 241

Corrections, The (Franzen), **I:** 139

Corso, Gregory, **I:** 184

Covey, Mr., **I:** 168–169, 174, 175, 176, 177, 178

"Covey the Negro Breaker" (Douglass), **I:** 174

Cowley, Malcolm, **I:** 138

Crane, Hart, **I:** 74

Crane, Stephen, **I:** 237–255, 275

Crisis (magazine), **I:** 282, 298

Criterion (literary review), **I:** 360

Crucible, The (A. Miller), **I:** 54, 55, 61

Cry of Jazz, The (Bland), **I:** 195

Cummins, Maria Susanna, **I:** 258, 261

Cunningham, Merce, **I:** 74

Custer, George Armstrong, **I:** 251

"Custom-House, The" (Hawthorne), **I:** 259, 260, 264–269, 271, 272, 274

Daisy Miller (H. James), **I:** 200, 215

Damnation of Theron Ware, The (Frederic), **I:** 135

Daniel Deronda (G. Eliot), **I:** 206

Dante Alighieri, **I:** 75–76, 104, 364, 370

Dar. See *The Gift* (Nabokov)

Dark Princess: A Romance (Du Bois), **I:** 282

Darkwater: Voices from within the Veil (Du Bois), **I:** 282, 288

Davis, Miles, **I:** 74

"Death by Water" (T. S. Eliot), **I:** 369

Death Comes for the Archbishop (Jewett), **I:** 144, 146

Death in the Afternoon (Hemingway), **I:** 331

Death of a Salesman (A. Miller), **I:** **53–69**

Débâcle, La (Zola), **I:** 241

"Decided Loss, A" (Poe), **I:** 340

Declaration of Independence (1776), **I:** 263, 288, 292, 293, 294

Declaration of Sentiments and Resolutions (1848; women's rights manifesto), **I:** 263

"Decline of the Magazine Short Story, The" (Norris), **I:** 148

Decline of the West (Spengler), **I:** 187

Defense, The (*Zashchita Luzhina*) (Nabokov), **I:** 90

Defoe, Daniel, **I:** 355

De Kooning, Willem, **I:** 74

DePrima, Diane, **I:** 195

Deren, Maya, **I:** 195

Desolation Angels (Kerouac), **I:** 184

Despair (*Otchayanie*) (Nabokov), **I:** 90

"Devil in the Belfry, The" (Poe), **I:** 350–351, 353, 355

Dickens, Charles, **I:** 348, 351, 352, 356, 360

Dickinson, Emily, **I:** 179, 180, 234, 239, 275

Dinesen, Isak, **I:** 38

Disraeli, Benjamin, **I:** 349

Divine Comedy (Dante), **I:** 364

Doctor Sax (Kerouac), **I:** 184, 185

Dodsworth (Lewis), **I:** 126

Doll's House (Ibsen), **I:** 211

Dostoyevsky, Fyodor, **I:** 187, 356

Douglass, Frederick, **I:** 163–182, 275

Douglass's Monthly (magazine), **I:** 165

Dowson, Ernest, **I:** 110

Doyle, Sir Arthur Conan, **I:** 339

Drabble, Margaret, **I:** 234

"Dream, A" (Poe), **I:** 340

Dreaming Emmett (Morrison), **I:** 20

Dreiser, Theodore, **I:** 144, 160, 329, 334

Du Bois, Burghardt, **I:** 287

Du Bois, W. E. B., **I:** 179, 281–301

"Duc De L'Omelette, The" (Poe), **I:** 340, 350

Dudley, Robert, earl of Leicester, **I:** 368

"Duluoz Legend, The" (Kerouac), **I:** 187

Dusk of Dawn (Du Bois), **I:** 282, 283, 290–291

Ecclesiastes, Book of, **I:** 322, 363

Echoes Down the Corridor (A. Miller), **I:** 67

Eggers, Dave, **I:** 51

Einstein, Albert, **I:** 365

Eisenhower, Dwight D., **I:** 222, 223

Eleven Tales of the Arabesque (Poe), **I:** 341

Eliot, George, **I:** 146, 199, 206, 339

Eliot, T. S., **I:** 72, 81, 103, 147, 215, 354, 359–374

Elizabeth I, queen of England, **I:** 368

Elmer Gantry (Lewis), **I:** 126

Emerson, Ralph Waldo, **I:** 75, 139, 145, 163–164, 172, 179, 180, 187, 206, 239, 240, 257, 272, 275, 361

Empty Mirror (Ginsberg), **I:** 74

Enchanter, The (Nabokov), **I:** 90

Endgame (Beckett), **I:** 56

Engels, Friedrich, **I:** 110

"Epimanes" (Poe), **I:** 353, 354

"Essentials of Spontaneous Prose" (Kerouac), **I:** 188

Eugene Onegin (Pushkin; Nabokov, trans.), **I:** 90

Exodus, Book of, **I:** 288–290

"Experiment in Misery, An" (S. Crane), **I:** 241

Eye, The (*Soglyadatay*) (Nabokov), **I:** 90

Ezekiel, Book of, **I:** 363

Fall of America, The (Ginsberg), **I:** 72, 85

"Fall of the House of Usher, The" (Poe), **I:** 344

Fanshawe (Hawthorne), **I:** 258

Farewell to Arms, A (Hemingway), **I:** 46, 322

Faulkner, William, **I:** 30–31, 140, 223, 234, 275

Faust (Goethe), **I:** 295

Fear and Loathing in Las Vegas (Thompson), **I:** 51

"Fenimore Cooper's Literary Offenses" (Twain), **I:** 3

Ferlinghetti, Lawrence, **I:** 74, 75, 195

Fern, Fanny, **I:** 258, 261

Fields, James T., **I:** 259

Finnegan's Wake (Joyce), **I:** 186

"Fire Sermon, The" (T. S. Eliot), **I:** 361, 367–369

FitzGerald, Edward, **I:** 297

Fitzgerald, F. Scott, I: 135, 223, 234, 321, 331

Fleurs du mal, Les (Flowers of evil) (Baudelaire), I: 364

Focus (A. Miller), I: 54

"Footnote to Howl" (Ginsberg), I: 82

Ford, Henry, I: 289

"Forest Walk, A" (Hawthorne), I: 273

"Forethought, The" (Du Bois), I: 284, 297

For Whom the Bell Tolls (Hemingway), I: 322, 323

Foster, George, I: 168

"Four Beasts in One—The Homo Cameleopard" (Poe), I: 353

Four Quartets (T. S. Eliot), I: 360

Fowles, John, I: 216

Francis of Assisi, Saint, I: 290

Francis Xavier, Saint, I: 304

Frank, Robert, I: 184

Franny and Zooey (Salinger), I: 35, 36

Franzen, Jonathan, I: 139

Frazer, James, I: 364, 372

Frederic, Harold, I: 135

Frederick Douglass's Paper (newspaper), I: 165

Free Air (Lewis), I: 126

French Lieutenant's Woman, The (Fowles), I: 216

Freneau, Philip, I: 172, 173

Freud, Sigmund, I: 149, 171, 172

From Ritual to Romance (Weston), I: 364, 367, 372

"Game of Chess, A" (T. S. Eliot), I: 360, 365–367

Garden of Earthly Delights, The (Bosch painting), I: 370

Garfield, James A., I: 165

Garrison, William Lloyd, I: 163, 164–165, 166, 167, 168, 169, 180

Gates of Wrath, The (Ginsberg), I: 74

Genet, Jean, I: 90

Georgics (Virgil), I: 147

Gift, The (Dar) (Nabokov), I: 90

Gillespie, Dizzy, I: 74

Ginger, Ray, I: 238

Ginsberg, Allen, I: 71–87, 184, 186, 187, 190, 195

Ginsberg, Louis, I: 73, 84, 85

Ginsberg, Naomi Livergant, I: 73, 79, 82, 83, 84–85

Girodias, Maurice, I: 90, 91

Giving Up America (Abraham), I: 216

Glass Menagerie, The (T. Williams), I: 304, 305, 306

Glory (Podvig) (Nabokov), I: 90

Go (Holmes), I: 73

Goethe, Johann Wolfgang von, I: 295

Golden Bough, The (Frazer), I: 364, 372

Golden Bowl, The (H. James), I: 200, 215

Gospel of Freedom (Herrick), I: 215

Gospel of Wealth, The (Carnegie), I: 283

Götterdämmerung (Wagner), I: 368

"Gradual Initiation into the Mysteries of Slavery" (Douglass), I: 173

Graham, Tom (pseudonym). See Lewis, Sinclair

Grant, Ulysses S., I: 239, 281, 282

Great Gatsby, The (F. Fitzgerald), I: 321

Greenstreet, Sydney, I: 103

Griswold, Rufus Wilmot, I: 339

Hamlet (Shakespeare), I: 63, 367

Hammarskjöld, Dag, I: 122

Handbook of Birds of Eastern North America (F. Chapman), I: 372

Hanna, Mark, I: 180

"Hans Phaall" (Poe), I: 354, 355

"Hapworth 16, 1924" (Salinger), I: 36

Hardy, Thomas, I: 157

Harris, Joel Chandler, I: 1

Hawkins, Coleman, I: 74

Hawthorne, Nathaniel, I: 147, 149, 234, 257–279

Hayes, Rutherford B., I: 165

Heartbreaking Work of Staggering Genius, A (Eggers), I: 51

"Heart of Darkness" (Conrad), I: 146, 172

"He Do the Police in Different Voices" (T. S. Eliot), I: 360

Hegel, Georg W. F., I: 288

Hemingway, Ernest, I: 16, 46, 159, 223, 321–337

Henry, Patrick, I: 177

Herrick, Robert, I: 215

Hike and the Aeroplane (Lewis), I: 126–127

Hinman, Wilbur F., I: 241

History of Woman Suffrage (Stanton), I: 263

Hitchcock, Alfred, I: 356

Hitchcock, Ripley, I: 244, 247

Hitler, Adolf, I: 363

Hit the Road (Kerouac), I: 188

Hoffmann, E. T. A., I: 343

Holmes, John Clellon, I: 73

Holmes, Oliver Wendell, Sr., I: 275

"Holy" (Ginsberg), I: 75

"Home Have Come Our Boys in Blue" (song), I: 251

Homer, I: 368

House of Seven Gables, The (Hawthorne), I: 258, 260, 269

Housman, A. E., I: 147

Howells, William Dean, I: 211, 275

"Howl" (Ginsberg), **I: 71–87**, 184

Howl and Other Poems (Ginsberg), I: 72, 75, 83

"How to Write a Blackwood's Article" (Poe), I: 351

Hughes, Howard, I: 178

Huncke, Herbert, I: 78, 82, 83, 186

Hutchinson, Anne, I: 270–271

Huxley, Aldous, I: 339

Ibsen, Henrik, I: 110, 122, 211

"I'm a Stranger Here Myself" (Lewis), I: 140

"Imp of the Perverse, The" (Poe), I: 343

Incident at Vichy (A. Miller), I: 55, 61

Inferno (Dante), I: 75–76, 364, 370

"In Memoriam" (A. Miller), I: 54

Innocents, The (Lewis), I: 126

In Russia (A. Miller), I: 55

Invisible Poet, The (Kenner), I: 372

Invitation to a Beheading (Priglashenie na kazn') (Nabokov), I: 90

I Rise in Flame, Cried the Phoenix (T. Williams), I: 310

Irving, John, I: 275

Irving, Washington, I: 343, 356

Isaiah, Book of, I: 174

It Can't Happen Here (Lewis), I: 126

Jackson, Andrew, I: 285, 353, 355

Jacobs, Harriet, I: 275

James, Alice, I: 199

James, Henry, I: 36, 147, 199–218, 234, 275, 332, 339

James, Henry, Sr., I: 199–200

James, William, I: 199, 252

Jane Eyre (C. Brontë), I: 149

Jazz (Morrison), I: 20

Jefferson, Thomas, I: 163, 164

Jenkins, Sandy, I: 175–177, 178, 179

Jennie Gerhardt (Dreiser), I: 160

Jesus, I: 80, 178, 353, 363, 365, 369, 370

Jewett, Sarah Orne, I: 144

Joans, Ted, I: 195

Job, The (Lewis), I: 126

Joffé, Roland, I: 275

Johnson, Joyce, I: 195

Johnson, Kay (Kaja), I: 195

John the Baptist, I: 365

Jones, Hettie, I: 195

Journey to the End of Night (Céline), I: 187

Joyce, James, I: 29, 74, 186, 365

Kaddish and Other Poems (Ginsberg), I: 72, 84

Kafka, Franz, I: 352, 356

Kamera Obscura. See *Laughter in the Dark* (Nabokov)

Kaufmann, Philip, I: 195

Keats, John, I: 72, 73, 350, 366

Kennedy, John F., I: 282

Kenner, Hugh, I: 372

Kerouac, Jack, I: 72–73, 75, 82, 83, 84, 183–197
Kesey, Ken, I: 84
Kierkegaard, Søren, I: 221, 222
King, Martin Luther, Jr., I: 71
King, Stephen, I: 339, 344, 356
King James Bible, I: 353
"King Pest" (Poe), I: 353
King, Queen, Knave (Korol', dama, valet) (Nabokov), I: 90
Kipling, Rudyard, I: 110, 136, 372
Korol', dama, valet. See King, Queen, Knave (Nabokov)
Kreutzer Sonata (Tolstoy), I: 146
Kropotkin, Peter, I: 110
Krutch, Joseph Wood, I: 139
Kubrick, Stanley, I: 105–106
Kupferberg, Tuli, I: 78
Lady of the Lake, The (Scott), I: 164
Lamantia, Philip, I: 75
Lamplighter (Cummins), I: 258, 260
Lang, Fritz, I: 81
Last Yankee, The (A. Miller), I: 55
Laughter in the Dark (Kamera Obscura) (Nabokov), I: 90
Lawrence, D. H., I: 310
"Lena Lingard" (Jewett), I: 144
Leopardi, Giacomo, I: 355
Letters to J. D. Salinger (collection), I: 51
Lewis, Sinclair, I: 125–141, 329, 334
Life and Opinions of Tristram Shandy, The (Sterne), I: 349
Life and Times of Frederick Douglass, The (Douglass), I: 165, 167
Life on the Mississippi (Twain), I: 3
"Ligeia" (Poe), I: 346, 347, 350
Lincoln, Abraham, I: 165, 180, 237, 238, 239, 252
Lindsay, Vachel, I: 138
"Lionizing" (Poe), I: 349, 355
"Literary Situation in 1895, The" (Cather), I: 147
"Little Annie's Ramble" (Hawthorne), I: 259
Little Women (Alcott), I: 149
Lolita (Nabokov), I: 89–108
Lolita: A Screenplay (Nabokov), I: 91, 106
"London" (Blake), I: 81
London, Jack, I: 185
Long Day's Journey into Night (O'Neill), I: 109–124
Longfellow, Henry Wadsworth, I: 258, 275
Look at the Harlequins! (Nabokov), I: 91
"Loss of Breath" (Poe), I: 340, 352
"Lost Generation, The" (Hemingway), I: 321

Lost Lady, A (Cather), I: 144, 151
Lost on the Road (Kerouac), I: 188
Lovecraft, H. P., I: 344, 356
Love on the Road (Kerouac), I: 188
"Love Song of J. Alfred Prufrock, The" (T. S. Eliot), I: 360
Lowell, James Russell, I: 275, 339–340
Lowell, Robert, I: 85
Lucian of Samosata, I: 354, 355
Luke, Gospel According to, I: 174
Lyly, John, I: 366
Lyne, Adrian, I: 106
Mabbott, Thomas Ollive, I: 342, 348
Macbeth (Shakespeare), I: 298–299
McClure, Michael, I: 75, 195
McClurg, Alexander, I: 237, 251
McEwan, Ian, I: 234
McInerney, Jay, I: 51
McKinley, William, I: 180
Maggie: A Girl of the Streets (S. Crane), I: 238, 240
Maggie Cassidy (Kerouac), I: 184, 185
Mailer, Norman, I: 178, 234, 335
Main Street (Lewis), I: **125–141**
Malina, Judith, I: 195
Mamet, David, I: 122
Mantrap (Lewis), I: 126
Man Who Had All the Luck, The (A. Miller), I: 54
Man Who Knew Coolidge, The (Lewis), I: 126
"Man Who Was Used Up, The: A Tale of the Late Bugaboo and Kickapoo Campaign" (Poe), I: 349–350
Many Loves of Dobie Gillis, The (television series), I: 195
Marble Faun, The (Hawthorne), I: 258, 261
"Marginalia" (Poe), I: 340, 341
Marvell, Andrew, I: 367
Marx, Karl, I: 110, 288
Mary (Mashen'ka) (Nabokov), I: 90
Mashen'ka. See Mary (Nabokov)
"Masque of the Red Death, The" (Poe), I: 345, 351
Maynard, Joyce, I: 35
Maysles, Albert, I: 195
Melville, Herman, I: 82, 223, 234, 260–261, 275
Memoirs (T. Williams), I: 304, 305, 306
Mencken, H. L., I: 138, 158, 159
Men Without Women (Hemingway), I: 327
Mérimée, Prosper, I: 96
Metamorphoses (Ovid), I: 368
Metropolis (film), I: 81
"Metzengerstein" (Poe), I: 340, 346, 353
Mexico City Blues (Kerouac), I: 184

Middlemarch (G. Eliot), I: 146, 206, 215
Middleton, Thomas, I: 365
Miller, Arthur, I: 53–69, 122
Milton, John, I: 214, 361
"Minister's Black Veil, The" (Hawthorne), I: 259
Misfits, The (A. Miller), I: 54
Mitchell, Isaac, I: 343
Modern Instance (Howells), I: 211
"Moloch" (Ginsberg), I: 75, 80–81
Monster and Other Stories, The (S. Crane), I: 238
Moore, Marianne, I: 72
Moore, Thomas, I: 346
Morath, Ingeborg, I: 54, 55
More, Thomas, I: 354
"Morella" (Poe), I: 346–347, 349
Morrison, Jim, I: 184
Morrison, Toni, I: 19–33
Moses (biblical person), I: 178, 290
Mott, Lucretia, I: 262–263
Moveable Feast, A (Hemingway), I: 329
"MS. Found in a Bottle" (Poe), I: 341, 344–345
Murder in the Cathedral (T. S. Eliot), I: 360
My Ántonia (Cather), I: **143–162**
My Bondage and My Freedom (Douglass), I: **163–182**
"Mystification" (Poe), I: 351
Nabokov, Vladimir, I: 89–108, 234, 339
Nabokov's Dozen (Nabokov), I: 90
Naked Lunch (Burroughs), I: 73, 184
Narrative of Arthur Gordon Pym, The (Poe), I: 340
Narrative of the Life of Frederick Douglass, An American Slave, Written By Himself (Douglass), I: 164–165, 166, 167, 168, 169, 175
Nature (Emerson), I: 145
Neal, John, I: 341
"Nebraska: The End of the First Cycle" (Cather), I: 144, 145
Nero, emperor of Rome, I: 362
New National Era, The (Douglass; periodical), I: 165
Nietzsche, Friedrich, I: 110, 115
Night of the Iguana, The (T. Williams), I: 305
Nikolai Gogol (Nabokov), I: 90
Nine Stories (Salinger), I: 35, 36
Norris, Frank, I: 147–148
North Star, The (Douglass; newspaper), I: 165, 166
Not under Forty (Jewett), I: 144, 159
"Novel Démeublé, The" (Cather), I: 151
Oakley, Annie, I: 138

Oates, Joyce Carol, **I:** 234

O'Connor, Flannery, **I:** 30–31, 275

Odyssey (Homer), **I:** 368

Oedipus Rex (Sophocles), **I:** 368

"Of Alexander Crummell" (Du Bois), **I:** 284

"Of Mr. Booker T. Washington and Others" (Du Bois), **I:** 284, 290, 291

"Of Noses" (Sterne), **I:** 349

"Of Our Spiritual Strivings" (Du Bois), **I:** 284, 286, 288, 289, 290, 292, 299

"Of the Black Belt" (Du Bois), **I:** 284, 289, 293

"Of the Coming of John" (Du Bois), **I:** 284

"Of the Dawn of Freedom" (Du Bois), **I:** 284, 293

"Of the Faith of the Fathers" (Du Bois), **I:** 284

"Of the Meaning of Progress" (Du Bois), **I:** 284

"Of the Passing of the First-Born" (Du Bois), **I:** 284

"Of the Quest of the Golden Fleece" (Du Bois), **I:** 282, 283, 284

"Of the Sons of Master and Man" (Du Bois), **I:** 284

"Of the Sorrow Songs" (Du Bois), **I:** 284

"Of the Training of Black Men" (Du Bois), **I:** 284, 289, 293–294, 297

"Of the Wings of Atalanta" (Du Bois), **I:** 284, 291–296

Old Man and the Sea, The (Hemingway), **I:** 322, 323

"Old Oaken Bucket, The" (Woodworth), **I:** 157

Old Testament, **I:** 80–81, 178, 288

"On a Book Entitled *Lolita*" (Nabokov), **I:** 89

O'Neill, Eugene, **I:** 109–124

One of Ours (Cather), **I:** 144, 159

"On Social Plays" (A. Miller), **I:** 62

On the Road (Kerouac), **I:** 73, 84, **183–197**

"Open Boat, The" (S. Crane), **I:** 240

Operette morali (Leopardi), **I:** 355

O Pioneers! (Cather), **I:** 144

Orlovsky, Peter, **I:** 74, 82, 83

Orpheus Descending (T. Williams), **I:** 304

O'Sullivan, John L., **I:** 264

Otchayanie. See *Despair* (Nabokov)

Othello (Shakespeare), **I:** 63

Our Mr. Wren (Lewis), **I:** 126

Our Mutual Friend (Dickens), **I:** 360

Out Cry (T. Williams), **I:** 315

Out of Africa (Dinesen), **I:** 38

Ovid, **I:** 368, 372

"Pact, A" (Pound), **I:** 359

Paine, Thomas, **I:** 172

Pale Fire (Nabokov), **I:** 90

Paradise (Morrison), **I:** 20, 21

Paradise Lost (Milton), **I:** 214

Parker, Charlie, **I:** 187

"Parsifal" (Verlaine), **I:** 367, 370

Pascal, Blaise, **I:** 225

Pater, Walter, **I:** 92

Paterson (W. C. Williams), **I:** 74

Patmore, Coventry, **I:** 149

Peacock, Thomas Love, **I:** 341, 349, 355

Pennebaker, Donn, **I:** 195

"Person-to-Person" (T. Williams), **I:** 315

Petronius, **I:** 362

Philadelphia Negro, The: A Special Study (Du Bois), **I:** 284

Picasso, Pablo, **I:** 371

Pickwick Papers, The (Dickens), **I:** 348

Pierce, Franklin, **I:** 258, 264

Pinter, Harold, **I:** 366

"Pit and the Pendulum, The" (Poe), **I:** 351

Planet News (Ginsberg), **I:** 72

Plath, Sylvia, **I:** 51, 85

Plato, **I:** 295, 341, 350

Plato Papers, The (Ackroyd), **I:** 356

Playing in the Dark: Whiteness and the Literary Imagination (Morrison), **I:** 20, 32

Plutonian Ode, and Other Poems (Ginsberg), **I:** 72

Pnin (Nabokov), **I:** 90

Podvig. See *Glory* (Nabokov)

Poe, Edgar Allan, **I:** 94, 96, 275, 339–358

Poems and Problems (Nabokov), **I:** 90

Poems of These States (Ginsberg), **I:** 72

Poetics (Aristotle), **I:** 110

Poetry and Tales (Poe), **I:** 355

"Poker Night, The" (T. Williams), **I:** 311

Pollock, Jackson, **I:** 74

Pompey the Great, **I:** 354

Pope, Alexander, **I:** 169, 365, 367

"Portrait of a Lady" (T. S. Eliot), **I:** 215

Portrait of a Lady, The (film), **I:** 216

Portrait of a Lady, The (H. James), **I:** **199–218**

Portrait of the Artist (Joyce), **I:** 186

Pound, Ezra, **I:** 72, 74, 359, 362, 372

"Predicament, A" (Poe), **I:** 351

Pride and Prejudice (Austen), **I:** 203

Priglashenie na kazn'. See *Invitation to a Beheading* (Nabokov)

"Prothalamion" (Spenser), **I:** 367

Protocols of the Elders of Zion, The (publication), **I:** 289, 299

Proust, Marcel, **I:** 99, 100

Pudd'nhead Wilson (Twain), **I:** 3

Pull My Daisy (Frank), **I:** 184

Pushkin, Alexander, **I:** 90

Rabbit Angstrom: A Tetralogy (Updike), **I:** 219, 220, 221, 234

Rabbit at Rest (Updike), **I:** 219, 220

Rabbit Is Rich (Updike), **I:** 219, 220

Rabbit Redux (Updike), **I:** 219, 220

Rabbit, Run (Updike), **I:** **219–236**

Radcliffe, Ann, **I:** 343

Raise High the Roof Beam, Carpenters and Seymour: An Introduction (Salinger), **I:** 35, 36

Rape of the Lock, The (Pope), **I:** 365

Raven and Other Poems, The (Poe), **I:** 340

Reality Sandwiches (Ginsberg), **I:** 72

Real Life of Sebastian Knight, The (Nabokov), **I:** 89, 90

Red Badge of Courage, The (S. Crane), **I:** **237–255**

Remembrance of Things Past (A la recherche du temps perdu) (Proust), **I:** 99–100

Rexroth, Kenneth, **I:** 74, 75, 84

"Rill from the Town Pump, A" (Hawthorne), **I:** 259

Rimbaud, Arthur, **I:** 74, 187

Rite of Spring (Le Sacre du printemps) (Stravinsky), **I:** 371

Rockefeller, John D., **I:** 283

Roderick Hudson (H. James), **I:** 200

Romeo and Juliet (Shakespeare), **I:** 44

Roosevelt, Eleanor, **I:** 63

Rossetti, Dante Gabriel, **I:** 110

Roudané, Matthew C., **I:** 56

Rousseau, Jean-Jacques, **I:** 96

Rubáiyát of Omar Khayyám (E. FitzGerald, trans.), **I:** 297

"Run-Away Plot, The" (Douglass), **I:** 177, 178

Rushdie, Salman, **I:** 234

Ruth Hall (Fern), **I:** 258

Sacre du printemps, Le. See *Rite of Spring* (Stravinsky)

Sacred Wood, The: Essays on Poetry and Criticism (T. S. Eliot), **I:** 360, 361

"Salesman at Fifty" (A. Miller), **I:** 67

Salesman in Beijing (A. Miller), **I:** 55, 66–67

Salinger, J. D., **I:** 16, 35–52

Sapphira and the Slave Girl (Jewett), **I:** 144, 159

Satyricon (Petronius), **I:** 362

Scarlet Letter, The (Hawthorne), **I:** 149, **257–279**

Schopenhauer, Arthur, **I:** 110

Scott, Sir Walter, **I:** 3, 164

"Scythe of Time, The" (Poe), I: 351, 352

Selby, Hubert, Jr., I: 30

Selected Poems, 1947–1995 (Ginsberg), I: 72, 85

Self-Consciousness (Updike), I: 220, 221

"Self-Reliance" (Emerson), I: 206

"Seven Tales of My Native Land" (Hawthorne), I: 257

Sevier, Valentine, I: 304

"Shadow—A Parable" (Poe), I: 345, 353

"Shadow of the Gods, The" (A. Miller), I: 61

Shadows on the Rock (Jewett), I: 144

Shakespeare, William, I: 9, 10, 44, 110, 117, 118, 119, 186, 298, 317–318, 365–366, 367, 371

Shaw, George Bernard, I: 110, 131, 136

Shelley, Percy Bysshe, I: 72, 73, 229

Shepard, Sam, I: 122

Shining, The (King), I: 344

"Significance of the Frontier in American History, The" (Turner), I: 145

"Signora Zenobia, The" (Poe), I: 351

"Silence—A Fable" (Poe), I: 353

Simpson, Louis, I: 78

Simpsons, The (television series), I: 339

Sinclair, Upton, I: 126

"Siope—A Fable" (Poe), I: 353–354

Sister Carrie (Dreiser), I: 144, 160

Small Craft Warnings (T. Williams), I: 306

Smart, Christopher, I: 75, 76

Smiley, Jane, I: 16

Smith, Gerrit, I: 165, 166, 180

Smith, Horace, I: 353, 354

Smith, James M'Cune, I: 168–169

Smith, Johnston (pseudonym). *See* Crane, Stephen

Snyder, Gary, I: 75, 184, 195

Socrates, I: 290

Soglyadatay. See The Eye (Nabokov)

Solomon, Carl, I: 74, 79, 82, 83

Song of Solomon (biblical book), I: 289

Song of Solomon (Morrison), I: 20

"Song of the Bride" (Wagner), I: 297

Song of the Lark, The (Cather), I: 144

Songs of Innocence and Experience (Blake), I: 85

Sophocles, I: 368

Souls of Black Folk, The (Du Bois), I: **281–301**

Speak, Memory: An Autobiography Revisited (Nabokov), I: 90, 99

Spengler, Oswald, I: 187

Spenser, Edmund, I: 367

Spoils of Poynton, The (H. James), I: 200

"Spring's Welcome" (Lyly), I: 366

Stanton, Elizabeth Cady, I: 180, 262–263

Stein, Gertrude, I: 321

Stendhal, I: 110

Sterne, Laurence, I: 349

Stevens, Thaddeus, I: 180

Stevens, Wallace, I: 72

Stirner, Max, I: 110

Stoddard, Elizabeth, I: 275

Stowe, Harriet Beecher, I: 16, 125, 177, 213, 260, 261, 275, 286

Strange Interlude (O'Neill), I: 110

Stravinsky, Igor, I: 371

Streetcar Named Desire, A (T. Williams), I: 56, **303–320**

Strindberg, August, I: 110, 122

Strong Opinions (Nabokov), I: 91, 92, 95, 99

Suddenly Last Summer (T. Williams), I: 311

Sula (Morrison), I: 20

Sumner, Charles, I: 180

Sumner, William Graham, I: 239–240

Sun Also Rises, The (Hemingway), I: **321–337**

"Sunflower Sutra" (Ginsberg), I: 83

"Supermarket in California, A" (Ginsberg), I: 83

Suppression of the African Slave Trade to the United States of America, 1638–1870, The (Du Bois), I: 284

Sweet Bird of Youth (T. Williams), I: 304, 305, 306, 314

Swift, Jonathan, I: 349, 354

Swinburne, Algernon Charles, I: 94, 110

Symposium (Plato), I: 341

"Tale in Imitation of the German, A" (Poe), I: 346

"Tale of Jerusalem, A" (Poe), I: 340, 353, 354

"Tale of Possessors, Self-Dispossessed, A" (O'Neill), I: 109

Tales of the Early Ages (H. Smith), I: 353

Tales of the Folio Club (Poe), I: 341, 345, 349

Tales of the Grotesque and Arabesque (Poe), I: **339–358**

Tamerlane and Other Poems (Poe), I: 340

Tar Baby (Morrison), I: 20

Tempest, The (Shakespeare), I: 366

Tennyson, Alfred Lord, I: 201, 372

Tess of the d'Urbervilles (Hardy), I: 157

Theater Essays of Arthur Miller, The (A. Miller), I: 55, 61, 62

"They Say It's Wonderful" (song), I: 138

Thirst, and Other One Act Plays (O'Neill), I: 110

Thompson, Hunter S., I: 51

Thoreau, Henry David, I: 139, 147, 187, 225, 275

Thus Spake Zarathustra (Nietzsche), I: 115

Ticknor, William D., I: 258, 259, 260

Tillman, Benjamin, I: 298, 299

Timebends: A Life (A. Miller), I: 54, 55, 56, 57, 61, 65

Titian, I: 204

"To a Nightingale" (Keats), I: 366

"To Elsie" (W. C. Williams), I: 75

"To His Coy Mistress" (Marvell), I: 367

Tolstoy, Leo, I: 146

Town and the City, The (Kerouac), I: 183, 184, 185, 186, 187, 188

"Tradition and the Individual Talent" (T. S. Eliot), I: 361

Trilling, Lionel, I: 73, 74, 95

Tristan und Isolde (Wagner), I: 363

"True History" (Lucian), I: 355

Turner, Frederick Jackson, I: 143, 144, 145

Turner, Nat, I: 165, 177

Turn of the Screw, The (H. James), I: 200

Twain, Mark, I: 1–17, 139, 178, 180, 223, 283, 285

Twice-Told Tales (Hawthorne), I: 257, 258, 259

Two-Character Play, The (T. Williams), I: 315

Ulysses (Joyce), I: 29, 365

"Ulysses" (Tennyson), I: 201

"Ulysses, Order, and Myth" (T. S. Eliot), I: 365

Uncle Remus: His Songs and His Sayings (Harris), I: 1

Uncle Tom's Cabin (Stowe), I: 16, 125, 177, 213, 260

Uncle Vanya (Chekhov), I: 315

"Unparalled Adventure of One Hans Pfaall, The" (Poe), I: 355

"Unwritten Drama of Lord Byron, An" (W. Irving), I: 343

Upanishads, I: 371

Updike, John, I: 139, 219–236

Up from Slavery (B. Washington), I: 290

Van Doren, Mark, I: 73, 74

Van Petten, John Bullock, I: 241

Veblen, Thorstein, I: 136

"Veille de Noel, Une" (Kerouac), I: 85–86

Verdenal, Jean, I: 363

Verlaine, Paul, I: 367

Verne, Jules, I: 354

Vesey, Denmark, **I:** 177

Vieux Carré (T. Williams), **I:** 305, 306

View from the Bridge, A (A. Miller), **I:** 62

"Village Virus, The" (Lewis), **I:** 126

Virgil, **I:** 75, 147

"Visionary, The" (Poe), **I:** 346

Visions of Cody (Kerouac), **I:** 186

Visions of Gerard (Kerouac), **I:** 184, 185

Vollmer, Joan, **I:** 191

Volshebnik (Nabokov), **I:** 89–90

"Von Jung" (Poe), **I:** 351–352

Vosburgh, R. G., **I:** 248

Wagner, Richard, **I:** 297, 363, 368

Waldman, Ann, **I:** 72, 85

Wallace, Lew, **I:** 138

Walpole, Horace, **I:** 343

Walpole, Hugh, **I:** 138

Warhol, Andy, **I:** 306

War Is Kind (S. Crane), **I:** 238

Warner, Susan, **I:** 260, 261

Warren, Henry Clarke, **I:** 372

Washington, Booker T., **I:** 283, 284, 287, 289–291, 294, 295, 296

Washington, Madison, **I:** 177

Waste Land, The (T. S. Eliot), **I:** 71, 81, **359–374**

Watch and Ward (H. James), **I:** 200

Webster, John, **I:** 364

Webster, Noah, **I:** 3

Wells, H. G., **I:** 354

Wells, Ida B., **I:** 165

Welty, Eudora, **I:** 147

West, Rebecca, **I:** 138

Weston, Jessie L., **I:** 364, 367, 372

Whalen, Philip, **I:** 75, 195

Wharton, Edith, **I:** 234

What Maisie Knew (H. James), **I:** 200

"What the Thunder Said" (T. S. Eliot), **I:** 362, 369–371

White, Thomas Willis, **I:** 340, 348

White, William Allen, **I:** 138

White Devil, The (J. Webster), **I:** 364

White Shroud (Ginsberg), **I:** 72

Whitman, Walt, **I:** 74, 75, 76, 80, 83, 85, 139, 172, 178, 179, 187, 234, 239, 241, 275, 285, 359, 361

Whittier, John Greenleaf, **I:** 275

Who's Afraid of Virginia Woolf? (Albee), **I:** 122

"Why the Little Frenchman Wears His Hand in a Sling" (Poe), **I:** 340, 352

Wide, Wide World, The (Warner), **I:** 260

Wilde, Oscar, **I:** 91, 92, 110, 356

Wilder, Thornton, **I:** 310

Williams, Rose Isabel, **I:** 304, 305, 306

Williams, Tennessee, **I:** 56, 122, 303–320

Williams, William Carlos, **I:** 74, 75, 77, 80, 83

"William Wilson" (Poe), **I:** 343–344, 352

Willis, N. P., **I:** 350

Wilson, Edmund, **I:** 342

Winfrey, Oprah, **I:** 32

Wings of the Dove, The (H. James), **I:** 200

Winner Take Nothing (Hemingway), **I:** 323

With Love and Squalor (essay collection), **I:** 51

Wolfe, Thomas, **I:** 186

Women, Beware Women (Middleton), **I:** 365

Woodworth, Samuel T., **I:** 157

Wordsworth, William, **I:** 72, 75

World So Wide (Lewis), **I:** 127

Wren, Sir Christopher, **I:** 372

Wright, Richard, **I:** 30

Wuthering Heights (E. Brontë), **I:** 157, 203

Yeats, W. B., **I:** 74, 365

Young, Lester, **I:** 87

"Young Folks, The" (Salinger), **I:** 36

"Young Goodman Brown" (Hawthorne), **I:** 259

"Youth" (Conrad), **I:** 146

Zangwill, Israel, **I:** 143

Zashchita Luzhina. See *The Defense* (Nabokov)

Zillah: A Tale of the Holy City (H. Smith), **I:** 354

Zola, Émile, **I:** 110, 241

A Complete Listing of Authors in
AMERICAN WRITERS

Acker, Kathy . . . . Supp. XII

Adams, Henry .Vol. I

Addams, Jane . . . . Supp. I

Agee, James . . . . .Vol. I

Aiken, Conrad .Vol. I

Albee, Edward .Vol. I

Alcott, Louisa May . . . . Supp. I

Algren, Nelson . . . . Supp. IX

Alvarez, Julia . . . . Supp. VII

Ammons, A. R. Supp. VII

Anderson, Sherwood . . . . .Vol. I

Angelou, Maya . . . . Supp. IV

Ashbery, John . . . . Supp. III

Auchincloss, Louis . . . . Supp. IV

Auden, W. H. Supp. II

Auster, Paul . . . . Supp. XII

Baldwin, James . . . . Supp. I

Baldwin, James . . . . .Retro. Supp. II

Bambara, Toni Cade . . . . Supp. XI

Banks, Russell . . . . Supp. V

Baraka, Amiri . . . . Supp. II

Barlow, Joel . . . . Supp. II

Barnes, Djuna . . . . Supp. III

Barth, John . . . . .Vol. I

Barthelme, Donald . . . . Supp. IV

Barthelme, Frederick . . . . Supp. XI

Bausch, Richard . . . . Supp. VII

Beattie, Ann . . . . Supp. V

Bell, Madison Smartt . . . . Supp. X

Bellow, Saul . . . . .Vol. I

Bellow, Saul . . . . .Retro. Supp. II

Benét, Stephen Vincent . . . . Supp. XI

Berry, Wendell . . . . Supp. X

Berryman, John . . . . .Vol. I

Bierce, Ambrose . . . . .Vol. I

Bishop, Elizabeth . . . . Supp. I

Bishop, Elizabeth . . . . .Retro. Supp. II

Blackmur, R. P. . . . . Supp. II

Bly, Robert . . . . Supp. IV

Bogan, Louise . . . . Supp. III

Bourne, Randolph . . . . .Vol. I

Bowles, Paul . . . . Supp. IV

Boyle, T. C. Supp. VIII

Bradbury, Ray . . . . Supp. IV

Bradstreet, Anne . . . . Supp. I

Brodsky, Joseph . . . . Supp. VIII

Brooks, Gwendolyn . . . . Supp. III

Brooks, Van Wyck . . . . .Vol. I

Brown, Charles Brockden . . . . Supp. I

Bryant, William Cullen . . . . Supp. I

Buck, Pearl S. . . . . Supp. II

Buechner, Frederick . . . . Supp. XII

Burke, Kenneth . . . . .Vol. I

Burroughs, William S. . . . . Supp. III

Butler, Robert Olen . . . . Supp. XII

Caldwell, Erskine . . . . .Vol. I

Cameron, Peter . . . . Supp. XII

Capote, Truman . . . . Supp. III

Carson, Anne . . . . Supp. XII

Carson, Rachel . . . . Supp. IX

Carver, Raymond . . . . Supp. III

Cather, Willa .Vol. I

Cather, Willa . . . . .Retro. Supp. I

Chabon, Michael . . . . Supp. XI

Chandler, Raymond . . . . Supp. IV

Cheever, John . . . . Supp. I

Chopin, Kate . . . . Supp. I

Chopin, Kate . . . . .Retro. Supp. II

Cisneros, Sandra . . . . Supp. VII

Clampitt, Amy . . . . Supp. IX
Coleman, Wanda . . . . Supp. XI
Cooper, James Fenimore . . . . .Vol. I
Coover, Robert . . . . Supp. V
Corso, Gregory . . . . Supp. XII
Cowley, Malcolm . . . . Supp. II
Cozzens, James Gould . . . . .Vol. I
Crane, Hart .Vol. I
Crane, Hart . . . . .Retro. Supp. II
Crane, Stephen . . . . .Vol. I
Creeley, Robert . . . . Supp. IV
Crèvecoeur, Michel-Guillaume
     Jean de . . . . Supp. I
Crews, Harry . . . . Supp. XI
Cullen, Countee . . . . Supp. IV
Cummings, E. E. . . . . .Vol. I
DeLillo, Don . . . . Supp. VI
Dickey, James . . . . Supp. IV
Dickinson, Emily . . . . .Vol. I
Dickinson, Emily . . . . .Retro. Supp. I
Didion, Joan . . . . Supp. IV
Dillard, Annie . . . . Supp. VI
Dixon, Stephen . . . . Supp. XII
Doctorow, E. L. . . . . Supp. IV
Doolittle, Hilda (H.D.) . . . . Supp. I
Dos Passos, John . . . . .Vol. I
Doty, Mark . . . . Supp. XI
Douglass, Frederick . . . . Supp. III
Dove, Rita . . . . Supp. IV
Dreiser, Theodore . . . . .Vol. I
Dreiser, Theodore . . . . .Retro. Supp. II
Du Bois, W. E. B. . . . . Supp. II
Dubus, Andre . . . . Supp. VII
Dunbar, Paul Laurence . . . . Supp. II
Dunn, Stephen . . . . Supp. XI
Eberhart, Richard . . . . .Vol. I
Edwards, Jonathan . . . . .Vol. I
Eliot, T. S. .Vol. I
Eliot, T. S. . . . . .Retro. Supp. I

Elkin, Stanley . . . . Supp. VI
Ellison, Ralph . . . . Supp. II
Ellison, Ralph . . . . .Retro. Supp. II
Emerson, Ralph Waldo . . . . .Vol. II
Epstein, Leslie . . . . Supp. XII
Erdrich, Louise . . . . Supp. IV
Fante, John . . . . Supp. XI
Farrell, James T. . . . . .Vol. II
Faulkner, William . . . . .Vol. II
Faulkner, William . . . . .Retro. Supp. I
Fitzgerald, F. Scott . . . . .Vol. II
Fitzgerald, F. Scott . . . . .Retro. Supp. I
Fitzgerald, Zelda . . . . Supp. IX
Ford, Richard . . . . Supp. V
Francis, Robert . . . . Supp. IX
Franklin, Benjamin . . . . .Vol. II
Frederic, Harold . . . . .Vol. II
Freneau, Philip . . . . Supp. II
Frost, Robert . . . . .Vol. II
Frost, Robert . . . . .Retro. Supp. I
Fuller, Margaret . . . . Supp. II
Gaddis, William . . . . Supp. IV
García, Cristina . . . . Supp. XI
Gardner, John . . . . Supp. VI
Garrett, George . . . . Supp. VII
Gass, William . . . . Supp. VI
Gibbons, Kaye . . . . Supp. X
Gilman, Charlotte Perkins . . . . Supp. XI
Ginsberg, Allen . . . . Supp. II
Glasgow, Ellen . . . . .Vol. II
Glaspell, Susan . . . . Supp. III
Goldbarth, Albert . . . . Supp. XII
Glück, Louise . . . . Supp. V
Gordon, Caroline . . . . .Vol. II
Gordon, Mary . . . . Supp. IV
Gunn Allen, Paula . . . . Supp. IV
Gurney, A. R. . . . . Supp. V
Haines, John . . . . Supp. XII
Hammett, Dashiell . . . . Supp. IV

Hansberry, Lorraine . . . . Supp. IV

Hardwick, Elizabeth . . . . Supp. III

Harjo, Joy . . . . Supp. XII

Harrison, Jim . . . . Supp. VIII

Harte, Bret . . . . Supp. II

Hass, Robert . . . . Supp. VI

Hawthorne, Nathaniel . . . . .Vol. II

Hawthorne, Nathaniel . . . . .Retro. Supp. I

Hayden, Robert . . . . Supp. II

Hearon, Shelby . . . . Supp. VIII

Hecht, Anthony . . . . Supp. X

Heller, Joseph . . . . Supp. IV

Hellman, Lillian . . . . Supp. I

Hemingway, Ernest . . . . .Vol. II

Hemingway, Ernest . . . . .Retro. Supp. I

Henry, O. . . . . Supp. II

Hijuelos, Oscar . . . . Supp. VIII

Hoffman, Alice . . . . Supp. X

Hogan, Linda . . . . Supp. IV

Holmes, Oliver Wendell . . . . Supp. I

Howe, Irving . . . . Supp. VI

Howe, Susan . . . . Supp. IV

Howells, William Dean . . . . .Vol. II

Hughes, Langston . . . . Supp. I

Hughes, Langston . . . . .Retro. Supp. I

Hugo, Richard . . . . Supp. VI

Humphrey, William . . . . Supp. IX

Hurston, Zora Neale . . . . Supp. VI

Irving, John . . . . Supp. VI

Irving, Washington . . . . .Vol. II

Jackson, Shirley . . . . Supp. IX

James, Henry . . . . .Vol. II

James, Henry . . . . .Retro. Supp. I

James, William .Vol. II

Jarrell, Randall . . . . .Vol. II

Jeffers, Robinson . . . . Supp. II

Jewett, Sarah Orne . . . . .Vol. II

Jewett, Sarah Orne . . . . .Retro. Supp. II

Johnson, Charles . . . . Supp. VI

Jones, James . . . . Supp. XI

Jong, Erica . . . . Supp. V

Justice, Donald . . . . Supp. VII

Karr, Mary . . . . Supp. XI

Kazin, Alfred . . . . Supp. VIII

Kennedy, William . . . . Supp. VII

Kenyon, Jane . . . . Supp. VII

Kerouac, Jack . . . . Supp. III

Kincaid, Jamaica . . . . Supp. VII

King, Stephen . . . . Supp. V

Kingsolver, Barbara . . . . Supp. VII

Kingston, Maxine Hong . . . . Supp. V

Kinnell, Galway . . . . Supp. III

Knowles, John . . . . Supp. XII

Kosinski, Jerzy . . . . Supp. VII

Kumin, Maxine . . . . Supp. IV

Kunitz, Stanley . . . . Supp. III

Kushner, Tony . . . . Supp. IX

LaBastille, Anne . . . . Supp. X

Lanier, Sidney . . . . Supp. I

Lardner, Ring .Vol. II

Lee, Harper . . . . Supp. VIII

Levertov, Denise . . . . Supp. III

Levine, Philip . . . . Supp. V

Levis, Larry . . . . Supp. XI

Lewis, Sinclair .Vol. II

Lindsay, Vachel . . . . Supp. I

London, Jack .Vol. II

Longfellow, Henry Wadsworth . . . . .Vol. II

Longfellow, Henry
      Wadsworth . . . . .Retro. Supp. II

Lowell, Amy . . . . .Vol. II

Lowell, James Russell . . . . Supp. I

Lowell, Robert .Vol. II

Lowell, Robert . . . . .Retro. Supp. II

McCarthy, Cormac . . . . Supp. VIII

McCarthy, Mary . . . . .Vol. II

McClatchy, J. D. . . . . Supp. XII

McCourt, Frank . . . . Supp. XII

McCullers, Carson . . . . .Vol. II
Macdonald, Ross . . . . Supp. IV
McGrath, Thomas . . . . Supp. X
McKay, Claude . . . . Supp. X
MacLeish, Archibald . . . . .Vol. III
McMurty, Larry . . . . Supp. V
McPhee, John . . . . Supp. III
Mailer, Norman . . . . .Vol. III
Mailer, Norman . . . . .Retro. Supp. II
Malamud, Bernard . . . . Supp. I
Marquand, John P. . . . . .Vol. III
Marshall, Paule . . . . Supp. XI
Mason, Bobbie Ann . . . . Supp. VIII
Masters, Edgar Lee . . . . Supp. I
Mather, Cotton . . . . Supp. II
Matthews, William . . . . Supp. IX
Matthiessen, Peter . . . . Supp. V
Maxwell, William . . . . Supp. VIII
Melville, Herman . . . . .Vol. III
Melville, Herman . . . . .Retro. Supp. I
Mencken, H. L. . . . . .Vol. III
Merrill, James . . . . Supp. III
Merton, Thomas . . . . Supp. VIII
Merwin, W. S. . . . . Supp. III
Millay, Edna St. Vincent . . . . .Vol. III
Miller, Arthur . . . . .Vol. III
Miller, Henry . . . . .Vol. III
Miller, Sue . . . . Supp. XII
Minot, Susan . . . . Supp. VI
Momaday, N. Scott . . . . Supp. IV
Monette, Paul . . . . Supp. X
Moore, Lorrie . . . . Supp. X
Moore, Marianne . . . . .Vol. III
Morison, Samuel Eliot . . . . Supp. I
Morris, Wright . . . . .Vol. III
Morrison, Toni . . . . Supp. III
Muir, John . . . . Supp. IX
Mumford, Lewis . . . . Supp. III
Nabokov, Vladimir . . . . .Vol. III

Nabokov, Vladimir . . . . .Retro. Supp. I
Naylor, Gloria . . . . Supp. VIII
Nemerov, Howard . . . . .Vol. III
Niebuhr, Reinhold . . . . .Vol. III
Nin, Anaïs . . . . Supp. X
Norris, Frank . . . . .Vol. III
Oates, Joyce Carol . . . . Supp. II
O'Brien, Tim . . . . Supp. V
O'Connor, Flannery . . . . .Vol. III
O'Connor, Flannery . . . . .Retro. Supp. II
Odets, Clifford . . . . Supp. II
O'Hara, John . . . . .Vol. III
Olds, Sharon . . . . Supp. X
Oliver, Mary . . . . Supp. VII
Olson, Charles . . . . Supp. II
O'Neill, Eugene . . . . .Vol. III
Ortiz, Simon J. . . . . Supp. IV
Ozick, Cynthia . . . . Supp. V
Paine, Thomas . . . . Supp. I
Paley, Grace . . . . Supp. VI
Parker, Dorothy . . . . Supp. IX
Parkman, Francis . . . . Supp. II
Patchett, Ann . . . . Supp. XII
Percy, Walker . . . . Supp. III
Pinsky, Robert . . . . Supp. VI
Plath, Sylvia . . . . Supp. I
Plath, Sylvia . . . . .Retro. Supp. II
Podhoretz, Norman . . . . Supp. VIII
Poe, Edgar Allan . . . . .Vol. III
Poe, Edgar Allan . . . . .Retro. Supp. II
Porter, Katherine Anne . . . . .Vol. III
Pound, Ezra . . . . .Vol. III
Pound, Ezra . . . . .Retro. Supp. I
Powers, Richard . . . . Supp. IX
Price, Reynolds . . . . Supp. VI
Proulx, Annie . . . . Supp. VII
Purdy, James . . . . Supp. VII
Pynchon, Thomas . . . . Supp. II
Rand, Ayn . . . . Supp. IV

Ransom, John Crowe ....Vol. III

Rawlings, Marjorie Kinnan .... Supp. X

Reed, Ishmael .... Supp. X

Rice, Anne .... Supp. VII

Rich, Adrienne .... Supp. I

Rich, Adrienne ....Retro. Supp. II

Ríos, Alberto Álvaro .... Supp. IV

Robbins, Tom .... Supp. X

Robinson, Edwin Arlington ....Vol. III

Roethke, Theodore ....Vol. III

Roth, Henry .... Supp. IX

Roth, Philip .... Supp. III

Roth, Philip ....Retro. Supp. II

Rukeyser, Muriel .... Supp. VI

Russo, Richard .... Supp. XII

Salinger, J. D. ....Vol. III

Salter, James .... Supp. IX

Sandburg, Carl ....Vol. III

Santayana, George ....Vol. III

Sarton, May .... Supp. VIII

Schwartz, Delmore .... Supp. II

Sexton, Anne .... Supp. II

Shapiro, Karl .... Supp. II

Shepard, Sam .... Supp. III

Shields, Carol .... Supp. VII

Silko, Leslie Marmon .... Supp. IV

Simic, Charles .... Supp. VIII

Simon, Neil .... Supp. IV

Simpson, Louis .... Supp. IX

Sinclair, Upton .... Supp. V

Singer, Isaac Bashevis ....Vol. IV

Singer, Isaac Bashevis ....Retro. Supp. II

Smiley, Jane .... Supp. VI

Snodgrass, W. D. .... Supp. VI

Snyder, Gary .... Supp. VIII

Sontag, Susan .... Supp. III

Southern, Terry .... Supp. XI

Stafford, William .... Supp. XI

Stegner, Wallace .... Supp. IV

Stein, Gertrude ....Vol. IV

Steinbeck, John ....Vol. IV

Stern, Gerald .... Supp. IX

Stevens, Wallace ....Vol. IV

Stevens, Wallace ....Retro. Supp. I

Stone, Robert .... Supp. V

Stowe, Harriet Beecher .... Supp. I

Strand, Mark .... Supp. IV

Styron, William ....Vol. IV

Swenson, May .... Supp. IV

Tan, Amy .... Supp. X

Tate, Allen ....Vol. IV

Taylor, Edward ....Vol. IV

Taylor, Peter .... Supp. V

Theroux, Paul .... Supp. VIII

Thoreau, Henry David ....Vol. IV

Thurber, James .... Supp. I

Toomer, Jean .... Supp. IX

Trilling, Lionel .... Supp. III

Twain, Mark ....Vol. IV

Tyler, Anne .... Supp. IV

Updike, John ....Vol. IV

Updike, John ....Retro. Supp. I

Van Vechten, Carl .... Supp. II

Veblen, Thorstein .... Supp. I

Vidal, Gore .... Supp. IV

Vonnegut, Kurt .... Supp. II

Wagoner, David .... Supp. IX

Walker, Alice .... Supp. III

Wallace, David Foster .... Supp. X

Warren, Robert Penn ....Vol. IV

Welty, Eudora ....Vol. IV

Welty, Eudora ....Retro. Supp. I

West, Nathanael ....Vol. IV

West, Nathanael ....Retro. Supp. II

Wharton, Edith ....Vol. IV

Wharton, Edith ....Retro. Supp. I

White, E. B. .... Supp. I

Whitman, Walt . . . . Vol. IV

Whitman, Walt . . . . Retro. Supp. I

Whittier, John Greenleaf . . . . Supp. I

Wilbur, Richard . . . . Supp. III

Wideman, John Edgar . . . . Supp. X

Wilder, Thornton . . . . Vol. IV

Williams, Tennessee . . . . Vol. IV

Williams, William Carlos . . . . Vol. IV

Williams, William Carlos . . . . . . Retro. Supp. I

Wilson, August . . . . Supp. VIII

Wilson, Edmund . . . . Vol. IV

Winters, Yvor . . . . Supp. II

Wolfe, Thomas . . . . Vol. IV

Wolfe, Tom . . . . Supp. III

Wolff, Tobias . . . . Supp. VII

Wright, Charles . . . . Supp. V

Wright, James . . . . Supp. III

Wright, Richard . . . . Vol. IV

Wylie, Elinor . . . . Supp. I

Yates, Richard . . . . Supp. XI

Zukofsky, Louis . . . . Supp. III